Foundations for the LPC

Foundations for the LPC

Professional Conduct
Imogen Clout, MA (Oxon), Solicitor, Lecturer in Legal Practice, University of Sheffield

Financial Services
Clare Firth, LLB, Solicitor, Director of Legal Practice, University of Sheffield and Pauline Laidlaw, LLB, Solicitor, Deputy Director of Legal Practice, University of Sheffield

EC Law
Rachel Cutts, BA (Hons), Solicitor, formerly Lecturer in Legal Practice, University of Sheffield and Zoe Ollerenshaw, LLB, Solicitor, Lecturer in Legal Practice, University of Sheffield

Revenue Law
Clare Firth, Pauline Laidlaw, George Miles, Paulene Denyer

Probate and Administration of Estates
George Miles, LLB (Exon), Solicitor, Associate Senior Lecturer, Faculty of Law (sometime Associate Dean, Head of Professional Legal Studies), University of the West of England, Bristol and Paulene Denyer, LLB (Hull), LLM (Lond), Solicitor, Senior Lecturer, Faculty of Law, University of the West of England, Bristol

Human Rights
Elizabeth Smart, Solicitor, Deputy Director of Legal Practice, University of Sheffield

OXFORD
UNIVERSITY PRESS

OXFORD
UNIVERSITY PRESS

Great Clarendon Street, Oxford OX2 6DP

Oxford University Press is a department of the University of Oxford.
It furthers the University's objective of excellence in research, scholarship,
and education by publishing worldwide in

Oxford New York

Auckland Bangkok Buenos Aires Cape Town Chennai
Dar es Salaam Delhi Hong Kong Istanbul Karachi Kolkata
Kuala Lumpur Madrid Melbourne Mexico City Mumbai Nairobi
São Paulo Shanghai Singapore Taipei Tokyo Toronto

Oxford is a registered trade mark of Oxford University Press
in the UK and in certain other countries

Published in the United States
by Oxford University Press Inc., New York

First published 1997
Second edition 1998
Third edition 1999
Fourth edition 2000
Fifth edition 2001
Sixth edition 2002

British Library Cataloguing in Publication Data
Data available

Library of Congress Cataloging in Publication Data
Data available

ISBN 0-19-925510-5

Typeset by Newgen Imaging Systems (P) Ltd., Chennai, India
Printed in Great Britain
on acid-free paper by
Ashford Colour Press Limited, Gosport, Hampshire

OUTLINE CONTENTS

DETAILED CONTENTS

PREFACE

This book provides foundations for study on the Legal Practice Course, containing materials relating to the Core and Pervasive areas (other than Accounts and Skills) identified in the Written Standards for the Course issued by the Legal Practice Course Board. Accounts and Skills are each the subject of a dedicated volume in the Legal Practice Course Guide series.

As with all the volumes in this series, the intention is to provide a text that can act as a 'bridge' between a set of 'notes' and other sources to which students on a Legal Practice Course can expect to be exposed as a preparation for the world of a solicitor's practice. The principles introduced here will be further developed in the context of the Compulsory and Elective Areas of the Course, and hopefully reference to this volume will aid the student's studies in those areas also.

The chapters on Revenue Law take into account the proposals contained in the Budget introduced by the Chancellor of the Exchequer in April 2002. However, they do not reflect any changes that may have been made to the Finance Bill since it was first published.

In Chapter 14, the forms of Oath for Executors, for Administrators with the will annexed and for Administrators are reproduced for teaching purposes only by kind permission of The Solicitors' Law Stationery Society Limited. Form IHT 200, the supplementary pages D1 to D18 inclusive and the form IHT(WS) are reproduced by kind permission of the Inland Revenue. Crown copyright is reproduced with the permission of the Controller of Her Majesty's Stationery Office.

The materials in Appendices 2 and 3 are reproduced from 'Professional Ethics Information Pack—Financial Services and Solicitors' by kind permission of The Law Society.

The authors are grateful for the support and assistance afforded to them by members of the Academic Division of Oxford University Press—and in particular by Jane O'Regan.

George Miles
Bristol
July 2002

TABLE OF CASES

TABLE OF STATUTES

European legislation

International legislation

TABLE OF SECONDARY LEGISLATION

European secondary legislation

Professional conduct

1

Professional conduct

'Legal ethics and professional responsibility are more than a set of rules, they are also a commitment to honesty, integrity and service in the practice of the law.'

(Cranston, Ross, *Legal Ethics and Professional Responsibilty*, Oxford: OUP, 1995)

INTRODUCTION

1.1 The Guide

The Guide to the Professional Conduct of Solicitors ('the Guide') with its supplements, is the essential book covering this part of the course and your future conduct as a solicitor. There would be little point in our paraphrasing the Guide, because the points that it covers are detailed and complex. Simplifying, or summarising them means that you lose the subtlety of them. This book is designed to be read in conjunction with the Guide.

Students starting the LPC in Autumn 2002 will receive the 8th edition of the Guide, published in 1999. Updates to this are published on the web at www.lawsociety.org.uk. Look under Guide Online for the text. Chapter 32 shows updates to the printed Guide.

The Guide is a thick book and at first sight looks rather daunting, but it is well set out, with clear statements of the principle and then illustrations of how it is to be applied. It contains the Solicitors Practice Rules 1990. These are added to from time to time by recommendations and by Council Directions. In due course, recommendations are sometimes 'upgraded' and become rules of practice.

The Law Society's *Gazette* has a regular section on Professional Conduct with questions and answers on Ethics. It is worth reading because it highlights many of the common problems that solicitors encounter in practice and demonstrates how the rules are applied.

1.2 How to use *The Guide to the Professional Conduct of Solicitors*

1.2.1 Structure of the Guide

At first sight the Guide is a complicated book. It has been divided into seven separate parts which do not seem to follow a particularly logical order:

I Solicitors in practice.

II International aspects of practice.

III Relationship with client.

IV Obligations to others.

V Particular areas of practice.

VI Financial regulations.

VII Complaints and discipline.

Part I is outlined in the rest of this chapter.

Part II which deals with international relations, is outside the scope of LPC.

Parts III and IV are covered in **1.3**, looking principally at the solicitor's relationship with the client.

Part V which focuses on particular aspects of practice, will be dealt with in **1.11** and also within each subject in which it has particular application, such as conveyancing and litigation and advocacy.

Part VI comes within the ambit of the Accounts Course in the LPC so is not dealt with in this book.

Part VII is covered at **1.6** which deals with complaints and discipline.

1.2.2 Rules

The Solicitors' Practice Rules 1990 are set out as Annex 1A to the first chapter of the Guide, and each rule is separately printed in the chapter which expounds that rule later in the Guide.

The Solicitors' Practice Rules are not the only rules that govern the conduct of solicitors. There are both statutory and non-statutory sources. These are listed in Chapter 1.03 of the Guide. The Law Society both interprets the rules and gives guidance as to how they are to be applied. Much of this guidance, which is authoritative and therefore should be followed, is in the Guide itself. If you are faced with a problem which does not seem to be covered by the text you can also telephone or write to the Professional Ethics Department at the Law Society who give confidential helpful advice.

1.3 Part I of the Guide

Part I of the Guide, '*Solicitors in Practice*', deals with the matters set out below.

Chapter 1 of the Guide tells you the sources for the rules, citing the statutory and other sources and the ones that apply to practising solicitors. It is worth noting section 1.08 which points out that a solicitor even in his private capacity is expected to act in such a way that the profession is not brought into disrepute and continues to be an officer of the Supreme Court even when not in practice.

Chapter 2 tells you all the formalities for becoming and remaining a solicitor, including the appropriate regulations for training and continuing education. In order to practise as a solicitor you must hold a practising certificate which is renewed each year on application. Normally, if you are in practice with a firm, the firm will organise the application form and the payment of the fee. You must complete the appropriate number of hours of Continuing Professional Development (i.e. courses and seminars) in order to qualify.

Chapter 3 tells you the rules that relate to the running of an office. These are not things that the trainee has much to do with at first but it is worth reading them through to see the matters that are of concern to the firm. The firm that you join may well have a handbook setting out its office procedures which you will need to read and comply with, especially if the firm has a 'kite mark' or is franchised by the Legal Services Commission.

Chapter 4 deals with the rules for solicitors who are employed by non-solicitors, 'in-house solicitors' as they are more often called. They may have particular difficulties because they, but not their employers, will be bound by the Code of Practice.

Chapter 5 deals with public funding (still referred to as legal aid in this edition), and you should read it whatever kind of work you are planning to do. It is very short. *All* clients have a right to know whether they are eligible for public funding whether or not the solicitor's firm actually offers publically funded work. This is a rule that is often overlooked, fudged, or ignored when firms of solicitors who do not offer public funding take instructions from clients. If it appears to you that a client's means are limited and he may come within public funding eligibility then you have a clear duty to tell the client so, and if your firm does not do publically funded work then you should be prepared to assist him to find a firm that does. The client may, of course, decide that somehow he will raise the money for your fees, but this decision should be made in the light of your advice. Note that the edition of the Guide predates the creation of the Community Legal Service and so the terminology needs updating; the principles remain the same.

This chapter also deals with the disclosure of information that would otherwise be confidential to the Legal Aid Board (now the Legal Services Commission) if you find out that the Board has been misled by the client, or if you believe that the client is insisting on litigation being conducted unreasonably so that the costs are being unnecessarily increased.

Chapter 6 deals with clients who are referred by a legal expenses insurer, and again is worth reading through so that you know what it covers. It too is very short.

Chapter 7 covers anti-discrimination, and you should read it carefully. In particular it is worth noting the position if a client wants to discriminate against a barrister on the grounds of race, colour, ethnic or national origins, sex or sexual orientation, or disability. (Like the client who said, when discussing the choice of barrister 'I don't care who he is as long as he isn't black.') In such a case the solicitor should cease to act if the client is insistent.

1.4 How this chapter of the book is divided

The first section of this part of the book will look at:

(a) What being a member of a profession means.
(b) What is meant by a professional standard of work—the distinction between bad work and negligence.
(c) Where complaints lie and what the sanctions are.

The second section will highlight some of the main areas of professional conduct that create dilemmas in the office and consider the ways of dealing with them. These chapters contain case studies and exercises that you can work through, thinking about the way in which the rules say you should approach such problems and what you think that you ought to do as a consequence. This will not always be the same as your gut reaction.

The third section turns to the way in which the professional rules impinge on particular aspects of legal work, such as conveyancing and litigation and looks at each in context. You will also encounter these when you are studying that particular subject.

1.5 What being a member of a profession means

1.5.1 Being members of a profession

When you become a student member of the Law Society, as you have to in order to take up a place on the Legal Practice Course, you are joining a profession, and this means that you are voluntarily submitting to the rules of professional conduct that govern the way in which members of that profession are expected to behave and conduct their business. This sounds rather portentous and daunting, deliberately, because the rules are strict, and are sternly enforced if they are breached. Even student members, who are not normally in contact with clients and so do not have to apply many of the rules, are still expected to behave in a way that does not bring the profession into disrepute in their personal conduct. For example, breaches of examination regulations would not only be offences in the context of your LPC institution, but also might be taken to be breaches of the rules of professional conduct.

From now on you should regard yourselves as being members of the profession, with the responsibilities and constraints on your behaviour that implies.

In all cases it is the spirit of the rules which is the guiding principle.

The rule that sets out the basic principles from which all the other rules derive is Practice Rule 1:

> A solicitor shall not do anything in the course of practising as a solicitor, or permit another person to do anything on his or her behalf, which compromises or impairs or is likely to compromise or impair any of the following:
>
> (a) the solicitor's independence or integrity;
> (b) a person's freedom to instruct a solicitor of his or her choice;
> (c) the solicitor's duty to act in the best interests of the client;
> (d) the good repute of the solicitor or the solicitors' profession;
> (e) the solicitor's proper standard of work;
> (f) the solicitor's duty to the Court.

This is the fundamental rule. All the others that we will be considering later in this chapter in this section owe their origins to this rule, and if there is any ambiguity in interpreting them, you go back to this rule to test out your proposed course of conduct. This does not mean that you should leave behind your own moral good judgement, but you must also apply and adhere to the professional standards.

1.5.2 Definition of a profession

What does being a member of a profession mean, and why do we need such institutions?

1.5.2.1 Closed shop

To those who feel that it is important that market forces should shape the way in which society and its institutions function the idea of a profession can seem unduly restrictive, because its members claim for themselves the right to monopolise a particular set of skills and the work associated with them and refuse to let other people earn their living in this way. Traditionally one of the reasons that people have been attracted to the practice of law was that it was 'a good job' and handsomely remunerated. The 'closed shop' is one aspect of a profession but it is not its distinguishing feature. 'Closed shops' exist in many other jobs. It should be the least important aspect.

1.5.2.2 Guarantee of standards

More importantly, the existence of a profession is a guarantee of standards to the members of the public who have to make use of the services provided by its members.

The Law Society now ensures, by the regulations that govern the teaching of the Legal Practice Course, that Professional Conduct forms part of the course and is assessed. Before the Law Society's Finals Course, it was not taught as a distinguishable subject, and trainee solicitors were expected somehow to absorb ethics as they learned the job. It is an indication of how seriously it is now taken that you have to learn it and this part of the book has been written.

Over the last 20 years the Guide has expanded from a slim paperback to the large blue book that you know. This indicates the way in which professional standards have come to be emphasised and made more and more explicit. Older solicitors may view this with distaste, taking the line that 'there was no need for it in my day ... it's the sort of people coming into the profession now ... '. It is more likely that the increase in emphasis has been in response to the general attitude of the public who are readier to complain and demand a high standard from members of professions generally. At one time people would have been very reluctant to complain about their doctor or solicitor. It was not the 'done thing' and there was a general impression that a complaint would not be properly dealt with in any event. Although professions may still be seen as closing ranks to protect their own, they are now much more conscious of their public image and the need to be seen to be serving and protecting their clients' interests.

1.5.2.3 Professional qualifications

From the point of view of the public (or what lawyers sometimes call 'the lay client') the most obvious function may be that the professional body oversees and therefore guarantees its members' level of professional skill, competence and knowledge. There are therefore very clear rules about how the people employed by solicitors' firms are 'held out' to members of the public, so that clients should know exactly whether the person who is dealing with their affairs is a solicitor or a trainee or a legal executive or a secretary.

1.5.2.4 Standard of care for the client

The most important function of the profession, however, is that the client should be guaranteed a standard of care from the solicitor which reflects the fact that the client's needs and interests should be paramount.

Although the members of the profession obviously join it in order to gain a livelihood, the money-making motive must be sublimated to the needs of the client in the event of a conflict between the two.

And this is why it is important to be aware of the distinction between the customer and the client. **The client is not a customer**.

In the case of a client, the client's needs must always come first, even though that may not be the most profitable enterprise for the solicitor. By contrast, in a purely business enterprise, the customer is there to be made money from. It may be that putting the customers' needs first is the best way to ensure that the customer comes back, but that is incidental.

These last two paragraphs may make it seem as though the client is somehow to be held at arms' length in a rather distant relationship, but this is not so. Clients will rate their satisfaction with the firm in terms of how they perceive your devotion to their interests. The biggest source of work for a firm is always its existing clients and their recommendations of new clients. You will want to foster this. The ethical framework in which you operate is an important guarantee to the client, and a sensible client will respect this and be the happier because of it.

Sadly, in times when the forces of the market are regarded as having pre-eminent importance, the pressures on solicitors to act profitably and only profitably are ever increasing, and many solicitors feel that professional standards are under threat as a result.

Drawing the distinction between the client and the customer can help us to think further about the solicitor/client relationship. The customer, we are told, is always right. But this is not the case with the client. One of the difficult parts of the job is that sometimes you have to tell the client that he is wrong and should not continue with the course of action that he wants. Some clients will take offence at this, taking the line that 'you are my solicitor so you have to do what I want'. At this point the professional code can be invoked to protect your integrity as a solicitor.

The duty to act in the best interests of the client is not necessarily the same as doing what the client may want you to do. This approach may displease the client, who wants to be treated as a customer, but you have to make that distinction. For example, in a matrimonial case you may have to act for a client who wants to use the proceedings as a way of taking revenge for an unhappy marriage and wants to insist on an adversarial approach throughout. You may well feel that this would only prolong proceedings, escalate costs and make everyone worse off financially and emotionally. You will have to explain your approach to the client. If you feel bound to deal with the case in a different way (as you may do if you are a member of the Solicitors' Family Law Association which has a code of practice for its members) you may have to decline to act if the client insists on pursuing his line of approach. The reason why you may sometimes have to refuse to carry out your client's wishes is because, as outlined in Rule 1, there are other constraints on a solicitor's behaviour that have to be balanced against the needs and wishes of the client.

The preamble to the CCBE Code of Conduct for Lawyers in the European Community puts it very well:

The function of the lawyer in society

In a society founded on respect for the rule of law the lawyer fulfils a special role. His duties do not begin and end with the faithful performance of what he is instructed to do so far as the law permits. A lawyer must serve the interests of justice as well as those whose rights and liberties he is trusted to assert and defend and it is his duty not only to plead his client's cause but to be his adviser.

A lawyer's function therefore lays on him a variety of legal and moral obligations (sometimes appearing to be in conflict with each other) towards:

- the client
- the courts and other authorities before whom the lawyer pleads his client's cause or acts on his behalf
- the legal profession in general and each fellow member of it in particular; and
- the public, for whom the existence of a free and independent profession, bound together by respect for rules made by the profession itself, is an essential means of safeguarding human rights in the face of the power of the state and other interests in society.

In the later part of this chapter we are going to look at how you balance and cope with these potential conflicts.

1.5.3 The implications of the Code in practice

The requirements of professional standards, which solicitors have to take very seriously, can create an internal tension in the management of solicitors' firms, particularly those who rely on legal aid for part of their income.

There is a constant pressure to make sure that work is carried out efficiently. From the firm's point of view this means doing the work as cheaply as possible within the requirements of the rules.

Solicitors have very high overheads because of the demands of the profession. There is a high ratio of staff: in most offices there will be one secretary to every fee earner and there are the other support staff as well, cashiers, switchboard operators, computer systems operators, outdoor clerks, gofers, receptionists. All have to be of high personal integrity and most of them have to be reasonably intelligent. This means that the cost of staff salaries is the major overhead in most practices.

Premises generally have to be fairly respectable. Firms need decent quality stationery and information technology. They need good security and safe storage of documents, including a huge amount of dead space for the storage of old files. This all costs a lot of money and public funding has not kept pace with inflation. Other fees have also been pared down to ward off the competition.

When you come into the office as trainee solicitor you will find that these constraints impinge directly on you. You will be used to keep costs down in areas where someone with legal knowledge is needed but the firm cannot afford to devote someone more expensive to this. You owe the same standard of care as the most experienced member of staff. 'I'm only the trainee' is no excuse. You are in the same position as a learner driver. Your inexperience does not allow you to deliver an inferior duty of care to your client. For this reason it is important that you start in practice already familiar with the rules of professional conduct.

All this may sound a bit one-sided; all in favour of the client. But the rules are there to protect you too. They give you a vital back-up when someone asks you to something that you should not.

Trainees (and qualified solicitors) are quite often asked by clients, or friends, or sometimes by colleagues to do things that general ethical standards and the rules forbid. Things like people asking you to sign passport photographs for them when you have not known them for the right length of time. Or certifying a copy of a document without being shown the original. Or writing a private letter on the firm's headed writing paper for someone who is not a client of the firm. You may feel that it is hard to refuse, especially friends. Clients can put a great deal of pressure on you to help them achieve what they want, which may not always be legal. You can use the back-up of the rules so that you can justify a refusal without letting it seem like a personal matter.

The rules also protect you as a member of the profession from the actions of solicitors who are not prepared to observe professional standards, which, regrettably, may happen from time to time.

As we have drafted this chapter and as a result, analysed the Rules which govern our conduct as solicitors, it has been borne in on us increasingly that good practice as a solicitor is a form of applied good manners, an ethical courtesy which we are expected to observe towards our clients and our fellow professionals. A century ago we could probably have summed this up by saying that we are expected to act as gentlemen. This is no longer a particularly apt phrase, and one might dismiss it as being old-fashioned, but we hope that by the time that you have worked your way through this part of the book you will agree that traditional core values in such things serve us well and should fulfil our clients' expectations of high standards and dedication to their needs.

1.6 Duties owed by the solicitor during the retainer

This section should be read in conjunction with Chapter 1 of the Guide: 'Rules and Principles of Professional Conduct' and Chapter 12: 'Retainer'. Chapters 17 and 19: 'Relations with Third Parties' and 'Relations with Other Solicitors' also provide useful background.

1.6.1 A professional standard of work

The points that have been made about your membership of a profession in **1.5** inform the way in which clients are entitled to be treated and the way in which their work is to be handled. We now look at the way in which you can fulfil the professional expectations that clients have of you. The duties imposed on you once the client has retained your services arise from a combination of sources. They relate both to the legal substance of the work you do—the quality of the advice you give and the effectiveness of the documents you draft—and to other more general aspects of the way in which you provide that service.

Principle 1.03 of the Guide refers to the statutory and non-statutory sources of the requirements of solicitors' professional conduct.

You will need to be aware of:

(a) guidance on professional conduct referred to in the Guide;

(b) obligations arising from the fiduciary nature of your relationship with the client;

(c) implied contractual terms, notably s 13 of the Supply of Goods and Services Act 1982;

(d) any express contractual terms, written or oral, incorporated into the firm's agreement with the client.

Other factors may also affect the expectations that clients or your principal may have of you. If the work you do is covered by kite mark ISO 9002 or takes place in the context of a Legal Services Commission franchise such regimes are intended to promote good management practices or tighter financial control and you will need to become familiar with specific criteria that you will have to keep to. This will also affect what is seen as 'the solicitor's proper standard of work'.

1.6.1.1 With reasonable skill and care

Practice Rule 1 refers to 'the solicitor's proper standard of work'. In asking yourself what this involves and what the client is therefore entitled to expect there are two useful starting points.

Principle 12.08 of the Guide says 'A solicitor must carry out a client's instructions diligently and promptly'.

Section 13 of the Supply of Goods and Services Act 1982 states: 'In a contract for the supply of a service where the supplier is acting in the course of a business, there is an implied term that the supplier will carry out the service with reasonable skill and care.'

The word 'reasonable' when applied to skill and care in the context of the solicitors' profession, does not imply a sort of genial averageness, but instead means a very high standard indeed. It is not enough for you to be possessed of the relevant skill; you must also be sure that you exercise it. This standard is picked up in Section 12.03: 'A solicitor must not act, or continue to act where the client cannot be represented with competence or diligence.'

It is a truism, often ruefully expressed by solicitors, that each client will behave as though he is the only client that you have and expect you to act accordingly. The pressing needs of other clients are not their needs. Each client expects to be first in priority.

Within your client list you have to make daily, sometimes hourly, decisions of whose work you attend to and where the priorities lie, but it is important that your clients do not feel that what they see as their pressing needs are being set aside because of other considerations. There is a delicate balance between being busy—which you need to be to earn the fees to justify your continued employment—and being so busy that actually nothing gets done because you never have time to do the work on a file that advances the case and eventually gets it to the point where a bill can be rendered.

Skill and care in solicitors' firms also covers the way in which work is delegated and subsequently supervised. The partners are ultimately responsible. Their assistants and trainees are supposed to be supervised by them to the extent that this is necessary to ensure that the client's interests are being properly looked after. In turn, if they delegate work to more junior members of staff they must make sure that they do the work properly. But it is not enough, if you are the trainee, or junior member of staff to whom things are delegated, to think that you can simply rely on the fact that it is ultimately your supervisor's responsibility. You have to make sure that you do the work properly, and if it is beyond your capacity and you feel that you are out of your depth, it is imperative that you seek help at an early stage, rather than allowing problems to escalate for lack of action on your part. Some actions, such as the giving of undertakings, you should not do without approval from your supervisor.

As a general rule, in cases where an issue of professional conduct arises, you should first consult the partner to whom you report or your immediate supervisor before taking any steps which involve you in an ethical or professional decision.

1.6.1.2 Fiduciary duty

As well as the positive things that should be done for the client in terms of the exercise of skill and care there are also things that should *not* be done to the client by the solicitor. Principle 12.09 sets this out. The client must not be exploited or taken advantage of. Clients must not be overcharged, or asked to pay more money on account than can be justified.

1.6.1.3 Contractual terms

Most solicitors now make the contract between themselves and the client explicit. The client will be asked to sign a copy of the 'client care letter' and return it to show that the terms are agreed. It is a moot point how often such letters are read in detail by clients or understood when first read. If your firm uses a standard client care letter you should read it to make sure that you know what it says and remind yourself to look at it from time to time to refresh your memory.

The Law Society has, in conjunction, with the Plain English Campaign, designed a number of letters that solicitors can use. These can be located on the web site by following the link under 'Members' on the home page to 'Practice Management', and then 'Client Care'. There are letters to cover contentious and non-contentious work.

1.6.1.4 Without negligence

It is easy to fall into the trap of thinking that provided you are not negligent you are doing a competent job. If you use reasonable skill and care then this should have the result of you not being negligent, but the reverse is not the case.

Most complaints about the way in which solicitors deal with matters are not about matters which have reached the pitch of negligence. Negligence is strictly defined for lawyers as a breach of duty which causes damage which results in the client's loss. Not all careless or inadequate practices by solicitors will result in this but the client will none the less be dissatisfied, and may feel that he has been disadvantaged or inconvenienced by the way in which the solicitor has acted. Clients will often regard something as 'negligent', using the word in layman's terms, because it is unacceptably careless. Although this may not be the tort definition of negligence pointing this out will not make the client feel better.

1.6.1.5 To the client's satisfaction

Solicitors tend to get a bad press. The good, competent things that we do are taken for granted and pass without comment, but as soon as there is a problem we are blamed and vilified. Part of the reason for this is that we are not good at explaining what it is we do, how legal process actually works and what clients may therefore fairly expect from the legal system. Many solicitors are very chary about giving general information to the public. They think that by explaining how the law works they will somehow lose their mystique and let members of the public think that there is nothing to it and in this way lose clients. Perhaps they feel that they could not justify their fees if they explained something so that a client could understand it; it would make it seem too simple.

As a result, we probably start at a disadvantage when it comes to providing a satisfactory service to the client who may be predisposed to be dissatisfied. This means that you have to be extra careful to provide a good service. When you analyse the common causes of complaints that are received by the Office for the Supervision of Solicitors a huge proportion stem from a failure on the part of the solicitor to explain what is happening and what is likely to happen in the case, and to make sure that the explanation is properly understood by the client.

As well as doing the job properly we have to make sure that the client understands what we are doing and when and why. Some of this is just a question of selling ourselves properly, and it may be that some solicitors neglect this because it does not fit easily with their idea of what they came into the profession to do; it seems too much like PR. However, many solicitors do not keep the client informed as they should.

Typical complaints are:

(a) not replying to phone calls;
(b) not replying to letters;
(c) delaying starting an action;
(d) not telling the client when costs have gone up;
(e) preparing documents full of mistakes;
(e) being patronising to the client;
(f) not telling the client what the client should be doing.

Typically complaints will arise when the solicitor is too busy, so that nothing gets done properly, or does not know what he is doing, so that nothing gets done properly, or simply neglects the basic courtesies of life and forgets to treat the client like a human being too.

1.6.2 Best practice

The term 'best practice' has evolved as a way of summing up the sorts of things that should be done in the office in order to make sure that things are done properly. Best practice is therefore more than the Rules set out in the Guide, though they naturally form its underpinning and *raison d'être*.

When you are thinking about what would constitute best practice you need to develop strategies for dealing with the volume of work which might otherwise threaten to overwhelm you, to look after yourself, in terms of your management of stress, and most importantly to think about how the client feels about what is happening to him during the time that you are acting.

The following is a list of tips which should help you to develop good practices. It is by no means exhaustive and you will doubtless develop your own practice rules as you gain experience.

(a) note every telephone or personal attendance in full in writing—preferably typed—on the file at the earliest possible opportunity;

(b) all filing should be done on a regular and frequent basis so that it is up to date;

(c) all files should be kept tidily and methodically (preferably in accordance with a house style) so that anyone can pick them up and find out what is happening;

(d) all time spent should be recorded on the file and accounted for centrally;

(e) all deadlines and time limits should be recorded somewhere prominent on the front of the file and in your diary;

(f) the client should be informed of each stage of the proceedings and each development;

(g) the client's instructions should be sought whenever there is a question as to how the matter is to proceed;

(h) all technical matters should be explained to the client in simple, straightforward terms;

(i) verbal explanations should always be confirmed in writing; and

(j) the solicitor should make sure that the client does understand what is happening.

1.6.3 Client care (complaints and how to deal with them)

This section should be read in conjunction with Chapter 13: *Client Care* and Chapter 14: *Professional Costs*, of the Guide.

1.6.3.1 The practice rule

The area of professional conduct known as 'client care' is governed by r 15 of the Solicitors' Practice Rules 1990:

> Solicitors shall: a) give information about costs and other matters, and b) operate a complaints handling procedure, in accordance with a Solicitors' Costs Information and Client Care Code made from time to time by the Council of the Law Society with the concurrence of the Master of the Rolls ... .

Costs and client care have been brought together in the Code, which is in the Guide at 13.02. This has been amended since the Guide was printed. The updated version is on the web site. Client care and complaints are covered by paragraph 7.

1.6.3.2 Dealing with complaints

'Client care letters' often tell the client how to complain before you have done any more than had the first interview with him. This is disconcerting for both client and solicitor.

Complaints will regularly happen in any solicitor's professional career. Sometimes this is because of the behaviour of the solicitor, sometimes it may be other circumstances which the solicitor cannot control, but the client is not aware of this. Sometimes the client is unhappy because of the whole context of the matter which has caused them to consult a solicitor in the first place, and so small problems assume a disproportionate importance.

Few complaints, however, will need to be dealt with by the Office for the Supervision of Solicitors, or even by the senior partner of the firm, provided they are dealt with early and swiftly, with punctilious courtesy.

If there is a mistake on the file this should be put right as soon as possible; you should tell the partner to whom you report, or your immediate supervisor, the client should be told and every effort should be made to correct it. If this is done it is far more likely to be susceptible of remedy and the client will appreciate what is being done and is much less likely to complain.

If the matter goes as far as a complaint it should be dealt with according to the office procedure as quickly, courteously and frankly as possible. In our experience, a sincere apology, coupled with clear efforts to put things right, disarms the angry client, who is much more prepared to accept that you too are human and sometimes errors will occur.

It is important that you are aware of the steps open to a client who is not satisfied with any aspect of the service they receive from you or the firm you work for. If you are familiar with the way in which the complaints system operates you may well be able to ensure that a client's worries or concerns do not escalate into formal complaints.

1.6.3.3 The Office for the Supervision of Solicitors

If a complaint goes outside the firm it will go to the Office for the Supervision of Solicitors which was set up by the Law Society on 1 September 1996. It replaced the Solicitors Complaints Bureau. It holds itself out as 'the organisation responsible for regulating the solicitors' profession, guarding professional standards and investigating complaints about solicitors' service and conduct.' In June 2000 the Legal Services Ombudsman criticized the complaints handling procedure and the Government issued a warning to the profession indicating that unless the service improved it would be taken out of the hands of the Law Society.

Ideally the OSS will refer complaints back to solicitors' firms so that they can be dealt with internally but sometimes matters will need to go further if there has been serious misconduct or the firm cannot or will not deal with the complaint in a satisfactory manner.

The powers of the OSS are set out at 30.04 in the Guide. Among others, it has the power to:

(a) reduce a solicitor's bill in whole or in part;

(b) order the solicitor to pay compensation up to £1,000;

(c) make a solicitor rectify a mistake at his own expense;

(d) discipline a solicitor for misconduct.

A complaint to the OSS is a very serious matter for any solicitor involved. It is noted in a solicitor's record if it is sustained and a solicitor seeking a public appointment may be asked about any complaints that have been made. The solicitor's firm too will have complaints noted against it, which may be a material factor in the grant or renewal of a public funding franchise.

Inevitably perhaps the largest proportion of the complaints that are made about solicitors deal with the question of costs, so the next section deals specifically with this topic.

1.6.4 Costs

1.6.4.1 What will your services cost?

As a trainee solicitor you are likely to be surprised by the hourly rate at which the firm charges time spent by you on client files. Do not let this lead to you be coy about money matters.

> Many solicitors never overcome their own embarrassment about the amount that they charge, though few go on to lower their fees. Instead a pattern of undercharging, half-hearted billing and poor cash flow is established. Ironically the amount eventually charged is still likely to come as a nasty shock for a client who has not yet confronted the financial realities of litigation. For these reasons alone the issue must be dealt with from the outset with as much information as is possible. (Walker, I., Know How for Personal Injury Lawyers)

The way in which costs should be dealt with is set out in paragraphs 3–6 of the Solicitors' Costs Information and Client Care Code. Paragraph 1 of the Code states:

> The main object of the code is to make sure that clients are given the information they need to understand what is happening generally and in particular on:
>
> (i) the cost of legal services both at the outset and as the matter progresses; and
>
> (ii) responsibility for clients' matters.

You should read the Code through carefully. Paragraph 3 covers how the information should be given, so that clients understand what they are being told. Paragraph 4 states what sort of information should be supplied to the client. Paragraph 5 deals with situations where litigation is contemplated and covers the additional information that should be supplied to publicly funded and privately paying clients. Paragraph 6 emphasises the need to keep the client regularly updated about the costs position.

1.6.4.2 How do you record your costs?

The trainee solicitor often finds time-recording one of the hardest parts of the job to come to terms with at first, partly because it seems so unnatural and partly because at first it is hard to appreciate its function in the solicitors' office. Initially it may seem to you that it is just a management practice designed to get every last minute's worth of work out of you. It may be used for this purpose but more importantly it is supposed to ensure that you are paid for every single thing that you have done in connection with a client's matter.

Time recording generally takes two forms. The first is the recording of the time that you spend in the office on a sheet (or on the computer on your desk) on which you log in the file name and number, and the number of minutes that you have spent working on the file. You may also be asked to categorise what you have done in those minutes in terms of a telephone or personal attendance, a letter or other document. Time is usually recorded in minimum units of five or six minutes. (Six is easier so that you can divide the hour by 10.) As a result it is permissible to charge six minutes for something, like a routine letter, which may have only taken you two minutes to draft. On a good day you may well have only been at your desk for seven hours, but your multiples of six-minute units may add up to far more. This is the reason why solicitors go prematurely grey!

Time sheets will be collated centrally and a record of the time, appropriately charged with your hourly rate, will be recorded against that client matter. You will be able to call up a computer printout which shows the running total of time spent and costs allocated on each matter. There should therefore be no excuse for not being able to tell the client at any given time what the costs amount to on the file. It is good practice, though you need streamlined office procedures to make it really effective, to produce a bill for the client at regular intervals, say every three months, so that he is not startled by the final accounting.

In addition, however, you will find that the printout for each matter is not enough. In litigation matters, where a bill is submitted to the scrutiny of the court—a process called 'taxation' before the Woolf reforms and now called 'assessment'—the printout is little help unless each action on the file has been recorded on the file itself. This means that every attendance, or time spent drafting, or perusing, or collating must be noted on the file, with the date when it was done and the length of time it took and a note of who did it.

It is easy to forget to do this and to assume that the entry on the time sheet will be enough, especially, say, when you have spent an hour reading a file that you have just taken over and putting the papers in order. But unless you write, or dictate, a note and stick it on the file to say what you were doing, and preferably, why, you will not get paid for it. Public funding matters are subjected to particularly tough scrutiny and as the profit margins are so low, you cannot afford to lose a penny. This means that you have to habituate yourself to the discipline of time-recording as soon as possible.

Litigation matters also pose particular problems when a running total is called for. This is because a bill is 'assessed' not simply on the basis of time spent at one hourly rate but by a more complicated scheme where different sorts of work are allocated different rates and routine letters and telephone calls are charged per item, not on the time spent. This means that the printout of your hours spent will not be instantly convertible into what the court will allow you to charge for your work on the case. You (or your costs draftsman) will need to do further calculations before you can give the client a reasonably accurate picture of the costs.

1.6.4.3 Publically funded clients

Clients who are publically funded still need proper information about costs. The application of the statutory charge and the contributions that clients are called upon to make mean that for only a few clients is the question of costs irrelevant. And even if the final bill of costs will not affect the client personally, you have to bear in mind your duty to the Legal Services Commission and consider whether the costs incurred cannot be justified in terms of the benefit that your client hopes to gain.

You will deal with the way in which the statutory charge works in Litigation on the Legal Practice Course, so we do not propose to go into it in detail here but you do need to bear the following matters in mind. Public funding is not supplied free in most cases. If the client 'recovers or preserves' property as a result of the legal action then the Legal Services Commission has first call on that money to repay the costs that it pays out to the solicitor. If the client ends up with money at the end of the case it is very difficult for it not to be deemed to have been recovered or preserved, so the charge will bite in nearly all successful cases unless costs can be recovered in full from the other side. (In matrimonial matters the client is allowed to keep the first £2,500.) Clients find this hard to understand at first, and because they are not having to find money to keep the action going during the case, it is easy for them to 'forget' or not be concerned by the fact that there will be a reckoning at the end of the case.

You have a duty to explain the statutory charge to every client who applies for public funding and you have to certify that you have done so on the application form. There is an information leaflet, supplied by the Legal Services Commission, which you must give to every applicant. Most firms who do publically funded work will also have a standard letter which they will send to all clients when an application is made, so as to reinforce the message. None of this absolves you from responsibility to get a clear message across to your client at the outset. It is probably easiest to explain the statutory charge to your client by saying that it is like a loan which is made to the client to fund the litigation but that they will have to pay back.

You also have the continuing responsibility during the currency of the case to keep an eye on the running costs total just as you would if you were acting for the client privately. Clients have to have a report of the accrued total of costs every six months, even in cases where the charge is not likely to apply.

You should also be clear that you have a responsibility to advise each and every client about the availability of public funding whether your firm offers it or not. If you think that the client's means would qualify them for public funding then they should be made aware of this. Some solicitors will take on a client with limited resources while they can afford to pay them privately but as soon as the money runs out seek to transfer them to a firm that will act for them on a publically funded basis. This seems to us a cynical and deplorable practice as it leaves the client facing a financial crisis and a change of solicitor at what is often a very stressful time. This may be a problem that is accentuated in the future when solicitors propose conditional fee agreements to their clients in circumstances in which the client would be eligible for public funding in any event.

WORKBOOK

1.7 The solicitor in context

This section is designed to be written on by you, contrary to anything that you may have had instilled in you about not writing in books. You should use it as a workbook. You will find that we have not supplied you with answers as such, but we have suggested the way in which your responses should be directed. These commentaries are set out at **1.14**. There are also Exercises, which are designed to get you to formulate your thoughts. These do not have a commentary, as it is important that the responses are your own thoughts, and not supplied for you.

1.8 The solicitor and the outside world

1.8.1 Obtaining instructions

This section should be read in conjunction with Chapter 11 of the Guide and the two annexes to that chapter, The Solicitors' Publicity Code 2001 and the Solicitors' Introduction and Referral Code 1990. You should look at the updated versions on the web site.

The rules that govern the way in which a solicitor obtains instructions are designed to guarantee that the client has full freedom of choice and that the mechanisms of that choice preserve the solicitor's integrity.

Practice rule 1 which has already been quoted at **1.5.1**, covers the point in section (b) and, indirectly in sections (c) and (d). Practice rules 2 and 3 take the matter further.

Practice rule 2

Solicitors may at their discretion publicise their practices or permit other persons to do so or publicise the businesses and activities of other persons, provided there is no breach of these rules and provided that there is compliance with a Solicitors' Publicity Code promulgated from time to time by the Council of the Law Society with the concurrence of the Master of the Rolls.

It is only comparatively recently that solicitors have been allowed to advertise and many solicitors are still uncomfortable with the idea. This partly stems from the fact that advertising makes it seem as if solicitors have a commodity to offer, rather than a service. When the rules on advertising were first relaxed solicitors were not allowed to state their particular expertise. Since the most cogent argument in favour of advertising is that allows the public easier access to legal services, this restriction has since been removed. Advertising also allows the client to find out more about what solicitors can offer and what prices they charge. Solicitors used to be very coy about their fees, but the rules of client care and the pressure of the market have meant that clients tend to be given more information. Over the last couple of years advertisements have become much bolder and explicit about money, particularly no-win-no-fee services.

Exercise 1

Look in your local Yellow Pages directory and find some advertisements for solicitors. Choose three with different styles. For each one answer the following questions:

- What do you think is good about the advertisement?
- What do you think is poor?
- Would it make you instruct the firm?
- If it doesn't attract you is it aimed at a different sort of clientele?
- What image of the firm does it project?

Exercise 2

Think about where advertisements for solicitors might be displayed. Some firms advertise on the back of hospital outpatients' appointment cards. Do you think that this is in poor taste?

- Would your view change if the firm stated that it specialised in personal injury?
- Would your view change if the firm stated that it specialised in clinical negligence?

Practice rule 3
Solicitors may accept introductions and referrals of business from other persons and may make introductions and refer business to other persons provided there is no breach of these rules and provided there is compliance with a Solicitors Introduction and Referral Code promulgated from time to time by the Council of the Law Society with the concurrence of the Master of the Rolls.

When you have read this try to formulate an answer to the two following questions:

Exercise 3

Why is it important that a client is free to instruct the solicitor of his own choice?

What protection do these rules offer to the solicitor, and why?

Now that you have thought about these matters consider the following scenario:

Problem 1

Facts

You are a trainee solicitor. You are walking to work one morning and you come to the scene of a traffic accident. The police and ambulance are in attendance and the road has just been cleared. You hover around to see if you can help and you recognise Mr Davis, an uninjured passenger who is giving his details. He is a neighbour of yours, living just down the road from you. You have spoken to him over the fence a few times when he has been gardening and say 'hello' when you meet him in the street. You realise that he is the father of the two children who have been injured in the crash and his wife was one of the drivers. He is very upset.

As a result of the crash you are late for work. You explain why you are late to your principal, who comments flippantly: 'It's a shame you haven't got your business cards yet; you could have handed them out at the scene!'

Problem 1: Question 1

Do you think that it would have been appropriate for you to have handed out your cards at the scene of the accident? Give your reasons for your view.

Problem 1: Question 2

You had been planning to pop in to see Mr Davis on your way home to find out how the family are doing.

- Do the Rules say that you should not do this?
- Should you take with you your firm's personal injury department brochure to give to him?
- Should you suggest that he contact the firm to get some legal advice?

Having thought about all these points, would you call in anyway as a good neighbour?

Problem 1: Question 3

You do not go round to see Mr Davis on the day of the accident but a few days later you bump into him at the local supermarket and you ask him how they all are. He knows what your job is and he asks you if you can recommend a local solicitor to him. You know that your personal injury department has a good reputation. What do you say to him?

1.8.2 Confidentiality

This section should be read in conjunction with Chapter 16 of the Guide and Annexes A–D to that chapter.

The principle of confidentiality is fundamental in the solicitor/client relationship. A solicitor is under a duty to keep confidential to his firm the affairs of clients and to ensure that the staff do the same. There are some clear exceptions in which this duty may be over-ridden but except where these apply this duty should be scrupulously observed.

A solicitor cannot be too careful in following this rule. Client's documents should not be left in a position in the office where other clients can see them. Even revealing the name of a client (which can happen if a file is left on a desk) and so indicating that you are acting for him can be a breach of the rules. All the solicitor's support staff need to have this rule impressed upon them. While it *may* be permissible to tell a story about a client without identifying him by name, you must be very careful not to include details which would allow someone else to identify who the client is indirectly. You do not always know what is and what is not a distinguishing factor. You should be careful about the company in which you tell such a story in case someone else who hears (or overhears) the story could identify your client.

The exceptions to the principle, which are set out in Section 16.02 of the Guide, fall generally within the scope of the criminal law. If a client wants a solicitor to help him in the commission of a crime, or an offence against children, a solicitor may disclose certain information to the appropriate authority, but such disclosure should only be made with caution and after you have checked the position carefully, consulting the Professional Ethics Department at the Law Society if necessary. As a matter of common sense, if you are faced with a situation where such disclosure seems appropriate this is a matter which should be discussed at the highest possible level in the firm, and not a decision which you should take on your own responsibility.

Problem 2

George Jones, a client of the firm, comes in to make a will and leaves his entire estate to a local charity. He tells you that his only living relative is his estranged wife Jane, whom he has not seen for several years.

He tells you that he is going abroad and he does not want anyone to know where he has gone and specifically that he does not want his wife to be told. He gives you his address in France on the strict understanding that you are not to pass it on to anyone.

A few months later a woman calling herself Jane Jones comes to your office and asks to see you. She says that she believes that her husband used to be a client of yours and asks you whether you know where he is.

What do you say to her?

Will your answer change if she says that it is extremely urgent that she gets in touch with him and wants you to help her?

Problem 3

Tom Slater, a long-standing client of yours who is a petty criminal with a history of minor thefts and disorderly behaviour, comes to see you while he is on bail in connection with a burglary. You are discussing sentencing policies when he tells you:

1. He is very relieved to have been granted bail as it means that he won't miss out on the 'big job' that he had been planning with some friends. They plan to hijack a coach load of teenage language students who will be arriving in the city next week and hold them to ransom.
2. He is also very relieved to see that someone else has been convicted of the armed robbery which he committed last summer.

Are you under any obligation to breach the duty of confidentiality that you owe to your client and pass on any of this information to the police?

Problem 4

You are a criminal practitioner. You are also an author in your 'spare' time and write articles for the local press on legal issues. You have a client called Marie Beechwood who has been charged with kidnap after stealing a new-born baby from the local hospital. She has had a 'difficult life'. She was molested as a child and battered by her former partner and has now at last settled down into what seems a stable relationship, but has had three miscarriages and her only baby died of a cot death when it was only two weeks old. She tells you, and the psychiatric reports confirm, that she was suffering from severe stress when she took the baby.

She feels that her story should be told because she wants the public to know what the terrible pressures are that can lead a woman like herself to commit this crime. She has already been approached by a national tabloid to sell her story.

She asks you to write her biography and to negotiate the sale to the press and to publishers.

Can you write the book and enter into these negotiations on her behalf?

1.9 The solicitor and the client

This section should be read in conjunction with Chapter 12: Retainer and Chapter 15: Conflict of Interests of the Guide.

1.9.1 Client care

We have looked at the way in which the solicitor attracts work from members of the public who then become clients (**1.8.1**) and then those clients' affairs become protected from the outside world (**1.8.2**).

In this section we will look at how the relationship with the client is formed, what the solicitor's duties are when the relationship begins, how long it lasts, and what happens if a conflict of interest arises between two clients of the same solicitor, so that the solicitor cannot continue to fulfil all his duties to both of them at the same time.

1.9.2 Retainer

The rules about retainer—the contractual relationship between solicitor and client—are set out in Chapter 12 of the Guide. They are clearly expressed. It is worth noting, however, that the solicitor is free to choose to accept instructions or not.

Rule 12.01 sets out the circumstances in which it would be right to refuse to accept instructions and what motivations for refusal are wrong. What it does not make clear is that there may be other reasons which would suggest to you that acting for the client would not be a good idea.

Problem 5

Write down some of the reasons which would make you refuse to take on a client:

Now examine the reasons given below and see how they match up to the commentary to r 12.01. Write your comments below each one.

Problem 6

- He wants to sue another solicitor who sends me a lot of work.
- He wants to sue another solicitor who is a friend of mine.
- I don't like the client.
- I like the client a lot.
- The client's a nutter.

Problem 7

> Write down a list of reasons that you think might motivate you to take on a case.
>
> Then, try to think what the pitfalls of such motivations might be.

The retainer does not start at the beginning of the first interview with the client, but at the point where both parties are satisfied that they want to enter into a contractual relationship. If a client makes an appointment to see you and you do not feel that you can act for him, the retainer does not start, any more than it does if the client decides that you are not the solicitor that he wants. However, if the first meeting is followed by an agreement to instruct and to act, the first meeting is covered by the rules that relate to retainer. Even if you or the client decide at the end of that first meeting that you will not continue with the relationship, the rules relating to confidentiality should be observed in respect of any information that you have learned during the meeting, as a matter of professional courtesy.

You do not have to give the client reasons for refusing to take on the case. Some potential clients do not realise that the decision to commence a retainer is a bilateral process and may react badly if you refuse to take on the case. Remember, however, that in turning down instructions, you should still be acting as a representative of the profession, you are still 'in role'. Clients should be refused with courtesy and pleasant firmness. If you think that they have a good case but other reasons prevent you taking the matter on it is good practice to try to recommend another solicitor (bearing in mind the client's freedom of choice), or give the client a list of other local solicitors, so that the client feels assisted by you, if only in a small way.

A slightly trickier situation arises when a client who is already being acted for by a solicitor comes to you because he is unhappy about the way in which the case is being handled and wants to change. Rule 12.07 makes it clear that you cannot accept instructions while another retainer exists, but this does not prevent you seeing the client for a preliminary appointment so that the client can decide whether he wants to change to you and you decided whether to accept those instructions. Effectively, you would be giving a second opinion.

It is only prudent to be extremely careful in giving such an opinion or in agreeing to take such a matter on. You need to see a great deal of the paperwork in order to form a proper view of the case, and this is not always provided. Further, the version of events that the client tells you may be partial, or deliberately edited. If the client has been badly treated by the other solicitor, the client may be very upset and it can be hard to distinguish a genuine grievance from an obsession. Some clients 'opinion-shop' until they find a solicitor who will tell them what they want to hear.

The bilateral nature of the start of the retainer contrasts with the termination of the retainer, where the client can end it at any time for any reason, but the solicitor must not terminate the retainer except with good reason and upon reasonable notice. You cannot simply get fed up with a client and ask them to go elsewhere. This is another reason for being careful when accepting instructions in the first place.

At the end of the retainer, the solicitor's professional discretion to the client remains, and a former client may well return to the firm for further advice in a different area of the law. The potential for a conflict of interest arising therefore exists during the existence of the retainer and thereafter, if a new client, whose interests might conflict with those of a former client, seeks to instruct the firm.

1.9.3 Conflicts of interest when accepting instructions

One of the strongest reasons for refusing to take on a client is that it would cause a conflict of interest or a potential conflict of interest with the affairs of another client or with the solicitor or the firm. Chapter 15 of the Guide sets out the guidelines about conflicts of interest.

At the point at which a new client makes an appointment it is good practice to run a 'conflict check' with the firm's records department to make sure that there is not a potential conflict which would prevent you accepting instructions.

You are unlikely to spot a conflict like this without such a check, unless the client tells you that his opponent is already a client of your firm or has instructed you in the past. Clients do not always know this. For instance, it is possible in the early days of a marriage breakdown for both husband and wife to consult the same firm of solicitors, each seeing a different solicitor. The conflict only becomes apparent when they each receive a letter from the other's solicitor and find that it is the same firm. Sometimes, even the firm's computer will not pick this conflict up, if both parties consult the same firm within a very short space of time.

Problem 8

Mr and Mrs Campbell have been your firm's clients for years, on and off. During this period they have moved house twice and each time your firm did the conveyancing. Mrs Campbell has been prosecuted for not paying her TV licence, some shoplifting and being drunk and disorderly. Mr Campbell has had two convictions for theft, the latter being an armed robbery. Your firm has represented them on all their court appearances, the last one was two years ago.

You are working in the matrimonial department and one morning you come in to find Mrs Campbell sitting in reception with a black eye and a split lip following a beating from Mr Campbell. She tells you that she wants you as her solicitor to get an injunction against Mr Campbell and file a divorce petition for her.

Can you act for her?

Does it affect your answer if we change the facts and say that all you have ever done for them in the past is deal with their conveyancing and the last time was five years ago?

Problem 9

> Your firm acts for Hallam Thursday, the town's biggest football club and have a long association with them which goes back over 25 years. The wife of Alan Whickersley, one of their star players this season, comes to see you and says that she wants a divorce.
>
> Do you accept her instructions?

1.9.4 Conflicts of interest during the retainer

Sometimes a conflict between two clients may arise during the time that you are acting for them because their circumstances bring them suddenly into conflict in a way which could not, at the beginning of the retainer, have been predicted. For instance, two commercial clients may fall out over a contract that they had made between themselves, or a husband and wife, for whom you are buying a property, may find that their marriage is splitting up. You could not be expected to foresee the future when you took these cases on.

In other cases, with hindsight, you realise that you may have created a situation where there is the potential for a conflict to develop. Part of your skill as a solicitor is recognising where there is a potential for a conflict and avoiding it in the first place. For instance, imagine that you are a family lawyer and you are about to see a new client. When you collect her from reception you find that she is accompanied by her mother who has come to give her 'moral support'. Your client is very unwilling to be parted from her mother and you do not want to cause a fuss at the beginning of the relationship so her mother comes into the interview. Two possible problems may later occur: the mother may ring up to find out what is happening on the case and take offence if you refuse to discuss your client's private affairs with her—she does not understand the distinction you are drawing between her sitting in and finding out what is happening later. Or, more seriously, your client and her mother may fall out and your client's mother may feel that she wants to intervene in the proceedings, say to make an application for residence of the children.

Another typical situation is where you are acting for someone who has been introduced to the firm by someone who is in a position of power over them. For instance, a long-standing client of the firm may ask that you act for his daughter who is buying a flat—he will pay the bill, too. You are acting for the daughter but her father keeps ringing up for a progress report. She may be happy for you to keep him informed, at the outset, but her view of what she wants and his may diverge, and you find yourself caught in the middle. If you had made the distinction clear at the outset and explained to the original client that his daughter's affairs would have to be kept confidential by you, you might not have got into difficulties.

Whenever you get instructions you need to be quite clear at the outset who exactly is your client and where your duties lie. Third parties may need treating with discretion and even caution. In a case like this it is a good idea to have a large note on the front of the file to remind not only you but other people who may have to deal with enquiries, such as your secretary, or anyone else working on the file.

1.10 The solicitor and other solicitors

This section should be read in conjunction with Chapter 19 of the Guide ('Relations with other solicitors').

1.10.1 Dealing with other solicitors

Dealings with other solicitors (in this context, solicitors in other firms) can be a source of worry and difficulty, particularly when you are new to the profession and you do not know yet what you may reasonably expect of 'the other side'.

Chapter 19 of the Guide seems too brief at first to give helpful guidelines; however, under the Principle 19.01, 'Duty of good faith', the notes amplify the statement and it may also be helpful to look at the Code of Practice of the Solicitors' Family Law Association which, under the heading 'Dealing with other solicitors' states:

12. In all dealing with other solicitors, you should show courtesy and try to maintain a good working relationship.
13. You should try to avoid criticising other solicitors involved in a case.

You need to be polite, but sometimes firm and to remember always that your client's interests must come first. Sometimes it is tempting to be seduced by the camaraderie of being in the same profession and to be too easy going or confidential with another solicitor in a way which probably does not best serve your client's interests.

Other solicitors should be polite to you too, and not seek to take advantage of your inexperience when you are first in practice. Sometimes you will meet with rudeness or bullying. In our experience, the only successful way to deal with this is to be as silkily polite and calm as you know how. And, if you are on the telephone, modulate your voice so that it is as softly spoken as possible. This often goes against your immediate instincts, but it means that quarrels and arguments do not escalate. When you are writing a letter, always bear in mind that it could (one day) be read out in court, and restrain your language and tone accordingly. You should always remember that you are going to have to have a continuing relationship with the solicitor on the other side, and probably not just in this matter but in future cases as well. You never know when you may have to rely on a fund of good will from your opponent.

If you have to complain about another solicitor, you should see whether this can be dealt with between firms before you think about involving the OSS. This should be reserved for serious matters, and before any such complaint is made it is a matter that you should discuss with senior solicitors in your firm. Not only will the OSS take a complaint seriously, but the firm that is complained about will note who has made the complaint and it may make relationships between the firms difficult. This, in turn, may not be in your clients' best interests.

Problem 10

Your client, Mrs Bradley, is instructing you in a claim for increased maintenance for her son. The solicitors for her former husband, Syrett & Co., who have been persistently aggressive and taken a number of cheap points against you in the case, send you a copy of a letter that Mr Bradley has had from another firm of solicitors, Egdon, Heath & Co., complaining on Mrs Bradley's behalf about his behaviour, and that of his 'mistress' during access visits. Syrett & Co. make a number of sarcastic remarks in their letter about your client's predilection for changing solicitors. What should you do? What should Egdon, Heath & Co. do?

Points to consider:

1. Should Egdon, Heath & Co. have taken Mrs Bradley's instructions?
2. Is the matter in which she has instructed them a separate matter from the things that you are doing for her?
3. Do you think that she has told Egdon, Heath & Co. about your existence?
4. Do you think that you can continue to act if they are dealing with this aspect of the matter?
5. What are you going to say to the client?
6. Is it any of Syrett & Co.'s business anyway?

Problem 11

You have a case on with Charles Pershore & Co. on the other side. You are bothered because they have not responded to your letters for some weeks now. The solicitor in question, Mr Chambers, seems impossible to get hold of by telephone; you leave messages, but none are returned. Their silence is holding everything up; your client is getting very vexed with you. There are no obvious steps you can take at court to resolve the issue. What should you do?

Points to consider:

1. Are Charles Pershore & Co. in breach of the professional code?
2. What can you do in practical terms to get a proper response?
3. What do you think might be the most effective tactic?
4. What would be in the best interests of your client?

Problem 12

> You are consulted by a client who is very agitated because what looks like a fairly self-evident case of negligence—industrial injury, which has left him unfit for work has been allowed to go out of time by his present solicitor, Mr Heath, of Egdon, Heath & Co. He wants you to take on the claim against Mr Heath as this now looks like the only way of getting him compensation. You know that Mr Heath is a great mate of the head of your department, John Clarke—they play golf together and Mr Heath is his daughter's godfather. What do you do?
>
> Points to consider:
>
> 1. Would there be a conflict of interests if you were to act for the client?
> 2. Do you think that in the circumstances it would be proper for you to act?
> 3. If you do act, what problems might arise at a later stage?
> 4. Would you tell the client about the relationship?
> 5. If you did, how would you put it to him? What factors would you want him to consider?
>
> Add any further comments which you think appropriate

1.10.2 Undertakings

This section should be read in conjunction with Chapter 18 of the Guide ('Professional undertakings'). You should read Chapter 18 of the Guide before proceeding with this section. We will look at undertakings in more detail in **1.11.2**. This subject will also be covered more fully on the Professional Skills Course. However, you should be aware of it. Though it does not exclusively occur in the context of solicitors dealing with other solicitors this is the context where it most commonly arises and so we have included it in this section of the book.

Principle 18.01 defines an undertaking as follows:

> any unequivocal declaration of intention addressed to someone who reasonably places reliance on it and made by:
>
> (a) a solicitor or a member of a solicitor's staff in the course of practice; or
>
> (b) a solicitor as 'solicitor', but not in the course of practice.

It is important to note that a declaration does not have to have the words 'undertake' or 'undertaking' in it to have the effect of an undertaking, though if you do use these words you are indicating the solemnity of the promise that you are making.

You have only to read Chapter 18 of the Guide to see that the term is strictly construed, against the person who purports to give the undertaking.

The trap that it is easiest to fall into, without having intended any dishonest or unfair conduct on your part, is to make a promise which you are not actually capable of keeping because the events that affect your ability to keep the promise are outside your control. The most obvious example of this is that you undertake to pay a sum of money by a due date but you do not have the money in your possession. You are relying on the money coming to you from a third party over whose actions you have no control. If the third party does not fulfil their obligation, you are sunk. You are still bound by your undertaking and you, or your firm, will have to draw on your own resources to fulfil it.

Most firms now will have a policy that an undertaking of any sort can only be given by a partner and that any undertaking should be recorded not only on the file but also in a separate log so that the partnership can check what commitments have been made. If your firm does not have a procedure like this it is nevertheless important that while you are still inexperienced you should check the terms of any undertaking that you propose to make with your principal, and, of course, only give such an undertaking on the express instructions of the client.

In the following four cases, consider what promises are being made. If there are undertakings in the letter, are they sensible ones or do they take the solicitors into any traps that they should avoid? If this is the case, how would you reword the letter?

Problem 13

Barnum & Stocker
Solicitors

40 Marsh Baldon Road
Oxford
OX1 4UU
01865 941587
(Fax 854322)

David Barnum LLB. Eileen Stocker M.A.

Your ref: pp/44
Our ref: ES/pw/442
Date: 2nd September 2002

To:
Carstairs & Co.
39 Carstairs Road
Sheffield
S10 5GX

Dear Sirs

Ross v Ross

We refer to our recent conversation on this matter.

Our client is prepared to hand over to your client the canteen of silver which was a wedding present from her grandmother, provided that your client returns to him his collection of Grateful Dead tapes and his Harley Davidson motorbike.

This exchange will take place at your client's home on 14th October at 10.00 a.m.

Yours faithfully,

Barnum & Stocker

BARNUM & STOCKER

Problem 14

Barnum & Stocker
Solicitors

40 Marsh Baldon Road
Oxford
OX1 4UU
01865 941587
(Fax 854322)

David Barnum LLB. Eileen Stocker M.A.

Your ref: pp/44
Our ref: ES/pw/442
Date: 2nd September 2002

To:
Carstairs & Co.
39 Carstairs Road
Sheffield
S10 5GX

Dear Sirs

149 The Gallop, Long Marston

We refer to our conversation between the writer, Mrs Stocker and your Michael White this morning.

We confirm our undertaking to hold the transfer of the above property to your order pending the completion of the purchase by Mr and Mrs Goldenberg which is scheduled for 7th September.

We will advise you by telephone as soon as we are about to complete.

Yours faithfully,

Barnum & Stocker

BARNUM & STOCKER

Problem 15

Barnum & Stocker
Solicitors

40 Marsh Baldon Road
Oxford
OX1 4UU
01865 941587
(Fax 854322)

David Barnum LLB. Eileen Stocker M.A.

Your ref: pp/44
Our ref: ES/pw/442
Date: 2nd September 2002

To:
Carstairs & Co.
39 Carstairs Road
Sheffield
S10 5GX

Dear Sirs

Leigh v Peters

We undertake to pay you the sum of £5,400 which our client will be sending to us from France, in settlement of your client's claims.

Kindly confirm that the matter may be settled on this basis and that there will be no order for costs.

Yours faithfully,

Barnum & Stocker

BARNUM & STOCKER

Problem 16

Barnum & Stocker
Solicitors

40 Marsh Baldon Road
Oxford
OX1 4UU
01865 941587
(Fax 854322)

David Barnum LLB. Eileen Stocker M.A.

Your ref: pp/44
Our ref: ES/pw/442
Date: 2nd September 2002

To:
Carstairs & Co.
39 Carstairs Road
Sheffield
S10 5GX

Dear Sirs

Towcester v Kaplan

We thank you for your letter of 14th August 2001 and apologise for the delay in replying due to the writer's being on holiday.

We undertake to pay your client's costs in this matter, and look forward to receiving your account and the draft consent order.

Yours faithfully

Barnum & Stocker

BARNUM & STOCKER

PROFESSIONAL CONDUCT ISSUES IN THE CORE SUBJECTS

Professional conduct runs through all the subjects that you will study on the Legal Practice Course. This section highlights for you the key issues in each of the core subjects. It is intended as an outline only; in each core subject you will need to look at these issues in greater detail. You need to remember the rules of professional conduct when writing an assessment or an examination when they are easily forgotten in a panic.

1.11 Litigation and advocacy

This section should be read in conjunction with Chapter 21 of the Guide, 'Litigation and Advocacy', and its Annexes A–I. You may also find Chapter 22, 'Alternative Dispute Resolution', interesting. It is very short. Principles 21.02, 21.04, and 21.06 have been amended since the Guide was printed.

1.11.1 An officer of the court

To a layman the obvious issue of professional conduct that arises in this area is the question of how the solicitor can honestly defend the guilty client. (For an answer see Principle 21.20 and its accompanying notes.) Though this is not the only issue in this area it highlights the potential difficulties that may arise. The chief issue of professional conduct which is likely to arise in matters of litigation, particularly in criminal matters, centres on the solicitor's role as an officer of the court, which has to be balanced with the duty to look after the client's best interests.

1.11.1.1 Duty not to mislead

The duties of the officer of the court mean that the solicitor must not mislead the court or be party to a deception. The notes make it clear that when you take your client's instructions you are not expected to do a forensic examination of the truth of your client's case in the way that you might expect the prosecution or the other side to do. You will not as the solicitor be treated as misleading the court if you put forward the client's story in good faith, relying on what he has told you as being the truth. On the other hand the notes make it plain that if there is something in the story which should arouse your suspicions you should check the truth of the statement as far as you are able on the basis that this is being put forward in proof to the court. In other words, don't be naive. If your client presents you with a story full of inconsistencies or holes, check it. You are, after all, doing a better job for your client if you point out the weakness of the story at an early stage rather than waiting for it to be shot down in flames in court.

1.11.1.2 Client's evidence must be checked by client

Any evidence which is put forward by you on your client's behalf, in the form of a statement or an affidavit, must be checked with the client before it is filed with the court or sent to the other side. It is not enough simply to have prepared it from the original instructions. It is important that you make it clear to the client that he must alter it so that it tells his story exactly. Too often, clients attribute a hallowed status to the statement prepared by the solicitor: 'If the solicitor wrote it it must be true. . . .', and do not appreciate that the document is their proof of evidence which will be tested in court.

1.11.1.3 Advocacy and eloquence

You will need to bear in mind the duty not to mislead the court particularly when learning advocacy skills. Eloquence and rhetoric on your client's behalf can lead you into exaggerating the facts, or even making them up in order to plead your client's case to the utmost. When you choose language to emphasise your points you need to be careful that the basic facts are not being distorted. Don't get carried away.

1.11.1.4 Respect for the court—undertakings

The solicitor must behave with respect to the court (and this includes your mode of dress). The solicitor must obey an order of the court and must keep to any undertaking givento the court. An undertaking to a court is a most solemn promise; its breach punishable by committal for contempt. Quite often a solicitor may be called upon to give an undertaking with little notice. It may seem impossible to refuse a request from a court, but unless you are absolutely sure that the undertaking can be fulfilled by you you should explain your difficulty and decline. For instance, you may be asked to undertake to hold a client's passport to the order of the court (meaning that you will not release it unless the court says that you may). This you could undertake to do without a problem, provided you had the passport in your possession. But you might be asked to undertake to produce a document to the court within a set time limit. Unless that document is within your immediate control and you know where it is, this would be a risk. You might get back to the office to find it gone. Without it, you could not fulfil your undertaking. It would have been better to say that you would 'use your best endeavours' to produce it.

1.11.1.5 Balancing your client's needs

On the other hand, this does not mean that the solicitor is the puppet of the court, doing its job in disguise. Principle 21.09 makes it plain that solicitors should not discuss cases privately with judges and the client's case must be put fairly. You have to preserve the balance between the dignity and propriety of the legal institution, and the needs of your client when faced with this daunting institution. Sometimes this can be an awkward straddle. Your client may feel that you are too much part of the establishment to represent him fairly. If you overcompensate to get the client's confidence, you may be in danger of bringing the profession, or your professional reputation, down.

1.11.1.6 Some other issues

The following are some other issues which are likely to arise in the context of litigation and advocacy. This is not an exhaustive list. We have already looked at some of the issues in Part II.

Conflict of interest

(a) Appointment of a litigation friend—the person appointed must not have interests which conflict with those of the person under a disability.

(b) Co-defendants—there is a potential for conflict if their stories implicate the other.

(c) A solicitor must not act as an advocate if he or a member of the firm may be called as a witness.

(d) A potential witness of fact (as opposed to an expert witness) should not sit in a meeting with a client at which the case is discussed, or a conference with Counsel.

Costs

(a) You need to remember that you have a duty to the Legal Services Commission as well as to your client.

(b) The Community Legal Service must be informed of a change in your client's circumstances that would take them outside the scope of public funding or increase their contribution.

(c) You must make sure that each step you take in a case is within the scope of the certificate that has been granted to you and extend or amend the certificate as appropriate.

1.12 Conveyancing

This section should be read in conjunction with Chapter 25 of the Guide, ('Conveyancing'), together with its Annexes A–H. You should also reread Chapter 18, 'Professional Undertakings'. Principles 25.01 and 25.08 have been amended since the Guide was printed.

1.12.1 Introduction

Much of a solicitors' practice depends on goodwill, not only with clients, but also in terms of relationships with other professions and institutions. A solicitor in a local practice (particularly if he deals with non-contentious work) builds up a considerable network of contacts within the business community, with banks and building societies, with insurance brokers and financial advisers. Conveyancing is still, despite the inroads on the solicitors' monopoly and the considerable reduction in fees that can be charged, the bread and butter of most local solicitors' practices.

The awkwardness of English property transactions is to a great extent smoothed by the goodwill and trust which is built up between solicitors and the financial community. This has disadvantages, however; rules can be bent, or even ignored on the basis that they are an unwarranted intrusion. It is perhaps because of this that there are very strict rules which have grown up to regulate professional practice in conveyancing transactions; without them, the scope for abuse would be considerable.

1.12.2 Conflicts of interest

Professional conduct problems in conveyancing centre round the potential conflicts of interest that may arise and how you deal with them. Whereas in contentious matters the existence of a conflict may be quite plain because you have parties who are on different 'sides', in non-contentious matters where the two (or more) parties are embarked on what might almost look like a joint enterprise—the conveyance of a property to their mutual satisfaction—it is easier to lose sight of the potential for conflict. The closeness of the professionals mentioned above may obscure this as well and the clients may not perceive any conflict either.

The rule that deals with this is practice rule 6 (avoiding conflicts of interest in conveyancing). The rule and its notes take up a good deal of Chapter 25 of the Guide, and we do not propose to reproduce them here, but you will need to study them carefully within the context of the subject. You should look at the amended rule 6 on the web site.

1.12.3 Undertakings

We have already looked at the question of undertakings in **1.10.2**. You will need to think about them further in conveyancing, and this is the context in which they most occur in the solicitor's office. This is because property transactions inevitably take place for the most part without a physical handover of deeds or money and so everybody's word has to be reliable and relied on. In cases where there is a mortgage you have three parties to deal with. Over recent years the practice of conveyancing has been more and more regulated by the use of formulae and protocols so that standard methods are used.

In the annexes you will find standard forms of undertaking:

(a) 25B—for use with building societies

(b) 25C—for use with banks.

1.12.4 Fraud

This area is one which is easily susceptible to fraud. Annex 25G reprints the Law Society's 'Green Card' which gives details of what might alert you to a property fraud being practised and the steps that you can take to minimise the risk. Obviously, you must not act if your client is trying to get you to breach the law or the rules of professional conduct.

1.12.5 Contracts

Practice rule 6A deals with the situation where there is more than one prospective buyer. This is often referred to as a 'contract race', because normally the property will be sold to the first buyer who can exchange contracts.

If you are instructed to deal with more than one prospective buyer the rule says that you must, provided your client consents, disclose the fact that there is a rival buyer to each prospective purchaser immediately. If your client will not give consent to this you must immediately cease to act.

You should note that though your client's consent is needed, the fact that you must refuse to act immediately if it is withheld gives your client little choice in the matter.

Rule 6A does not, however, fix any other rules for the contract race, so though the expectation would be that the first buyer to be ready to exchange will win, your client can choose which buyer to go with. As a matter of good practice, you will need to establish with your client what the rules of the race will be, and, if instructed, inform all buyers.

1.13 Business law and practice

There is no particular chapter of the Guide which has special relevance to the subject of business law and practice. This is not because issues of professional conduct do not arise or because a company, as an entity is entitled to any less in the exercise of professional etiquette than an individual client. Rather, the issues that you will meet span all aspects of professional conduct.

The chief area where you are likely to find some difficulty is in identifying exactly who your client is. Once you have done this the normal duties that you owe, of confidentiality and the avoidance of conflict, should fall into place.

A company has a legal persona, so does an individual person. In every case you must work out whether you are acting for someone in his individual personal capacity, or for him as a representative of a company or other organisation. Sometimes a client will have two roles; for instance, you may be acting for him in a divorce, and at the same time acting for the company of which he is the managing director. A client with a management role in a company may instruct you to do something for that company but you need to check whether he has the authority of the board to give you those instructions, or is acting on his own initiative. If you are the solicitor for the company, you will need to make sure that it is the decision of the company that you should take this action. This is not always easy to work out when you are new to a business environment, so you need to remind yourself to be alert to these considerations. It may not always be clear to the client either. The client may not recognise that as far as you are concerned he has different 'hats' and your response to instructions may vary accordingly.

There is an obvious potential for conflicts of interest where people wear different 'hats' or where people are engaged in joint enterprises—such as partnerships or companies—and then fall out. If you have been acting for the joint enterprise you may find that one or other client is suddenly trying to claim your services in a dispute between them. In such circumstances the firm has to cease to act for both or all of them.

There are also potential problems regarding confidentiality. If information comes into the solicitor's possession which is relevant to the client's affairs, the client should be told about it (principle 16.06). The private affairs of a client may sometimes impinge on the interests of the business which is also the solicitor's client. In some circumstances this may lead to the solicitor being caught between the demands of the two retainers with the result that the solicitor probably has to cease to act for both. Note 8 to principle 16.06 deals with such a situation in a conveyancing context but you can see how it can extend to a business situation.

1.14 Commentary to problems

(*Problems set out at **1.8**.*)

Problem 1

Questions 1 and 2

Points for consideration

- You should have borne in mind the Rules that are in the Solicitors' Publicity Code, paragraph 1(*d*). Note that the prohibition about publicity in bad taste in the 1990 Code, is no longer contained in the 2001 Code.
- Mr Davis and his family have a right to privacy and not to be hassled. Do you think that this can be balanced by the argument that people need to know their legal rights (it is estimated that up to 70 per cent of compensatable accidents in this country are not pursued by the victims)?
- Do you think that an approach such as that outlined in the questions might in any event be counter-productive?

Questions 3 and 4

Points for consideration

- You must bear in mind the principle that the client must be free to instruct a solicitor of his own choice.
- If you recommend your firm you should make it clear that there are other firms who do the work.
- Libraries and Citizens Advice Bureaux will have lists of local solicitors and so will Yellow Pages.
- You do not have to be falsely modest if you know that your firm is good at what it does, but you should avoid a hard-sell approach.

Problem 2

The answer in principle is in 16.04. The client's address must not be disclosed. Further, it is a breach in these circumstances even to reveal that the Mr Jones is your client. This might not seem to be a problem in this case, but in other circumstances, where you were holding money for the client for instance, this knowledge might enable his opponent to obtain an injunction freezing the money in your possession.

- What form of words would you employ to indicate that a message, or letter left with you, would be passed on?
- Is it in your client's interests to know what his wife wants to tell him? (It might be that he wishes to avoid service of divorce papers, for instance.)

In any event you should contact your client and tell him what has happened (see the Guide at 16.06).

Problem 3

This problem tends to arouse strong feelings. As solicitors we feel that we should be committed to justice. The rules about client confidentiality are firm, though, and our client must come first. It is important to recognise that the role of the solicitor as an officer of the court does not mean that you are the assistant to the police force, whose function and interests are different.

Look again at the problem and consider what sort of person you are dealing with. Do you really believe what your petty criminal client is saying?

If you do, in Question 1, see the notes to 16.02, comments 1, 3 and 13. You would have to be not only convinced that the client was going to take part but also have enough information from the client to do something about it. In practice, if the client started to talk about a plan like this you would tell him not to tell you anything about it.

With the second question, the likelihood of it being the truth seems even more remote. But note that none of the exceptions in 16.02 apply so even if you thought it true you would be under a duty to keep your client's confidence.

This may seem completely unpalatable to you.

Nobody said that being a solicitor was going to be easy.

Problem 4

Section 16.02 note 2 says that you can breach the client's confidentiality with her consent. So there would seem to be no problem here.

But other things should concern you:

- If she is under stress, is she in a position to give you proper instructions? Might she change her mind later on and regret her decision?
- Might a conflict of interests arise between you as author and her if you are negotiating on her behalf?
- Would it look as if you were unfairly trying to profit from your client's misfortune (see 16.05)?
- What impression would it give to members of the public?

As a cautionary tale look at the real life case of the solicitor for Frederick West:

> Published in *The Electronic Telegraph* on Friday 1 March 1996, © Telegraph Group Limited.
>
> **WEST SOLICITOR CLEARED OVER MURDER BOOK DEAL**
>
> by Toby Harnden
>
> A SOLICITOR who acted for Frederick West was found guilty of conduct likely to bring his profession into disrepute at a disciplinary hearing yesterday but was cleared of trying to make money from the case.
>
> Howard Ogden, 42, who was West's legal adviser for five months after his arrest in February 1994, was suspended from practising for a year and ordered to pay half the estimated costs of £5,000.
>
> The solicitors' disciplinary tribunal had heard that Mr Ogden was so committed to his client that he took him videos and fruit and would wash his underwear. He also looked after West's goldfish for several months.
>
> West said in a statement taken before he was found dead in his cell on New Year's Day 1995, that Mr Ogden's 'main concern was to get information from me to provide material for a book and he was not concerned with my defence'.
>
> West was awaiting trial accused of 12 murders, including that of his daughter, Heather, and stepdaughter, Charmaine.

Mr Ogden admitted two allegations of acting in a way likely to bring his profession into disrepute and allowing a conflict of interest to arise. The tribunal found him not guilty of entering into an improper commercial deal with West.

During West's time on remand at Gloucester police station, the tribunal heard, Mr Ogden and others would regularly discuss how his life story could be made into a book and then a film.

'One police officer, Det. Con. Hazel Savage, was a dead ringer for Glenda Jackson. I was a larger version of Danny de Vito.'

'One way of relieving the horror of it all was through humour,' said Mr Ogden. 'There would be a lot of talk about who would play who, who would be which role.'

There was apparently no discussion about which actors could play Frederick and Rosemary West, who was to be found guilty of 10 murders.

Janet Leach, who sat in on interviews as an 'appropriate adult', was unable to appear before the tribunal because of ill-health. In two statements, however, she described West's relationship with Mr Ogden.

'There was never any evidence that Mr Ogden was seeking to profit from the book. Fred wanted to be famous. He sacked Mr Ogden because he was too close to the truth.'

Three months after West's arrest Mr Ogden asked him to sign an agreement which started: 'Mr Howard Ogden . . . may write a book about my case.'

In August 1994, the tribunal heard, West decided to dispense with Mr Ogden's services and instructed other solicitors. A statement written by West a month before his death was read out.

It said: 'It became clear to me that Mr Ogden's main concern was to get information from me to provide material for a book.'

Andrew Gregg, for Mr Ogden, said that such language would not have been used by West, who was almost illiterate.

Mr Ogden was close to tears as he described the dealings over the confidentiality contract and stopped to sip water.

He said the tapes of 39 hours of interviews he held with West contained the 'unexpurgated version' of his life. The Rosemary West trial 'only touched on the worst aspects of the case'.

Mr Ogden said that when the police decided to brick up West's house at 25 Cromwell Street, he was asked to look after furniture and a wooden drinks bar West had made. 'He wanted me to have the bar and there was a tank full of goldfish. I kept them until they were collected by his children.'

Philip Hodson, chairman of the tribunal, said: 'In the extraordinary circumstances of the West case it is important to take care with all these matters and to observe scrupulous professional standards.

'This he failed to do and has admitted that he has brought the entire profession into disrepute.'

After the hearing, Mr Ogden said he intended to appeal against the sentence.

(*Problems set out at **1.9**.*)

Problem 5

We thought that the following might be included:

- This client cannot afford the fees that this firm charges, and legal aid is not available.
- This client is obviously a 'difficult person' and I am not experienced enough to deal with him without coming to grief.

- This client is not being honest with me and so acting for him is going to be fraught with difficulties.
- This client is very upset but he does not have a case which can be brought to law successfully.

These would all be valid reasons for not starting a retainer.

Problem 6

• He wants to sue another solicitor who sends me a lot of work.	At first sight a refusal might seem to offend against 12.01 note 2, but you might feel that there was a possibility of later embarrassment or that the client might perceive a conflict of interests even if one did not arise in fact. Note the point that you should try to find the client a solicitor who can act without embarrassment. It is proper for you to assist the client in this way without this being a breach of the rules
• He wants to sue another solicitor who is a friend of mine.	More obviously, because of a conflict of interest, this would be an appropriate reason for refusing to take on the case. Note the point that you should try to find the client a solicitor who can act without embarrassment.
• I don't like the client.	This sounds too frivolous to be a good reason. You don't have to like the client and indeed, it would be foolish to assume that you will like them all. Are you denying the client access to justice by your refusal? On the other hand, is your dislike so strong that it is going to affect your performance on behalf of that client? Check that your dislike is not based on a prejudice as set out in commentary to note 1.
• I like the client a lot.	This might not seem a good reason, but there is a danger in identifying too closely with the client so that you lose your professional detachment. The extreme example of this is where you feel a sexual attraction to the client (see 15.04 note 9 of the Guide).
• The client's a nutter.	This may be an honest, if not charitable response. Clients are likely to be nervous at a first interview and this leads some of them to behave in a peculiar fashion. The law does seem to attract, particularly in litigation, an appreciable number of people who have mental or behavioural problems of one form or another. If the client genuinely lacks mental capacity then you should follow r 24.04. More often, you will encounter the client with personality problems, who is odd or eccentric. Some have good cases, but are obviously going to be hard work as clients. Some don't, and you have to use your judgment as to the strength of the case and your ability to cope. If you feel that it is too difficult for you, as a matter of professional courtesy you should try to help them to find a solicitor who can; whether a colleague of yours or someone at another firm.

Problem 7

We thought that your reasons might include the following:

- I dislike (or even, hate) their opponent. Watch out—do you have enough detachment to deal with the case professionally?
- This client has a lot of money and the case will bring in a lot of costs. Watch out—you need to earn fees, but you must act in the client's best interests and not inflate the bill just because you know that he can pay for it.
- This client is a famous person. Watch out—it may bring you in new work if it gets known that you have acted but famous people are often very demanding of your time and resources. Are you so dazzled by fame that you are not assessing the merits of their claim properly?
- I feel sorry for the client. Watch out—all the compassion in the world will not turn a bad case into a good one.
- The client needs justice. Watch out—the law allows people to claim damages, not justice, and they do not always coincide.
- No-one else is willing to act. Of course, everyone should be able to find a lawyer to represent them but watch out—have all the other lawyers that the client has consulted spotted the flaw in the case or the client that you haven't yet seen?

Problem 8

Although you have no current retainer with either client you cannot now act for Mrs Campbell because you have in the past acquired relevant information about Mr Campbell which would create a conflict.

If the case alters you might not have relevant information so that problem would not arise, but you ought to get his consent as a matter of courtesy, because, after all he probably still thinks of you as his solicitor and may therefore be very put out if you now act against him. Also, although you may not think that you have information relevant to the present crisis of the domestic violence, you may have in terms of the financial arrangements between the parties when they bought and sold the matrimonial home. It is probably best to err on the side of caution rather than cause embarrassment to arise later.

Problem 9

There isn't a conflict here as such. The club is one entity and its players are another so Alan Whickersley is not your client and you could act for his wife against him.

However we leave it to your imagination to conjure the scene when he gets a letter from you and goes to see his manager, and the manager ('it's a family club') rings up your senior partner and tells him what he thinks about you putting his lad off his game . . .

It might have been more prudent if you had suggested that she instruct someone else.

(*Problems set out at **1.10**.*)

Problem 10

1. No. If they knew that you were instructed they should not have taken instructions from the client (Guide 12.07).
2. No. Although the client may think that, it is because it seems to be a different issue to her. But it will all be dealt with at the court under the same case number and some of the issues will be related.

3. Highly unlikely given principle 12.07. They would have been most unprofessional to have taken her instructions in these circumstances. So she has either lied to them or been 'economical with the truth'.
4. One of you is going to have to stop acting. It ought to be the firm that came to the case last—Egdon, Heath & Co., unless the client has decided that she wants to change solicitors and has just been slow about telling you.
5. You will have to ask her to be frank about whom she intends to instruct. It would be easy to get quite cross but this will do neither of you any good. Instead, it may be a useful tactic to show her the Guide and explain that it puts both firms in some difficulties.
6. Yes, because they need to know whom they are dealing with. On the other hand there is no need for them to be sarcastic about it and they could have written a much nicer letter. But writing a cross one back will not help you either. It is always worth bearing in mind that one day a letter from you might be read out in court. Are you sure that its tone will withstand scrutiny months or years later and out of context? Don't do something that you will blush for once you have cooled down.

Problem 11

1. Yes. Principle 12.10 states that solicitors should deal promptly with communications relating to the matter of a client, and as a matter of good manners and professional courtesy you should have had a response. There may be a number of reasons, however, why you are getting no response: their client may have given no instructions, their client may have stopped paying them so that there is a dispute as to whether they are still acting, their client may have given them instructions to give you no response, the person acting in the matter may be ill, or may be going through a breakdown. Professional courtesy would still suggest that you are given an indication about why there is no response but you can see why there might be good reasons why this is not forthcoming.

2. and 3. You could threaten a formal complaint, but this might be unproductive at this stage. You could try someone more senior in the firm. Someone in your firm might know someone in their firm who could find out whether there is a problem. You could write to the senior partner and request a proper response. If there is a problem that is personal to Mr Chambers this should have the effect of revealing it.

4. You do not want to make a complaint which will cause a grievance with the other solicitor and rub off onto the way in which he conducts the litigation. Your client has enough problems as it is. Make it clear that you are taking action to protect your client's interests.

Problem 12

1. We have already encountered a similar sort of dilemma in Problem 9 (above) and in thinking about the reasons that might prevent you taking a client's instructions. There is no conflict here in terms of you personally acting, or indeed between your firm and Egdon, Heath & Co.

2. and 3. You have to think about the consequences and look and what the problems might be in the future. Do you think that pressure, however discreet, might be put upon you?

3. It might be sensible to go straight to John Clarke and talk to him about it and to voice your concerns at this stage. You need to be subtle; you don't want him to think that you think that he would act unprofessionally towards you, do you?

4. If you didn't and he later found out, do you think that he would think that you had deliberately concealed it from him? Might he then suspect your ability in other ways?
5. You need to assure your client that he has your complete devotion to his interests at all times. You must assure him that you would do your very best for him. Is he going to be confident in you? If he thinks that he might not be at some point in the future it is probably best not to start the relationship.

Problem 13

The promise about the exchange is not an undertaking. It is a promise being made by the client which is being relayed by the solicitors, who cannot themselves guarantee the exchange.

In drafting such a statement of agreement you need to be careful not to phrase it so that the normal use of 'we' includes the client and so the promise becomes yours.

Problem 14

This is a good example of an undertaking.

The writer confirms a conversation in which an undertaking was given. This should always be done, as speedily as possible.

The precise terms and timescale are set out, thus avoiding arguments about ambiguities.

The further confirmation indicated in the last paragraph should ensure that no later misunderstandings occur.

Problem 15

There is an obvious danger in the letter. The writer is undertaking to pay a sum of money which is not within the writer's control. It may be that he means to say that he will pay it over when he receives it, and only then, but this is not the way in which the first paragraph has been worded.

Problem 16

Unless the solicitors have been ordered to pay the costs personally, which is unusual, the payment of the other party's costs is not their liability so they should not be giving an undertaking about it.

They do not appear to know what the costs are, either. If they do, the amount should have been inserted to avoid misunderstandings. If the amount is still at issue, they should be trying to limit the liability to a finite sum. A phrase such as 'to be assessed if not agreed' would have this effect.

2

Financial services

GENERAL INTRODUCTION TO THE REGULATION OF FINANCIAL SERVICES

2.1 Introduction

The first part of this chapter is a general introduction to the regulation of financial services. The Financial Services and Markets Act 2000 (FSMA 2000) is put into context and the need for authorisation under the Act is explained. What is covered by the general prohibition is considered, as are the meanings of 'regulated activity and specified investment'.

The second part discusses the position of solicitors, specifically those who are regulated by the Law Society, a 'designated professional body'.

In the final part of this chapter, what constitutes money laundering and the relevance of the legislation to solicitors is considered.

2.1.1 Investments

To appreciate the legislation and its effect fully it is helpful to understand what the legislation affects. The FSMA 2000 uses the term 'investment'. It helps, initially, to consider the word in its wider meaning, rather than in the narrower meaning which is given to it under the legislation.

A dictionary definition of 'investment' is 'monies *invested* for income or profit'. The definition of the verb 'to invest' is 'to commit monies to a particular use in order to earn a financial return'.

The meaning which is given to the word 'investment' in the FSMA 2000 does not include all investments in the wider meaning. (The meaning of the word for the purposes of the FSMA 2000 is considered at **2.1.3.2**.)

2.1.1.1 Financial return

The financial return—the income or profit—can be a return of income or capital, income being a recurring return and capital being a one-off benefit.

So an investment is something which will, it is hoped, bring in a return. Monies can be invested in a number of different ways. There are investments which will bring in solely income; investments which will bring in solely capital; and investments which will bring in a combination of both. The return received on an investment generally reflects the risk involved in making the investment.

2.1.1.2 The risk

The risk attached to an investment is the chance of the original money invested being lost to the investor. Some investments carry little (if any) risk, and the return on these is usually predictable and on the low side. For example, a building society deposit account. A deposit account pays a lower rate of interest than that paid on the more usual building society account people invest in—a building society share account—but the deposit account has the advantage that should the society find itself in difficulties the account holder is guaranteed first repayment from the funds available and so the chances of the investor losing his capital are negligible.

Other investments carry a much higher risk, for example, shares on the Stock Market. The chance of a high return, by way of income (dividends) or capital growth, is there, but there is always a chance of the original investment being lost if, for example, the company goes into liquidation. An investor should always be aware of the risk attached to a particular investment, and investors should invest in those investments which carry a degree of risk only if they can afford to lose their original investment.

The diagram below shows various investments building up the layers in a pyramid. The higher in the pyramid, the more risky the investment. A lottery, with no real chance of the stake being returned, floats above the pyramid.

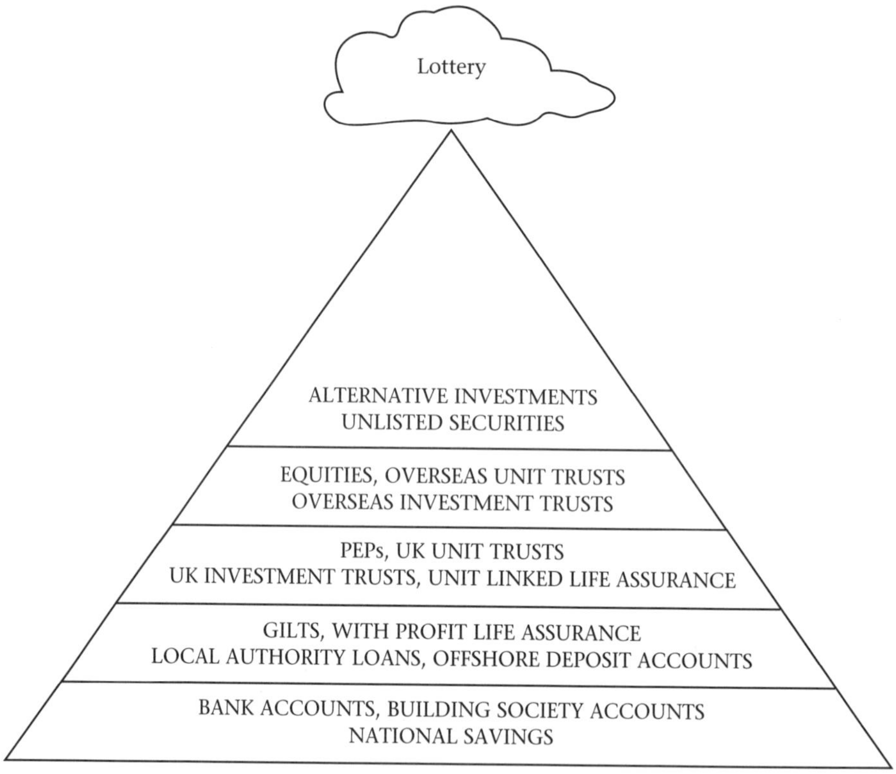

2.1.1.3 Other considerations

There are a great number of investments on the market—bank or building society accounts, gilts, equities, unit trusts—and which investment a person makes depends very much on the investor's individual circumstances and requirements. Risk is not the only factor to be taken into account on making an investment; other considerations are:

(a) will the capital be needed with only a short period of notice;

(b) are there tax advantages which should be considered; and

(c) one consideration which should not be overlooked, what will give the investor peace of mind?

Appendix 1 to this book gives details of a number of investments. It also contains an explanation of some of the 'jargon' used in the financial services sector, with which it is useful to be familiar.

2.1.2 The background to the Financial Services and Markets Act 2000

With so many products on the market, investors often look for advice on which investment to make. Who can investors turn to?

Historically, and until 29 April 1988, investors could look to anyone for advice. The financial services industry was left to self-regulation with no one agency in overall control of the field. There was no requirement on financial advisers to have any qualifications, or for them to be registered or authorised. Anyone could advise a person about investments. This was found to be inadequate and gave rise, in the late 1970s and early 1980s, to a number of scandals in the investment sector, in which a number of investors lost considerable sums of money through poor advice. In addition the investment markets were rapidly changing. In 1981, the then Secretary of State appointed Professor L.C.B. Gower to carry out a review of the law on investor protection.

This review resulted in the Financial Services Act 1986, an Act which introduced measures to regulate 'investment business' and those who gave investment advice (or, in the words of the Act, those who carried on investment business). It achieved this by prohibiting a person from carrying on investment business in the UK unless that person was authorised under the Act, or was an exempt person (s 3, 1986 Act). The Financial Services Act 1986 came into force on 29 April 1988 and, until 1 December 2001, any investment business carried on after that date was caught by that Act.

At midnight on 30 November 2001, the FSMA 2000 came into force, repealing the Financial Services Act 1986. It is this Act which provides the framework for the current statutory regime.

2.1.2.1 The effect of the act

Under this regime there is a single regulator for the financial services industry. This single regulator is known as the Financial Services Authority (FSA). It has sole responsibility and powers for authorising, regulating, investigating, and disciplining authorised persons.

2.1.2.2 FSA's general duties

Set out in the FSMA 2000 are the four regulatory objectives that guide the FSA: market confidence; public awareness; the protection of consumers; and the reduction of financial crime (FSMA 2000, s2). The public awareness objective is 'promoting public understanding of the financial system' (FSMA 2000, s4). The understanding is of the benefits and risks associated with different kinds of investments or financial dealings. One of the aims of the FSA in meeting the protection of consumers objective is to secure the appropriate degree of protection for consumers having regard to the differing degrees of risk involved with different kinds of investment. In addition, the differing degrees of experience and expertise that different consumers may have in relation to different kinds of regulated activity are to be taken into account. One concept to which the FSA will also have regard is the general principle that consumers should take responsibility for their own decisions (FSMA 2000, s5).

2.1.2.3 The general prohibition

The FSMA 2000, s19 prohibits a person from carrying a regulated activity unless that person is authorised under the Act, or is an exempt person. Section 19(2) refers to this prohibition as 'the general prohibition'.

2.1.2.4 Sanctions

The FSMA 2000 sets out the sanctions for breaching the general prohibition. It is a criminal offence (FSMA 2000, s23). In addition, any agreement made by a person in contravention of the general prohibition is unenforceable, and action can be taken to recover money or property paid or transferred and for compensation for any loss (FSMA 2000, s26). The amount of compensation to be paid is set out in s28 of the Act. Further, it is a criminal offence to make a false claim to be, or falsely to hold oneself out as, an authorised or exempt person.

2.1.2.5 Authorisation and exemption

To be able to carry on a regulated activity without contravening the general prohibition a person must be either an authorised person or an exempt person.

Section 31 sets out the categories of authorised persons for the purposes of the FSMA 2000. There are four categories, but this chapter is concerned only with the first—that of being a 'person' who has been authorised by the FSA to carry on one or more regulated activities. The 'person' may be an individual, a body corporate, a partnership, or an unincorporated association (FSMA 2000, s40). To become authorised an application is made to the FSA. If granted authorisation the authorised person is regulated by the FSA and is subject to the rules and regulations made by the FSA. These rules and regulations are set out in the FSA Rule Book.

The FSMA 2000, s38 provides for the Treasury to permit specified persons or those falling within a specified class to be exempt from the general prohibition. An order has been made by the Treasury (the Financial Services and Markets Act 2000 (Exemption) Order 2001 (SI 2001 No. 1201)) which provides for various persons to be exempt from the general prohibition. The exemptions are not comprehensive. However, the detail of the order is beyond the scope of this chapter.

The provision of relevance to most solicitors is that contained in FSMA 2000, Part XX. This grants an exemption from the general prohibition to members of the professions. This is explained in detail at **2.2** below.

2.1.3 The need for authorisation

When is a person carrying on a regulated activity with the consequence that authorisation under the Act is required?

The FSMA 2000, s 22 provides:

> 22.—(1) An activity is a regulated activity for the purpose of this Act if it is an activity of a specified kind which is carried on by way of business and—
>
> (a) relates to an investment of a specified kind; or
>
> (b) in the case of an activity of a kind which is also specified for the purposes of this paragraph, is carried on in relation to property of any kind.
>
> (2) ...
>
> (3) ...
>
> (4) 'Investment' includes any asset, right or interest.
>
> (5) 'Specified' means specified in an order made by the Treasury.

For the activity to be a regulated activity and caught by the general prohibition it must generally:

(a) be an activity of a specified kind;

(b) be carried on by way of business; and

(c) relate to an investment of a specified kind.

There are some activities which do not have to relate to a specified investment (FSMA 2000, s 22(1)(b)).

Regulated activities and investments of a specified kind warrant further explanation (see **2.1.3.1** and **2.1.3.2** below).

2.1.3.1 Regulated activities

The FSMA 2000 does not itself define what activities are regulated activities. This is left to secondary legislation, in that the Act provides for the Treasury to make an order specifying activities that are to be included in the definition of 'regulated activities' (FSMA 2000, s 22(5)). To date the Treasury has made one order specifying the kind of activities which are regulated activities—the Financial Services and Markets Act 2000 (Regulated Activities) Order 2001 (SI 2001 No. 544) (the RAO).

The specified activities listed at present include:

(a) dealing in investments as agent;

(b) arranging deals in investments;

(c) managing investments;

(d) advising on investments;

(e) entering as provider into a funeral plan contract;

(f) entering into or administering regulated mortgage contracts.

2.1.3.1.1 Dealing in investments as agent

This involves the buying, selling, subscribing for or underwriting of securities or contractually based investments as agent.

2.1.3.1.2 Arranging deals in investments

This could also be described as making arrangements for another person to *deal*. Simply recommending an investor to a broker would not be arranging. There must be some active participation.

2.1.3.1.3 Managing investments

This requires involvement in addition to just holding the investments, e.g., receiving dividends on shares which form part of a trust fund which a solicitor is administering; or on a trust fund which a solicitor is administering, deciding whether or not a rights issue for shares, offered by a company in whom the trust has shares, should be taken up.

2.1.3.1.4 Advising on investments

This involves giving advice to an investor on the merits of making a particular investment. It may be distinguished from the giving of generic advice on investments. For example, giving advice on the benefits of a repayment mortgage compared with an endowment mortgage is generic advice and is not caught by the Act.

2.1.3.1.5 Entering as provider into a funeral plan contract

A funeral plan contract is a contract under which, in return for the customer making a payment, the provider undertakes to provide a funeral in the United Kingdom for the customer (or another person). Where it is expected, or intended, that the funeral will take place within one month of the contract then the funeral plan contract is not caught by the legislation.

2.1.3.1.6 Entering into or administering regulated mortgage contracts

The provisions governing regulated mortgage contracts are not expected to come into force until 2004.

2.1.3.1.7 Excluded activities

In addition to listing the specified activities, the RAO also sets out exclusions that are applicable. Where an exclusion applies (and this can be defined by the investment subject to the activity, or by the activity itself) the activity does not fall under the FSMA 2000 and so no authorisation is required. The person can engage in the activity without fear of prosecution. Examples include: dealing with or through authorised persons (RAO, Article 22), unless a commission is received for which he does not account to the client; arranging deals with or through authorised persons (RAO, Article 29), unless a commission is received for which he does not account to the client; funeral contract plans where the plan is covered by insurance or trust arrangements (RAO, Article 60).

In addition to the exclusions set out as applicable to individual activities the RAO also sets out a number of exclusions that apply to several specified kinds of activity. Two exclusions which will be of relevance to solicitors are 'Trustees, nominees and personal representatives' (RAO, Article 66) and 'Activities carried on in the course of a profession or non-investment business' (RAO, Article 67). (See **2.4.1.**)

2.1.3.2 Specified investments

As with regulated activities, the Act does not itself define what investments are specified investments. This is also dealt with in the RAO (RAO, Part III). The investments listed in the RAO as specified investments include:

(a) deposits;

(b) contracts of insurance;

(c) shares;

(d) instruments creating or acknowledging indebtedness;

(e) Government and public securities, but excluding National Savings products;

(f) instruments giving entitlement to investments;

(g) certificates representing certain securities;

(h) units in a collective investment scheme;

(i) options;

(j) futures;

(k) funeral plan contracts;

(l) regulated mortgage contracts.

Some investments which are not included, and consequently are not regulated by the Act, are:

(m) land;

(n) currency;

(o) tangible assets, e.g., art, classic cars, etc.

2.2 Relevance to solicitors

So far as solicitors are concerned, the FSMA 2000 impacts on them. They are carrying on a business; their work involves investments specified under the FSMA 2000 (shares in an estate which the solicitor is administering; an endowment policy being cancelled on the sale of a property and the redemption of the mortgage); and solicitors frequently engage in a specified activity—dealing, arranging, managing or advising. Furthermore, it is unlikely that the activity will be excluded under the Act. They are carrying on regulated activities. Consequently solicitors, on the face of it, need to be authorised to engage in their work which may fall to be regulated under the FSMA 2000.

2.2.1 The Law Society as a designated professional body

The regulated activities that most solicitors engage in are those which arise out of their main work as solicitors; they are incidental to their main work. For example, selling shares in an estate that the solicitor is administering. Under the new regime these activities will be referred to as 'non-mainstream regulated activities'. Some solicitors do engage in regulated activities that are not incidental to their main work; for example, advising a client on what investments to make with an inheritance received. Such activities will be termed 'mainstream regulated activities'.

The majority of solicitors do not engage in mainstream regulated activities but in non-mainstream regulated activities. While it is accepted by the Law Society that consumers need protection, the Society's view is that all solicitors are regulated by the Law Society, their professional body. For solicitors carrying on only non-mainstream regulated activities the requirement also to be regulated by the FSA would not be in a consumer's best interests. The dual regulation would be onerous and expensive. The Treasury accepted this argument and FSMA 2000, Part XX was added to the FSMA 2000 while it was still a Bill.

This Part of the FSMA 2000 contains provision for members of a professional body who are engaging only in non-mainstream regulated activities to be exempt from the requirement to be authorised persons in order to carry out certain regulated activities. It grants an exemption from the general prohibition.

There are a number of conditions before the exemption is available:

(a) the professional body must be a designated professional body (DPB);

(b) the professional body must also supervise and regulate the way in which its members carry on non-mainstream investment business.

2.2.2 Designated professional bodies

The Treasury has the power to designate such bodies, and by SI 2001 No. 1226, eight professional bodies, including the Law Society, were designated for the purposes of FSMA 2000, Part XX. Other professional bodies designated include the Law Society of Scotland, the Law Society of Northern Ireland, the Institute of Chartered Accountants in England and Wales, and the Institute of Actuaries.

2.2.3 The scope rules

The Law Society supervises and regulates the way in which the non-mainstream regulated activities are carried on by new practice rules, known as the Scope Rules. These fill in the detail of the DPB regime and are subject to approval by the FSA. The Scope Rules are considered in Part II below.

2.2.4 Additional conditions to be satisfied

In order for the carrying on of the non-mainstream regulated activities to be exempt certain conditions need to be met (FSMA 2000, s327). These conditions include the following:

(a) The person carrying on the regulated activities must be a member of a profession.

(b) That person must not receive a commission from a third party in respect of the regulated activities, unless he accounts to his client for the commission.

(c) The regulated activity must be provided in a way that is incidental to the provision of professional services.

(d) The investment to which the regulated activity relates must not be an investment specified in an order by the Treasury for the purposes of FSMA 2000, s327(6).

This last condition means that there will some regulated activities that do not come under the exemption to the general prohibition. Members of DPBs will not be able to undertake these activities, even though they appear to fit within the DPB regime. The Treasury has made an order under FSMA 2000, s327(6), the Financial Services and Markets Act 2000 (Professions) (Non-Exempt Activities) Order 2001 (SI 2001 No. 1227) (NEAO). The detail of the NEAO is beyond the scope of this chapter.

2.2.5 Solicitors carrying on mainstream regulated activities

Such solicitors will be subject to dual regulation. The regulated activities they undertake will not be covered by the DPB exemption and so they will need to apply to the FSA for permission to carry on regulated activities. Once granted authorisation they will then be subject to the FSA Rule Book.

The authorisation can be for different types of regulated activities. Which activity will determine what 'permission' is required from the FSA. If the application is made in the name of a firm, approved person(s) will be named. The authorisation will also dictate what controlled functions the approved persons can undertake.

The detail of the application for authorisation by the FSA and the appropriate regulations to which authorised persons are subject to are beyond the scope of this chapter.

2.3 The regulatory regime

A diagrammatic representation of the regulatory regime and the role of the regulatory bodies is set out below.

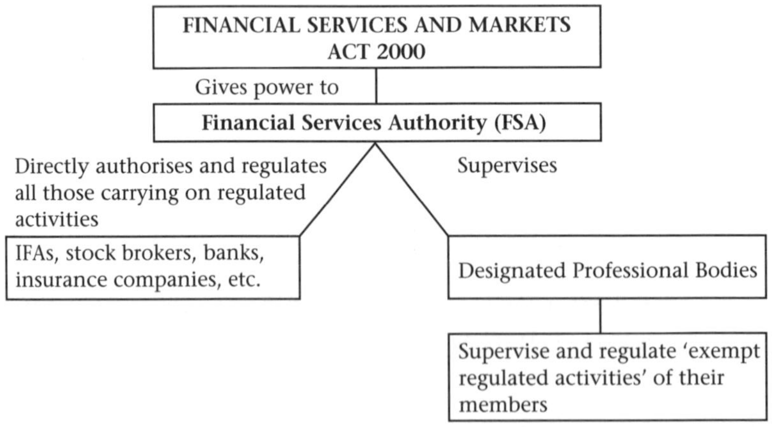

2.4 Financial promotions

In addition to the regulated activities regime and the general prohibition, the FSMA 2000 also sets out a second regime governing financial promotions. Section 21(1) states: 'A person ('A') must not in the course of business, communicate an invitation or inducement to engage in investment activity.' As with the regulated activities regime, the detail of the financial promotions regime is set out in secondary legislation—the Financial Services and Markets Act 2000 (Financial Promotion) Order 2001 (SI 2001 No. 1335) (FPO).

The terminology used in the financial promotions regime differs from that used in the regulated activities regime. For example, it uses the term 'controlled' rather than 'specified'. The activities and investments which fall within the legislation relating to financial promotions are similar to those falling within the regulated activities regime, but they are not identical.

The FPO defines 'communication' and distinguishes between 'real time communications'—those made in a face-to-face situation or in a telephone conversation—and 'non-real time communication'—which would include communications in writing (a letter, a publication or a web site) or by e-mail.

The Part XX DPB regime does not cover financial promotions, and so solicitors undertaking non-mainstream regulated activities could still be caught by the financial promotions regime as they are not authorised by the FSA. There are several exemptions. Those relevant to solicitors engaging in exempt regulated activities under the DPB regime are discussed in more detail at **2.5.2.3** below.

SOLICITORS AND THE FINANCIAL SERVICES LEGISLATION

2.5 Solicitors regulated by the Law Society

The purpose of this part of the chapter is to explain in more detail the ways in which solicitors can comply with the financial services legislation.

There are three methods of complying with the legislation:

(a) seeking authorisation from the FSA directly (see **2.2.5**);

(b) ensuring that the only activities undertaken are those which are classified as excluded under the legislation;

(c) taking advantage of the Part XX exemption, and ensuring that the only regulated activities undertaken are those deemed exempt regulated activities under the regulation of the Law Society in its role as a DPB.

The majority of solicitors will undertake only non-mainstream regulated activities and so the first method will be inappropriate. The second and third of these methods are discussed in **2.5.1** and **2.5.2** below.

2.5.1 Excluded activities

The effect of carrying on only excluded regulated activities is that the activities do not come within the legislation and so no authorisation is needed. There are two types of excluded activities: those which apply depending on the investment which is subject to the activity; and those of a general application, which apply notwithstanding the investment. Examples of the first type are set out at **2.1.3.1.7.** Examples of the second type include trustees and personal representatives (RAO, Article 66) and provision of non-investment services (RAO, Article 67). These two exclusions are important to solicitors as many of the activities solicitors are engaging in on a day-to-day basis will come within their scope.

2.5.1.1 Trustees and personal representatives

Article 66 of the RAO provides for certain activities carried out by trustees and personal representatives to be excluded from the general prohibition. This means that solicitors acting in these capacities do not have to worry about authorisation. The activities excluded include arranging, managing, safeguarding and administering, and advising. There is a proviso to the exclusion. The solicitor must receive only his costs for acting as trustee or personal representative; no additional remuneration must be received by him. In addition, the arranging or advising must be for or to a fellow trustee or personal representative, or for or to a beneficiary under the trust or will, or on intestacy.

2.5.1.2 Provision of non-investment services

The activities of dealing as agent, arranging, safeguarding and administering, and advising, when carried on in the course of a profession and when such that they might reasonably be regarded as a necessary part of other services provided in the course of that profession, are excluded from the general prohibition. As with the exclusion for trustees and personal representatives, the solicitor must not receive additional remuneration for the activity. This exclusion will apply, for example, when arranging the assignment of an endowment policy in connection with a conveyancing transaction, or when arranging the sale of all the assets in an estate when administering it. However, where a decision has to be made as to which assets should be sold and which retained, it would be advisable to seek the advice of an authorised person.

2.5.2 Solicitors regulated by the Law Society as a designated professional body

The Law Society is a designated professional body (DPB). As such it takes on the responsibility for regulating and supervising the way in which its members carry on non-mainstream regulated activities.

The Solicitors' Financial Services (Scope) Rules 2001 (the Scope Rules) and the Solicitors' Financial Services (Conduct of Business) Rules 2001 (the Conduct of Business Rules) set out the framework for the regulation. The Scope Rules set out the scope of the regulated activities which may be undertaken by solicitors. The Conduct of Business Rules regulate the way in which the exempt regulated activities are carried on.

2.5.2.1 Scope Rules

The Solicitors' Financial Services (Scope) Rules 2001 are reproduced in **Appendix 2**. The Scope Rules have been clearly drafted and are, with the Conduct of Business Rules, perhaps the most easily understood part of the financial services legislation affecting solicitors undertaking non-mainstream regulated activities. In addition, the Law Society has issued guidance notes for the Rules. These should be read with the Rules and are also reproduced in **Appendix 2**.

The Scope Rules set out the conditions and restrictions with which solicitors' firms seeking to rely on the DPB regime must comply when carrying on regulated activities. They also prohibit solicitors from carrying on certain regulated activities and set out the effect of a breach of the Rules.

The Scope Rules and their guidance notes should be read in full. However, three of the conditions warrant specific mention. A firm which carries on any regulated activities must ensure that:

(a) the activities arise out of, or are complementary to, the provision of a particular professional service to a particular client;

(b) the manner of the provision by the firm of any service in the course of carrying on the activities is incidental to the provision by the firm of professional services;

(c) the firm accounts to the client for any pecuniary reward or other advantage which the firm receives from a third party. (Scope Rules 4(a), (b), (c))

Guidance notes 1, 2, and 3 explain the implications of these three conditions (see **Appendix 2**).

At **2.2.4** it was pointed out that FSMA 2000, s327 sets out additional conditions which need to be met in order for the carrying on of the non-mainstream regulated activities to be exempt. Compliance with the Scope Rules will ensure that these additional conditions are also met.

2.5.2.2 Conduct of Business Rules

The Solicitors' Financial Services (Conduct of Business) Rules 2001 are reproduced in **Appendix 3**. As with the Scope Rules (see **2.5.2.1** above), the Law Society has issued guidance notes which should be read with the Rules. These are also reproduced in **Appendix 3**. The Conduct of Business Rules are easy to understand and are almost minimalist in nature, the approach of the Law Society being that exempt regulated activities should be covered so far as possible by the existing professional conduct rules.

As with the Scope Rules, the Conduct of Business Rules and their guidance notes should be read in full. They set out what information clients must receive, how transactions should be effected, what records must be kept (including records of the transactions and any commissions received), and details of the safekeeping of clients' investments.

The Conduct of Business Rules apply only to solicitors relying on the DBP regime. However, it is recommended that firms relying on an exclusion to ensure that they are not breaching the FSMA 2000 also comply with the Rules as the distinction between the two methods of compliance is very fine.

2.5.2.3 Financial promotions

Solicitors carrying on exempt regulated activities under the DBP regime must be aware of the implications of the financial promotions regime as regulated by the Financial Promotions Order (SI 2001 No. 1335 as amended) (FPO: see **2.4**). As they are not authorised by the FSA they will be subject to the restriction on financial promotions. They will have to ensure either that the content of the communication is approved by an authorised person (if it is not a real time communication, as authorised persons are prohibited from approving real time communications for unauthorised persons), or that the communication comes within an exemption. There are two relevant exemptions, one dealing with real time communications and the second dealing with non-real time communications. Together these two exemptions should cover most communications to clients.

2.5.2.3.1 Real time communications

The exemption covering these communications is contained in Article 55 of the FPO. Briefly, the communication will be exempt provided the solicitor is relying on the DPB exemption; the person to whom the communication is made is an existing client; and the activity to which the communication relates is incidental to the provision of professional services and either is excluded under Article 67 of the RAO (provision of non-investment services: see **2.5.1.2**) or is an exempt regulated activity by virtue of the DPB exemption.

2.5.2.3.2 Non-real time communications

The exemption covering these communications is contained in Article 55A of the FPO as amended. Where non-real time communications are concerned, the communication will be exempt provided the solicitor is relying on the DPB exemption and the communication includes a specified statement. The statement is set out in guidance note 3.5 to the Solicitors' Financial Services (Conduct of Business) Rules 2001 (reproduced in **Appendix 3**).

2.6 Conclusion

Where a solicitor is carrying on regulated activities the flow chart that follows sets out the questions to be asked to determine whether the activities come within the financial services regime, whether they are excluded and so no authorisation is required, or whether they will be exempt regulated activities under the DPB regime.

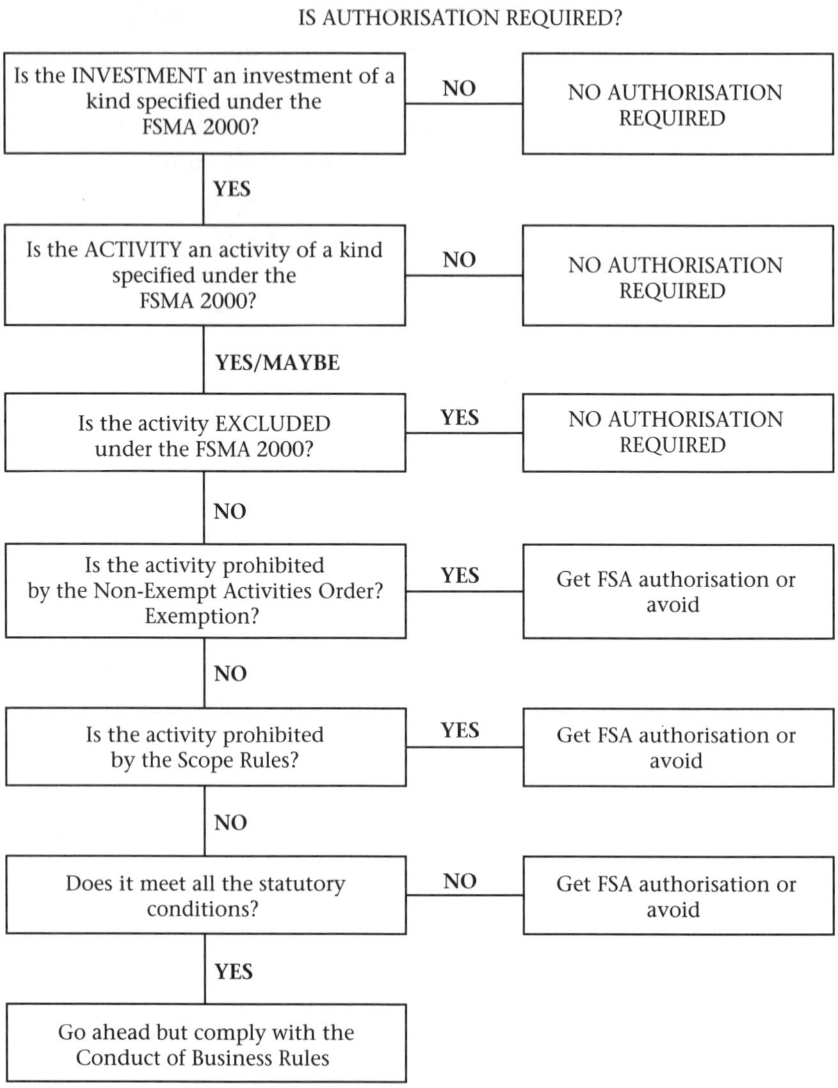

MONEY LAUNDERING

2.7 Money Laundering Regulations 1993

It is important for all solicitors to be aware of their potential to be involved, usually unwittingly, in a money laundering scheme. The Criminal Justice Act 1993 (CJA 1993) contains detailed provisions making it a criminal offence to assist anyone whom you know or suspect to be laundering money generated from crime. The substantive details of the relevant provisions of CJA 1993 and the other legislation to which it relates are contained in the Guide Annex 16B.

It is also important to be aware of other substantive legislation contained in the Criminal Justice (International Cooperation) Act 1990, the Northern Ireland (Emergency Provisions) Act 1991, the Proceeds of Crime Act 1995 (as it amends the Criminal Justice Act 1988), and the Anti-Terrorism, Crime and Security Act 2001.

Additionally, a solicitor who becomes involved in money laundering may become a constructive trustee of the proceeds and, as such, liable to any loser. The Court of Appeal has also given guidance on how to deal with monies where there is a suspicion of money laundering (*Governor and Company of the Bank of Scotland v A Limited and Others* [2001] 3 All ER 182). Details of the guidance contained in Lord Woolf's judgment are outside the scope of this book.

Solicitors should be conversant with the Money Laundering Regulations 1993 SI 1993 No. 1933 (MLR) which came into effect on 1 April 1994. The MLR are part of a concerted effort to make it more difficult for the proceeds of crime to be laundered. Essentially they set out rules to be followed by anyone engaging in 'relevant business' within the definition of the MLR.

2.7.1 Money laundering

Before looking at details of the MLR it is helpful to understand what is meant by money laundering. Essentially it is the process by which 'dirty' monies, i.e. the proceeds of crime, are 'washed' to give them the appearance of 'clean' money.

There are three stages in a money laundering transaction: placement, layering, and integration.

2.7.2 Stage one: Placement

This is the stage at which the cash proceeds of the crime are put into a non-cash asset, for example, buying investments with cash or buying a property with cash. Alternatively the money may be initially paid into a series of bank accounts. This stage will be the most difficult for the criminal because he will be disposing of cash. The initial cash may also be taken and invested 'off shore', i.e. taken out of the country and reintroduced to the country at the layering stage. This asset is then sold, or the money withdrawn from the bank, to enable layering to take place.

2.7.3 Stage two: Layering

To avoid the money being readily traceable, the money will be passed through many transactions to create a trail which is not easily followed by the authorities. Money launderers may seek to pass money through a solicitor's client account as part of 'layering'. Law Society guidance makes it clear that money should be passed through the client account only where there is 'a genuine underlying legal transaction or some other valid reason to hold clients' money'.

2.7.4 Stage three: Integration

The final stage is for the money to pass into a legitimate business or investment. By this stage, from the criminal's point of view, the proceeds will, it is hoped, not be readily traceable back to the proceeds of the original crime.

2.7.5 Blue card warning

The Law Society has issued a warning to all solicitors alerting them to circumstances in which they might be assisting money laundering ('blue card warning', the Guide

Annex 16D). The warning signs highlighted on the blue card warning include:

(a) unusual settlement requests, for example payment for a property with large sums of cash or by a third-party cheque (not being a cheque from a recognisable institution), or money being transferred from a third party;

(b) unusual instructions, for example long-distance clients who have no apparent reason for instructing your firm;

(c) requests to hold large sums of cash for no apparent reason, particularly where you are asked to issue a cheque to return the cash, or are asked to transmit the funds to a third party for no apparent reason;

(d) secretive clients, for example clients who are reluctant to provide their details of identity, and in particular where you have not met the client;

(e) suspect territory, for example where a client is introduced by an overseas bank or third party based in a country where drug trafficking may be prevalent.

2.7.6 Matters of conduct

Principle 3.16 of the Guide requires all principals in private practice to 'consider what procedure should be instituted to comply with the MLR'. In particular it recommends procedures which should be implemented to reflect the requirements of the MLR.

It is also important to remember that a solicitor's duties of confidentiality and disclosure are varied by the statutory provisions relating to money laundering (the Guide, Principle 16.07).

As the Guide points out, the legislation requires solicitors to be alert to the possibilities of money laundering and to make further enquiries of clients, if appropriate. It does not require solicitors to suspect their clients of money laundering without cause. Where there is suspected money laundering the legislation does require it to be reported to the appropriate authority (see the CJA 1993 and MLR, reg 14). If a solicitor is aware a report has been made to the authorities, or that an investigation into money laundering is being made, he must not disclose this to the client without the consent of the appropriate authority. If he does disclose such information to the client without consent he may be guilty of an offence under the appropriate legislation (the Guide Annex 16B).

2.7.7 The Money Laundering Regulations 1993

The MLR are set out in full in the Guide Annex 3B. The MLR apply to anyone who carries on 'relevant financial business' and where there is a 'business relationship' or a 'one-off transaction'.

2.7.8 Relevant financial business

Regulation 4 of the MLR sets out what constitutes 'relevant financial business'. There are two paragraphs with which solicitors need to be particularly concerned. These are reg 4(1)(f) and (h).

Regulation 4(1)(f) defines 'relevant financial business' as 'investment business within the meaning of the Financial Services Act 1986'. The implementation of the FSMA has led to the definition being amended to certain 'regulated activities'. Most firms of solicitors will fall within the scope of the regulations even if they only conduct non-mainstream investment business.

Regulation 4(1)(h) includes within the definition 'any of the activities in points 1 to 12, or point 14, of the annex to the Second Banking Coordination Directive.' Of these points those of particular relevance to solicitors are:

(a) point 1: acceptance of deposits and other repayable funds from the public;

(b) point 4: money transmission services;

(c) point 9: advice to undertakings on capital structure, industrial strategy and related questions and advice and services relating to mergers and the purchase of undertakings; and

(d) point 14: safe custody services.

2.7.9 Business relationship

Regulation 3(2) defines 'business relationship' as 'any relationship between one or more persons where:

(a) the purpose of the arrangement is to facilitate the carrying out of transactions between the persons concerned on a frequent, habitual, or regular basis; and

(b) the total amount of any payment or payments to be made by any person to any other in the course of that arrangement is not known or capable of being ascertained at the time the arrangement is made'.

To fall within the scope of 'an arrangement' at least one party must be acting in the course of a business.

2.7.10 One-off transaction

Regulation 2(1) defines a 'one-off transaction' as 'any transaction other than a transaction carried out in the course of an established business relationship formed by a person acting in the course of relevant financial business.'

Having established that solicitors carry on relevant financial business it is clear to see that in their everyday dealing they will be involved in both business relationships and one-off transactions for the purposes of the Regulations. Accordingly they will be required to comply with the rules.

2.7.11 Compliance with the MLR

Regulation 5 of the MLR contains the main thrust of the Regulations, but it is important to be fully conversant with the Regulations as a whole.

Regulation 5 of the MLR requires the implementation of the following procedures:

(a) identification procedures, e.g. on the introduction of a new client the production of evidence of the client's identity in the form of a passport, driving licence, birth certificate or other documentary evidence. Clearly the best form of identification will be in the form of something not easily forged and which contains a photograph. If the client is a limited company then, unless it is listed on the Stock Exchange, it may be appropriate to carry out a company search to establish full details of its identity. The full requirements for identification are set out in regs 7 and 9. Regulation 10 give details of certain exemptions to the identification requirements;

(b) *record-keeping procedures*. These are set out in reg 12 and include keeping full details of evidence of identity and of all relevant transactions for a period of at least five years from the date of completion of the relevant business;

(c) *internal reporting systems*. Regulation 14 sets out in detail the reporting requirements, which include appointing an appropriate person to whom reports of suspicions or knowledge of money laundering should be made. It also includes details of procedure to be followed and information to be made available to the responsible person. Of most importance is the requirement to make the information available to a constable (who is anyone so designated by the Customs and Excise). Currently this is satisfied by reporting to the Financial Unit at the National Criminal Intelligence Service. The Law Society has recommended that as a matter of best practice all firms should appoint a Money Laundering Reporting Officer even if they are not currently required to have one;

(d) other appropriate internal control and communication procedures;

(e) an obligation to make employees aware of their duties in handling relevant financial affairs and the applicable legislation; and

(f) an obligation to train employees in the recognition of potential money laundering transactions.

Failure to comply with reg 5 of the MLR is a criminal offence, although the regulation sets out factors that may be taken into account by the court in determining whether the accused has complied with the Regulations.

The implementation of the FSMA 2000 has also led to changes for solicitors. Solicitors who conduct mainstream financial services and who are regulated directly by the FSA must also comply with the FSA's Money Laundering Sourcebook.

2.7.12 The future

The Second European Money Laundering Directive, which has yet to be introduced into UK legislation, and the Proceeds of Crime Bill will further extend solicitors' obligations in relation to money laundering.

EC law

3

EC Law

THE COMMUNITY, ITS INSTITUTIONS AND EC LAW

3.1 Introduction

It is imperative that all lawyers today have an understanding of the law of the European Community as it impacts on many areas of current law and failure to advise on European law could open solicitors to negligence claims and disciplinary actions.

3.2 The origins of the European Community

Although the European Economic Community came into being following the signing of the Treaty of Rome in 1957, the origins can be traced back to 1946 when Winston Churchill called for European unity following the end of the Second World War. In 1948, 16 west-European countries signed a treaty creating the Organisation of European Economic Cooperation. This was followed in 1949 by the signing of the North Atlantic Treaty Organisation. The Treaty of Rome came into force on 1 January 1958. It was signed by the six original member states: Belgium, The Netherlands, Luxembourg, Italy, France and Germany. These six states were already signatories to the European Coal and Steel Community Treaty in Paris in 1951, the ECSC being the role model for the EEC. The ECSC created a single market for coal and steel only and the EEC was designed to create an economic community not covered by the other communities, namely ECSC and Euratom. Euratom (European Atomic Energy Committee) was created to raise living standards through the establishment and growth of nuclear industries and was signed at the same time as the Treaty of Rome. In 1965, the Merger Treaty effectively merged the institutions of the EEC and ECSC. The EEC Treaty is essentially a 'framework' treaty as it sets out in broad principles the aims, leaving the political institutions of the Community to fill the gaps with secondary legislation. In 1973, the UK, Ireland and Denmark joined the Community. Norway was also meant to join but a national referendum showed that a majority of the electorate was opposed so Norway pulled out. The Treaty of Accession was incorporated into UK law by the European Communities Act 1972. In 1979, Greece signed an Act of Succession and was followed by Spain and Portugal in 1986 bringing the total number of member states to 12. In 1986, there was an important development when the 12 member states signed the Single European Act. The purpose of this Act was to eliminate the remaining barriers to achieve a single internal market and it also introduced a number of procedural changes to accelerate the community decision-making process. In 1991, the Treaty on European Union was signed at Maastricht. Briefly it:

(a) extends the scope of Community competence;

(b) contains common foreign and security policy through inter-governmental cooperation including a pledge by member states to full economic and monetary policy;

(c) contains provisions on justice and home affairs, for example, a common policy on asylum, judicial cooperation in criminal matters, international fraud and drug trafficking; and

(d) increases the powers of the European Parliament by creating a procedure called 'codecision' which gives it the power of veto in some matters.

Also in 1991, the European Economic Area Treaty was created which extends the single market to the EFTA (European Free Trade Association) countries of Finland, Sweden, Norway, Austria, Iceland and Liechtenstein. In 1995, Austria, Finland and Sweden joined the EC.

The Amsterdam Treaty came into force on 1 May 1999. It is part of the ongoing process to update the Treaties of Europe. It builds on the European integration achieved so far and follows on from the Single European Act and the Maastricht Treaty.

The Amsterdam Treaty provides new powers for the EU in a range of areas to protect the citizens of Europe and to improve our standards of living by looking at a variety of areas. Broadly, there are new measures to tackle the problems of crime and drugs, workers' rights, discrimination, equality and unemployment. The protection of the environment has become a core objective of the EU in addition to establishing consumer protection as a priority. The EU is committed to a high level of human health and has been given new powers to combat poverty.

In addition, Article 12 of the Amsterdam Treaty renumbers the various Articles of the EC Treaty and the Treaty on European Union in an effort to simplify the various different references. The previous and new numbering equivalents are set out in **3.30** below in so far as are relevant to these chapters.

3.3 The institutions

The European Union is made up of the following institutions:

(a) the European Commission (**3.3.1**);

(b) the Council of the European Union (**3.3.2**);

(c) the European Parliament or Assembly (**3.3.3**);

(d) the European Court of Justice (**3.3.4**);

(e) the European Court of Auditors (**3.3.5**);

(f) the European Investment Bank (**3.3.6**);

(g) the Economic and Social Committee (**3.3.7**);

(h) the Committee of the Regions (**3.3.8**);

(i) the European Ombudsman (**3.3.9**); and

(j) the European Monetary Institute (**3.3.10**).

The Council and the Commission provide the main day-to-day impetus in the Community's decision-making process. The Commission makes policy proposals after consulting a wide range of experts or interested parties; the Council takes the final decision after consulting the European Parliament and the Economic and Social Committee and after discussions in the Committee of Permanent Representatives (COREPER).

3.3.1 The European Commission

The Commission is made up of 20 members who are appointed jointly by the member governments for a five-year renewable term. The bigger countries such as France and the

UK have two members and the smaller states, one. The Commission is headed by a President chosen by the Commissioners and appointed for a two-year renewable term. Once appointed, the Commissioners become independent of their national government and are required to act in the interests of the Union as a whole. Each Commissioner is responsible for a particular area of Community policy, e.g., the environment or competition law.

The Commission has four main functions:

(a) to initiate Community action;

(b) to act as a watchdog and in the last resort take member states, firms or individuals to the European Court for infringements of EC law;

(c) to ensure that policy decisions taken by the Council are implemented; and

(d) to act as a mediator between governments steering its policy decisions through the Council.

Decisions within the Commission are taken on a simple majority vote and the Commission is collectively answerable to the European Parliament.

3.3.2 The Council of the European Union

The Council of the European Union or the Council of Ministers as it is more usually known is the decision-making body of the European Union and the principal forum for negotiating legislation. It consists of one representative from each member state appointed by governments. Its composition will depend on the matter under discussion. The Presidency is held for a term of six months and is rotated alphabetically through the member states as spelt in their own language. The Single European Act requires the Council to meet twice a year. The Council receives proposals from COREPER (see **1.3**). Items on the agenda are divided into 'A' and 'B' issues. 'A' items are where there are no controversial issues and therefore require only formal approval. 'B' items require Council discussion. The Council has to decide on these proposals. Voting can be by simple majority, qualified majority or unanimity. Where vital national interests are at stake, a member state may insist on a unanimous vote. Otherwise, measures can be agreed by a qualified majority which requires 62 votes and a combination of large and small countries in favour of the proposal.

3.3.3 The European Parliament

This is the only Community Institution which meets and debates in public. Its Members are directly elected by the citizens of each member country. Each MEP serves for a five-year term. Members sit in political groups of which there are currently eight, not in national delegations. The number of MEPs which each member state has depends on its size. Each MEP is required to vote on an individual and personal basis. The main task of the Parliament is to monitor the work of the Council and the Commission. It has to be consulted on most Commission proposals before the Council gives its final approval. The Parliament must respond to the proposal within a reasonable time and the Council must take its responses into account but is not bound by them. The Maastricht Treaty provides for a joint decision-making procedure in certain areas and the right to initiate legislation, though it is limited to a narrow range of decisions. The Parliament has three other powers:

(a) it can dismiss the Commission by a two-thirds majority, although it has never done so;

(b) it is responsible for drawing up the preliminary draft budget; and

(c) it has the right to bring actions before the European Court of Justice.

The Amsterdam Treaty has extended the range of policies in which the Parliament will take decisions jointly with the Council of Ministers and Parliament now has the right to approve or reject the nomination of the Commission President.

3.3.4 The European Court of Justice

There are 15 independent judges assisted by eight Advocates-General and a President of the Court. They are all appointed jointly by member states for six-year renewable terms. The President is elected from amongst the judges for a three-year term. The function of an Advocate-General is to assist the judges in reaching their decision. He will present his submissions being a detailed analysis of the relevant issues of law and fact together with his recommendations. The Court is not bound to follow these but they are useful for understanding the reasoning behind the Court's decision. Situated in Strasbourg, the Court deals with disputes between member states, member states and community institutions, community institutions and firms, individuals or Community officials. It can hear appeals from member states, the Commission, the Council, or from an individual, on all of whom its rulings are binding. At the request of national courts it can give preliminary rulings on the interpretation of Community law. The Single European Act provided for the setting up of a new Court of the First Instance which commenced proceedings on 1 September 1989. Its jurisdiction is limited to disputes between the Community and its servants, competition law cases and applications for judicial review and damages in respect of certain matters. There is a right of appeal on matters of law to the Court of Justice.

3.3.5 The European Court of Auditors

This was set up in 1977 to examine the revenue, expenditure and accounts of the Community and also to establish links with national audit bodies. Situated in Strasbourg, it comprises 12 members appointed by the Council for six years. The Court produces reports showing the management of the Union's finances which are a source of pressure on the institutions and others with administrative responsibility to manage them soundly.

3.3.6 The European Investment Bank

This is the Union's financing institution. It provides loans for capital investment promoting the Union's balanced economic development and integration. Its annual lending of ECU 20 billion makes it the largest international financing institution in the world.

3.3.7 The Economic and Social Committee

The Committee advises the Commission, the Council and the European Parliament. Its members are divided into the three groups of workers, employers and various interests which represent the different categories of economic and social activity in the Union. It draws up opinions on draft Community legislation and the main issues affecting society.

3.3.8 The Committee of the Regions

This is the Union's youngest institution. There is now a legal obligation to consult this committee of representatives of local and regional authorities on a variety of matters that concern it directly.

3.3.9 The European Ombudsman

As each citizen of each member state is both a national and a European citizen, each has the right to apply to the European Ombudsman if he is a victim of an act of 'maladministration' by the EU institutions or bodies. The Ombudsman has wide-ranging powers of enquiries, for example, the Community institutions and bodies are required under certain conditions to provide all evidence he may request. The Ombudsman may also make recommendations to EU institutions and he can refer the case to the European Parliament for it to draw political conclusions from it if appropriate.

3.3.10 The European Monetary Institute

The function of the EMI is to make monetary unification possible by making the necessary preparations for the establishment of the European System of Central Banks, the conduct of a single monetary policy and for the creation of a single currency.

3.4 The sources of EC law

The law of the European Community is not the same as the law of the European Union. EC law was created by or under the international treaties. EU law results from the Maastricht Treaty. It is EC law which is part of each member state's domestic legal system, not EU law.

The sources of EC law are set out below:

3.4.1 The treaties

The following treaties are a source of EC law:

(a) Treaty of Rome;
(b) Merger Treaty—EEC and ECSC merged;
(c) Accession Treaties;
(d) Budgetary Treaties;
(e) Single European Act;
(f) European Economic Area Treaty—extended to EFTA countries;
(g) Treaty on European Union—Maastricht; and
(h) Amsterdam Treaty.

3.4.2 EC secondary legislation

EC secondary legislation consists of:

(a) regulations;
(b) directives;
(c) decisions;
(d) recommendations; and
(e) opinions.

The legislative powers of the Community are laid down in Art 249. This lists the five kinds of acts (secondary legislation) set out in the list above and also contains a short statement of the characteristics of each kind of act.

A regulation shall have general application. It is binding in its entirety and directly applicable in all member states, i.e. a member state does not need to pass any legislation implementing the contents of the regulation. In fact, national implementing measures are deemed improper unless the regulation requires member states to take action to implement it.

A directive shall be binding as to the result to be achieved, upon each member state to which it is addressed, but shall leave to the national authorities the choice of form and methods, i.e. a directive lays down an objective and allows each national government to achieve it by the means they regard as most suitable. Directives require implementation by member states before being fully effective in law.

A decision shall be binding in its entirety upon those to whom it is addressed i.e. it does not require implementing legislation and is binding on member states and individuals.

A recommendation and an opinion are not binding at all although they have been seen to have been of persuasive authority in certain cases.

3.4.3 International agreements with non-member states

International agreements with non-member states are a source of EC law.

They have effect in Community law and are applied by the European Court which has declared them to be 'an integral part of Community law', e.g. the Community is bound by the General Agreement on Trade and Tariffs (GATT) which was concluded before the establishment of the Community and all member states are party to it.

3.4.4 General principles of Community law which encompasses the entire jurisprudence of the European Courts

General principles of Community law are an important source of law. They are derived from a number of sources but the most important are the Community treaties and the legal systems of the member States.

THE RELATIONSHIP BETWEEN EC AND NATIONAL LAW

3.5 The concept of direct effect

3.5.1 Meaning

The EC Treaties were incorporated into UK law by the European Communities Act 1972 whereby Community law became directly applicable, i.e. part of our internal system. But the wording 'directly applicable' has created a problem because this phrase also covers provisions of Community law capable of application by national courts at the suit of individuals. The definition of a regulation provides that it is ... 'directly applicable and can be relied on by an individual litigant ... '. Therefore, we use the term 'directly effective' where a provision grants rights to individuals which must be upheld by the national courts.

Whether a particular provision will have direct effect is a matter of construction and each member state will apply criteria such as clarity of language and the extent to which the provision has been incorporated into national law. Unfortunately, member states are not always consistent. It is important to know whether a provision is directly effective because if it is, domestic courts must apply it and in priority over any conflicting provisions of national law.

Section 2(1) of the ECA provides that:

> All such rights, powers, liabilities, obligations and restrictions from time to time created or arising by or under the Treaties, and all such remedies and procedures from time to time provided for by or under the Treaties, as in accordance with the Treaties are without further enactment to be given legal effect or used in the United Kingdom shall be recognised and available in law, and be enforced, allowed and followed accordingly; and the expression 'enforceable Community right' and similar expressions shall be read as referring to one to which this subsection applies.

3.5.2 Treaty articles

The doctrine of 'direct effect' was first developed in the case of *Van Gend en Loos v Nederlandse Administratie der Belastinge* (26/62) [1963] ECR 1 when a Dutch firm sought to invoke a provision of Community law against Dutch Customs Authorities. The firm had imported ureaformaldehyde from Germany into the Netherlands and had been charged a customs duty. This breached the EC rules on free movement of goods and the firm sought reimbursement from the Dutch government. A Dutch tribunal requested the ECJ to determine whether Art 25 could be relied upon by an individual rather than a member state. The ECJ held that the Article was directly effective, i.e. it gave rise to rights or obligations which individuals may enforce before their national courts. A provision will be directly effective provided it meets certain criteria:

(a) it must be sufficiently clear and precise; and
(b) it must be unconditional and leave no room for the exercise of discretion in implementation by member states or Community institutions.

Van Gend dealt with an individual invoking an Article against an organ of the state and this is known as 'vertical' direct effect. But what about an individual invoking a Treaty Article against another individual or 'horizontal' direct effect?

This was dealt with in *Defrenne v Sabena* [1976] ECR 455. Ms Defrenne was an air hostess with Sabena Airlines. She brought an action based on Art 141 EC Treaty which provides that men and women should receive equal pay for equal work. Sabena were in breach of this provision as male stewards were paid more for the same work. Sabena argued that Art 141 was not directly effective as it is concerned with the relationships between individuals and not between member states and individuals. The ECJ disagreed and provided that Treaty provisions could have 'horizontal' direct effect provided they met the same criteria, i.e. clear and precise obligations with no discretion left to member states as to implementation.

3.5.3 Directives

The problem with directives is that they require implementation by member states unlike regulations and therefore it was thought that they could not have direct effect. The ECJ disagreed in *Grad Finanzamt Traunstein* (9/70) [1971] CMLR 1 where a haulage company sought to challenge a tax levied by the German authorities which the company claimed was in breach of an EC Directive. The German government argued that only regulations were directly applicable and directives required implementation. The ECJ disagreed. The fact that only regulations were described as directly applicable did not mean that other binding acts were incapable of such effects.

This decision was confirmed in *Van Duyn v Home Office* (41/74) [1974] ECR 1337. Ms Van Duyn was a Dutch national and a member of the Church of Scientology. She wanted to enter the UK to work for the Church. The UK Government had decided that the Church was undesirable and tried to exclude her on the ground of public policy. The Dutch government had implemented a directive dealing with the grounds for exclusion which were based on the personal conduct of the individual. Ms Van Duyn argued that it was not her personal conduct. The ECJ held that Ms Van Duyn was entitled to invoke the directive directly before her national court, thus confirming that directives can be directly effective. However, a directive will still have to satisfy the criteria set down in the Treaty cases. Remember that a directive has to be implemented by the member state and, therefore, it cannot be directly effective until the time limit for implementation has expired. This was considered in the *Ratti* case where S. Ratti, a solvent manufacturer, labelled his solvents in line with an EC directive. This was contrary to the old Italian law and he was prosecuted for infringing national law. The ECJ ruled that once the time limit for the implementation of a directive has expired, a member state may not apply internal law to someone who has complied with a directive. S. Ratti was able to rely on one directive as that time limit had expired but not on the one that for which the time limit was still running.

These cases illustrate 'vertical' direct effect, i.e. individual v state, but what about 'horizontal' direct effect, i.e. can an individual invoke a directive against another individual?

3.5.3.1 Horizontal direct effect

There are many cases discussing the horizontal direct effect, the first of which was *Marshall v Southampton and South-West Hampshire Area Health Authority* (152/84) [1986] ECR 723. Mrs Marshall sought to challenge the AHA's compulsory retirement age of 65 for men and 60 for women as discriminatory. The ECJ held that the AHA was acting in its capacity as an 'emanation of the State' and so Mrs Marshall was able to recover damages, i.e. the AHA was not seen as an individual. In *Foster v British Gas plc* (188/89) [1990] ECR I-3313 a claim was made in respect of different retirement ages. The ECJ held that a directive might be relied on against organisations or bodies which were 'subject to the authority or control of the state or had special powers beyond those which result from the normal relations between individuals and which is carrying out a public service'. This therefore extended the concept of direct effect to a body or organisation with special powers carrying out a service or controlled by the state.

However, this spread of the concept of direct effect of a directive was halted in *Rolls Royce v Doughty* [1987] IRLR 447. Here, although the plaintiff was in the same situation as Mrs Foster, the ECJ held that Rolls Royce did not exercise any special powers, unlike British Gas, and Mrs Doughty was unsuccessful. The public services which it provided e.g. defence, were provided to the state and not to the public. In 1995, in *Griffin v South West Water Services* [1995] IRLR 15, a privatised water company was held to be within the *Foster* definition. The case of *Faccini Dori v Recreb Srl* (C-91/92) [1994] ECR I-325 concerned door-step selling and here, the ECJ halted the concept of 'horizontal' direct effect. 'A directive cannot itself impose obligations on an individual and cannot therefore be relied on by an individual'.

3.5.3.2 Indirect effect

Meanwhile, the Court has tried various solutions to the problem of 'horizontal' direct effect. The first one of these was suggested in *Von Colson and Kamann v Land Nordrhein-Westfalen* (14/83) [1984] ECR 1891 which was based on a directive concerning equal treatment. Ms von Colson was employed in the prison service as a social worker. The authorities at a totally male prison would not engage her because of her sex on the grounds that it would cause too many problems and be too risky. The matter was referred to the ECJ. Instead of dealing with the vertical/horizontal problem, the ECJ turned instead to Art 10 of the EC Treaty. This provides that national courts should interpret national law in such a way as to give effect to a directive by ensuring its objectives are met. The result of this case is that although Community law is not directly effective, it may still be applied indirectly as domestic by means of interpretation. This gave rise to the concept of 'indirect effect'. However, the success of this principle depends on the member state's discretion to interpret national law. In *Marleasing SA v La Comercial Internacional de Alimentacion SA* (106/89) [1990] ECR I-4135, the Spanish Court was confronted with a national law on the constitution of companies which conflicted with an EC directive not implemented in Spain. The ECJ ruled specifically and without qualification that national courts were 'required' to interpret domestic law in such a way as to ensure that the objectives of the directive were achieved.

3.5.4 Regulations

Regulations will have direct effect provided they are sufficiently precise.

3.5.5 Decisions

Decisions may be directly effective provided the criteria for direct effect are satisfied.

3.5.6 Recommendations and opinions

These are non-binding measures and it is thought that at best they can only be taken into account in order to resolve ambiguities in domestic law.

3.6 Supremacy

We have seen that the courts are supposed to interpret domestic law so as to ensure the objectives of a Directive are met, but what if there is a conflict between community law and national law? The EC Treaty is silent on this therefore it has been developed through case law. The question needs to be considered from the perspective of the EC and from that of the UK.

3.6.1 EC

In 1964, the Court made a very brave ruling in *Costa v ENEL* (6/64) [1964] ECR 585 which concerned the compatibilty with EC law of the nationalisation of the Italian electricity industry. It was very brave because the foundations of EC law were barely established. The Court held that Community law must be supreme over conflicting national law. This was cited in *Van Gend en Loos* and the Court went further to state that a member state, by joining the Community, had limited its sovereign rights and Art 10 of the EC Treaty underlined the member state's commitment to observe Community law. The conflict went further in *Internationale Handesgesellschaft mbH v Einfuhr- und Vorratsstelle für Getriede und Futtermittel* (11/70) [1970] ECR 1125 where there was a conflict between a regulation concerning the requirement under the Common Agricultural Policy for an export licence which conflicted with an Article in the German Constitution on German fundamental rights. The ECJ ruled that the provisions of Community law will always prevail over the provisions of national law no matter what has passed earlier. The Court went further in *Simmenthal SpA v Commission* (92/78) [1979] ECR 777 where a number of regulations provided for the common organisation of the market in veal and beef by controlling the price of frozen beef. Here it was suggested that Community law is to be given priority over national law as soon as it comes into force, otherwise there can be no uniformity throughout the Community. Where a conflict exists, a judge should shut his eyes to national law and must not wait for it to be changed.

3.6.2 UK

Problems arise with the concept of supremacy from a UK perspective because, firstly, the UK has a dualist attitude, i.e. international and national law are different, and secondly, it has a largely unwritten constitution. In 1979, the case of *Macarthys Ltd v Smith* (129/79) [1980] ECR 1275, which concerned equal pay reached the Court of Appeal where it took the European view, i.e. that 'the courts have a bounden duty to give priority to Community law'. This was followed in 1983 by *Garland v British Rail Engineering Ltd* (12/81) [1982] ECR 359 which concerned sex discrimination, where the House of Lords adopted the 'rule of construction' approach. It said that the words of a statute passed after the Treaty are to be construed, if reasonably capable of bearing such a meaning, as to be intended to carry out the obligation which is imposed by the Treaty, and not to be inconsistent with it. In *R v Secretary of State for Transport, ex parte Factortame* (C-213/89) [1991] 1 AC 603, the House of Lords was confronted with the Merchant Shipping Act which was enacted to stop Spanish fishermen's quota-hopping measures. The Spanish fishermen said that it discriminated on the grounds of nationality. The House of Lords went further to suggest that if a British Act is in breach of a claimant's directly effective Community rights, these would prevail over the contrary provisions of the Act. In a further case, *Webb* (279/80) [1981] ECR 3305, which concerned discrimination based on pregnancy, the House of Lords, after making an application for a ruling, held that it should construe domestic legislation so as to accord with a directive.

These cases dealt with directly effective provisions but in *Duke v GEC Reliance Ltd* [1988] AC 618, there was a clash between a statute and a non-directly effective provision. The Court acknowledged that it ought to interpret the statute in line with the directive even though it was not directly effective but went on to set aside the directive and apply the UK statute even though it was contrary to EC law. Therefore, unless a provision is directly effective it will have no force in the UK courts unless it is given effect by UK Parliament.

REMEDIES

3.7 Article 234 reference procedure

Under Art 234 the ECJ can give preliminary rulings on the following:

(a) interpretation of the Treaty;

(b) validity and interpretation of acts of Community institutions; and

(c) interpretation of statutes of bodies established by an act of Council.

The purpose of the procedure was commented on in *Rheinmühlen-Dusseldorf v Einfuhr-und Vorratsstelle für Getriede und Futtermittel* (146/73) [1974] ECR 139. This case concerned an attempt by a German cereal importer to obtain an export rebate under Community law. A question was raised as to whether Art 234 gave an unfettered right for national courts to refer or whether it is subject to national provisions whereby lower courts are bound by the judgments of superior courts. The ECJ replied quite strongly that 'Article 234 is essential for the preservation of the Community character of the law established by the Treaty and has the object of ensuring that in all circumstances the law is the same in all States in the Community.'

There are two situations where the Art 234 procedure works:

(a) Where a case is being heard before a court from which there is no appeal, the national court must make a reference if it believes clarification of Community law is required to decide the case. It is not necessary to make a reference where the point is so obvious as to leave no scope for reasonable doubt. This latter point was made in *CILFIT Srl v Ministry of Health* (283/81) [1982] ECR 3415 and is known as the doctrine of *acte claire*. This case concerned a dispute between wool importers and the Italian Ministry of Health over payment of an inspection levy in respect of wool imports from outside the EC.

(b) Where a case is being heard by a court or tribunal which is exercising a judicial function, that court or tribunal has the discretion to make a reference. The ECJ's opinion must be required to decide the case. In *R v Bouchereau* (30/77) [1977] 2 CMLR 800 the magistrates' court made a reference. M. Bouchereau, a French national, was convicted of possessing a small quantity of drugs. He was fined £35 but the magistrate was minded to recommend deportation. The ECJ ruled that the crime was not sufficient to justify deportation.

Once the Court has given its judgment, it is too late to ask for a reference. Article 234 relies on willingness to refer and there has been only one occasion on which the ECJ has refused to give a ruling, the case of *Foglia v Novello* (No. 1) (104/79) [1980] ECR 745 and *Foglia v Novello* (No. 2) (244/80) [1981] ECR 3045 which was seen as a policy case. Foglia, a wine producer, agreed to sell some wine to Mrs Novello who was an exporter. It was agreed that Foglia would not bear the cost of any duties levied by the French in breach of EC law. He eventually had to pay them and sought reimbursement from Mrs Novello. On a reference, the ECJ stated that it had no power to rule on national law and it should not be used as a method for testing the compatibility of EC and national law.

3.8 Judicial review

Article 234 is not the only way to challenge the legality of a Community act. Article 230 provides that the Court has a duty to review the legality of:

(a) acts adopted jointly by the European Parliament and Council;

(b) acts of the Council, Commission and European Central Bank; and

(c) acts of the European Parliament intended to produce legal effects *vis-à-vis* third parties.

There are four grounds of review:

(a) lack of competence or *ultra vires*;.

(b) infringement of essential procedural requirement or procedural *ultra vires*, for example, failure to give reasons;

(c) infringement of a Treaty or any rule of law relating to it which includes 'non-discrimination and human rights; and

(d) misuse of power or using power for an improper or illegitimate purpose.

An applicant must:

(a) have the right personally to challenge a decision, i.e. it must be of direct and individual concern to the addressee (otherwise Community acts can only be challenged by member states/Council/Commission); and

(b) bring the action within two months of the date of publication of the measure or notification to the claimant or in the absence thereof, the date on which it came to the knowledge of the latter.

But Art 241 does allow persons who are affected by a regulation to challenge it indirectly, i.e. where, for example, a person is subject to a later decision based upon the regulation. In addition, Art 232 provides that the ECJ may bring an action against a Community institution (for example, where it has failed to act). Articles 235 and 288 provide that an institution may be sued where one of its servants has acted wrongfully in the performance of its functions or the institution itself has so acted. Rather than bring an action directly against a defendant, an applicant may make a complaint to the Commission. This procedure is free but it does take rather a long time.

3.9 Enforcement of law against member states

The Commission has the power to commence proceedings against a member state for failure to implement Community law under Art 226. It has to deliver a *reasoned opinion* on the matter after giving the state concerned an opportunity to submit its observations. If the state does not comply within the time period set down by the Commission, the matter is taken before the European Court of Justice.

Other member states can bring an action against another defaulting member state by reason of Art 227. Again, the Commission gives a reasoned opinion to which the offending state can submit its observations. If the Commission has not delivered an opinion within three months, the matter can still go before the European Court of Justice. The absence of an opinion does not matter.

Although member states have been reluctant to use Art 227, the Commission is increasingly using Art 226 as part of the process of achieving a single market.

3.10 Seeking a remedy in the National Courts

The European Court of Justice has recently become more concerned about the effectiveness of remedies applied in the national courts for breach of Community law. Originally, it held in *Comet BV v Produktschap voor Siergewassen* (45/76) [1976] ECR 2043, which concerned payments made by Comet to the defendant on the export of plants and bulbs for which it sought reimbursement that such a remedy should be 'no less effective' than that available to deal with a breach of national law. However, the Court's view has changed over the years such that in the recent *Factortame* case, it held that a national court should create an appropriate legal remedy if none exists.

An injunction can be obtained in an English court for breach of Community law.

An interim order was considered in the *Factortame* case which concerned a group of Spanish fishermen who owned British registered trawlers. The Merchant Shipping Act had the effect of preventing these fisherman from fishing in British waters. This conflicted with Community legislation and so the fishermen applied for judicial review of the Act. Such a reference to the European Court of Justice would take two years. In the meantime, the fishermen would lose their livelihood. Therefore, they applied for interim relief pending a judgment disapplying the Merchant Shipping Act. The House of Lords refused the application stating that they could not obtain an injunction against the Crown. A reference under Art 234 was made and the ECJ disagreed and stated that the House of Lords must set aside the national law which precluded the granting of interim relief. Therefore, the House of Lords had to suspend the Merchant Shipping Act.

Claims for damages arise in actions against member states for non-implementation (direct effect) and also between private individuals for breach of Treaty provisions.

In *Bourgoin v MAFF* [1986] QB 716, the UK banned French turkeys in the run up to Christmas 1981 on health grounds although the real reason was to protect the home market. Some French turkey breeders sued the Minister of Agriculture but the Court of Appeal held that there could be no action against a Minister of the Crown for innocently exercising his legislative powers. However, in the case of *Francovich v Republic of Italy* (C-6 & 9/90) [1991] ECR I-5357, the Italian government was obliged to make good the damage suffered as a result of the non-implementation of a directive. In this case, an Italian company went into liquidation leaving its employees with unpaid salary arrears. A directive was in existence which required member states to set up a compensation scheme to deal with this situation but Italy had not complied. S. Francovich sought compensation from the Italian court. This finding was upheld in *Factortame* with the result that a person who has suffered loss as a result of a breach of Community law by a public body is not obliged to go down the judicial review route with its three-month time limit provided that the result pursued by the Directive involved the conferring of rights for the benefit of individuals, the content of those rights could be determined by reference to the Directive and there was a causal link between the failure to implement the Directive and the harm suffered by the individual. The case of *Factortame* added a further point that a national court must set aside national procedural laws that represent an obstacle to the implementation of EC law. From the case of *Garden Cottage Foods v Milk Marketing Board* [1984] AC 130 it is clear that where there is a directly effective provision and an individual has suffered loss, he can claim for damages against the individual who caused the loss. This case concerned an application for an interlocutory injunction to restrain the defendants from refusing to supply milk to the plaintiffs. The refusal was alleged to be an abuse of a dominant position by the Milk Marketing Board. The compensation must be proportionate and where national measures do not allow for adequate compensation, they should be ignored. This has particular relevance in sex discrimination cases.

FREE MOVEMENT OF GOODS

3.11 EC treaty provisions

One of the main points of the internal market is free movement of goods and as such it is a 'corner stone' of the Community. Its aim is to create a single market free of all restrictions on trade. This is achieved through a number of EC Articles:

(a) Art 3: the elimination as between member states of customs duties and quantitative restrictions (quotas) on the import and export of goods and all measures having equivalent effect.

(b) Arts 23–24: the creation of a Customs Union providing for the free circulation of goods throughout the EC whatever their place of origin once they are within the EC. A Common Customs Tariff is applies to all products imported into the Community from outside the EC.

(c) Art 25: the internal aspects of Common Customs Tariff: member states should not introduce any new customs duties.

(d) Arts 26 and 27: external aspects of Common Customs Tariff, i.e. how it works. Products are divided into lists which have applicable tariff rates (tariff rates are average of duties applied in four customs areas).

(e) Art 28: prohibits quantitative restrictions on imports and measures having equivalent effect.

(f) Art 30: exceptions to Art 28 where restrictions are justified on the grounds of public morality, public policy, public health, public security, protection of national treasures and protection of intellectual property rights.

(g) Art 31: requires member states to adjust any state monopolies to ensure that no discrimination as to the conditions under which goods are procured and marketed exists between nationals of member states.

The meaning of 'equivalent effect' depends on whether it is in relation to customs duties or quantitative restrictions.

3.12 Customs duties

Customs duties come in many guises and are often called a tax. An example was given in the Gingerbread case of *Commission v Luxembourg and Belgium* (2, 3/62) [1962] ECHR 425. These member states put a tax on imported gingerbread. They claimed the tax was to compensate for tax on rye (an ingredient of gingerbread). The ECJ held that the charge jeopardised the objectives of the Community and was a result of a unilateral decision. When applied to import but not to similar national product it has same effect as a customs duty and is unlawful.

3.13 Quantitative restrictions

This is the rule in *Dassonville*, i.e. 'all trading rules enacted by member states that are capable of hindering, directly or indirectly, actually or potentially, intra-Community trade' have the same effect as quotas (*Procureur du Roi v Dassonville* (8/74) [1974] ECR 837). In this case, a Belgian importer of Scotch whisky was prosecuted for selling it with false certificates of origin. He had imported the whisky from France and it was difficult to obtain certificates. He argued that Belgian law made it more difficult to import whisky if it came from a state other than the state of origin and this therefore breached Art 28.

Examples of measures which fall within this this rule, i.e. are not allowed, include:

(a) a requirement that a certificate or licence be obtained prior to import or export, for example, a certificate of origin;

(b) measures encouraging purchase of national products on the basis of national origin. For example, in *Commission v Ireland* (248/81) [1982] ECR 4005, a 'buy Irish' campaign was not allowed as it discouraged the purchase of other goods rather than merely drawing a consumer's attention to the specific qualities of the products; or

(c) measures which affect the domestic product as well. The leading case in this area is *Cassis de Dijon (Rewe-Zentral AG v Bundesmonopolverwaltung für Branntwein* (120/78) [1974] ECR 649) where a French company wanted to export blackcurrant liqueur to Germany. The liqueur had an alcohol content of 15–20 per cent. German law set down a minimum alcohol content of 25 per cent for fruit liqueurs and therefore the Germans sought to prevent the importation of the French product. The ECJ applied *Dassonville* and found the German law to be in breach of Art 28.

3.14 Exceptions to Article 28

3.14.1 The 'rule of reason'

It is important to identify whether a measure affects the equivalent domestic product as well as the imported one as certain measures, although within *Dassonville*, will not breach Art 28 if they are 'necessary to satisfy mandatory requirements'. This is known as the rule of reason. Therefore goods which have been lawfully marketed in one member state are entitled to move throughout the rest of the Community. Mandatory requirements include the:

(a) protection of public health;

(b) fairness of commercial transactions;

(c) defence of consumer; and

(d) protection of environment.

However, in order for the measure to be necessary, it must be proportionate to the aim. In *Cassis*, the German government argued the defence of 'protection of the consumer' but the ECJ held that the measure was disproportionate to the aim as clear labelling was an acceptable alternative.

3.14.2 Article 30

3.14.2.1 Public morality

This will be a matter for individual states but restrictions must not constitute a means of arbitrary discrimination against the import or a restriction on trade. Therefore, the exception can only be used where such a measure would affect a home-produced product in the same way. In *R v Henn & Darby* (34/79) [1979] ECR 3795 the defendants were convicted of being 'knowingly' concerned in the fraudulent evasion of the prohibition on the importation of indecent or obscene articles. These consisted of boxes of obscene films and magazines which were illegal. In *Conegate v Customs & Excise Commissioners* (121/85) [1986] ECR 1007 the goods consisted of sex dolls which could be sold lawfully throughout the UK.

3.14.2.2 Public policy

This can only be used where there is a serious threat to the fundamental interests of society. In *R v Thompson and others* (7/78) [1978] ECR 2247 the defendants traded in coins, some of which were no longer legal tender. They were convicted of being knowingly concerned in the fraudulent evasion of the prohibition on the importation of gold coins into the UK.

3.14.2.3 Protection of the health and life of humans, animals and plants

Again this is a matter for individual states and must not constitute arbitrary discrimination. Such discriminatory measures include import bans, import licences, health inspections and prior-authorisation requirements. The actual measure must be considered carefully as it may not be for the protection of health but may actually constitute discrimination. In *Commission v UK* (40/82) [1982] ECR 283, the UK government prohibited the import of poultry from France which adopted a policy of vaccination rather than slaughter. This was ostensibly to prevent the spread of Newcastle Disease. The ECJ ruled that the ban was unnecessarily restrictive and not part of a well-thought-out health policy but rather a measure to protect the UK poultry industry.

3.14.2.4 Public security

This cannot be readily called upon as a defence to a breach of Art 28. In *Campus Oil Ltd v Ministry for Industry and Energy* (72/83) [1983] ECR 2727 the Irish government required petrol importers to buy 35 per cent of their needs from an Irish refinery at government-fixed prices. This was so as to preserve the national refinery. The ECJ ruled that the measure was justified on the grounds of public security to maintain the national stocks in times of crisis.

3.14.2.5 Protection of national treasures

This ground has not yet been successfully revoked but it was suggested in *Commission v Italy* (7/68) [1968] ECR 423 that a wish by a member state to prevent an art treasure from leaving that country may have been acceptable even though it may constitute a quantitative restriction.

3.14.2.6 Protection of industrial and commercial property

Intellectual property covers both industrial property and artistic property. 'Industrial property' means rights related to the production and distribution of goods such as trade marks and patents. 'Artistic property' means literary and artistic property such as copyrights. Intellectual property rights provide for the enjoyment of valuable property rights as against the world. It has usually been left to the national authorities to grant their own rights which relate to each national territory. Such individuality is really contrary to the spirit of the Community and therefore, the ECJ has restricted the use of this as a defence to a breach of Art 28. It has distinguished between the ownership of these rights and their exercise. National rules must not constitute abritrary discrimination or a restriction on the free movement of goods. The Court will consider the 'specific subject matter' of the right. For example, the specific subject matter of a patent is 'to use an invention with a view to manufacturing industrial products and putting them into circulation for the first time' (*Centrafarm BV v Sterling Drug Inc.* (15/74) [1974] ECR 1147). Sterling Drug Inc. held the British and Dutch patents for a drug called NEGRAM. This drug was marketed either by Sterling Drug Inc. or companies licensed to do so. Centrafarm, an independent Dutch company, bought supplies of the drug in Britain and Germany where it was much cheaper and resold it in the Netherlands. Sterling Drug Inc. and its subsidiaries invoked their patent and trade mark rights before the Dutch court to prevent NEGRAM being marketed in the Netherlands by Centrafarm. The ECJ held that once the patented goods are circulated in another member state the right to exclude those goods is 'exhausted' and the patentee cannot prevent the import of the patented product. A similar approach has been adopted for trade marks and copyright.

Therefore, when dealing with free movement of goods:

(a) Look to see whether the measure falls within Art 28. If no, don't worry.
(b) If yes, look for defence with rule of reason or Art 30.
(c) If neither apply, the measure will be unlawful.

FREE MOVEMENT OF PERSONS

Article 17 of the EC Treaty now states that every EC national shall now be a citizen of EU. Each Union citizen has the right to move and reside freely within the member state, subject to the limitations in the treaty and in other legislation.

3.15 Workers

Article 39 provides for free movement of workers within the Community, but what is a 'worker'? Article 39 gives a vague definition as 'a wage-earner or assimilated worker'. In the case of *Sotgiu v Deutsche Bundespost* (152/73) [1974] ECR 153 the German Post Office's decision to pay increased separation allowances only to workers living away from home was held to be capable of breaching Art 7 (now repealed). The Court referred to a worker as 'a person engaged in activities of an economic nature'. In *Lawrie-Blum v Land Baden-Württemberg* (66/85) [1986] ECR 2121 the applicant was a trainee teacher employed by the Minister of Education with the status of a civil servant. A worker was defined as someone who 'provides services of some economic value, for and under the direction of another person, for which he receives remuneration'.

3.15.1 Workers' rights

In *Levin v Staatssecretaris van Justitie* (53/81) [1982] ECR 1035, Mrs Levin was a British national married to a South African national. She was refused a residence permit by the Dutch authorities because she was not in gainful employment. The Court was asked to give a definition of a 'worker' which it did by referring to the four basic rights of the worker:

3.15.1.1 Right to migrate

Member states no longer have the discretion to grant passports but the UK does have a discretion under royal prerogative. A worker can go to another member state for the purpose of seeking employment. In the UK, immigration rules allow a person to stay for this purpose for six months. Directive 68/360 provides a right to enter a member state on the production of a valid ID card or passport.

3.15.1.2 Right to reside

The right to reside is conferred upon production of two documents:

(a) the document with which the individual entered the country; and
(b) confirmation of engagement from employer or certificate of employment.

Residence permits are granted for five years, are automatically renewable, and a break of six months' residence justifies withdrawal of the permit, except where the person is unemployed for 12 consecutive months within five years when the break can be of up to one year (could be looking for job in other member state).

3.15.1.3 Right to remain

A worker has the right to remain, i.e. to stay when retired. This is extended to:

(a) retired workers who have reached national retirement age and have worked in a member state for at least one year and have resided there for at least three years;
(b) permanently incapacitated workers who have resided in a member state for at least two years. If the incapacity is due to a work injury, the period is irrelevant; and
(c) frontier workers.

3.15.1.4 Right to equal treatment

Workers have a right to equal treatment, i.e. not to be discriminated against on grounds of pay, sex or nationality. A migrant worker is also entitled to the same tax and social advantages as a national worker, whether or not these are attached to the contract of employment. These were defined in *Ministère Public v Even* (207/78) [1979] ECR 2019 as 'those rights and advantages granted to workers because of their status as workers or residence'. There is a limitation as full equality of treatment is only available to those lawfully resident by virtue of obtaining employment rather than temporary rights of residence.

3.16 Families of workers

A 'family' is defined in Art 10(1) of reg 1612/68 as:

(a) a spouse and descendants under 21 or dependants; or
(b) dependent relatives in ascending line of worker and spouse.

The rights of residence of spouses do not depend on continuing cohabitation. In *Diatta v Land Berlin* (267/83) [1985] ECR 567, the ECJ held that the right of residence subsisted as long as the marriage continued irrespective of whether or not the parties to the marriage were still together. Once the marriage was dissolved, the rights of residence of the spouse terminated. This view was upheld in *R v Sectretary of State for the Home Department, ex parte Sandhu, The Times*, 10 May 1985 case but should be read in line with Article 8 of the European Convention on Human Rights.

3.16.1 What about 'cohabitee'?

This was discussed in the case of *Netherlands v Reed* (59/85) [1986] ECR 1283 where the member state decided that Reed was not entitled to remain as a spouse and she was not a worker. But, aliens in a stable relationship with Dutch nationals are entitled to remain. Therefore, she was being discriminated against and the ECJ decided that she was entitled to remain as a cohabitee.

3.16.2 What about dependants?

Dependants have the same rights as a worker even after a divorce and this includes children of the family even though they may not be decendants. They have the right to work in the host state if they have the necessary qualifications. In *Gü v Regierungspräsident Düsseldorf* (131/85) [1986] ECR 1573, a Turkish Cypriot doctor was married to an

Englishwoman who was employed as a hairdresser in Germany. He was refused permission to practice medicine. This decision was overturned by the ECJ. Dependants are also entitled to be admitted to educational, apprenticeship and vocational training courses. In *Casagrande v Landeshauptstadt München* (9/74) [1974] ECR 773, it was also added that dependants should be entitled to 'general measures to facilitate attendance', e.g. grants.

This latter point was discussed in a number of cases beginning with *Brown v Secretary of State for Scotland* (197/86) [1988] ECR 3205. He was of dual nationality but domiciled in France. He won a place at Cambridge University to read engineering. He also won a sponsorship from Ferranti and eight months pre-term work in Scotland as preparation. He was refused a grant on the grounds that he was unable to claim it as a social advantage because he was not a worker. However, the ECJ held that he was entitled to non-discriminatory access to education because he had worked in preparation for his degree but that he could not claim the grant as a social advantage because Brown had only acquired the status of 'worker' as a result of being accepted into university.

This was contrasted in *Lair v University of Hanover* (39/86) [1989] ECR 3161 where the member state decided Lair was entitled to claim a grant as a social advantage as she had come to UK a few years earlier and acquired the status of a worker. Also, her work was unconnected with her degree.

3.17 Exceptions to Article 39

Article 39 is not applicable to employment in public service. This has been exploited by member states and so has been limited to 'posts involving the exercise of official authority and functions related to safeguarding the general interests of the State'. Article 39 also contains certain restrictions so that a member state can deny residence on the grounds of:

(a) public policy;

(b) public security; or

(c) public health;

For all these grounds it must be the personal conduct of the individual that is relied on for the purposes of the exception.

13.17.1 Public policy

There are a number of cases which illustrate the working of this exception. The first is *Van Duyn* where it was said that there must be a 'genuine and sufficiently serious threat to public policy affecting one of the fundamental interests of society'. In *Adoui and Cornuaille v Belgium* (115, 116/87) [1982] ECR 1665 it was added that 'membership of an organisation may constitute conduct but must be such that the government has recently taken steps to curb such activities'. In this case, Adoui and Cornaille worked in a Belgian cafe with a rather questionable reputation. They were refused residency on the ground of public policy. In *Rutili v Minister for the Interior* (36/75) [1975] ECR 1219, the ECJ held that, to use the public policy restriction, there must be a total ban and the fundamental interests of society must be affected. Only in exceptional cases will past conduct in itself justify deportation. This is also to be borne in mind when using the grounds, as a former terrorist will be allowed entry provided he is no longer a threat. In *Rutili*, he had been involved in trade union and political activities. He was an Italian working in France and the French government tried to restrict his movements to certain areas of France without success.

It must be the personal conduct of the individual concerned. In *Bonsignore v Oberstadtdirektor of the City of Cologne* (67/74) [1975] ECR 297, the applicant, who was an Italian working in Germany, was found guilty of causing the death of his brother by the negligent handling of a firearm. He was directed to be deported for its deterrent effect. The ECJ said that a member state could not use a Community worker as a 'scapegoat'.

Finally, previous criminal convictions do not in themselves constitute a ground for expulsion or exclusion. In *R v Bouchereau* (30/77) [1977] 2 CMLR 800, the authorities sought to deport Bouchereau, a French national working in the UK, on the ground of his conviction for the unlawful possession of drugs. The conviction must constitute a serious threat to the fundamental interests of society.

13.17.2 Public security

Although border controls are being reduced, member states are still entitled to take such measures as are considered necessary for the purpose of combating terrorism, crime, the traffic of drugs and illicit trade in works of art.

When using the grounds of public policy or security, adequate reasons must be given for the exclusion (*Rutili*).

13.17.3 Public health

The diseases to fall within the ground of public health must be highly infectious or contagious, e.g. TB.

FREEDOM OF ESTABLISHMENT AND PROVISION OF SERVICES

3.18 Introduction

Articles 43 to 55 extend the freedom of movement of workers to include the free movement of the person who is self-employed to establish himself in another member state or to provide services there. These rights do not just apply to a person but also extend to companies.

3.19 Freedom of establishment

Articles 43 to 48 cover the right of establishment. This means the right to 'set up shop' in another member state either permanently or semi-permanently. Article 43 provides for the restrictions on establishment of a national in another member state to be progressively abolished. It includes the right to take up and pursue self-employed activities and to set up and manage undertakings, companies and firms under the conditions laid down by the law of the country where such establishment is effected. Companies or firms are defined in Art 48 as 'companies or firms constituted under civil or commercial law, including cooperative societies, and other legal persons governed by public or private law, save for those which are non profit making.' Therefore, a UK company wishing to set itself up in Germany can do so provided it is properly constituted under UK law. If its main office is outside the EC it must have an effective link with a member state.

3.20 Freedom to provide services

Articles 49 to 55 deal with the right to provide services such that restrictions on providing services are to be abolished. The 'right to provide services' means the provision of services by an individual in another member state without residing there. Services are defined as those 'normally provided for remuneration, in so far as they are not governed by the provisions relating to freedom of movement for goods, capital and persons'.

3.21 Limitations

The freedom of establishment and the freedom to provide services are not absolute rights. They can be moderated on the grounds of public policy, security or health. In addition, they do not apply to activities connected with the exercise of official authority in that member state. A further limitation is that the freedom of establishment can only be exercised 'under the conditions laid down for its own nationals by the law of the country where such establishment is effected; or under the same conditions as are imposed by that state on its own nationals'. The problem for a non-national trying to establish himself or provide a service in another member state is that he may not comply with the conditions laid down in that particular state for the practice of the particular trade or profession he wants to exercise. He may not be suitably qualified according to that member state. The relevant conditions are those laid down by a trade or professional body relating to education, training and professional conduct. These vary from state to state and have proved to be a barrier.

3.21.1 Education and training

Article 47 envisaged a series of directives for the mutual recognition of qualifications from hairdressers to lawyers. Unfortunately, the issue of directives has proved to be a slow and difficult task. Since the rights of establishment and provision of services appeared to be conditional on the issuing of directives, it was thought those rights could not be invoked by individuals until the directives were issued. This point was tested in the *Reyners v Belgium* (2/74) [1974] 2 CMLR 305. Mr Reyners was a Dutchman born, educated and resident in Belgium. He was a doctor of Belgian law but was refused admission to the Belgian Bar because he was not a Belgian national. He claimed that this decision was in breach of Art 43. The Belgian Government argued that Art 43 was not directly effective, it could not be relied on by an individual as against a member state, because it depended on the issuing of directives under Art 47. The Court held that the Article was in itself directly effective and that the provisions of Art 47 were complementary to Art 43 and not a necessary precondition. The same principle was applied in the context of services in *Van Binsbergen v Bestuur van de Bedrijfsvereniging voor de Metaalnijverheid* (33/74) [1974] ECR 1299. Here, Van Binsbergen, a Dutchman, qualified as an advocate in Holland. He had been living and working there but then moved to Belgium. He challenged a rule of the Dutch Bar that persons representing clients before certain tribunals must reside in the state in which that service is supplied. He argued that this rule was in breach of Arts 43 and 50. Again, no harmonising directives had been enacted. The Court held he was entitled to rely on the Articles which were directly effective.

The harmonisation process has been extremely slow and therefore, the Commission approved Directive 89/48 which was implemented by the European Communities

(Recognition of Professional Qualifications) Regulations 1991. The effect of this is that where entry into a particular profession depends on possession of a diploma awarded on the completion of professional education and training of at least three years' duration, an individual is entitled to pursue that profession in the Community on the same terms as apply to nationals in the host state. If there are substantial differences, the candidate is to follow an adaptation period or take an aptitude test, whichever the applicant chooses. However, where the profession requires knowledge of national law, the state may stipulate whether the candidate is to take an aptitude test or follow a period of adaptation.

A further directive has since been issued for the mutual recognition of post-secondary educational and training courses. Now, where a profession is subject to the possession of a diploma, a host state cannot refuse to allow a non-national to take up occupation on the same conditions as those that apply to its own nationals.

3.21.2 Professional conduct

In addition to the rules governing training and education, there are also rules of professional conduct for certain professions. These can constitute barriers to the free movement of persons. In *Van Binsbergen*, it was acknowledged that professional rules of conduct relating to the legal profession do not infringe Arts 49 and 50 provided they do not discriminate against a non-national. In *Gullung v Conseils de l'ordre des advocats du barreau de Colmar et de Saverne* (292/86) [1988] ECR 111, a registration requirement with the German Bar for all barristers wishing to establish themselves in Germany was held to be permissible as such registration was required of its own nationals. However, there is still a problem for lawyers seeking to establish themselves in France. A law was passed in 1990 requiring foreign lawyers to become a member of a local Bar before being able to provide legal services even where French law does not require compulsory assistance of the lawyer. This would seem to contradict the directives for mutual recognition, however, it is still the intention in France that all lawyers must qualify under the French system. A foreign lawyer must present himself before an appropriate local Bar before he is free to practise.

In December 1997, the Council of Ministers passed the lawyers' Rights of Establishment Directive which member states now have two years to implement. This gives EU lawyers a permanent right of establishment under their home title in another EU country.

3.22 Freedom to receive services

The freedom to provide services under Arts 49 and 50 has now been extended to receive services. In *Luisi & Carbone v Ministero del Tesoro* (286/82) [1984] ECR 377 which concerned a breach of Italian currency regulations, the Court interpreted Art 49 to include the freedom for recipients of services to go to another state to receive that service there. Recipients were held to include tourists, persons receiving medical treatment and persons travelling for the purposes of education and business. This equality principle was developed in the case of *Cowan v French Treasury* (186/87) [1989] ECR 195. This concerned a British tourist who was the victim of a criminal assault while on holiday in Paris. His claim for compensation from the French Criminal Injuries Compensation Board was rejected as he was not a French national. On a reference under Art 234 the Court held that he was entitled to receive compensation as a recipient of services. Compensation could not be denied on the ground of nationality. The principle of non-discrimination has been extended to education and vocational training. In the case of *Gravier v City of Liege* (293/83) [1985] ECR 593, the issue of access to education was considered. In this case, a French woman was asked to pay an additional fee to attend a course in Belgium because she was a non-national. The Court held that she did not have to pay such a fee provided the course represented vocational training. As a result of this case and subsequent cases, EC nationals must be granted access to courses which generally are vocational on the same terms as those granted to nationals of the host country, even when those courses are subsidised by the state.

COMPETITION LAW

3.23 Introduction

As has been seen, one of the main objectives of the Community is the creation of a common market. Although competition is generally seen as a benefit to the Community as it stimulates economic activity and provides freedom of choice, it can impede the freedom of businesses to trade between member states. Where competition is not properly controlled, the markets are divided. Article 3(f) of the EC Treaty requires the institution of a system ensuring competition does not distort the common market. Articles 28 and 30 covering the free movement of goods and Arts 49 to 55 concerning the right to provide services are added to by Arts 81 and 82. Article 81 deals with anti-competitive practices and Art 82 concerns abuse of a dominant position.

3.24 Article 81

Article 81 prohibits:

> all agreements between undertakings, decisions by associations of undertakings and concerted practices which may affect trade between member states and which have as their object or effect the prevention, restriction or distortion of competition within the common market.

Examples of agreements which fall within Art 81 are set out in the Article and include price fixing, controlling production or markets and sharing sources of supply.

In order to fall within the ambit of Art 81, the wording of the Article needs to be considered more carefully.

3.24.1 Agreement

Although not defined by the Treaty, the word 'agreement' has been widely defined to include not only contracts but also formal and informal understandings and gentlemen's agreements whether written or oral. In *BMW Belgium v Commission* an attempt was made by BMW's subsidiary in Belgium to limit car dealers there from selling cars to other member states. BMW Belgium issued a circular to the Belgian BMW dealers asking them not to make such sales. The dealers were to signal their assent by signing and returning a copy of the circular although it was made clear to them that this would not constitute a contract. However, the ECJ decided otherwise and it was held to be an agreement under Art 81. The Court will look at the intention of the parties when considering whether there is an agreement or not.

3.24.2 Undertakings

Again this is not defined by the Treaty but has been widely interpreted to include any entity engaged in economic or commercial activity regardless of its legal status or the way it is financed (*Höfner and Elser v Macrotron GmbH* [1993] 1 CMLR 306). Examples of undertakings include companies, individuals engaged in sporting or cultural activities, trade associations, state-owned corporations, public authorities engaged in commercial activities, transport organisations and non-profit making organisations.

Agreements between undertakings which form a single economic unit will not infringe Art 81 so an agreement between a parent company and a subsidiary will not amount to a decision between undertakings unless the subsidiary acts independently of the parent. Commission guidelines have also made it clear that genuine agents will not be considered a separate undertaking from their principal and therefore agency agreements will generally fall outside Art 81. The Commission considers an agent to be a genuine agent unless the agent accepts a significant financial or commercial risk.

3.24.3 A decision by an association of an undertaking

The most common association aimed at by Art 81 is a trade association. Such trade associations are often used, for example, for promotional campaigns or to set standards. However, where such an association co-ordinates its activities, for example, by standardising pricing or by imposing standards which are designed to exclude competitors, this may have an anti-competitive effect. The decision of the association does not have to be binding. Recommendations from an association to its members may be sufficient to be in breach of Art 81—for example a non-binding recommendation in terms of a publishers' code of conduct (*Re the Application of the Publishers' Association* [1989] 4 CMLR 825).

3.24.4 Concerted practice

This occurs where there is some co-ordinated action between businesses in the same sector which distorts competition in the market place, for example, agreeing to raise prices at the same time or exchanging information on future price increases. In *Imperial Chemical Industries v Commission* (48/69) [1972] ECR 619, the ECJ defined a concerted practice as a form of cooperation between undertakings where there is no formal agreement but they have 'knowingly substituted practical cooperation ... for the risks of competition'. In the *ICI* case, ICI was one of ten major dyestuffs producers who between them produced 80 per cent of the dyes sold in the EC. ICI announced a price increase which was shortly followed by the others. There was evidence of collusion such as messages from parent companies to subsidiaries within hours of each other. The ECJ, upholding the decision of the Commission, agreed that there had been a concerted practice between undertakings which contravened Art 81 and the companies were fined heavily. Parallel behaviour will amount to a concerted practice if it leads to competition which does not correspond to the normal conditions of the market.

3.24.5 Effect on trade between member states

The agreement or concerted practice must effect intra-community trade or be capable of having such an effect. Therefore an agreement which effects only non-member states will not breach Art 81.

The test for whether an agreement is within Art 81 was set out in *Société Technique Minière v Maschinenbau* (56/65) [1966] ECR 235 which concerned an exclusive right for STM to sell earth-moving equipment provided STM did not sell competing machinery:

> It must be possible to foresee with a sufficient degree of probability on the basis of a set of objective factors of law or fact that the agreement in question may have an influence, direct or indirect, actual or potential, on the pattern of trade between member states.

Such an intra-community effect can occur even where the parties are based outside the EC provided the agreement or practice is implemented within the EC. The *Wood Pulp* cases [1985] 3 CMLR 474 concerned forestry practices in Finland, Sweden and Canada which had an effect on the wood pulp prices in the Community.

Even agreements which relate to one member state can contravene Art 81 if they have the effect of shutting off the national market from competitors or potential competitors from other member states or if they reinforce the division of the common market. An example of the latter was a scheme to fix the price of cement in the Netherlands. In *Vereeniging van Cementhandelaren v Commission* (8/72) [1972] ECR 977 the Netherlands Cement Dealers Association introduced a purely national cartel whereby the price of cement was fixed for sales of less than 100 tonnes and a target price applied for larger sales.

3.24.6 The object or effect of distorting competition

The scope of Art 81 is very wide and looks at the object of or effect any agreement has on competition rather than the form in which it is expressed. If an agreement distorts competition then, whether or not that was its intention, there will be a breach of Art 81. If the agreement or arrangement is not intended to restrict competition then a full market analysis of its actual effects will be required to establish whether or not it is anti-competitive.

Even if an agreement is likely to increase trade it may still be in breach of Art 81. This was considered in the important case of *Etablissements Consten SA v Commission* (56 & 58/64) [1966] ECR 299 where a German manufacturer (Grundig) appointed a sole distributor (Consten) for France who was granted exclusive use of the Grundig trade mark in France. Consten agreed not to sell the goods outside France. Similar restrictions applied to other Grundig distributors appointed for other territories. Consten brought a trade mark infringement action to prevent the resale in France of Grundig products bought by a French company in Germany. Consten and Grundig argued that the effect of Consten's appointment as distributor was to increase trade not to reduce it. The ECJ upheld the Commission's view that the agreement breached Art 81 as it had been used to divide the market and to prevent parallel trade.

3.24.7 Agreements likely to breach Article 81

Both vertical agreements and horizontal agreements may potentially fall foul of Art 81. A vertical agreement is an agreement between undertakings which operate at different levels of the production or distribution chain. For example, an agreement between a manufacturer and a distributor or a manufacturer and a customer or a distributor and a retailer. Examples of vertical agreements include distribution, supply, franchising and purchasing agreements. Very often such agreements will include provisions which breach Art 81 in order to make the agreements commercially viable. For example, exclusive customer groups, geographic territories, or exclusive supply or purchase obligations.

A horizontal agreement is an agreement between undertakings that are at the same level in the production or distribution chain. For example, an agreement between one manufacturer and another or between a number of retailers. Examples of such agreements include research and development agreements, specialisation agreements and information sharing agreements. Such agreements often include provisions in breach of Art 81 to make them commercially viable, for example, agreements to share markets, fix trading conditions, or joint buying and selling arrangements.

Generally, the Commission and the ECJ have looked more favourably on vertical agreements recognising that their pro-competitive effect outweighs the effects of the provisions in breach of Art 81.

3.24.8 De Minimis Notice

Only agreements which affect competition to an appreciable extent will fall foul of Art 81 even if they intend to restrict competition. The Commission has issued a Notice on Agreements of Minor Importance which provides that certain agreements will not breach Art 81 provided:

(a) the undertakings' combined market share must not exceed 10 per cent for horizontal agreements or 15 per cent for vertical agreements. If in doubt as to the category of the agreement the 10 per cent threshold applies;

(b) the thresholds in (a) above are reduced to 5 per cent in the case of parallel networks of agreements affecting more than 30 per cent of the relevant market in the EU; and

(c) certain so called 'hard core' restrictions are not contained in the agreements, depending on whether the agreement is a vertical or horizontal agreement as the case may be. (These hard core restrictions mirror those imposed in the relevant block exemptions for vertical and horizontal agreements (see **3.25.2** below).)

The Notice also makes it clear that agreements between small and medium-sized undertakings are rarely capable of appreciably affecting trade between member states. Small and medium-sized undertakings are currently defined as undertakings with fewer than 250 employees and either an annual turnover of less than 40 million Euro, or an annual balance sheet value of 27 million Euro or less.

The Notice should be treated with caution as it is not legally binding, and therefore it would be better to rely on exemptions (see **3.25** below).

3.24.9 Sanctions for breach of Article 81

Any agreement which is in breach of Art 81 is void by Art 81(2) and therefore unenforceable. The Commission has the power to impose fines of up to 1 million Euros or 10 per cent of the annual turnover of the relevant undertakings, whichever is the greater. Lastly, aggrieved third parties who are adversely affected by the anti-competitive behaviour can seek an injunction against the undertakings concerned to prevent the behaviour and/or to claim damages.

The Commission has and does use its powers to fine heavily. In 2001, the Commission imposed fines of 1.4 billion Euro (source: *In Competition*, December 2001). To discourage cartels seeking to fix prices or share markets illegally, the Commission has adopted a leniency policy encouraging 'whistle-blowing' and cooperation with the competition authorities by cartel members. This abolishes or reduces liability to fines on a decreasing basis depending on whether a cartel member first notified the Commission of the cartel and the order in which cartel members began to cooperate with the Commission.

3.25 Exemptions to Article 81

As the scope of Art 81 is so wide it can catch many commercial agreements, even those intended to increase competition. The potential sanctions for being in breach of Art 81 are heavy. It is therefore necessary when advising on commercial agreements to ensure that they fall outside Art 81 or that an exemption is available. Generally, an exemption will be granted where the anti-competitive effects are outweighed by the economic benefits to the consumer or the public at large. Exemption can either be by way of an individual application to the Commission, or by way of a block exemption. At the moment, only the Commission has the power to grant individual and block exemptions.

3.25.1 Individual exemptions

An individual undertaking can apply informally with the Commission issuing a 'comfort letter' stating that the agreement, in its opinion, does or does not infringe Art 81. As with the De Minimis Notice (see **3.24.8** above), such comfort letters are non-binding on the Commission and the European Courts and should therefore be treated with caution.

Alternatively, the undertaking can make a formal application to the Commission for exemption under Art 81(3). The grant of an exemption will depend on the applicant satisfying four conditions laid down in the article:

(a) the agreement must contribute to improving the production or distribution of goods or to promoting technical or economic progress;

(b) the agreement must allow consumers a fair share of the resulting benefit;

(c) there must be no unnecessary restrictions; and

(d) there must be no elimination of competition.

Exemptions may be granted only for specific periods, conditions may be attached and the exemption may be renewed or revoked.

3.25.2 Block exemptions

Due to the enormous number of applications for individual exemption, the Commission has increasingly relied on its power to grant block exemptions. These are a series of regulations issued for certain types of agreement considered to be generally beneficial rather than anti-competitive. Where an agreement falls within a block exemption, an undertaking need not notify it to the Commission for individual exemption.

3.25.2.1 Old style block exemptions

In the past, the Commission adopted a formulistic and regulatory approach to the drafting of block exemptions which prescribed the form agreements could take, the restrictions which could be included, and the restrictions which were prohibited. If an agreement fell outside the terms of the block exemption then it was presumed to be illegal under Art 81. Undertakings to such agreements would normally notify them and apply for individual exemption to ensure enforceability and to avoid liability to fines.

Existing industry-specific and other, more general, block exemptions continue to follow this approach. For example, the block exemption on technology transfer agreements.

3.25.2.2 New style block exemptions

The Commission is now moving away from the prescriptive approach to an economics-based approach, which uses market effect and, in particular, market share as the criteria for intervention.

The block exemptions on vertical agreements, specialisation agreements, and research and development agreements are examples of this approach. In these exemptions, certain agreements falling below specified market share thresholds are presumed to fall within Art 81(3) provided certain prohibited restrictions are not included. Above the relevant market share thresholds, such agreements are not covered by the relevant block exemption, but they are not necessarily presumed illegal under Art 81.

Guidelines to accompany the market-based block exemptions have been issued by the Commission. They provide guidance as to whether or not to notify agreements falling outside the new style block exemptions. Some also consider the application and interpretation of the exemptions themselves. In effect, the onus of regulating agreements has shifted away from the Commission to the undertakings. Businesses, and their advisers, must decide for themselves whether an agreement and its restrictions have an anti-competitive effect on the market having regard to any relevant guidelines and competition case law. They cannot simply notify an agreement whenever there is doubt as to whether it falls within a market-based block exemption.

It should be noted that specific rules still apply to certain sectors. For example, distribution agreements for motor vehicles are excluded from the block exemption on vertical agreements. It should also be remembered that the benefit of a block exemption (old style or new style) may be withdrawn from an agreement falling within it if the authorities consider that the agreement has, on balance, an anti-competitive effect.

3.25.2.3 Market share

As market share is becoming increasingly important, it is necessary to be able to correctly identify relevant markets. This is considered in more detail in **3.27.1** below.

The detailed terms of the Commission's block exemptions are beyond the scope of this book.

3.26 Rule of reason

As the scope of Art 81 is so wide, the ECJ and the Commission have, when applying it, struck a balance between the anti-competitive effects of agreements and their pro-competitive effects. Agreements which, on balance, promote market integration or product distribution, or produce economic or technical benefits, will be permitted. For example:

(a) a reasonable post-contractual restriction in a franchising agreement (*Pronuptia de Paris GmbH v Pronuptia de Paris Irmgard Schillgalis* (161/84) [1986] ECR 353);

(b) an exclusive plant breeder licence for maize seed where otherwise the new technology involved would not have reached the market (*Nungesser KG & Eisele v Commission* (258/78) [1982] ECR 2015); and

(c) agreements between manufacturers of dishwashers and domestic water heaters designed to improve energy efficiency (*CECED Dishwasher, Notice Number 2001/C 250/2 and CECED Water Heaters, Notice Number 2001/C 250/3*).

3.27 Article 82

Article 82 regulates the activities of undertakings in a dominant position. It provides that:

Any abuse by one or more undertakings of a dominant position within the common market or in a substantial part of it shall be prohibited as incompatible with the common market in so far as it may affect trade between member states.

An example of such abuse would be directly or indirectly imposing unfair purchase or selling prices or other unfair trading conditions. As with Art 81, it is important to consider the wording carefully, as for a breach of Art 82 three elements must be established. These are as follows:

(a) a dominant position;

(b) an abuse of that position; and

(c) the abuse must affect trade between member states.

3.27.1 Dominant position

A dominant position was defined in *United Brands v Commission* (27/78) [1978] ECR 207 as 'a position of economic strength enjoyed by an undertaking which enables it to hinder the maintenance of effective competition on the relevant market by allowing it to behave to an appreciable extent independently of its competitors and customers and ultimately of consumers'.

The question of whether an undertaking holds a dominant position needs to be considered in the context of the relevant market for the goods or services in question. It is only when the relevant market has been correctly defined that it can be established whether or not an undertaking has a dominant position in that market. The Commission has issued a notice on the definition of the relevant market for the purposes of competition law which provides useful guidance on defining the relevant market.

The Commission's notice makes it clear that it is necessary to define the relevant product and geographic market. The relevant product market is determined by reference to the product in question and the goods or services which are interchangeable or substitutable for them by reason of their characteristics, price and intended use. There are two kinds of product substitution: demand-side substitution and supply-side substitution. Demand-side substitution is the extent to which a consumer can obtain alternative goods. Supply-side substitution is the extent and ease with which other undertakings can supply alternative goods in competition with the undertaking in a dominant position.

In the *United Brands Case* the Commission decided the relevant product market in question was bananas and not the fruit market and that United Brands had abused a dominant position within that market. At the time of the case, United Brands was a conglomerate which handled 40 per cent of the EC trade in bananas. United Brands had argued that it did not enjoy a dominant position in the fruit market and this was the proper context for examining its position. The Commission disagreed and contended that there is a demand for bananas which is separate from the demand for other fresh fruit. The consumer buys bananas specifically for their nutritional and other qualities and would not readily accept other fresh fruit as a substitute. In particular, bananas cannot be easily substituted for other fruit due to their suitability for the young and elderly. Therefore, the Commission found the market to be bananas and not fresh fruit generally. The ECJ upheld the Commission's position.

The relevant product market can sometimes be quite small. In *Hugin Kassaregister AB v Commission* (22/78) [1979] ECR 1869, Hugin was held to be in breach of Art 82 as it refused to supply spare parts for independent repair of cash registers. The Commission defined the relevant product market as consisting of spare parts for Hugin machines for which Hugin was the sole supplier. This was upheld by the ECJ despite arguments from Hugin that such a definition was too narrow.

It is also necessary to consider the relevant geographic market. The geographic market will be influenced by factors such as costs and feasibility of transport and consumer preferences. It extends to the area within which consumers are likely to search for alternatives.

Once the relevant market has been determined it is necessary to establish whether the undertaking has a dominant position within that market. To help decide whether the undertaking holds a dominant position, a number of factors will be considered:

(a) market share of undertaking;
(b) market share of competitors;
(c) financial and technical resource;
(d) control of production and distribution;
(e) conduct and performance; and
(f) strength of customers' bargaining position.

3.27.2 Abuse of a dominant position

It is acceptable to hold a dominant position but not to abuse it. Unfair trading practices will amount to an abuse under Art 82. Examples of abuse would include the following:

(a) Unfair prices: such a price would be where the price bears no relation to the economic value of the product or service, whether excessively high or low;
(b) Discriminatory prices, where different customers are charged different prices without objective justification;
(c) Refusal to supply: in *United Brands*, the undertaking had refused to supply a previous customer which had participated in an advertising campaign for a rival undertaking; or
(d) Tying practices: obliging customers to take unrelated products or ancillary products for no objectively justifiable reason, or using volume discounts, fidelity rebates or fidelity penalties to discourage customers from taking competitors' products.

3.27.3 Affecting trade between member states

This phrase has the same meaning as for Art 81 such that the effect of the abuse would be to partition the markets in the Community.

3.27.4 Merger control

Abuse of dominant position under Art 82 will extend to mergers which eliminate competition. Some undertakings have attempted to reinforce their position by having, for example, tying agreements between an undertaking and its subsidiary. Although this may not constitute a breach of Art 81, it may constitute a breach of Art 82 if it has the effect of driving competition from the market. In addition, a merger between two or more undertakings which brings them under common control may amount to a breach of Art 82.

Regulations have been issued that provide that the Commission will investigate mergers considered to have a community dimension. Whether or not a merger has a community dimension is determined by reference to the turnover of the undertakings involved and is decided by reference to two alternative criteria. The terms of the merger regulations, the procedures involved, and the notices issued by the Commission to explain them are complicated and are therefore beyond the scope of this book.

3.27.5 Exemptions and sanctions

Lastly, there are no exceptions to Art 82 equivalent to those under Art 81. The sanctions for breach of Art 82 are similar to those for breach of Art 81. The Commission can impose fines and aggrieved third parties can claim damages and/or seek injunctive relief.

3.28 Modernisation of the EC competition system

The Commission is in the process of modernising its competition law procedures. It is proposed that the powers to grant individual exemptions be delegated to the competition authorities of the member states. The Commission will instead determine competition policy, grant new block exemptions and issue guidance for businesses and national competition authorities so that they can decide whether agreements or practices breach competition law. The detailed modernisation proposals are beyond the scope of this book.

THE EUROPEAN CONVENTION ON HUMAN RIGHTS

3.29 The ECHR and EC law

The European Convention on Human Rights and Fundamental Freedoms was drawn up under the direction of the Council of Europe in 1950. It came into force in 1953, which was before the European Community, and as a result is not just limited to the countries of Western Europe but includes those of Eastern Europe amounting to 32 parties. Its aim is to safeguard fundamental rights, both civil and political. Although it does not specify what those rights are, it is generally held to include sexual equality, freedom of religion, the right to a fair hearing and freedom of expression, to name but a few.

This new doctrine was announced in *Stauder v City of Ulm* (26/69) [1969] ECR 419, which concerned a Community scheme to provide cheap butter for recipients of war benefits. Herr Stauder received war victim benefits and therefore was entitled to cheap butter. He had to provide a coupon with his name and address on which he felt to be humiliating and a violation of fundamental human rights and that therefore the Community decision requiring this was invalid. The Court held that this measure did not require the production of a person's name and address. 'Interpreted in this way the provision at issue contains nothing capable of prejudicing the fundamental human rights enshrined in the general principles of Community law and protected by the Court'. This judgment recognised that fundamental human rights are a general principle of Community law.

In *Internationale Handelsgesellschaft* (11/70) [1970] ECR 1125, the Court went one step further such that the concept of human rights applied by the Court, while deriving its validity solely from Community law, is nevertheless 'inspired' by national constitutional traditions. *Nold (J.) KG v Commission* (4/73) [1974] ECR 491 concerned a decision under ECSC which provided that coal wholesalers could not buy German Ruhr coal direct from the selling agency unless they purchased a certain minimum quantity. Herr Nold could not do this and claimed the decision was a violation of human rights and deprived him of a property right and partly infringed his right to the free pursuit of an economic activity. The Court recognised these rights but said they were subject to limitations:

(a) A Community measure in conflict with fundamental rights as expressed in the constitutions of member states will be annulled.

(b) International Treaties can supply guidelines which should be followed within the framework of Community law.

The issue of human rights has been brought up to date by Maastricht, as Art F of the Union Treaty provides that the Union shall respect fundamental rights as guaranteed by the Convention on Human Rights and Fundamental Freedoms and as they result from constitutional traditions common to member states.

For a discussion of the European Convention and the Human Rights Act 1998, see **Chapter 16**.

FURTHER INFORMATION

3.30 Renumbered Articles

Previous numbering	New numbering	Previous numbering	New numbering
Article 3	Article 3	Article 23	Repealed
Article 5	Article 10	Article 24	Repealed
Article 7	Repealed	Article 25	Repealed
Article 8	Article 17	Article 26	Repealed
Article 9	Article 23	Article 27	Repealed
Article 10	Article 24	Article 28	Article 26
Article 11	Repealed	Article 29	Article 27
Article 12	Article 25	Article 30	Article 28
Article 13	Repealed	Article 36	Article 30
Article 14	Repealed	Article 48	Article 39
Article 15	Repealed	Article 52	Article 43
Article 16	Repealed	Article 54	Article 44
Article 17	Repealed	Article 55	Article 45
Article 18	Repealed	Article 56	Article 46
Article 19	Repealed	Article 57	Article 47
Article 20	Repealed	Article 58	Article 48
Article 21	Repealed	Article 59	Article 49
Article 22	Repealed	Article 60	Article 50

Previous numbering	New numbering	Previous numbering	New numbering
Article 61	Article 51	Article 169	Article 226
Article 62	Repealed	Article 170	Article 227
Article 63	Article 52	Article 173	Article 230
Article 64	Article 53	Article 175	Article 232
Article 65	Article 54	Article 177	Article 234
Article 66	Article 55	Article 178	Article 235
Article 85	Article 81	Article 184	Article 241
Article 86	Article 82	Article 189	Article 249
Article 119	Article 141	Article 215	Article 288

3.31 BIBLIOGRAPHY AND FURTHER READING

Mark Furse, *Competition Law of the UK & EC* (2000) Blackstone Press.

T.C. Hartley, *The Foundations of European Community Law* (1998) Oxford University Press.

Penelope Kent, *Law of the European Union* (2001) Longman.

Alison Jones & Brenda Sufrin, *EC Competition Law: Text, Cases and Materials* (2001) Oxford University Press.

D. Lasok, *Law & Institutions of the European Union* (2001) Butterworths.

David Medhurst, *A Brief and Practical Guide to EU Law* (2001) Blackwell Science.

J. Steiner & L. Woods, *Textbook on EC Law* (2000) Blackstone Press.

Sweet & Maxwell and Linklaters & Alliance, *In Competition* (May 2001 to April 2002).

C. Vincenzi & J. Fairhurst, *Law of the European Community* (1996) Longman.

Stephen Weatherill, *Cases & Materials on EC Law* (2000) Blackstone Press.

Richard Whish, *Competition Law* (2001) Butterworths.

Revenue law

4

An introduction to revenue law

4.1 The history of taxation

For centuries monarchs and, later, governments have had and used the power to raise money by way of taxes. This 'revenue' was originally required to fund the cost of maintaining an army and a navy and a relatively small amount of other public expenditure. Over the last century we have seen a vast increase in the amount of government expenditure on the provision of a wide range of services including healthcare, housing, education and roads and the provision of financial benefits like social security payments and pensions.

In order to pay for these services and benefits, governments raise money by imposing a number of different taxes and other payments. We would commonly associate taxes with, for example, income tax, but in the past there have been other, more unusual, taxes. Window tax, for example, was imposed at one time on the basis of the number of windows in a building. A less obvious tax which still exists and which you will consider in the LPC is stamp duty.

4.2 Changing taxes

Taxes have changed over the years. Income tax was imposed as a temporary measure in 1842 and has been with us ever since. However, each year it is customary for the Chancellor of the Exchequer to announce the government's financial requirements and proposed taxation measures for the forthcoming year in his annual Budget speech in November. These proposals then form the basis of the Finance Bill for that year which later becomes the Finance Act.

4.3 Taxes in the LPC context

The study of 'Revenue Law', as it is often called as an alternative to 'Taxation', forms an integral part of the LPC. It is termed a 'Core Subject' because it should not be studied in isolation. It pervades many of the Compulsory Subject and Elective Subject areas.

4.4 The main taxes

The main taxes and their common abbreviations are:

(a) Income tax (IT)

(b) Capital gains tax (CGT)

(c) Corporation tax (CT)
(d) Inheritance tax (IHT)
(e) Value added tax (VAT).

4.5 The EC dimension

Membership of the European Community has meant the acceptance of measures which affect the extent to which a member state can impose taxation and customs duties. It has also meant the harmonisation of indirect taxation and, in particular, the introduction of VAT in all member states.

4.6 Sources of tax law

4.6.1 Statute and statutory instrument

The rules governing the taxes that you will be concerned with on this course are mainly contained in various Acts of Parliament but are also to be found in statutory instruments.

In the case of each tax there is a principal charging Act but, on occasions, provisions will also be contained in other Acts or statutory instruments which either contain administrative provisions or which amend the earlier legislation.

The principal charging Acts and their common abbreviations are as follows:

Income tax	Income and Corporation Taxes Act 1988	ICTA
Capital gains tax	Taxation of Chargeable Gains Act 1992	TCGA
Corporation tax	Income and Corporation Taxes Act 1988	ICTA
Inheritance tax	Inheritance Tax Act 1984	IHTA
Value added tax	Value Added Tax Act 1994	VATA

Many of the administrative provisions relating to income tax, corporation tax and capital gains tax are contained in the Taxes Management Act 1970 (TMA). Similar provisions relating to VAT are contained in the Customs and Excise Management Act 1979.

4.6.2 Case law

Regard must also be had to case law which may assist in determining the meaning and extent of the statutory provisions.

4.6.3 Inland revenue statements

4.6.3.1 Statements of practice

Statements of practice indicate what view the Inland Revenue will take of the practical application of particular tax provisions.

4.6.3.2 Extra-statutory concessions

If a taxpayer satisfies the terms of an extra-statutory concession, then the Revenue will waive its right to collect tax which would otherwise be due.

4.7 Administration of income tax, capital gains tax and corporation tax

4.7.1 Treasury

Broadly, all taxation is under the control of the Chancellor of the Exchequer. He is a politician and is not necessarily an expert in either taxation or economic matters. He relies heavily on his permanent civil servants who are members of the Treasury.

4.7.2 Board of the Inland Revenue

The members of the Board are known as the Commissioners of the Inland Revenue. They must not be confused with Special Commissioners and General Commissioners who are involved in the appeals system which is considered later at **5.12**. The Commissioners of the Inland Revenue are permanent civil servants appointed by the Treasury. The Board regulates the administration of direct taxation in the UK. It is the Board who issue statements of practice and extra-statutory concessions.

4.7.3 Tax districts and HM inspectors of taxes

The country is divided into tax districts, each headed by a District Inspector. The inspector is responsible for examining the returns of individuals, unincorporated businesses and companies and computing the tax that is due. A notice of assessment is then raised and sent to the taxpayer showing the amount of tax that is due.

4.7.4 Collectors of taxes

Just as the country is divided into tax districts, so it is divided into areas served by a smaller number of Accounts and Collection Offices. Each Office operates under the authority of a Collector of Taxes. As the name suggests, the Collector is responsible for the collection of tax, if necessary, through the courts.

4.7.5 General and special Commissioners

See **5.12** for the role of the Commissioners in the appeal process.

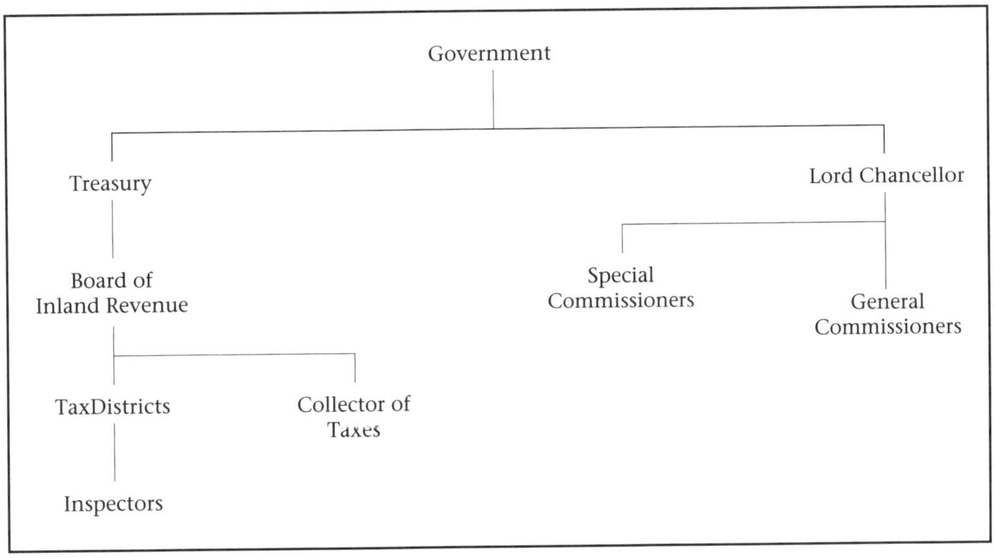

Figure 4.1 Administration of direct taxation in the UK.

4.8 Administration of inheritance tax

4.8.1 Treasury

See **4.7.1**.

4.8.2 Board of inland revenue

See **4.7.2**.

4.8.3 Capital taxes office

Unlike the taxes we have considered in **4.7** above, the Capital Taxes Office administers inheritance tax for the Board of Inland Revenue. It also deals with the actual collection of the tax.

4.8.4 Special commissioners

The appeal process is similar to that in respect of the other taxes mentioned at **4.7**.

4.9 Administration of value added tax

4.9.1 Treasury

See **4.7.1**.

4.9.2 Commissioners of Customs and Excise

The Commissioners of Customs and Excise have a headquarters in London and a VAT Centre in Southend which deals with the issue of VAT returns and the administration of payments. In addition, there are a number of VAT offices around the country which deal with registration and investigation work.

4.9.3 VAT tribunals

Appeal against a decision of the Commissioners is made to the VAT Tribunal.

4.10 Who pays tax?

The following are potentially taxable in respect of the following taxes:

4.10.1 Individuals

Income tax on income.

Capital gains tax on chargeable gains.

Value added tax if the individuals carry on a business and register for VAT or become liable to pay VAT.

4.10.2 Partnerships

Income tax on income.

Capital gains tax on chargeable gains.

Value added tax if the partnership registers for VAT or becomes liable to pay VAT.

4.10.3 Personal representatives

The deceased's outstanding income tax and income tax chargeable during the administration of the deceased's estate.

Capital gains tax on any chargeable gain arising during the administration of the estate.

VAT if they carried on the deceased's business and this was registered for VAT purposes.

Inheritance tax on the value of the deceased's estate.

4.10.4 Trustees

Income tax on the income produced by the trust fund.

Capital gains tax on any chargeable gain arising.

VAT if the trustees carry on a business and this is registered for VAT purposes or they become liable to pay VAT.

4.10.5 Companies

Corporation tax on income profits.

Corporation tax on capital gains.

Value added tax if the company is registered for VAT or becomes liable to pay VAT.

Inheritance tax in certain very limited circumstances.

4.11 Tax planning

Solicitors and accountants are frequently asked to advise clients on ways in which to reduce their tax liability. Even if the client does not actually ask them to do so, potentially they will be negligent if they fail to take account of the tax implications of a certain course of action when giving other advice. In giving this advice, it is important to understand the difference between tax avoidance and tax evasion.

4.11.1 Tax avoidance

Tax avoidance is a legitimate exercise by which the potential taxpayer seeks to organise their affairs in such a way as to ensure either that no tax will be payable in respect of something which might otherwise have given rise to a tax liability, or that the amount of the liability is reduced to the lowest possible level by the use of the available tax concessions and reliefs.

4.11.2 Tax evasion

Tax evasion involves the taxpayer ignoring a tax liability or concealing it, for example, by failing to disclose the liability to the relevant authority by making a false return. Tax avoidance is legitimate; tax evasion is not.

5

Income tax

5.1 Basic structure of income tax

5.1.1 Sources of income tax law

Sources of income tax law are:

(a) Statute: The principal charging act is the Income and Corporation Taxes Act 1988 (ICTA 1988). The annual Finance Acts have made changes to ICTA. Income tax is renewed annually by parliament.

(b) Case law and Inland Revenue statements of practice and extra-statutory concessions.

5.1.2 Income

There is no statutory definition of income. But as income tax is charged on income and not capital profits, income needs to be distinguished from capital profits. Income profits are subject to income tax. Capital profits are not subject to income tax, but may give rise to a capital gains tax liability (see **6.1.2**). Generally, income is of a recurrent nature, e.g. salary received each month, interest regularly paid on a bank or building society account every quarter, or the annual profits of an unincorporated business.

5.1.3 Who pays income tax?

The following pay income tax:

(a) individuals (including minors);

(b) partnerships;

(c) personal representatives; and

(d) trustees.

5.1.4 Income tax year

The income tax year runs from 6 April to 5 April and is called the 'tax year' or 'year of assessment'. It is referred to by the calendar years which it straddles—e.g. the tax year beginning on 6 April 2002 is referred to as the tax year 2002/03.

5.1.5 Collection of tax

There are two methods of collection of income tax. These are:

(a) deduction at source (see **5.1.5.1**); and

(b) self assessment (**5.1.5.2**).

5.1.5.1 Deduction at source

Certain types of income are said to be paid 'net of tax, i.e., subject to deduction of income tax at source. Examples of types of this income are:

(a) dividends;

(b) salaries (Pay As You Earn 'PAYE');

(c) trust income;

(d) interest paid by banks and building societies (except by the National Savings Bank);

(e) debenture interest (loan interest payments paid by companies).

The payer of the income effectively acts as a tax collector by deducting the tax from the payment and handing the tax to the Inland Revenue. (The recipient is given credit for the tax paid.) The payer then hands over the net amount to the recipient.

To prevent a multiplicity of claims for repayment of income tax by non-taxpayers there is a procedure whereby, if an investor meets certain criteria, he can register with the payer (e.g. the bank or building society) for the interest to be paid without deduction of any tax. This is done by filling in form R85. (See **Example 1**.)

5.1.5.2 Self assessment

The second method of collection of tax is self assessment which will affect anyone whose income is not subject to deduction of tax at source. Examples of persons who will have to file income tax returns to the Inland Revenue are:

(a) self-employed;

(b) partners;

(c) company directors;

(d) individuals having more than one source of income;

(e) individuals in receipt of investment income the receipt of which may make them liable to tax at thc higher rate.

EXAMPLE 1

An investor has an account with a bank or building society on which interest of £100 gross is due. He will receive £80 from the bank/building society, the bank/building society having deducted tax at the savings rate (technically known as the lower rate) (20% in the year 2002/03) of £20 to hand to the Inland Revenue.

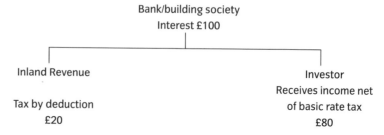

Bank/building society
Interest £100

Inland Revenue
Tax by deduction
£20

Investor
Receives income net
of basic rate tax
£80

If he is a basic rate taxpayer, then he will have no further liability for tax on this income.

If the taxpayer's circumstances are such that he is not liable for tax, then he will be able to make a repayment claim to the Inland Revenue for the £20 paid on his behalf by the bank/building society

Bank/building society
Interest £100

Inland Revenue		Investor
Tax by deduction		Receives income net of basic rate tax
£20		£80
	Reclaims	
(20)	➡	20
nil		£100

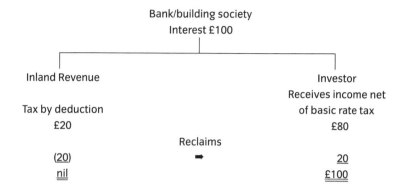

If the taxpayer is a starting rate taxpayer he will be able to reclaim the difference between the tax which would have been paid at the starting rate and the tax payable at the savings rate i.e. £10.00

However, if he is a higher rate taxpayer, then he will be liable for a further £20 tax on this income.

Bank/building society
Interest £100

Inland Revenue		Investor
Tax by deduction		Receives income net of basic rate tax
£20		£80
	Additional liability	
(20)	⬅	20
£40		£60

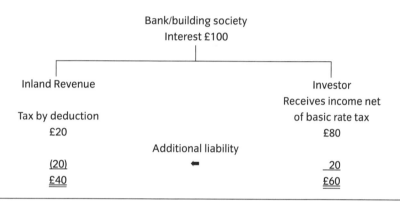

5.2 Calculation of income tax

Income tax is charged on an individual's taxable income.

There are a number of steps that must be followed to determine an individual's liability to income tax. These are as follows:

Step 1 You need to identify all sources of statutory income (see **5.4** and **5.5**).

Step 2 Next you must ascertain total income by deducting any charges on income (see **5.6**).

Step 3 Once you have deducted charges on income you must deduct personal allowances treated as tax deductions to ascertain taxable income (see **5.7**).

Step 4 Having ascertained taxable income you can now apply the appropriate rates of tax (see **5.8**). You must remember that there are rules as to the order in which different sources of income are taxed. (see **5.5, 5.8**, and **Example 13**).

Step 5 Having applied the rates of tax you should identify and apply any allowances treated as tax reductions (see **5.9**).

Step 6 Lastly, you must deduct any tax deducted at source (see **5.10**).

To summarise the above using the terms:

Statutory income
less
Charges on income
=
Total income
less
Personal reliefs (personal allowance and blind person's allowance only)
=
Taxable income

We will be looking at each of the elements for calculating taxable income. It is *important* that you learn this formula.

5.3 Rates of tax

5.3.1 The rates and tax bands

Income tax is charged at starting, basic and higher rates. For the tax year 2002/03 the rates of tax are as follows:

Slice of taxable income	*Rate*	*Referred to as:*
£1–£1,920	10%	starting rate
£1,921–29,900	22%	basic rate
£29,901 and above	40%	higher rate

Therefore, the starting rate of 10 per cent is charged on the first £1,920 of taxable income, the basic rate of 22 per cent is charged on the next £27,980 of taxable income and the higher rate of 40 per cent is charged on all taxable income above £29,900.

EXAMPLE 2

An individual has *taxable* income of £31,000. His tax liability is computed as follows:

Slice of taxable income	*Rate*	£
£1,920	at 10%	192.00
£27,980	at 22%	6,155.60
£1,100	at 40%	440.00
Tax liability		6,787.60

5.3.2 Exceptions

5.3.2.1 When calculating the tax liability of a taxpayer whose income includes savings and dividend income, the savings income and the dividend income must be treated as the top slices of income. This is looked at in more detail in **5.5**.

Dividend income attracts both a starting and basic rate of 10 per cent. However, if the taxpayer is a higher rate taxpayer the dividend income will attract tax at 32.5 per cent. For this reason dividend income is treated as the top slice of income after savings income.

5.3.3 Personal representatives

Personal representatives are liable to the basic rate of tax only, 22 per cent for the tax year 2002/03. On savings income, where the basic rate is 20 per cent there is no additional liability to income tax.

5.3.4 Trustees

Trustees are liable to either the basic rate of tax, or the rate applicable to trusts. (See **6.2.1.3** and **11.4.2**.)

5.4 Statutory income

5.4.1 Calculating statutory income

Looking back at the calculation of taxable income (**5.2**), it can be seen that the first step is to calculate the individual's statutory income.

'Statutory income' is the total of an individual's income computed according to the rules contained in the various Schedules set out in ICTA 1988. Each schedule relates to a particular form of income and has rules for determining how much of the income from that source goes into the computation of statutory income.

An individual may have (and often does have) more than one source of income which fall into different schedules. The schedules are set out in detail below.

However, certain types of income are exempt from income tax (exempt income), i.e. they are not included in calculating statutory income. These items include:

(a) child benefit and certain other social security benefits;

(b) the first £70 of National Savings Bank interest each year;

(c) interest on National Savings Certificates;

(d) scholarships;

(e) interest on damages for personal injuries or death;

(f) certain maintenance received;

(g) interest on a Tax Exempt Savings Account (TESSAs);

(h) dividends paid on a Personal Equity Plan (PEPs);

(i) all interest and dividends paid on Individual Savings Account (ISA);

(j) gross income up to £4,250 p.a. from renting a room (subject to certain conditions being satisfied).

5.4.2 The schedules

Schedule	*Source of income*	*Basis of assessment*
A	Rent and other receipts from land in the UK. Furnished lettings	CYB
D Case I	Profits of a trade in the UK.	CYB
D Case II	Profits of a profession or vocation in the UK.	CYB
D Case III	Interest, annuities and other annual payments.	CYB
D Case VI	Income not taxable under another Schedule.	CYB
E	Offices, employments and pensions, chargeable benefits under social security legislation (sick pay, maternity payments).	CYB
F	Dividends and certain other distributions by companies.	CYB

CYB = current year basis.

5.4.2.1 Basis of assessment

The basis of assessment for each Schedule determines which income is taxable in a particular tax year, i.e. whether the income to be taxed in a particular year is the income earned in that year or for an accounting period ending in that tax year.

5.4.2.2 Current year basis

Tax is charged on the income received in that tax year, e.g. Schedule E—for the tax year 2002/03, the taxpayer will be charged to tax on salary received between 6 April 2002 and 5 April 2003 (inclusive).

5.5 Grossing up

Certain types of income will be received by the taxpayer net of tax. (Remember collection of tax by deduction at source at **5.1.5.1**.) In order to calculate the taxpayer's liability to tax, it is necessary to include the gross amount of that particular source of income in the taxable income calculation.

The reason for this is that except in the case of salary, tax will only have been deducted at the savings rate of income tax, however, it may well be that the particular circumstances of this taxpayer are such that his taxable income attracts tax at the higher rate as well as the starting and basic rates. It is therefore necessary to add the gross amount of this source of income to the taxpayer's other income in order to calculate the exact amount for which the taxpayer is liable. However, credit is then given for the tax deducted at source. The balance is the amount which the taxpayer must pay to the Inland Revenue.

Dividend income is treated differently from savings income in that the taxpayer will receive a tax credit of 10 per cent of the gross dividend as if tax had been deducted at that rate at source.

In order to calculate the gross income where tax has been deducted at source, the formula is as follows:

$$\text{Gross amount} = \text{Net amount} \times \frac{100}{(100 \text{ less the rate at which tax has been deducted})}$$

Grossing up should be applied to trust income, interest paid by banks and building societies (except the National Savings Bank), debenture interest (all of which are known as savings income) and dividend income.

Schedule E income should not be grossed up because, under the PAYE system, income tax at all rates will have been deducted by the employer using tables and information supplied by the Inland Revenue and taking into account the taxpayer's personal reliefs. A certificate of tax paid (Form P60) is given by the employer to the employee on a yearly basis showing the gross figure. If the taxpayer has other sources of income apart from salary, then he will put this figure in his tax return for the purposes of assessing what further tax liability (if any) he has.

Therefore, in order to calculate the gross amount which goes into the computation of statutory income, the formula is as follows for savings income:

$$\text{Gross amount} = \text{Net amount} \times \frac{100}{(100 - 20)} = \text{Net amount} \times \frac{100}{80}$$

The formula for grossing up dividend income is as follows:

$$\text{Gross amount} = \text{Net amount} \times \frac{100}{(100 - 10)} = \text{Net amount} \times \frac{100}{90}$$

EXAMPLE 3

Maria receives dividend income of £900.

The calculation to gross up the dividend income is:

$$\text{Gross dividend} = 900 \times \frac{100}{90} = £1{,}000$$

In the example above, once Maria's income tax liability is calculated she will be entitled to a credit of the income tax deducted at source. This is referred to as a tax credit. In this case she will be entitled to a tax credit of £100 against her final liability (i.e. the tax paid on the gross dividend of £1,000 at the rate of 10 per cent).

As stated earlier, at **5.3.1**, the basic rate of tax is normally 22 per cent. However, savings income is an exception in that it attracts a basic rate of tax of 20 per cent, not 22 per cent. Therefore, if the taxpayer is a starting or basic rate taxpayer, the tax paid by the body paying the interest will satisfy the taxpayer's liability to tax. If the shareholder receiving savings income is a non-taxpayer he will be able to make a repayment claim to the Inland Revenue for the tax paid by the relevant body. However, if he is a higher rate taxpayer, then he will be liable to pay tax on the gross amount of the savings income at 40 per cent less the tax credit for the tax paid on his behalf by the relevant body.

The full amount of the savings income is treated as a top slice of income (but before dividend income). When the rates of tax are applied to the taxable income (which, do not forget, will include the gross amount of savings income) it is necessary to treat the full amount of the savings income included in the taxable income as a top slice of income and calculate the tax on it before calculating the tax on dividend income.

Dividend income attracts a basic rate of tax of 10 per cent, not 22 per cent. Therefore, if the taxpayer is a starting or basic rate taxpayer the tax deemed to be paid by the company paying the dividend will satisfy the taxpayer's liability to tax. If the shareholder is a non taxpayer or is unable to utilise the tax credit in full there is no right to make a repayment claim. If the taxpayer is a higher rate tax payer then he will be liable to tax on the gross amount of the dividend income of 32.5 per cent less the tax credit.

Trustees are taxed on dividend income at the rate of 25 per cent.

EXAMPLE 4

Daniel's taxable income has been calculated at £32,000. This includes gross savings income of £6,000. This means that his non-savings income is £26,000 (£32,000 – £6,000).

Ignoring reliefs/charges on income for the purposes of this exercise, applying the rates of tax and using the non-savings income first:

Slice of taxable income	*Rate*	*Tax £*
£1,920 of non-savings income	at 10%	192.00
£24,080 of non-savings income	at 22%	5,297.60

(i.e. £26,000 of non-savings income, leaving £3,900 of the basic rate band still available) then continuing to apply the rates of tax to the savings income, remembering that savings income attracts a basic rate of tax of 20%, not 22%:

£3,900 of savings income	at 20%	780.00
£2,100 of savings income	at 40%	840.00
Tax liability		7,109.60
less tax credit		(1,200.00)
Tax to be paid to the collector		£5,909.60

If instead of savings income the £6,000 had all been dividend income then the calculation would be as follows:

Slice of taxable income	*Rate*	*Tax £*
£1,920 of non-dividend income	at 10%	192.00
£24,080 of non-dividend income	at 22%	5,297.60

then continuing to apply the rates of tax to the dividend income, remembering that dividend income attracts a basic rate of 10%, not 22% and a higher rate of tax of 32.5%:

£3,900 of dividend income	at 10%	390.00
£2,100 of dividend income	at 32.5%	682.50
Tax liability		6,562.10
less tax credit		(600.00)
Tax to be paid to the collector		£5,962.10

5.6 Charges on income

Once statutory income has been calculated, the next step is to calculate total income. Total income is derived by deducting from statutory income what are known as 'charges on income'. Charges on income are a form of relief because they remove sums of money from the income tax calculation.

Charges on income are deducted from the taxpayer's income for the tax year in which they are paid. The type of charges within the scope of this book are payments of interest on qualifying payments.

Most interest payments do not attract tax relief and must be paid out of taxed income (e.g. credit card and overdraft interest). However, in certain cases, tax relief is available for interest paid on money borrowed. The qualifying payments for income tax purposes within the scope of this book are:

(a) a loan to invest in a partnership;

(b) a loan to invest in a close trading company;

(c) a loan to personal representatives to pay IHT (inheritance tax)

You should, of course, bear in mind that there are other types of charges on income. We will look at those with which we are concerned in more detail below.

5.6.1 Loan to invest in a partnership

The loan must be for a qualifying purpose. These are:

(a) to buy a share in a partnership; or

(b) to make a loan to a partnership provided the money is used for the purposes of its trade, profession or vocation; or

(c) to add to a partner's capital.

There is also a condition which must be satisfied. This is that the partner must be a partner (or become a partner) when the loan is made and must still be a partner when the interest is paid.

EXAMPLE 5

Sally is a partner in a firm of solicitors. Her statutory income is £30,000. She borrows £10,000 to make a loan to the partnership. This loan is to be used to buy new office equipment. Interest is charged on the loan at the rate of 10% per annum. This means that she will pay interest of £1,000 each year on that loan.

As the interest on the loan is for a qualifying purpose (i.e. it is a loan to her partnership and the money is to be used for the purposes of its profession) and as she is a partner when the interest is paid, the interest paid will be treated as a charge on income.

Therefore, Sally will calculate her total income as follows:

	Statutory income	£30,000
less		
	Charges on income	£1,000
equals		
	Total income	£29,000

5.6.2 Loan to invest in a close trading company

The loan must be for a qualifying purpose. These are:

(a) to purchase shares in a close trading company; or

(b) to lend money to a close trading company.

A close company is a company which is controlled by:

(a) five or fewer participators (i.e. shareholders); or

(b) participators (however many) who are also directors.

'Control' lies in the hands of those holding more than one-half of the votes at a general meeting of shareholders (i.e. a majority shareholding). Therefore, if a company has nine or fewer shareholders, then it will always be a close company. Whatever the distribution of shareholdings, there must always be five who, between them, own a majority of the shares. In assessing 'control', rights of shareholder's 'associates' (e.g. spouse, children) are also taken into account.

There also some conditions which must be complied with. These are:

(a) The company must carry on a trade, and

(b) The borrower must either:

 (i) own or acquire at least 5 per cent of the shares in the company; or

 (ii) be a shareholder and work for the greater part of his time in the management or conduct of the company.

EXAMPLE 6

Colworth Engineering Ltd has nine shareholders, one of whom is Stephanie. She is also a full-time working director of the company.

Stephanie takes out a loan of £5,000 to lend to Colworth Engineering Ltd. Interest on the loan is charged at 10% per annum. Therefore the annual interest paid by Stephanie is £500.

Colworth Engineering Ltd is a close trading company. It is a close trading company because it has only nine shareholders.

We do not know Stephanie's shareholding but as she is a full-time working director she meets the condition that 'the borrower is a shareholder and works for the greater part of her time in the conduct of the company'.

This means that the loan is for a qualifying purpose and the interest paid will be treated as a charge on income.

Stephanie will be able to deduct the £500 interest as a charge on income.

5.6.3 A loan to personal representative to pay inheritance tax

Personal representatives (PRs) are liable to income tax on the income received by the estate during the administration period at the basic rate of 22 per cent (or 10 per cent in the case of dividend income from companies). They are not liable to pay income tax at any higher rates but neither do they qualify for any allowances.

You will see in **Chapter 13** on entitlement that PRs often have to pay inheritance tax (IHT) in respect of part of the deceased's estate before they obtain a grant. The PRs, however, need to obtain the grant before they can dispose of assets in the estate which will then enable them to pay the IHT. The PRs will often need to take out a loan to pay this part of the IHT. If a loan is taken out then income tax relief is available to them to the extent that the loan was to pay IHT on personal property in the UK.

5.7 Personal reliefs treated as income tax deductions

Once total income has been calculated, the next step is to deduct personal reliefs in order to compute the taxpayer's taxable income. It is important to differentiate between a tax deduction and a tax reduction (see **5.9**) because the treatment will make a difference to the amount of tax ultimately payable. Only tax deductions are taken into account at this stage.

5.7.1 Personal representatives and trustees

Personal representatives and trustees are not entitled to any personal reliefs.

5.7.2 Tax deductions

There are only two reliefs which are dealt with as tax deductions:

(a) the personal allowance (including the personal age allowance), and

(b) the blind person's allowance.

The remaining reliefs are dealt with as income tax reductions. These are dealt with in more detail in **5.9**.

Personal reliefs treated as deductions from total income are looked at in more detail below.

5.7.2.1 Personal allowance (PA)

Each individual is entitled to a personal allowance. For 2002/03 this is £4,615.

The personal age allowance is also treated as a tax deduction (see **5.9.1.2**).

Husband and wife are taxed separately and are each entitled to a personal allowance. If one spouse has a surplus personal allowance, the surplus cannot be transferred to the other spouse, nor can it be carried forward and used in a later year. However, if one spouse has an unused personal allowance, a tax saving can be made by transferring assets producing income to that spouse.

5.7.2.2 Blind person's allowance

A registered blind person can claim a relief in addition to his other allowances. The full relief may be claimed even if the blind person was so registered for only part of the tax year for which the claim is made.

For 2002/03, the relief is £1,480.

5.8 Applying the rates of tax to statutory income

Having ascertained taxable income, the next step is to apply the rates of tax. Before this, the taxable income must be split down into non-savings income, savings income, and dividend income. This is because the rates of tax must be applied in the following order:

(a) Non-savings income.

(b) Savings income.

(c) Dividend income.

Savings income and dividend income are treated as the top two slices of income. (See **Example 4, Example 8,** and **5.5.**)

5.9 Personal reliefs treated as income tax reductions

Certain personal reliefs only attract tax relief at a particular rate. For the tax year 2002/03, the rate is 10 per cent. These reliefs are treated as income tax reductions.

The reliefs dealt with in this way relevant to this course are:

(a) children's tax credit,

(b) married couples' age allowance, and

(c) qualifying maintenance payments.

If the reliefs were dealt with as a deduction, in the same way as the personal allowance and the blind person's allowance, then relief would be obtained at the taxpayer's highest rate, i.e. 40 per cent, 22 per cent or 10 per cent according to the taxpayer's individual circumstances, and not at the prescribed rate of 10 per cent of the relevant relief. Therefore, the reliefs are instead treated as income tax reductions. That is, the amount of the taxpayer's liability to tax for the relevant tax year is reduced by an amount equal to 10 per cent of the relevant relief.

The reduction can only reduce the taxpayer's tax bill to nil—there cannot be any repayment of tax.

The reliefs are covered in more detail at **5.9.1.1** to **5.9.1.3**.

5.9.1.1 Children's tax credit

A new children's tax credit was introduced in the tax year 2001/02. This relief may be claimed for a child, stepchild, adopted child or child looked after at the taxpayer's expense who is under 16 at the start of the tax year and living with the taxpayer for at least part of the tax year. There is only one credit for each family irrespective of the number of children living with the taxpayer.

The relief for the tax year 2002/03 is £5,290. The tax reduction is limited to 10 per cent of this sum (£529.00). However, this is the maximum amount that can be claimed and in the circumstances set out below the relief will be reduced.

From the tax year 2002/03 the children's tax credit is increased by £5,200 to £10,490 for the tax year in which a child is born.

For a couple living together, if neither pays higher rate tax then either can have the whole tax credit or they can opt to share the credit equally between them. With the consent of both parties the credit can be allocated to the lower wage earner. It is also possible for any unused part of the tax credit to be transferred to the other partner at the end of the tax year.

However, if either partner is a higher rate taxpayer the partner earning the highest income must claim the credit. The relief (£5,290) is reduced by £2.00 for every £3.00 of taxable income that the taxpayer earns in excess of the basic rate tax band.

There are special rules for allocation of the credit in the year of marriage, commencement of cohabitation, splitting up or if the child only lives with the parent for part of the tax year. These rules are beyond the scope of this book.

5.9.1.2 Age allowances

Individuals are entitled to higher personal (see **5.7**) and married couples' allowances (MCA) if they are of a certain age at the end of the tax year:

Personal allowance		
Aged 65 to 74	For tax year 2002/03	£6,100
Aged 75 and over	" "	£6,370
Married couple's allowance		
Aged 65 to 74	For tax year 2002/03	£5,465
Aged 75 and over	" "	£5,535

A man who is married and living with his wife for any part of a tax year is entitled to the married couple's allowance for that year in addition to his personal allowance. However to qualify for the allowance at least one of the couple must have reached the age of 65 before 6 April 2000.

The MCA is automatically allocated to the husband but:

(a) The married couple may jointly elect that the MCA be allocated wholly to the wife. (The election must be made before the beginning of the appropriate tax year.) *or*

(b) The wife may elect independently that half of the MCA be allocated to her. (Again, the election must be made before the beginning of the appropriate tax year.)

(c) If any part of the MCA cannot be used fully by either the husband or wife then that spouse may give notice to the Inland Revenue to transfer the unused part to the other spouse. This election must be made within five years of 31 January next following the appropriate tax year.

There are special rules relating to the MCA for the year of marriage, separation and death which are outside the scope of this book.

Income limit for age related allowances

The full age allowances are only available if the taxpayer's total income does not exceed £17,900 (2002/03). Above this limit:

(a) the PA is reduced by £1 for every £2 of the taxpayer's total income over £17,900 until it equals the normal PA.

(b) The MCA is similarly reduced by £1 for every £2 of the husband's total income above £17,900 less any reduction in his PA under (a) above until it equals £2,110, which will be the minimum MCA. The tax reduction is limited to 10 per cent of this sum (£211.00).

EXAMPLE 9

Henry is a married man aged 78 with a total income of £22,900. As Henry is over 75 he is entitled to the higher personal allowance of £6,370. As he is also married, he is also entitled to the higher MCA of £5,535. However, as his total income exceeds £17,900, a reduction in the PA and MCA must be made for the excess income.

To calculate the PA and MCA available to Henry we first calculate the reduction for the excess income. The excess income is calculated by deducting from his total income the limit of £17,900, giving a figure of £5,000. This is then halved as the reduction is £1 for every £2 of excess income, giving a reduction of £2,500.

We then look at the amount of PA available:

Personal allowance

	£
Age allowance	6,370
less	
reduction for excess	(2,500)
	3,870

As this is below the normal PA of £4,615 the reduction is limited to £1,755, the difference between the age allowance and the normal PA. Henry gets relief equal to the normal PA of £4,615.

The amount of MCA available to him is then calculated:

	£
Married couple's allowance	
Age allowance	5,535
less	
reduction for excess (the unused reduction, £2,500 – £1,775)	(725)
	4,810

MCA age allowance available: £4,180

As this is higher than the minimum MCA of £2,110 the higher figure of £4,810 is taken. Relief is limited to 10 per cent of this figure i.e. £481.00.

5.9.1.3 Maintenance payments

Tax relief for maintenance payments was withdrawn from the tax year 2000/01 unless one or both of the parties was born before 6 April 1935. Further consideration of maintenance payments is outside the scope of this book.

5.10 Deduction of tax deducted at source

The last step is to deduct any tax deducted at source (see **5.1.5.1** and **5.5**). This is to ensure that taxpayer does not account again for the tax already deducted by, for example, the bank or building society. It is also important to remember that most employees will have had tax deducted under the PAYE system.

5.11 Date for payment

5.11.1 Taxpayers not subject to deduction of tax at source

For anyone not subject to deduction of tax at source, e.g. sole traders or partners, tax is payable in three tranches.

(a) an interim payment on 31 January during the relevant tax year;

(b) a further interim payment on 31 July following the end of the relevant tax year;

(c) a balancing payment/repayment on 31 January following the end of the relevant tax year.

For the tax year 2002/03 tax will be payable as follows:

(a) first interim payment 31 January 2003;

(b) second interim payment 31 July 2003;

(c) a balancing payment/repayment on 31 January 2004.

The amounts of each of the 'interim payments' will normally be based on half of the income tax liability (less any tax deducted at source) for the preceding tax year. However, the taxpayer will have the right to reduce payments on account where he believes that the amounts due for the current year will be less. Payments on account will not be required when substantially all of a taxpayer's income is subject to deduction of tax at source, for example PAYE, or where the amount is below a threshold to be determined by the Treasury from time to time.

Interest will run on tax from the date it is due to the date it is paid. The Inland Revenue will pay interest on amounts overpaid from the date of payment (or the due date, if later), to the date of repayment.

In addition, if a tax liability for a tax year is not paid by 28 February following the tax year, a surcharge of 5 per cent of the outstanding tax will be charged. There will be a right of appeal against the surcharge on the grounds of reasonable excuse.

The taxpayer has a choice of when the tax return is submitted. If the taxpayer includes all information on the tax return and forwards this to the Inland Revenue no later than 30 September in the following tax year, the Inland Revenue will calculate the assessment on his behalf. Otherwise the filing deadline is 31 January following the tax year (or two months after the Inland Revenue have required him to make a return, if later) and the taxpayer must calculate the amount of the assessment. In either case the Inland Revenue may later amend the assessment if it was incorrect.

5.11.2 Deduction at source

Where income is received after deduction of income tax at source (e.g. dividends, interest) and the taxpayer is a higher-rate taxpayer, the extra tax is due on 31 January following the tax year.

So far as Schedule E income is concerned (i.e. salary), tax is deducted and paid to the Inland Revenue under the PAYE system at lower, basic and higher rates at the time the salary is paid. It is computed by use of personal tax codes, issued by the Inland Revenue to employers and employees, and deduction tables supplied to employers. If the taxpayer has no other sources of income, then the correct amount of tax should have been paid. However, if the taxpayer has other sources of income, then the taxpayer will need to complete a tax return.

Overdue tax will attract interest.

5.12 Appeals

An appeal against an assessment must be made within 30 days of the issue of a notice of assessment. The appeal is made in writing to the local Inspector stating the grounds of appeal.

If there is no settlement, then the appeal will be listed for hearing before the General Commissioners unless the taxpayer elects to appeal to the Special Commissioners. He can do so in nearly all cases but appeals relating to personal reliefs must be heard by the General Commissioners. If an appeal is on certain technical matters, then the appeal must be dealt with by the Special Commissioners.

An appeal does not defer the date for payment or affect the amount due unless the taxpayer specifically applies for postponement of an amount of tax which the taxpayer considers to be excessive. Provided that the amount for which postponement is requested is agreed by the Inspector, the tax not disputed becomes payable 30 days after the Inspector's agreement to the postponement unless this is before the normal due date. When the appeal is determined, the postponed tax is payable 30 days after the issue of the notice by the Inspector of the amount finally agreed or the normal due date if later.

The Commissioners' decision on fact is final, but on a point of law appeal lies to the High Court provided that immediate dissatisfaction with the decision is expressed by the taxpayer. Further appeal lies to the Court of Appeal and, with leave, to the House of Lords. However, tax cannot be postponed beyond the date of the Commissioners' determination. If further appeal is to be made and the tax is found not to be payable, it will be repaid.

5.13 Back duty cases

A back duty case arises when the Revenue discovers that a taxpayer has evaded tax, usually by not disclosing his true income, by supplying inaccurate information or by claiming reliefs and allowances to which he is not entitled.

On discovery of a back duty case, the Revenue can commence criminal proceedings and/or make assessments for the lost tax plus interest and/or claim penalties. However, criminal proceedings are rarely taken and the Revenue prefer to reach some settlement with the taxpayer.

5.14 Income tax calculation

EXAMPLE 8

Thomas is a partner in a firm of architects. He borrowed £15,000 to invest in the partnership on which he pays annual interest of 9%.

In June 2001 Thomas' first wife died. He remarried his new wife Elizabeth on 12 September 2001. His income from the partnership for the tax year 2002/03 is £33,000. He also receives during the tax year 2002/03 dividend income of £3,250, net interest from the Rutland Building Society of £1,200 and net interest of £300 from the Hallam Bank plc.

Thomas' wife Elizabeth is employed as a solicitor. She receives a salary of £29,500. She has two daughters from her previous marriage who live with her. During the tax year 2002/03 she receives net interest of £5,000 from White Rose Bank; she also receives dividend income of £400 and net interest from the Rivelin Building Society of £350.

Calculate Thomas' income tax bill for 2002/03:

	Net £	*Gross* £
Calculate statutory income		
Trade profits (Schedule D Case 1)		33,000.00
Dividend income $\frac{(3{,}250 \times 100)}{100-10}$	3,250.00	3,611.11
Bank interest $\frac{(300 \times 100)}{100-20}$	300.00	375.00
Building society interest $\frac{(1{,}200 \times 100)}{100-20}$	1,200.00	1,500.00
Statutory income		38,486.11
Deduct: charges on income		
Interest on loan from Hallam Bank plc £15,000 × 9%	1,350.00	1,350.00
Total Income		37,136.11

Deduct personal allowances			
Personal allowance			(4,615.00)
Taxable income			£32,521.11

Before the rates of tax can be applied Thomas' income must be divided into dividend, savings and non-savings income. This is because dividend and savings income are always treated as the top slices of income with dividend income being taxed last. His savings income is £1,875, i.e. gross bank interest of £375 plus gross building society interest of £1,500. His dividend income is £3,611.11. His non-savings income which is taxable is £27,035.00 (£32,521.11 − £5,486.11).

Apply the rates of tax			
Taxable non-savings income is £27,035 (£32,521.11 − £5,486.11)			
	£1,920.00	@10%	192.00
	25,115.00	@22%	5,525.30
Savings income £1,875*	£1,875.00	@20%	375.00
Dividend income £3,611.11**	£990.00	@10%	99.00
	£2,621.11	@32.5%	851.86
Total tax			7,043.16
Less children's tax credit***			354.26
Total tax			6,688.90
Deduct tax deducted at source			
Bank interest		75.00	
Building society interest		300.00	
Dividend income		361.11	
		736.11	(736.11)
			£5,952.79

*All his savings income will be taxed at 20% because he has not exhausted his basic rate tax band.

**The first £990 of his dividend income will be taxed at 10% because he has not exhausted his basic rate tax band. The remaining £2,621.11 will fall to be taxed at the higher rate which for the purposes of dividend income is 32.5% as opposed to the higher rate of 40% for all other types of income.

***Both Thomas and Elizabeth are higher rate taxpayers, however because Thomas is the higher earner he must claim the children's tax credit. The credit will be reduced by £2,00 for every £3.00 of taxable income exceeding the basic rate tax band. £2,621.11 of Thomas's income falls to be taxed at the higher rate. The tax credit of £5,290 will be reduced by £1,747.41 (£2,621.11 × 2/3) to £3,542.59. The credit is limited to 10% of this amount, i.e. £354.26.

Elizabeth's tax bill will be calculated as follows:

	Net	Gross
	£	£
Calculate statutory income		
Salary (Schedule E)		29,500.00
Dividend income $\frac{(400 \times 100)}{100-10}$	400.00	444.44
Bank interest $\frac{(5{,}000 \times 100)}{100-20}$	5,000.00	6,250.00
Building society interest $\frac{(350 \times 100)}{100-20}$	350.00	437.50
Statutory income		36,631.94
Deduct charges on income		Nil
Total income		36,631.94

Deduct personal allowances			
Personal allowance			4,615.00
Taxable income			32,016.94
Apply the rates of tax			
Non-savings income £24,885.00 (£32,016.94 – £7,131.94)			
	1,920.00	@10%	192.00
	22,965.00	@22%	5,052.30
Savings income £6,687.50	5,015.00	@20%	1,003.00
	1,672.50	@40%	669.00
Dividend income £444.44	444.44	@32.5%	144.44
Total tax			7,060.74
Deduct tax deducted at source			
Dividend income		44.44	
Building society interest		87.50	
Bank interest		1,250.00	
		1,381.94	1,381.94
Less PAYE			£5,678.80

6

Capital gains tax

6.1 Basic structure of capital gains tax

6.1.1 Sources of capital gains tax law

The sources of capital gains tax law are:

(a) Statute: the principal charging Act is the Taxation of Chargeable Gains Act 1988 (TCGA).

(b) Case law and Inland Revenue statements of practice and extra-statutory concessions.

6.1.2 Capital profits

There is no statutory definition of capital profits. Capital profits need to be distinguished from income profits because capital profits may give rise to a charge to capital gains tax (CGT) as opposed to a charge to income tax. Generally capital profits are of a non-recurring nature. The consequence of this is, usually, there will be no charge to CGT where there has been a charge to income tax.

6.1.3 Collection of taxes

CGT is subject to self-assessment in the same manner as income tax. This system has been discussed in more detail at **5.1.5.2**.

6.1.4 Payment of CGT

The normal due date for payment of CGT is 31 January following the end of the year of assessment in which the gain arose. Therefore if a capital asset is disposed of in the tax year ending 5 April 2003, i.e. 2002/03, the tax falls due to be paid by 31 January 2004. Overdue tax attracts interest.

6.1.5 Appeals and back duty cases

See **5.12** and **5.13**.

6.2 Who pays CGT?

6.2.1 Chargeable persons

The following are liable to CGT:

(a) individuals;

(b) partners;

(c) personal representatives; and

(d) trustees.

6.2.1.1 Individuals

Individuals are liable to CGT.

6.2.1.2 Partners

Where there is a disposal of a partnership asset which results in a CGT liability, each partner is separately assessed for CGT upon his share of the partnership gains, i.e. a partner is liable for his share of the tax only—there is no joint and several liability.

For the tax year 2002/03 individuals and partners pay CGT at a rate of 10 per cent (in the case of starting rate taxpayers), 20 per cent (in the case of basic rate taxpayers) and 40 per cent (in the case of higher rate taxpayers).

6.2.1.3 Personal representatives and trustees

Personal representatives may incur a liability to CGT during the administration period when they dispose of chargeable assets. Trustees may also incur a CGT liability if they dispose of chargeable assets from the trust fund. However, unlike individuals and partners, personal representatives and trustees pay tax on any chargeable gains arising at the 'rate applicable to trusts'. The rate applicable to trusts for the tax year 2002/03 is 34 per cent.

6.2.2 Non-chargeable persons

The following are not liable to CGT:

(a) companies;

(b) charities.

6.2.2.1 Companies

Companies do not pay CGT. They pay corporation tax on both their income and capital profits. The principles for calculating the company's capital profits which are liable to corporation tax are the same as for calculating what gains are liable to CGT in the case of an individual.

NB Shareholders who are not companies are liable to CGT when they dispose of their shares in a company.

6.2.2.2 Charities

Charities are exempt from paying CGT.

6.3 The charge to CGT

CGT is charged on the amount of chargeable gains accruing to the taxpayer on the disposal of chargeable assets in a year of assessment. The year of assessment equates to the income tax year, i.e. 6th April to the following 5th April (see **5.1.4**). Where a taxpayer disposes of an asset a number of steps need to be followed to determine a taxpayer's liability to CGT. These steps are:

Step 1 You need to identify whether the relevant asset is a chargeable asset. If the asset does not come within the definition of chargeable asset there is no liability to CGT and the subsequent steps may be ignored.

Step 2 Next you should identify whether there has been a disposal for CGT purposes of the relevant asset. If there has been no disposal for CGT purposes there is no liability to CGT, and the subsequent steps may be ignored.

Step 3 Once you have identified that there has been a disposal of a chargeable asset the gain realised by the taxpayer on that disposal needs to be calculated.

Step 4 Consider what, if any, exemptions or reliefs are available, other than taper relief and annual exempt amount.

Step 5 When calculating the gain, on some occasions it may transpire that the taxpayer has not made a gain but has suffered a capital loss. You should remember that there are rules as to how these losses are taken into account.

Step 6 Having taken into account any capital losses, if the taxpayer has made an overall gain you should utilise any taper relief and/or annual exempt amount.

Step 7 Having followed these steps you will have determined the taxpayer's net chargeable gain for the relevant year of assessment. The liability to CGT on this net chargeable gain is calculated by applying the appropriate rates of tax.

To summarise, the steps are:

Step 1 Is the asset a chargeable asset?
Step 2 Has there been a disposal?
Step 3 Calculate the gain.
Step 4 Utilise any exemptions and reliefs other than those mentioned at Step 6.
Step 5 Utilise any losses.
Step 6 Utilise taper relief and annual exempt amount.
Step 7 Apply the appropriate rates of tax.

The remainder of this part of the book looks at these steps in more detail.

6.4 Chargeable assets

The basic rule is that all assets are chargeable assets unless they fall within an exemption.
Exempt assets include:

(a) private motor cars (including certain vintage and veteran cars);
(b) UK sterling (i.e. cash);
(c) wasting assets (i.e. assets with a predictable life of less than 50 years). Examples are TV's, washing machines and other consumer goods;

(d) tangible moveable property (e.g. antiques) if the disposal consideration is £6,000 or less.

Chargeable assets are divided into two categories; business assets and non-business assets. It is important to determine into which category an asset falls as different levels of taper relief will apply (see **6.8.4.1** and **6.8.4.2**).

6.5 Disposal

A disposal occurs:

(a) on the sale of the whole or part of an asset which is not an exempt asset;

(b) on the gift of the whole or part of an asset which is not an exempt asset;

(c) on the receipt of a capital sum resulting from the ownership of an asset which is not an exempt asset (even if the person paying the capital sum does not acquire the asset). An example of this would be if a valuable painting (i.e., worth more than £6,000) was destroyed by fire and the owner received a payment of its value under an insurance policy.

6.5.1 Death

On death, there is no disposal by the deceased and therefore no CGT liability. However, there is a deemed acquisition by the personal representatives for CGT purposes. They are deemed to acquire the deceased's assets at their market value at the date of death. A future disposal by the personal representatives may give rise to a CGT liability on any gains arising between the date of death and the date of the disposal. The effect of this rule is to wipe out any gains which accrued during the deceased's lifetime.

6.5.2 Spouses

Where spouses are living together, a disposal between them is treated as producing neither a gain nor a loss. There will therefore be no CGT payable on the transfer. However, the gains arising before the date of transfer are not wiped out. The payment of CGT on those gains is merely deferred. When the donee spouse later disposes of the asset, then he will be charged to tax not only on his gain, but on the gains accrued during the period of ownership by the other spouse as well (see **6.9.2**).

6.5.3 Relevant date of disposal

Where the disposal is by way of sale, the disposal occurs on exchange of contracts and not on completion of the contract. This is important for determining into which year of assessment the disposal falls.

For example, where Colin is selling a building plot and exchanges contracts on 30 March 2002 with completion on 21 April 2003, any gain made would fall to be taxed within the tax year 6 April 2001 to 5 April 2002.

6.6 Calculation of the gain

Once you have identified that there has been a disposal of a chargeable asset during the year of assessment, the next step is to calculate the gain arising from the disposal.

6.6.1 The gain

The gain arising on the disposal is the consideration for the disposal less allowable expenditure.

6.6.2 Consideration for the disposal

6.6.2.1 Sales at arm's length

Normally, where there is a sale and the sale is at arm's length (i.e. not between connected persons), then the sale price is taken to be the consideration for CGT purposes. If an asset is sold for payments by way of instalments, then the consideration is the aggregate of the payments.

6.6.2.2 Sales at an undervalue

If the sale is at an undervalue then the sale for CGT purposes is deemed to be at the market value of the asset on the date of disposal (see **6.5.3**). The actual consideration paid is ignored. However, if it can be shown that the low sale price was only as a result of a bad bargain, then the actual sale price will be taken.

As will be seen when dealing with inheritance tax, a gift or sale at an undervalue may also lead to a charge to inheritance tax if the donor dies within seven years of the disposal. If the charge to inheritance tax does occur, then the inheritance tax attributable to the value of the asset can be treated as an expense which is deductible in calculating the gain on the donee's disposal.

However, the deduction of the inheritance tax can only reduce the donee's gain to nil; it cannot create a loss which the donee is then able to use to reduce other gains in the same tax year or carry forward to future tax years.

6.6.2.3 Sales between connected persons

If the sale is not at arm's length (i.e. it is between connected persons), then the gain, if any, will be calculated by reference to the market value of the asset on the date of the disposal. The actual consideration agreed between the parties is ignored. The purpose of the rules is to prevent taxpayers avoiding CGT by fixing an artificially low sale price which will correspondingly produce an artificially low gain.

Connected persons include:

(a) spouse*;

(b) relatives (brothers, sisters, parents, grandparents, children, grandchildren, i.e. lineal descendants);

(c) spouses of any connected person;

(d) business partners (except where partnership assets are disposed of under a *bona fide* commercial arrangement).

*Note that transfers between spouses are a special category and the transfer is treated as being on a no gain/no loss basis (see **6.5.2** and **6.9.2**).

6.6.2.4 Gifts

If there has been a gift, then for CGT purposes, the consideration is the market value of the asset on the date of disposal.

6.6.2.5 Market value

Market value is the price the asset might reasonably be expected to fetch on the open market.

6.6.3 Allowable expenditure

Allowable expenditure is the total of the:

(a) initial expenditure;
(b) subsequent expenditure; and
(c) incidental costs of disposal.

6.6.3.1 Initial expenditure

'Initial expenditure' is:

(a) the acquisition cost of the asset or where there is a disposal between connected persons the market value of the asset at the date of acquisition; and
(b) the incidental costs of acquisition (e.g. legal and valuation fees, stamp duty, etc.); or
(c) (if the asset was created rather than acquired) expenditure wholly and exclusively incurred in creating the asset (e.g. the cost of building a weekend cottage).

6.6.3.2 Subsequent expenditure

Subsequent expenditure is:

(a) expenditure wholly and exclusively incurred for the purposes of enhancing the value of the asset, otherwise known as enhancement expenditure, i.e. expenditure which is reflected in the state or nature of the asset at the date of disposal (e.g. cost of building an extension but not the cost of routine maintenance or insurance); and
(b) expenditure wholly and exclusively incurred for the purposes of defending title to the asset (e.g. legal fees in resolving a boundary dispute).

6.6.3.3 Incidental cost of disposal

Incidental cost of disposal is the cost incurred in disposing of the asset (e.g. legal and estate agent's fees, advertising costs).

EXAMPLE 1

David bought his holiday cottage in 1990, from his father, for £50,000. The market value of the cottage as at that date was £70,000. During the purchase, David incurred legal fees of £800 and stamp duty of £500. Since he purchased the cottage, David has spent £1,500 having double-glazing put in the cottage and £600** on decorative repairs.

David now sells the cottage for £100,000, incurring legal fees of £700 and estate agent's fees of £1,400.

What is David's gain on the sale of the cottage?

		£
Consideration		100,000
Less: Allowable expenditure:		
Initial expenditure:		
Acquisition cost (market value*)	£70,000	
Incidental costs of acquisition:		
Legal fees	£800	
Stamp duty	£500	
Subsequent expenditure:		
Improvements	£1,500	
Incidental costs of disposal:		
Legal fees	£700	
Estate agent's fees	£1,400	(74,900)
Gain		£25,100

* The acquisition cost is deemed to be market value because David bought the cottage from a connected person, his father.

** The decorative repairs do not form part of the allowable expenditure because they are a cost of routine maintenance.

6.7 Capital losses

It may be that the consideration received on the disposal is less than the cost of the asset. If so, there will be a capital loss arising from the disposal.

A capital loss is created when the cost of the asset is greater than the consideration received.

6.7.1 Setting losses against gains

If a loss arises on a transaction chargeable to CGT, it is first offset against other chargeable gains arising in the same tax year ('carry across' relief). Therefore, it is necessary to calculate the gain or loss on each disposal made during the tax year, using the principles which have been covered above. Once this has been done, the gains are added together to calculate the total gains for the tax year. Similarly, the losses are added together to calculate the total losses for the tax year. The total losses are then deducted from the total gains to calculate the gains (losses) for the tax year.

Since 6 April 1998 losses are deducted before applying taper relief and the annual exempt amount (but after deducting other reliefs) and are allocated in the manner most beneficial to the taxpayer.

6.7.2 Carry forward of losses

If, having offset the losses against other gains in the same tax year, there is still an unrelieved balance of loss, this can be carried forward. The losses can be set off to reduce gains to the level of the annual exempt amount. The loss can be carried forward in this way indefinitely until all the loss has been relieved in subsequent tax years ('carry forward' relief).

6.8 Exemptions and reliefs

There are a number of exemptions and reliefs that should be considered before the amount to be taxed can be determined. The main exemptions and reliefs are contained in paragraphs **6.8.1** to **6.8.8**.

It is important to realise that the exemptions and reliefs can interact with each other in different ways. The various interactions are highlighted and explained in the paragraphs dealing with the exemptions and reliefs. It is advisable to identify all appropriate exemptions and reliefs for any given scenario. Once the appropriate exemptions and reliefs have been identified, and the interaction between them determined, the exemptions and reliefs can be properly applied.

6.8.1 Annual exempt amount

6.8.1.1 Individuals

There is an exempt band available for each tax year, i.e. gains up to that limit are not liable to CGT. For the tax year 2002/03, the annual exempt amount is £7,700. The exemption or any unused part of it cannot be carried forward.

6.8.1.2 Personal representatives and trustees

Personal representatives and trustees have an annual exempt amount. For personal representatives the annual exempt amount for gains accruing in the year of death and the two following years of assessment are the same as for an individual (i.e. for the tax year 2002/03, £7,700). Beyond the third year they have no annual exempt amount. All chargeable gains are chargeable to CGT. For trustees the annual exempt amount is an amount equal to one-half of the individual's annual exempt amount (i.e. for the tax year 2002/03, £3,850).

6.8.2 Tangible moveable property

It has already been stated (see **6.4(d)**) that tangible moveable property (e.g. antiques) is exempt from CGT where the consideration on the disposal is £6,000 or less.

Where the consideration on the disposal exceeds £6,000, the chargeable gain is either the actual gain or 5/3 of the difference between £6,000 and the value of the consideration, whichever is the lesser amount. (Obviously, it would be unfair if a disposal were wholly liable to CGT whereas if the consideration had been slightly less, the disposal would have been completely exempt.)

Where a loss is made on the disposal of a tangible asset sold for less than £6,000 the sale price is deemed to be £6,000 to ensure that no capital loss is created.

6.8.3 Private dwelling house

A gain on the disposal by an individual of a dwelling house, including grounds of up to half a hectare, will be completely exempt provided it has been occupied as the taxpayer's only or main residence throughout his period of ownership (TCGA, ss 222–226). For the purposes of calculating an individual's period of ownership the following may be ignored:

(a) the first year of ownership;

(b) the last three years of ownership;

(c) certain periods of absence for job-related activities.

A married couple may only have one main residence. If more than one residence is owned then an election must be made as to which is the main residence. The election may be backdated up to two years from the date of acquisition of the second residence. If no election is made the Inland Revenue will decide which is the main residence. Similar rules apply for any individual who owns more than two properties.

6.8.4 Taper relief

For all chargeable assets disposed of on or after 6 April 1998 the chargeable gain may be reduced by the application of taper relief. The rules relating to the taper relief were revised with effect from 6 April 2000, and further revised with effect from 6 April 2002. The pre-April 2002 rules are outside the scope of this book.

* – Do these after unused losses, not when look at other Reliefs!

Taper relief operates by charging a reduced percentage of the gain. The percentage of the gain which is chargeable is determined by the length of time the asset has been owned (the qualifying holding period). The relevant percentage is set out in the table below (Table 1) which reflects the position for disposals after 6 April 2002.

Table 1

Gains on disposals of business assets		Gains on disposals of non-business assets	
Number of whole years in qualifying holding period	Percentage of gain chargeable	Number of whole years in qualifying holding period	Percentage of gain chargeable
1	50	—	—
2 or more	25	—	—
		3	95
		4	90
		5	85
		6	80
		7	75
		8	70
		9	65
		10 or more	60

To use the table to arrive at the relevant percentage it is necessary to determine the following:

(a) Is the chargeable asset a business asset or a non-business asset? and

(b) What is the qualifying holding period?

6.8.4.1 Business assets

A business asset includes:

(a) an asset used for the purposes of a trade carried on by that individual, whether alone or in partnership or by a qualifying company of that individual;

(b) an asset used for the purposes of any office or employment to which that individual was at that time required to devote substantially the whole of his time;

(c) shares or securities held by an individual in a qualifying company.

A company will be a qualifying company if it is a trading company, or the holding company of a trading group, where either the company is unlisted (including any company listed on the Alternative Investment Market) or the taxpayer is an officer or employee of the company or a company within the same group, or the taxpayer holds shares which entitle him to exercise not less than 5 per cent of the voting rights.

6.8.4.2 Non-business assets

If an asset does not fall within the above definition it is not a business asset.

It is possible that an asset may have been both a business asset and a non-business asset during the period of ownership. In such circumstances there are special rules which apportion the taper relief. These rules are beyond the scope of this book.

6.8.4.3 Qualifying holding period

The qualifying holding period is the number of whole years after 5 April 1998 for which the chargeable asset is held. A whole year is any continuous period of 12 months and does not have to coincide with a tax year.

The maximum reduction in the amount of the gain chargeable to tax as a result of taper relief is reached once the asset has been owned for a qualifying holding period of ten years.

6.8.4.4 Assets held on 17 March 1998

For non-business assets only, where an asset was held on the 17 March 1998 an additional one year is added to the qualifying holding period, to the maximum qualifying holding period of ten years.

6.8.4.5 More favourable treatment of business assets

As can be seen from **Table 1** taper relief is more generous on the disposal of a business asset. A business asset needs to be held for only one whole year before taper relief applies; a non-business asset must be held for a minimum of three whole years to benefit from the relief. In addition, the amount of the gain chargeable to tax is smaller in the case of a business asset than in the case of a non-business asset. For example; where a business asset is held for a qualifying holding period of nine whole years only 25 per cent of the gain is taxable. Where a non-business asset is held for a qualifying holding period of nine whole years 65 per cent of the gain is taxable.

6.8.4.6 Taper relief and the annual exempt amount

Taper relief is taken before an individual's annual exempt amount.

EXAMPLE 2

Carlos, aged 35 and in good health, has shares which entitle him to 20% of the voting rights in Scientific Trading Limited. He is a full-time working director of the company and has a taxable income of £32,000 per annum. He acquired the shareholding, for which he paid the market value of £56,000, on 27 June 1998. He disposes of the shareholding on 6 September 2002 for which he receives consideration of £102,000. The sale is not to a connected person. He has disposed of no other chargeable assets in the tax year 2002/03. He has no capital losses from previous tax years to be relieved by carry forward relief.

To determine the taxable amount you need to work through the six steps (see **5.3**). As a reminder those steps are:

Step 1 Is the asset a chargeable asset?

Step 2 Has there been a disposal?

Step 3 Calculate the gain.

Step 4 Utilise any exemptions except those mentioned at Step 6.

Step 5 Utilise any losses.

Step 6 Utilise taper relief and the annual exempt amount.

Step 7 Apply the appropriate rates of tax.

Applying those steps:

Step 1 The asset is a chargeable asset because it does not fall within the definition of an exempt asset.

Step 2 Carlos has sold the whole of the asset and so a disposal has occurred.

Step 3 Calculate the gain:
(Ignoring incidental costs of acquisition, subsequent expenditure and incidental costs of disposal.)

	£
Consideration for the disposal	102,000
Less: Allowable expenditure:	
Acquisition cost	(56,000)
Gain	46,000

Step 4 There are no exemptions or reliefs available.

Step 5 You are told he has disposed of no other chargeable assets during the year of assessment, so there are no losses to be relieved by setting them against these gains (carry across relief). You are also told that there are no unrelieved losses from previous tax years.

Step 6 From the information supplied there are no other exemptions or reliefs available to Carlos except for taper relief and the annual exempt amount. The taper relief must be applied before the annual exempt amount.

To apply taper relief:

(a) Ascertain whether the asset is, for the purpose of taper relief, a business asset or a non-business asset. The asset is shares which are held in a qualifying company, i.e. a company in which he owns shares carrying at least 5 per cent of the voting rights and he is a full-time working officer of that company; and

(b) Ascertain the qualifying holding period. This is four whole years. The part year of ownership is disregarded.

Looking at **Table 1** only 25% of the gain will be chargeable. The gain net of taper relief is:

£46,000 × 25% = £11,500

The annual exempt amount should now be deducted.

Gain net of taper relief	11,500
Less: Annual exempt amount	(7,700)
Taxable amount	£3,800

Step 7 Carlos has taxable income of £32,000. All the gain will be taxed at the higher rate:

£3,800 × 40% = £1,520

CGT to pay = £1,520

6.8.5 Hold-over relief (gifts and sales at an undervalue)

Hold-over relief is available where there has been a gift or a sale at an undervalue (TCGA, s 165). Where the disposal is a sale at an undervalue, the relief is available, but only in respect of that part of the gain which is attributable to the 'gift' element. It is available in respect of business assets only.

Business assets include:

(a) goodwill;

(b) assets used in the business (including assets owned personally but used in the business);

(c) shares of a trading company not quoted on the Stock Exchange or the Alternative Investment Market;

(d) shares in a trading company which is a personal company. A personal company is one where the taxpayer owns at least 5 per cent of the voting shares in that company.

Both donor and donee must elect for the relief as the effect is to postpone payment of tax and shift liability to the donee. The donor's gain arising from the disposal will not be charged to CGT but will be 'held over' until the donee's eventual disposal of the asset. The gains are not wiped out. Liability for the donor's gains during his period of ownership of the asset shifts to the donee in that when the donee eventually disposes of the asset, he will be charged to CGT on both gains, subject to any exemptions or reliefs available to the donee at that time.

If the donee does not dispose of the asset until his death, then the donor's gain will escape CGT altogether (as will as the donee's gain). This is because there is no disposal (and therefore no charge to CGT) on death (see **6.5.1**). The donor's chargeable gain which is to be held over is calculated in the usual way.

The donee is deemed to acquire the asset at market value less the donor's chargeable gain. The effect of this is that when the donee eventually disposes of the asset, his gain will include the donor's gain.

The donor is not able to reduce the gain to be held over by applying his annual exempt amount. The effect of this rule is that unless the donor has other gains in the tax year against which he can use his annual exempt amount, that amount will be unused. Therefore, if the donor is not expected to make any other disposals in the tax year and the gain arising from the disposal is the same as or only marginally exceeds his annual exempt amount, then the donor and donee may decide not to elect for this relief so as to obtain a greater tax saving.

EXAMPLE 3 (hold over relief)

Martin transfers his business to his son when the market value of the business is £50,000. Martin purchased the business on 1 April 1982 for £10,000. Ignoring indexation and any other exemptions and reliefs:

The net gain to be held over will be calculated as follows:

	£
Market value	50,000
Less: Acquisition cost	(10,000)
Net gain held over	£40,000

If Martin's son later sells the business for £60,000 net of expenses of the sale, the net gain on disposal will be calculated as follows:

	£
Sale price (net)	60,000
Less: Acquisition cost*	(10,000)
Chargeable gain	£50,000

* Acquisition cost is the market value at date of his acquisition less the held over gain:

£50,000 − £40,000 = £10,000

6.8.6 Roll-over relief on replacement of qualifying business assets

This relief encourages expansion and investment in business assets by enabling the sale of those assets to take place without an immediate charge to CGT provided the sale proceeds are invested in other business assets within a certain period (TCGA, s 152). The charge to

CGT is postponed until the disposal of the new asset. There is a similar relief for companies (see **8.6.1.2**).

The relief is available to an individual who disposes of a qualifying asset used in or by a trade, profession or vocation. For these purposes the definition of 'trade' includes a trade carried on by a personal company (i.e. a company in which the individual has not less than 5 per cent of the voting rights).

There are other circumstances which may qualify for relief but these are beyond the scope of this book.

Qualifying assets include:

(a) fixed plant and machinery not forming part of a building;

(b) land and buildings occupied for the purposes of a trade (NB the trade must not be the development of land);

(c) goodwill;

(d) milk quotas and potato quotas;

(e) ewe and suckler cow quotas;

(f) ships, aircraft and hovercraft.

There are other qualifying assets for the purpose of roll-over relief (TCGA, s 155).

It is important to remember that both the 'old' and 'new' asset must be qualifying assets although not necessarily of the same kind. For example, a farmer could sell land occupied for the purpose of his business and roll over his gain into milk quota.

The replacement asset must be acquired within a period commencing one year before and ending three years after the disposal of the 'old' asset.

The 'old' asset must also have been used in the taxpayer's business throughout its ownership otherwise the roll-over relief will be apportioned *pro rata* to the period of such use.

The effect of roll-over relief is that the gain will be effectively postponed until either the disposal of the 'new' asset or or any gain is no longer rolled over into the purchase of a further qualifying asset.

As with hold-over relief, the whole of the gain arising on the disposal of the business asset must be rolled over. Again, this means that unless the taxpayer has other disposals in the same tax year, his annual exempt amount will be wasted if he elects for the relief. This relief may be used in conjunction with taper relief. However, there are special rules as to the application of taper relief in these circumstances which are beyond the scope of this book.

6.8.7 Retirement relief

This relief is available to an individual who disposes of a business interest when aged 50 years or over, or when he is less than 50 years old but retiring on the ground of ill-health at the time of the disposal (TCGA, ss 163–164).

To qualify for the relief the disposal must be of a business or part of a business or be a disposal of assets used for the purpose of the relevant business at the date of cessation of that business. For these purposes a business encompasses a sole trader, a partnership or a personal company, i.e., a company in which the disponor holds at least 5 per cent of the voting rights. The disponor must also be a full-time working officer or employee of the company in a management or technical capacity. Generally the Inland Revenue will regard a full working week as 30 hours. If, however, an individual subsequently wishes to reduce his working hours then, provided he works a minimum of 10 hours a week in a management or technical capacity, then the benefit of the relief can be preserved. Only the period of full-time employment will be taken into account in determining whether the individual is entitled to any or full relief.

To obtain any relief the relevant business or asset must have been owned for at least one year prior to the disposal. To obtain full relief the business or asset must have been owned for at least 10 years prior to disposal. If the business or asset has been owned for between one and 10 years then the relief will be applied *pro rata*.

For the tax year 2002/03 full relief is available on gains of up to £50,000 and on 50 per cent of gains between £50,000 and £200,000, i.e. on the next available £150,000. The maximum relief available is £125,000 i.e. £50,000 + (1/2 × £150,000). The relief available will no longer be available from the tax year 2003/2004. The following table (**Table 2**) shows the maximum relief available for the tax year 2002/03.

Table 2

Year	100% relief up to and including	50% relief between
2002–03	£50,000	£50,000 and £200,000

Unlike hold-over relief and roll-over relief on the replacement of business assets it is possible to use this relief in conjunction with taper relief and the annual exempt amount. It is, however, important to remember that until retirement relief is phased out the relief must be applied before taking into account taper relief and the annual exempt amount. This means that any gains qualifying for retirement relief which are not wholly absorbed by that relief will further benefit from taper relief.

EXAMPLE 4

Margot, aged 60, has shares which entitle her to 50% of the voting rights in Frost Interiors Limited. She is the full-time working managing director of the company and has a taxable income of £100,000 per annum. She acquired the shareholding, for which she paid the market value of £30,000, on 10 January 1986. Margot disposes of the shareholding on 6 July 2002 for which she receives consideration of £1,200,000. The sale is not to a connected person. She has disposed of no other chargeable assets in the tax year 2002/03. She has no capital losses from previous tax years to be relieved by carry-forward relief.

To determine the CGT payable you need to work through the six steps (see **6.3**). As a reminder those steps are:

Step 1 Is the asset a chargeable asset?

Step 2 Has there been a disposal?

Step 3 Calculate the gain.

Step 4 Utilise any exemptions and reliefs other than those mentioned at Step 6.

Step 5 Utilise any losses.

Step 6 Utilise taper relief and the annual exempt amount.

Step 7 Apply the appropriate rates of tax.

Applying those steps:

Step 1 The asset is a chargeable asset because it does not fall within the definition of an exempt asset.

Step 2 Margot has sold the whole of the asset and so a disposal has occurred.

Step 3 Calculate the gain:
(Ignoring indexation (see **6.11**) incidental costs of acquisition, subsequent expenditure and incidental costs of disposal.)

	£
Consideration for the disposal	1,200,000
Less: Allowable expenditure:	
Acquisition cost	(30,000)
Gain	1,170,000

Step 4 From the information supplied, Margot will be potentially eligible for retirement relief. She will also be eligible for taper relief and the annual exempt amount. Retirement relief must be applied before the taper relief and the annual exempt amount (see **6.8.4.6**).

To ascertain what retirement relief is available:

(a) Ascertain her age. She is aged 60.

(b) Ascertain whether the asset is eligible. The asset is shares in a personal company (i.e. she owns shares carrying more than 5% of the voting rights) and she is a full-time employee of the company in a management capacity.

(c) Ascertain the period she has held the shares. The shares have been held for 13 years. Margot will be eligible for full retirement relief which is available as follows:

The first £50,000 of the gain @ 100%	£50,000
The second £150,000 of the gain @ 50%	£75,000
Total retirement relief available	£125,000

The amount of the gain remaining unrelieved after retirement relief will be:

£1,170,000−£125,000 = £1,045,000

Step 5 You are told she has disposed of no other chargeable assets during the year of assessment, so there are no losses to be relieved by setting them against these gains (carry-across relief). You are also told that there are no unrelieved losses from previous tax years.

Step 6 Taper relief can now be applied.
To apply taper relief:

(a) Ascertain whether the asset is, for the purpose of taper relief, a business asset or a non-business asset. The asset is shares which are held in a qualifying company, and

(b) Ascertain the qualifying holding period. This is 4 whole years. The part year of ownership is disregarded.

Looking at **Table 1** (see **6.8.4**) she is entitled to four years relief and only 25% of the gain will be chargeable. The gain net of taper relief is:

£1,045,000 × 25% = £261,250.00

The annual exempt amount should now be deducted.

	£
Gain net of taper relief	261,250.00
Less: Annual exempt amount	(7,700.00)
Taxable amount	£253,550.00

Step 7 Margot has taxable income of £100,000. All the gain will be taxed at the higher rate:

£253,550 × 40% = £101,420
CGT to pay = £101,420

6.8.8 Roll-over relief on incorporation of a business

The relief is available when an individual transfers an unincorporated business as a going concern to a limited company either wholly or partly in consideration for the issue of shares in that company (TCGA, s 162). The relief will be restricted if the consideration is only partly provided by the issue of shares. This relief may be used in conjunction with taper relief. However, there are special rules as to the application of taper relief in these circumstances which are beyond the scope of this book.

6.8.9 Life policies

Gains accruing on disposal of a life policy (which occurs on assignment, surrender or maturity) are exempt unless the disponor is not the original beneficial owner and acquired their rights or interest for consideration in money or money's worth.

6.9 Taxation of the chargeable gain (the applicable rates of tax)

6.9.1 Individuals

As has been stated previously, individuals are charged to CGT on their chargeable gains at rates equivalent to the rates of income tax which would apply if the gains were treated as their top slice of income. It is therefore necessary to consider the taxpayer's income tax position when deciding what rate or rates of CGT to apply.

So if Khaled's taxable income is £30,000 and, after his annual exempt amount of £7,500, he has chargeable gains of £2,500 then his gains will be charged at 40 per cent. £29,400 of his taxable income will have used up his starting and basic rate tax bands. The last £600 of his taxable income will be charged at 40 per cent as will his chargeable gain of £2,500. The £2,500 is charged as the top slice of his income.

EXAMPLE 5

Laura has a taxable income of £20,000. After taking into account her annual exempt amount she has chargeable gains of £10,000. Applying the rates of tax to calculate the CGT payable.

£		£
9,900 (29,900 − 20,000)	at 20%	1,980
100 (10,000 − 9,900)	at 40%	40
CGT payable		£2,020

NB the first £20,000 of the starting and basic rate bands have already been absorbed by Laura's taxable income of £20,000. Therefore the first £9,900 of the chargeable gain will be taxed at the 20% rate, leaving £100 to be taxed at 40%.

6.9.2 Husband and wife

A husband and wife are taxed separately for CGT purposes. They each have an annual exempt amount of £7,700. A disposal between spouses does not give rise to CGT.

The disposal is treated as neither producing a gain nor a loss. However, the gain is not wiped out altogether. When the donee spouse disposes of the asset, then that spouse will be charged to CGT not only on the spouse's own gain but also on the donor spouse's gain. The donee spouse is deemed to acquire the asset at donor spouse's acquisition cost.

EXAMPLE 6

Andrew acquires a plot of land in June 1983 for £6,000. On 25 December 1985 he transfers the plot to his wife Ellen. Ignoring any other exemptions or reliefs.

On 10 June 1992 Ellen sells the plot for £20,000.

On the transfer from Andrew there will be no CGT payable because of the spouse exemption. When Ellen disposes of the property CGT will be calculated as follows:

Her cost of acquisition is the price at which Andrew bought the land, i.e. £6,000.

Ellen's net gain will be calculated as follows:

	£
Consideration	20,000
Less: Allowable expenditure:	
Acquisition cost	6,000
Net gain	£14,000

6.9.3 Personal representatives and trustees

Personal representatives and trustees pay CGT at the rate applicable to trusts whatever the size of their gains. For the tax year 2002/03 this is 34 per cent (see **6.2.1.3**).

6.10 Instalment option

There is an option to pay CGT by instalments in two cases:

(a) undue hardship (**6.10.1**);

(b) gifts of land and certain shareholdings (**6.10.2**).

6.10.1 Undue hardship

If the consideration is payable by instalments over a period exceeding 18 months from the date of disposal and the Revenue are satisfied that the taxpayer would otherwise suffer undue hardship, the CGT may also be paid by instalments.

The Inland Revenue directs the period (not exceeding eight years) over which the CGT can be paid and what constitutes undue hardship.

6.10.2 Land and certain shareholdings

Where the disposal is a gift of:

(a) land;

(b) a controlling shareholding in any company;

(c) a minority holding in an unquoted company;

then the CGT may be paid by ten equal annual instalments *but* the option is only available provided hold-over relief is not available on the disposal. This applies even if hold-over relief is available but not claimed.

Interest on these instalments runs from the normal date for payment unless the gift is of agricultural property.

6.11 Assets held at 5 April 1998 (indexation allowance)

When calculating the gain (see **6.6** above) an allowance (indexation allowance) is made to some elements of the allowable expenditure. This allowance is made to remove from the charge to CGT any increase in the value of the asset which is solely due to the effects of inflation since the asset was acquired or the expense incurred. The effect of inflation on the value of the asset, or expenditure incurred, is calculated by using the Retail Prices Index (RPI) which is published monthly by the government.

The indexation allowance is only taken in account when calculating the gain on assets held at 5 April 1998. If an asset was acquired after that date no allowance is made for indexation.

The table below (**Table 3**) gives details of the multiplier, the indexed rise, which is to be applied to the relevant item of allowable expenditure by reference to the month in which that expenditure was incurred.

Table 3 **Capital gains tax indexation allowance: April 1998**

RI Year	Jan	Feb	Mar	Apr	May	Jun	Jul	Aug	Sep	Oct	Nov	Dec
1982	—	—	2.047	2.006	1.992	1.987	1.986	1.985	1.987	1.977	1.967	1.971
1983	1.968	1.960	1.956	1.929	1.921	1.917	1.906	1.898	1.889	1.883	1.876	1.871
1984	1.872	1.865	1.859	1.834	1.828	1.823	1.825	1.808	1.804	1.793	1.788	1.789
1985	1.783	1.769	1.752	1.716	1.708	1.704	1.707	1.703	1.704	1.701	1.695	1.693
1986	1.689	1.683	1.681	1.665	1.662	1.663	1.667	1.662	1.654	1.652	1.638	1.632
1987	1.626	1.620	1.616	1.597	1.596	1.596	1.597	1.593	1.588	1.580	1.573	1.574
1988	1.574	1.568	1.562	1.537	1.531	1.525	1.524	1.507	1.500	1.485	1.478	1.474
1989	1.465	1.454	1.448	1.423	1.414	1.409	1.408	1.404	1.395	1.384	1.372	1.369
1990	1.361	1.353	1.339	1.300	1.288	1.283	1.282	1.269	1.258	1.248	1.251	1.252
1991	1.249	1.242	1.237	1.222	1.218	1.213	1.215	1.213	1.208	1.204	1.199	1.198
1992	1.199	1.193	1.189	1.171	1.167	1.167	1.171	1.171	1.166	1.162	1.164	1.168
1993	1.179	1.171	1.167	1.156	1.152	1.153	1.156	1.151	1.146	1.147	1.148	1.146
1994	1.151	1.144	1.141	1.128	1.124	1.124	1.129	1.124	1.121	1.120	1.119	1.114
1995	1.114	1.107	1.102	1.091	1.087	1.085	1.091	1.085	1.080	1.085	1.085	1.079
1996	1.083	1.078	1.073	1.066	1.063	1.063	1.067	1.062	1.057	1.057	1.057	1.053
1997	1.053	1.049	1.046	1.040	1.036	1.032	1.032	1.026	1.021	1.019	1.019	1.016
1998	1.019	1.014	1.011									

If an asset was held on 5 April 1998, the indexation allowance to that date must be calculated before taper relief is applied.

The elements of the allowable expenditure to which indexation applies are:

(a) the acquisition cost;

(b) the incidental costs of acquisition; and

(c) any subsequent expenditure.

Indexation is not applied to the incidental costs of disposal.

Each element of the allowable expenditure to which indexation applies must be indexed separately. Each item of expenditure is multiplied by the indexed rise relevant to the month in which that expenditure was incurred. As has already been mentioned, the indexed rise is ascertained by reference to **Table 3**.

The Indexation allowance cannot be used to create a capital loss.

EXAMPLE 7

Bharti buys a holiday cottage in January 1990 for £80,000. In May 1993 she builds a conservatory onto that cottage. The cost of building the conservatory is £6,000.

The indexed gain up to 5 April 1998 will be calculated as follows:

(a) The indexed rise for January 1990, the month of acquisition of the cottage, is ascertained from **Table 3**. This is 1.361. This multiplier is applied to the acquisition cost of £80,000 to give the indexed acquisition cost of £108,880.

(b) The indexed rise for May 1993, the month in which the subsequent expenditure was incurred, is also ascertained from **Table 3**. This is 1.152. This multiplier is applied to the subsequent expenditure of £6,000 to give the indexed subsequent expenditure of £6,912.

The gain is then calculated in the usual way.

Using the above facts the calculation will be:

Allowable expenditure:	£
Acquisition cost (acquisition cost + indexation allowance)	108,880
Subsequent expenditure (subsequent expenditure + indexation allowance)	6,912
Total allowable expenditure to 5 April 1998	£115,792

6.12 Assets held at 31 March 1982

There are also special rules for assets owned on the 31 March 1982.

Where there is a disposal on or after 6 April 1998 of a chargeable asset which was acquired by the taxpayer before 1 April 1982 the indexation allowance is calculated by reference to further special rules. These rules are beyond the scope of this book.

6.13 Disposals of part

When the disposal is of only part of the asset, the initial and subsequent expenditure must be apportioned when calculating the gain on the disposal of part.

To find out what proportion of the initial and subsequent expenditure is deductible in calculating the gain on the disposal of part, the formula is as follows:

$$\frac{A}{A + B}$$

where A = consideration received for the part disposed of, and B = market value (at the date of disposal) of the part retained.

EXAMPLE 8

Jill bought a large plot of land in 1985 for £400,000 including her costs of acquisition. She now sells part of it for £100,000. The market value of the retained part is £400,000. Her costs of disposal are £2,000. What is her gain on the disposal? Ignoring indexation and any other reliefs.

Proportion of initial expenditure deductible (there is no subsequent expenditure):

$$\frac{£100{,}000}{£100{,}000 + £400{,}000} = 1/5$$

In calculating the gain on the disposal of part, Jill is able to deduct 1/5 of the total initial expenditure.

		£
Consideration		100,000
Less: Allowable expenditure:		
Add:		
Initial expenditure (1/5 × £400,000)	80,000	
Incidental costs of disposal	2,000	(82,000)
Gain		£18,000

6.14 Tax planning

6.14.1 Using the annual exempt amounts of both spouses

Remember that both spouses will be entitled to an annual exempt amount. Therefore, it may be worthwhile transferring assets to the other spouse or into the joint names of both, so as to make use of both exemptions. There will be no charge to CGT on the transfer.

6.14.2 Using the lower and basic rate bands of tax of both spouses

If one spouse pays income tax at the higher rate but the other only pays income tax at the lower or basic rate, then it will probably be beneficial to transfer assets into the name of the less wealthy spouse. When the less wealthy spouse disposes of the asset, then at least part of the gain will be charged to CGT at a lower rate.

EXAMPLE 9

Harry acquired a plot of land in 1988 for £2,000. He sells the land in June 2002 for £25,000. His taxable income is £30,000. Ignoring any exemptions or reliefs other than the annual exempt amount:

	£
Consideration	25,000
Less: Allowable expenditure:	
Acquisition cost	(2,000)
Gain	23,000
Less: Annual exempt amount	(7,700)
Chargeable gain	£15,300

All of Harry's gain will be charged at 40% because he is a higher rate taxpayer and the chargeable gain is treated as the top slice of income. He will pay CGT of £6,120.

Harry's wife Margaret, however, has a taxable income of £5,000. If Harry transfers the land to her she will acquire it (because of the spouse exemption) at Harry's acquisition cost. If she disposes of the property her chargeable gain will be calculated as follows:

	£
Consideration	25,000
Less: Allowable expenditure:	
Acquisition cost	(2,000)
Gain	23,000
Less: Annual exemption	(7,700)
Chargeable gain	£15,300

Because Margaret has not yet used all of her basic rate tax band of 20% the whole of the gain will be charged at the basic rate. She will pay CGT of £3,060.

The tax saving for Harry and Margaret will be £3,060 which represents £6,120 (i.e. Harry's potential tax bill) less £3,060 (i.e. Margaret's potential tax bill).

When you are considering whether to transfer assets, however, remember that the cost of legally transferring the asset to the spouse may be more than the potential tax saving. This must be taken into account. You must remember also that you cannot utilise any unused income tax allowances when calculating the CGT liability on the chargeable gain.

7

Inheritance tax

7.1 Basic structure of inheritance tax

7.1.1 Sources of inheritance tax

Sources of inheritance tax (IHT) law are:

(a) Statute: The principal charging Act is the Inheritance Tax Act 1984 (IHTA 1984). (The true name of the statute is the Capital Transfer Tax Act 1984 but s 100, Finance Act 1986 provides that it may be known as the Inheritance Tax Act 1984 and it is by this title that it is generally referred to.) However, as for income and capital gains tax, annual Finance Acts have made changes to the Act.

(b) Case law and Inland Revenue statements. Again, as for income and capital gains tax, these may be relevant as sources of IHT law.

7.1.2 Administration

IHT is a direct tax and is administered in the same way as income and capital gains tax.

7.1.3 Collection of tax

7.1.3.1 Lifetime transfers

Tax due in respect of lifetime transfers liable to IHT is collected by direct assessment.

7.1.3.2 Death

Tax due on the death of a person is also collected by direct assessment. A form of self assessment is used.

7.1.4 Appeals and back duty cases

The same regime applies as for income tax and you should refer to **5.12** and **5.13**.

7.2 The charge to inheritance tax

Section 1 of the Inheritance Tax Act 1984 (IHTA 1984) states that 'Inheritance tax shall be charged on the value transferred by a chargeable transfer.' This raises two questions, what is a *chargeable transfer* and how is the *value transferred* calculated?

7.2.1 Chargeable transfers

7.2.1.1 The legislation

Section 2 of IHTA 1984 expands on s 1 and explains that, 'A chargeable transfer is a *transfer of value* which is made by an individual but is not . . . an *exempt transfer*.' The Act then goes on to expand this further stating what is meant by a transfer of value (IHTA 1984, s 3) and what is meant by an exempt transfer. (See **7.5.2** and **7.6.3**.)

A transfer of value:

> is a disposition made by a person (the transferor) as a result of which the value of the transferor's estate immediately after the disposition is less than it would be but for the disposition; and the amount by which it is less is the value transferred by the transfer. (IHTA 1984, s 1(3)).

The Act excludes some assets from the charge to tax and also details dispositions which are not transfers of value.

7.2.1.2 Excluded assets

Excluded assets

Categories of excluded property are set out in ss 6, 47 and 48 of IHTA 1984. Section 6 includes property situated outside the UK where the person beneficially entitled to it is domiciled outside the UK. Sections 47 and 48 deal with reversionary interests in settled property. The term reversionary interest is used to describe the situation where X leaves some property in a settlement so that Y enjoys the income from that settlement during his lifetime, but, on Y's death, the property goes to Z absolutely. Prior to Y's death, Z's interest in the settled fund is referred to as a 'reversionary interest'. This interest is excluded property so far as Z is concerned. In some cases the reversionary interest will not be excluded property. One example would be if it was purchased for money or money's worth.

7.2.1.3 Dispositions which are not transfers of value

Gratuitous benefit

A disposition is not a transfer of value if the transferor had no intention to confer a gratuitous benefit. This principle is relevant where there has been a sale at an undervalue. If the transferor can prove that he made a bad bargain (for example, through not recognising how much the asset was really worth) and had no intention of conferring a gratuitous benefit on the transferee, then the loss resulting to the transferor's estate arising from the bad bargain will not have any IHT implications.

Dispositions for family maintenance (IHTA 1984, s 11)

Payments by a transferor to spouses, children and dependent relations which result in a loss to the transferor's estate are not chargeable in the following circumstances:

(a) if the payment is by one spouse for the maintenance of the other. (This provision includes any disposition for maintenance made on the occasion of a divorce); or

(b) if the payment is for the maintenance, education or training of a child of the marriage (or of any other child not in the care of its parents); or

(c) if the payment represents reasonable provision for the care and maintenance of a dependent relative.

7.3 Potentially exempt transfers

In addition to excluded assets and dispositions which are not transfers of value, some transfers of value made during a person's lifetime are classified by the Act as 'Potentially Exempt Transfers' (PETs) (IHTA 1984, s 3A). If a transfer of value is a PET, then if it is made seven years or more before the transferor dies it is an exempt transfer, otherwise, i.e. if the transferor dies within seven years of making the transfer, it is a chargeable transfer. Whilst the transferor is alive, it is thus potentially exempt.

A PET is a *lifetime* transfer of value made on or after 17 March 1986 to one of the following:

(a) another individual; or

(b) the trustees of an interest in possession trust made on or after 16 March 1987;or

(c) the trustees of an accumulation and maintenance trust; or

(d) the trustees of a trust for the benefit of the disabled.

The majority of lifetime transfers are PETs. One exception to be aware of is a lifetime transfer into a discretionary trust. Such a transfer will be a lifetime chargeable transfer (LCT).

7.4 The transfer of value on death

There is a deemed transfer of value on death. This means that when a person dies they are treated as if immediately before their death they made a transfer of value.

7.5 The occasions to tax

There are, then, three occasions on which IHT is charged:

(a) on a chargeable transfer made during a person's lifetime (a lifetime chargeable transfer, LCT);

(b) on a PET or LCT when the transferor does not survive seven years from the date of the transfer; and

(c) on death.

Having identified that there has been a chargeable transfer, to calculate the IHT payable on a chargeable transfer there are five basic steps to follow:

(1) Calculate the value transferred.

(2) Identify any available exemptions and deduct them from the value transferred.

(3) Identify any available reliefs and deduct them from the value transferred.

(4) Calculate the transferor's cumulative total as at the date of the transfer and the amount of the nil rate band remaining.

(5) Calculate the IHT payable by applying the appropriate rate (or rates) of tax to the value of the transfer for IHT purposes. (The rate (or rates) will depend on whether the tax is being paid on the date of the transfer or on the death of the transferor.)

The five basic steps remain the same regardless of the occasion on which the tax is being charged. Depending on which occasion is the relevant one, there are additional steps to go through. These are set out later when examples of calculating the tax are worked through for each of the three occasions on which IHT is charged.

Points which are common to all three occasions are discussed at each step below.

7.5.1 Step 1: Calculate the value transferred

The value transferred is usually the market value of the asset at the date of the transfer. Two provisos to this are set out below. There are other provisos to this which are set out when each occasion is looked at individually.

7.5.1.1 Related property

Some assets are worth more when valued together, as a set for example, than they would be if they were owned by more than one person. For example, six dining chairs could be worth £3,600 as a set, giving an individual value of £600. However, if they are not kept as a set the value of each chair would be only £200, giving a total value of only £1,200. A transferor could use this to his advantage. For example, Mr Evans owns a pair of antique side tables. The market value of the pair is £50,000 but if they were separated they would each be worth only £15,000. Mr Evans wants to give the side tables to his daughter. If he made a gift to her of the pair then he would have made a PET of £50,000 (ignoring any exemptions or reliefs). However, if Mr Evans were to give away one of the side tables to his wife the loss to his estate would be £35,000 (£50,000 less £15,000 being the value of the side table he retained). As the gift was to his wife it would be exempt for IHT purposes (see **7.5.2.1**). Mr Evans could then gift the remaining side table to his daughter, this would be a PET of £15,000 as the side table is no longer one of a pair and so has a lower value. His wife could gift the side table she received to their daughter, also making a PET of £15,000. The potential liability to IHT is therefore smaller than it would have been had Mr Evans made the gift to his daughter of both of the side tables.

Section 161 of IHTA 1984 prevents transferors from avoiding IHT in this way. Property in one spouse's estate is related to property in the other spouse's estate. Where any property in one spouse's estate would be worth more if valued together with related property in the other spouse's estate, the property is valued as a proportion of the related property valued together.

This means that, on the facts of Mr Evans above, when he makes the gift of one side table to his daughter the side table is valued with the side table in his wife's estate, as the related property rules apply, and so the loss to his estate is $1/2 \times$ £50,000 = £25,000, rather than £15,000.

Shareholdings are a good example of assets affected by the related property rules. The related property rules apply mainly to property in the estates of spouses but the rules do cover other situations where the transferor makes gifts to other exempt transferees, for example charities, and stands to benefit from a similar tax advantage.

7.5.1.2 Joint property

When an individual has only a share in an asset it is more difficult to sell the share than it would be to sell the whole. To take account of this difficulty the value of the individual's share in the asset is reduced by between 10 per cent and 15 per cent. For example, Joan and Ruth own a house as tenants in common, in equal shares. The house has a market value of £64,000. The value of Joan's share in the property for IHT purposes is in the region of £28,800 (one-half of the property is worth £32,000; 10 per cent of this is £3,200, and so the discount leaves a value of £28,800). This can be an advantage to the transferor if the transferor's share in a property is gifted to another, or the transferor dies; the loss to the transferor's estate is smaller because of the discount. However, if a transferor owns an asset outright and chooses to gift a share in the asset, the loss to the transferor's estate is higher as the value of the share of the asset retained must be discounted before ascertaining the loss to the estate. For example, if Joan owned the house outright and chose to gift a half share to Ruth the loss to Joan's estate would not be £32,000, one-half of the value of the house. It would be £35,200, as the value of the share she has retained is worth only £28,800, after taking into account the discount.

When the joint owner is the transferor's spouse the related property rules apply and no discount is given.

7.5.2 Step 2: Identify any available exemptions and deduct them from the value transferred

A transfer of value made by an individual will not be a chargeable transfer if it is an exempt transfer. There are a number of exemptions available, some cause the whole transfer to be exempt, others cause part of the transfer to be exempt with the remainder of the transfer being a chargeable transfer or a PET.

The transfer of value may qualify for exemption by virtue of the fact that it is a disposition to an exempt transferee (these are applicable on lifetime dispositions *and* on death) or because it comes within one of a number of limited *lifetime* transfers which qualify for exemption.

7.5.2.1 Exemptions available on lifetime transfers and on death

Given below is a list of the main exemptions available both on lifetime dispositions and on death. The statutory reference is given for the exemptions and the relevant section should be consulted for the full conditions applicable.

Exemptions available on lifetime dispositions only are set out at **7.6.3**.

(a) *Transfers between spouses* (IHTA 1984, s 18): Transfers between spouses are exempt provided that the gift is immediate, i.e. the gift takes effect immediately. However, it is common for a spouse to state in his will that his estate will pass to the other spouse only if the other spouse survives for a specified period. As long as the specified period does not exceed 12 months the spouse exemption will still apply.

Provided both the transferor and the spouse are domiciled in the UK there is no limit on the amount of the exemption. However, the exemption is limited if the transferor was domiciled in the UK but the spouse was not. The current limit to the exemption is these circumstances is £55,000.

(b) *Gifts to charities* (IHTA 1984, s 23).

(c) *Gifts to political parties* (IHTA 1984, s 24).

(d) *Gifts for national purposes* (e.g. to British Museum or National Trust) (IHTA 1984, s 25).

(e) *Gifts for public benefit* (IHTA 1984, s 26).

7.5.3 Step 3: Identify any available reliefs and deduct them from the value transferred

Applicable reliefs available both on lifetime transfers and deemed transfers of value on death are business property relief (BPR) and agricultural property relief (APR).

Generally, any exemption is deducted before any available relief. However if the disposition is a lifetime disposition and BPR or APR is available at 50 per cent the relief is given before deducting the annual and other exemptions. This ensures that the exemptions are maximised.

7.5.3.1 Business property relief

BPR relief operates to reduce the value transferred by a transfer of relevant business property by either 100 per cent (i.e. no charge to IHT) or 50 per cent. To qualify for the relief the transferor must have owned the relevant business property for two years prior to the transfer. However, if the relevant business property is a replacement for other relevant business property, then the relief will be available if the combined period of ownership is two years or more.

7.5.3.2 Relevant business property

The following categories of property qualify for BPR:

(a) a business or interest in a business, e.g. the business of a sole proprietor or a partner's interest in a business;

(b) shares in an unquoted company;

(c) shares in a quoted company which give the transferor control of the company; or

(d) land or building, machinery or plant used for the purposes of a business carried on either:

  (i) by a company (unquoted or quoted) of which the transferor has control; or

  (ii) by a partnership of which the transferor was a partner.

The reduction in the value transferred is 100 per cent for business property coming within categories (a) and (b) and 50 per cent for business property coming within categories (c) and (d).

7.5.3.3 Related property

Under the related property rules (see **7.5.1.1**), holdings of husband and wife are treated as one holding and if their total holding gives control then either will have control for the purposes of the relief. See **Example 3** below.

7.5.3.4 Additional rule for lifetime transfers

Where a lifetime transfer is made (either a lifetime chargeable transfer or a PET where the transfer does not survive by seven years) and IHT (or additional IHT) becomes payable because the transferor dies within seven years, then the relief is not available unless the property originally transferred (or replacement property which qualifies as relevant business property) is still owned by the transferee at the date of the transferor's death (or transferee's death, if earlier).

EXAMPLE 1

William has shares in a quoted company giving him control of the voting. The other shares are held by unrelated parties. He gives his holding away. It is valued at £240,000. William dies one year after the gift.

The gift is a PET when it is made. As William dies within seven years of making the gift it becomes a chargeable transfer. The shares are relevant property for the purposes of BPR (category (c) at **7.5.3.2**) and so BPR is available. The value transferred is reduced by 50%. Ignoring other exemptions which may be available, the value transferred is 50% of the value of the shares at the date of the transfer; 50% × £240,000 = £120,000.

EXAMPLE 2

At the time of his death Mr Slater was the owner of a building used by an unquoted company in which he had a controlling shareholding. The value of the land at the date of his death is £350,000. The shareholding in the company has a value of £450,000.

On his death there is a deemed transfer of value. The shares are relevant property for the purposes of BPR (category (b) at **7.5.3.2**) and so BPR is available. Their value transferred is reduced by 100%. The value transferred is nil.

As Mr Slater has a controlling interest in the company, the building is also relevant property for the purposes of BPR (category (d) at **7.5.3.2**) and so BPR is available. The value transferred is reduced by 50%. The value transferred is 50% × the value of the buildings at the date of death; 50% × £350,000 = £175,000.

EXAMPLE 3

Mr Exton holds 40% of the shares in a quoted trading company. His wife holds 20% of the shares in the same company. Mr Exton gives his holding to his son.

This gift is a PET. Should Mr Exton die within seven years of making the gift then the PET will become a chargeable transfer. Due to the related property rules Mr and Mrs Exton's shareholdings are treated as one. Mr Exton is deemed to have a holding of 60% and so has control of the company. The shares are relevant property for the purposes of BPR (category (c) at **7.5.3.2**) and so BPR is available. Their value transferred is reduced by 50%.

7.5.3.5 Agricultural property relief

This relief operates in a similar way to BPR. It reduces the value transferred by a transfer of agricultural property by either 100 per cent (i.e. no charge to IHT) or 50 per cent. Agricultural property is defined in the IHTA 1984 and, basically, is agricultural land or pasture and farm buildings situated in the UK, the Channel Islands or the Isle of Man. The agricultural value of the property is taken as the value at which the property would be valued if it was subject to a perpetual covenant prohibiting its use otherwise than as agricultural property.

To qualify as agricultural property, the property must have been:

(a) occupied by the transferor for agriculture throughout the two years immediately before the transfer. (There is no condition on the time of ownership. The transferor may have rented the property initially and only purchased the property shortly before selling it. The transferor will still qualify for APR provided the total period of occupation was at least two years.); or

(b) owned by the transferor for seven years before the transfer and occupied by someone for agriculture throughout that seven-year period.

Relief at 100 per cent is available for transfers on or after 10 March 1992 if:

(i) the transferor was the owner or tenant in possession; or

(ii) the transferor had the right to obtain possession within 12 months. (By concession if the transferor has the right to obtain vacant possession within 24 months relief at 100 per cent is also given); or

(iii) where the transfer is after 1 September 1995, the transferor's interest fails to come within either of classes (i) or (ii) because of a new tenancy granted on or after 1 September 1995.

There also rules governing the position where a tenancy is inherited.

Relief at 50 per cent is available on any other qualifying agricultural property.

7.5.3.6 Additional rule for lifetime transfers

Where a lifetime transfer is made (either a lifetime chargeable transfer or a PET where the transfer does not survive by seven years) and IHT (or additional IHT) becomes payable because the transferor dies within seven years, then the relief is not available unless the property originally transferred (or replacement property which qualifies as relevant agricultural property) is still owned by the transferee at the date of the transferor's death (or transferee's death, if earlier) and the property qualifies for the relief at the date of the transferor's death.

EXAMPLE 4

Joe owns his farm, which he works, and has done so for many years. The agricultural value of his farm is £160,000. If Joe were to gift the farm, or on his death, agricultural property relief at 100% is available. The agricultural value of the farm in Joe's estate is reduced to nil.

EXAMPLE 5

Alistair owns a farm which has been let to a tenant farmer for the past nine years. The agricultural value of the farm subject to the tenancy is £200,000. If there were to be a disposal by Alistair agricultural relief would be available at 50% and the value of the property would be reduced to £100,000 for IHT purposes.

7.5.4 Steps 4 and 5

Step 4: Calculate the cumulative total of the transfers at the date of the transfer and the amount of the nil rate band remaining.

Step 5: Calculate the IHT payable by applying the rate (or rates) of tax to the value of the transfer for IHT purposes.

These two steps require some further explanation.

7.5.4.1 The rates of IHT

IHT is currently charged at two rates. For the tax year 2002/03 the first £250,000 is taxed at 0 per cent, the nil rate band (NRB), the amount above £250,000 is taxed at 40 per cent. (See the example on a lifetime chargeable transfer for the rate which applies to LCTs at the time they are made.) **All calculations shown here have assumed that the current rates have always applied.** This is not the case. The rates usually alter with each tax year, following an announcement in the budget by the Chancellor. Tax tables should be consulted to determine the rates of tax which were applicable at any given date.

7.5.4.2 The principle of cumulation

IHT operates on a cumulative basis, the cumulation period being seven years. The rate (or rates) of tax applicable to a chargeable transfer depends on the cumulative total of all chargeable transfers made by the transferor in the seven years preceding the transfer currently being charged. As a consequence of the cumulation principle, the transfer is taxed as the top slice of the aggregate of the cumulative total and the transfer. The cumulative total eats into the NRB. To calculate the rate (or rates) of tax at which the chargeable transfer is to be taxed, the cumulative total is deducted from the NRB. If, after deducting the cumulative total from the NRB, there is some NRB remaining then the amount of the transfer equal to the NRB remaining is taxed at 0 per cent and the remainder of the transfer is taxed at the rate applicable to the occasion of the charge.

It is important to emphasise that the cumulative total is relevant only in determining the rate (or rates) of tax. Once this has been determined, the rate(s) is then applied only to the value transferred by the current chargeable transfer. It is not applied to the cumulative total.

To calculate the transferor's cumulative total at the date of the current transfer it is necessary to look back over the seven years preceding the date of the transfer and identify the chargeable transfers, if any, which the transferor made during that period. Having identified the chargeable transfers the next step is to calculate the net value of those transfers for IHT purposes. This is achieved by following Steps 1 to 3 inclusive.

Both examples below assume that current rates apply.

EXAMPLE 6

Isabelle dies, her estate is valued at £275,000 for IHT purposes. Three to four years before she died she gifted cash of £100,000 to her daughter, Jasmine. She made no other gifts.

When made, the gift to Jasmine was a PET. As Isabelle has died within seven years of making the gift it is a chargeable transfer. There are no other chargeable transfers within the seven years preceding Isabelle's death.

Ignoring any exemptions and reliefs which may be available on the gift to Jasmine the value transferred was £100,000. Isabelle's cumulative total at the date of her death is £100,000.

Deducting the cumulative total from the NRB, i.e. subtracting £100,000 from £250,000 leaves an amount of £150,000 of the NRB remaining. When the rate(s) of tax are applied to the value of the estate on Isabelle's death, there is £150,000 of the NRB available.

The rates of tax applied will be £150,000 taxed at 0% and the remaining £125,000 of the estate (total £275,000) taxed at 40% giving a total of £50,000 of IHT to pay.

EXAMPLE 7

Ignoring exemptions and reliefs. Philip makes a gift to a discretionary trust of £320,000. This is a lifetime chargeable transfer and is chargeable to IHT.

If this is the only gift Philip has made in the last seven years, Philip's cumulative total at the time of making the gift is nil, meaning that all of the NRB is available. The rates of tax applied will be £250,000 taxed at 0% and the remaining £70,000 taxed at 20%, giving a total of £14,000 of IHT to pay when the gift is made. (See **7.6.1**.)

However, if, in the previous seven years, Philip has made chargeable transfers of £146,000, then the IHT payable is different. Philip's cumulative total is £146,000. Deducting this from the NRB leaves an amount of £104,000 of the NRB remaining. The rates of tax applied will be £104,000 taxed at 0% and the remaining £216,000 taxed at 20%, giving a total of £43,200 IHT to pay.

7.5.4.3 Summary

Steps 4 and 5 can be summarised as the following sub-steps:

(a) Identify any chargeable transfers in the seven years preceding the current transfer.

(b) Calculate the value of those chargeable transfers for IHT purposes, i.e. find their net value for IHT. This is done by following Steps 1, 2 and 3.

(c) Calculate the transferor's cumulative total at the date of the current transfer, by adding together the net value of all chargeable transfers made in the preceding seven years.

(d) Calculate the balance of the NRB remaining, if any, by deducting the cumulative total from the NRB.

(e) Apply the rates of tax to the current transfer.

7.6 The charge to tax and a lifetime chargeable transfer

In addition to the points mentioned above, when following the five steps to calculate the IHT payable on a chargeable transfer, some additional points should also be taken into account when the occasion is a lifetime chargeable transfer. These are identified as each step is considered.

7.6.1 The rates of tax

One matter which is best dealt with at this point is a mention of the rates of IHT charged on a LCT. Provided the transferor survives seven years from the date of the transfer then the rates of tax applicable to the transfer are one-half of the usual rates, that is 0 per cent on the NRB and 20 per cent on values exceeding the NRB. However, should the transferor fail to survive the seven-year period then the usual rates of tax apply to the transfer, that is the NRB at 0 per cent and 40 per cent on values exceeding the NRB. The way this works in practice is that at the time of the LCT, IHT is paid at the reduced rates. If the transferor then dies within the seven-year period the additional tax is paid. The five basic steps are applied to a LCT at the time of the transfer.

7.6.2 Step 1: Calculate the value transferred

For lifetime dispositions the value transferred is the amount by which the value of the transferor's estate is reduced by the disposition. That is the loss to the transferor's estate. The value transferred is normally determined by reference to market value. In the case of a gift, the loss will usually be the market value of the asset transferred. In the case of a sale at an undervalue, the loss will usually be the market value of the asset less the consideration received on the sale.

It is important to note that the loss to the transferor's estate will not always equal the gain to the transferee's estate.

EXAMPLE 8

Peter owns 51% of the issued share capital of Crookesmoor Ltd. The total issued share capital amounts to 10,000 shares. Peter is able to pass an ordinary resolution at a shareholders' meeting on his own (an ordinary resolution is arranged by 51% of the vote) and, because of this, his holding is deemed to carry control of the company and is valued accordingly. Peter's 51% holding in the company is valued at £11 per share.

Peter wishes to give 200 of his shares (i.e. 2% of the company), to his son, David. A stake of that size, being a very small minority holding in the company (i.e. one which does not carry control), is worth only £3 per share.

Assume that a 49% holding in Crookesmoor Ltd, because it no longer carries control, is only worth £7 per share.

The diminution in Peter's estate is:

	£
Value of estate before gift (5,100 at £11)	56,100
Less value of estate after gift (4,900 at £7)	34,300
	£21,800

This is a very different result from the £600, which is the value to David of the shares actually gifted (200 at £3).

7.6.2.1 Related property

Do not overlook the effect of the related property rules (see **7.5.1.1**)

7.6.2.2 Grossing-up

As mentioned earlier, the value transferred is the amount by which the transferor's estate is reduced by the disposition. The transferor is primarily liable for any IHT due on a lifetime chargeable transfer, but the transferee can pay. Usually it is the transferee who pays the IHT. This means that the loss to the transferor's estate is limited to the value of the gift itself. However, if the transferor pays the IHT due on a lifetime chargeable transfer then the loss to the transferor's estate will be the total of the gift and the IHT due on the transfer. The value of the gift must be grossed-up to find the value transferred. If the transferor is paying the IHT then the property gifted is generally described as the *net chargeable transfer* and the loss to the transferor's estate is described as the *gross chargeable transfer*, being the net chargeable transfer plus the attributable tax. The steps to follow when grossing-up a transfer are:

(a) Calculate the net chargeable transfer (NCT); i.e. from the chargeable transfer deduct any exemptions or reliefs which may be available, e.g. the annual exemption, spouse exemption, BPR or APR.

(b) Calculate the amount of the net chargeable transfer exceeding the transferor's NRB at the date of the transfer. To do this calculate how much of the transferor's NRB is available by calculating the transferor's cumulative total at the date of the transfer and deducting it from the full NRB. This will give the amount of the NRB available. Subtracting this amount from the NCT will leave the amount of the NCT exceeding the NRB.

(c) Calculate the IHT payable. The formula to use is:

IHT = 1/4 × amount of NCT exceeding NRB

This formula applies when the lifetime rate of IHT is 20 per cent. For periods when the rate of tax differed consult tax tables.

(d) Calculate the gross chargeable transfer (GCT). This is done by adding the net chargeable transfer to the IHT payable. GCT = NCT + IHT. This is the loss to the transferor's estate.

EXAMPLE 9 (grossing up (assumes that the current rates apply))

Mr Teal transfers £160,000 into a discretionary settlement. He is to pay the IHT. He has made chargeable transfers in the last seven years amounting to £275,000 for IHT purposes.
Working through the steps:

(a) Calculate the net chargeable transfer (NCT). On the facts given here the only exemption or relief available is the annual exemption for the tax year in which the gift is made (see **7.6.3.1**). *Assume that the previous year's annual exemption was used elsewhere*. The NCT is £157,000 (i.e. £160,000 − £3,000 annual exemption).

(b) Calculate amount of the net chargeable transfer exceeding Mr Teal's NRB. Mr Teal has a cumulative total £275,000. His nil rate band is used up and this means that all of the current chargeable transfer exceeds the NRB.

(c) Calculate the IHT payable. Applying the formula: IHT = 1/4 × £157,000 = £39,250.

(d) Calculate the gross chargeable transfer. The gross chargeable transfer is the total of the NCT and IHT, which is £196,250 i.e. (£157,000 + £39,250).

The loss to Mr Teal's estate is the amount of the gross chargeable transfer, £196,250.

EXAMPLE 10 (grossing up (assumes that the current rates of tax apply))

Mrs Francis transfers £285,000 into a discretionary settlement. She is also to pay the IHT. She has made no chargeable transfers in the last seven years.

(a) Calculate the net chargeable transfer (NCT). On the facts given here the only exemption or relief available is the annual exemption for tax year in which gift is made. *Assume that the previous year's annual exemption was used elsewhere*. The NCT is £282,000 (i.e. £285,000 − £3,000 annual exemption).

(b) Calculate amount of the net chargeable transfer exceeding Mrs Francis's NRB. Subtracting the full NRB of £250,000 from the NCT leaves an amount of £32,000 exceeding the NRB.

(c) Calculate the IHT payable. Applying the formula: IHT 1/4 × £32,000 = £8,000.

(d) Calculate the gross chargeable transfer. The gross chargeable transfer is the total of the NCT and IHT, which is £290,000 i.e. (£282,000 + £8,000).

The loss to Mrs Francis's estate is the amount of the gross chargeable transfer, £292,000.

EXAMPLE 11 (grossing up (assumes that the current rates of tax apply))

Mr Frost transfers £266,000 into a discretionary settlement. He is to pay the IHT. He has made chargeable transfers in the last seven years amounting to £69,000 for IHT purposes.

(a) Calculate the net chargeable transfer (NCT). On the facts given here the only exemption or relief available is the annual exemption for tax year in which gift is made. *Assume that the previous year's annual exemption was used elsewhere*. The NCT is £263,000 (i.e. £266,000 − £3,000 annual exemption).

(b) Calculate amount of the net chargeable transfer exceeding Mr Frost's NRB. To do this calculate how much of the transferor's NRB is available by calculating the transferor's cumulative total at the date of the transfer and deducting it from the full NRB. This will give the amount of the NRB available. Subtracting this amount from the NCT will leave the amount of the NCT exceeding the NRB.

Mr Frost has a cumulative total of £69,000. This leaves £181,000 of his nil rate band available for this transfer. Subtracting the £181,000 from the NCT leaves an amount of £82,000 exceeding the NRB.

(c) Calculate the IHT payable. Applying the formula: IHT = 1/4 × £82,000 = £20,500.

(d) Calculate the gross chargeable transfer. The gross chargeable transfer is the total of the NCT and IHT, which is £283,500 i.e. (£263,000 + £20,500).

The loss to Mr Frost's estate is the amount of the gross chargeable transfer, £283,500.

Note: If transferor pays the tax, should the transferor make other gifts or die within the next seven years the *gross* figure must be brought forward as part of the cumulative total.

7.6.2.3 Incidental expenses of transfer and CGT

There may be expenses incurred in connection with the gift, or a sale at an undervalue (e.g. legal costs, stamp duty, etc.). There may also be a liability to CGT as well as to IHT. The rules for deduction of expenses or CGT from the value transferred are as follows:

(a) If the expenses or CGT are paid by the transferor, they do not reduce the value transferred.

(b) If they are paid by the transferee they reduce the value transferred.

7.6.3 Step 2: Identify any available exemptions and deduct them from the value transferred

In addition to the exemptions detailed at 7.5.2 there are additional exemptions to be taken into account. These are available for lifetime dispositions only.

7.6.3.1 The annual exemption

The first £3,000 of transfers made by a transferor in any one tax year are exempt. Where the transfers of value exceed £3,000, the first £3,000 is taken to be exempt. If the total transfers fall short of £3,000, the unused part of the exemption may be carried forward to the following tax year. However, in the following tax year the £3,000 exemption for that year must be used before the amount brought forward. There is no further carry forward if the amount brought forward cannot be used in the following tax year. The exemption is applied chronologically if there is more than one transfer of value in a tax year. If there are several gifts on one day the exemption is apportioned between them in proportion to the values transferred.

EXAMPLE 12

In the tax year 1996/97 Maria makes transfers of value of £1,800. In the tax year 1997/98 she makes transfers of value of £3,500. In the tax year 1998/99 she makes transfers of value of £6,000. She has not made any other gifts. The transfers of value made in the tax year 1996/97 fall within the annual exemption for that year and so are exempt for IHT purposes. Maria has used £1,800 of the annual exemption for that tax year, she has £1,200 of the annual exemption unused.

In the tax year 1997/98 she will have to use the annual exemption for that year, 1997/98. If some of the transfers are unrelieved after applying the annual exemption, she can utilise the unused exemption from 1996/97:

1997/98

	£
Transfers of value	3,500
Less exemption (1997/98)	(3,000)
Chargeable transfers	500
Less balance of unused AE 1996/97	500
Total chargeable transfers	Nil

In 1998/99 Maria can only use the annual exemption for that year. £3,000 of the transfers of value made in that year will be chargeable transfers and will form Maria's cumulative total.

1998/99

	£
Transfers of value	6,000
Less exemption (1998/99)	(3,000)
Chargeable transfers	£3,000

The unused balance of the annual exemption from the tax year 1996/97 (£700) will be lost.

7.6.3.2 Small gifts exemption

A transferor is allowed to make any number of gifts of up to £250 provided they are to different of people, without affecting the cumulative total (IHTA 1984, s 20). The gifts must be outright and not by way of settlement. The gift itself must be no more than £250 — the exemption cannot be used to cover the first £250 of a larger gift, i.e. if the gift is greater than £250, it is not an exempt transfer.

7.6.3.3 Gifts in consideration of marriage

Gifts in consideration of marriage are exempt up to certain limits (IHTA 1984, s 22). The limits are dependent on the relationship of the donor to the parties to the marriage. If the value of the gift exceeds the limit, the excess is chargeable. The limits are:

(a) £5,000 if the gift is by a parent of one of the parties to the marriage;

(b) £2,500 if the gift is by a remoter ancestor of one of the parties to the marriage, e.g. a grandparent or great-grandparent;

(c) £2,500 if the gift is by one of the parties to the marriage; or

(d) £1,000 if the gift is by any other person (e.g. a guest).

The gift must be:

(a) before a specific marriage and conditional on it, i.e. the donor must have a right to recover the gift if the marriage does not take place; or

(b) on or contemporaneously with the marriage; or

(c) after the marriage provided it was given in satisfaction of a prior legal obligation.

The gift must also be an outright gift to either of the parties to the marriage or, if settled, it must comply with the conditions set out in s 22 of IHTA 1984.

Where the marriage exemption is available, it should be deducted before the annual exemption, so that the annual exemption can be used elsewhere, if required.

7.6.3.4 Normal expenditure out of income

Transfers of value are exempt if they can be proved to be part of the normal expenditure of the transferor, made out of income and of such a size that, after allowing for all such transfers, the transferor is left with sufficient income to maintain the standard of living which the transferor is used to (IHTA 1984, s 21).

Example: Life policy written in trust

The most likely example of expenditure which falls into this exemption is where the transferor takes out a policy which assures the transferor's own life for the benefit of, say, the transferor's children. When the policy matures (on the death of the transferor), the proceeds of the life policy do not pass through the transferor's estate (and thus do not attract IHT), but instead they go directly to the children. The transferor is deemed to make a gift to the children every time a premium on the policy is paid. However, the transferor will frequently be able to establish that such a gift does not represent a transfer of value because it can be exempted under the 'normal expenditure out of income' provisions. The transferor is paying the premiums out of income and is left with sufficient income to maintain the transferor's usual standard of living. As the premiums are paid regularly the payments are part of the transferor's normal expenditure.

7.6.4 Step 3: Identify any available reliefs and deduct them from the value transferred

The only reliefs available are those set out at **7.5.3**. Do not forget the additional rules applicable to lifetime transfers for both BPR (**7.5.3.4**) and APR (**7.5.3.6**).

7.6.5 Steps 4 and 5

Calculate the transferor's cumulative total as at the date of the transfer and the amount of the nil rate band remaining and calculate the IHT payable by applying the rate (or rates) of tax to the value of the transfer for IHT purposes.

As stated at **7.6.1**, lifetime chargeable transfers are initially charged at half the rates in force at the time of the transfer. The current 2002/03 rates of tax are 0 per cent for the first £250,000 and 20 per cent for the balance over that amount. As before the rate or rates of tax applicable will depend on the cumulative total of all previous chargeable transfers made in the last seven years. When a transferor makes a LCT the amount of IHT payable is calculated by following the five steps. The position if the transferor dies within seven years of making the transfer, with the result that the full rates of IHT are chargeable, is discussed at **7.7**.

EXAMPLE 13 (assumes that the current rates of tax apply)

On 5 June 2002 Zac transfers a cash payment of £275,000 into a discretionary settlement. He has made no previous lifetime transfers. Any IHT is to be paid by the trustees of the settlement. Calculate the IHT payable on the transfer.

Zac has made a lifetime chargeable transfer. Following the five steps:

Step 1: the value transferred is the amount of the cash payment, £275,000.

Step 2: one exemption available is the annual exemption for the tax year in which the gift is made, 2002/03. This means that the transfer is reduced by £3,000 to £272,000. As this is the first chargeable transfer Zac has made he also has available his annual exemption for the previous tax year, 2001/02. This reduces the transfer to £269,000.

Step 3: there are no reliefs which are available to Zac.

Step 4: Zac's cumulative total is nil as he has made no chargeable transfers in the seven years preceding the transfer on 5 June 2002.

Step 5: as this is a LCT the rates of tax are one-half of the official rates, the NRB at 0% and the balance of the transfer at 20%. Applying the rates of tax, the first £250,000 is taxed at 0% and the remaining £19,000 is taxed at 20%. The trustees of the discretionary settlement have £3,800 of IHT to pay.

EXAMPLE 14 (with cumulation (assumes that current rates of tax apply))

On 28 February 2001 Mr Martin transfers a cash sum of £177,000 into a discretionary settlement and the trustees are to pay any IHT due as a result of the transfer.

Mr Martin had made a transfer into the settlement of £150,000 on 17 November 1993, just over seven years prior to the present gift.

He also made a cash payment into the settlement of £122,000 on 9 May 1994, between six and seven years prior to the present gift. The tax on each of those transfers was paid by the trustees of the settlement.

In addition to these LCTs Mr Martin also made a gift of £70,000 cash to his daughter on 1 March 2000. He made no other lifetime transfers. Any IHT is to be paid by the trustees of the settlement. Calculate the IHT payable on the transfer.

Mr Martin has made a lifetime chargeable transfer. Following the five steps:

Step 1: the value transferred is the amount of the cash payment, £177,000.

Step 2: one exemption available is the annual exemption for the tax year in which the gift is made, 2000/01. This means that the transfer is reduced by £3,000 to £174,000. (The annual exemption for the previous tax year will not be available to Mr Martin as it will have been used on the gift made on 1 March 2000.)

Step 3: there are no reliefs which are available to Mr Martin.

Step 4: going back for seven years from 28 February 2001 Mr Martin made one chargeable transfer, the transfer to the settlement on 9 May 1994. The transfer on 17 November 1993 was made more than seven years before the transfer in 2001. The gift to his daughter on 1 March 2000 was a PET. As Mr Martin is still alive the PET is treated as (potentially) exempt and so can be ignored for the purposes of calculating his NRB. The value of the transfer made on 9 May 1994 was £122,000. The only exemption available will be the annual exemption for the tax year in which the gift was made. This reduces the transfer to £119,000. (The annual exemption for the previous tax year will not be available to Mr Martin as it will have been used on the gift made on 17 November

1993.) There are no reliefs which are available to this transfer. The value of the transfer for IHT purposes is £119,000. Mr Martin's cumulative total on 28 February 2001 is £119,000.

Step 5: Mr Martin has £131,000 of the NRB available to him. The remainder of the transfer, £43,000, is taxed at 20%. There is IHT of £8,600 for the trustees to pay.

7.7 The charge to tax and a lifetime chargeable transfer where the transferor dies within seven years of the lifetime chargeable transfer

At **7.6.1** it was pointed out that, provided a transferor survived seven years from the date of making an LCT the rate of IHT charged on values exceeding the NRB was reduced to 20 per cent. If the transferor failed to survive the seven-year period then IHT is charged at the full rate, 40 per cent. IHT at the reduced rate is paid at the time of the transfer and any additional liability is paid at the time of the transferor's death. In practice this means that if a transferor dies within the seven-year period there has to be a second calculation of IHT. The full calculation needs to be carried out as, not only is the IHT payable at the full rates, but also due to the transferor's death the transferor's cumulative total at the date of the LCT may have changed and so the amount of the NRB available may have altered. This would be the case if the transferor had made a PET within the seven years preceding the date of the LCT which was not included in the transferor's cumulative total at the time of the LCT because it was, at that time, a PET. If the PET was made within seven years of the transferor's death then it will now be a chargeable transfer and so its value will be included in the transferor's cumulative total at the date of the LCT (see **Example 15**, below).

On occasions the value of the property gifted by the LCT may fall between the date of the gift and the date of the transferor's death. If this is case then, usually, the lower (date of death) value is used to calculate the additional tax payable (IHTA 1984, s 131). The lower value is not used if the property gifted was a lease with less than 50 years unexpired, or if the gift was of tangible movable property which was a wasting asset (see **Example 18**, below).

The lower value is only used to calculate the additional charge to IHT as a result of the donor's death. The original date of gift value is used in all other calculations, for example the calculation of the donor's cumulative total.

In addition to the five basic steps there are two other steps which may be relevant.

7.7.1 Step 6: Taper relief

Although IHT is charged at the full rates if the transferor dies within the seven-year period, there is some relief provided the transferor survived at least three years from the date of the gift. The relief is given by only a percentage of the IHT calculated being payable. The amount of the relief depends on how long the transferor survived after making the LCT.

If the transfer is made within three to four years of the transferor's death only 80 per cent of the IHT calculated is payable. If the period between the transfer and the death is four to five years 60 per cent of the IHT is payable; five to six years, 40 per cent; and six to seven years, only 20 per cent. This relief is known as taper relief, or tapering relief, as the amount of IHT payable tapers off the longer the transferor survives (see **Example 16**, below).

It is important to understand that taper relief reduces the IHT attributable to the transfer, it does not reduce the value transferred.

7.7.2 Step 7: Taking into account any IHT paid at the date of the LCT

After applying taper relief account is taken of any IHT that was paid at the date of the transfer. Full credit is given for tax paid at the time of the transfer. However, if the amount of tax paid at the date of the transfer exceeds the amount of IHT payable due to the death of the transferor within the seven-year period then the balance of IHT payable is reduced to nil. There will be no refund of tax.

EXAMPLE 15 (effect of death on a LCT made within seven years of the transferor's death assuming that the current rates of tax apply throughout)

Using the facts in **Example 14**, above, Mr Martin dies on 10 August 2001. The LCT made by Mr Martin on the 28th February 2001 was within the seven years preceding his death. IHT is now chargeable on the LCT at the full rates. The full calculation needs to be repeated.

Following the five steps:

Step 1: the value transferred is the amount of the cash payment, £177,000.

Step 2: one exemption available is the annual exemption for the tax year in which the gift is made, 2000/01. This means that the transfer is reduced by £3,000 to £174,000. (The annual exemption for the previous tax year will not be available to Mr Martin as it will have been used on the gift made on 1 March 2000.)

Step 3: there are no reliefs which are available to Mr Martin. (As before.)

Step 4: going back for seven years from 28 February 2001 Mr Martin made one chargeable transfer, the transfer to the settlement on 9 May 1994. The transfer on 17 November 1993 was made more than seven years before the transfer in 2001. The gift to his daughter on 1 March 2000 was a PET.

As Mr Martin has died within seven years of the PET it is no longer a PET, it becomes chargeable.

The value of the transfer made on 9 May 1994 was £122,000. The only exemption available will be the annual exemption for the tax year in which the gift was made. This reduces the transfer to £119,000. (The annual exemption for the previous tax year will not be available to Mr Martin as it will have been used on the gift made on 17 November 1993.) There are no reliefs which are available to this transfer. The value of the transfer for IHT purposes is £119,000.

The value of the transfer made on 1 March 2000 was £70,000. The only exemption available will be the annual exemption for the tax year in the gift was made, 1999/00. This reduces the transfer to £67,000. As he had made no chargeable transfers in the preceding tax year, 1998/99, he also has available his annual exemption for that year.

This reduces the transfer to £64,000. Mr Martin's cumulative total on 28 February 2001 is £183,000 (i.e. £119,000 + £64,000).

Step 5: Mr Martin has £67,000 of the NRB available to him. The remainder of the transfer, £107,000 is taxed at 40%. There is IHT of £42,800 for the trustees to pay.

Step 6: as Mr Martin died within three years of the LCT, taper relief is not available.

Step 7: IHT of £8,600 was paid at the time of the transfer. Credit is given for this payment. The amount of IHT payable by the trustees of the settlement due to Mr Martin's death within the seven-year period is £34,200.

EXAMPLE 16: (with taper relief)

On the same facts as **Example 14**, above, Mr Martin dies on 9 July 2005. The steps up to and including Step 5 remain as in **Example 15**, above. At Step 6, as the LCT was made within 4 to 5 years of his death taper relief is available. Only 60% of the IHT is payable, 60% of £42,800, giving an amount due of £25,680.

Step 7: IHT of £8,600 was paid at the time of the transfer. Credit is given for this payment. The amount of IHT payable by the trustees of the settlement due to Mr Martin's death within the seven year period is £17,080.

EXAMPLE 17

On the same facts as **Example 14**, above, Mr Martin dies on 9 July 2007. The steps up to and including Step 5 remain as in **Example 15**. At Step 6, as the LCT was made within six to seven years of his death taper relief is available. Only 20% of the IHT is payable, 20 per cent of £42,800, giving an amount due of £8,560.

Step 7: IHT of £8,600 was paid at the time of the transfer. Credit is given for this payment. The amount of IHT payable by the trustees of the settlement due to Mr Martin's death within the seven-year period is reduced to nil. There will be no repayment of the additional tax paid at the time of the transfer.

EXAMPLE 18: (effect of death on a LCT made within seven years of the transferor's death where the value of the property gifted has fallen and assuming that the current rates of tax apply throughout)

On 15 November 2000 Jason makes a gift of a freehold property worth £444,000 to a discretionary settlement and the trustees are to pay any IHT due as a result of the transfer. He has made no previous lifetime transfers.

Jason dies on 10 February 2005. On that date the property has a value of only £384,000.

A: IHT on the occasion of the LCT
Following the five steps:

Step 1: the value transferred is the value of the property on the date of the transfer, £444,000.

Step 2: one exemption available is the annual exemption for the tax year in which the gift is made, 2000/01. This means that the transfer is reduced by £3,000 to £441,000. As this is the first chargeable transfer Jason has made he also has available his annual exemption for the previous tax year, 1999/00. This reduces the transfer to £438,000.

Step 3: there are no reliefs which are available to Jason.

Step 4: Jason's cumulative total is nil as he has made no chargeable transfers in the seven years preceding the transfer on the 15 November.

Step 5: as this is a LCT the rates of tax are one-half of the official rates, the NRB at 0% and the balance of the transfer at 20%. Applying the rates of tax, the first £250,000 is taxed at 0% and the remaining £188,000 at 20%. The trustees of the discretionary settlement have £37,600 of IHT to pay.

B: Supplementary charge
As the transfer was within the seven years preceding his death IHT is now chargeable on the LCT at the full rates. The full calculation needs to be repeated.
Following the five steps:

Step 1: the value transferred is the value of the property on the date of the transfer, £444,000. However, as the value of the property has fallen, the date of death value can be used to calculate the additional tax payable (IHTA 1984 s 131). The value of the property is £384,000.

Step 2: one exemption available is the annual exemption for the tax year in which the gift is made, 2000/01. This means that the transfer is reduced by £3,000 to £381,000. As this is the first chargeable transfer Jason has made he also has available his annual exemption for the previous tax year, 1999/00. This reduces the transfer to £378,000.

Step 3: there are no reliefs which are available to Jason.

Step 4: Jason's cumulative total is nil as he has made no chargeable transfers in the seven years preceding the transfer on the 15 November.

Step 5: Jason has available to him the full NRB, the balance of the transfer is taxed at 40%. Applying the rates of tax, the first £250,000 is taxed at 0% and the remaining £128,000 at 40%. There is IHT of £51,200 for the trustees to pay.

Step 6: as Jason died within four to five years of the LCT taper relief is available. Only 60% of the IHT is payable, 60% of £51,200, giving an amount due of £30,720.

Step 7: IHT of £37,600 was paid at the time of the transfer. Credit is given for this payment. The amount of IHT payable by the trustees of the settlement due to Jason's death within the seven year period is reduced to nil. There will be no repayment of the additional tax paid at the time of the transfer.

NB: The lower value of the property is used only to calculate the additional IHT payable by the trustee as a result of the donor's death. The original value is used when calculating the donor's cumulative total at the date of death (which in this case will be £438,000).

NB: Similar principles apply when calculating the IHT payable by the donee of a PET when the donor dies within seven years of the gift. Thus, if in Example 18 Jason's original transfer had been a PET rather than an LCT, there would have been no charge to tax at the time of the gift. On his death within 7 years, the PET would have become chargeable. The calculation described in Steps 1–6 of paragraph B above would be undertaken to establish the donee's liability to tax on the former PET. Jason's cumulative total of lifetime transfers, however, would remain at £438,000.

7.8 The charge to tax and a PET

IHT is charged on a PET when the transferor does not survive for a period of seven years from the date of the PET. If the transferor dies within that period the transfer becomes a chargeable transfer and IHT is payable at the full rates at the date of death.

If a PET becomes a chargeable transfer then the steps to follow to calculate the IHT payable are the five basic steps, taking note of the matters mentioned when the charge to IHT and a LCT was considered, and, in addition, Step 6, set out at **7.7.1.** (Step 7 is not applicable as there will have been no IHT payable at the time of the PET.) Looking at the steps as applicable to a PET which becomes chargeable:

7.8.1 Step 1: Calculate the value transferred

The comments made when looking at Step 1 in the charge to tax and a lifetime chargeable transfer (**7.6.2**), the related property rules (**7.5.1.1**) and the comments on incidental expenses of transfer and CGT (**7.6.2.3**) are all relevant here. Also relevant are the comments at **7.7** on a fall in value of the gifted property between the date of the gift and the date of the transferor's death. The lower value, subject to the exceptions set out at **7.7**, is used in the calculation of IHT payable as a result of the donor's death within seven years of the date of the gift.

7.8.2 Step 2: Identify any available exemptions and deduct them from the value transferred

As with LCTs, in addition to the exemptions set out at **7.5.2.1**, the exemptions available for lifetime dispositions, set out at **7.6.3**, are all available to reduce the value transferred by a PET.

7.8.3 Step 3: Identify any available reliefs and deduct them from the value transferred

Only business property relief and agricultural relief are available. Again, do not overlook the additional rules applicable to lifetime transfers at **7.5.3.4** and **7.5.3.6** respectively.

7.8.4 Steps 4 and 5

Calculate the transferor's cumulative total as at the date of the transfer and the amount of the nil rate band remaining and calculate the IHT payable by applying the rate (or rates) of tax at the date of death to the value of the transfer for IHT purposes.

If a PET becomes a chargeable transfer then IHT is charged at the full rates of tax. The transferor's cumulative total at the date the PET was made must be calculated to determine the applicable rate or rates of tax.

EXAMPLE 19 (assumes that the current rates of tax apply throughout)

(Taking the facts from **Example 6**, above, and expanding them.) Isabelle dies on 15 June 2002. Her estate is valued at £275,000 for IHT purposes. She gifted cash of £100,000 to her daughter, Jasmine, on 21 December 1998. This was in addition to a gift of cash of £176,000 she made on 5 November 1993 to the trustees of a discretionary settlement. The trustees paid any IHT. She made no other gifts.

When made, the gift to Jasmine was a PET. As Isabelle has died within seven years of making the gift it is a chargeable transfer. There are no other chargeable transfers within the seven years preceding Isabelle's death.

Step 1: calculate the value transferred. As the gift was of cash the value transferred is £100,000.

Step 2: identify any exemptions and deduct them from the value transferred. One exemption available is the annual exemption for the tax year in which the gift is made, 1998/99. This reduces the transfer to £97,000. As Isabelle had made no lifetime gifts in the previous tax year, 1997/98, the annual exemption for that year is also available. This reduces the transfer to £94,000.

Step 3: identify any reliefs and deduct them from the value transferred. There are no reliefs available as the gift is cash.

Step 4: calculate the transferor's cumulative total at the date the gift is made and the amount of the NRB remaining. Going back seven years from 21 December 1998, the date of the PET which has become chargeable, Isabelle made one chargeable transfer, the gift to the settlement. This was an LCT. (Although the LCT has to be taken into account when calculating Isabelle's cumulative total in December 1998, no additional tax is payable on it as it was made more than seven years before her death.) To calculate Isabelle's cumulative total Steps 1 to 3 have to be applied to the LCT. The value transferred was £176,000. The exemptions available will be the annual exemption for the tax year in which the gift was made, 1993/94. This reduces the value transferred to £173,000. As she had made no transfers during the previous tax year, 1992/93, that year's annual exemption is also available reducing the value transferred to £170,000. No other exemptions are available and there are no reliefs available. The value of the LCT for IHT purposes is £170,000. Isabelle's cumulative total on 21 December 1998 is £170,000. She has £80,000 of the NRB available to her.

Step 5: calculate the IHT payable by applying the rate (or rates) of tax to the value of the transfer for IHT purposes. £80,000 of the transfer falls within the NRB. The remainder of the transfer will be taxed at 40%. There will be IHT of £5,600 to pay on the transfer. See **7.8.5.1** below for the final step in the calculation.

7.8.5 Step 6: Taper relief

The final step to be taken is to apply taper relief, if applicable. This applies to PETs which become chargeable in exactly the same way in which is applies to the additional charge to IHT on LCT where the transferor dies within seven years of the transfer. See **7.7.1**.

7.8.5.1 Continuing Example 19

As the gift was made three to four years before Isabelle's death only 80 per cent of the tax is payable. The amount of tax to pay is £4,480.

7.9 The charge to tax and death

As stated at **7.4**, there is a deemed transfer of value on death. Again the five basic steps need to be gone through to calculate the IHT payable on the occasion of a person's death. There are some additional points to be taken into account and these are mentioned as the five steps are considered.

7.9.1 Step 1: Calculate the value transferred

On death, the value transferred is the value of the deceased's *estate* immediately *before* the deceased's death (IHTA 1984, s 4).

7.9.1.1 The estate

The deceased's estate is the aggregate of all property to which, immediately prior to death, the deceased was beneficially entitled to, other than excluded property. This includes not only assets which the deceased owned as sole owner, but also the deceased's share of any property owned jointly, either as beneficial joint tenants or as tenants in common.

The deceased's estate also includes the value of any interest which the deceased had in settled property. Only property in which the deceased had an interest in possession is included. An example of a deceased having an interest in possession is where the deceased was the sole life tenant of a trust fund. The capital value of the trust fund will be aggregated with the deceased's estate for the purposes of calculating any liability to IHT.

Also included in the value of the deceased's estate will be the value of any property subject to a reservation of a benefit (see **7.10**).

7.9.1.2 Liabilities

The value of the estate is the total value of the assets which make up the estate, less any liabilities of the estate.

7.9.1.3 Excluded property

As mentioned at **7.2.1.2**, some assets are excluded for IHT purposes. Do not forget that a reversionary interest in settled property is excluded property.

7.9.1.4 The value of the estate

The general rule is that assets are to be valued at their market value immediately before death. The date-of-death value is usually referred to as the probate valuation. There are exceptions to the market value rule and these are set out below.

7.9.1.5 Related property

Do not overlook the effect of the related property rules (see **7.5.1.1**). A provision which should not be overlooked is the provision contained in s 176 of IHTA 1984. This gives some relief to the related property rules. If property in the deceased's estate is valued as related property and is sold within four years of the date of death, then, provided the sale meets the conditions set out in the section, s 176 of IHTA 1984 allows the property to be revalued without it being treated as related property. This means that the lower value can be substituted for IHT purposes.

7.9.1.6 Value immediately before death

Section 4 of IHTA 1984 states that 'the value transferred is the value of the deceased's estate immediately *before* death.' However, some assets are valued immediately *after* death in order that any changes in the value of the asset by reason of the death can be taken into account. One example would be a life policy. Where the deceased has taken out a life policy and the proceeds to be paid out on death form part of the estate, it is the policy proceeds which are taxable even though the proceeds are not due immediately before death, they are only due as a result of the death and the insurance company does not in fact pay out until after death! Another example is the loss of goodwill. Where the deceased was a proprietor of a business it will frequently be the case that the business will suffer as a result of the deceased's death through loss of goodwill and, consequently, the value of the business will fall. The legislation permits this factor to be taken into account when valuing the business at the date of death, even though the goodwill is not in fact lost until some time later.

7.9.1.7 Sale of land within four years of death

The usual market value rules apply to land held in a deceased's estate. However, if an interest in land is sold within four years of the date of death for less than the probate value the lower value can, in certain circumstances, be substituted for the probate value (IHTA 1984, ss 190–198).

7.9.1.8 Sale of qualifying shares within 12 months of death

Again, the usual market value rules apply to shares held in a deceased's estate. If the shares are shares in a company which is quoted on a recognised stock exchange or holdings in an authorised unit trust (qualifying shares) and are sold within 12 months of the date of death for less than the probate value the lower value can, in certain circumstances, be substituted for the probate value (IHTA 1984, ss 178–189). When calculating the overall loss to the estate by virtue of the qualifying shares being sold for less than the probate value, it is the aggregate, or net, loss to the estate taking into account the proceeds of sale of all qualifying shares sold during the 12 months.

7.9.2 Step 2

Identify any available exemptions and deduct them from the value transferred.

The only exemptions available are the ones set out at **7.5.2.1**. Do not forget that the ones set out when looking at a LCT are *not* available on death.

7.9.3 Step 3

Identify any available reliefs and deduct them from the value transferred.

In addition to the reliefs set out at **7.5.3** there are two other reliefs available on death.

7.9.3.1 Woodlands relief

If the deceased's estate included land in the UK which was not eligible for agricultural property relief but on which trees and underwood are growing, woodlands relief may be available (IHTA 1984, s 125). The deceased must have been beneficially entitled to the land throughout the five years preceding the date of death or must have been beneficially entitled to the land otherwise than for consideration in money or money's worth (i.e., had been given or inherited the land on the death of another.

The relief operates in a different way to BPR and APR. Those reliefs operate by including the value of the asset in the value of the estate and applying a relief calculated as a percentage of the value of the asset. Woodlands relief operates by excluding the value of the woodlands from the estate. Any liability to IHT is deferred until there is a disposal of the woodlands.

For the relief to operate the beneficiary of the woodlands must elect to the Inland Revenue for the relief.

7.9.3.2 Quick succession relief

Quick succession relief offers some relief where a person dies within five years of receiving a chargeable transfer (IHTA 1984, s 141). For it to apply, the deceased's estate must have been increased by a chargeable transfer (either a lifetime gift or one which occurred on death) made to the deceased within five years of the deceased's death ('the first transfer'). In addition, IHT must have been paid on the first transfer. (For the relief to be applicable there is *no* requirement that the property the deceased received as a result of the first transfer still forms part of the deceased's estate at the date of death.)

The relief operates by giving a tax credit which then reduces the IHT payable on death ('the second transfer').

There are two stages to calculating the tax credit. First the calculation:

$$\frac{(G - T)}{G} \times T$$

where G is the gross amount of the first transfer and T is the amount of IHT paid on the first transfer.

A percentage of the figure arrived at is allowed as the tax credit, the percentage depending on the amount of time which has elapsed between the two transfers. The percentages are:

100% if the first transfer was one year or less before death.
80% if the first transfer was one to two years before death.
60% if the first transfer was two to three years before death.
40% if the first transfer was three to four years before death.
20% if the first transfer was four to five years before death.

The amount of the tax credit cannot result in a refund of IHT.

EXAMPLE 20 (assume that the current rates of tax apply throughout)

Ignoring exemptions and reliefs

Gladys dies in August 2002. She leaves her estate, valued at £427,000, to her daughter, Barbara. Gladys made no lifetime gifts. The IHT payable on Gladys' estate is £70,800 (i.e. £250,000 @ 0% and £177,000 @ 40%). Barbara dies suddenly in October 2002. She has made no lifetime gifts. Her estate is valued at £511,000 and she leaves this to her sister. As Barbara dies within 5 years of inheriting her mother's estate QSR is available.

The amount of the QSR is:

Stage One:

$$\frac{(G - T)}{G} \times T \qquad \frac{(427{,}000 - 70{,}800)}{427{,}000} \times 70{,}800 = 59{,}060$$

Stage Two:

As Gladys died one to two years before Barbara's death 80% of this figure is available, 80% × 59,060 = £47,248.

The IHT payable on Barbara's estate is £104,400 (£250,000 @ 0% and £261,000 @ 40%) less the QSR of £47,248, leaving IHT to pay of £57,152.

7.9.4 Steps 4 and 5

Calculate the transferor's cumulative total as at the date of the transfer and the amount of the nil rate band remaining and calculate the IHT payable by applying the rate (or rates) of tax to the value of the transfer for IHT purposes.

On death, the transferor's estate is liable to IHT. The rate or rates of tax will depend on the cumulative total of all chargeable transfers made by the transferor in the seven years before death. It must be remembered that the cumulative total will include all PETs which have now become chargeable transfers as a result of the transferor's death within seven years.

EXAMPLE 21 (assumes that the current rates of tax apply throughout)

James dies on 31 May 2002. The value of his estate is £60,000, there are no exemptions or reliefs available to his estate. During his lifetime James made only one gift. He made a gift, on 1 April 1997, of £152,000 cash into a discretionary settlement with the trustees paying any IHT due as a result of the transfer.

Following the five steps to calculate the IHT payable on the estate:

Step 1: the value transferred is the value of the estate, £60,000.

Step 2: there are no exemptions available.

Step 3: there are no reliefs available.

Step 4: there is one transfer made in the seven years preceding his death which will make up his cumulative total. The value of the transfer made on 1 April 1997 was £152,000. One exemption available will be the annual exemption for the tax year in which the gift was made, 1996/97. This will reduce the value of the gift to £149,000. The annual exemption for the previous year, 1995/96, is also available and will reduce the value of the gift to £146,000. There are no reliefs which are available to this transfer.

James' cumulative total on the date of his death is £146,000.

Step 5: there is £104,000 of James' NRB remaining. All the estate, £60,000, will be taxed at 0 %. There is no IHT to pay.

EXAMPLE 22 (assumes that the current rates of tax apply throughout)

James dies on 31 May 2002. The value of his estate is £60,000, there are no exemptions or reliefs available to his estate. During his lifetime James made several gifts. He made a gift, on 1 April 1997, of £152,000 cash into a discretionary settlement with the trustees paying any IHT due as a result of the transfer.

On 25 June 1998 he made a gift of £90,000, cash, to his daughter.

The only other gift he made was a gift of £40,000 cash on 4 July 1999 to his son. Following the five steps to calculate the IHT payable on the estate:

Step 1: the value transferred is the value of the estate, £60,000.

Step 2: there are no exemptions available.

Step 3: there are no reliefs available.

Step 4: there are three transfers made in the seven years preceding his death. James' cumulative total will equal the total of the value for IHT purposes of each of the three transfers. The value of the transfer made on 1 April 1997 was £152,000. One exemption available will be the annual exemption for the tax year in which the gift was made, 1996/97. This will reduce the value of the gift to £149,000. The annual exemption for the previous year, 1995/96, is also available and will reduce the value of the gift to £146,000. There are no reliefs which are available to this transfer.

The value of the gift made on 25 June 1998 was £90,000. Again, one exemption available will be the annual exemption for the tax year in which the gift was made, 1998/99. This will reduce the value of the gift to £87,000. The annual exemption for the previous year, 1997/96, is also available and will reduce the value of the gift to £84,000. There are no reliefs which are available to this transfer.

The value of the gift made on 4 July 1999 was £40,000. Again one exemption available will be the annual exemption for the tax year in which the gift was made, 1999/00. This will reduce the value of the gift to £37,000. The annual exemption for the previous year, 1998/99 has already been used. There are no reliefs which are available to this transfer.

James' cumulative total on the date of his death is £267,000 (146,000 + 84,000 + 37,000).

Step 5: all the NRB has been used. The estate, £60,000, will all be taxed at 40%. There is IHT of £24,000 to pay.

7.9.5 LCTs and PETs made in the seven years preceding the date of death

Do not overlook the fact that when a person dies not only may there be a charge to IHT on the deceased's estate, there may also be additional IHT to pay on any LCT made in the seven years preceding the date of death. This is because, at the time of the LCT, IHT is paid at half the rates applicable on death, with the balance of any IHT being due if the transferor dies within seven years of the date of the transfer.

There may also be a liability to IHT on any PET made in the seven years preceding the date of death. This is due to the fact that a PET is treated as an exempt transfer at the time it is made and only becomes a chargeable transfer if the transferor dies within seven years of making the PET.

EXAMPLE 23 (assumes that the current rates of tax apply throughout)

Jonathon dies on 17 February 2001. His estate comprises of a house he owns jointly, in equal shares, with his sister. The market value of the house is £90,000. He also owned at the date of his death an interest in a partnership, his interest having a market value of £100,000. The other assets in his estate have a value of £100,000. By his will he has left a legacy of £10,000 to the Royal National Institute for the Blind (a registered charity) and the remainder of his estate passes to his sister.

During his lifetime he made the following gifts. On 24 September 1992 a gift of £50,000 cash to one of his nieces, Jane. On 15 May 1994 a gift of £83,000 cash to his nephew, Mark, on the occasion of Mark's wedding. On 10 November 1995 a gift of £180,000 cash to the trustees of a discretionary settlement, on which he agreed to pay any IHT due. In addition to these gifts, on 2 June 1998 he gifted a building which was used by the partnership to his nephew, Mark. The building was owned solely by Jonathon and had a market value of £100,000. Mark still owned the building at the date of his uncle's death.

What IHT was payable during Jonathon's lifetime and what IHT is payable on his death?

During his lifetime only one of the gifts made was a LCT, the gift to the discretionary settlement. The other gifts were gifts to individuals and so were PETs.

Following the five steps to calculate the IHT payable when the LCT was made on 10 November 1995:

Step 1: the value transferred is the amount of the cash payment, £180,000.

Step 2: one exemption is available, the annual exemption. Jonathon has available the annual exemption for the tax year in which the gift is made, 1995/96; this reduces the value of the gift to £177,000. (The annual exemption for the previous tax year will not be available as it will have been used on the gift made on 15 May 1994.)

Step 3: there are no reliefs available.

Step 4: Jonathon's cumulative total is nil as he has made no chargeable transfers in the seven years preceding this transfer. (The gifts on 24 September 1992 and 15 May 1994 are PETs.)

Step 5: the whole of Jonathon's NRB is available. The value transferred, £177,000, falls within the NRB: there is no IHT payable when the gift is made.

When Jonathon dies not only will there be a charge to IHT on his estate; there may also be additional IHT to pay on any LCT made in the seven years preceding his death and a charge to IHT on any PETs made in the seven years preceding his death. The gift made on 15 May 1994 was made in the seven years preceding his death, as was the LCT on 10 November 1995 and the PET on 2 June 1998. Beginning with the earliest gift:

Following the five steps:

Step 1: the value transferred was the value of the cash gift, £75,000.

Step 2: the gift was made in consideration of Mark's marriage. The first £1,000 is exempt, reducing the value transferred to £82,000. The annual exemption for the tax year in which the gift was made is also available, reducing the transfer to £79,000. The annual exemption for the previous tax year is also available, reducing the transfer to £76,000.

Step 3: there are no reliefs available.

Step 4: Jonathon's cumulative total on 15 May 1994 was nil. The gift made on 24 September 1992 was a PET. As it was made more than seven years before Jonathon died it is not chargeable.

Step 5: all the NRB is available and so there is no IHT to pay on the occasion of Jonathon's death on the gift made on 15 May 1994.

Looking next at the LCT made on 10 November 1995: Repeating the steps taken above when calculating the IHT payable at the time the gift was made:

Step 1: the value transferred is the amount of the cash payment, £180,000.

Step 2: one exemption is available, the annual exemption. Jonathon has available the annual exemption for the tax year in which the gift is made, 1995/96; this reduces the value of the gift to £177,000.

Step 3: there are no reliefs available.

Step 4: Jonathon's cumulative total is £76,000, which is the value of the transfer made on 15 May 1994.

Step 5: £174,000 of Jonathon's NRB is available. £174,000 of the value transferred is taxed at 0%, the remainder, £3,000, is taxed at 40%, giving a total of £1,200 IHT. As this is a calculation of the additional IHT due on a LCT due to the death of the transferor within seven years of the making of the gift.

Step 6: provides for taper relief to be applied, if appropriate. The gift was made within five to six years of Jonathon's death and so only 40% of the IHT is payable, £480.

Step 7: there was no IHT payable at the time the transfer was made and so the IHT due on the LCT as a result of Jonathon's death within seven years of the transfer is £480.

Following the steps for the transfer made on 2 June 1998: Step 1: the value transferred is the market value of the building, £100,000. Step 2: the annual exemption for the tax year in which the gift was made, 1998/99, is available, as is the annual exemption for the preceding tax year, 1997/98. However, Step 3: as the building was used for the purpose of the business carried out by the partnership of which Jonathon was a partner, the building qualifies for BPR at 50% **(7.5.3.2)**. The BPR is given before deducting the annual exemptions **(7.5.3)**, leaving a value transferred of £44,000. Step 4: Jonathon's cumulative total on 2 June 1997 was £253,000 (£76,000 + £177,000). There is no NRB remaining and the whole £44,000 will be taxed at 40%, making IHT of £17,600. Step 6: as the gift was made within two to three years of Jonathon's death there is no taper relief. (Step 7 is not applicable as the transfer was a PET when originally made and so there will have been no IHT paid at the time of the gift.)

The liability to IHT on the estate remains to be calculated.

Step 1: the value of the estate is the value of Jonathon's share in the house, which, as it was jointly owned will have the joint owner's discount applied, giving a value of £45,000 − (10% of £45,000) = £40,500. The remainder of the estate was valued at £200,000. The value of the estate is £240,500.

Step 2: there is one exemption, the gift to the charity of £10,000 is exempt, reducing the value transferred to £230,500.

Step 3 the interest in a partnership qualifies for BPR at 100%, reducing the value of the estate to £130,500.

Step 4: the total value for IHT purposes of each of the chargeable transfers made in the seven years preceding the date of death will form Jonathon's cumulative total. At the date of his death this total is £297,000 (£76,000 + £177,000 + £44,000).

Step 5: all Jonathon's NRB has been used, all the estate, £130,500, will be taxed at 40%, giving IHT of £52,200 to pay.

The IHT due on the gift made on 10 November 1995 to the discretionary settlement, £480, is payable by the trustees of the settlement, out of the trust monies.

The IHT due on the gift made on 2 June 1998 to Mark, £17,600, is payable by Mark.

The IHT due on the estate, £52,200, is payable by Jonathon's personal representatives from the monies in his estate.

7.10 Gifts subject to a reservation

A gift of property is subject to a reservation if, after gifting the property, some benefit is still enjoyed or retained by the transferor. It would be tempting under the IHT legislation for the transferor to give away property to another individual but to continue to retain an interest in it. That way, the property would not form part of the transferor's estate liable to IHT on death. Also, provided the transferor survived seven years from the date of the gift the property would escape IHT altogether. (Even if the transferor died within seven years of making the gift then, provided the value of the gift fell within the transferor's NRB at the date the gift was made, and the rates of IHT remain the same, then no more IHT would be payable on the death than would have been paid had the gift not been made and the asset still formed part of the deceased's estate. If the transferor died within the seven-year period and the value of the property transferred exceeded the available NRB then taper relief would operate to reduce the amount of IHT payable.) A good example of a gift where a benefit is retained would be a parent who makes a gift of a holiday home to a child but continues to use the holiday home frequently throughout the year without paying any rent to the child.

There is legislation to prevent taxpayers trying to avoid IHT in this way (Finance Act 1986, s 102).

The original gift of the asset will be a lifetime transfer, a LCT or a PET depending on the recipient of the gift. In addition, if the property is still subject to a reservation at the transferor's death, then the property, at its value at the date of death, will be included in the transferor's estate and will be taxed as part of the transferor's estate on death. If the original gift was made in the seven years preceding the transferor's death, IHT or additional IHT may be payable on the original gift as a result of the death.

If, in the above example of the gift of a holiday home, the parent was still enjoying visits to the property at the time of death, which was six years after the original gift, the original PET would become chargeable as a result of the death. In addition, the value of the property would also be included in the value of the parent's estate at the date of death. There would be a double charge to IHT.

If the reservation ceases before death, then the transferor will be treated as making a PET on the date the reservation ceases. In the earlier example, if the parent ceased using the property five years after having made the original gift, there would be a PET at the date the parent stopped using it. The value of the PET would be the value of the property at that date. If the parent died one year after ceasing to use the property both PETs would become chargeable as they would have been made in the seven years preceding the parent's death.

As the making of a gift with a reservation can result in a double charge to IHT there are provisions giving some relief for this.

Care should be taken to avoid giving advice to a client which could result in a gift with a reservation being made.

7.11 Liability, burden and payment of tax

The question of liability is concerned with who will actually be required to send to the Revenue any IHT that is due: burden is concerned with who ultimately bears the tax (a matter of no concern to the Revenue but of considerable interest to, for example, the beneficiaries of a deceased's estate).

7.11.1 Lifetime chargeable transfers

7.11.1.1 Due date for payment

IHT due on the value transferred by a chargeable lifetime transfer normally falls due six months after the end of the month in which the transfer takes place. However, if the chargeable transfer occurs between 6 April and 30 September (inclusive) in the tax year, then the IHT is due on 30 April in the following year.

Overdue IHT attracts interest.

7.11.1.2 Liability and burden

The primary liability for (and burden of) IHT due in respect of a lifetime chargeable transfer lies with the transferor. However, it is possible for the transferee to agree to pay the tax instead of the transferor.

As stated above, there is only likely to be a lifetime chargeable transfer where there has been a transfer into a discretionary trust. If the tax is not paid by the transferor by the due date, then the trustees become liable. If the trustees are unable to pay the tax, then the Revenue have power to seek payment from persons who have an interest in the settlement.

7.11.1.3 Additional tax due on death

Where a person dies within seven years of making a lifetime chargeable transfer, additional tax may become payable. If so, then this is due six months after the end of the month in which death occurred.

The primary liability for this additional tax lies with the transferee (i.e. the trustees). However, if the tax remains unpaid after the due date, the Revenue can seek payment from persons who have an interest in the settlement and, as a final recourse, from the personal representatives of the transferor's estate.

7.11.2 PETs which become chargeable

7.11.2.1 Due date for payment

IHT falls due six months after the end of the month in which the transferor's death occurs.

Overdue tax attracts interest.

7.11.2.2 Liability and burden

The transferee is primarily liable (and bears the burden of the tax). In the case of a trust, the transferee will be the trustees (and the burden will fall on the trust property (effectively on the beneficiaries)). If the tax remains unpaid 12 months after the date of death, then the personal representatives of the deceased's estate are liable, leaving them to try to recover the tax from those who have primary liability.

7.11.3 Death

7.11.3.1 Due date for payment

IHT due on death is due six months after the end of the month in which death occurs.

Overdue tax attracts interest.

7.11.3.2 Liability and burden

This depends on the property bearing the IHT.

7.11.3.3 Deceased's free estate

The PRs are liable for the IHT on the deceased's free estate. If the will is silent as to burden, tax on the free estate in the UK is normally borne by the residue (in the case of foreign property, by that property itself). If the testator has specifically provided that particular gifts in the will are to bear their own tax that direction will normally prevail.

7.11.3.4 Settled property in which the deceased had an interest

If IHT is due as a result of the death on assets in a trust fund in which the deceased had an interest, then the trustees of the settlement are liable for the IHT due. The burden falls on the trust property.

7.11.3.5 Property passing other than under the deceased's will or intestacy

If property passed outside the will, for example, the deceased's share of a house owned as beneficial joint tenants with the deceased's sister, then the beneficiary of the asset, the sister, bears the burden for the IHT attributable to it although the liability falls on the PRs.

7.11.4 Instalment option

In certain cases, IHT may be paid by ten equal annual instalments, the first instalment due on the normal due date for payment.

Only certain assets qualify for the instalment option. These are:

(a) land and buildings; or

(b) shares or securities giving control immediately before the transfer; or

(c) unquoted shares or securities of a company which did not give the transferor control provided the Inland Revenue are satisfied that the attributable to their value cannot be paid in one sum without undue hardship;

(d) unquoted shares (but not securities) of a company which did not give the transferor control where the value transferred attributable to the shares exceeds £20,000 *and* either the nominal value of the shares is not less than 10 per cent of the nominal value of all the shares of the company at the time of the transfer, *or* the shares are ordinary shares and their nominal value is not less than 10 per cent of the nominal value of all ordinary shares of the company at that time;

(e) (where the transfer is on death) unquoted shares or securities of a company which did not give the transferor control where the tax on the holding and on any other shares or securities qualifying for the instalment option comprises at least 20 per cent of the tax payable by a particular person;

(f) a business or interest in a business.

7.11.5 Entitlement

The instalment facility is available in respect of:

(a) transfers on death; or

(b) lifetime chargeable transfers where the transferee pays the IHT (the transferor is primarily liable); or

(c) a PET which becomes chargeable, provided the transferee pays the IHT and still owns the property at the date of the transferor's death. If the property is sold, then the whole amount of IHT remaining becomes payable immediately.

EXAMPLE 24

Colin dies on 20 November 2001. Part of his estate comprises 20,000 shares in a quoted company which gave Colin control of the company. The shareholding is valued at £75,000 at the date of Colin's death. The IHT payable in respect of shares is, say, £27,400.

If the instalment option is not opted for, IHT falls due on 31 May 2002.

However, if instalment option is opted for, £2,740 (1/10 × £27,400) is payable on each 31 May from 31 May 2002 until 31 May 2011.

7.11.6 Interest

Where land is concerned (other than land on which agricultural property relief is available), interest accrues on the balance of IHT outstanding from the date when the first instalment becomes due for payment.

However, in respect of the other categories of property qualifying for the instalment option, the general rule is that no interest is payable provided that each instalment is paid by the due date.

7.12 Tax planning

7.12.1 Lifetime gifts and taper relief

As a general principle, tax will be saved by making a transfer during one's lifetime rather than on death. This is due to the seven year cumulation period.

If the transferor survives seven years after making the gift, then no tax will be payable on the gift if it was a PET and tax at only half the official rates will have been paid if it was a lifetime chargeable transfer.

Even if death occurs within seven years, the full charge to IHT may be mitigated by taper relief. However, it is important to understand that taper relief reduces the *IHT* attributable to the chargeable transfer *not* the value of the chargeable transfer itself. Therefore, taper relief is only applicable if IHT is payable on the chargeable transfer.

IHT will only be payable on the chargeable transfer if the value of the transfer, taking into account the transferor's cumulative total at the date the transfer was made, exceeds transferor's NRB. If the chargeable transfer (taking into account the cumulative total at the date of the gift) does not exceed the NRB available at the date of chargeable transfer no IHT is payable and so taper relief is inapplicable.

7.12.2 Appreciating assets

An asset which has potential for capital appreciation should be considered before other assets if the transferor is thinking of making lifetime gifts. This is because the value of the asset at the *date of transfer* is taken for IHT purposes. Should the asset remain in the estate its value at the date of death will have been higher (it is an appreciating asset) and a higher liability to IHT could result.

The instalment option may be available to reduce the burden of any IHT on lifetime gifts (and hold over relief may be available to hold over any CGT).

However, it may be not within the taxpayer's means to give away his assets several years before his death.

7.12.3 Utilising exemptions

7.12.3.1 Exemptions generally

Full use should be made of the available exemptions, of which the annual exemption is the most important. It allows property to be handed down tax-free over a period of time.

7.12.3.2 Spouse exemption

Each spouse is liable for IHT. It may be worthwhile for the more wealthy spouse to transfer property to the other spouse to enable both spouses to make full use of their annual exemptions and nil rate band. For example, if the estates are of sufficient size, it will be beneficial for spouses to arrange their estates such that each has an estate at least equal to the nil rate band. This will mean that they will each be able to give away the maximum amount without paying tax.

8

Corporation tax

8.1 Introduction: The charge to corporation tax

Corporation tax (CT) is charged on the profits of companies resident in the UK by reference to their taxable profits arising in each accounting period.

A company is not charged to income tax or capital gains tax; it is charged to CT on its profits. 'Profits' means both its income profits and capital gains.

This difference between companies and individuals is not as fundamental as first appears. The income profits of a company liable to CT are calculated in the same way as an individual's statutory income is calculated for income tax purposes (see **5.4**). The capital gains of a company liable to CT are calculated on the basis of similar principles to those which apply to CGT for individuals (see **Chapter 6**, above although there are a number of differences).

8.2 Taxable profits

The company's taxable profits are the figure upon which it pays CT.

Taxable profits are calculated by deducting what are known as 'charges on income' from the company's total profits.

The company's total profits are the aggregate of its income profits and its capital gains for the relevant accounting period.

8.3 Calculation of income profits

A company's income profits liable to CT are calculated in the same way as an individual's statutory income (see **5.4**). That is, the company's income is assessed to tax under the rules of the relevant Schedules set out in the Income and Corporation Taxes Act 1988 (ICTA 1988). The assessments under the various Schedules are then added together to calculate the net income profits liable to CT.

The major source of the company's income is likely to be from a trade of one sort or another. Therefore, Schedule D Case I, which assesses the profits of a trade in the UK, is likely to be the most relevant Schedule.

It is important not to ignore the fact that a company may have other sources of income apart from trading income and that other Schedules may be relevant in the calculation of income profits. For example, the company may well have investments from which it derives rental income. If so, Schedule A will be relevant in assessing that rental income.

Another source of income may be bank and building society interest which is assessed to tax under Schedule D Case III. There is one important difference in the tax treatment of interest in relation to companies. Whereas individuals receive the interest net of income tax at the 20 per cent rate, companies receive interest gross. There is therefore no need to gross up the interest received in calculating the company's taxable profits.

8.3.1 Schedule D Case I

Schedule D Case I assesses the profits of a trade in the UK.

The rules for assessment are the same for both companies and sole traders/trading partnerships. The trading profits liable to CT are those profits actually arising in the chargeable accounting period.

The profits liable to tax are the chargeable receipts less deductible expenditure.

8.3.1.1 Chargeable receipts

Chargeable receipts are those which:

(a) *derive from the trading activity.*
The receipt must derive from the trading activity rather than from circumstances not directly connected with the trade, e.g. sales or compensation received for cancellation of a trading contract, but not a gratuitous sum received on termination of a trading relationship as a gesture of goodwill.

(b) *and which are of an income nature.*
Income receipts must be distinguished from capital receipts. This distinction is very important in the case of sole traders and partnerships in view of the fact that capital receipts attract CGT, not income tax. It is less so in the case of companies because both capital receipts and income receipts are charged to CT.

If an item is purchased for the purpose of resale at a profit, the proceeds of sale will be of an income nature, e.g. stock. On the other hand, if the asset is purchased for the benefit or use of the business on a more permanent basis as opposed to resale, then the receipt will be of a capital nature, e.g. purchase of machinery for a factory or office equipment.

8.3.1.2 Deductible expenditure

Expenditure is deductible if it is:

(a) *of an income nature;*
If expenditure is incurred for the purpose of enabling the company/trader to resell the item at a profit, then the expenditure will be of an income nature, e.g. the expense to a company in buying its stock but not its expense in buying its permanent assets such as office equipment.
Another test is whether the expenditure is recurrent rather than once-and-for-all expenditure. If recurrent, it will generally be of an income nature, e.g. overheads (electricity, rent, telephone, interest paid on an overdraft). On the other hand, once-and-for-all expenditure such as the purchase of fixed assets (e.g., cars, office equipment), will generally be of a capital nature and not deductible.

(b) *and if it has been incurred wholly and exclusively for the purposes of the trade.*
Expenditure is not 'wholly' incurred for the purposes of the trade if it is excessively large such that it partly represents a gift, e.g. excessive remuneration to a director.
Expenditure is not 'exclusively' incurred for the purposes of the trade if the motive for incurring the expenditure includes an element of personal enjoyment,

e.g. a trip to the USA partly for business purposes but also for a holiday, will not be a deductible business expense.

8.3.2 Calculation of income profits

The steps required are:

(a) take total chargeable receipts (income);

(b) deduct expenditure which is allowable;

(c) deduct capital allowances

8.4 Capital allowances

Companies like sole traders/partnerships may be able to reduce their trading profits by claiming capital allowances on expenditure on machinery and plant and on industrial buildings. The capital allowances system works in a similar way for both companies and sole traders/partnerships (see **Chapter 10**, below).

8.5 Trading loss relief

It may well be that after deduction of trading expenses and capital allowances, that a trading loss is produced under Schedule D Case I. If so, then loss relief may be available in respect of that loss. It may also be that although a trading profit has been made in the current accounting period, that there have been trading losses in previous accounting periods for which loss relief is available in this accounting period.

For companies, there are two types of loss relief available. If available, they are taken before charges on income are deducted. To the extent that charges on income incurred for trading purposes are unrelieved in consequence, these may be carried forward and treated in the same way as trading losses (ICTA 1988, s 393(9) and see **8.5.2**).

8.5.1 Carry across and carry back relief for trading losses

A company's trading loss for an accounting period can be carried across to be deducted from profits (income or capital) from any source for the same accounting period (ICTA 1988, s 393A).

If the income profits or capital gains of the same accounting period are insufficient to absorb the loss (either wholly or in part), then the unrelieved loss can be carried back to be deducted from income or capital profits from the 12 months immediately preceding the accounting period in which the loss was made, provided that the company was then carrying on the same trade. This provision applies to losses incurred in any accounting period ending on or after 2 July 1997 and which require time apportionment in respect of an accounting period which starts before and ends after that date. In respect of losses arising prior to 2 July 1997 the carry-back may be effected and deduction made against income or capital profits during the previous three years, providing the company was carrying on the same trade. The loss must be set against the profits of the later accounting periods first. Again, if the carry-back would involve setting the losses against profits of an accounting period commencing earlier than a date three years previously the profits must be time-apportioned.

If carry-back relief is taken, then it will mean that the company will recover CT previously paid.

EXAMPLE 1

A company makes its accounts up to 31 December in each year. In the year ended 31 December 2001 it makes a profit of £80,000 and chargeable gains of £10,000. In the year ended 31 December 2002 it makes a trading loss of £160,000 and chargeable gains of £60,000. It has charges on income incurred for trading purposes of £10,000 for each period and only carries on the same trade during each period.

Its profits chargeable to corporation tax will be:

Year ended 31 December 2002	
Trading profit for year	Nil
Chargeable gains	£60,000
Less: s 393 A carry-across relief	£60,000
Taxable profit for year	Nil

Unrelieved losses to carry back of £160,000 − £60,000 = £100,000

Year ended 31 December 2001	
Trading profit for year	£80,000
Chargeable gains	£10,000
	£90,000
Less: s 393 A carry-back relief	£90,000
Taxable profit for year	Nil

Unrelieved losses to carry forward of £100,000 − £90,000 = £10,000

Unrelieved charges on income to carry forward for year ended 31 December 2001 of £10,000 and for year ended 31 December 2002 of £10,000.

8.5.2 Carry-forward relief for trading losses

Alternatively, or to the extent that a loss is not relevant under s 393A, above, a company's trading loss for an accounting period can be carried forward to be deducted from the first subsequent profits which that trade produces (ICTA 1988, s 393(1)).

This relief is not available against non-trading income or against capital gains. Further, if the company has two or more trades, then the relief can only be taken against the profits of the trade which produced the loss.

8.6 Calculation of chargeable gains

8.6.1 Normal CGT principles apply

A charge to CT may arise when the company disposes of a chargeable asset in the accounting period which results in a chargeable gain.

The chargeable gain is calculated in the same way as for individuals, but as the company is not an individual, it is not entitled to an annual exemption. Unlike an individual, a company is not entitled to taper relief. Instead, for companies only, Indexation Relief (see **6.11** above) continues to apply after 5 April 1998. Accordingly, indexation tables for this purpose (see **6.11** above) will continue to be published in respect of periods after that date.

The only CGT reliefs to which the company may be entitled are:

(a) capital loss relief;

(b) roll over relief on replacement of qualifying business assets.

8.6.1.1 Capital loss relief

If a company makes a capital loss, then it may be set off against capital gains of the same accounting period. If the loss is unrelieved, either wholly or in part, then the loss may be carried forward and set off against capital gains of later accounting periods.

8.6.1.2 Roll over relief on replacement of qualifying business assets

This relief is also available to sole traders and partnerships. See **Chapter 10**, below, for further details.

If a company disposes of a qualifying business asset used for the purposes of its trade and reinvests all of the proceeds in the purchase of another qualifying business asset, then the gain is not taxable at the time of the disposal but is deducted from the acquisition cost of the new asset. (See **6.8.6.**)

The main types of qualifying business asset are:

(a) land and buildings;

(b) fixed plant and machinery;

(c) goodwill;

(d) ships, aircraft and hovercraft.

Both the old and the new assets must be qualifying business assets. The new assets must have either been acquired within one year before or three years after the disposal of the old asset.

The relief operates by deferring the payment of tax on the gain arising from the disposal. However, the charge to tax is not escaped altogether. The gain arising on the disposal is deducted from the acquisition cost of the new asset. When the new asset is disposed of, unless roll over relief is further available to defer the payment of tax, the company will be charged to tax on the gain arising from the disposals of both the old and new assets.

The Budget in April 2002 contained new provisions for the tax treatment of intangible assets such as goodwill. This will impact on the application of roll over relief for intangible assets acquired after 1 April 2002. A new form of roll over relief will apply in relation to those assets. Further details of the new tax treatment are beyond the scope of this book.

8.7 Charges on income

A company's income profits and capital gains for an accounting period will be added together to produce the company's total profits for the accounting period. Charges on income are then deducted to arrive at the taxable profits, which is the figure upon which CT is paid.

Note that charges on income can be deducted from income profits from all sources and from capital gains, whereas trading expenses can only be deducted from trading receipts under Schedule D Case I. Therefore, it is important not to confuse those expenses which qualify as charges on income and those which are merely trading expenses. See also **Chapter 10**.

The main charges on income are:

(a) certain charitable donations;

(b) patent royalties.

Charges on income are payable by the company subject to deduction of income tax at the basic rate. This tax is paid to the Inland Revenue and the recipient of the payments will be assessed on the grossed up amount but will receive a tax credit for the income tax already paid.

8.8 Rates of tax

CT rates are fixed by reference to financial years, being the period from 1 April in one year to the following 31 March. This is marginally different from the income tax year which runs from 6 April to 5 April in the following year.

It is important to appreciate that CT is calculated by reference to each accounting period of the company. An accounting period is normally 12 months ending with the company's accounting date, i.e. the date to which the company's accounts are made up.

In view of the fact that rates of tax are fixed for financial years, if the accounting period does not match the financial year and the rates of tax change, then in order to calculate the company's CT liability, the profits of the accounting period must be apportioned on a time basis between the two financial years.

EXAMPLE 2

A company makes up its accounts to 31 December in each year.

Its profits for the accounting period ending 31 December 1999 are £1,650,000.

The full rate of CT for the financial year 1998 (i.e. 1 April 1998 to 31 March 1999) is 31% but the rate changes to 30% for the financial year 1999, CT will be payable as follows:

	£
3/12 × £1,650,000 × 31%	127,875
9/12 × £1,650,000 × 30%	371,250
	£499,125

Rates of tax for the financial year 2002 (i.e. 1 April 2002 to 31 March 2003) are:

	£	%
Starting rate	0–10,000	0
Lower marginal rate	10,001–50,000	23.75
Small companies' rate	50,001–300,000	19
Upper marginal rate	300,001–1,500,000	32.75
Standard rate	Over 1,500,000	30

8.8.1 Standard rate

This applies where the company's profits are equal to or exceed the upper limit of £1,500,000. The standard rate applies to all of the taxable profits.

EXAMPLE 3

Company has taxable profits of £2,000,000.
Taxable profits exceed upper limit.
All £2,000,000 taxed at standard rate (30%) = £600,000.

8.8.2 Small companies' rate

This will apply to all of the taxable profits if they do not exceed the lower limit of £300,000.

EXAMPLE 4

Company has taxable profits of £250,000.
Taxable profits between £50,000 and below £300,000.
All profits taxed at small companies' rate (19%) = £47,500.00

The marginal rate applies if the company's profits fall between the relevant limits namely, £300,001 and £1,500,000.

For these companies, there is an effective marginal rate of 32.75 per cent, the profits up to the lower limit being taxed at the small companies' rate and the profits above that amount being taxed at the upper marginal rate. For the financial year 2002, the first £300,000 will be taxed at 19 per cent and the balance up to £1,500,000 at 32.75 per cent.

The reason why the upper marginal rate is higher than the standard rate is because the first band (£300,000) is taxed at only 19 per cent. Therefore, it is necessary to apply to the balance of the profits a rate higher than the standard rate so that the combined average of both rates will progressively approach the standard rate as the profits reach the upper limit.

EXAMPLE 5

Company has taxable profits of £1,000,000.
Taxable profits between lower and upper limits.
First £300,000 taxed at small companies' rate (19%) and balance at upper marginal rate (32.75%)

CT = £300,000 × 19%	£ 57,000
£700,000 × 32.75%	£229,250
	£286,250

8.8.3 Starting rate

This will apply to all the taxable profits if they do not exceed the limit of £10,000.

EXAMPLE 6

Company has taxable profits of £8,000
Taxable profits below £10,000
All profits taxed at the starting rate (0%) = zero

The lower marginal rate applicable to small companies applies if the company's profits fall between the relevant lower and upper limits namely, £10,001 and £50,000.

For these companies the lower marginal rate is 23.75 per cent, the profits up to the lower limit being taxed at the starting rate and the profits above that amount being taxed at the lower marginal rate. For the financial year 2002, the first £10,000 will be taxed at 0 per cent and the balance up to £50,000 at 23.75 per cent.

EXAMPLE 7

Company has taxable profits of £40,000.
Taxable profits between lower and upper limit
First £10,000 taxed at the starting rate of 0% and balance at lower marginal rate of 23.75%

CT = £10,000 × 0%	Nil
£30,000 × 23.75%	£7,125
	£7,125

The reason why the lower marginal rate is higher than the starting rate is because the first band up to £10,000 is only taxed at 0 per cent. Therefore it is necessary to apply to the balance of the profits up to £50,000 a rate higher than the starting rate so that the combined average will progressively approach the small companies rate as the profits reach the upper limit.

8.9 Distributions of profit

8.9.1 Distributions of profit: The old rules

Until 5 April 1999, if a company paid a dividend or other distribution of profit to its shareholders, it had to pay advance corporation tax (ACT) to the Revenue. Therefore, on top of the dividend, the company also had to pay the ACT. For the tax year 1998/99, the rate of ACT was 25 per cent of the amount of the actual dividend paid. For example, if a company paid a dividend of £800, then it would additionally have to pay ACT of £200.

The ACT paid by the company was treated as satisfying the individual shareholder's income tax liability on the dividend payment at rates up to and including the standard rate, so only taxpayers who were liable to income tax at the higher rate would have additional tax to pay.

The ACT paid by the company on dividends paid during its accounting period was, subject to certain limits, deductible from the amount of CT payable on the profits for that accounting period (known as 'mainstream CT' or 'MCT'). The rules relating to the set off of ACT against MCT are outside the scope of this book. They are relevant to all companies in relation to accounting periods ending on or before 5 April 1999. Companies who have been unable to set off that ACT in full are deemed to have 'surplus ACT'. Special rules govern the ability to set off surplus ACT against MCT and are outside the scope of this book. They remain relevant in respect of accounting periods ending after 5 April 1999 for companies having surplus ACT which they were unable to set off against MCT in respect of accounting periods ending on or before that date.

If a company paid a dividend to a shareholder which was another company, it had to pay ACT in the usual way unless both companies were members of the same group and an election had been jointly made by the companies and accepted by the Inland Revenue, enabling the dividend to be paid without ACT being payable. Dividends paid to a company which were subject to ACT are known as 'franked investment income'. This was not taxable in the hands of the recipient company and was free from any further charge to CT. If the recipient company made a distribution to its own shareholders out of that income, it did not have to pay ACT. The reason for this rule is that it would be unfair to tax the same profits twice.

8.9.2 Distributions of profit: The new rules

No payment of ACT is required in respect of dividends or other distributions of profit made on or after 6 April 1999.

A distribution of profit will normally be by way of dividend but if a company buys back or redeems its shares for a price over and above the original allotment price, it may also be treated as making a distribution of profit of the excess over and above the allotment price, which will then be treated as if it was a dividend.

Although ACT was abolished with effect from 6 April 1999, individual shareholders will still be entitled to some reduction in the rate of tax payable on dividends received, to reflect the fact that those dividends are being paid by the company out of profits which have themselves already been subject to CT. The dividends will be taxed at a rate of 10 per cent or at 32.5 per cent in respect of higher rate taxpayers (See **5.5**). Shareholders receiving dividends who are themselves companies no longer have the benefit of any reduction in the rate of CT payable on their own profits.

8.10 Calculating the liability

The steps to be followed are:

(a) Calculate income profits = trading receipts less trading expenses.

(b) Calculate chargeable capital gains

(c) Calculate taxable profits = Total profits (income profits + chargeable gains) less charges on income.

(d) Apply the appropriate rate or rates of tax.

(See the example at **8.14**.)

8.11 Payment of CT

8.11.1 CT

CT is normally payable nine months after the end of the company's accounting period to which it relates. A 'pay and file' system applies. Under this system, companies make their own assessments of their liability to CT. Companies are required to complete a CT return (Form CT200) in which the company calculates its own CT liability. The return must be delivered to the Revenue within 12 months of the end of the period to which it relates. There are graduated penalties for late filing of returns. A new self-assessment regime was put into effect for accounting periods ending on or after 1 July 1999. Companies with taxable profits exceeding £1.5 million now have to pay CT quarterly.

8.11.2 Interest

Unpaid or underpaid CT which is overdue, attracts an interest charge payable in addition. This interest cannot be treated as a charge on income.

8.12 Close companies

A close company is a company which is controlled by five or fewer 'participators' (shareholders) or by 'participators' (however many) who are also directors.

'Control' effectively means a majority shareholding. Remember that in assessing control, the rights of 'associates' must be added to the rights of the participator. 'Associates' include, amongst others, spouse, parents, remoter forebears, children, remoter issue, brothers and sisters.

Nearly all private companies will be close companies. Indeed, if a company has nine or fewer shareholders, then it will always be a close company, whatever the respective shareholdings, since it must be under the control of some five of them, even if none of them are related to each other.

Close companies are subject to special tax rules which are designed to prevent their use as a vehicle for tax avoidance.

8.12.1 Loans to participators or their associates

When a close company makes a loan to a participator or his associate, a charge to CT is imposed. For the financial year 2001, the company must pay the Revenue CT equivalent to 25 per cent of the amount of the loan.

The charge will only be refunded if and when the loan is repaid, written off or released.

In the recipient's hands, the loan is not taxable so long as it remains a loan. If and when the loan is written off, it is treated as if a dividend in the recipient's hands, i.e. the CT paid by the company is treated as satisfying the recipient's income tax liability save in so far as the recipient is a higher rate taxpayer. A shareholder who is not even liable for starting rate income tax is not able to make a repayment claim to the Revenue to recover the tax paid by the company.

8.12.2 Exceptions

The charge to CT does not arise if:

(a) the loan is made in the ordinary course of a money lending business, e.g. a finance company making a loan on commercial terms to someone who just happens to hold shares in the company;

(b) if the loan (together with any outstanding loan to the same person), does not exceed £15,000, the borrower works full time for the company and owns less than 5 per cent of the shares.

8.12.3 Gifts and other transfers of value by close companies

Inheritance tax is generally only charged on transfers of value made by individuals. However, if a close company makes a transfer of value, then this is deemed to be a gift by all the participators in the company in proportion to their shareholdings.

Each shareholder is then treated as having personally made a gift of the appropriate fraction of the company's gift. Unless covered by a relief and/or exemption available to that individual, the gifts will be taxed as though they were chargeable transfers. The rules relating to potentially exempt transfers (see **Chapter 7** above), meaning that there would be no liability to inheritance tax if the donor survives for a full seven years and with a sliding scale of liability for lesser periods, do not apply. Therefore, inheritance tax becomes payable immediately.

The company is primarily liable for the IHT due. This is one exception to the general rule that companies are not liable for inheritance tax.

This provision does not apply if the transfer is a dividend or a benefit in kind provided to a director or employee of the company. The aim of the legislation is to ensure that gifts or other transfers or value do not escape tax. However, dividends are already assessed to tax under Schedule F and benefits in kind to directors and employees under Schedule E.

8.12.4 Provision of benefits in kind to a participator or associate

If close companies provide benefits in kind (e.g. living accommodation) for a participator or his associate, then the company will be treated as making a distribution. The cost to the company of providing that benefit in kind will be treated for tax purposes as though it were a dividend. The recipient will be assessed to income tax under Schedule F.

This provision will not apply, however, if the participator or his associate is a director or employee of the company.

Again, the aim of the legislation is to ensure that benefits in kind are assessed to tax. If the participator or associate is a director or employee of the company, then the benefit is already assessed to tax under Schedule E.

8.12.5 Close investment holding companies: Rates of tax

A 'close investment holding company' is a company which exists purely for the purposes of holding investments. If a company is a 'close investment holding company', then the small companies' rate of CT will not be available and the company will pay CT on all of its taxable profits at the standard rate.

This only applies to close companies which exist purely for the purposes of holding investments. Trading companies or companies which deal in land, shares or securities and companies carrying on investment on a commercial basis or group holding companies which hold investments by way of shares in their own subsidiary companies are not affected by these anti-avoidance provisions.

8.13 Steps to calculate CT including chargeable gains

1. Calculate income profits for CT purposes:
   - 1.1 Calculate income profits from main activity.
   - 1.2 Deduct capital allowances and/or apply any balancing charges or allowances.
   - 1.3 Deduct any available trading losses.
   - 1.4 Add any income from other sources.

2. Add together all the chargeable gains for the accounting period calculated as follows:
   2.1 Take the disposal consideration.
   2.2 Deduct allowable expenditure being:
   - acquisition cost
   - costs of acquisition
   - subsequent improvements
   - indexation allowance on the above three items only
   - costs of disposal
   2.3 Deduct any capital losses for the accounting period.
   2.4 Deduct any capital losses carried forward (if utilised).
   2.5 Deduct any available trading losses.
3. Deduct charges on income from the aggregate of 1 + 2.
4. Apply the appropriate rate or rates of tax.

8.14 Example of CT calculations

EXAMPLE 8

Moorcroft Ltd has five shareholders. It has profits and losses as follows:

Accounting period ended	*Trading profits*	*Other income profits*	*Capital gains*
31 March 2001	(£100,000)	£10,000	Nil
31 March 2002	£50,000	£10,000	(£20,000)
31 March 2003	£100,000	£10,000	£30,000

NB: figures in brackets denote income/capital losses

Moorcroft Ltd has no charges on income in any accounting period.

In 2002/2003, Moorcroft Ltd:

Declares a dividend of £5,000 (£1,000 paid to each of the five shareholders).
Makes a loan of £10,000 to a shareholder, Sally Barnett, who is a part-time employee.
Claims capital allowances of £20,000

Calculate Moorcroft Ltd's corporation tax liability for each of these years. Assume for this example that CT rates remain the same as in 2001/02 for all three years.

Year ended 31 March 2001:

Taxable profits:

Trading income	Nil
Other income	£10,000
Capital gains	Nil
	£10,000
Less trading losses carried across	(£100,000)
	(£90,000)

No corporation tax liability.
Unrelieved trading losses of £90,000 to carry forward.

Year ended 31 March 2002:

Taxable profits:

Trading income	£50,000	
Less trading loss b/f**	(£90,000)	Nil
Other income		£10,000
Capital gains		Nil
		£10,000

Corporation tax due = nil (£10,000 × 0%)

* Capital losses cannot be set against income. Capital loss of £20,000 will be carried forward.

** Trading losses can only be brought forward against income profits of the same trade and not other income profits.

Year ended 31 March 2003:

Total profits:

	£	£
Trading income	100,000	
Less capital allowances	20,000	80,000
Less trading losses b/f	(40,000)	40,000
Other income		10,000
		50,000
Capital gains	30,000	
Less capital losses b/f	(20,000)	10,000
		£60,000

Taxable profits:

Taxable profits exceed £50,000 but less than £300,000 so all profits taxed at 19%

Corporation tax due = £11,400 (£60,000 × 19%)

CT paid on loan* = £2,500 (25% × £10,000)

* Moorcroft Ltd is a close company and so must pay CT on the loan in addition to CT on the taxable profits.

9

Value added tax

9.1 Introduction to VAT

Value added tax (VAT) is a tax levied on supplies of goods and services made by a supplier who is or is required to be registered for VAT purposes. It was introduced into the UK in 1973. It is also applied by all other EC member states under various names, although the rates of tax and the types of goods and services to which it applies do vary between member states.

It is payable on taxable supplies of goods or services made in the UK by a 'taxable person' in the course of business. It is also charged on imports of goods into the UK from outside the EC and on goods and some services obtained elsewhere in the EC.

9.2 Sources of VAT law

The principal charging statute is the Value Added Tax Act 1994 (VATA 1994). Detailed provisions relating to implementation of the Act are contained in a large number of statutory instruments. Many of these deal with the effect of VAT in very specific situations. Because of the complexity of the VAT legislation, the practitioner faced with a VAT issue will have to research all of this legislation to determine the application of VAT in particular circumstances. This book only deals with the basic principles of VAT which are of general application.

Additionally, HM Customs and Excise issue VAT Notices. Whilst they lack legal force, they express the views of HM Customs and Excise on the law as it applies to specific transactions. These can be a valuable source of information.

Like income tax and capital gains tax, VAT is subject to a number of extra-statutory concessions where Customs and Excise allow relief from VAT on an extra-statutory basis.

EC Directives 67/227 and 77/338 are also relevant sources, VAT having been introduced in 1973 in order to bring UK law in line with European Community law.

9.3 Administration of VAT

VAT is administered by HM Commissioners of Customs and Excise and not by the Inland Revenue.

They operate from a headquarters in London, a central accounts and computer centre in Southend and a number of local VAT offices throughout the country.

Apart from the submission of periodic returns of VAT to the central office in Southend, most of a VAT-registered trader's dealings will be with the local offices who deal with matters concerning registration and compliance with VAT legislation. They also have teams of officers who carry out what are known as 'control visits', inspecting the records of businesses to ensure they are properly recording all transactions and implementing VAT correctly.

In addition, there are teams of specialists who carry out investigations work where there are believed to be more serious breaches of VAT legislation. These officers often carry out lengthy and detailed investigation and surveillance work before using their powers to seize relevant records.

Appeal from a decision of the Customs and Excise is made to an independent VAT Tribunal. Appeals from decisions of the VAT Tribunals can be made to the High Court or direct to the Court of Appeal with the consent of the Tribunal.

9.4 Classifications of supply

In order to understand the operation of VAT it is important to recognise that goods and services fall into four distinct categories:

(a) standard rated: these are subject to VAT at the standard rate of 17.5 per cent.

(b) lower rated: these are subject to VAT at lower rate of 5 per cent.

(c) zero rated: these are technically subject to VAT but a rate of 0 per cent.

(d) exempt: these are not subject to VAT at all.

9.4.1 Standard rated supplies

Standard rated supplies comprise anything which does not fall within one of the other categories.

9.4.2 Lower rated supplies

Supplies of domestic heat and power attract VAT at a lower rate, currently 5 per cent. However, the lower rate does not apply to supplies for non-domestic purposes.

9.4.3 Zero rated supplies

Full details of supplies which will be zero rated for VAT purposes are contained in sch 8 to VATA 1994. Zero-rated supplies include the following:

(a) food, other than non-essential food (e.g. chocolate) and food supplied in the course of catering (e.g. restaurant food or hot take-away food);

(b) water and sewerage services;

(c) construction of buildings, but not alterations or repairs to existing buildings;

(d) books and newspapers;

(e) exports made outside the EC;

(f) public transport;

(g) children's clothing and footwear and supplies of protective safety helmets and boots.

9.4.4 Exempt supplies

Full details of supplies which will be exempt from VAT are contained in sch. 9 to VATA 1994. The principal categories of exempt supplies are as follows:

(a) Supplies of land (including buildings) or of any interest in land or any rights over land. (This does not apply to certain matters such as car parking rights or the letting of holiday cottages. It is also possible to waive the exemption in respect of supplies of land and so to elect to charge VAT.)

(b) Provision of insurance or reinsurance.

(c) Postal services provided by the Post Office.

(d) Betting, gaming and lotteries (which are usually subject to betting licence duty).

(e) Finance (which covers a wide range of transactions such as banking, money lending and the sale and purchase of shares).

(f) Education and vocational training provided by non-profit making establishments.

(g) Provision of health services.

(h) Burial and cremation.

(i) Trade unions and similar bodies providing they are non-profitmaking.

(j) Sports competitions and physical education (basically, provided the organisation is non-profitmaking and returns all fees as prizes).

(k) Certain works of art.

(l) One-off fund-raising events by charities and other similar bodies.

9.5 Inputs and outputs

The idea underlying VAT is that it is a tax on the value added to goods at each stage in the production process or on the whole value of services provided. In other words, a VAT registered business will be able to reclaim the VAT paid on the goods or services which it purchases ('input tax') and will only pay VAT on the value of the goods it sells ('output tax').

The VAT which it actually pays to the Customs and Excise will be as follows:

Output tax minus input tax = tax payable.

There are certain restrictions on the reclaiming of input tax, which is not recoverable in respect of the following:-

(a) Motor vehicles unless they are used exclusively for business purposes. If there is any element of non-business use, no VAT is recoverable. However if the vehicle is leased then 50 per cent of the VAT on the leasing payment can be recovered if there is non-business use.

(b) Business entertainment or hospitality.

(c) Certain fittings acquired by a builder for a new dwelling.

EXAMPLE 1

A VAT-registered business purchases standard rated goods and services of £174,000 plus VAT and zero rated supplies of £2,000. It makes sales of £620,000, all of which are standard rated items. The VAT which it pays over to Customs and Excise at the end of the relevant VAT period will be:

			£
Output tax	£620,000 × 17.5%		108,500
Less: Input tax	£174,000 × 17.5%	£30,450	
	£2,000 × 0%	£0	30,450
Net VAT payable			£78,050

9.6 The charge to VAT

VAT is charged on the taxable supply of goods and services by a taxable person (see **9.7.1**) in the course of a business carried on by him. The amount on which the tax is charged is the value of the supply.

9.6.1 Taxable supply

All supplies of goods and services are taxable supplies except those supplies which are exempt supplies.

9.6.2 Supply of goods

A supply of goods takes place in any transaction where the whole property in the goods is transferred (e.g. sale or even a gift of goods exceeding £50 in value, such as a business giving a Christmas hamper to a customer) or where the agreement expressly contemplates that the property will be transferred, as in the case of a hire-purchase agreement. In addition to goods in the more obvious sense, the definition includes the supply of any form of power, heat, refrigeration or ventilation or the grant, assignment or surrender of a major interest in land (i.e. the freehold or a lease for a term exceeding 21 years).

9.6.3 Supply of services

Generally any supply which is not a supply of goods (as defined above) and which is done for consideration, is a supply of services (e.g. solicitors' services). However, gifts of services are not considered to be a supply.

9.6.4 Taxable person

A taxable person is any individual, partnership or company making or intending to make taxable supplies and registered, or required to be registered for VAT.

Note that taxable person includes any person who ought to be registered but has failed to take the necessary steps to register.

9.6.5 Business

'Business' is a wide term which covers any trade, profession or vocation. It includes the disposal of a business or any of its assets. It would include, for example, a supply of services by a firm of solicitors who are registered for VAT. If that firm were then to sell their old office computers, they would also have to charge VAT on the sale price because there would be a sale of business assets, although not a common transaction for that particular business.

9.6.6 Value of supply

VAT is charged on the value of the supply of goods or services. This is what the goods or services would cost were VAT not charged. Often, the value of the supply is given as part of the price. For example, a service may be advertised as costing £100 plus VAT, £100 being the value of the supply.

On the other hand, the price of the supply quoted may be the VAT-inclusive amount. If so, then the value of the supply will be the total price less the VAT element. To find this amount multiply the gross amount by the appropriate VAT fraction, namely 7/47 for the standard rate of 17.5 per cent.

For instance, the total price is £1,000 then £1,000 × 7/47 = VAT element × £148.94.

A price is always deemed to include VAT, unless the contrary is stated.

If the supply is one of goods and is not for a consideration (i.e. a gift), then the value of the supply is the market value of the gift.

9.7 Registration

9.7.1 Taxable persons

VAT is only charged on persons who are registered or required to be registered for VAT. It is the person (i.e. individual, company or partnership) and not the business who is required to register for VAT. That person's VAT registration will cover all his business activities and he is taxable on all his taxable supplies, however diverse his different business interests may be. Where, however, there are separate business entities, separate registrations will be allowed. For example, a person trading as a sole trader is separate from a limited company of which he is a director and majority shareholder, or from a partnership in which he is a partner with others.

In the case of groups of companies, a group VAT registration is normally effected under which one of the companies is designated as the 'representative member' to be responsible for all VAT returns and payments for the whole group, with the other companies remaining jointly and severally liable for payment. Individual companies which have several separate trading divisions are able to seek separate registration for each trading division.

9.7.2 Compulsory registration

Under sch 1 to VATA 1994, a person is required to register for VAT at the end of any month if the value of his taxable supplies (including zero rated supplies) in the past 12 months has exceeded a certain threshold. Further, a person is required to register for VAT at any time if there are reasonable grounds for believing that the value of his taxable supplies in the next 30 days will exceed that threshold.

The registration threshold from 1 April 2002 is £55,000. If, however the annual limit has been exceeded but Customs and Excise are satisfied that taxable turnover will not exceed £53,000 in the following 12 months, registration will not be needed.

Registration is effected by submitting form VAT1 to Customs and Excise. In the case of registration of a partnership form VAT2 must also be submitted, giving details of all of the partners. On registration, the taxable person is issued with a VAT registration number.

9.7.3 Voluntary registration

It is possible for persons who make or intend to make taxable supplies of less than the current compulsory registration threshold to register for VAT voluntarily.

9.7.3.1 Advantages of voluntary registration

The main reason why a business may wish to register for VAT voluntarily is to enable it to reclaim VAT charged to it by its suppliers. If the business is not registered, then it is not able to do so.

9.7.3.2 Disadvantages of voluntary registration

When deciding whether to register voluntarily, the business must consider the disadvantage that VAT may affect its selling position in that it will have to charge its customers higher prices including the VAT element. This will not be a problem if the customers are themselves exclusively VAT registered persons as all VAT charged can be reclaimed by them. It will also not be a problem if the business makes predominantly zero-rated supplies. However, it may affect the selling position of a small business which is not currently VAT registered and is able to undercut its larger rivals who are obliged to charge VAT, where the customers are not themselves VAT registered or are otherwise unable to reclaim the input VAT by virtue of making only exempt supplies (see **9.7.3.3**).

The business should also not ignore the additional administrative costs associated with accounting for VAT.

9.7.3.3 Exempt and zero-rated suppliers

It is not possible for a person who makes or intends to make only exempt supplies to register for VAT voluntarily. That person falls wholly outside the VAT net. He makes no charge to customers for VAT but at the same time, because he is unable to register for VAT, cannot reclaim the VAT charged by suppliers.

Therefore, although zero-rated and exempt suppliers are similar in that the customer does not actually pay any VAT, the distinction is important in the sense that a zero-rated supplier can register for VAT and reclaim VAT charged on his supplies. An exempt supplier is not able to do so.

9.8 Rates of tax and tax points

9.8.1 The tax point

The tax on a supply of goods and services becomes chargeable at a definite time which is known as the 'tax point'. The rate of tax charged is the rate applicable at the date of the tax point and the tax must be accounted for in the tax period into which the tax point falls (see **9.9.1**).

So far as goods are concerned, the basic rule is that the tax point is the date on which the goods are removed to give affect to the transaction (i.e. the date of despatch). If goods are not actually removed (e.g. machines built on site), the tax point is the date on which they are made available to the customer.

In the case of services, the basic rule is that the tax point is the date on which the services are performed. In practice, this means the date on which the services are completed.

However, the basic tax point can be altered by invoicing and payment arrangements:

(a) If the supplier issues a tax invoice or receives payment before the basic tax point, then the tax point can be brought forward to the date of the invoice or date of payment (whichever is earlier).

(b) If the supplier issues a tax invoice within 14 days after the basic tax point, then the tax point can be delayed to the date when the invoice is issued.

9.8.2 Rates of tax

For the financial year 2002/03 (i.e. 1 April 2002 to 31 March 2003), the rates of tax are as follows:

Standard rate:	17.5%
Lower rate:	5%
Zero rate:	0%

9.9 Accounting for VAT

9.9.1 Tax invoices

When a registered person supplies goods or services taxable at a positive rate (i.e. any supply other than one which is zero rated) to another taxable person, he must, within 30 days of the time of the supply, issue a 'tax invoice' to that person obtaining certain specified details. The tax invoice is an important document, since it is the principal evidence available to the customer to support a claim for the reclaim of input tax. The customer must keep the original, and the supplier must retain a copy.

It is not necessary to issue a tax invoice for zero-rated supplies (except if the customer is in another EC member state), or for supplies to customers who are not taxable persons, although such persons may request one.

The tax invoice must clearly show the following:

(a) a number identifying the tax invoice;

(b) date of supply, i.e. the tax point;

(c) supplier's name, address and VAT registration number;

(d) customer's name (or trading name) and address;

(e) type of supply;

(f) description sufficient to identify the goods or services supplied;

(g) for each description, the quantity of goods or the extent of the services, the rate of tax and amount payable (excluding VAT).

(h) rate of any cash discount offered;

(i) the total tax chargeable at each rate, with the rate of tax to which it relates;

(j) the total amount of tax chargeable.

If there is more than one date on a tax invoice, the tax point must be clearly identified.

9.9.2 VAT records

The taxable person must record in books of account all output tax charged by him and all input tax reclaimed by him in each three month period (known as the 'tax period').

There are special rules which allow businesses to deal with their VAT accounting on a monthly basis if they so wish.

9.9.3 Due date for payment

Within one month of the end of the tax period, the taxable person must submit a VAT return in form VAT 100 for the tax period together with a cheque for the VAT due.

9.9.4 The amount of VAT payable

The amount of VAT payable is the VAT charged on all supplies of goods and services made in the course of the business (output tax) less any VAT paid in the course of the business (input tax).

Where input tax exceeds output tax, a repayment of the difference will be made by Customs and Excise.

When a person makes both exempt and taxable supplies, special rules provide that only part of his input tax will be deductible from the output tax charged on the taxable supplies.

There are also special rules concerning self-supply of goods and services. For example, if an insurance company (exempt and therefore unable to recover input tax) also has its own printing business to supply it with printing upon which it would pay VAT if it purchased the supplies elsewhere, there will be a potential charge to VAT on the supply made.

EXAMPLE 2 (periodic VAT calculation)

Hallam Wholesale Ltd operate a cash and carry warehouse, selling both food and household goods. They are a VAT registered supplier. Their sales in the last VAT quarter amounted to £2,500,000 net of VAT of which £1,500,000 was zero-rated and £1,000,000 was standard-rated. Their purchases in this period were zero-rated food of £1,100,000 and other standard-rated goods for resale of £700,000 plus VAT. In addition they have, in the same period, received invoices for the following sums plus VAT where appropriate, from VAT registered suppliers:

Accountants	£15,000
Solicitors	£1,500
Telephone	£1,000
Electricity	£2,000
Water charges	£2,400
Buffet lunch for customers	£1,400

The VAT payment which should accompany Hallam Wholesale's VAT return in respect of this period will be calculated as follows:

Output tax:	£
£1,500.000 × 0%	0.00
£1,000.000 × 17.5%	175,000.00

Less Input tax:	£	
Goods £1,100,000 × 0%	0.00	
Goods £700,000 × 17.5%	122,500.00	
Accountants £15,000 × 17.5%	2,625.00	
Solicitors £1,500 × 17.5%	262.50	
Telephone £1,000 × 17.5%	175.00	
Electricity £2,000 × 17.5%	350.00	
Water £2,400 × 0%	0.00	125,912.50
Net VAT due		£49,087.50

Electricity is for non-domestic use and is charged at standard rate.
Water charges are zero rated.
Buffet lunch is entertainment and so input tax is not allowable.

The return must be submitted and VAT paid within 30 days of the end of the period.

9.10 Penalties

A person who fails to comply with the VAT legislation is liable to a range of criminal and civil penalties in addition to being required to pay any unpaid tax with interest. The main penalties are as follows:

9.10.1 Late notification of liability to register

Where a person who is liable to register for VAT fails to do so, he will be liable to a civil penalty of the greater of £50 and a percentage of the net tax for which he was liable during the period when he should have been registered (in addition to the tax itself plus interest). This percentage rises according to the period of delay and is:

5 per cent for a period of up to 9 months;
10 per cent between 9 and 18 months;
15 per cent where the failure lasts more than 18 months.

9.10.2 Default surcharge

If a registered person submits a return late or submits the return on time but fails to pay the VAT on time, Customs and Excise can apply a default surcharge which can range from £30 to 15 per cent of the tax due. The detailed provisions are outside the scope of this book.

9.10.3 Serious misdeclaration penalty

Serious misdeclaration penalty applies when the VAT liability is understated on the return or where Customs and Excise assess less than the total tax which should be due and the taxpayer fails to point this out to them within 30 days. In order to attract the penalty, the underdeclaration or overstatement of repayment must exceed the lesser of £1,000,000 or 30 per cent of the relevant amount for the period. The rate of penalty is 15 per cent of the tax underdeclared.

9.10.4 Persistent misdeclaration penalty

Persistent misdeclaration penalty is at the rate of 15 per cent of the tax due and relates to circumstances where there is a material inaccuracy, namely an underdeclaration which exceeds the greater of £500,000 and 10 per cent of the gross amount of VAT for the period. Again the detailed rules are outside the scope of this book.

9.10.5 Interest on VAT unpaid

Interest is also payable on VAT which is unpaid, the rate currently being 2.5 per cent in excess of the average of bank base lending rates. This is not treated as an allowable expense for the purposes of calculating liability of the business to income tax or to corporation tax.

10 Introduction to the taxation of sole proprietors and partnerships

10.1 Introduction

Taxable income is calculated by deducting charges on income and personal reliefs from the taxpayer's statutory income. The taxpayer's statutory income is the total of his income computed according to the rules to the various Schedules set out in the Income and Corporation Taxes Act 1988 (see **Chapter 5** above).

So far as sole traders and trading partnerships are concerned, the most relevant Schedule in computing the sole trader's or partner's statutory income will, in the case of traders, be Schedule D Case I which assesses the profits of a trade. For professionals such as solicitors or accountants, whether they are a sole trader or partnership, the most relevant Schedule will be Schedule D Case II which assesses the profits of a profession or vocation. The rules for assessing income under Schedule D Cases I and II are almost identical and are set out below. As the provisions relating to sole traders also apply to partnerships and *vice versa*, the provisions of this Part relate to both unless stated to the contrary.

It is assumed for the purposes of this Chapter that the sole trader or partnership has no other income apart from its trade or vocation income. When calculating the income tax liability of a sole trader or partner, it is important to appreciate the fact that the sole trader/partner may well have other sources of income apart from income from the business/partnership. For example, the sole trader/partner may receive bank or building society interest which is assessed to tax under Schedule D Case III or dividend income which is assessed under Schedule F. That income must also be included in the statutory income calculation.

Details of the charges on income and personal reliefs to which the sole trader/partner may be entitled and for more detail on the calculation of income tax, are contained in **Chapter 5**, above.

10.2 Income tax liability of partnerships

10.2.1 Liability

Each individual partner is required to includc his share of the partnership income in his own tax return and will be separately assessed for income tax on that partnership income on an individual basis. The partners are not jointly and severally liable for the tax due in respect of the partnership income. An individual partner is liable for the tax due on his share of the partnership income only.

10.2.2 Calculation of trading profits

The rules for assessing a sole trader's/partnership's trading profits liable to income tax under Schedule D Cases I or II are, briefly, that the trading profits are calculated by deducting deductible expenditure and capital allowances from the sole trader's/partnership's chargeable receipts.

10.2.2.1 Chargeable receipts

Chargeable receipts are those which:

(a) *derive from the trading activity.*
The receipt must derive from the trading activity rather than from circumstances not directly connected with the trade, e.g. sales, or compensation received from cancellation of an order, would be a trading receipt, but this would not apply to a gratuitous sum received on termination of a trading relationship as a gesture of goodwill.

(b) *are of an income nature.*
Income receipts must be distinguished from capital receipts. This distinction is very important in the case of sole traders and partnerships because capital receipts attract CGT and not income tax. If an item is purchased for resale at a profit, the proceeds of sale will be an income receipt, e.g. purchase and sale of stock by an antique dealer. If the asset is purchased for the benefit or use of the business on a more permanent basis, as opposed to resale, the receipt will be of a capital nature, e.g. purchase and sale of shelves and counters in a shop.

10.2.2.2 Deductible expenditure

Expenditure will be deductible if it:

(a) *is of an income nature.*
If the expenditure is incurred for the purposes of enabling the business to resell the item at a profit, the expenditure will be of an income nature, e.g. the purchase of stock but not the cost of buying permanent assets like office equipment.
Another test is whether the expenditure is recurrent rather then once-and-for-all expenditure. If recurrent, it will generally be of an income nature. Examples would be rent, rates, telephone and interest on an overdraft. Once-and-for-all expenditure like the purchase of cars or office equipment will not be deductible as it is of a capital nature.

(b) *has been wholly, exclusively ~~and necessarily~~ incurred for the purposes of the trade.*
Expenditure is not wholly incurred for the purposes of the trade if it is excessively large, so that it is, effectively, in part a gift. Expenditure is not exclusively and necessarily incurred if it has a dual purpose, e.g. a trip to America which is part business and part holiday and will not be an allowable deduction.

10.2.2.3 Capital allowances

These are explained at **10.9**.

10.3 Basis of assessment: Accounting basis

The business will have to produce accounts on a consistent basis each year. In respect of accounting periods ending on or before 5 April 1999 there were three ways in which the accounts of a sole trader or partnership could be prepared and the method used will have to be agreed with the Revenue. The bases which could be used to determine trading profit (loss) were:

10.3.1 Earnings basis

Accounts include all income earned whether or not it is actually received and all expenses incurred whether or not actually paid. There is no requirement for invoices to have been issued or received. The value of stock and work in progress at the end of the accounting period is taken into account.

This method is used by a trader or trading partnership (Schedule D Case I) and the Revenue normally insisted on this method being used by professionals (Schedule D Case II) for the first three years. In respect of accounting periods beginning on or after 6 April 1999 all businesses will have to use this basis to comply with the requirement that the accounts show 'a true and fair view' of the profits for the accounting period.

10.3.2 Cash basis

Accounts include only the items actually received and paid. Income earned but not paid and expenses incurred but not paid are not included. The value of work in progress at the end of the accounting period is not taken into account. Some solicitors operated on this basis. With limited exceptions for barristers during early years of practice, the cash basis of assessment was abolished with effect from 6 April 1999. Special adjustment rules apply to the transition but these are outside the scope of this book. The resulting additional income tax charge may be spread over ten years.

10.3.3 Bills delivered basis

Accounts include all bills delivered to customers or clients and all invoices received whether or not actually paid. Other items such as the value of work in progress are often disregarded. This basis was commonly used by solicitors. Like the cash basis, this basis ceased to apply in respect of accounting periods commencing on or after 6 April 1999. Special adjustment rules and the ability to spread the additional tax charge over ten years apply as for the cash basis.

10.4 Basis of assessment: Taxation basis

The basis of assessment determines the basis period for the relevant tax year, that is, the period in respect of which trading profits will be assessed to tax in that particular tax year. A sole trader/partnership is assessed to income tax under Schedule D Cases I or II on the current year basis (CYB), that is, on the profits of the accounting period ending in the current tax year (the 'basis period').

EXAMPLE 1

A partnership makes up its accounts to 31 May in each year. Its trading profits are as follows:

1999	£10,000
2000	£15,000
2001	£20,000
2002	£30,000
2003	£35,000

The Schedule D Case I or II income for income tax purposes is as follows:

Tax Year	*Schedule D Case I or II income*
1999/00	£10,000
2000/01	£15,000
2001/02	£20,000
2002/03	£30,000

Income tax becomes payable in three instalments as follows:

(a) First interim payment on 31 January during the tax year in which the accounting period ends.

(b) Second interim payment on 31 July immediately following the end of the tax year.

(c) Final payment/repayment on 31 January following the end of that tax year or 30 days following assessment (if later).

The interim payments will be estimated by the Revenue and based on the income tax payable in respect of the previous tax year but it is possible for the taxpayer to have the figures amended if there has been a significant change in the income which has not had income tax deducted at source.

10.5 Starting a new business: The opening year rules

There are special rules which apply to determine the basis of assessment under Schedule D Cases I and II in the early years of the business.

10.5.1 The rules

For the purposes of this book, it is assumed that the sole trader's/partnership's first accounts are made up to a date which falls in either the first or second tax year of the trade and that the business does not change its accounting date. If not, then the opening year rules are more complex and are outside the scope of this book.

The opening year rules are as follows:

Tax year	*Basis of assessment*
Year of commencement	Profits from date of commencement to following 5 April.
Second year	Profits for 12 months ending with accounting reference date in second tax year *or* if the period from commencement to that date is less than 12 months, the actual profits of first 12 months' trading.
Third and subsequent years	Current year basis (i.e. normal basis).

Always find out what tax year you are concerned with and the accounting period applicable. Do not forget that it is rare for a business to have an accounting year, which coincides with the tax year. If profits are taxed twice under these rules then this will be corrected later (see **10.7** overlap relief).

10.5.2 Apportionment of profits on a time basis between accounting periods

Where, under the opening year rules, the profits to be assessed in a particular tax year are the actual profits arising in a given period, the profits are calculated by apportioning the profits of one or more accounting periods on a time basis. For the sake of simplicity in the examples, apportionment will be on a monthly basis although, in practice, the calculation will be done upon a daily basis.

EXAMPLE 2

Mark starts his business on 1 November 2002, making up accounts to 31 October in each year. The tax year in which he starts business is therefore the tax year 2002/03.

His trading profits are as follows:

Year ended	*Profits*
31/10/03	£18,000
31/10/04	£39,000
31/10/05	£44,000

His Schedule D Case I assessments are as follows:

Tax year	*Basis of assessment*	*Basis period*	*Schedule D Case I Income*
2002/03	Actual from commencement to 5/4/03	1/11/02–5/4/03 (approx. 5 months)	£7,500 (5/12 × £18,000)
2003/04	12 months to a/c ref date in tax year	1/11/02–31/10/03	£18,000
2004/05	CYB	1/11/03–31/10/04	£39,000
2005/06	CYB	1/11/04–31/10/05	£44,000

EXAMPLE 3

Anne starts in business on 1 July 2002. She makes up her first set of accounts for the six months ended 31 December 2002 and then for calendar years thereafter. The tax year in which she starts her business is the tax year 2002/03.

Her trading profits are as follows:

6 months ended 31/12/02	£3,000
Year ended 31/12/03	£7,600
Year ended 31/12/04	£8,200
Year ended 31/12/05	£6,400

Her Schedule D Case I assessments are as follows:

Tax year	*Basis of assessment*	*Basis period*	*Schedule D Case I income*
2002/03	Profits from commencement to 5/4/03	1/7/02–5/4/03	£4,900 (£3,000 + [3/12 × £7,600])
2003/04	12 months to a/c ref date in tax year	1/1/03–31/12/03	£7,600
2004/05	CYB	1/1/04–31/12/04	£8,200
2005/06	CYB	1/1/05–31/12/05	£6,400

10.6 Ceasing business: The closing year rules

As for the opening years of business, there are special rules which apply in the final years of a business

10.6.1 The rules

The closing year rules are as follows:

Tax year	*Basis of assessment*
Final year	Actual profits from day after end of basis period in penultimate tax year to date of discontinuance
Penultimate and previous years	CYB

EXAMPLE 4

Peter is in partnership with Tim and Bob. Peter takes 4/10 of the profits (both income and capital) with the balance being shared equally between Tim and Bob. Partnership accounts are made up to 31 July in each year.

Peter retires with effect from the end of the current accounting period, 31 July 2002. The partnership's profits for the last two years are as follows:

Accounting period (Year ending)	*Profits*
31/7/01	£70,000
31/7/02	£100,000

The partners' Schedule D Case I assessments for 2001/02 and 2002/03 will be as follows:

2001/02
Tax year before retirement:
For all partners:
Basis of assessment: CYB. Profits = £70,000

Peter (4/10)	£28,000
Tim (3/10)	£21,000
Bob (3/10)	£21,000

2002/03
Tax year of retirement:
Peter:
Basis of assessment: Actual profits from day after last basis period (i.e. 1/8/01) to retirement (31/7/02)

Profits = £100,000
Peter (4/10): £40,000

Tim and Bob
Basis of assessment: CYB. Profits = £100,000

Tim (3/10)	£30,000
Bob (3/10)	£30,000

10.6.2 Apportionment of profits on a time basis between accounting periods

As for the opening year rules, if the profits to be assessed in a tax year under the closing year rules are the actual profits arising in that period, then if necessary, the profits are calculated by apportioning the profits of one or more accounting periods on a time basis. Again, for the sake of simplicity in this book, apportionment will be done on a monthly rather than daily basis.

10.7 Overlap relief

The intention under the rules is that over the lifetime of the business, its profits should be taxed in full once and once only. However, the Revenue recognises that during the first two years of a business under the opening year rules, the sole trader/partnership will have some of its profits taxed more than once if it makes up its accounts to a date other than 5 April in each year. To compensate, the new legislation has introduced a form of relief whereby the profits that have been taxed more than once in the opening years of the business can be deducted from profits in the final tax year. This form of relief is known as 'overlap relief'. If the overlap relief is greater than the profits from which it is deducted in the final tax year, then the Revenue will allow the excess overlap relief to be treated as a loss.

EXAMPLE 5

Jane starts business on 1 August 1999, making up her accounts to 31 July in each tax year. She ceases to trade on 31 July 2003. Jane's trading profits for the first accounting period to 31/7/00 are £15,000.

In her first tax year of trade (1999/00), Jane will be assessed to tax under the opening year rules on her actual profits from the date of commencement (1/8/99) to 5/4/00 (i.e. actual profits during that eight-month period).

Jane's Schedule D Case I assessment for 1999/00 will therefore be £10,000 (8/12 × £15,000).

In her second tax year (2000/01), Jane will be assessed to tax under the opening year rules on her actual profits of the first 12 months of trade (i.e. the 12-month period from 1/8/99–31/8/00). This corresponds with Jane's first accounting period.

Jane's Schedule D Case I assessment for 2000/01 will therefore be £15,000.

It can be seen that the profits of the period 1/8/99–5/4/00 have been assessed to tax in both the tax years 1999/00 and 2000/01. Therefore, when Jane ceases to trade, she will be entitled to deduct £10,000 (the profits for that period) from her assessment for her final tax year (2003/04).

If, for example, her assessed profits in the final tax year are £30,000, then overlap relief will operate to reduce her Schedule D Case I income to £20,000.

10.8 Changes in the membership of a partnership

10.8.1 Introduction

Where there is a change in the composition of the partnership and there is at least one person who is common to both the old and the new firms, there will be a deemed automatic continuation of the partnership for income tax purposes. However, the new opening/closing year rules will apply, on an individual basis, to the partner who is joining/leaving the partnership.

10.8.2 New partner(s): Opening year rules apply

New partner(s) only will be treated for income tax purposes in the tax year in which they are admitted as though they have just started to trade as sole traders. The opening year rules (see **10.5**) will therefore apply to the new partner(s) only for the tax year in which they are admitted and for the following tax year, as follows:

Tax Year	*Basis of assessment*
Year of admission	Profits from date of admission to following 5 April.
Tax year after admission	Profits for 12 months ending with accounting year end in tax year after admission *or* if the period from commencement to that date is less than 12 months, the actual profits of first 12 months trading.
Third and subsequent tax years	CYB.

The new partner will be assessed in the opening years on his share of profits for the relevant basis period (i.e. the period which is assessed to tax in the relevant tax year). This will be determined by the relevant profit-sharing ratio for that basis period.

EXAMPLE 6

Angela and Brian have been in partnership for many years sharing profits equally. They make up their accounts to 31 December in each year. On 1 January 2003, they admit Clare as a partner. Thereafter, Angela, Brian and Clare share profits equally. The partnership's profits are as follows:

Accounting period (Year ending)	*Profits*
31/12/02	£20,000
31/12/03	£30,000
31/12/04	£45,000
31/12/05	£60,000

2002/03
Tax year of admission
Angela and Brian will be assessed to tax as follows:
Basis of assessment: CYB (i.e. 1/1/02–31/12/02)
Profits = £20,000
Angela (1/2) £10,000
Brian (1/2) £10,000
Clare will be assessed to tax as follows:
Basis of assessment: Profits from date of admission to following 5 April (i.e. 1/1/03–5/4/03)
Profits = £7,500 (3/12 × £30,000)
Clare (1/3) = £2,500

2003/04
Tax year following admission
Angela and Brian will be assessed to tax as follows:
Basis of assessment: CYB (i.e. 1/1/03–31/12/03)
Profits = £30,000
Angela (1/3) £10,000
Brian (1/3) £10,000
Clare will be assessed to tax as follows:
Basis of assessment: Profits of 12 months ending with a/c ref date in 2003/04 (i.e. 1/1/03–31/12/03)
Profits = £30,000
Clare (1/3) = £10,000

2004/05
Third tax year
Angela Brian and Clare will be assessed to tax as follows:
Basis of assessment: CYB (i.e. 1/1/04–31/12/04)
Profits = £45,000
Angela (1/3) £15,000
Brian (1/3) £15,000
Clare (1/3) £15,000

10.8.3 Retiring/expelled/deceased partners: Closing year rules apply

Similarly, retiring, expelled or deceased partner(s) only, will be treated for income tax purposes in the tax year in which they leave as though they have just ceased trading as sole traders. The closing year rules will apply to the outgoing partner(s) only for the tax year in which they leave.

Tax year	*Basis of assessment*
Tax year of leaving	Actual profits from day after last basis period to date of leaving
Penultimate and previous tax years	CYB

As on admission of a new partner, the retiring/expelled/deceased partner will be assessed in the closing years on his share of the profits for the relevant basis period for that tax year. His share will be calculated by reference to the relevant profit-sharing ratio for that basis period.

EXAMPLE 7

Stephen, Mary and Sarah have been in partnership for many years, sharing profits equally and making up their accounts to 31 December in each year. On 31 December 2002, Sarah retires as a partner. Thereafter, Stephen and Mary continue to share profits equally. Sarah retires therefore in the tax year 2002/03.

The partnership's profits are as follows:

Accounting period (Year ended)	*Profits*
31/12/01	£30,000
31/12/02	£45,000

Sarah will be assessed to tax as follows:

2001/02
Tax year prior to retirement
Basis of assessment: CYB
Profits = £30,000
Sarah (1/3) = £10,000

2002/03
Tax year of retirement:
Basis of assessment: Actual profits from day after last basis period (i.e. 1/1/02) to date of retirement (31/12/02)
Profits = £45,000
Sarah (1/3) = £15,000

10.9 Capital allowances

Ordinarily, expenditure which is of a capital, as opposed to income, nature, is not deductible in calculating the sole trader's/partnerships trading profits liable to tax under Schedule D. However, certain types of assets, principally plant and machinery and industrial buildings, do attract relief in the form of capital allowances. The provisions relating to capital allowances are contained in the Capital Allowances Act 1990 (as amended). The effect is that, in each accounting period, a proportion of the value of the asset is deductible when calculating the taxable profits of the trade when Statutory Income is calculated.

10.9.1 How the allowances are given

Capital allowances for sole proprietors and partnerships and also for limited companies are given by reference to accounting periods. This means that the business will calculate its entitlement to capital allowances by reference to capital expenditure and capital disposals arising in each accounting period of the business and will deduct them when calculating the trading profits of each accounting period. Balancing charges, which are explained below, will also now be treated as a trading receipt of the relevant accounting period, i.e. added to trading profits for the relevant accounting period.

10.9.2 Plant and machinery (except cars which are not used solely for business purposes and long life assets)

10.9.2.1 The writing down allowance

If expenditure is incurred on an item of plant and machinery within this category, it will qualify for a 'writing down allowance' (WDA) of 25 per cent of the acquisition cost in the first accounting period and, in subsequent accounting periods, a WDA of 25 per cent of the written-down value on a reducing balance basis. This is increased to a 40 per cent WDA during the first year only for all expenditure on relevant plant and machinery incurred between 2 July 1998 and 1 July 2003. The business must be able to satisfy at least two of the following conditions for the year in which the expenditure is incurred or the preceding year:

(a) turnover does not exceed £11.2 million;

(b) assets of the business do not exceed £5.6 million;

(c) business does not have more than 250 employees.

'Written down value' (WDV) means the original cost of the asset less any capital allowances already given. If the criteria for the increased first year allowance are not satisfied then the normal 25 per cent WDA will apply.

EXAMPLE 8

Mr Evans has been in business for many years as a baker, preparing accounts to 31 December in each year. On 1 October 2002, Mr Evans purchases some machinery for £10,000. It is assumed, for the purposes of this example, that Mr Evans has no other items of plant and that he qualifies for the increased first year WDA.

The accounting period ending 31 December 2002 will fall to be assessed in the tax year 2002/03 (CYB). For this accounting period, Mr Evans is entitled to a WDA of 40 % of the cost of the machinery less any capital allowances already given (WDV).

His capital allowance for this accounting period will be:

40 % × WDV (£10,000 − nil) = £4000

The above capital allowance is deducted in calculating Mr Evans' trading profits for the accounting period ending 31 December 2002.

His capital allowance for the accounting period ending 31 December 2003 will be:

25 % × £6,000 (£10,000 − £4,000) = £1,500

If, as is likely, the sole trader/partnership owns more than one item of plant and machinery, then the position is more complicated. For the purposes of calculating the WDA, the assets are aggregated in a 'pool' of assets and treated as if they are all one asset. Therefore, the amount of the WDA (subject to any increased first year allowance) will be up to 25 per cent of the total of expenditure on machinery and plant less all allowances so far claimed (i.e. the written down value of the 'pool' of capital assets).

EXAMPLE 9

Mr Sinclair has been in business for many years as a garage proprietor, preparing accounts to 31 December in each year.

On 1 November 2002, Mr Sinclair purchased some machinery for £6,000 and on 1 November 2003, he purchased some more equipment for £1,000. He has never purchased any other items of plant or machinery. He qualifies for temporary increased first year WDA.

Accounting period ending 31 December 2002
Written-down value of 'pool' b/f = Nil
Written-down value of 'pool' = £6,000 (£6,000 addition + Nil b/f)
WDA = £2,400 (40 % of £6,000)
Written-down value of 'pool' c/f = £3,600 (£6,000 − £2,400)

Accounting period ending 31 December 2003
Written-down value of 'pool' b/f = £3,600
Written-down value of 'pool' = £4,600 (£3,600 + £1,000)
WDA = £1,150 (25 % of £4,600)
Written-down value of 'pool' c/f = £3,450 (£4,600 − £1,150)
b/f = brought forward (from last period)
c/f = carried forward (to the next period)

10.9.2.2 Disposals: balancing allowances and balancing charges

When an asset is sold (or on cessation of trade) there will be a balancing adjustment to be made to ensure that the business does not get tax relief for more than has actually been lost by depreciation in the value of the asset.

If the business has just one item of plant and machinery, the position is relatively straightforward:

(a) If the asset is sold for less than the written-down value, there will be a balancing allowance (effectively an additional WDA) of an amount equal to the difference between the sale price and the written-down value. This will be deducted from trading profits in the same way as for other capital allowances.

(b) If, on the other hand, the asset is sold for more than the written-down value, there will be a balancing charge of the amount equal to the difference between the sale price and the written-down value. A balancing charge is added to trading profits and is therefore effectively a negative capital allowance clawing back part of the capital allowance already received. However, the balancing charge will be restricted to the amount of the allowances which have been given on the asset. Therefore, if the sale price exceeds the original cost of the asset, then the original cost of the asset is substituted for the sale price in computing the charge. The excess of the sale price over the original cost will be liable to be taxed as a capital gain and so liable to CGT in the case of individuals and partnerships.

EXAMPLE 10

Mrs Johnson has been in business for many years, preparing accounts to 31 December in each year. On 1 September 2002, she purchased some machinery for £2,000 which she sells on 1 September 2003 for £800. She qualifies for the increased first year WDA.

Accounting period ending 31 December 2002
Capital expenditure = £2,000
WDA = £800 (40 % of £2,000)
Written-down value c/f = £1,200 (£2,000 – £800)

Accounting period ending 31 December 2003
Written-down value b/f = £1,200
Disposal for £800 (i.e. less than written-down value)
Balancing allowance = £400 (£1,200 – £800)

If the asset had been sold for £2,500 instead of £800, then the position would have been as follows:

Written-down value b/f = £1,200
Disposal for £2,500 (i.e. greater than written-down value)
Sale price exceeds original cost: in calculating balancing charge, original cost substituted for sale price.
Balancing charge = £800 (£2,000 – £1,200)
Excess of sale price over cost (£500) liable to CGT.

If, on the other hand, there is a general 'pool' of assets, then:

(a) The sale price of the item disposed of is deducted from the written-down value of the 'pool' brought forward from the previous accounting period. This will be done before the WDA is calculated on the remaining assets. The effect of the deduction of the sale price of the asset which is sold is that smaller allowances will be available on the 'pool' in that and subsequent accounting periods.

(b) As for a single item, the sale proceeds deducted from the 'pool' cannot exceed the original cost of the asset sold. Any excess of sale proceeds over original cost represents a capital gain that will be liable to be taxed as a capital gain.

(c) If the sale price is greater than the balance brought forward on the 'pool' (the WDV of the 'pool'), then a balancing charge is made, restoring the 'pool' value to zero.

(d) On cessation of trade, the difference between the total sale proceeds of the assets and the WDV of the 'pool' will give rise to a balancing charge or balancing allowance as appropriate.

10.9.3 Motor cars not used solely for business purposes

These are subject to special rules which mean that:

(a) Motor cars which are used for private as well as business purposes qualify for a 25 per cent WDA. (Note that the temporary 40 per cent first year allowance will not apply.)

(b) The maximum allowance in any year is calculated on the basis that the original cost of the car was £12,000 and is therefore £3,000.

(c) The WDA is calculated on a reducing balance basis.

(d) The Revenue will only allow a percentage of the WDA to be used, this being the percentage calculated to reflect the amount of use made of the vehicle for business purposes as opposed to the use for private purposes.

(e) Cars are not treated as being part of the general 'pool' of capital assets. Each car is treated separately as if it was the only asset owned by the business.

10.9.4 Industrial buildings

A writing down allowance of 4 per cent of the original cost of construction or purchase of an industrial building can be claimed for every accounting period when the building is in use. As the WDA is a percentage of the original cost of the building, (unlike the reducing balance basis applied to other assets), full relief is obtained after 25 accounting periods.

If the building is sold (or when trade ceases), a balancing adjustment will need to be made. If the building has been sold for less than the WDV, a balancing allowance will be given. If the building is sold for more than the WDV, a balancing charge will be imposed. However, as for plant and machinery, if the building is sold for more than the original cost, the balancing charge cannot exceed the amount of the allowances which have been given. The excess of the sale price over the original cost is liable to be taxed as a capital gain.

When the building is sold, the purchaser can claim a writing down allowance on the building. The purchaser is entitled to a WDA on the 'residue of expenditure' on the balance of the 25-year period. The commencement of the 25-year period is when the building was originally built or purchased by the first claimant. The 'residue of expenditure' is the WDV at the date of sale plus or minus any balancing adjustment. However, the rate of the WDA which the purchaser can claim is not limited to 4 per cent and special rules apply which are outside the scope of this book.

EXAMPLE 11

Alan buys a factory for £100,000 and claims the WDA of 4 % for the first 10 accounting periods of ownership. He then sells the factory to David for £70,000. David retains the factory for the next 30 accounting periods.

The capital allowances position of Alan and David is as follows:

Alan

During 10 accounting periods of ownership, Alan can claim WDA of 4% of cost of building for each accounting period.

WDA = £4,000

Total WDA over 10 accounting periods = £40,000 (10 × £4,000)

WDV at date of sale = £60,000 (£100,000 − £40,000)

Disposal for sum greater than WDV.

Balancing charge = £10,000 (£70,000 − £60,000)

David

Balance of 25 accounting periods = 15 accounting periods (25 − 10)

Residue of expenditure = WDV + balancing charge = £70,000

David will be able to claim a WDA on £70,000 over the next 15 accounting periods.

10.10 Partnerships: Allocation of profits/losses between partners

In the case of partnerships, once the partnership's trading profits (loss) under Schedule D Cases I or II have been calculated, the next step is to allocate these profits (losses) between the partners in the firm in the relevant profit (or loss) sharing ratio.

The profit (loss) ratio to be applied in allocating the profit (loss) between the partners for a particular tax year, will be determined by reference to the ratio for the accounting period which is assessed in that tax year.

EXAMPLE 12

An existing business makes up its accounts to 31 December in each year. For the tax year 2002/03, under the current year basis, the business will be assessed on the profits for the accounting period ending 31 December 2002. The profit (loss) sharing ratio for that accounting period will govern how the profits (losses) are allocated amongst the partners in the tax year 2002/03.

10.11 Trading loss relief

It may well be that the partnership or sole trader has suffered a trading loss under Schedule D Cases I or II. This may be because deductible expenditure is greater than chargeable receipts or because, even though trading profits have been made, the deduction of capital allowances creates a trading loss. Under the current year basis, it will generally result in a nil assessment for the current tax year.

However, in addition, relief for the trading loss made in that accounting period is given in a number of ways. If a partnership makes a loss, each partner can choose what type of loss relief to claim in respect of his share of the loss.

10.11.1 'Carry across' against other income

Under s 380(1) of ICTA 1988, the loss made in that accounting period may be set off against any of the taxpayer's other income taxable in the year of the loss, if the taxpayer so elects – 'carry across'.

The 'year of the loss' is the tax year in which the loss-making period of account ends. For example, if a taxpayer makes a loss in his accounting year ending 31 December 2002, that loss will be treated as arising in the tax year 2002/03, since that is the tax year in which the loss-making accounting period ends. Under s 380(1), the loss made can be set off against any income of the taxpayer which falls to be assessed in the tax year 2002/03.

If a trading loss is not fully relieved under s 380(1), either because the taxpayer did not elect to take the relief or because the taxpayer's other income in the year of the loss was insufficient, then the taxpayer may elect to set off the loss (or unrelieved loss) against any income taxable in the preceding tax year (i.e. 2001/02).

Note that use of either relief means a deduction from total income (i.e. statutory income less charges on income) and so can result in a loss of allowances which are treated both as a deduction (e.g. personal allowance) and as a reduction (e.g. CA).

EXAMPLE 13

Alan has been in business since 1996, making up his accounts to 30 September each year. His trading profits for the two years ended 30 September 2002 were:

Year ended 30 September 2001: Profit £60,000
Year ended 30 September 2002: Loss (£48,000)
In addition, he has dividend income which amounts to £9,800 (gross) annually.

The year of the loss is the tax year in which the loss-making period of account ended i.e. 2002/03.

Therefore he can make a claim under s 380(1) of ICTA 1988 to offset his loss of £48,000 against any of his income for that tax year, as follows:

2002/03

	£
Schedule D Case I (CYB)	Nil
Dividend	9,800
	9,800
Less s 380(1) loss relief	9,800
	Nil

Unclaimed loss £ £38,200 (£48,000 − £9,800)

He can then elect to set the balance of his loss against any of his income taxable in the previous tax year (i.e. 2001/02) as follows:

2001/02

	£
Schedule D Case I (CYB)	60,000
Dividend	9,800
	69,800
Less s 380(1) loss relief	38,200
	£31,600

The loss is now fully relieved.

10.11.2 'Carry across' and 'carry back' against capital gains

Under s 72 of the Finance Act 1991, any trading loss remaining after a s 380 claim has been made may be set off against the taxpayer's net capital gains (i.e. capital gains before the annual exemption is taken) for the tax year of the loss and/or the preceding tax year, provided that the trade which gave rise to the loss is still being carried on.

10.11.3 'Carry forward' against future profits

If s 380 relief is not claimed (or is claimed but there is still an unrelieved balance of loss), then the loss (or unrelieved balance) may, if the taxpayer so elects, be carried forward and set off against the first available profits of the same trade (ICTA 1988, s 385). There is nothing to prevent the taxpayer leaving a gap of several years before the year in respect of which the relief is first claimed.

Once the election has been made in respect of a tax year, there are two important points to note:

(a) Under s 385, losses can only be offset against profits from the *same trad*e, not against non-trading income or trading income other than from the trade which produced the loss.

(b) The loss must be set against profits for the year in respect of which the election is made and then the next year in which there are those profits and so on until all the loss is relieved.

10.11.4 Terminal loss relief

A loss sustained in the final 12 months' trading can be carried back and set against profits of the same trade for the three tax years preceding the tax year of discontinuance, taking later years before earlier years (ICTA 1988, s 388). Note that s 388 does not allow relief against non-trading income or capital gains, or trading income other than income from the trade which produced the loss. The loss must be set against the profits from later years before earlier years.

10.11.5 Start up loss relief

Losses made in the first four tax years of a new business may be carried back and set against other income of the taxpayer (not capital gains) for the three tax years preceding the tax year of the loss (ICTA 1988, s 381). Unlike s 388, income from earlier years must be relieved before later years.

10.11.6 Carry-forward relief on incorporation of business

When an unincorporated business is transferred to a company in consideration wholly or mainly in exchange for the allotment of shares in the company to the former proprietor(s), he/they can set off their unabsorbed trading losses against any income (e.g. dividends, salary) which they receive from the company for any year throughout which they own such shares (ICTA 1988, s 386).

10.12 Statutory income

Once the sole trader's/partner's Schedule D income has been assessed, it is then necessary to calculate the sole trader's/partner's statutory income. If the sole trader/partner has other sources of income apart from Schedule D Case I or II income, then his statutory income will be the total of his Schedule D Case I or II income added to his other sources of income which will have been assessed under the relevant Schedules to ICTA 1988 (e.g. dividend income will have been assessed under Schedule F).

If the sole trader/partner has made a trading loss under Schedule D Cases I or II, then he will be entitled to set off that loss against his other income under s 380(1) of ICTA 1988 as mentioned above. This will have the effect of reducing his statutory income.

10.13 Taxable income

Once the sole trader's/partner's statutory income has been calculated then, as normal, any charges on income attracting full relief to which the sole trader/partner is entitled are deducted to calculate total income. Personal reliefs attracting full relief are then deducted to calculate taxable income. Once the taxpayer's tax liability has been calculated, reductions are made for any personal reliefs attracting relief at 15 per cent only and for any tax which has been collected at source. For a more detailed consideration of these principles see **Chapter 5**, above.

11

Introduction to the taxation of trusts and settlements

11.1 Background

Settlements may be created by settlors in their lifetime, or by will, or they may arise under the intestacy rules. It is our purpose here to consider the tax implications of such settlements from the viewpoint of both the trustees and the beneficiaries.

The three main taxes to be considered are inheritance tax, capital gains tax and income tax. Each tax must initially be considered separately as there is no overall integrated approach to the taxation of trusts. As we will see, the term 'settlement' has a different meaning for each tax, and may also be different from the use of the term in other contexts.

Again, there is no consistency in the method of taxing the trust, even within the individual taxes. In some cases the trust itself is taxed as if it were a separate entity from the beneficiaries (for instance, the inheritance tax treatment of discretionary trusts; the capital gains taxes treatment where the property is 'settled'). In other cases the trust is taxed by reference to the way in which the beneficiaries deal with their interests, almost as if the trust did not exist (for instance, the inheritance tax treatment of interest in possession trusts; the capital gains tax treatment of property which is excepted from the definition of 'settled property'). A variety of approaches can be identified in the income tax treatment of trusts, where both the trustees and the beneficiary may be liable to tax.

11.2 Inheritance tax

Statutory references in this section are to Inheritance Tax Act 1984 (as amended) unless otherwise indicated.

11.2.1 Definition of 'settlement'

For the purposes of inheritance tax, the term 'settlement' is defined by s 43(2). It includes a disposition whereby property is for the time being:

(a) held in trust for persons in succession (e.g., 'to Lesley for life, remainder to Rosalind');

(b) held for a person subject to a contingency (e.g., 'to Charles provided he attains the age of 25');

(c) held on trust to accumulate the whole or part of the income, or to make payments from income at the discretion of the trustees or some other person;

(d) charged or burdened with the payment of an annuity.

There is no settlement for inheritance tax purposes where property is held behind a trust for sale as beneficial joint tenants or tenants in common, nor where it is held in a bare trust.

The charging regime for settlements basically draws a distinction between those settlements where there is a beneficial interest in possession (**11.2.3**) and those where there is not (**11.2.4**). Certain 'privileged' trusts where there is no interest in possession are excepted from the charging rules described in **11.2.4**; the most important example is the accumulation and maintenance settlement, which is considered in **11.2.5**.

Where chargeable events occur, the primary liability for the payment of the tax lies with the trustees—the burden falling upon the trust property. In appropriate cases, the instalment option will be available if the charge arises on a death or, in other situations, if qualifying property remains settled.

11.2.2 Creation of a settlement

Prima facie, this constitutes a transfer of value by the settlor and its chargeability will be determined in the normal way. Unless covered by an exemption, therefore, when property is put into a settlement *inter vivos* there will be either a PET or an LCT. If this is done on death (either by the terms of the will or the operation of the intestacy rules) the property involved is part of the transfer deemed to take place on death and so chargeable (unless, again, covered by an exemption).

11.2.3 Settlements with a beneficial interest in possession

There is no statutory definition of an interest in possession. The basic test is the immediate right to the income from, or the use or enjoyment of, the property.

Generally, it will not be difficult to identify whether there is an interest in possession, and a life tenant *prima facie* has such an interest (unless only contingently entitled).

On the other hand, remaindermen and beneficiaries under discretionary trusts do not have the immediate right to receive any income (etc.) from the property and thus do not have an interest in possession. The same is true of beneficiaries with contingent interests (though the position of minor beneficiaries with contingent interests is noted at **11.2.3.1**(*c*) below).

11.2.3.1 Particular cases

(a) Where there is a power to accumulate income

Generally, this will be interpreted as a power to withhold the income from the beneficiary (so that no interest in possession can exist) unless the accumulations must be held for the beneficiary or his or her personal representative.

(b) Minors with vested interests in capital

Such a minor will not have the right to the income as it arises, and at first sight would appear not to have an interest in possession. Trustee Act 1925, s 31, (unless excluded or modified by the trust instrument) will, however, enable the trustees to apply the income for the minor's benefit and requires them to accumulate the income not so applied (see **15.3.10**). As such accumulations, together with his capital entitlement, must be paid to the minor on attaining 18, (or if he dies whilst a minor, to his personal representatives) such a minor does have an interest in possession during minority.

(c) Minors with contingent interests in capital

Here again it is important to bear in mind the terms of Trustee Act 1925, s 31. We will see (at **15.3.10**) that a beneficiary whose interest in capital does not vest at 18 nonetheless effectively obtains at that age a vested interest in the income. Thus, if the disposition is 'to Anna provided she attains the age of 21', Anna is entitled to receive the income from age 18—at which point she has, therefore, a beneficial interest in possession.

11.2.3.2 Charging basis (s 49)

A beneficiary who has a beneficial interest in possession is treated as if beneficially entitled to the property in which that interest subsists. In other words, if Lincoln is the life tenant entitled to the income from a trust fund whose capital is valued at £500,000, that capital value is treated as part of his estate for tax purposes. (If he were entitled to half of the income from the fund then £250,000 would be deemed to be part of his estate.)

This, incidentally, is why a reversionary interest (a remainderman's future interest) is normally excluded property for inheritance tax purposes (see **7.2.1.2**). All the value of the property is for tax purposes attributed to the life tenant's estate; the future interest is therefore 'ignored' in considering the remainderman's estate.

11.2.3.3 Chargeable events

These occur whenever, and to the extent that, the interest in possession terminates—since this will (effectively) be treated as a disposition of the property by the person with the interest in possession.

(a) Death of the life tenant—a chargeable event

Thus, the deemed transfer on the death of the life tenant includes the trust property. The trustees are primarily liable for the tax attributable to this part of the estate, and the burden of that tax will fall upon the trust property. However, the tax payable on both the unsettled and settled estate will be affected by the need to cumulate both with any chargeable lifetime transfers made by the life tenant in the seven years prior to the death to fix the rate(s) of tax payable.

(b) Termination during the lifetime of the life tenant—chargeable events

The termination may occur during the lifetime of the life tenant—e.g., on the sale, gift or surrender of the life interest, or the consent by the life tenant to the advancement of the remainderman. Normally, unless exempt, such lifetime terminations will be treated as PETs made by the life tenant and thus only actually chargeable to tax if the life tenant dies within the next seven years.

Notice that a tax charge may arise on a sale of the life tenant's interest. A transfer of value will occur even if the sale has been for the full market value of the life tenant's interest—because the life tenant has been treated as 'owning' the property, whereas the value of the life interest will be determined on an actuarial basis.

EXAMPLE 1

Lisa is the life tenant of a fund of £100,000 and she sells her life interest to Penelope for £25,000 (its full actuarial value). There will be a transfer of value (normally a PET) of the amount by which her estate goes down in value—£75,000. (This demonstrates the fact that inheritance tax is not merely a tax on gifts or transactions at an undervalue.)

(c) Termination during the lifetime of the life tenant—no chargeable event

If on the termination of the interest in possession the life tenant becomes absolutely entitled to the settled property, no charge will arise. This is because the value of the life tenant's estate does not change, and so there can be no transfer of value. Thus suppose that trustees advance £10,000 from capital to the life tenant under a power given to them by the trust instrument (this would not, of course, be possible under the general law). Prior to the advancement, this sum would have been deemed to be part of the life tenant's estate; it now is the life tenant's absolutely.

Again, no charge will arise on a partition of the settled property to the extent of the property taken by the life tenant under the arrangement.

EXAMPLE 2

Lucas is the life tenant and Roger the remainderman of a settled fund worth £500,000, and they agree to break the settlement on terms that Lucas will take £100,000 absolutely and Roger the remaining £400,000. The amount taken by Lucas does not affect the value of his estate; however, there is a transfer of value (normally a PET) by Lucas of the amount taken by Roger.

However, if the life tenant purchases a reversionary interest, special rules apply to prevent avoidance of tax.

EXAMPLE 3

Lois is the life tenant under a settlement of £500,000. Ronald is the remainderman, and Lois agrees to purchase his reversion for its full actuarial value of (say) £100,000. Her estate both before and after the transaction includes the value of the settled property, but the estate of Lois has now been depleted by the £100,000 paid to Ronald. She has, in effect, bought something which was already regarded as hers for tax purposes and reduced the value of her estate in the process. By s 55 she is prevented from gaining any tax advantage from such a deal: she will be deemed under this provision to have made a transfer of value (normally a PET) of the amount paid to Ronald.

11.2.3.4 Exemptions and reliefs

In the main, the availability of exemptions and reliefs will be determined by reference to the circumstances of the life tenant, the 'deemed owner' of the property for tax purposes. Thus, if on the termination of the interest in possession the former life tenant's spouse then becomes entitled (either absolutely or to a life interest), the spouse exemption will apply. On a lifetime termination, although the small gifts and normal expenditure exemptions are not available, the life tenant may claim any available annual exemption and marriage exemption.

Where the settlement includes property which might qualify for business property or agricultural property reliefs, their availability will be determined by whether the life tenant fulfils the various conditions.

There is a special version of quick succession relief (s 141) which operates in a broadly similar manner to the general quick succession relief described in **7.9.3.2**.

There is also an exemption in certain circumstances where, on the termination of the interest in possession the property reverts to the settlor (s 141). Thus, if Stanley settles property on Lancelot for life but fails to deal with the remainder interest, the property will revert to Stanley's estate on Lancelot's death—with no charge to tax. The exemption will also apply if the property were to revert to the settlor's spouse or widow (if the settlor is dead) provided this occurs within two years of the settlor's death. However, the exemption will not be available if the settlor or the settlor's spouse had acquired the reversionary interest for consideration in money or money's worth. Thus, if Stanley had settled the property on Lancelot for life with remainder to Roberta, the exemption would not apply on the death of Lancelot if Stanley or his wife had meanwhile purchased Roberta's interest.

11.2.3.5 Reversionary interests

As we have already seen, in **7.2.1.2**, these are normally excluded property for inheritance tax purposes. The effect is that a disposition of any such interest cannot lead to a charge to tax.

However, there are certain situations where, to prevent avoidance of tax, reversionary interests are not excluded property. We have already encountered one of these—where the reversionary interest is sold to the life tenant (s 55—see **11.2.3.3** above). The other cases include (s 48):

(a) Where the reversionary interest has at any time been acquired for a consideration in money or money's worth. By removing the reversion's excluded property status once it has been the subject of a sale, s 48 prevents potential tax avoidance.

EXAMPLE 4

Romeo sells his reversionary interest under a settlement to Xavier (who is not another beneficiary under the trust) for £50,000. Romeo is disposing of excluded property so that no tax liability can arise. If it were not for s 48, Xavier would have replaced a chargeable asset (£50,000) with excluded property which would not be taxable as part of his estate on his death—and which he could give away *inter vivos* without fear of a tax charge.

The effect of s 48 is that Xavier's reversionary interest will be part of his estate for inheritance tax purposes.

(b) Where either the settlor or the settlor's spouse is, or has been, beneficially entitled to the reversionary interest. Were it not for this rule, it would be possible to avoid tax by this sort of device.

EXAMPLE 5

Suppose Sarah settles property worth £500,000 on her mother Mildred (aged 90). Sarah retains the reversionary interest which she then gives to her daughter Doreen. The settlement giving Mildred the life interest would be a PET of (in practice) a relatively small sum (the loss to Sarah's estate being the difference between the value of the property settled and the value of the reversionary interest in it subject to the life interest of an elderly life tenant). The subsequent gift of the reversionary interest escapes tax as a disposition of excluded property. However, by s 48 its excluded status is effectively removed so that there is a transfer of value (a PET) on that occasion. There will also, of course, be a charge to tax on the settled property on the death of Mildred!

11.2.4 Settlements without an interest in possession

Discretionary and accumulation trusts clearly fall into this category, but remember that for inheritance tax purposes it also includes any case where a minor beneficiary is only contingently entitled. Unlike those cases where there is an interest in possession, there is no one to whom the value of the settled property can be readily attributed for tax purposes.

Rather, it is the property itself which is effectively taxed, though the basic intention of the charging regime is to achieve some sort of parity with what happens where there is an interest in possession (and indeed in the case of unsettled property)—i.e., the equivalent of one full tax charge every generation.

Tax is charged on 'relevant property', which is defined (s 58) as settled property (other than excluded property) in which there is no qualifying interest in possession—one to which (normally) an individual is beneficially entitled. Certain special cases—including accumulation and maintenance settlements (see **11.2.5** below)—are excepted.

It is not our purpose here to discuss the charging scheme in all its complexity; rather, we will attempt only an outline explanation so as to assist a clearer understanding of the special treatment afforded to accumulation and maintenance settlements and other favoured trusts excepted from the scheme.

11.2.4.1 Creation of the settlement

This will generally be a transfer of value by the settlor. As we saw (in **7.3** and **7.6**) the *inter vivos* creation of a discretionary settlement is an LCT, chargeable at half the rate(s) which would have applied on a death at that time, with the possibility of a supplementary charge should the settlor then die within seven years. Grossing-up will apply on creation, unless the settled fund pays the tax. There are special rules which apply where a settlor creates 'related settlements' (basically, several settlements on the same day) and where property is subsequently added to the settlement.

If the settlement with no interest in possession is created by the terms of the settlor's will, the property concerned will be part of the estate deemed to be transferred on the settlor's death.

11.2.4.2 Subsequent chargeable events

These basically fall into two categories:

(a) The periodic charge. This is imposed at ten-yearly intervals, the first occasion of the charge normally being the tenth anniversary of the creation of the trust. Basically, the charge is upon the value of 'relevant property' in the settlement at the time.

(b) The 'exit charge'. This is imposed when capital 'leaves' the settlement during the first ten years or between periodic charges (e.g., because the trustees exercise a discretion to distribute capital; or a beneficiary fulfils a contingency and becomes absolutely entitled; or someone becomes entitled to an interest in possession in the settled property). The value to be charged is the value leaving the settlement. However, no exit charge will apply where the capital leaves the settlement within three months of the creation of the trust or of a periodic charge (s 65); or if it does so within two years of the creation of the settlement where this happened on death (s 144).

11.2.4.3 Rates of tax and cumulation

The periodic charge is levied at 30 per cent of the lifetime rate of inheritance tax—i.e., at a maximum rate of 6 per cent (30 per cent of 20 per cent). The exit charge is levied at a proportion of the charge which would have been levied on a periodic charge had it occurred at the time—the precise method of calculation depending upon whether the exit charge arises before the trust's first ten-year anniversary or subsequently.

In all cases, in calculating the tax payable the settlor's cumulative total of chargeable lifetime transfers in the seven years prior to the creation of the settlement is the starting point of the settlement's cumulative total. This is so however long the settlement has been in existence.

11.2.5 Accumulation and maintenance settlements and other favoured trusts

These are all trusts without an interest in possession but to which the usual periodic and exit charges do not apply.

11.2.5.1 Accumulation and maintenance settlements (s 71)

Such a settlement must satisfy all of the following conditions:

(a) One or more of the beneficiaries, on or before attaining a specified age not exceeding 25, will become entitled to, or to an interest in possession in, the settled property or part of it.

It is not necessary that the beneficiaries should attain a vested interest in the capital by the specified age; the acquisition of an interest in possession is sufficient. Thus, this condition is met in the case of a gift of capital at age 30 because the beneficiary becomes entitled under s 31, Trustee Act 1925 to the income (and thus an interest in possession) at 18, notwithstanding that the capital does not then vest.

There may be difficulties in satisfying the condition that beneficiaries 'will' attain such an interest where the settlement gives the trustees overriding powers of advancement or appointment. However, as long as such powers can only be exercised amongst the existing beneficiaries and cannot postpone entitlement (to income at least) beyond 25, the condition is met. Thus, for example, there is no problem if the trust provides for property to be held for a class of beneficiaries in equal shares contingent upon their attaining the age of 25, with a power given to the trustees (expressed to be exercisable until a beneficiary attains 25) to appoint the fund to one or more of the class as they think fit. The trust property will vest either in the beneficiaries (or those selected by the trustees) no later than age 25.

(b) No interest in possession subsists in the settled property (or part) and the income therefrom is being accumulated so far as not applied for the maintenance, education or benefit of a beneficiary who will become entitled on or before age 25.

(c) Either:

  (i) not more than 25 years have elapsed since the creation of the settlement (or, if later, since the (latest) time when conditions (a) and (b) were satisfied); or

  (ii) all the beneficiaries are/were either grandchildren of a common grandparent or are the children or widow(er)s of such grandchildren who were beneficiaries but who died before attaining an interest in possession.

The inheritance tax consequences on the creation of an accumulation and maintenance settlement are determined in the ordinary way (remember that the lifetime creation of such a settlement is a PET). Thereafter, there is generally no periodic or exit charge. However, tax will become payable (on a special basis) if at the end of 25 years the settlement still satisfies conditions (a) and (b) but the beneficiaries are not all within (c)(ii).

11.2.5.2 Charitable and similar trusts

Trusts for charitable and similar purposes and those for the benefit of mentally disabled persons and those in receipt of an attendance allowance are not subject to the rules described in **11.2.4** above. Nor are pension fund trusts (s 151), employee trusts (s 86), or protective trusts even after forfeiture (ss 73 and 88).

11.2.5.3 Survivorship clauses

These are commonly included in wills for a variety of tax and succession reasons. A standard provision of this kind is 'To Benedict provided he survives me for 28 days but if he fails to do so then to Clarissa'.

Because Benedict's interest is contingent, a settlement with no interest in possession arises on the death of the testator. At the end of the survivorship period (or on Benedict's earlier death) this will come to an end because Benedict (or Clarissa) becomes absolutely entitled to the property. In principle, therefore, an exit charge should then arise. However, provided the survivorship period does not exceed six months, this will not happen (s 92).

11.3 Capital gains tax

Statutory references in this section are to Taxation of Chargeable Gains Act 1992 unless otherwise stated.

11.3.1 The basic position

As we shall see, the creation of a settlement is a disposal for the purposes of the tax. Thereafter, so long as the property remains within the definition of 'settled property'—with the possibility of an 'exit charge' when it ceases to do so—it is subject to a special charging regime. Disposals (actual or notional) by the trustees of the trust property may trigger a charge to tax; disposals by the beneficiaries of their beneficial interests generally do not.

11.3.2 Definition of 'settled property'

The Act does not define the term 'settlement'; rather, it talks of 'settled property', which is defined (s 68) as 'any property held in trust' except in those situations excepted from the definition by s 60. This excludes from the definition property held by a person:

(a) as nominee for another person; or

(b) as trustee for another person who is absolutely entitled as against the trustee (i.e., someone who has the exclusive right—subject only to the payment of trust expenses—to direct how the property should be dealt with). Such a situation (sometimes called a 'bare trust') might arise where a remainderman has become absolutely entitled on the death of the life tenant, or a beneficiary has fulfilled a contingency; or

(c) as trustee for any person who would be absolutely entitled as against the trustees but for infancy or other disability. This must be the only reason why the person concerned is not able to call immediately for the property to be 'handed over'—i.e., that person's interest must be vested. If a contingency (e.g., attaining 18) still has to be fulfilled, the property remains settled property.

Where one of the three exceptions applies, the trust property is for tax purposes dealt with as if it were vested in the beneficiary concerned, and acts of the nominee or trustee are treated as those of the beneficiary.

If two or more persons hold property as joint tenants or tenants in common, the property is not 'settled property' for the purposes of capital gains tax provided they are together absolutely entitled to the property.

11.3.3 Settlor's liability

This will depend upon whether the settlement is created in the lifetime or on death.

11.3.3.1 Lifetime settlement

Whenever property is transferred to trustees, there is a disposal for capital gains tax purposes by the settlor to the trustees. This is so whether the settlement is revocable or irrevocable, and even if the settlor (or the settlor's spouse) is a trustee (even the sole trustee) or a beneficiary.

The disposal (and corresponding acquisition by the trustees) is at the then market value of the property concerned. Any gain or loss will essentially be computed in the ordinary way. However, as the settlor and the trustees are connected persons (s 18(3)) any loss can only be relieved by setting it against gains made on subsequent disposal(s) to the trustees. If hold-over relief (s 165) is available (either because the assets are put into the trust by a transfer which is an LCT for inheritance tax purposes, or are business assets), it may be claimed by the election of the settlor alone.

11.3.3.2 Settlement created on death

Here, there will be no disposal (in line with the general scheme of the Act that death is not a chargeable event for capital gains tax purposes). The deceased's personal representatives will (as we have seen in **6.5.1**) be deemed to acquire the assets concerned at their market value at the date of death, and this will also be the value at which the trustees will be deemed to have acquired them, subject to the benefit of any indexation allowance available to the personal representatives at the date of handover to the trustees.

11.3.4 Liability of trustees

As in the case of income tax, trustees are a single and continuing body for tax purposes; thus a change of trustees is not a chargeable event for capital gains tax purposes. For all gains arising on or after 6 April 1998 trustees pay capital gains tax at the rate applicable to trusts see **6.2.1.3**). For the tax year 2002/03 the applicable rate is 34 per cent. There are anti-avoidance rules (in ss 77 and 78) whereby if the settlor or the settlor's spouse has any interest in a settlement, any gains are taxed as gains of the settlor and not of the trustees.

11.3.4.1 Actual disposals

Where the trustees sell trust assets, any chargeable gain or allowable loss is calculated in the normal way. The exemptions and reliefs to which they may be entitled include:

(a) *Annual exempt amount* (s 3 and sch 1). This is available normally at half the rate to which an individual is entitled in the year in question (for the tax year 2002/03 it is £3,850). However, where the same settlor has created more than one settlement, the available exempt amount is divided equally between them—subject to the proviso that each trust is entitled to a minimum exemption of 10 per cent of the exemption available to individuals (for the tax year 2002/03, therefore, £770).

(b) *Taper relief*. This is basically the same as for individuals.

(c) *Main residence* (s 225). Trustees may claim this exemption on the disposal of a property which has been the only or main residence of a person entitled to occupy it under the terms of the settlement.

(d) *Retirement relief* (s 164). Trustees of an interest in possession settlement which includes a business or shares in a family company may claim this relief on a 'material disposal' provided the various conditions are met by reference to the life tenant.

(e) *Roll over relief* (s 152). This will be available only if the trustees are carrying on an unincorporated business.

Where trustees incur a loss on the disposal, it can be relieved against any gains which they have in the same tax year, with any surplus being carried forward to future years.

11.3.4.2 Notional disposals (s 71)

When someone becomes absolutely entitled to (any part of) the trust property as against the trustees (or would become so entitled but for infancy or other disability) such property (or part) ceases to be 'settled property'. This may occur, for example, where the trustees exercise a power of advancement—though not where cash is advanced, since sterling is an exempt asset for tax purposes; when a beneficiary obtains a vested interest on fulfilling a contingency; where the remainderman becomes absolutely entitled on the *inter vivos* termination of a life interest (e.g., on the surrender of the life tenant's interest).

On the happening of any such event, the trustees are deemed to dispose of the property concerned and immediately reacquire it (as nominee of the beneficiary) at its then market value. Any chargeable gain or allowable loss is calculated in (essentially) the ordinary way. Hold-over relief may be claimed in appropriate circumstances on a joint election by the trustees and the beneficiary; in this case, the disposal is deemed to be not at market value but at the trustees' allowable expenditure at the date of disposal.

If the trustees incur an allowable loss for which they are unable to obtain relief, the loss may effectively be transferred to the beneficiary who becomes absolutely entitled.

Where the event causing the property to cease to be 'settled property' is the death of the life tenant, there is no chargeable disposal; but (as is generally the case for capital gains tax purposes on death) there is nonetheless a deemed disposal and reacquisition by the trustees at the then market value of the property (s 73). The effect is that the remainderman acquires the property at this value. However, tax must now be paid on any gain held over when the property was put into the settlement.

If on the death of the life tenant the property remains settled property (e.g., because another life tenant becomes entitled, or because a remainderman is only contingently entitled), the position is governed by s 72. There is again no chargeable disposal, but there is a deemed disposal and reacquisition of the property by the trustees which will form the basis of any future charge. However, tax will again be payable on any gain held over when the property was put into the settlement.

11.3.5 The beneficiaries

The tax position of the beneficiaries will depend upon whether the trust property is within the definition of 'settled property' or not.

11.3.5.1 Settled property (s 76)

On the disposal by a beneficiary of the beneficial interest there is no chargeable event—unless that beneficial interest was acquired by the beneficiary or a predecessor in title for consideration in money or money's worth (other than consideration consisting of another interest under the settlement).

11.3.5.2 Bare trust

If the property has ceased to be 'settled property', the beneficiary is effectively treated as already the 'owner' of the property. The result is that any subsequent disposals by the trustees are treated and taxed as if made by the beneficiary.

11.4 Income tax

Statutory references in this section are to Income and Corporation Taxes Act 1988 (as amended, in particular by Finance Act 1995) unless otherwise stated.

11.4.1 The basic position

As we will see, income arising under a trust will normally suffer tax in the hands of the trustees in a manner not dissimilar (in general terms) to that applicable to personal representatives. Beneficiaries under the trust may have to include trust income in their tax returns, thus perhaps (according to their circumstances) enabling them to make a repayment claim or causing them to be liable to higher rate tax.

However, in relation to certain *inter vivos* trusts there are anti-avoidance provisions which effectively require the income from the settlement still to be taxed as part of the settlor's income. These provisions (found in ss 660A to 688) affect (broadly) the following categories of settlement, a term which is for these purposes very widely defined:

(a) where the settlor has made a settlement under which the settlor's minor children benefit;

(b) where the settlor or the settlor's spouse have retained an interest in the settlement, whether or not actual benefits are received by them;

(c) where the settlor, the settlor's spouse, or minor child have received a capital payment or benefit from the settlement.

These provisions, which do not apply to trusts arising on death, are complex and are not further discussed in this book.

11.4.2 Liability of trustees

11.4.2.1 Generally

Trustees (who are for tax purposes a single and continuing body) are liable to income tax at the basic rate on all of the income arising to the trust (other than dividends where the rate is 10 per cent and interest on savings where the rate is 20 per cent), without any deduction for any trust expenses. Their statutory income is calculated in essentially the same way as that of individual taxpayers; they cannot, however, claim personal reliefs—but are not liable to higher rate tax.

11.4.2.2 Trustees 'special rate' (The rate applicable to trusts)

For the tax year 2002/03 this is 34 per cent and is payable on all income which (under s 31, Trustee Act 1925 or the trust instrument) is to be accumulated, or is payable at the discretion of the trustees or some other person—and (in either case) is not to be treated (before distribution) as the income of either the settlor (see above) or a beneficiary (see **11.2.3** above).

In practice, the liability to pay tax at this special rate applies to those cases where there is an accumulation and maintenance settlement for inheritance tax purposes, and to most other cases where there is for the purposes of that tax a settlement without an interest in possession (see **11.2.4** and **11.2.5** above).

The special rate is in effect only levied on the amount of trust income actually available for accumulation or for the exercise of the discretion, since the trustees are able to deduct expenses 'properly' chargeable to income under the general law (whatever the trust instrument may actually provide). Such expenses must, however, be claimed against dividends in priority to other income.

Where any of the net income of the trust is paid to, or applied for the benefit of, a beneficiary, the trustees must provide a tax deduction certificate for the tax paid by them.

11.4.3 Beneficiaries with a right to trust income

In cases where beneficiaries have a vested interest in the income of the trust it will be taxed as part of their income when it arises, whether it is accumulated, applied for their benefit, or distributed to them.

A beneficiary who has a vested interest in the capital will (unless the trust instrument otherwise provides) normally also have a vested interest in the income—even if under 18. A beneficiary whose right to capital is contingent on attaining an age greater than 18 will (unless s 31, Trustee Act 1925 has been excluded or modified by the trust instrument) effectively receive a vested interest in the income at 18. From that age until either the capital vests or the interest fails (e.g., because the beneficiary dies before fulfilling the contingency), the trustees (under s 31) must pay the income to the beneficiary. It must be returned, therefore, as part of the beneficiary's statutory income.

Where beneficiaries have vested interests, it is their share of the income (after trustees' expenses have been met) grossed up at basic rate which must be included in their returns. They have tax credits for the tax paid by the trustees.

Capital payments by the trustees will, in principle, not be liable to income tax. However, where the beneficiary is entitled to have income augmented from capital such 'topping-up' payments will be taxed in the hands of the beneficiary—*Brodie's Will Trustees v IRC* (1933) 17 TC 432; *Cunard's Trustees v IRC* [1946] 1 All ER 159.

11.4.4 Beneficiaries with no right to trust income

This situation arises where the beneficiary's entitlement to the income depends upon the fulfilment of a contingency, or the exercise of a discretion in the beneficiary's favour.

In these cases, the trust income will be taxed at the rate applicable to trusts, for the tax year 2002/03 34 per cent, in the hands of the trustees as it arises. If such income is simply accumulated, it is not taxable as part of the beneficiary's income; and the accumulations, when finally paid over to the beneficiary, are effectively capital and therefore not then liable to income tax. The fact that such accumulating income cannot (where the beneficiary is only contingently entitled) be treated as the beneficiary's income is really the reason why this special rate is payable in such cases. By taxing the income at an effective rate of 34 per cent the Revenue makes such contingent accumulation trusts less attractive compared with those cases where (because the income is to be treated as belonging to the beneficiary) they have the chance to tax the income at the higher rate of 40 per cent.

However, if any of the income is advanced to, or applied for the benefit of, the beneficiary the amounts so paid or applied (grossed-up at the rate paid by the trustees) are then treated as part of the beneficiary's income for tax purposes—with the benefit of a tax credit for the total tax effectively already paid by the trustees.

Probate and administration of estates

12

Introduction to probate and administration of estates

12.1 Introduction

The aim of this part of the book is to provide you with a basis for understanding the practice and procedure of obtaining a grant of representation and the administration of an estate.

When someone dies, his relatives or friends will usually have dealt with the most pressing matters—registering the death and arranging the funeral—before consulting a solicitor. In simple cases, or where the deceased has left little property, it may well be that a solicitor is not consulted at all. Commonly, however, the advice of a solicitor will be sought as to who is entitled to the deceased's property, as to the liability of the estate to tax and generally as to 'what has to be done' in order to pass the deceased's property to those now entitled to it. We have broken down the consideration of our task as follows:

(a) *Chapter 13 Entitlement to the estate:* To a large extent, who is entitled to the deceased's property will depend upon whether or not there is a valid will (**13.1**). To the extent that there is not, the intestacy rules apply (**13.10**). Some property, however, passes independently of the will or the operation of the intestacy rules (**13.17**). Sometimes, relatives or dependants may be able to make a claim for provision to be made for them which if successful would have the affect of 'varying' the dispositions made in the deceased's will or taking effect under the intestacy rules (**13.22**).

(b) *Chapter 14 Application for a grant of representation:* We begin this chapter with a consideration of the nature and effect of grants of representation (**14.1**). The requirements of the court are then considered (**14.11**), followed by those of the Revenue (**14.18**). This Chapter ends with a summary of the practice involved in obtaining a grant (**14.24**).

(c) *Chapter 15 Post-grant practice:* The duties and powers of personal representatives are considered first (**15.1**). The administration of the estate begins in earnest with the collection/realisation of the assets, following which the debts and other liabilities must be discharged (**15.5**). The final steps involve the distribution of the estate to those entitled (**15.13**).

13

Entitlement to the estate

13.1 Wills

In the following paragraphs we are assuming that a person has died leaving a will. You may have been instructed by a relative or friend of the deceased who has been appointed as executor by the will, or your firm may have been appointed. The role of executors is, in effect, to manage the deceased's estate until it can be distributed to those entitled. Normally, these entitlements will be determined by the deceased's will, but this is subject to a number of important provisos, i.e. that:

(a) the will is valid (**13.2**); that is, that the deceased (the testator) was both capable of and had the intention to make this will, and that it was properly executed. If the will is invalid it will be wholly ineffective, and the deceased's property will pass to those entitled under the intestacy rules (see **13.9** to **13.14**);

(b) the will has not been revoked (**13.3**). If so, again the deceased's property will pass to those entitled on intestacy;

(c) where the will has been altered, whether such alterations are effective (**13.4**);

(d) that if the will refers to any other documents, whether these documents have been 'incorporated' and thus become part of the will (**13.5**);

(e) that the will effectively deals with the whole of the deceased's estate capable of passing by will. Any such property that does not pass under the will, because, for example, the clause dealing with the residue of the deceased's estate fails (**13.6**), again passes under the intestacy rules;

(f) certain of the deceased's property may not have been capable of being disposed of by will, but will pass as of right to those entitled (**13.17** and **13.18**);

(g) that the will has not been varied after the testator's death. This may seem a surprising concept, but it is possible for the court to vary entitlements under a will if a successful claim is made under the Inheritance (Provision for Family and Dependants) Act 1975 (**13.22** to **13.29**). It is also possible for beneficiaries under a will (and those entitled under the intestacy rules) to vary their entitlements by consent, and indeed to reject outright gifts which would otherwise pass to them (**13.11**).

13.2 Validity of wills

13.2.1 Generally

English law will generally recognise a will as valid (Wills Act 1963) if it accords with the internal law of either:

(a) the country in which it was executed; or

(b) the country in which the deceased was domiciled or of which he was a national—either at the time of its execution or of the deceased's death.

So far as English domestic law is concerned, a valid will requires that the testator should have the *capacity* and *intention* to make the will, and compliance with the prescribed *formalities*.

13.2.2 Capacity

At the date of making the will, the testator must not (normally) have been under the age of 18. (Being of age is, however, not a requirement if the testator was in a position to make a 'privileged' will as a soldier on actual military service or a seaman at sea). Additionally, the testator must have had the necessary mental capacity.

13.2.2.1 The basic test

The test for mental capacity was laid down in *Banks v Goodfellow* (1870) LR 5; QB 549. Testators must have understood three things:

(a) the nature of the act (i.e. the making of a will) and its effects;

(b) the extent of their property; and

(c) the claims to which they ought to give effect.

Generally, it must be shown that the requisite understanding existed at the date of execution of the will. However, the rule in *Parker v Felgate* (1883) 8 PD 171 lays down an acceptable alternative where this cannot be done. Under this rule, it will be sufficient to show that:

(a) the requisite capacity existed at the date of giving instructions for the preparation of the will;

(b) the will was prepared in accordance with those instructions;

(c) at the time of execution the testator understood that he was signing a will for which instructions had previously been given (though it is not necessary for the testator at that time to be able either to remember what those instructions were, or to understand the will if read over to him).

13.2.2.2 Proof

The onus of proving the existence of the necessary mental capacity lies with the propounder of the will (i.e. the person seeking to prove it—to have it accepted by the court as valid: the process is described at **14.13** and **14.14**). In this context, there are two rebuttable presumptions:

(a) Rational will. Capacity is presumed where a duly executed will (i.e. one complying with the formality requirements) appears to be rational. If it does not so appear, the propounder will then have to prove capacity.

(b) Mental illness continues. Where the testator generally lacked capacity, there is a presumption that this state of affairs continues. This may be rebutted by evidence showing that the testator had recovered, or that the will was made in a lucid interval.

EXAMPLE 1

Ann, aged 80, made a will shortly before her death. She was known to be suffering from Alzheimer's disease. Generally, then, she would be presumed to be incapable of making a valid will. In this case, however, Ann's solicitor obtained her consent to consult her doctor who confirmed that Ann was only suffering from a mild form of the disease, and that there were times when Ann would have the necessary mental capacity to make a will. The doctor agreed to be present when the will was executed, and supplied the solicitor with a short note confirming that (at that time) Ann was capable of understanding the nature and effect of the will. The solicitor also kept an attendance note of the circumstances at the time of execution. It is likely that the court would be prepared to admit the will to probate (i.e. accept it as a valid will) in the light of this evidence, even if contested.

13.2.2.3 Lack of capacity

Where capacity is not presumed or proven, the will cannot be admitted to probate.

For completeness, you should note that where a person lacks the necessary mental capacity to make a valid will for themself, the Court of Protection is able (under the provisions of s 96 of the Mental Health Act 1983) to make a 'statutory will' on behalf of that person.

13.2.3 Intention

13.2.3.1 The requirement

The testator must have had a general intention to make a will, and a specific intention to make the particular will. Put another way, the testator must know and approve the contents of the will. To the extent that such knowledge and approval are lacking, the will cannot be admitted to probate.

The necessary knowledge and approval must normally have existed at the date of the execution of the will: however, the rule in *Parker v Felgate* (**13.2.2.1**) also applies in this context.

13.2.3.2 Proof

Again, the onus of proof lies on the propounder of the will. There is generally a rebuttable presumption that a testator with the necessary mental capacity executed the will with the requisite knowledge and approval of its contents. Those who seek to challenge the will would have to prove that the testator made the will (or perhaps a particular provision in it) as a result of force, fear, fraud or undue influence; or that the necessary knowledge and approval were lacking because of a mistake.

There is no such presumption of knowledge and approval in two situations:

(a) The testator is blind or illiterate, or someone has signed the will on the testator's behalf. As we will see (**13.2.4.2**) a suitably drafted attestation clause will assist in supplying the necessary evidence of knowledge and approval.

(b) There are suspicious circumstances—in particular where the will substantially benefits the person who prepared it (or a close relative of that person). In such cases, evidence will be required of the testator's knowledge and approval of the contents of the will, otherwise the gift will fail.

13.2.4 Formalities

13.2.4.1 Section 9 of the Wills Act 1837 (as substituted by s 17 of the Administration of Justice Act 1982)

This section provides that:

> No will shall be valid unless—
>
> (a) it is in writing, and signed by the testator, or by some other person in his presence and by his direction; and
>
> (b) it appears that the testator intended by his signature to give effect to the will; and
>
> (c) the signature is made or acknowledged by the testator in the presence of two or more witnesses present at the same time; and
>
> (d) each witness either—
>
> (i) attests and signs the will; or
>
> (ii) acknowledges his signature,
>
> in the presence of the testator (but not necessarily in the presence of any other witness), but no form of attestation shall be necessary.

The section does not apply to privileged wills, which can be made informally—even orally. Nor does it apply to statutory wills under the Mental Health Act 1983, for which that Act lays down special rules.

13.2.4.2 Attestation clause

Most wills will contain an attestation clause (hopefully all those professionally drawn will do so), although it is not a requirement for validity. If so, your task in proving the formal validity of the will is straightforward, as it will be presumed that the will has been executed in accordance with s 9 of the Wills Act 1837, i.e. there is a presumption of due execution.

There are a number of different forms of attestation clauses in common use, but all should show (as a minimum) compliance with the statutory requirements.

EXAMPLE 2

Hugh Jones has died. At the end of his typewritten will there is an attestation clause; the signatures are in ink.

SIGNED by Hugh Jones as his } last will in our joint presence } and then by us in his }	Hugh Jones
Jean Fredericks *18, Westway, Barchester* *Alan Price* *2, The Grove, Barchester*	

Unless there is evidence to the contrary, the will is presumed to be formally valid.

Where the testator was blind or illiterate, or someone else signed on behalf of the testator, we saw (in **13.2.3.2**) that there is no presumption of knowledge and approval and that this will have to be established if the will is to be admitted to probate. The simplest way of doing this is by the inclusion of a special attestation clause showing that:

(a) the will was read over to the testator in the presence of the witnesses;

(b) that the testator understood and approved the will;

(c) that the testator then signed the will or that it was signed by another in the testator's presence and at his direction; and

(d) that the witnesses attested the will as before.

If the will does not include an attestation clause (or only an inadequate one) compliance with the requirements of s 9 will have to be proved. This will also be necessary if there is something on the face of the will, for example, the testator's signature is not complete, to show that there were unusual circumstances at the time of execution. The 'mechanics' of how this is done is discussed at **14.16**, but it is convenient to consider below the requirements of s 9 in greater detail.

13.2.4.3 In writing

A will may be typed or handwritten (in ink or pencil—though the use of both will raise a rebuttable presumption that the parts written in pencil are 'deliberative only' and they will only be admitted to probate if there is evidence that the testator intended them to be final). There is no restriction as to the material upon which a will may be written, nor as to the language used: it may even be written in code, provided there is evidence available enabling it to be deciphered.

13.2.4.4 Signature

The testator's usual signature is ideal, but any mark (e.g. a thumbprint or rubber stamp) made by the testator and intended to be a signature will suffice. One of the leading cases on this point is *In the Goods of Chalcraft* [1948] P 222; 1 All ER 700, where a dying testatrix managed to sign 'E. Chal' but was unable to complete her full signature. It was held that this was sufficient; the testatrix intended what she had written (as much as she could manage in the circumstances) to be her signature. In another case, *In the Estate of Cook* [1960] 1 WLR 353; 1 All ER 689, the will began with the name of the testatrix and ended with the words 'Your loving mother'. The court accepted that the testatrix intended this to be her signature.

However, testators do not need to sign their own wills; the Act allows signature by another—at the testator's direction and in the testator's presence. The person so signing (who may be one of the witnesses) may sign their own name or that of the testator, and ideally, as noted above, the attestation clause should recite this.

13.2.4.5 With intent to give effect to the will

It is usual (and logical) for the signature to appear at the end of the will, but this need not necessarily occur. In *Wood v Smith* [1993] Ch 90, the testator had made his signature at the beginning of the will, intending this to give effect to his will, but written before he had made any provisions disposing of his estate. The Court of Appeal held that this could constitute a valid execution of the will provided the signing and the subsequently written dispositions all formed part of one transaction.

13.2.4.6 Signature made/acknowledged in the presence of two or more witnesses present at the same time

Where the testator is (as is usually the case) signing the will, the signature must be completed in the presence of at least two witnesses, present at the same time. The witnesses do not need be able to see the contents of the will, or even to know that the testator is signing a will. They must, however, be able to see the testator writing the signature (for this reason a blind person cannot act as a witness), though it is not necessary for them to see the signature itself. Alternatively, the testator may sign the will and then acknowledge that signature (by words or conduct) in the presence of the (two or more) witnesses, who must be present at the same time and be able to see the signature. Again, ideally, this will be recited in the attestation clause. There are no special rules as to the capacity of the witnesses, but they must be bodily and mentally present (not, e.g. drunk or asleep). Although, by s 15 of the Wills Act 1837, a beneficiary will normally lose a gift under a will where that beneficiary or their spouse has witnessed the will (**13.6.5**), this does not affect the formal validity of the will.

13.2.4.7 Witnesses attest and sign (or acknowledge their signatures) in the presence of the testator

Attestation is, in effect, the validation of the testator's signature. The witnesses need not sign (or acknowledge) in each other's presence, though in practice this is what usually happens. However, the presence of the testator (bodily and mentally) is required when the signature/acknowledgement is made.

13.2.5 Codicils

A codicil is used to add to, amend or partially revoke the terms of an existing will. The requirements for a valid codicil are the same as those required for a valid will.

13.3 Revocation of a will

13.3.1 The general position

Provided a testator retains testamentary capacity, a will is revocable at any time during the testator's lifetime. This is so even if the testator has entered into a contract not to revoke the will (though if the will is revoked the estate may be liable for the breach of contract).

13.3.1.1 Circumstances in which revocation may occur

Revocation may occur:

(a) automatically by operation of law:
   (i) marriage (see **13.3.1.3**);
   (ii) divorce or nullity (see **13.3.1.4**);
(b) by deliberate act of the testator:
   (i) later will or codicil (see **13.3.1.5**);
   (ii) destruction (see **13.3.1.6**).

Sometimes, revocation is regarded as conditional only. This is considered in **13.3.2**.

The law relating to alterations is discussed in **13.4**.

13.3.1.2 Mutual wills

A qualification to the principle of revocability is the equitable doctrine of mutual wills. This may be invoked to impose a constructive trust on the property of the testator where:

(a) there is an agreement between (say) husband and wife to confer benefits upon each other by their respective wills and an intention then to benefit the same ultimate person(s) (e.g. their children);

(b) there is an agreement that the survivor shall be bound by the arrangement;

(c) an event has occurred to cause the arrangement to become binding. This will happen when the first of the parties dies not having revoked their will believing that (b) still applies—or perhaps when the survivor accepts the benefit under will of the first to die.

Where these conditions are all met, although the survivor's will must remain revocable, any purported disposition of the property bound by the trust will be ineffectual. This is because the beneficial interests of those claiming under the trust have priority over those of the beneficiaries claiming under the new will or the intestacy rules on the death of the survivor.

It should be noted that such wills can be problematic and are not 'popular' with practitioners.

13.3.1.3 Marriage

If the testator has married after executing a will, that marriage will generally revoke that will (Wills Act 1837, s 18 (both in its original form and as substituted by Administration of Justice Act 1982)).

The scope of the exceptions to this general rule depend upon whether the will was made before 1983 or after 1982. Normally wills are dated at the time of execution, and we shall only deal here with wills made after 1982. The principal exceptions are found in s 18(3) and (4) of the Wills Act 1837 (as substituted).

(a) Section 18(3) provides that where '... it appears from the will that at the time it was made the testator was expecting to be married to a particular person and that he intended that the will should not be revoked by the marriage, the will shall not be revoked by his marriage to that person'.

(b) Section 18(4) provides that where '... it appears from a will that at the time it was made the testator was expecting to be married to a particular person and that he intended that a disposition in the will should not be revoked by his marriage to that person ...' then that particular disposition will not be revoked by the marriage, and the rest of the dispositions will also be 'saved' unless the contrary appears from the will.

Only intrinsic evidence is admissible to establish the testator's expectation and intention, and an express declaration included in the will covering the points will prevent revocation.

EXAMPLE 3

John Kent married Avril Brown in September 1994, and died in April 1997. His will, dated 8 August 1994, contained the following declaration:

> 'I DECLARE that I make this will in the expectation of my marriage to Avril Brown and that I intend that this will shall not be revoked by that marriage.'

John's will is effective despite his marriage.

It is possible for a testator to make a will conditional upon marriage, i.e. the will does not take effect unless and until the marriage takes place. Clearly, in such cases the question of revocation by subsequent marriage does not arise.

13.3.1.4 Divorce/nullity

The statutory provisions have been the subject of recent amendment, and we shall only deal here with the position where the testator died after 1995.

Here, the new s 18A(1) of the Wills Act 1837 provides (subject to contrary intention in the will) for a sort of 'limited revocation' on a decree absolute of divorce or nullity. Any provisions in the will as to the appointment of the former spouse as executor or trustee take effect as if the former spouse had died on the date upon which the marriage is dissolved or annulled, and will thus be ineffective. Further, any property which is given by the will to the former spouse passes as if that spouse had died on that day, and will thus not pass to the former spouse.

By s 4 of the Act (again, subject to expressed contrary intention) an appointment of the former spouse as guardian of the testator's children is similarly 'revoked'.

Note that these provisions do not apply on separation, nor do they affect any provisions of the will other than those indicated.

13.3.1.5 Later will/codicil

By s 20 of the Wills Act 1837 a will is revoked (wholly or partially) by a later will or codicil; or 'by some writing declaring an intention to revoke the same and executed in the manner' of a will—as in *Re Spracklan's Estate*, [1938] 2 All ER 345, where the Court of Appeal held that a letter (signed by the testatrix and duly attested) to her bank manager asking him to destroy the will which the bank was keeping for her satisfied this requirement.

A later will or codicil impliedly revokes an earlier testamentary disposition only to the extent that it is inconsistent with or merely repeats the terms of the earlier document. However, it is common—and helpful for the avoidance of doubt—for a will to contain an express revocation clause, such as, 'I hereby revoke all previous wills and codicils made by me'.

Clearly, a codicil to a will should not contain such a revocation clause!

The doctrine of conditional revocation may apply (see **13.3.2**).

13.3.1.6 Destruction

By s 20 of the Wills Act 1837 a will is also revoked by 'burning tearing or otherwise destroying the same by the testator or by some person in his presence and by his direction with the intention of revoking the same'.

There are thus two essential elements for an effective revocation:

(a) *An act of destruction*. An act of destruction is necessary; merely writing 'cancelled' or 'revoked' across the will is not enough. Nor is putting a line through parts of the will, or even the signature of the testator (though it will be otherwise if there has been an effective obliteration). In *Re Adams (Dec'd)* [1990] Ch 601, the testator's signature had been heavily scored through with a ball-point pen so as to render it illegible. The court held that a material part of the will had been destroyed with the intention to effect a revocation of the whole. Where part only of the will is destroyed, this may amount to a revocation of that part of the will only, or of the whole will if of a sufficiently substantial or vital part (e.g. the testator's or witnesses' signatures, *Hobbs v Knight* (1838) 1 Curt 769).

The court will admit extrinsic evidence of the testator's intention in determining the extent of any revocation, and may infer this from the state of the will at the date of death.

A destruction by someone other than the testator must, to be effective, be done in the testator's presence and at the testator's direction; if not, it is not possible for the testator subsequently to 'ratify' the act.

(b) *An intention to revoke*. The testator must have the intention to revoke at the time of the will's destruction. The necessary mental capacity is the same as that required for the making of a will (see **13.2.3**). Accidental revocation is, therefore, an impossibility; so is one based upon a mistaken belief that the will is invalid or has already been revoked. If a will is found mutilated at the date of death, this will be rebuttably presumed to have been done by the testator with the intention of revoking it (wholly or partially, depending upon the extent of the mutilation). There is a further rebuttable presumption that a will last known to have been in the testator's possession, but which cannot be found at the date of death, has been destroyed by the testator with the intention of revoking it.

The doctrine of conditional revocation may again apply (see **13.3.2** below).

13.3.2 Conditional revocation

This topic is generally beyond the scope of this book. Suffice it to say that we were considering above the situation where a testator has an absolute intention to revoke an existing will, in which case the revocation is immediately effective (assuming the other essential elements are present). There may be evidence, however, that the intention to revoke is conditional only, when the revocation will not be effective unless and until the condition is met. The condition might be, for example, the validity of a new will. Difficult questions may arise in such cases, both as to admissibility of evidence and as to construction (especially where revocation clauses appear to have been mistakenly included in wills or codicils) and specialist practitioner's books should be consulted.

The doctrine of conditional revocation may also apply in the context of alterations (see **13.4.1.3**).

13.4 Alterations in wills

13.4.1 Section 21 of the Wills Act 1837

This lays down the basic rule, which is that:

> . . . no obliteration, interlineation, or other alteration made in any will after the execution thereof shall be valid or have any effect, except so far as the words or effect of the will before such alteration shall not be apparent, unless such alteration shall be executed in like manner as hereinbefore is required for the execution of a will . . .

13.4.1.1 Effective alterations

An alteration will be effective if:

(a) it is made (or is presumed to have been made without evidence to the contrary) before execution. An unattested alteration is rebuttably presumed to have been made after execution (except where the 'alteration' is the filling in of a blank space, when the rebuttable presumption is that this was done prior to execution). Either presumption is rebutted by intrinsic or extrinsic evidence to the contrary;

(b) it is made after the will but duly executed. In practice, it is sufficient if the testator and the witnesses initial the alteration;

(c) the original wording or effect of the will is, as a result of the 'alteration', not apparent (i.e. is not decipherable by natural means, see **13.4.1.3**(b)).

13.4.1.2 Ineffective alterations

An alteration will be ineffective if:

(a) it is unattested and made by the testator after (or it cannot be established to have been made before) execution and does not amount to an obliteration;

(b) it is made by someone other than the testator and without his knowledge and approval;

(c) it is made by the testator without an intention to revoke.

13.4.1.3 Consequences of invalid alteration

This will depend upon whether the original wording is 'apparent' or not. The wording is apparent if it can be deciphered by 'natural means'—such as holding up to the light or using a magnifying glass) without resort to 'forbidden' methods (such as the use of chemicals, infra red photography or extrinsic evidence).

(a) If the original wording is so apparent, it will be admitted to probate.

(b) If it is not so apparent, the will is *prima facie* admitted to probate with a blank space where the obliteration has occurred. However, where there has been an attempted substitution in place of what has been obliterated the doctrine of conditional revocation may apply; this will allow the courts to employ any of the forbidden methods mentioned above in an attempt to ascertain and give effect to the original wording.

13.4.2 Precautions

It is clearly sensible to have all alterations (even those made before execution of the will) initialled by the testator and the witnesses. Further, testators should be discouraged from attempting to make their own 'adjustments' to their wills.

13.5 Incorporation by reference

As we have seen (**13.2.4**) for a document to be admitted to probate it must be executed in accordance with the requirements of s 9, of the Wills Act 1837. However, a document not so executed may, in effect, become part of the will under the doctrine of incorporation by reference.

For this to happen, three conditions must be met:

(a) The document must be clearly identified in the will.

(b) The document must already exist at the date of the will. The onus of proving this fact lies with the person seeking incorporation of the document.

(c) The document must be referred to in the will as already in existence at the time of execution. If this is not the case (e.g. because the statement is equivocal or the reference is to a document to be prepared in the future) the document in question cannot be incorporated.

EXAMPLE 4

Clause 3 of a recently deceased testator's will (made in 1995) states 'I leave £10,000 to be held on the trusts set out in clause 5 of the Trust Deed dated 8 March 1992 and made between myself of the one part and Daniel Thomas and Ruth Brown of the other part'. The deceased's executor, Daniel Thomas, tells you that he has the trust deed mentioned in the will at home in his safe. It would seem that all the requirements for incorporation are satisfied; the gift under the will is *prima facie* valid. The trust deed would thus be submitted to probate with the will (see **14.16**).

13.6 Failure of gifts by will

There are a number of reasons why gifts contained in wills may fail. We shall only deal at **13.6.2** with three of those reasons, and with the consequences of failure at **13.6.4**. You should additionally note, however, that a gift will fail if the wording is uncertain, as do gifts contrary to public policy. In the last category, for example, a person convicted of murdering the testator is not permitted to take a benefit under the victim's will (or intestacy). Again, a beneficiary of a gift under a will is entitled to refuse that gift (i.e. to disclaim it), and a gift offending the rules against perpetuity and accumulation will also fail. None of these issues is considered further here.

First, a mention of terminology that you may encounter in wills. Technically, a 'legacy' is a gift of personalty (e.g. money, shares, chattels) and a devise is a gift of realty (e.g. freehold land). The term 'legacy' is, commonly used to encompass both types of gift, as we will in the remainder of this chapter.

Legacies can further be classified as specific, general, demonstrative or residuary (**13.6.2**), relevant when considering whether a legacy fails and the consequences of failure. Before considering the 'hallmarks' of these legacies we should briefly note two rules of construction as to the date from which the will speaks.

13.6.1 Date from which the will speaks

Unless there is a contrary intention in the will, then:

(a) as to property, the will speaks and takes effect 'as if it had been executed immediately before the death of the testator' (Wills Act 1837, s 24). Thus a gift of the contents of the testator's house will *prima facie* be construed as a gift of the contents as at the date of death (rather than at the date of the will).

The use of words such as 'my', 'now' or 'at present' in describing the gift may be sufficient to indicate a contrary intention. For example, a gift of 'my 500 shares in ABC plc' would probably be construed as a gift of the shares owned at the date of the will. On the other hand, a gift of 'all my shares in ABC plc' would *prima facie* pass the shares owned at the date of death; the subject matter of the gift here is generic and so described as to be capable of increase or decrease between the date of the will and the date of death.

(b) as to the objects of the gift (i.e. the beneficiaries) the will speaks from the date of execution. In other words, s 24 does not apply (unless a contrary intention appears from the will). As a result, a gift to 'the vicar of St Luke's Church Barchester' is *prima facie* a gift to the person fulfilling that description at the date of the will. This rule does not apply to 'class gifts' or to identified gifts to each member of a class (see further at **13.7.2**).

gift of personalty ie Money etc But commonly used to describe and gifts of land.

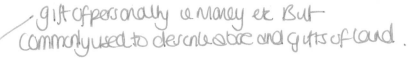

13.6.2 Legacies: Specific, general, demonstrative, pecuniary or residuary

13.6.2.1 Specific legacy

This is a gift of particular property owned by the deceased distinguished from any other property of the same kind which may be owned by the deceased, e.g. 'my 500 shares in XYZ plc', 'my freehold property Greenacre'. Such gifts are subject to the doctrine of ademption if the testator does not own the property concerned at the date of death (see **13.6.3**).

13.6.2.2 General legacy

This is a gift of property not distinguished by the testator from other similar property, e.g. '500 shares in XYZ plc'. This constitutes a gift of any 500 shares in the company (even if that was the number which the testator owned at the date of the will). Such gifts are not subject to the doctrine of ademption, so that if in the example the testator did not own any XYZ plc shares at the date of death, the beneficiary is entitled to require estate funds (provided these are sufficient) to be used to buy 500 such shares.

13.6.2.3 Demonstrative legacy

Such legacies (not commonly encountered today) are essentially general in character, but a specific source is identified from which it is to be paid, e.g. '£1,000 to Ambrose to be paid from my Newtown Building Society Account'. Such legacies are not adeemed if the account has been closed during the testator's lifetime, or there is insufficient in the account at the date of death to pay the legacy in full. In such circumstances, the beneficiary is entitled to any balance at that time, and to have the deficiency paid as a general legacy.

13.6.2.4 Pecuniary legacy

This is a gift of money, and usually is general in character, e.g. a gift of '£5,000'. However, it may be specific (e.g. a gift of 'the £5,000 which I keep in my safe' or 'the £5,000 which Xavier owes me'); or demonstrative (e.g. '£5,000 payable from my current account at Newtown Bank').

13.6.2.5 Residuary legacy/devise

Residuary gifts embrace all the rest of the deceased's property (i.e. not disposed of by any specific, general or demonstrative gifts).

13.6.3 Failure of legacies: Ademption

To the extent that a testator no longer owns the property which is the subject of a specific legacy at the date of death, the gift is adeemed, i.e. it fails, and the disappointed beneficiary is not entitled to any compensation. Ademption may occur because the testator has sold the property, or given it away before death.

EXAMPLE 5

Clause 3 of Paul's will states, 'I give my 800 shares in PQR plc to my brother Robert'.It is likely that this will be construed as a specific gift of the 800 shares that Paul owned at the date of the will in PQR plc. If Paul sold 300 of those shares before he died, Robert would only take the remaining 500 shares.

Ademption can also occur where there has been a change is substance (i.e. in the very nature of the property) as opposed to a mere change in name or form. This distinction is not always easy to see.

EXAMPLE 6

Clause 4 of Paul's will provides 'I give my 100 shares in BCD plc to my sister Susan'. Again this is likely to be construed as a specific gift. Suppose before Paul died BCD plc subdivided its shares so that one original share was represented by five new shares. It is likely that this would be construed as a mere change in the form of the shares, and Susan would take the 500 (new) shares in BCD plc. If, however, BCD plc were taken over by another company (say FGH plc), and FGH plc issued shares in FGH plc to replace those held in the original company, it is likely that this would be seen as a change in substance (i.e. shares in an entirely different company) and the gift of the BCD plc shares to Susan would fail.

Note that ademption only applies to specific legacies; it has no application to general legacies (e.g '500 shares in XYZ plc', see **13.6.2.2**) or where the subject matter of the gift is ascertained at the date of death (e.g. 'the contents of my house', see **13.6.1**)

13.6.4 Failure of legacies: Lapse

13.6.4.1 Beneficiary dying before testator

As a general rule, a beneficiary must survive the testator in order to take a gift under that testator's will, otherwise the gift lapses—in which event (unless there is an effective substitutional provision, see **13.6.4.3**) the subject matter of the intended gift will fall into residue, or (if itself a share of residue) pass under the intestacy rules (see **13.6.6**).

We saw at **13.3.1.4** that if the testator's marriage has been dissolved, then, unless the will provides otherwise, gifts in the will to the former spouse will in effect lapse.

A class gift (see **13.7.2**) only lapses if all members of the class predecease the testator: the rule is similar in the case of gifts to beneficial joint tenants.

13.6.4.2 *Commorientes*

Usually there is no problem in determining who died first—the testator or the beneficiary—and thus whether the gift has lapsed. What, however, if they die in a common accident (e.g. a plane crash), and the order of death is uncertain? Unless the will provides that the beneficiary must survive the testator for a certain period (28 days is common) the *commorientes* rule (Law of Property Act 1925, s 184) applies. Under this rule, where there is no evidence as to the order in which deaths have occurred then, for succession purposes, the younger is deemed to have survived the elder. Thus a gift in the younger's will to the elder would lapse, but not *vice versa*. The *commorientes* rule generally applies both where there is a will, and where there is no will so that the estate will be distributed under the intestacy rules (see **13.11**).

13.6.4.3 Substitutional gifts

Although it is not possible to prevent the operation of the doctrine of lapse, the will may specifically provide as to what is to happen to the gifted property if the original beneficiary dies before the testator. This is particularly common so far as residuary gifts are concerned.

EXAMPLE 7

Della's will leaves, '£2,000 to my niece Jane and the rest of my estate to my husband Neil but if he fails to survive me then to my son Mark'. Only Della's son Mark survives her; the gifts to Jane and Neil therefore lapse. Jane's gift will thus fall into residue, and Mark will take Della's entire estate.

13.6.4.4 Substitution by statute

Section 33 of the Wills Act 1837 in effect provides a sort of statutory substitutional clause—but only to benefit the testator's grandchildren (or their children, etc.). This section applies where:

(a) a will contains a gift to the child or issue (i.e. remoter descendant) of the testator; and

(b) the intended beneficiary dies before the testator, leaving issue; and

(c) issue of the intended beneficiary are living (including *en ventre sa mère*) at the testator's death.

If these conditions are met then, in the absence of a contrary intention shown by the will, the gift takes effect as a gift to such issue, who take (in equal shares if more than one) the gift which their parent would have taken. It is not clear whether if the original gift is contingent the gift 'substituted' by s 33 is subject to the same contingency.

The section also applies (in the absence of a contrary intention in the will) to a class gift to the testator's children or remoter issue. It is important to appreciate that s 33 cannot prevent the failure of gifts in favour of beneficiaries who predecease but who are not issue of the testator. Thus in the example of Della's will at **13.6.4.3**, s 33 would not operate to save the gift of £2,000 for any of Jane's children who survived Della. However, if Mark had also predeceased but his two children survived Della, then under s 33, Della's entire estate would pass to those two children in equal shares.

13.6.5 Failure of gifts to witnesses

A gift in a will fails if the beneficiary or the beneficiary's spouse witnesses the will, though the validity of the will as such is not affected (Wills Act 1837, s 15). However, the gift will not fail if, ignoring the attestation by the beneficiary or spouse, the will is duly executed, i.e. because there are at least two other witnesses who are not beneficiaries or their spouses. Further, a gift within the terms of s 15 may be 'saved' if the will is subsequently confirmed by a codicil which is independently witnessed.

If the will appoints solicitors (or other professionals) to act as executors it will invariably also contain a charging clause, enabling them to be paid for their work in administering the estate. On a death prior to 1 February 2001, s 15 would cause the charging clause to fail if a member of the firm appointed was one of the (two) witnesses to the will. However, where the deceased died after 31 January 2001, by virtue of s 28(4)(a) of the Trustee Act 2000, such a provision is treated as remuneration for services (and not as a gift) so that the charging clause would not fail in such circumstances.

Where the beneficiary's spouse has witnessed the will, s 15 applies only if the beneficiary and the witness were married at the date of the execution of the will; there will be no problem where they married after that date.

13.6.6 Consequences of failure of legacies

If the gift fails then clearly the original intended beneficiary will not take. Who will take instead?

13.6.6.1 Alternative provision in will or by statute

First, it is necessary to consider whether the will itself has made alternative provision in the event of failure of the original gift. Thus, in the case of ademption, has the testator provided that the beneficiary is to receive alternative property if the original gifted property is no longer in the estate at death? In the case of lapse, does the will contain an effective substitutional clause (**13.6.4.3**)? Alternatively, is the gift saved by statute (see Wills Act 1837, s 33, **13.6.4.2**) or the saving provisions of s 15 of the Wills Act 1837 or s 28(4) of the Trustee Act 2000?

13.6.6.2 No alternative provision

Save where the gift has adeemed, the property which was the subject matter of the failed gift will form part of the deceased's estate. Who is now entitled to this property? The answer will depend on the type of gift which has failed. Unless the failed gift was a gift of residue, then (assuming there is an effective residuary gift) the gifted property will 'fall into residue', i.e. swell the property that would otherwise pass under the residuary legacy.

If a gift of residue wholly fails, the entire residuary estate will pass to those entitled under the intestacy rules (see **13.9** to **13.14**). If, however, the gift of residue only fails in part, there is a 'partial intestacy' as to the property comprised in the failed gift: this part will again pass to those entitled on the deceased's intestacy. A partial intestacy will also arise where the will contains effective non-residuary gifts, but either there is no gift of residue or it fails wholly or in part.

EXAMPLE 8

Jack's will contains the following gifts, '£1,000 to my godson Stephen Smith and the residue of my estate to be divided equally between my daughter Harriet and my late wife's son Keith Jones'. Both Stephen and Keith have predeceased Jack, but Harriet and Keith's daughter Rachel survive.

The pecuniary legacy lapses, and this sum will now form part of the residuary estate. Harriet will take one-half of the residue in accordance with the will. Section 33 of the Wills Act 1837 will not save the remaining one-half share for Rachel (because Keith is not Jack's issue). Jack is thus partially intestate, and the failed gift will pass to those entitled on Jack's intestacy.

In this example, a partial intestacy would have been avoided if:

(a) the will had included an express substitutional gift in favour of Keith's issue in the event of the gift to Keith failing; or

(b) the will had provided that the residue was to be divided 'equally between such of my daughter Harriet and my late wife's son Keith Jones as survive me'. In this case, the effect would have been to pass the whole of the residuary estate to Harriet;

(c) the will had left the residuary estate to Harriet and Keith 'jointly' rather than 'equally'. Here again the effect would have been that Harriet would take the whole of the residuary estate.

If Jack's daughter had also died before him leaving no children alive at the date of his death, then Jack's entire estate would pass under the intestacy rules.

13.7 Gifts to children in wills

We do not intend to cover the law on construction of wills—a major topic in itself. Gifts to children are so common in wills, however, that it is worth noting a few points of construction in relation to such gifts.

13.7.1 Meaning of 'children'

In the absence of contrary intention in the will, gifts to a person's 'children' (whether that person is the testator or anyone else) will include all children of that person (whether legitimate, illegitimate or adopted by them). It will not include a natural child of that person who has been adopted by someone else. Relevant legislation includes the Legitimacy Act 1976, the Adoption Act 1976 and (for wills made after 3 April 1988), Family Law Reform Act 1987.

13.7.2 Class gifts

Class gifts are particularly used in wills to leave property to children where it is not desired to name the children individually. Class gifts do raise a number of construction issues. You will be relieved to know that we do not intend to explore the complex cases, but merely to explain briefly the basic rules and highlight points that may need further research.

13.7.2.1 How to recognise a class gift

A class gift is a gift of property to be divided amongst beneficiaries who fulfil a general description, for example, '£50,000 to the children of Zoe', '£50,000 to the children of Zoe who attain the age of 18'. In such cases, the total value of the gift is clear: the problem is to know how to share it amongst those entitled. This will obviously depend upon how many people fit the description. In the examples given, it would not be possible to answer this question with certainty at least until the death of Zoe; in the meantime, no distribution would be possible.

A similar problem arises where the gift in the will takes the form of an individual gift to the members of a class, e.g. '£5,000 to each of the children of Zebedee'. Here, what the prospective beneficiaries are to take is identified but until the death of Zebedee it cannot be known how many children will qualify.

13.7.2.2 Class closing rules

The courts have invented 'class closing rules' to overcome these problems and allow distribution at an earlier date. The various rules (which one applies to a given case depends upon the type of gift involved) determine when the class will close. In principle, this will generally happen when there is one person fitting the description who has a vested interest. At whatever point the class closes, it does so to the exclusion of any potential beneficiary not then 'living'—a term which includes a child conceived and subsequently born alive. This is obviously 'unfair' to those thus excluded from benefit; but this disadvantage is considered to be outweighed by the advantage of earlier distribution.

The class closing rules may be excluded by a clear provision in the testator's will, such as 'to the children of Zoe living at my death', 'to the children of Zebedee whenever born'.

As indicated above, the rules (if not so excluded) differ in detail according to the type of gift involved. We shall only mention here the types of class gift most commonly encountered.

(a) Immediate vested gift, e.g. '£5,000 to the children of Arthur'. The class closes at the date of the testator's death if there is any child of Arthur then living. If there are none, the class remains open until the death of Arthur.

(b) Immediate contingent gift, e.g. '£5,000 to the children of Arthur who attain the age of 18'. Here the class closes at the testator's death if any such child has already reached the age of 18. The class will include any of Arthur's children who are 18 plus any others then living who subsequently attain that age. If a 'class member' dies before 18, then they will not share in the gift. If at the date of the testator's death no child of Arthur has fulfilled the contingency (i.e. attained 18), the class remains open until one does; the class will then close around that child and any others then living who subsequently attain the age of 18.

(c) Individual gift to members of a class, e.g. '£5,000 to each of the children of Arthur,' £5,000 to each of the children of Arthur who attain the age of 18'. In these cases, unless there is a contrary intention in the will, the class will close at the date of the testator's death. If there are no children of Arthur then living, the gift fails.

13.8 Wills: Checkpoints

1. Formal validity:
   (a) Is the will signed by the testator and two witnesses (**13.2.4.1**)?
   (b) Does the will contain an appropriate attestation clause (**13.2.4.2**)?
   (c) If no/inadequate attestation clause, has s 9 of the Wills Act 1837 been complied with (**13.2.4.3** to **13.2.4.7**)?
   (d) Is there any suggestion that the testator lacked capacity (**13.2.2**)? Note presumptions (**13.2.2.2**).
   (e) Is there any suggestion that the testator did not know and approve of the contents of the will (**13.2.3**)? Note presumptions (**13.2.3.2**).
2. Revocation:
   (a) Is the will the most recent one (**13.3.1.5**)
   (b) Does it contain a revocation clause (**13.3.1.5**)
   (c) Has the testator married (**13.3.1.3**) or divorced (**13.3.1.4**) since the date of the will?
   (d) Is there evidence that the will has otherwise been revoked (**13.3.1.6** and **13.3.2**)?
3. Alterations:
   (a) Are any alterations effective (**13.4.1.1**)?
   (b) Are any alterations ineffective (**13.4.1.2**)?
4. Incorporation:
   (a) If the will refers to another document, has that document been incorporated and is it available (**13.5**)?
5. Failure of gifts:
   (a) Does the testator's estate include property specifically gifted by the will (**13.6.3**)?
   (b) Have any named beneficiaries predeceased the testator (**13.6.4.1**)?

(c) If so, is there an effective substitutional gift (**13.6.4.3**) or is the gift saved by s 33 of the Wills Act 1837 (**13.6.4.4**)?

(d) Has a beneficiary or their spouse acted as witness (**13.6.5**)?

6. Class gifts

(a) Does the will contain class gifts (**13.7.2.2**)?

(b) If so, have the class closing rules (**13.7.2.2**) been excluded by the terms of the will?

(c) If not:

(i) Does the will contain an immediate vested class gift and, if so, is any person within the class alive at the date of the testator's death?

(ii) Does the will contain an immediate contingent class gift and, if so, has any person fulfilled the contingency at the date of the testator's death?

(iii) Does the will contain an individual gift to members of a class and, if so, is any person within the class alive at the testator's death?

13.9 Intestacy

We have already made reference to the 'intestacy rules'. Distribution of a deceased's estate is governed by these rules when the deceased has died either:

(a) wholly (or totally) intestate, i.e. without having effectively disposed of any of their property by will. This may be because the deceased never made a will or the will is invalid; or

(b) partially intestate, i.e. having made a valid will but this does not dispose of the whole of the estate. This situation may arise where the will contains no residuary gift, or where there is a gift of residue but this has wholly or partly failed (e.g. because a residuary beneficiary has predeceased the testator, and there is no effective substitutional gift (either in the will or by the operation of s 33 of the Wills Act 1837—see **13.6**).

In the first case, the distribution of the whole of the deceased's succession estate will be in accordance with the intestacy rules: in the second, these rules will only apply to such of the deceased's property as does not pass under the will. In both cases, however, certain types of property will pass on death quite independently of the intestacy rules (see **13.18**), for example, property held by the deceased as a beneficial joint tenant.

13.10 Intestacy: The basic position

Where the deceased left a will, its effective provisions will be implemented. To the extent that the estate is not disposed of by will, its distribution is governed by the rules in Part IV of the Administration of Estate's Act 1925 (as amended).

13.10.1 Section 33(1) of the administration of estates act 1925 (as amended)

Section 33(1) provides that the personal representatives hold the intestate's estate not disposed of by will on trust with a power to sell. The personal representatives must pay the funeral, testamentary and administration expenses, debts and other liabilities of the deceased out of the intestate's ready money and from the net proceeds of any part of the estate which is sold.

The residuary estate (what is left after all the liabilities and expenses have been discharged) is then to be shared amongst those entitled according to the statutory rules.

13.10.2 Entitlement

As we will see, the position of a spouse (provided that spouse survives the intestate by 28 days) is considered first under the intestacy rules. The surviving spouse may take the whole of the intestate's estate. If not, or the spouse does not so survive, the rules then set out in order of entitlement categories of the deceased's relatives who are entitled to (or to a share in) the intestate's estate. Earlier classes take to the exclusion of later classes of relatives, and generally children of a predeceasing relative take their parent's share. If the deceased was partially intestate, the surviving spouse or some of these relatives may also benefit under the will, but this will not affect any entitlement that they may have under the intestacy rules.

13.10.3 The statutory trusts

In the case of certain classes of relatives—namely, issue, brothers and sisters, uncles and aunts—it will be seen that the class takes 'on the statutory trusts'. Section 47 of the Administration of Estates Act 1925 defines this expression as meaning:

(a) equally for all members of the class of relatives concerned living or *en ventre sa mère* (i.e. conceived) at the date of the intestate's death who attain the age of 18 or marry under that age;

(b) the issue of any class members who predecease take *per stirpes* their parent's share provided they (i.e. the issue) attain 18 or marry earlier.

Where the potential beneficiary dies before the intestate (regardless of whether that person had attained the age of 18 or was married), but leaves issue, then the substitution referred to in (b) above applies. Where, however, the potential beneficiary is living at the date of the intestate's death ((a)) but subsequently dies before attaining a vested interest (i.e. before attaining the age of 18 or earlier marriage), the estate will be dealt with as if that person had never existed (even if survived by their issue).

Thus it is important to note whether the potential beneficiary dies before or after the intestate, as **Example 9** illustrates.

13.11 Entitlement where there is a surviving spouse of the intestate

Where the death occurs after 1995 the spouse (i.e. a person to whom the intestate was lawfully married at the date of death) must survive the intestate by 28 days. There is no entitlement under the intestacy rules for a divorced spouse (i.e. after decree absolute) or one who is judicially separated.

We noted in **13.6.4.2** that the *commorientes* rule (where the order of death is uncertain) relates also to cases where there is a total or partial intestacy. So far as intestate succession between spouses is concerned, the spouse must (if the death is after 1995) survive the deceased by 28 days, so that the point cannot arise. In the case of intestate succession between other relatives, the *commorientes* rule will apply in the usual way, as there is no requirement that they survive the deceased by 28 days in order to become entitled.

Assuming that the deceased's spouse so survives, that spouse's entitlement will depend on whether the deceased's issue also survive, and if not, whether certain of the deceased's other close relatives survive.

EXAMPLE 9

Ian has recently died intestate, leaving the following issue:

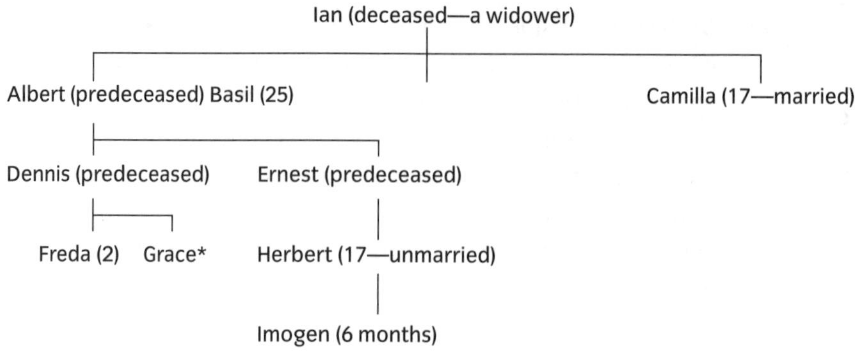

* Grace was *en ventre sa mère* at the date of Ian's death.

Ian's estate will pass to his issue on the statutory trusts. As he had three children it will *prima facie* be divided into three shares.

Both Basil and Camilla will take a vested one-third share each—they have satisfied the contingency. Note that Camilla, although she has fulfilled the contingency, is under 18 and so will not be able to give an effective discharge to the personal representatives. The capital of her share will have to be held for her until she attains her majority. She will, however, be entitled to receive the income in the meantime, as a married infant can give a good receipt for income. Were she to die before attaining 18, her one-third share would pass as part of her estate to those entitled on her intestacy.

Albert's share will pass under the statutory trusts to his issue, i.e. his one-third share will be sub-divided into two equal shares. The (one-sixth) share which Dennis would have inherited had he survived Ian, will be held on the statutory trusts for Freda and Grace; Ernest's one-sixth share will similarly be held for Herbert (he does not obtain a vested interest because he is not married).

If both Freda and Grace were to die before attaining vested interests (e.g. they both die aged 15) their one-sixth share would accrue to Herbert, provided he in turn survives to attain a vested interest. If he also fails to do so, the estate will be distributed as if Freda, Grace and Herbert had never existed. The whole of Albert's share will therefore accrue to Basil and Camilla, since these will be the only interests under the statutory trusts which vest. Imogen will not be entitled as her father (Herbert) was alive at the date of Ian's death.

13.11.1 Spouse alone

Where there are no issue, parents, or brothers or sisters of the whole blood (or their issue), the personal representatives hold the whole of the residuary estate for the surviving spouse absolutely.

13.11.2 Spouse and issue

13.11.2.1 The spouse

The spouse is entitled to:

(a) the personal chattels absolutely;

(b) statutory legacy of £125,000, free of tax and costs, with interest (currently at 6 per cent) from the date of death until payment;

(c) life interest in one-half of the residuary estate. Thus, if anything remains after the personal chattels and the statutory legacy have been paid, the spouse is entitled to the income for life from one-half of the balance of the estate.

When Dies capital goes to other entitled and is Distributed.

13.11.2.2 The issue

The issue are entitled (on the statutory trusts, see **13.10.3**) to the other half of the residuary estate and to the remainder interest in that half in which the spouse has a life interest. no need to invest can get straight away

13.11.2.3 Personal chattels

The term 'personal chattels' is defined by s 55(1)(x) of the Administration of Estates Act 1925 as including:

> . . . carriages, horses, stable furniture and effects (not used for business purposes), motor cars and accessories (not used for business purposes), garden effects, domestic animals, plate, plated articles, linen, china, glass, books, pictures, prints, furniture, jewellery, articles of household or personal use or ornament, musical and scientific instruments and apparatus, wines, liquors and consumable stores, but do not include any chattels used at the death of the intestate for business purposes nor money or securities for money.

In spite of this definition showing signs of its age, it is clear that it is intended to cover items of personal and domestic use and ornament. In most cases there is unlikely to be much difficulty in determining whether a particular item, by its nature, falls within the definition. However, user is sometimes relevant: assets used for business purposes are excluded, so that it would appear that a car used for both business and private purposes falls outside the definition.

The phrase '. . . articles of household or personal use . . .' has been held to include, for example:

(a) a 60-foot yacht used by the deceased for pleasure (*Re Chaplin* [1950] Ch 507; 2 All ER 155);

(b) a stamp collection made by the deceased as a hobby (*Re Reynold's Will Trusts* [1966] 1 WLR 19; 3 All ER 686);

(c) a collection of watches worth some £50,000 out of an estate of approximately £80,000 (*Re Crispin's Will Trusts* [1975] Ch 245; [1974] 3 WLR 657; [1974] 3 All ER 772).

13.11.3 Spouse, no issue but parent(s) or brothers/sisters of the whole blood (or their issue)

In this case, the spouse takes:

(a) the personal chattels absolutely;

(b) statutory legacy of £200,000, free of tax and costs and with interest (as before);

(c) one-half of the residuary estate (i.e. the capital) absolutely.

The other half of the residuary estate passes to the intestate's parent(s) or, if neither survives, to the brothers and sisters of the whole blood or their issue on the statutory trusts.

13.11.4 Special rules applying to spouses

There are two possible elections which may be open to the surviving spouse and, if exercised, will affect the distribution described above. These relate to the surviving spouse's life interest and to the matrimonial home.

13.11.4.1 Redemption of life interest

Where the surviving spouse has a life interest in the residuary estate an election may be made, in writing, to the personal representatives to capitalise that life interest (Administration of Estates Act 1925, s 47A). If the spouse is the sole personal representative, the election is made to the Senior District Judge of the Family Division. The time limit for making the election is 12 months from the date of the grant, but the court can, in its discretion, extend the time limit.

The effect of making the election is that, instead of receiving the income only from one-half of the residuary estate for life, the spouse takes a capital sum (inevitably less than half of the residuary estate) absolutely. The balance of the residuary estate (after the deduction of the costs of the capitalisation) will then be held for the issue on the statutory trusts.

There is a complex statutory formula for arriving at the capitalised value. However, if the issue are all *sui juris* the figure may be arrived at instead by agreement between the spouse and the issue.

13.11.4.2 Appropriation of the matrimonial home

Schedule 2 to the Intestates' Estates Act 1952 enables the surviving spouse, in effect, to purchase the matrimonial home (or the deceased's interest in it where they were beneficial tenants in common). The election is not necessary where the deceased and the surviving spouse were beneficial joint tenants because the deceased's interest accrues automatically to the survivor, independently of the intestacy rules.

The 'matrimonial home' is defined as that in which the surviving spouse was resident at the date of death of the intestate; it does not matter whether the deceased was also so resident.

The Act gives the spouse the right to require the personal representatives to appropriate the matrimonial home (at its value at the date of appropriation, see *Re Collins* [1975] 1 WLR 309; [1975] 1 All ER 321) in partial or total satisfaction of the spouse's statutory legacy and/or absolute or capitalised life interest in the residuary estate. If these are not adequate to 'purchase' the deceased's interest, the deficiency may be made up out of the spouse's own resources.

This election too must be made in writing to the personal representatives within 12 months of the grant (the court having again a discretion to extend the time limit). Normally, during this period the personal representatives cannot sell the matrimonial home without the spouse's consent. If the spouse is one of two or more personal representatives, the notice should be given to the others. The schedule does not say what is to happen if the spouse is the sole personal representative.

In four cases, the consent of the court is required before the election can be made. Broadly, this would be when the home was only part of a building owned by the deceased, or if the home was part of a farm or other business premises, and specialist texts should be consulted in these circumstances.

The general power of appropriation (**15.3.2.1**) is also available to the surviving spouse if also the personal representative of the intestate—but note the 'self-dealing' rule mentioned in **15.3.2.3**.

13.12 Issue of the intestate

Subject to the entitlement of any surviving spouse, the residuary estate is held for the issue of the intestate on the statutory trusts.

Effectively, children take to the exclusion of remoter issue, except where a child predeceases the intestate leaving issue, when, as we have seen, the issue take their parent's share on the statutory trusts.

An adopted child is treated as a legitimate child of its adoptive parent(s) and not as the child of its natural parents (Adoption Act 1976, s 39). A legitimated child is treated as if born legitimate (Legitimacy Act 1976, ss 5 and 10).

Section 18 of the Family Law Reform Act 1987 provides that (on a death on/after 4 April 1988) the distribution of assets on intestacy is to be determined without regard to whether the parents of a particular person were (or were not) married to each other. In other words, illegitimacy is ignored—and this applies not only to the intestate's issue but to all other relatives who may be entitled under the intestacy rules. (On a death before 4 April 1988 different rules applied.)

The Family Law Reform Act 1987 provides no special protection for personal representatives who distribute in ignorance of illegitimate claimants. However, under s 18(2) there is a presumption that an illegitimate child is not survived by its father, or any person related to that child only through its father, unless the contrary is shown.

13.13 Other relatives of the intestate

If there are no surviving spouse or issue, the order of entitlement to share in the estate is as follows:

(a) parents (equally if both alive); but if none then

(b) brothers and sisters of the whole blood (i.e. who share the same parents as the deceased) on the statutory trusts; but if none then

(c) brothers and sisters of the half blood (i.e. who share only one parent with the deceased) on the statutory trusts; but if none then

(d) grandparents (equally if more than one); but if none then

(e) uncles and aunts of the whole blood (i.e. brothers and sisters of the whole blood of one of the intestate's parents) on the statutory trusts; but if none then

(f) uncles and aunts of the half blood (i.e. brothers and sisters of the half blood of one of the intestate's parents) on the statutory trusts. It is blood relatives of the intestate who are entitled, not those related only by marriage.

Apart from parents or grandparents, members of each class take on the statutory trusts. For example, Harry (a bachelor) dies intestate. His only surviving relative is a niece, Isla, the daughter of his late sister Gwen. Isla will be entitled to all of Harry's estate provided she attains 18 (or marries under that age). Of course, if Gwen had survived Harry, Isla would have no entitlement.

13.14 The Crown

If the intestate is not survived by any relatives qualifying to share in the estate in any of the above categories then the Crown takes the residuary estate as *bona vacantia*. If the intestate died resident within the Duchy of Lancaster or in Cornwall, the Duchy or Duke of Cornwall respectively take as *bona vacantia*.

Section 46 of the Administration of Estates Act 1925 gives the Crown, etc. a discretion in such cases to make provision for the intestate's dependants (who need not be related to the deceased) and for 'any other person for whom the intestate might reasonably have been expected to make provision'

13.15 Inheritance tax and intestacy

It is not our purpose here to go into this topic in any detail, but merely to stress that any property passing to the deceased's spouse under the intestacy rules will be wholly exempt from inheritance tax (as it will be covered by the spouse exemption which you will have already encountered).

13.16 Intestacy: Checkpoints

1. Does any of the deceased's estate pass by will (**13.10**)?
2. As to property undisposed of by any will and passing under the intestacy rules:
   (a) Has the deceased's spouse survived by 28 days?
   (b) If so, see Table 1 below and **13.11**.
   (c) If the surviving spouse does not take the entire residuary estate, is:
      (i) redemption of life interest;
      (ii) appropriation of matrimonial home;
      relevant or necessary (**13.11.4**)
3. If spouse does not survive for 28 days:
   (a) Are there issue (**13.12**)? (NB the statutory trusts (**13.10.3**).)
   (b) If not, are there other relatives qualifying to share in the estate (**13.13**)? (NB the statutory trusts (**13.11.3**).)

Table 1 **Destination table where intestate's spouse survives by 28 days**

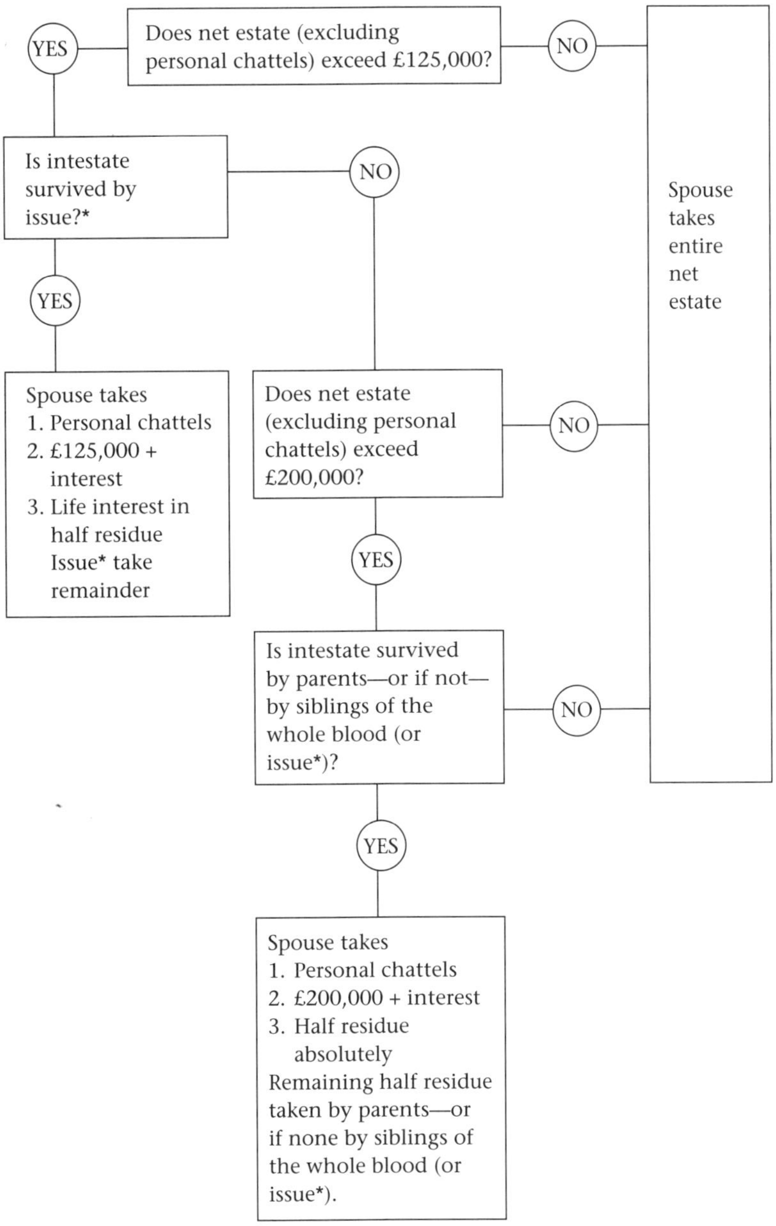

*on statutory trusts

13.17 Property not passing under the will or the intestacy rules

We noted above that certain property passes on death quite independently of the will (if any) or intestacy rules. This is the case even if the will purports to gift such property, as it is simply not capable of being passed by will. The value of such property may well be significant, and knowledge of how such property passes will be relevant when advising on entitlements to property owned by the deceased. Depending on the type of property, it may or may not be part of the deceased's taxable estate chargeable to inheritance tax on death (see **7.9**). Although not of immediate concern, for ease of reference, such property is listed at **13.19** and **13.20**.

13.18 Property passing outside the will or intestacy rules

The property listed below does not form part of the deceased's 'succession estate' and therefore is not payable to the deceased's personal representatives.

13.18.1 Property owned by the deceased as beneficial joint tenant

Where the deceased was a beneficial joint tenant of any property, the deceased's interest accrues automatically on death to the surviving joint tenant(s). This is the case whether the property is personalty (e.g a bank account) or land (e.g the matrimonial home).

Where the jointly owned property is held as beneficial tenants in common, however, the share of each joint owner will pass under their will (or the intestacy rules).

EXAMPLE 10

Joyce and John, who are not married, live together with their daughter Kelly (aged 18) who is Joyce's only child. Joyce has a joint bank account (beneficial joint tenancy) with John, and they jointly own their home as tenants in common. Joyce dies intestate, survived by John and Kelly. Joyce's share of the money in the bank account will pass by survivorship to John, and can be claimed by producing a copy of her death certificate to the bank. Her share in the home, however, will form part of her succession estate, which here passes under the intestacy rules to Kelly.

13.18.2 Trust policies

If the deceased had taken out life assurance on his own life, then the sum assured may, under the terms of the policy, be payable to the deceased's estate. If so, the proceeds payable on death will be paid to the deceased's personal representatives as part of the estate passing under the will or intestacy rules.

Alternatively, the life policy may be held for the benefit of other person(s) either as a result of an express assignment or trust of the policy, or as a result of being written under s 11, Married Womens' Property Act 1882. The latter case is only applicable if the intended beneficiaries are the life assured's spouse and/or children; in other cases, an express assignment or trust of the policy will be required. In either case, the policy 'belongs' to the beneficiaries and the policy monies are payable directly to them (or trustees for them) on proof of death, by sending a death certificate and completed claim form to the insurance company.

it doesn't say held on trust for beneficiary
presume passes to estate

EXAMPLE 11

Peter has taken out two policies of life assurance. The Eversure Assurance Co. policy is written in trust for his wife, Pam. The other policy, which is with the Longlife Assurance Co., is payable to his estate. Peter's will leaves his estate to his wife and children in equal shares. Pam survives Peter and is able to obtain the proceeds of the Eversure policy shortly after Peter's death. She finds this sum a useful means of support, pending the distribution of her late husband's estate (which includes the proceeds of the Longlife policy) in accordance with the will.

13.18.3 Pension scheme benefits

Many occupational pension schemes are drafted in such a way that a lump sum payable on death 'in service' does not form part of the estate of the deceased member of the scheme. This is achieved by making any such sum payable to family members entirely at the discretion of the trustees of the scheme—though usually the member is allowed to make a (non-binding) 'nomination' of his preferred recipient—not to be confused with the sort of nomination discussed at **13.18.4**. The deceased has no interest in such lump sum (and thus it cannot form part of his succession estate). The trustees of the scheme only require proof of death to enable payment to be made.

Again, it must be stressed that not all pension schemes operate in this way; frequently, any 'death in service' benefit is part of the estate of the deceased passing under the terms of the will or the intestacy rules.

13.18.4 Statutory nominations

In the case of certain investments, a person who is aged 16 or over may pass the property concerned on death under a statutory nomination made in writing and attested by one witness. Such a nomination is revoked by subsequent marriage, a later nomination, or if the nominee predeceases the nominator: however, it is unaffected by any subsequent will.

It is now only possible to make such a nomination of monies deposited in friendly societies and industrial and provident societies, up to a limit in each case of £5,000. It used to be possible to nominate funds in trustee savings banks (withdrawn 1 May 1979) and National Savings Certificates and the National Savings Bank (withdrawn 1 May 1981). However, nominations made before these dates remain effective (unless revoked).

If property capable of nomination in this way is not so nominated, it forms part of the property passing on death under the terms of the deceased's will or the intestacy rules.

13.18.5 *Donationes mortis causa*

You will no doubt have encountered this type of gift in earlier studies of trust law and you will recall that they are gifts made in contemplation of death. We do not intend to go into further detail here, but only to mention that property passing under a valid *donatio mortis causa* passes directly to the donee on death.

13.18.6 Life interests in trust property

Where the deceased was possessed of such an interest at the date of death, the trust property will pass in accordance with the terms of the trust instrument.

13.18.7 Gifts with the reservation of benefit

This is an inheritance tax concept—it basically means that the deceased has given away property in their lifetime, but has retained some benefit in the gifted property. Regardless of the tax position, if the property has been effectively gifted in their lifetime, it will no longer belong to the deceased for succession purposes.

13.19 Property not forming part of the succession estate but forming part of the deceased's estate for inheritance tax purposes

Although the following property is not payable to the deceased's personal representatives, it nevertheless must be included in calculating the value of property passing on death for inheritance tax purposes, i.e. it forms part of the deceased's taxable estate:

(a) Property held by the deceased as beneficial joint tenant—the value of the deceased's share only, not the whole value of the property. Thus in the example at **13.18.1**, only the value of Joyce's share of money in the bank account would be included in her estate for tax purposes. The value of her interest in the house (part of her succession estate) would, of course, also form part of her taxable estate on death.

(b) Nominated property (**13.18.4**).

(c) *Donationes mortis causa* (**13.18.5**).

(d) Life interests in trust property (**13.18.6**).

(e) Gifts with a reservation of benefit (**13.18.7**).

13.20 Property not forming part of the deceased's estate for succession or inheritance tax purposes

These are:

(a) Trust policies (**13.18.2**). Policies payable to the deceased's estate would, however, form part of the taxable estate.

(b) Pension scheme benefits payable at the discretion of the pension trustees (**13.18.3**). If the lump sum benefit is payable to the deceased's estate, again it will be included in the estate for inheritance tax.

13.21 Property not passing under the will or the intestacy rules: Checkpoints

1. Is there property which does not pass as part of the deceased's succession estate (**13.18**)?
2. If so, does such property:
   (a) form part of the deceased's taxable estate (**13.19**)?
   (b) not form part of the deceased's taxable estate (**13.20**)?

13.22 Provision for family and dependants

In this section we will consider, in outline, how a successful claim under the Inheritance (Provision for Family and Dependants) Act 1975 may alter the distribution of property that would otherwise be in accordance with the deceased's will, the operation of the intestacy rules, or a combination of both in the case of partial intestacy. In some cases, orders can be made which affect certain types of property which pass outside the deceased's succession estate, or even property disposed of by the deceased in the lifetime.

The Act enables certain classes of persons to apply for provision from the deceased's estate on the basis that the deceased's will or intestacy fails to make adequate financial provision for them, and only applies if the deceased dies domiciled in England and Wales.

You may be asked to advise a potential applicant under the Act, or to advise the personal representatives about the merits of a claim made against the deceased's estate. In the latter case, any statements by the deceased (or, indeed, any other evidence) as to why no provision was made for the claimant should be carefully preserved; such statements will be relevant if the claim goes to court, and may be useful in negotiations with the claimant.

All statutory references in the remainder of this Part of the chapter are to the Inheritance (Provision for Family and Dependants) Act 1975 unless otherwise stated.

13.23 The basis of the claim for provision

In order to succeed an applicant must:

(a) apply within the time limit (**13.24**);

(b) fall within one of the categories of applicant set out in s 1(1) (as amended) (**13.25**); and

(c) satisfy the court that the will or intestacy fails to make reasonable financial provision for the applicant (**13.26**).

The court may then order financial provision to be made out of the deceased's net estate (**13.28**). The deceased may have anticipated that a claim might be made under the Act and may have disposed of property prior to death in an attempt to defeat such a claim. The Act contains anti-avoidance provisions (ss 10 and 11) enabling an order to be made relating to such property in limited circumstances, although this is not further discussed here.

The Act also sets out certain guidelines which the court must take into account both when deciding whether or not reasonable financial provision has been made for the applicant, and if not, whether any order should be made (**13.27**).

13.24 The application

13.24.1 The time limit for making applications

Applications should normally be made within six months from the grant of representation (the document which confirms or grants authority to act as personal representatives) to the deceased's estate. A late application is only permitted if the court gives leave.

13.24.2 Protection of personal representatives from personal liability

Linked to the six-month time limit is the protection against personal liability granted by the Act to the personal representatives. If no claim has been made within the time limit, then the personal representatives may distribute the deceased's estate, and will not be liable personally even if the court allows a late application. Until the time limit has expired, the personal representatives run the risk of personal liability if the claim is successful and property distributed to beneficiaries has been dissipated by them. As claims can only be made against the net estate, the deceased's debts can, however, safely be paid.

13.24.3 Ascertaining whether a grant of representation has been issued

A claimant under the Act will need to know whether a grant of representation has been issued to enable the application to be made within the time limit. There is a procedure, known as a standing search, which will enable an applicant to find this out, and to obtain a copy of the grant. Specialist texts should be consulted for details of the procedure.

13.25 The applicant

13.25.1 Categories of applicant

The onus is on applicants to show that they come within one of the categories set out in s 1(1) in order that they can apply for an order to be made in their favour.

Applications under the Act are personal actions. If the applicant dies before the matter is determined by the court, then the application cannot proceed.

13.25.1.1 The deceased's spouse (s 1(1)(*a*))

The marriage must have subsisted at the time of the deceased's death. A judicially separated spouse can apply, unless an order has been made under s 15 by the matrimonial court, preventing an application under the Act.

13.25.1.2 The former spouse of the deceased who has not remarried (s 1(1)(*b*))

The marriage may have ended by decree of divorce or nullity. Again, no claim can be made if the matrimonial court has barred an application under the Act (s 15 and 15A) by the former spouse—commonly part of a 'clean break' order.

13.25.1.3 A cohabitant (s 1(1)(*ba*))

This provision enables a claim to be made by a person who has lived in the same household as the deceased, as their husband or wife, throughout the two-year period immediately prior to the deceased's death.

13.25.1.4 A child of the deceased (s 1(1)(*c*))

Note that adult children can apply, but are unlikely to be successful if the applicant is able-bodied and in employment.

13.25.1.5 A person who has been treated as a child of the family in relation to any marriage of the deceased (s 1(1)(*d*))

In effect, the Act is here usually referring to step-children of the deceased, although the relevant 'treatment' may occur when that child is an adult. Again, claims by adult step-children are possible, but unlikely to be successful unless something more is shown.

13.25.1.6 A dependant (s 1(1)(*e*))

A dependant is any person (not included in the foregoing paragraphs) who immediately before the death of the deceased was being maintained, either wholly or partly by the deceased.

Broadly, this category allows claims by those financially dependent on the deceased. The Act lays out a two stage test (s 1(3)) which must be satisfied by an applicant to come within this category. Suffice it to say here that the applicant must demonstrate that the financial support received was in excess of the value of any consideration provided by the applicant in return for such support.

EXAMPLE 12

Joy's aunt provides her with rent-free board and lodging while she is completing her LPC course. In return, Joy, helps her with some housework. The aunt dies. It is likely that Joy would be able to establish that she comes within s 1(1)(*e*), although this of itself does not mean that her claim will succeed.

EXAMPLE 13

Two widowed brothers decide to pool their resources and live in the same house. Ted pays the rent, but Tom pays for their food. If the value of their contributions to running the house are roughly equal, then neither would be able bring a claim under s 1(1)(e) against the estate of the other.

13.26 Reasonable financial provision

The Act (in s 1(2)) sets out a two-stage process:

(a) Has the will or the intestacy rules, or in appropriate cases a combination of the two, failed to make reasonable financial provision for the applicant?

(b) If so, the court considers what would amount to such reasonable financial provision.

What amounts to reasonable financial provision will depend on who is making the application, as the Act sets out two standards. One is applicable to an application by the surviving spouse, and the maintenance standard applies to other categories of applicant.

13.26.1 The surviving spouse standard (s 1(2)(*a*))

13.26.1.1 The surviving spouse

If the applicant is the surviving spouse, the standard is such financial provision as would be reasonable in all the circumstances, whether or not that provision is required for maintenance.

This standard is thus more generous than the maintenance standard (below). The intention is that the surviving spouse will have a claim on the family assets at least equivalent to that of a divorced spouse, and the court is directed to have regard to the provision which would have been awarded in divorce proceedings (s 3(2), see **13.27.2.1**).

13.26.1.2 Discretion to apply surviving spouse standard to judicially separated spouses and former spouses

By s 14 the court has a discretion to apply the surviving spouse standard to judicially separated and former spouses if the death occurs within 12 months of the final decree in the judicial separation or divorce proceedings—and no final order has been made (or refused) in those proceedings.

13.26.2 The maintenance standard

The standard is such provision as would be reasonable in all the circumstances for the applicant to receive for maintenance (s 1(2)(*b*)). Case law establishes that reasonable provision for maintenance is such that enables the applicant to live decently and comfortably according to his situation.

13.26.3 The test

The question for the court, judged objectively on the basis of facts known at the time of the hearing (s 3(5)) is whether the will or intestacy makes reasonable financial provision for the applicant. The court is not bound by testators' views as to whether they felt they were acting reasonably in making no, or only limited, provision for the applicant.

13.26.3.1 Evidence of a testator's reasons

If there is evidence (including hearsay evidence) of the reasons why a testator has not made provision in the will for an applicant, however, this is admissible (s 1, Civil Evidence Act 1995 and see **13.27.1.5**). For instance, the testator may have placed a written statement with the will, giving reasons as to why no provision has been made for an adult child. The court will judge what weight should be given to this evidence. It will clearly be given more weight if it is considered judgement (e.g. 'my son has a well-paid job; my daughter's accident has prevented her earning her own living'), but the court will also take into account those childrens' circumstances at the time of the hearing.

The will, once admitted to probate, is a public document, and thus open to inspection. A written statement of reasons, placed with the will and not referred to in it, will not be admitted to probate, and thus remains confidential.

13.27 The guidelines

The court must take into account the guidelines in s 3(1), both when determining whether the applicant has established that no reasonable financial provision has been made (**13.26.3**), and in determining what order, if any, should be made under s 2 (**13.28**). It is entirely in the court's discretion as to whether any order should be made at all.

Some of the guidelines are relevant to all applicants; some only relate to a particular category of applicant.

13.27.1 Guidelines relevant to all applicants

13.27.1.1 Financial resources and needs of the applicant, any other applicant and any beneficiary whether now or in the foreseeable future

The court will assess the relative financial position of persons with any claim on the estate. Thus a needy applicant will have greater prospects of success if the beneficiaries are well off. In *Re Collins* [1990] Fam 56, it was held that the fact that the applicant was in receipt of social security benefits did not preclude the court from making an order out of her mother's estate.

13.27.1.2 Any moral obligation of the deceased to any applicant or beneficiary

In *Re Callaghan* [1984] Fam 1, for example, a claim was made by an adult child of the family against his step-father's estate. The step-father died intestate and his estate passed to his three sisters whom he had not seen for ten years. The court held that the deceased's greatest obligation was owed to the applicant who had kept in close touch with him and looked after him in his last illness. The court also took into account that many of the assets of the estate came from the applicant's mother who had died some years previously, and ordered a lump-sum payment of £15,000 to the applicant to enable him to buy his council house outright.

13.27.1.3 The size and nature of the net estate of the deceased

The larger the estate the easier will it be for the court to order reasonable provision for an applicant. Conversely, as costs will usually be awarded out of the estate, the court will discourage claims where the estate is small (*Re Coventry* [1980] Ch 461 above).

The source of the deceased's estate may be relevant, as in *Re Callaghan* (**13.27.1.2**).

13.27.1.4 Physical or mental disability

Any physical or mental disability of any applicant or beneficiary will be taken into account.

13.27.1.5 Any other relevant matter including the conduct of the applicant or any other person

Clearly the court has a wide discretion as to the matters it can take into account under this heading. As already mentioned, any statement (whether oral or written) by the deceased as to the reasons for the disposition of the estate can be considered (**13.26.3.1**). In *Re Callaghan* (**13.27.1.2**) the caring conduct of the applicant assisted his claim.

13.27.2 Guidelines relevant to particular categories of applicant

In addition to the factors set out above, the court must also take into account the following:

13.27.2.1 Where the applicant is the surviving spouse (s 3(2))

The following factors are relevant:

(a) the age of the applicant and the duration of the marriage;

(b) the applicant's contribution to the welfare of the deceased's family;

(c) the provision which the applicant might reasonably have expected to receive if, at the date of death, the marriage had instead been terminated by divorce.

Note that the likely provision on divorce is only a starting point; a different award may be appropriate on a financial provision application. For instance, the divorce court will have to consider the future needs of both parties—clearly this will no longer be relevant.

13.27.2.2 Where the applicant is a former spouse (s 3(2))

The guidelines (a) and (b) set out at **13.27.2.1** apply. Guideline (c) (what the divorce court would order) only applies if the court exercises its discretion to apply the surviving spouse standard (see **13.26.1.2**). Even if an application by a former spouse has not been barred by the matrimonial court (**13.25.1.2**), the Court of Appeal has indicated that only rarely would post-decree applications be successful. This is because the matrimonial court will have already considered the issues of maintenance and the allocation of assets between the parties.

13.27.2.3 Where the applicant is a cohabitant (s 3(2A))

The following factors are relevant:

(a) The age of the applicant and how long they have lived in the same household as husband or wife of the deceased.

(b) The applicant's contribution to the welfare of the family of the deceased, including by looking after the home or caring for the family.

13.27.2.4 Where the applicant is a child (s 3(3))

Here the court must consider the manner in which the applicant was being or might be expected to be educated or trained.

13.27.2.5 Where the applicant is a child of the family (s 3(3))

As well as considering the education guideline (in **13.27.2.4**) the court must also consider:

(a) whether the deceased had assumed any responsibility for the applicant's maintenance and, if so, the extent and the basis upon which the deceased assumed responsibility and for how long;

(b) whether in assuming and discharging that responsibility the deceased did so knowing that the applicant was not his own child; and

(c) the liability of any other person to maintain the applicant.

13.27.2.6 Where the applicant was maintained by the deceased (s 3(4))

Here the court must in addition to the general guidelines consider the extent to which and the basis upon which the deceased assumed responsibility for the applicant.

13.28 Family provision orders

5.29.1 Types of financial provision orders

The court must take into account the guidelines set out in **13.27** in deciding whether to make an order under s 2 and, if so, the type of order. The most common order is for a lump-sum payment, either in cash or by way of a transfer of a particular asset, but periodical payments orders (e.g. £200 per month) can also be made. Interim periodical payment orders are possible pending the determination of the final order.

13.28.2 Inheritance tax

How is the inheritance tax position affected if the court makes an order varying the disposition of the deceased's estate? The Act provides (s 19(1)) that for all purposes, including inheritance tax, the variation is deemed to be effective as from the deceased's death. In effect, the order is 'read back', as if the deceased had made the provision ordered by the court. If, for example, the court orders that provision be made for a surviving spouse, the estate's liability for inheritance tax will be reduced. This is because the property passing to the surviving spouse will be exempt from inheritance tax.

If an award is made the court can direct whether any inheritance tax is to be borne by the applicant or the estate.

13.29 Property available for financial provision orders

The deceased's 'net estate' from which any order for financial provision orders is made is widely defined in s 25(1). It comprises the following:

(a) All property of the deceased owned at the date of death and which could have been disposed of by will, less:
   (i) funeral testamentary and administration expenses;
   (ii) debts and liabilities; and
   (iii) inheritance tax.

(b) The deceased's severable share of a joint tenancy (which normally passes by survivor-ship, see **13.18.1**) but only if the application is made within the six-month time limit (**13.24.1**) and the court so orders (s 9).

(c) Any property which the court has ordered under the anti-avoidance provisions to be available (under s 10 or 11, which are not further discussed here).

(d) any property in respect of which the deceased made a statutory nomination (**13.18.4**), a *donatio mortis causa* (**13.18.5**), or which the deceased could have appointed in lifetime under a general power of appointment which has not been exercised.

13.30 Family provision: Checkpoints

1. Advising the personal representatives:
   (a) Has notice of any claim under the Act been received within the prescribed time limit (**13.24**)?
   (b) Does the claimant *prima facie* fall within any of the categories within s 1(1) of the Act (**13.25**)?
      (i) If so, do the dispositions taking effect on death make any provision for the claimant and could this be regarded as reasonable financial provision (**13.26**) to the relevant standard (**13.26.1** and **13.26.2**)?
      (ii) Is there any evidence as to why the deceased failed to make more generous provision for the claimant (**13.26.3.1**)?
      (iii) Do any of the general or special guidelines have any particular relevance to the claim (**13.27**)?

2. Advising the claimant:

   (a) Has a grant been issued and, if so, how long ago (see **13.24**)?

   (b) Does the claimant *prima facie* fall within any of the categories within s 1(1) of the Act (**13.25**)?

   (c) If so, do the dispositions taking effect on death make any provision for the claimant and could this be regarded as reasonable financial provision (**13.26**) to the relevant standard (**13.26.1** and **13.26.2**)

   (d) Is there any evidence as to why the deceased failed to make more generous provision for the claimant (**13.26.3.1**)?

   (e) Do any of the general or special guidelines have any particular relevance to the claim (**13.27**)?

14

Application for a grant of representation

14.1 Grants of representation

In **14.1** to **14.10** we begin our consideration of the practice and procedure relating to the issue of a grant of representation to the personal representatives of someone who has died. Such grants are court orders and are evidence of the personal representative's title to deal with the deceased's estate.

We will begin by examining briefly the court's jurisdiction in probate matters (**14.1.1**) and the responsibilities of solicitors instructed to act in the administration of an estate (**14.2**). We will then consider the effect of grants (**14.3**) and those cases where a grant is not necessary (**14.4**). The principal types of grant will then be examined (in **14.5**). The concluding paragraphs (**14.6** to **14.10**) will look at various aspects of the position of personal representative.

14.1.1 Background

14.1.1.1 Probate jurisdiction

The probate jurisdiction of the court is concerned with three issues:

(a) whether a document may be admissible to probate;
(b) who is entitled to a grant of representation;
(c) should a grant already made be revoked.

Most probate business is non-contentious (in the probate lawyer's jargon, 'common form') business and is exclusively the province of the Family Division of the High Court. Where there is a dispute concerning any of the above issues, the matter becomes contentious. Contentious (or 'solemn form') business is conducted in the Chancery Division, the County Court having a concurrent jurisdiction where the value of the estate is below the County Court limit at the date of death (currently this is £30,000). However, even in these cases, once the dispute is resolved the grant issues from the Family Division.

A grant is normally made by the English courts where the deceased left property situate in England and Wales (Administration of Justice Act 1932, s 2).

14.1.1.2 Non-contentious business

Common form business is mostly conducted in either the Principal Registry of the Family Division in London (headed by a senior district judge and a number of district judges) or in one of the District Probate Registries (or sub-Registries attached to most of them), each headed by a registrar. The jurisdiction of the Registries is not restricted to any geographical area. On the death of someone living (say) in Bristol there is no reason why the grant should not be applied for in Newcastle-upon-Tyne (or indeed anywhere else). However, it will normally in practice be more convenient to use the local Registry.

Application for a grant may be made by a personal representative in person or through a practising solicitor.

Non-contentious business is regulated by the Non-Contentious Probate Rules 1987, as amended by the Non-Contentious Probate (Amendment) Rules 1991. For convenience, these are hereafter referred to as 'the Rules' or 'NCPR'.

14.2 Responsibilities of solicitors instructed by personal representatives

It is not essential for personal representatives to instruct solicitors to act for them in obtaining a grant or in the administration of the estate. However, where a solicitor is instructed it is important to appreciate that the personal representatives are the solicitor's clients. Clearly, there is a potential for a conflict of interest if the solicitor also advises members of the family or the beneficiaries—especially if any hint of a dispute emerges.

It is also important to remember that the personal representatives will often be close relatives of the deceased and therefore (particularly initially) experiencing a degree of distress. The solicitor acting must be sensitive to this in dealings with the client, tempering efficiency with sympathy and understanding of the client's feelings.

14.2.1 Initial duties

On receiving instructions, the solicitor's first responsibilities will relate to the obtaining of the grant. There are basically three types of grant, which are discussed in more detail in **14.5**:

(a) *Probate.* This normally only issues to an executor duly appointed by the will or a codicil.

(b) *Letters of Administration with will annexed.* This grant is appropriate where there is a will but for some reason it is not possible to make a grant of probate to an executor.

(c) *Letters of Administration.* This grant, often called 'simple administration', is issued where the deceased died intestate.

Whichever is the appropriate grant, details will be required of the various assets and liabilities of the estate so that their value can be established. If there is a will, this will need to be obtained and its validity and admissibility to probate considered. Any application for a grant has to be supported by certain papers which will have to be prepared. These include the appropriate Oath and in some cases other affidavit evidence (see **14.16**); and (where required) an Inland Revenue Account (see **14.18**).

Once all the documentation is complete and any tax has been paid, application for the grant is made by lodging the various papers (including any will and codicils) at the selected Registry, either in person or by post, together with a cheque for the appropriate court fees. On receipt by the Registry, the papers are examined to check that they are in order and any testamentary documents are photocopied. The court records are searched to check *inter alia* that no grant has already been made and that no application has been made to another Registry. If all is in order, the grant is prepared, signed by a duly authorised signatory and sealed with the seal of the Family Division or of the District Registry.

The grant is then sent, together with any office copies requested on making the application, to the 'extracting solicitor'—usually some 10 to 14 days after the application is lodged.

14.2.2 Later duties

Once the grant has been obtained, it will be necessary to advise the personal representatives as to their powers and duties. The various assets will need to be realised and the liabilities discharged. There may be a need to advise on a variety of matters, including beneficial entitlement, interim distribution and possible changes in the disposition of the estate, before the estate can be finally wound up. These matters are considered in **Chapter 15**.

14.3 The effect of the issue of a grant

A grant of representation issued by the court is conclusive evidence as to the terms and due execution of any will (and codicil), or that the deceased died intestate.

From the viewpoint of the personal representatives, the effect of the grant depends upon whether they are executors or administrators.

14.3.1 Executors

An executor's title to act derives from the will (or codicil). The deceased's property vests in the executor on death, and the executor has full authority to deal with it without a grant. An executor may even commence court proceedings prior to the issue of a grant, though it may be necessary to obtain a grant before judgment.

The grant of probate, then, merely confirms the executor's title to act. However, a grant (or an office copy) is the only acceptable proof of the executor's title, and except in cases considered in **14.4** below will in practice always be required to enable the executor to deal with the deceased's property.

14.3.2 Administrators

Whether the grant is with will annexed or of simple administration, the issue of the grant actually confers authority to act upon the administrator; prior to this not even the person with the best right to a grant has any authority to act. It is only on the issue of the grant that the deceased's property vests in the administrator; in the interim it has been vested in the Public Trustee. What is more, the grant once made does not relate back to the date of death so as to confirm any action taken in the interim—except for the limited purpose of protecting the deceased's estate from wrongful injury in that period.

14.4 Grant not necessary

As we saw in **13.18** to **13.21** there are a number of situations where property passes on death directly to those entitled and not through the hands of the personal representatives; in these cases, since the personal representatives do not need to make title to the assets, a grant is not necessary.

It may also sometimes be possible for property which does pass to the personal representatives to be obtained or dealt with by them without the need for a grant.

14.4.1 Small sums due to the estate

Under the Administration of Estates (Small Payments) Act 1965, it may be possible for the personal representatives to obtain payment of sums due to the estate on production of a copy of the death certificate. However, where orders have been made under this Act, there is an upper limit (currently £5,000) in respect of each item—and if this is exceeded a grant will be necessary to establish title to the whole sum, not just the excess. The Act allows such payment to be made to the person appearing to be entitled to the grant or to be beneficially entitled to the asset concerned. The Act merely permits payment without a grant, however; it is not obligatory. Monies which are covered by orders under this Act include:

(a) money held in the National Savings Bank, National Savings Certificates or Premium Savings Bonds (NB small balances in accounts with the high street clearing banks are not covered by orders under the Act);

(b) monies payable on the death of a member of a trade union, industrial or provident society or a friendly society;

(c) civil servants' salaries, wages or superannuation benefits;

(d) service pensions, police and firemens' pensions.

Similar provisions apply under the Building Societies Act 1986 to funds invested in a building society.

14.5 Types of grant

We have already identified the three types of grants. Entitlement to these will now be more fully considered.

14.5.1 Probate

This grant can only be made to an executor, who is usually expressly appointed by the will or a codicil. If a firm of solicitors is appointed, unless the will clearly provides to the contrary (as it should) it will be the partners at the date of the will (or codicil containing the appointment) who are entitled to act. The appointment of an executor may be implied (in which case the appointee is described as 'executor according to the tenor of the will') where the will shows an intention that a particular person should perform the functions of an executor.

Appointments of executors are usually 'unlimited' as to property and time. However, it is possible for the appointment to be limited in either of these respects, e.g. 'I appoint X to be executor as to my business of ...'; 'I appoint Y to be executor until my son Z attains his majority'. A grant issued to any such executor will be similarly limited.

14.5.2 Letters of administration with will annexed

This grant is appropriate where there is a valid will but it is not possible to make a grant of probate in favour of an executor. It may be that the will fails to appoint an executor, or that those appointed are dead or are unwilling or unable to act. Other situations where this grant will issue include cases where the appointed executors are minors or otherwise incapable of taking a grant (see **14.6** below).

14.5.2.1 Rule 20 of the NCPR

This governs the order of entitlement to a grant where the deceased left a valid will. At the head of the list is an executor (who as we have seen is entitled to a grant of probate). Where such a grant is not possible, the rule lays down the order of entitlement to a grant of letters of administration with will annexed. For a person in a later category to establish title to the grant it will be necessary to account satisfactorily for all those (including executors) who would have a better right (see **14.14.3**).

Under r 20 the full order is:

(a) An executor.

(b) A trustee of the residuary estate.

(c) Any other residuary beneficiary (including one for life), or (where there is a partial intestacy because the residue is not wholly disposed of by the will) anyone entitled to share in the undisposed of residue. Normally, a residuary beneficiary whose interest is vested will be preferred to one whose interest is contingent only.

(d) The personal representative of anyone in (c) other than a life tenant of residue.

(e) Any other beneficiary (including a life tenant or one holding as a trustee) or a creditor. Again, a person with a vested interest is normally preferred to one whose interest is contingent only.

(f) The personal representative of anyone in (e) other than a life tenant or person holding as a trustee.

As can be seen, the order mainly depends upon entitlement to the deceased's property under the terms of the will, with the residuary interest being treated as the principal interest, whatever its value in relation to the other gifts under the will.

14.5.2.2 Rule 21 of the NCPR

Where a gift in a will fails by virtue of s 15 of the Wills Act 1837 (because the beneficiary or the beneficiary's spouse has witnessed the will, see **13.6.5**), that beneficiary loses the right to a grant under r 20 as a beneficiary named in the will—though may still claim in any other capacity (e.g. as a person entitled on intestacy or as a creditor).

14.5.3 Letters of administration

A grant of 'simple administration' is appropriate where there is no valid will.

The order of entitlement to the grant is governed by r 22 of the NCPR, which as will be seen broadly follows the order of entitlement to share in the estate of the intestate (discussed at **13.9** to **13.16**). Again, for anyone in a lower category to be able to establish title to the grant it will be necessary to satisfactorily account for all those with a better right (see **14.15.2**).

14.5.3.1 Rule 22 of the NCPR

The order under r 22 is:

(a) The surviving spouse.

(b) The children of the deceased and the issue of any child who has predeceased.

(c) The deceased's parents.

(d) The deceased's brothers and sisters of the whole blood and the issue of any who have predeceased.

(e) The deceased's brothers and sisters of the half blood and the issue of any who have predeceased.

(f) Grandparents.

(g) Uncles and aunts of the whole blood and the issue of any who have predeceased.

(h) Uncles and aunts of the half blood and the issue of any who have predeceased.

(i) The Treasury Solicitor where the Crown claims *bona vacantia*.

(j) A creditor of the deceased.

14.5.3.2 Personal representatives

Basically, the personal representatives of a person have the same right to a grant as the deceased whom they represent. This is subject to r 27 of the NCPR (**14.7**) and to r 22(4) which gives preference to persons within categories (b) to (h) in **14.5.3.1** over the personal representative of a surviving spouse who has died before obtaining a grant—unless the spouse was beneficially entitled to the whole estate.

14.5.4 Limited grants

There are a number of situations in which a limited grant may be appropriate. These include grants where the only person entitled to a grant is a minor or suffering from mental incapacity (**14.8**).

14.5.5 Special grants

The most commonly encountered special grant is administration *de bonis non*. Such a grant is made to allow the completion of the administration of the deceased's estate following the death of the sole, or last surviving, personal representative to whom a grant has been issued who has died leaving part of the estate unadministered. It is also the appropriate grant following the revocation of a previous grant.

A *de bonis non* grant is not necessary where one of several proving personal representatives has died; the remaining grantees have full authority to complete the administration of the estate. Nor is it appropriate on a death before a grant has been issued; a *de bonis non* grant is always a 'second grant'.

Further, it will not be necessary to obtain such a grant where the so-called 'chain of representation' exists. This occurs where a sole, or last surviving, proving executor (i.e. one to whom a grant of probate has been issued) dies and that executor's executor duly takes a grant of probate.

EXAMPLE 1

Suppose that Toby dies appointing Tabitha to be his executor. Tabitha proves the will but dies before completing the administration of Toby's estate, appointing Trevor to be her executor. By proving Tabitha's will, Trevor automatically becomes also the executor by representation of Toby and able to complete the administration of Toby's estate. The 'chain' only operates through proving executors. If, in the example, Tabitha had failed to appoint an executor, or if Trevor had renounced or died before taking a grant to Tabitha's estate, or either Toby or Tabitha had died intestate, there would have been no chain and a grant *de bonis non* would have been needed to complete the administration of Toby's estate.

The order of entitlement to a *de bonis non* grant is governed by r 20 (**14.5.2**) if the original grant was of probate or administration with will annexed; or r 22 (**14.5.3**) where it was a grant of simple administration.

14.6 Personal representatives: Capacity

In principle, a testator is free to appoint anyone as executor. Equally, any person who under r 20 or r 22 of the NCPR has the right to a grant is entitled to apply for a grant of letters of administration. There is no rule automatically debarring (say) someone who is insolvent or who has a criminal record. However, there are a number of qualifications to this general principle: these include the following.

14.6.1 Minors

A minor cannot take a grant. If the minor is one of several executors or potential administrators, the practice is to make a grant immediately to the adult executors or administrators, with, in the case of a grant of probate, power being reserved to the minor to apply for a grant of 'double probate' on attaining 18. Where the minor is the only or last surviving executor or potential administrator, a grant of letters of administration (with will annexed if there is a will) is made (normally to the minor's parent or guardian) for the use and benefit of the minor until age 18, when it automatically terminates and a grant can then be made to the executor/administrator now entitled.

14.6.2 Mental incapacity

Where executors or potential administrators are suffering from mental incapacity such as to render them incapable of managing their own affairs, the position is broadly similar to that applying in the case of minors, and where it is the only executor/potential administrator who is so incapacitated a grant for the use and benefit of that person will be made to the persons specified in r 35 of the NCPR.

14.6.3 Section 116 of the Supreme Court Act 1981

Section 116 gives the court a discretion, where it considers that 'by reason of any special circumstances' it is necessary or expedient, to issue a grant to someone other than the person who is *prima facie* entitled under the Rules. A grant in these circumstances may be issued to anyone (not necessarily the person with the 'next best right'), and may be general or limited in any way in which the court sees fit.

This power has been used, for example, to pass over a potential grantee shown to be unfit to administer the estate (e.g. because bankrupt) or otherwise unsuitable or unable to act (e.g. because in prison; or missing and whereabouts unknown).

14.6.4 Section 50 of the Administration of Justice Act 1985

This allows the court to remove any existing personal representative and appoint a substitute. Such substitute will be an executor if replacing an executor; otherwise the grantee will be an administrator.

14.7 Personal representatives: Several claimants

14.7.1 Probate

On an application for a grant of probate, all the executors appointed by the will or any codicil (and whose appointments have not been revoked by a later codicil) must in some way be accounted for. How this is achieved will be discussed **14.13**. Subject to this, the grant may issue to any one or more of them, up to the limit imposed by s 114 of the Supreme Court Act 1981 (**14.8**). Rule 27 of the NCPR requires that notice of the application shall normally be given to any executors to whom power is being reserved (see **14.9.2**).

14.7.2 Administration

When a grant of letters of administration with will annexed or simple administration is applied for, all those having a better right to a grant than the applicant(s) must be 'cleared off' (i.e. accounted for). We will consider how this should be done at **14.14** and **14.15**. Where there are several potential grantees in the same degree of priority, r 27 allows the grant to be made (again, subject to the limits imposed by s 114 of the Supreme Court Act 1981) to any one or more of them, but this time without any requirement for notice to the others entitled in the same degree.

However, r 27 further provides that preference should normally be given to:

(a) an adult rather than someone on behalf of a minor entitled in the same degree;

(b) a living person rather than the personal representative of a deceased person who, if living, would have been entitled in the same degree.

14.8 Personal representatives: Number

14.8.1 Executors

A sole executor always has full authority to act, even in cases where minority or life interests arise (contrast the position of administrators at **14.8.2**).

A testator can appoint any number of executors, but a grant of probate cannot issue to more than four (Supreme Court Act 1981, s 114). Those who have not predeceased the testator or renounced have 'power reserved' to them (see further **14.9.2**).

However, s 114 does not prevent the possibility of a grant to a maximum of four executors in respect of part of the deceased's estate and another grant to four different executors in respect of another part. Thus, if the deceased had appointed four executors to deal with his business and four further executors to deal with the rest of the estate, two grants in respect of the different parts of the estate can be made to them all.

14.8.2 Administrators

Here, whether the grant is with will annexed or simple administration, s 114 again provides for a maximum of four grantees. However, in certain cases, it also requires that there should normally be a minimum of two (or a trust corporation, such as the Public Trustee or a bank). This minimum requirement arises whenever, under any will or on the intestacy, a beneficiary is an infant or there is a life interest. However, if a grant is made to two grantees as a result of this requirement and one of them then dies, there is no requirement for a replacement to be appointed: the survivor has full authority to act henceforth alone (though the court may on application appoint a 'replacement').

14.8.3 Additional personal representatives

14.8.3.1 Rule 25 of the NCPR

A person entitled to a grant of administration may, without leave, apply for a grant together with a person entitled in a lower degree, provided there is no other person entitled in priority to the person to be joined—or, if there are any such persons, they have all renounced. If the person sought to be joined does not have any (or any immediate) right to a grant, an *ex parte* application to a district judge or registrar will normally be required.

14.9 Personal representatives: Renunciation/power reserved

No one can be forced to accept office as an executor or administrator, though a person entitled to a grant can be forced to make up their mind whether to take a grant or not. Executors or administrators are free to renounce their rights to a grant provided they have not accepted office. As an alternative to renunciation, an executor who does not wish to act in the administration may have 'power reserved' (see **14.9.2**).

14.9.1 Executors: Renunciation

An executor accepts office, thus losing the right to renounce, by taking a grant, or even before this by 'intermeddling' in the estate, i.e. by doing something which shows an intention to accept office. Acts of charity, humanity or necessity are not sufficient to constitute such acceptance. Thus, for example, arranging the funeral will not be enough; but writing to request payment of monies due to the estate will.

A renunciation must be in writing, signed by the renouncing executor, and containing a statement that the executor has not intermeddled. It becomes effective on being filed at the Registry (usually with the papers to lead the grant to some other person).

An executor cannot generally renounce part of the office. The office must be accepted in full, or renounced in full.

Under r 37 of the NCPR, a renunciation by an executor of the right to a grant of probate does not operate as the renunciation of any rights that person may have to a grant of letters of administration (whether as beneficiary or creditor), unless there is also an express renunciation of those rights.

14.9.2 Executors: Power reserved

Rather than renounce, one of several executors appointed by the will/codicil who does not wish to act in the administration can instead have 'power reserved' (see further **14.13.7.3**). This, in effect, means that the executor concerned will not be involved in the application for the grant and thus will not be entitled/required to take part in the process of dealing with the testator's affairs. However, if circumstances change (e.g. a proving executor falls ill or dies, or the non-proving executor changes his mind) the executor to whom power has been reserved can apply for a grant at a later stage—and thereafter be involved with the administration.

14.9.3 Administrators: Renunciation

An administrator accepts office only by taking a grant: no amount of 'intermeddling' prior to this will constitute acceptance. Renunciation is again effected in writing, signed by the renouncing 'administrator' (no declaration that there has been no intermeddling being required in this case), and this is filed (usually) with the other papers to lead the grant to someone else. Rule 37(2) provides that an administrator who has renounced in one capacity (e.g. as a residuary beneficiary) can claim a grant in another (e.g. as a creditor).

14.10 Grants of representation: Checkpoints

1. Effect of the issue of a grant (**14.3**).
2. Is a grant necessary (**13.8** and **14.4**)?
3. If yes, which one is appropriate:
   (a) Is there a will?
      (i) If so, probate (**14.5.1**) or letters of administration with will annexed (**14.5.2**).
      (ii) Entitlement to grant governed by r 20 of the NCPR (**14.5.2.1**).
   (b) If no will:
      (i) Letters of administration (**14.5.3**).
      (ii) Entitlement to grant governed by r 22 of the NCPR (**14.5.3.1**).
4. Are any potential grantees
   (a) Minors (**14.6.1**)?
   (b) Mentally incapable (**14.6.2**)?
5. Is more than one person entitled to the grant (**14.7**)?
6. How many may/must apply (**14.8** and **14.9**)?
7. May a potential applicant renounce (**14.9**)?

(*See further* ***Table 1***.)

Table 1 **Application for a grant of representation**

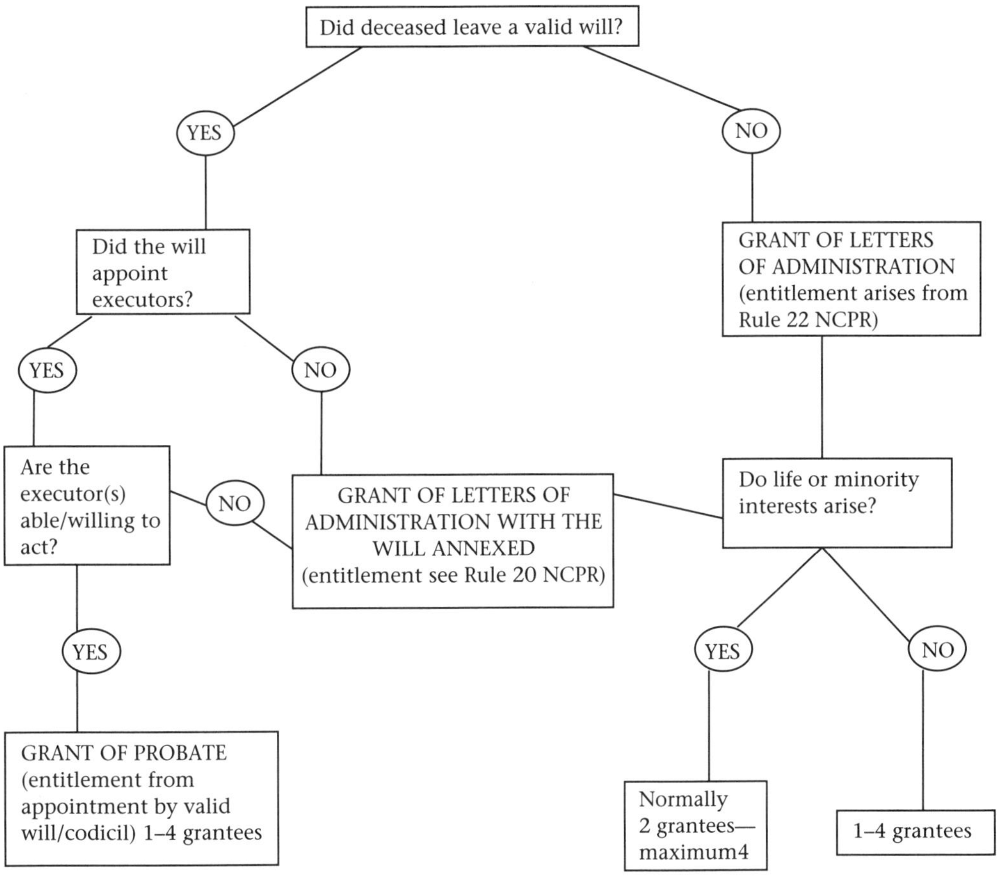

14.11 The court's requirements

Every application for a grant of representation must be supported by an Oath—in effect, evidence in the form of an affidavit—sworn or affirmed by the personal representatives, usually before a solicitor holding a current practising certificate and who is not a partner or employee of the firm preparing the Oath.

The essential purposes of the Oath are:

(a) to identify the applicants and the deceased;

(b) (in the case of a grant of letters of administration) to account for those who have a better right to a grant under r 20 or r 22 of the NCPR;

(c) to establish the applicant's title to the grant sought.

14.12 The requirements generally

Increasingly, firms are now using commercial software packages to produce 'customised' Oaths for the particular case in which they may be acting. Alternatively, pre-printed forms are completed and adapted to meet the circumstances of the particular case: in this event, it is important to make sure that the 'finished document' reads as a piece, i.e. it should make proper sense in the same way as if it had been specifically drafted for the case concerned.

There are a number of different versions of pre-printed forms available from Law Stationers, which may vary slightly, e.g. in the order in which information is presented, or in what is actually pre-printed, but whose basic structure is essentially similar. They all contain marginal notes to assist in their completion. In cases of doubt or difficulty the guidance of the court should be sought.

We will here consider the completion of Oaths for executors (**14.13**); for administrators with will annexed (**14.14**); and for administrators (**14.15**). In **14.16** we will consider some of the situations in which it may be necessary to provide the court with further affidavit evidence. In all cases, the heading will be the same:

IN THE HIGH COURT OF JUSTICE
FAMILY DIVISION
THE PRINCIPAL REGISTRY (or)

THE DISTRICT PROBATE REGISTRY AT ....
In the estate of......................... deceased (see **14.13.1**).

The details of the extracting solicitor should also be given: the Registry will then address any correspondence or queries to the solicitor rather than the personal representatives. It will be convenient (especially in the case of larger firms) for the solicitor's reference also to be given: this will then appear on the grant when issued and thus make it easier to identify who is dealing with the matter when this is received in the extracting solicitor's office.

14.13 Oath for executors

This is the appropriate Oath where a grant of probate is sought by an executor appointed by the will or a codicil.

14.13.1 'In the estate of ... deceased'

This is, in effect, the final part of the heading. The true full name of the deceased should be entered here. In most cases, this will present no difficulty.

However, sometimes it may be necessary to include an alternative 'alias' name, for example, because the will was not executed in the deceased's full name; because the deceased's name has changed since making the will; or because the deceased held property in different names.

The inclusion of an 'alternative' name will not, however, be necessary unless one of the indicated circumstances applies. Thus the fact that the deceased was named 'John' but was habitually called 'Jack' does not require any reference or explanation in the oath, unless, for example, he made his will in the name of Jack, or held property in that name.

Whenever an alias is necessary, the deceased (wherever his name is to be mentioned in the Oath) should be described by the true full name, followed by the alternative(s), e.g. 'John Edward Smith otherwise John Smith'. To comply with the requirements of r 9 of the NCPR it will also be necessary to furnish an explanation for the 'alias'.

Oath for Executors

IN THE HIGH COURT OF JUSTICE

Family Division

Extracting Solicitor ....

Address ....

†"Principal" or "District Probate". If "District Probate" add "at ....".
*If necessary to include alias of deceased in grant add "otherwise (alias name)" and state below which is true name and reason for requiring alias.
(1) "I" *or* "We". Insert the full name, place of residence and occupation, or, if none, description of the deponent(s) adding "Mrs", "Miss", as appropriate, for a female deponent.

The † Registry

IN the Estate of* deceased.

(1)

(2) *Or* "do solemnly and sincerely affirm".
(3) Each testamentary paper must be marked by each deponent, and by the person administering the oath.
(4) "with one, two (or more) Codicils", as the case may be.

make Oath and say (2) that
(1) believe the paper writing now produced to and marked by (3)
to contain the true and original last Will and Testament (4)

of*
of

formerly of

deceased,

(5) This should be the date of birth as shown in the Register of Deaths.
(6) If exact age is unknown, give best estimate.
(7) Where there are separate legal divisions in one country, the state, province, etc., should be specified.
(8) Delete "no", if there was land vested in deceased which remained settled land notwithstanding his or her death.
(9) Settled land may be included in the scope of the grant provided the executors are also the special executors as to the settled land; in that case the settlement must be identified.

who was born on the day of (5) and
who died on the day of
aged years (6) domiciled in (7)
and that to the best of knowledge, information and belief there was (8) [no]
land vested in the said deceased which was settled previously to h death (and
not by h Will (4))
and which remained settled land notwithstanding h death (9)

And (1) further make oath and say (2)
that notice of this application has been given to

(10) Delete or amend as appropriate. Notice of this application must be served on all executors to whom power is to be reserved unless dispensed with by a Registrar under Rule 27 (3).

the executor(s) to whom power is to be reserved, [save
]. (10)

And (1) further make Oath and say (2)
that (11) (12)

(11) "I am" *or* "we are". Insert relationship of the executors to the deceased only if necessary to establish title or identification.
(12) "The sole", *or* "the surviving", *or* "one of the", *or* "are the", *or* "two of the", etc.

Execut
named in the said

(13) If there was settled land and the grant is to include it, insert "including settled land" but, if the grant is to exclude the settled land, insert "save and except settled land".

and that (1) will (i) collect, get in and administer according to the law the real and personal estate (13) of the said deceased; (ii) when required to do so by the Court, exhibit on oath in the Court a full inventory of the said estate (13)
and when so required render an account of the administration of the said estate to the Court; and (iii) when required to do so by the High Court, deliver up the grant of probate to that Court; and that to the best of knowledge, information and belief

(14) Complete this paragraph only if the deceased died on or after 1 April 1981 and an Inland Revenue Account is not required; the next paragraph should be deleted.

(15) The amount to be inserted here should be in accordance with the relevant figure shown in paragraph 1 of the PEP List.

(16) The amount to be inserted here should be in accordance with the relevant figure shown in paragraph 2 of the PEP List.

(17) Complete this paragraph only if an Inland Revenue Account is required and delete the previous paragraph.

N.B. The names of all executors to whom power is to be reserved must be included in the Oath.

(14) [the gross estate passing under the grant does not exceed (15) £
and the net estate does not exceed (16) £ , and that this is not a case in which an Inland Revenue Account is required to be delivered]

(17) [the gross estate passing under the grant amounts to £
and the net estate amounts to £].
*

SWORN by the above-named
Deponent

at

this day of

Before me,

A Commissioner for Oaths/Solicitor.

1999 Edition
5.99 F36582
5073580
★ ★ ★ ★ ★

14.13.1.1 The true full name

Normally, this will be the name on the birth certificate or, in the case of a married woman, the name of her husband (assuming she had adopted his surname). Similar principles will *prima facie* apply in the case of a divorced woman.

14.13.1.2 Common problems

Will in 'incorrect' name. This might arise, for example, because the deceased whose full name is Jane Elizabeth Smith has made her will in the name of Jane Smith. In such a case, she should be described as 'Jane Elizabeth Smith (otherwise Jane Smith)'. It will also be necessary to swear, in the Oath (at the end of the printed form) or in a separate affidavit, that 'the true name of the deceased is Jane Elizabeth Smith but that she made and executed her will in the name of Jane Smith'. In such a case, the grant will normally issue in the true name only. *Property in different names.* Where the deceased held property in different names, again the full true name should be given first, followed by the 'alias'. It will also be necessary, at the end of the Oath form or in a separate affidavit, to indicate which is the true name and to include a statement that the deceased held property in the alternative name(s)—identifying (at least one item of) property held in the alternative name(s). For example, at the end of the pre-printed form might be added 'And that the true name of the deceased was Jonathan Smith and that he held Blackacre in the name of John Smith'. The grant will then be issued showing both names.

14.13.2 The applicants

The first paragraph of the Oath identifies those who are applying for the grant. The order should be the same as that in the will, but, in practice, if it is desired to change the order (e.g. to place a solicitor who has been appointed first) this can be done.

14.13.2.1 Names

The true full name of each applicant should be given. If this differs from the name in the will/codicil containing the appointment, an explanation will be required.

If the discrepancy is slight, the matter is usually easily dealt with, e.g. 'Susan Jones (in the will called Sue Jones)'. If the name has been misspelt, again the solution is simple, e.g. 'Jonathan James (in the will written Jonathon James)'. If the name has changed on marriage the explanation (e.g.) 'Ann Evans, married woman (formerly and in the will called Ann Brown, spinster)' will suffice.

Sometimes, the Registry may require further proof of the identity of an applicant. This might arise, for example, where the will appoints 'my wife' without naming her. In such a case, the (short) further evidence needed can usually be incorporated into the Oath (e.g. by including a statement that the applicant 'was the lawful wife of the deceased at the date of the will').

14.13.2.2 Addresses

The full postal address (including postcode, where known) of the true place of residence of each applicant should be given. Solicitors (and others acting in a professional capacity) may give their business addresses. Former addresses need not be given unless relevant in establishing the executor's identity (where this is an issue).

14.13.2.3 Occupations or descriptions

The occupation of each applicant, male or female, should be given (e.g. 'schoolteacher' or, if retired, 'retired schoolteacher'). If the applicant has no occupation, this should be stated: in the case of a woman, her marital status should be given.

14.13.3 '... Make oath and say ...'

It is not necessary for the Oath to be sworn. Applicants may, instead, affirm—in which event, the words 'make Oath and say' whenever they appear should be deleted and replaced with 'do solemnly and sincerely affirm'. It will also be necessary to alter the jurat at the end of the form (in some prints this appears on the back of the form) by deleting the word 'SWORN' and substituting 'AFFIRMED'.

14.13.4 ... That [I/We] believe the paper writing now produced to and marked by [Me/Us] to contains the true and original last will and testament ...

The purpose of this statement is to identify the document(s) which are being put forward as admissible to probate. This is achieved by 'marking' the document(s) concerned: the deponents (the applicants for the grant swearing the oath or making the affirmation) and the solicitor administering the oath or taking the affirmation sign the documents, thus exhibiting them to the affidavit evidence which the Oath comprises. If there is a codicil, after the word 'testament' there should be added 'with (one) (two, or as the case may be) codicil(s)'.

14.13.5 Details of the deceased

This part of the form requires basic information regarding the deceased testator. This must now include their date of birth and gender.

14.13.5.1 Name

As already discussed (in **14.3.1**) the deceased's full true name should be given here, with any alias.

14.13.5.2 Address

The last residential (postal) address (including post code, where known) of the testator should be given. If this is different from the address in the will or codicil, the previous address should be added after the words 'formerly of ...' (any intervening changes of address are ignored). If the addresses are the same, the words 'formerly of' should be deleted.

14.13.5.3 Date of birth and death

Usually, the birth and death certificates will give the relevant dates; however, it is not normally necessary to submit copies of the certificates.

14.13.5.4 Age

The testator's age should be stated (the best estimate being sufficient where this is uncertain).

14.13.5.5 Domicile

Normally, the deceased's domicile at the date of death must be included in the Oath. Where the deceased died domiciled in England or Wales domicile should be sworn as 'England and Wales'. The sworn domicile will appear in the grant: this may have important consequences in relation to the recognition of grants within the different jurisdictions in the UK.

14.13.6 Settled land

You will not often in practice encounter an estate where the deceased had an interest in settled land governed by the Settled Land Act 1925: this is even more unlikely now that no new strict settlements can be created (Trusts of Land and Appontment of Trustees Act 1996). However, in all cases the personal representatives must state whether there is/is not any settled land. It is quite wrong simply to delete the whole paragraph where there is no such land in the estate. In fact, the only permissible deletion is of the word '(no)' where there is, in fact, such land—for which a separate grant will be needed. In this event, it is enough to disclose in the Oath its existence: it is not necessary to give details of the settlement.

14.13.7 Executor's title

This purpose of this part of the form is to establish the 'capacity' in which the proving executors claim to be entitled to the grant. The discussion which follows indicates some of the more commonly met situations.

14.13.7.1 Relationship to the deceased

As we have seen (**14.3.1**), an executor's 'title' essentially depends upon appointment as executor by the will or codicil, the grant strictly only being required as evidence of that title. The fact that an executor is related to the deceased is therefore normally immaterial and need not be stated. However, it will be necessary to state the applicant's relationship to the deceased where identity is an issue: for example, if the will appoints 'my daughter' without naming her. If the will appoints 'my wife' or 'my husband' without naming the spouse concerned, the Oath should include a statement to the effect that the applicant is the lawful widow(er) and was lawfully married to the deceased at the time of the making of the will.

14.13.7.2 Where all appointed are applying

The wording to be used to describe the title of the proving applicant(s) will obviously depend upon the circumstances of the particular case. For example:

Only one appointee	*the sole executor/executrix.*
All male, or female	*the executors.*
All female	*the executrixes.*
Implied appointment	*the executor according to the tenor.*

14.13.7.3 Not all applying

Again the wording to be used to describe the entitlement of those applying will depend upon the circumstances. For example:

Some have died	*the surviving executor(s)/executrixes.*
Some have renounced	*one (or two, etc.) of the executors/executrixes*

In this case it is not necessary to recite the fact of renunciation by the other executor(s), but it helps the Registry if this is done. However, the renunciation itself must be filed with the papers to lead the grant.

Power is to be reserved	*one (or two, etc.) of the executors/executrixes*

In this situation, the name(s) of the executor(s) to whom power is to be reserved must be indicated: further, the Oath must normally also state (NCPR, r 27) that notice of the application for the grant has been given to such executor(s).

14.13.7.4 Partners in a firm

Where partners in a firm (e.g. of solicitors) are appointed by name and some have pre-deceased or renounced, or power is to be reserved to one or more of the named partners, the procedures described in **14.13.7.3** above should be followed.

Where, however, the appointment is of partners in a firm without naming them (e.g. 'the partners at the date of my death in Solicitor & Co.') and not all of them wish to apply, it is sufficient for the Oath to contain a statement that the applicant is/was a partner (or the applicants are/were partners) at the appropriate date. Power can be reserved to 'the other partners' without naming them, and notice need not be given to those not wishing to act (NCPR, r 27(1A)).

14.13.8 Duties of the personal representatives

In practice little needs to be done with this paragraph of the Oath, except where there is settled land (see **14.13.6**), when it will be necessary to insert the words 'save and except settled land'.

14.13.9 Value of the estate passing under the grant

There are two paragraphs relating to the value of the gross and net estate passing under the grant. One of these must be completed and the other deleted.

14.13.9.1 The estate passing under the grant

This is the deceased's free estate (i.e. unsettled property) in the UK in respect of which the grant is needed as evidence of the personal representatives' title. Property which does not pass to the personal representatives (i.e. in that capacity) is not relevant here (see **13.17** to **13.21**).

14.13.9.2 First paragraph

This should be completed (and the second paragraph therefore deleted) only if the estate is an excepted estate for inheritance tax purposes (see **14.19**). Where it is appropriate to complete this paragraph, the gross and net figures are not stated precisely, but rather as not exceeding the upper limit of the appropriate band. In respect of a death on or after 6 April 2000, the figure for the gross estate will be £210,000. As a result of a Practice Direction in March 2002, from 15 April 2002 the net value of the estate is to be stated rounded up to the next whole thousand and expressed as 'not exceeding £...'.

EXAMPLE 2

If the estate is an excepted estate and the value of the estate passing under the will is £105,000 (gross) and £94,500 (net), the figures to be inserted in the first paragraph would be £210,000 (gross) and £95,000 (net).

14.13.9.3 Second paragraph

This paragraph should be completed (and the first one deleted) in all other cases, i.e. whenever an Inland Revenue Account is required. In such cases, the figures to be shown in the Oath are the gross and net figures derived from the probate summary (form D18—see **14.21.18**.)

Oath for Administrators with the Will

Extracting Solicitor ....

Address ....

IN THE HIGH COURT OF JUSTICE

Family Division

*"Principal" or "District Probate". If "District Probate" add "at______".

† If necessary to include alias of deceased in grant, add "otherwise (alias name)" and state below which is true name and reason for requiring alias.

(1) "I" *or* "We". Insert the full name, place of residence and occupation or, if none, description of the deponent(s).

(2) *Or* "do solemnly and sincerely affirm".

(3) Each testamentary paper must be marked by each deponent, and by the person administering the oath.

(4) "With one, two (or more) Codicils", as the case may be.

(5) This should be the date of birth as shown in the Register of Deaths

(6) If exact age is unknown, give best estimate.

(7) Where there are separate legal divisions in one country, the state, province, etc., should be stated.

(8) Complete both blanks. When either such interest arises, two grantees may be required

(9) Delete "no", if there was settled land vested in deceased which remained settled land notwithstanding his death.

(10) If there was settled land such land may be included in the scope of the grant, but the settlement must be identified and all the applicants must show that they are also entitled to a grant in respect of the

(11) Here state manner in which all prior rights are satisfied, e.g., residuary legatees/devisees must show that no executors were appointed, or that those appointed either died before deceased or survived him and have since died without taking probate, or that they have renounced probate, or have failed to take a grant after being cited so to do *(the order*

(12) "I am" or "we are" and state title of applicants to the grant, including their relationship to the deceased only if necessary to establish title or

(13) If there was settled land and the grant is to include it, insert "including settled land", but, if the grant is to exclude the settled land, insert "save and

(14) Complete this paragraph only if the deceased died on or after 1 April 1981 and an Inland Revenue Account is not required; the next paragraph should be deleted.

(15) The amount to be inserted here should be in accordance with the relevant figure shown

(16) The amount to be inserted here should be in accordance with the relevant figure shown

(17) Complete this paragraph only if an Inland Revenue Account is required and delete the previous paragraph.

The* Registry

IN the Estate of †

deceased.

(1)

make Oath and say (2) that
(1) believe the paper writing now produced to and marked by (3)
to contain the true and original last Will and Testament (4)

of †

of

formerly of

deceased,

who was born on the day of (5) and

who died on the day of

aged years (6) domiciled in (7)

and that there is (8) minority and (8) life interest in the estate of the said deceased; and that to the best of knowledge, information and belief there was (9) [no] land vested in the deceased which was settled previously to h death (and not by h Will (4)) and which remained settled land notwithstanding h death (10)

and (1) further make Oath and say (2)
that (11)

100

that (12)

; and that

(1) will (i) collect, get in and administer according to the law the real and personal Estate (13) of the said deceased; (ii) when required to do so by the Court, exhibit on oath in the Court a full inventory of the said Estate, (13) and when so required render an account of the administration of the said Estate to the Court; and (iii) when required to do so by the High Court, deliver up the grant of letters of administration with Will annexed to that Court; and that to the best of knowledge, information and belief.

(14) [the gross estate passing under the grant does not exceed (15) £ , and the net estate does not exceed (16) £ , and that this is not a case in which an Inland Revenue Account is required to be delivered]

(17) [the gross estate passing under the grant amounts to £
and the net estate amounts to £].
*

SWORN by the above-named
Deponent

at

this day of

Before me,

A Commissioner for Oaths/Solicitor.

14.13.10 Other matters

The blank space at the end of the printed form can be used to provide any further information which might be required, e.g. as to an alias (see **14.13.1**); as to the identity of the applicant (see **14.13.2**); or as to the notice required under r 27 of the NCPR (see **14.13.7.3**) if not dealt with earlier. If the matter cannot be dealt with concisely, it will be necessary to file a separate affidavit.

14.13.11 Jurat

Each deponent must swear, or affirm, the Oath before an independent solicitor (or Justice of the Peace). It is not necessary for the names of all the deponents to be inserted if they are all swearing or affirming at the same time. Otherwise, a separate jurat should be drawn and completed for each deponent.

14.14 Oath for administrators with will annexed

As we saw in **14.5.2**, a grant of letters of administration with will annexed is appropriate whenever there is a will and a grant is for some reason not going to be made to an executor (because, perhaps none were appointed, or those appointed are all dead, or have renounced).

Many of the points discussed at **14.13** above regarding the completion of an Oath for executors apply equally to the Oath for administrators with the will. In this section we will concentrate upon the points of difference.

14.14.1 The applicants

Entitlement to apply for a grant of administration with will annexed is determined by r 20 of the NCPR (see **14.5.2.1**). The order in which the applicants' names appear in the Oath should follow that order.

14.14.2 Minority and life interests

We have already seen (in **14.8.2**) that if a minority or life interest arises, a grant of letters of administration (whether or not with will annexed) will normally only issue to two grantees (or a trust corporation). An oath for administrators with will annexed must contain a statement as to whether or not there are minority or life interests arising—either under the terms of the will, or under the intestacy rules where the deceased died partially intestate. This part of the Oath form must, therefore, always be appropriately completed.

14.14.3 Clearing

The Oath must always 'clear off'—in effect, account for—all those who under r 20 of the NCPR have a 'better right' to the grant than the applicant(s). There is no need to account for anyone else in the same category as the applicant(s), nor to give notice of the application to any such person(s). All oaths for administration with will annexed will, therefore, have to account for the fact that no executor is applying by showing (as the case may be) that no executors were appointed, or that they are all dead or have renounced.

What further clearing is required will then depend upon how far down the list the applicant comes. Where there is a partial intestacy and an applicant is seeking a grant as a person entitled to share in the undisposed of property under the intestacy rules, anyone under r 22 of the NCPR having a 'better' claim than the applicant will also have to be cleared. Thus, in the second example in **14.14.4** below, it would be necessary to account for the fact that the deceased's spouse (who would have a better right under r 22 than his children) was not applying.

14.14.4 Capacity

The Oath must then state the precise capacity in which the applicant claims to be entitled to the grant. This, remember, depends essentially upon entitlement to share in the estate rather than relationship to the deceased. Thus, for example:

(a) 'the residuary legatee and devisee under the said will';

(b) 'the daughters of the deceased and two of the persons entitled to share in the undisposed of estate of the said deceased';

(c) one of the specific legatees and devisees named in the said will'.

14.15 Oath for administrators

The grant of simple administration is appropriate where the deceased died wholly intestate. The entitlement to the grant essentially depends (as we saw in **14.5.3.1**) upon the applicant's relationship to the deceased. Many of the comments made in explanation of the practice in completing the Oath for executors (**14.13**) and the Oath for administrators with will annexed (**14.14** above) are equally relevant in this case also. Again, we will here concentrate upon the differences.

14.15.1 The applicants

The order in which the names of the applicants are set out in the Oath should follow the order of priority in r 22 of the NCPR (see **14.5.3.1**). In the case of simple administration, no question of a discrepancy with the will can, of course, arise.

14.15.2 Clearing off

Following the words '*... domiciled in ... Intestate'* it is necessary to account for those with a better right to the grant than the applicant. Specifically, three matters must here be addressed:

14.15.2.1 Status of the deceased

The deceased's marital status must first be indicated: for example,

(a) 'a bachelor/spinster'

(b) 'a married man/woman'

(c) 'a widow/widower'

(d) 'a single man/woman' (where the deceased's marriage had been ended by a decree absolute of divorce). The details of the divorce (including the name of the court and the date of the decree) must be recited and it must also be sworn or affirmed that the deceased had not remarried.

Oath for Administrators

Extracting Solicitor..........

Address..........

IN THE HIGH COURT OF JUSTICE

Family Division

*"Principal" or "District Probate". If "District Probate" add "at..........".

†If necessary to include alias of deceased in grant, add "otherwise (alias name)" and state below which is true name and reason for requiring alias.

(1) "I" *or* "We". Insert the full name, place of residence and occupation or, if none, description of the deponent(s).

(2) or "do so solemnly and sincerely affirm".

(3) This should be the date of birth as shown in the Register of Deaths.

(4) If exact age is unknown, give best estimate.

(5) Where there are separate legal divisions in one country, the state, province, etc., should be stated.

(6) Here give the status of deceased- "a spinster","a widower" etc., and where necessary clear off the classes entitled in order of priority to applicant, e.g., "without issue or parent".

(7) The words which follow clear illegitimate, legitimated and adopted children and should be deleted if application made by surviving spouse (unless in the special circumstances it is necessary to clear issue) or a child. If appropriate substitute "without" for "or".

(8) Complete both blanks. When either such interest arises two grantees may be required unless a trust corporation is applying.

(9) Delete "no", if there was land vested in deceased which remained settled land notwithstanding his or her death.

(10) If there was settled land such land may be included in the scope of the grant, but the settlement must be identified and all the applicants must show that they are also entitled to a grant in respect of the settled land.

(11) "I am" or "we are".

(12) Show applicant's title, e.g., "brother of the whole blood and one of the persons entitled to share in the estate".

(13) If there was settled land and the grant is to include it, insert "including settled land", but, if the grant is to exclude the settled land, insert "save and except settled land".

(14) Complete this paragraph only if the deceased died on or after 1 April 1981 and an Inland Revenue Account is not required; the next paragraph should be deleted.

(15) The amount to be inserted here should be in accordance with the relevant figure shown in paragraph 1 of the PEP List.

(16) The amount to be inserted here should be in accordance with the relevant figure shown in paragraph 2 of the PEP List.

(17) Complete this paragraph only if an Inland Revenue Account is required and delete the previous paragraph.

The* **Registry**

IN the Estate of † deceased.

(1)

make Oath and say (2)
that

of deceased,

born on the day of (3) and

died on the day of

aged years (4) domiciled in (5)

Intestate (6)

(7) or any other person entitled in priority to share in h estate by virtue of any enactment and that (8) minority (8) life interest arises under the intestacy; and that to the best of knowledge, information and belief there was (9) [no] land vested in the said deceased which was settled previously to h death and which remained settled land notwithstanding h death (10)

And (1) further make Oath and say (2) that (11) the (12)

of the said Intestate, and that (1) will (i) collect, get in and administer according to the law the real and personal Estate (13) of the said deceased; (ii) when required to do so by the Court, exhibit on oath in the Court a full inventory of the said Estate (13) and when so required render an account of the administration of the said Estate to the Court; and (iii) when required to do so by the High Court, deliver up the grant of letters of administration to that Court; and that to the best of knowledge, information and belief

(14) [the gross estate passing under the grant does not exceed (15) £ , and the net estate does not exceed (16) £ , and that this is not a case in which an Inland Revenue Account is required to be delivered]

(17) [the gross estate passing under the grant amounts to £ and the net estate amounts to £].

SWORN by the above named Deponent

at

this day of

Before me,

A Commissioner for Oaths/Solicitor.

14.15.2.2 Clearing of those entitled under r 22 of the NCPR

It is not necessary to clear anyone entitled under this Rule in the same category as the applicant (nor is it necessary to give notice of the application to any such person). Thus, for example, if the deceased had four children, an application may be made by one of them (two if a minority or life interest arises) without reference to the others. However, it is essential to account for all those who might have a better right to the grant. This is, in effect, normally done by showing that the deceased was not survived by any relative(s) in the categories higher than that of the applicant(s), or that any survivors have since died or renounced.

In the simplest case, i.e. where there are no surviving relatives with a better right to the grant, the wording used is as follows:

To clear	*Swear that deceased died*
Spouse	a bachelor, spinster, widow(er), single man/woman
Children/issue	without issue
Parents	(or) parent
Brothers/sisters/their issue	(or) brother or sister of the whole [or half] blood or issue thereof (or) grandparent
Grandparents	or uncle or aunt of the whole
Uncles/aunts/their issue	[or half] blood or issue thereof

Where a relative in a higher category has survived but has since died/is not seeking a grant (e.g. having renounced) the wording of the Oath must deal with this, for example: '... Intestate leaving ... his lawful widow and the only person entitled to his estate him surviving who has since died/duly renounced letters of administration'. (In the latter case, the renunciation must be lodged with the papers to lead the grant.)

14.15.2.3 Clearing of 'any other person entitled in priority ... by virtue of any enactment'

These words are designed to clear any illegitimate, legitimated and adopted children and remoter issue of the deceased: they cannot be used as a 'short cut' formula for clearing those entitled under r 22.

If the application is being made by the surviving spouse or children/issue of the deceased, these words should normally be deleted.

If the applicant is from any category in r 22 below children or other issue, the words 'or any other person entitled ... by virtue of any enactment' must always be left in.

14.15.3 Minority and life interests

The Oath for administrators must (as with the application for a grant with will annexed) contain a statement as to whether or not any such interests arise. A minority interest may of course arise whenever a beneficiary entitled to a share under the intestacy rules is under 18. A life interest will arise under the intestacy rules where the deceased is survived by a spouse and issue and the value of the estate is greater than the spouse's statutory legacy (see **13.11**).

14.15.4 Capacity in which grant sought

Essentially, as we have seen, the applicant's title depends upon relationship to the deceased and entitlement to the estate. The Oath must contain a precise statement as to both these matters.

14.15.4.1 Relationship

Some of the more commonly met descriptions to be used here are:

Spouse	*lawful husband/lawful widow*
Child	*son/daughter*—note that this is the appropriate description whether the child's parents were (or were not) married at the time of its birth.
Adopted child	*lawful adopted son/daughter*—note that the Oath should contain a statement giving details of the adoption order and that it is still subsisting.
Grandchild	*grandson/granddaughter*—note that the Oath will have to show that the grandchild's parent had predeceased so as to give the grand-child a beneficial interest under the statutory trusts.
Brother or sister	*brother/sister of the whole [or half] blood.*
Nephew or niece	*nephew/niece of the whole [or half] blood*—again, it will be necessary for the Oath to show that the applicant's parent has predeceased so as to give the applicant a share of the estate.
Parent	*father/mother*
Grandparent	*grandfather/grandmother*
Uncle or aunt	*uncle/aunt of the whole [or half] blood*
Cousin	*cousin german of the whole [or half] blood*—again, the Oath must show that the applicant's parent has predeceased so as to give the cousin a share of the estate.

14.15.4.2 Entitlement to the estate

The Oath must show the applicant(s) entitlement to the estate. For example: 'the only person(s) entitled to the estate'; 'one [two, etc.] of the persons entitled to share in the estate'.

Where a surviving spouse is solely entitled, it should be stated in the Oath that the net estate does not exceed (as the case may be) £125,000 or £200,000 (see **13.11.2.1** and **13.11.3**).

14.16 Further affidavit evidence

In the vast majority of cases, a properly completed Oath is the only affidavit evidence that the court will require. Sometimes, however, the district judge or registrar will require further affidavit evidence to be submitted before issuing a grant. Some of the situations where such additional evidence may be required are considered briefly below: in such circumstances you will need to consult relevant practitioner works and perhaps the court itself as to the nature of the evidence required.

14.16.1 Due execution (r 12 of the NCPR)

We saw in **13.2.4.2** that the inclusion in a will of an attestation clause *prima facie* showing compliance with the requirements of s 9 of the Wills Act 1837 raises a presumption of due execution. If no attestation clause is included, or that included is insufficient, due execution will have to be proved—as it will if there is any reason for possible doubt as to the will's due execution (e.g. where the signature is imperfect or appears in an unusual position). Evidence of due execution may also be required where the deceased was blind, or executed the will with a mark, or where the will was signed by someone on behalf of the testator, though in all these cases the matter is in practice most effectively dealt with by an adjustment to the attestation clause in the will. If this has not been done, an affidavit as to knowledge and approval will also be required (see **14.16.2** below).

Ideally, the evidence of due execution should be given by one of the attesting witnesses or (failing this) anyone else present at the time of execution.

14.16.2 Knowledge and approval (r 13 of the NCPR)

Where a will has been signed by a blind or illiterate person, or by someone else on the testator's behalf, or for any reason (e.g. signs of extreme feebleness in the signature) there is a possible doubt as to whether the testator had the necessary knowledge and approval of the contents of the will (see **13.2.4**), the court must be satisfied on these points before the will can be admitted to probate. These matters are (as we have already seen) best dealt with by appropriate adjustments to the attestation clause; if this has not been done, affidavit evidence will be required to support the application for the grant.

14.16.3 Terms, condition and date of will (r 14 of the NCPR)

The more commonly met possibilities here are set out below.

14.16.3.1 Alterations

We discussed the problems connected with alterations in **13.4**, where we saw that (except in the case of the filling in of a blank space) any unexecuted obliteration, interlineation or other alteration is presumed to have been made after execution of the will and thus to be inadmissible. Where a will contains any such unexecuted alterations, etc. it will normally be necessary (unless the district judge or registrar decides that the alteration is of no practical importance) for affidavit evidence to be provided as to whether or not each and every such alteration existed at the date of the execution of the will: ideally this should be given by one of the witnesses or (failing this) by anyone else present at the time of execution. A copy of the will, omitting any inadmissible alterations (and showing a blank space where an obliteration has rendered the original wording not apparent) will have to be prepared and lodged with the other papers to lead the grant.

14.16.3.2 Incorporation

Where a will refers to another document in such terms as to suggest that it should be incorporated in the will (see **13.5**) the document will have to be produced and identified by (usually) affidavit evidence.

14.16.3.3 Date

Where there is doubt as to the date upon which a will was executed affidavit evidence will normally be required (ideally from one of the witnesses or anyone else present at the time) to establish the date of its execution. If possible, this should establish the exact date of execution; however, if this is not possible it should seek to establish execution between two definite dates.

14.16.4 Attempted revocation (r 15 of the NCPR)

Where there are circumstances which suggest the possibility of attempted revocation (whether by burning, tearing or otherwise destroying, or by possible later will or codicil, e.g. suggested by the presence of pin or staple marks) the court must (in effect) be satisfied that the will has not been revoked. To this end, an affidavit of 'plight and condition' will often be required.

14.17 The court's requirements: Checkpoints

1. Oath for executors:
   (a) Are there any 'alias' problems (**14.13.1**)?
   (b) Are there any problems in identifying the applicant(s) (**14.13.2**)?
   (c) Do any of the applicants wish to affirm rather than swear (**14.13.3**)?
   (d) What was the deceased's domicile (**14.13.5.5**)?
   (e) What is the position regarding settled land (**14.13.6**)?
   (f) How should the title of the applicant(s) be stated (**14.13.7**)?
   (g) Have all non-proving executors been accounted for in some way and any required notices given (**14.13.7.3** and **14.13.7.4**)?
   (h) Which of the statements relating to the estate passing under the grant should be included (**14.13.9**)?
2. Oath for administrators with will annexed:
   (a) Are there any 'alias' problems (**14.13.1**)?
   (b) Are there any problems in identifying the applicant(s) (**14.13.2**)?
   (c) Do any of the applicants wish to affirm rather than swear (**14.13.3**)?
   (d) What was the deceased's domicile (**14.13.5.5**)?
   (e) Are there any minority or life interests—if so, minimum of two applicants normally needed (**14.14.2**)?
   (f) What is the position regarding settled land (**14.13.6**)?
   (g) Have those with a better right under r 20 been cleared off (**14.14.3**)?
   (h) How should the title of the applicant(s) be described (**14.14.4**)?
   (i) Which of the statements relating to the estate passing under the grant should be included (**14.14.9**)?
3. Oath for administrators:
   (a) Are there any 'alias' problems (**14.13.1**)?
   (b) Do any of the applicants wish to affirm rather than swear (**14.13.3**)?
   (c) Have those with a better right under r 22 been cleared off (**14.15.2**)?
   (d) What was the deceased's domicile (**14.13.5.5**)?
   (e) Are there any minority or life interests—if so, minimum of two applicants normally needed (**14.14.2** and **14.15.3**)?
   (f) What is the position regarding settled land (**14.13.6**)?
   (g) How should the title of the applicant(s) be described (**14.15.4**)?
   (h) Which of the statements relating to the estate passing under the grant should be included (**14.13.9**)?

4. Further affidavit evidence:

Are there any circumstances which may call for further evidence to be submitted, for example:

(a) query as to due execution of will (**14.16.1**);
(b) query as to knowledge and approval of contents of will (**14.16.2**);
(c) alterations in will (**14.16.3.1**);
(d) incorporation (**14.16.3.2**);
(e) query as to date of will (**14.16.3.3**);
(f) query as to attempted revocation of will (**14.16.4**).

14.18 The Revenue's requirements

*Before studying the material in this section (**14.18** to **14.22**), you will find it helpful to have considered **Chapter 7** on inheritance tax, and especially **7.9**, which relates to the charge to tax on death.*

Unless the estate is an 'excepted estate' (see **14.19** below), it will not normally be possible for the personal representatives to obtain a grant of representation until they have submitted an Inland Revenue Account, giving details of all the property in the deceased's taxable estate and its value, and (subject to the instalment option) paid any inheritance tax for which they are liable (Supreme Court Act 1981, s 109). The personal representatives are under a duty to deliver an account (normally) within 12 months after the end of the month of death. However, they will in practice want to be in a position to do so much earlier than this, because:

(a) until they have paid the tax due on the delivery of the account they will be unable to obtain the grant and thus will be unable effectively to deal with the estate;
(b) interest will begin to run six months after the end of the month of death.

The account form currently in use is known as **IHT 200**, which comprises a core account (considered in **14.20**) supported by supplementary pages as required in the circumstances of each particular case (considered in **14.21**). The steps involved in the actual calculation of the tax are discussed in **14.22**.

In order to satisfy the Revenue's requirements, it will be necessary for the solicitor acting for the personal representatives to obtain details of the various assets and liabilities of the estate, including property which passes on the death otherwise than through them (see **13.17** to **13.21**). The value of all such assets and liabilities as at the date of death must be established. This is a straightforward enough process in many cases, simply involving correspondence (e.g. with the bank, building society, insurance company, etc.) to ascertain the amount due to/from the estate. In other cases, expert assistance may be required (e.g. from an accountant, surveyor or stockbroker) in order to establish the open market value of the property concerned at the date of death.

In ascertaining the extent and value of the estate, the personal representatives (and the solicitor acting for them) are required to make the fullest enquiries that are reasonably practicable in the circumstances—failure to do so may lead to penalties being imposed. Where an account is required, this must be completed to the best of the personal representatives' knowledge and belief. Again, there may be penalties (and even the liability to prosecution) for failure to disclose property on which tax may be payable.

The system is essentially one of 'self assessment' of the taxable estate and calculation of any tax payable. The values shown in the account will ultimately have to be 'agreed' with the Capital Taxes Office (in the case of land with the local District Valuer), but this is usually done after the grant has been issued. Where tax is payable, this must be calculated by the solicitor acting for the personal representatives, who should then send the completed account (together with all necessary supplementary pages—including the Probate Summary (Form D18—see **14.21.18**)—and a cheque for the amount of the tax (plus any interest) due from the personal representatives) to the Capital Taxes Office. When Form D18 is returned, it is lodged at the selected Registry with the other papers to lead the grant (see **14.29**). [If no tax is payable, Form D18 is lodged with the other papers to lead the grant, and at the same time the Form IHT 200 and supplementary pages are sent to the Capital Taxes Office].

14.19 Excepted estates

If the estate is an 'excepted estate' there is no requirement to file an account in order to obtain a grant of representation, unless:

(a) the Capital Taxes Office so requires by notice in writing within 35 days of the issue of the grant; or

(b) it is subsequently discovered that the estate is not, after all, an excepted estate, in which event an account must be filed within six months of that discovery.

An 'excepted estate' is (in the case of someone dying on or after 6 April 2000) one where all the following conditions are met:

(a) the deceased died domiciled in the UK; and

(b) the estate comprises only property which passes under the deceased's will or under the intestacy rules, or by a statutory nomination, or beneficially by survivorship; and

(c) not more than £50,000 of that gross value is attributable to property situated outside the UK; and

(d) the deceased had not made any chargeable transfers (including former PETs) during the seven years prior to death, other than 'specified transfers' not exceeding in aggregate £75,000; and

(e) the total gross value of such property, including 'specified transfers', did not exceed £210,000.

'Specified transfers' are chargeable transfers (including former PETs) consisting only of cash and/or quoted shares or securities. Thus (for example) if the estate of the deceased includes trust property, or the deceased has an existing cumulative total at the date of death exceeding £75,000, the estate cannot be an excepted estate. In deciding whether the final condition is met, where the deceased was a beneficial joint tenant only the value of the deceased's interest is taken into account.

14.20 Form IHT 200

14.20.1 Introduction

Where the estate is not an excepted estate, this account must be completed in all cases, together with any appropriate supplementary pages, which will always include the Probate Summary—Form D18 (see **14.21.18**). However, it may not always be necessary to deliver a fully detailed account of the estate (see **14.20.2** below).

The current version of the account is an eight-page document. The Capital Taxes Office has issued a guide 'How to fill in Form IHT 200' (IHT 210), the notes in which are numbered to match the various boxes in the form.

Form IHT 200 is reproduced at pp 303–310 below.

The form contains a number of questions that must be answered: where there is nothing to be recorded in a particular box insert a dash or write in the figure '0'.

In showing the value of assets and liabilities and in identifying the taxable estate on the form, pence are ignored. Thus, for example, an asset or a liability of £5.75 would both feature in the form as £5. However, when it comes to the actual calculation of tax (and any interest) due, pence are not ignored!

14.20.2 Delivery of a reduced inland revenue account

Where there is no inheritance tax to pay because most/all of the estate is exempt, it may not be necessary to deliver a fully detailed account of the estate.

A reduced account may be submitted where:

(a) the deceased was domiciled in the UK at the date of death; and

(b) most of the assets passing under the will or the operation of the intestacy rules pass to an exempt beneficiary—broadly, a UK charity, a body such as the National Gallery, British Museum, the National Trust etc., or a surviving spouse; and

(c) the gross value (i.e. before deducting liabilities and any exemptions or reliefs) of assets passing to non-exempt beneficiaries *plus the value of*:

  (i) any other assets chargeable on death (including jointly owned assets passing by survivorship to someone other than the deceased's spouse); assets held in trust under which the deceased had the right to benefit (unless the assets now pass to an exempt beneficiary); assets the subject of a gift with reservation of benefit; foreign assets not passing under a UK will or intestacy rules) *and*

  (ii) the chargeable value (i.e. after deducting any exemptions or reliefs) of any gifts in the seven years before the deceased died

is less than the inheritance tax threshold.

Where all the conditions are met, IHT 19 (not reproduced) summarises how to complete IHT 200:

(a) PAGE 1 (see **14.20.3** below)—should be completed in full.

(b) PAGE 2 (see **14.20.4** below)—all questions should be answered, but it may not be necessary to complete all the supplementary pages.

It will be necessary to complete the relevant supplementary page(s) where there is a 'Yes' answer to any of the questions D1–D6.

A 'Yes' answer to any of questions D7–D16 will not necessitate completion of the relevant supplementary page(s) where **all** of the assets concerned pass to an exempt beneficiary.

(c) PAGES 3–5 (see **14.20.5** to **14.20.7** below)—should be completed as normal.

(d) PAGES 6 and 7 (see **14.20.8** and **14.20.9** below)—should be completed as normal, notwithstanding that there should not be any tax to pay.

(e) PAGE 8 (see **14.20.10** below)—should be completed in full, save that items with an estimated value that pass to exempt beneficiaries should not be included in box L3.

(f) Form D18 (see **14.21.18** below)—should be completed as normal.

14.20.3 Page 1

This page (which must be completed in full in all cases) contains Sections A, B and C and deals with a number of formal matters: its completion should normally present few difficulties. The following should be noted:

14.20.3.1 Boxes B8, B9 and B10

A tick should be placed in the appropriate box if any relatives in the specified categories survive the deceased.

14.20.3.2 Boxes B11 and B12

Enter the number of children/grandchildren surviving the deceased.

14.20.3.3 Box B13

Tick this box if the address shown in **B7** is that of a nursing home or other residential care home.

14.20.4 Page 2

Section D contains a series of questions, all of which must be answered by ticking the appropriate box. If the answer to any question is 'Yes ' it will be necessary (unless a reduced account is being submitted—**14.20.2** above) to complete the supplementary pages indicated. The following should be particularly noted.

14.20.4.1 Gifts and other transfers of value

The answer to this question is 'No' (and no details need be provided on Form D3) if the *only* gifts made by the deceased were:

(a) to their spouse (covered by spouse exemption);

(b) outright gifts to any individual not exceeding £250 in any tax year (covered by small gifts exemption);

(c) outright gifts to any individual of money or quoted stocks or shares which are *wholly* covered by the annual exemption and/or normal expenditure exemption.

If the deceased had made any other gifts/transfers of value—including transfers into settlement or payments of premiums under a policy of life insurance for the benefit of another person (other than the deceased's spouse)—the appropriate answer is 'Yes' and Form D3 must be completed.

14.20.4.2 Life insurance and annuities

A 'Yes ' answer will be required, and Form D9 must be completed, if the deceased paid premiums for (*inter alia*):

(a) insurance policies payable to the estate;

(b) a mortgage protection policy;

(c) insurance policies that are payable to beneficiaries under a trust and do not form part of the estate;

(d) joint life insurance policies under which the deceased was one of the lives assured but which remain in force after the deceased's death;

(e) insurance policies on the life of another person but under which the deceased was to benefit.

A 'Yes' answer and the completion of Form D9 will also be required if the deceased was in receipt of payments under an annuity which continue after their death, or under which a lump sum becomes payable as a result of their death.

14.20.5 Page 3

14.20.5.1 Section E

This section is only applicable where the deceased died domiciled in Scotland and is not further considered in this book.

14.20.5.2 Section F

This section is concerned with the deceased's estate in the UK, passing under the will or the intestacy rules (for which the grant of representation is required to enable the personal representatives to make title), where tax cannot be paid by instalments: as we shall see (in **14.20.7**) where the instalment option is available (see **7.11.4**) in respect of any such property, the details should be recorded in Section G.

The deceased's interest in property held as a beneficial joint tenant (and which therefore accrues by survivorship) should not be included in this section (because it passes outside of the will or the intestacy rules (**13.18.1**). However, the value of the deceased's interest as a beneficial tenant in common would be appropriately included here.

The totals for the various categories of assets listed (brought forward from the relevant supplementary pages) are entered in boxes F1 to F23—with a dash or the figure '0' inserted where no entry is required—and then totalled in box F24.

In most cases, the form is reasonably self-explanatory as to the information required. The following should be noted.

14.20.5.3 Box F13

In this box it is necessary to include the income from settled property to which the deceased was entitled where the trustees had received the income but had not yet paid it over to the deceased prior to the death.

14.20.5.4 Box F14

This box should include any income that had arisen from any such settled property but had not actually been received by the trustees at the date of the deceased's death.

14.20.5.5 Box F15

This box should include (*inter alia*) any outstanding salary, wages, directors' fees or pension arrears.

14.20.5.6 Box F17

This box should include payments due to the deceased under private medical insurance to cover hospital or other health charges incurred prior to death.

14.20.5.7 Box F22

A reversionary interest is normally 'excluded property' for inheritance tax purposes (**7.2.1.2**), so no tax will actually be payable on its value. However, it must nonetheless be disclosed (details being given on Form D17—see **14.21.17**).

14.20.5.8 Box F23

This box should include (with details also being given on form D17—see **14.21.17**)(*inter alia*) money due to the deceased from the sale of land where contracts had been exchanged but the sale had not been completed at the date of the deceased's death; and any other assets not included elsewhere.

14.20.6 Page 4

Section F continues on this page with a summary of the liabilities and funeral expenses deductible from, and any exemptions and reliefs claimed against, the value of the assets listed on the previous page.

14.20.6.1 Liabilities

The deceased's liabilities at the date of death for which deduction may be claimed here should not (normally) include a mortgage secured on land, or business debts both of which 'belong' in Section G. However, if the debts etc. disclosed in Section G exceed the value of the assets recorded in that section, the 'excess' may properly be claimed as a deduction here. The liabilities are totalled in box F25.

14.20.6.2 Funeral expenses

A deduction may be claimed for reasonable funeral expenses and a reasonable deduction for the mourning expenses of the close family of the deceased. It is also permissible to claim for the (reasonable) cost of a tombstone. The various allowable expenses are totalled in box F26.

14.20.6.3 Net total of assets

Boxes F25 and F26 should be added together and the total entered in box F27. The total of liabilities and funeral expenses is then deducted from the figure in box F24 and the resultant figure entered in box F28. [If this figure is a minus figure (i.e., because the liabilities exceed the value of the assets) the figure '0' should be recorded in box F28 (and in box F30) and the excess (i.e., the deficit) should be carried forward and included in the total recorded in box G15. If there are not enough assets in Section G to cover the deficit, the balance may be deducted from the value of any foreign property owned by the deceased—see Form D15 (**14.21.15**)].

14.20.6.4 Exemptions and reliefs

The exemptions and reliefs claimed should be identified and the amount claimed entered in the spaces indicated. Where any asset listed in boxes F1 to F23 is 'excluded property'—for example, a reversionary interest—this should also be identified and claimed as a deduction here. The total of all exemptions, reliefs and exclusions should then be entered in box F29.

14.20.6.5 Chargeable value of assets in the UK where tax may not be paid by instalments

The total in box F29 is deducted from the total in box F28, and the resultant figure entered in box F30. [There cannot be a deficit here: deducting exemptions etc can only reduce the figure in F28 to '0'].

14.20.7 Page 5

Section G is concerned with the deceased's estate in the UK (passing under the will or the intestacy rules and for which the grant of representation is required to enable the personal

...tatives to make title) where tax may be paid by instalments (see **7.11.4**). The totals for the assets in the listed categories, brought forward from the relevant supplementary pages, must be included in boxes G1 to G12 and totalled at G13. Whether or not the option is to be exercised must be indicated by ticking the appropriate box at the top of the page.

The deceased's interest in property held as a beneficial joint tenant (and which therefore accrues by survivorship) should not be included in this section because it passes outside of the will or the intestacy rules (**13.18.1**). However, the value of the deceased's interest as a beneficial tenant in common would be appropriately included here.

The following should be particularly noted.

14.20.7.1 Land and buildings

All real, leasehold and other immovable property owned by the deceased in the UK should be included in boxes G1 to G6, and form D4 (if appropriate—see **14.21.4**) and supplementary Form D12 (see **14.21.12**) should be completed. If a professional valuation has been obtained a copy should be attached.

14.20.7.2 Business interests

The net value (i.e., after taking into account business debts) of the deceased's business interests should be disclosed in boxes G7 to G9 and supplementary form D14 will need to be completed (see **14.21.14**).

14.20.7.3 Stocks and shares

The value of such assets qualifying for the instalment option (**7.11.4**) should be included in boxes G10 to G12.

14.20.7.4 Mortgages

Money secured by a mortgage on land included in Section G should be shown in box G14 and details given in supplementary Form D16 (see **14.21.16**). Where the deceased had a mortgage protection policy, the mortgage should be included here and the policy monies due to the estate shown in box F16.

14.20.7.5 Other liabilities

These would include deficits from Section F (see **14.20.6**) or in relation to foreign property included in supplementary form D15 (see **14.21.15**).

14.20.7.6 Net total of assets

The figure to be inserted in box G16 is arrived at by deducting from box G13 the sum of boxes G14 and G15. [If this figure is a minus figure (i.e., because the liabilities exceed the value of the assets) the figure '0' should be recorded in box G16 (and in box G18) and the excess (i.e., the deficit) should be carried back and included in the total recorded in box F25. If there are not enough assets in Section F to cover the deficit, the balance may be deducted from the value of any foreign property owned by the deceased—see Form D15 (**14.21.15**)].

14.20.7.7 Exemptions and reliefs

Any such claims for deduction against the value of property included in this section should be identified and totalled at box G17.

14.20.7.8 Chargeable value assets of assets in the UK where tax may be paid by instalments

The figure in box G17 is deducted from that in box G16, and the resultant total entered in box G18. [Again, there cannot be a deficit here: deducting exemptions can only reduce the figure in G18 to '0'].

14.20.8 Page 6

Section H is a summary of the chargeable estate and consists of entries in the various H1 to H15 that are copied from the boxes WS1 to WS15 in the Inheritance Tax Worksheet (Form IHT(WS) discussed in **14.22.1**) that is used to calculate the tax due on the chargeable estate.

14.20.9 Page 7

14.20.9.1 Section J

This section is concerned with calculating the tax liability.

First, the total tax payable is calculated, using figures brought forward from boxes WS16 to WS22 on Form IHT(WS)—see further **14.22.1**).

Second, the tax payable on the delivery of the account (which must be paid to enable the grant of representation to be issued) is calculated, again using figures from IHT(WS)—see **14.22.1**).

14.20.9.2 Section K

If a repayment of tax becomes necessary, the cheque will normally be made out in the names of all those signing the form (usually the personal representatives). If no bank account exists in those names there may be some difficulty in cashing the cheque. In this section there is the opportunity to indicate to whom such a cheque might conveniently be made payable e.g., the solicitors' firm acting for the personal representatives.

14.20.10 Page 8

The personal representatives delivering the account must complete and sign the Declaration set out on this page.

14.20.10.1 Box L1

The type of grant of representation for which application is being made should be indicated.

14.20.10.2 Box L2

The supplementary pages that (with Form IHT 200) make up the account should be listed in this box.

14.20.10.3 Box L3

Any boxes (in Form IHT 200 or any supplementary page) that contain a provisional estimate of value should be listed here.

Inland Revenue
Capital Taxes Office

Inland Revenue Account for Inheritance Tax

Fill in this account for the estate of a person who died on or after 18 March 1986. You should read the related guidance note(s) before filling in any particular box(es). The notes follow the same numbering as this form, so section headings are shown by capital letters and the items in each section are on a dark background.

A Probate Registry, Commissary Court or Sheriff Court District

Name A1 ______ Date of Grant ______

B About the person who has died

Title B1 ______ Surname B2 ______

First name(s) B3 ______

Date of birth B4 / / Date of death B5 / /

Marital status B6 ______

Last known usual address B7 ______ Postcode

Surviving relatives

Husband/Wife B8

Brother(s)/Sister(s) B9

Parent(s) B10

Number of

Children B11

Grandchildren B12

Nursing / Residential home B13

Domicile B14

Occupation B15

National Insurance number B16

Income tax district B17

Income tax reference or self assessment reference B18

C Solicitor or other person to contact

Name and address of firm or person dealing with the estate

C1 ______ Postcode

DX number and town

C2 DX

Contact name and reference

C3 ______

Telephone number

C4 ______

Fax number

C5 ______

For CTO use

IHT 200

R2H4114CTO11/99

D Supplementary pages

You must answer all of the questions in this section. You should read the notes starting at page 10 of form IHT 210 before answering the questions.

If you answer "Yes" to a question you will need to fill in the supplementary page shown. If you do not have all the supplementary pages you need you should telephone our Orderline on 0845 2341000

		No	Yes	Page
● **The Will**	Did the deceased leave a Will?	☐	☐	))))➤ D1
● **Domicile outside the United Kingdom**	Was the deceased domiciled outside the UK at the date of death?	☐	☐	))))➤ D2
● **Gifts and other transfers of value**	Did the deceased make any gift or any other transfer of value on or after 18 March 1986?	☐	☐	))))➤ D3
● **Joint assets**	Did the deceased hold any asset(s) in joint names with another person?	☐	☐	))))➤ D4
● **Nominated assets**	Did the deceased, at any time during their lifetime, give written instructions (usually called a "nomination") that any asset was to pass to a particular person on their death?	☐	☐	))))➤ D4
● **Assets held in trust**	Did the deceased have any right to any benefit from any assets held in trust or in a settlement at the date of death?	☐	☐	))))➤ D5
● **Pensions**	Did the deceased have provision for a pension, other than the State Pension, from employers, a personal pension policy or other provisions made for retirement?	☐	☐	))))➤ D6
● **Stocks and shares**	Did the deceased own any stocks or shares?	☐	☐	))))➤ D7
● **Debts due to the estate**	Did the deceased lend any money, either on mortgage or by personal loan, that had not been repaid by the date of death?	☐	☐	))))➤ D8
● **Life insurance and annuities**	Did the deceased pay any premiums on any life insurance policies or annuities which are payable to either the estate or to someone else or which continue after death?	☐	☐	))))➤ D9
● **Household and personal goods**	Did the deceased own any household goods or other personal possessions?	☐	☐	))))➤ ■
● **Interest in another estate**	Did the deceased have a right to a legacy or a share of an estate of someone who died before them, but which they had not received before they died?	☐	☐	D11
● **Land, buildings and interests in land**	Did the deceased own any land or buildings in the UK?	☐	☐	))))➤ D12
● **Agricultural relief**	Are you deducting agricultural relief?	☐	☐	))))➤ D13
● **Business interests**	Did the deceased own all or part of a business or were they a partner in a business?	☐	☐	))))➤ D14
● **Business relief**	Are you deducting business relief?	☐	☐	))))➤ D14
● **Foreign assets**	Did the deceased own any assets outside the UK?	☐	☐	))))➤ D15
● **Debts owed by the estate**	Are you claiming a deduction against the estate for any money that the deceased had borrowed from relatives, close friends, or trustees, or other loans, overdrafts or guarantee debts?	☐	☐	))))➤ D16

E Domicile in Scotland

- Has any claim for legal rights been made or discharged? No ☐ Yes ☐
- How many children are under 18 ☐ or 18 and over ☐

F Estate in the UK where tax may not be paid by instalments

	Box	£
Quoted stocks, shares and investments *(box SS1, form D7)*	F1	£
UK Government and municipal securities *(box SS2, form D7)*	F2	£
Unquoted stocks, shares and investments	F3	£
Traded unquoted stocks and shares	F4	£
Dividends or interest	F5	£
Premium Bonds	F6	£
National Savings investments *(show details on form D17)*	F7	£
Bank and building society accounts *(show details on form D17)*	F8	£
Cash	F9	£
Debts due to the deceased and secured by mortgage *(box DD1, form D8)*	F10	£
Other debts due to the deceased *(box DD1, form D8)*	F11	£
Rents due to the deceased	F12	£
Accrued income	F13	£
Apportioned income	F14	£
Other income due to the deceased *(box IP4, form D9, box PA1 form D6)*	F15	£
Life insurance policies *(box IP3, form D9)*	F16	£
Private health schemes	F17	£
Income tax or capital gains tax repayment	F18	£
Household and personal goods *(sold, box HG1, form D10)*	F19	£
Household and personal goods *(unsold, box HG2, form D10)*	F20	£
Interest in another estate *(box UE1, form D11)*	F21	£
Interest in expectancy (reversionary interest)	F22	£
Other personal assets in the UK *(show details on form D17)*	F23	£
Total assets *(sum of boxes F1 to F23)*	F24	£

3

- Liabilities

Name	Description of liability	

Total liabilities F25 £

- Funeral expenses

Total of funeral expenses F26 £

Total liabilities and funeral expenses *(box F25 plus box F26)* F27 £

Net total of assets less liabilities *(box F24 less box F27)* F28 £

- Exemptions and reliefs

Total exemptions and reliefs F29 £

Chargeable value of assets in the UK where tax may not be paid by instalments *(box F28 less box F29)* F30 £

G Estate in the UK where tax may be paid by instalments

Do you wish to pay the tax on these assets by instalments? No ☐ Yes ☐

• Deceased's residence				G1	£
• Other residential property				G2	£
• Farms				G3	£
• Business property				G4	£
• Timber and woodland				G5	£
• Other land and buildings				G6	£
	Interest in a business		Interest in a partnership		
• Farming business	G7.1	£	G7.2 £	G7	£
	Interest in a business		Interest in a partnership		
• Other business interests	G8.1	£	G8.2 £	G8	£
	Farm trade assets		Other business assets		
• Business assets	G9.1	£	G9.2 £	G9	£
• Quoted shares and securities, control holding only				G10	£
	Control holding		Non-control holding		
• Unquoted shares	G11.1	£	G11.2 £	G11	£
	Control holding		Non-control holding		
• Traded unquoted shares	G12.1	£	G12.2 £	G12	£
			Total assets *(sum of boxes G1 to G12)*	G13	£

Liabilities, exemptions and reliefs

- Name and address of mortgagee — G14 £
- Other liabilities

Total of other liabilities G15 £

Net total of assets less liabilities *(box G13 less boxes G14 and G15)* G16 £

- Exemptions and reliefs

Total exemptions and reliefs G17 £

Chargeable value of assets in the UK where tax may be paid by instalments *(box G16 less box G17)* G18 £

H Summary of the chargeable estate

You should fill in form IHT(WS) so that you can copy the figures to this section and to section J. If you are applying for a grant without the help of a solicitor or other agent and you do not wish to work out the tax yourself, leave this section and section J blank. Go on to section K.

Assets where tax may not be paid by instalments

• Estate in the UK *(box WS1)*	H1	£
• Joint property *(box WS2)*	H2	£
• Foreign property *(box WS3)*	H3	£
• Settled property on which the trustees would like to pay tax now *(box WS4)*	H4	£
Total of assets where tax may not be paid by instalments *(box WS5)*	H5	£

Assets where tax may be paid by instalments

• Estate in the UK *(box WS6)*	H6	£
• Joint property *(box WS7)*	H7	£
• Foreign property *(box WS8)*	H8	£
• Settled property on which the trustees would like to pay tax now *(box WS9)*	H9	£
Total of assets where tax may be paid by instalments *(box WS10)*	H10	£

Other property taken into account to calculate the total tax

• Settled property *(box WS11)*	H11	£
• Gift with reservation *(box WS12)*	H12	£
Chargeable estate *(box WS13)*	H13	£
Cumulative total of lifetime transfers *(box WS14)*	H14	£
Aggregate chargeable transfer *(box WS15)*	H15	£

J Calculating the tax liability

Calculating the total tax that is payable

• Aggregate chargeable transfer *(box WS16)*	J1	£
• Tax threshold *(box WS17)*	J2	£
• Value chargeable to tax *(box WS18)*	J3	£
Tax payable *(box WS19)*	J4	£
• Tax (if any) payable on lifetime transfers *(box WS20)*	J5	£
• Relief for successive charges *(box WS21)*	J6	£
Tax payable on total of assets liable to tax *(box WS22)*	J7	£

Calculating the tax payable on delivery of this account

• Tax which may not be paid by instalments *(box TX4)*	J8	£
• Double taxation relief *(box TX5)*	J9	£
• Interest to be added *(box TX7)*	J10	£
Tax and interest being paid now which may not be paid by instalments *(box TX8)*	J11	£
• Tax which may be paid by instalments *(box TX12)*	J12	£
• Double taxation relief *(box TX13)*	J13	£
• Number of instalments being paid now J14 / 10 *(box TX15)*		
• Tax now payable *(box TX16)*	J15	£
• Interest on instalments to be added *(box TX17)*	J16	£
• Additional interest to be added *(box TX18)*	J17	£
Tax and interest being paid now which may be paid by instalments *(box TX19)*	J18	£
Total tax and interest being paid now on this account *(box TX20)*	J19	£

K Authority for repayment of inheritance tax

In the event of any inheritance tax being overpaid the payable order for overpaid tax and interest in connection with this estate should be made out to

L Declaration

I/We wish to apply for a L1 ____________________

To the best of my/our knowledge and belief, the information I/we have given and the statements I/we have made in this account and in supplementary pages L2 ____________________ attached (together called "this account") are correct and complete.

I/We have made the fullest enquiries that are reasonably practicable in the circumstances to find out the open market value of all the items shown in this account. The value of items in box(es) L3 ____________________ are provisional estimates which are based an all the information available to me/us at this time. I/We will tell Capital Taxes Office the exact value(s) as soon as I/we know it and I/we will pay any additional tax and interest that may be due.

I/We understand that I/we may be liable to prosecution if I/we deliberately conceal any information that affects the liability to inheritance tax arising on the deceased's death, OR if I/we deliberately include information in this account which I/we know to be false.

I/We understand that I/we may have to pay financial penalties if this account is incorrect by reason of my/our fraud or negligence, OR if I/we fail to remedy anything in this account which is incorrect in any material respect within a reasonable time of it coming to my/our notice.

I/We understand that the issue of the grant does not mean that

- I/we have paid all the inheritance tax and interest that may be due on the estate, or
- the statements made and the values included in this account are accepted by Capital Taxes Office.

I/We understand that Capital Taxes Office

- will only look at this account in detail after the grant has been issued
- may need to ask further questions and discuss the value of items shown in this account
- may make further calculations of tax and interest payable to help the persons liable for the tax make provision to meet the tax liability.

I/We understand that where we have elected to pay tax by instalments that I/we may have to pay interest on any unpaid tax according to the law.

Each person delivering this account, whether as executor, intending administrator or otherwise must sign below to indicate that they have read and agreed the statements above.

Full name and address *Signature* *Date*	*Full name and address* *Signature* *Date*
Full name and address *Signature* *Date*	*Full name and address* *Signature* *Date*

Printed by St Ives Direct, St Ives plc, R2H4114 CTO11/99

14.21 Supplementary pages

There are some seventeen supplementary pages, (D1 to D17) which may require completion according to the circumstances of the individual case—see **14.21.1–14.21.17**. Form D18 must be completed in all cases where an IHT 200 must be submitted—see **14.21.18**. For the requirements where a reduced account is being submitted, see **14.20.2** above.

Forms D1 to D18 are reproduced at pp 322–350 below.

The Capital Taxes Office has issued explanatory notes to assist the completion of the respective supplementary sheets. These notes are numbered to match the respective forms.

The deceased's full name and the date of death should be inserted in the boxes at the beginning of each form.

14.21.1 Form D1 (p 322)

This supplementary form is only required if the deceased left a valid will: all the questions must be answered.

If the answer to Questions 1 and 2 is 'Yes' (or in the case of Question 2 'N/A') and the gross value of the estate is below the tax threshold (currently £234,000) it is not necessary to provide a copy of the will. In all other cases, a *copy* of the will (and any codicils) must be attached to the form.

If there has been a variation or disclaimer (see **15.11**) then a *copy* of the will plus a *copy* of the instrument of variation or disclaimer should be attached to form D1 whatever the size of the estate.

14.21.1.1 Box 1

If the deceased's address in the will differs from that shown on page 1 of IHT 200 a brief explanation is required. Thus, if the deceased had moved, it should be explained that the property in the will has been replaced by the property shown as the deceased's address at the date of death (if the deceased had moved several times between the date of the will and the date of death there is no need to recite the complete 'chain'). If the deceased had sold the property but not replaced it, it should indicate where in the estate the proceeds are included.

14.21.1.2 Box 2

If there are no specific bequests in the will the N/A box should be ticked. Otherwise, it is necessary to tick the appropriate box and if the answer to the question is 'No' a brief explanation of what happened to any item that does not feature in the estate at death should be given. Thus, if an item has been given away, the date of the gift, the name of the donee and the value of the item concerned at the time of the gift should be stated. If it has been sold, the date of sale and an indication of which assets included in IHT 200 represent the sale proceeds should be given.

14.21.1.3 Box 3

Where the answer to this question is 'No' because some/all of the estate passes to exempt beneficiaries, details should be given here (or on Form D17—see **14.21.17**) and the appropriate exemption claimed on IHT 200 and/or the appropriate supplementary page(s).

14.21.2 Form D2 (p 323)

This form must be completed if the deceased was domiciled outside the UK at the date of death. The Channel Islands and the Isle of Man are considered part of the UK for this purpose.

A person is usually regarded as domiciled in the country in which they have their main home. However, for inheritance tax purposes a person domiciled abroad may sometimes be treated as if they were domiciled in the UK. Thus if a person:

(a) has been regarded as resident for income tax purposes for at least 17 of the 20 years ending with the tax year in which they die; or

(b) was domiciled in the UK under English law at any time in the three years prior to their death.

they may be treated as domiciled in the UK at the date of their death.

Where the deceased was domiciled (or treated as domiciled) in the UK, inheritance tax may be charged on the deceased's worldwide estate (though double taxation relief may be available in the event of foreign tax also being payable). If the deceased was domiciled outside the UK at the time of death, any foreign assets will not be liable to UK inheritance tax.

14.21.3 Form D3 (p 325)

This supplementary form relates to gifts and other lifetime transfers of value made by the deceased.

There is no need to complete Form D3 (and the answer to the question about gifts on page 2 of IHT 200 is 'No') if the *only* gifts made by the deceased were:

(a) to their spouse (covered by spouse exemption);

(b) outright gifts to any individual not exceeding £250 in any tax year (covered by small gifts exemption);

(c) outright gifts to any individual of money or quoted stocks or shares which are *wholly* covered by the annual exemption and/or normal expenditure exemption.

In other cases, the questions in Form D3 must be answered and any further information given.

14.21.3.1 Box 1

There are four questions relating to gifts during the seven years prior to death, all of which must be answered. If the answer to any of them is 'Yes' the table in this section of the form must be completed.

Note that the value of the gifted property at the date of gift should always be shown in column 3. Any available exemption(s) should be identified and quantified in column 4 and any remaining chargeable value indicated in column 5.

The net value of the gift(s) after exemptions is totalled in box LT1 and the figure copied to box WS14 on Form IHT(WS).

14.21.3.2 Box 2

Two questions must be answered both concerning gifts with reservation. If the answer to either of them is 'Yes' the table in this section of the form must be completed.

In this case, the value of the gifted property for tax purposes will be the value at the date of death (see **7.10**). Note that neither the annual exemption nor the normal expenditure exemption can be claimed in relation to such gifts.

The net value of the gift(s) after exemptions is totalled in box LT2, and the figure copied to box WS12 on Form IHT(WS).

14.21.3.3 Box 3

The final section of the form is concerned with 'earlier' transfers—those made within the seven years prior to the earliest gift in Box 1 or Box 2. Remember that although any such transfer will no longer itself be in the deceased's cumulative total at the date of death (because the death has occurred more than seven years after the earlier transfer), it will be part of the cumulative total for the purposes of charging tax on any lifetime gifts etc made in the seven years following that earlier transfer (see **7.5.4, Step 4**).

The existence of such earlier transfers, therefore, does not affect the calculation of tax due in respect of the estate on death. However, the information provided here may be relevant in relation to the tax due for any chargeable lifetime transfers. The Capital Taxes Office will consider this issue after the grant has been issued.

14.21.4 Form D4 (p 327)

This must be completed where the deceased owned assets in the UK jointly with other people, or had made a statutory nomination in respect of any of their estate (see **13.18.4**). Details of any jointly owned foreign property should be given on Form D15 (see **14.24.15**) and of any business assets owned jointly by a partnership on form D14 (see **14.24.14**).

A separate form is required where the deceased owned property jointly with different people. Where the deceased owned a number of assets jointly with the same person and the circumstances of their ownership were the same in each case the relevant details may all be included on the same form. However, where some such assets were owned as beneficial joint tenants and some as tenants in common separate forms should be completed.

14.21.4.1 Boxes 1 and 2

The information to be included in Box 1 relates to joint property where tax cannot be paid by instalments. Box 2 is concerned with such property where the instalment option is available.

If the money in the joint account or used to buy the joint property was entirely provided by the deceased and the value of the whole asset is included on Form D3, it is only necessary to give the name of the joint owner, a description of the asset and its value. No further information regarding the history of the joint ownership is required.

If the property concerned was owned as beneficial joint tenant with the deceased's spouse (and thus accrues to the spouse by survivorship) it is only necessary to give the name of the spouse, a brief description of the asset and its approximate value.

Otherwise, the information requested regarding the history etc of the joint ownership should be included in the appropriate box. For Box 2, whether or not the option is to be exercised should be indicated.

14.21.4.2 Assets owned as beneficial joint tenants

The value of the deceased's share of joint assets listed in Box 1 is totalled at JP1 and of any liabilities relating to such property at JP2. The value of the net assets (JP1 less JP2) is then entered in JP3. [If this is a minus figure, JP4 should not be completed and '0' should be entered at JP5].

Any exemptions and reliefs claimed against the value of assets listed in Box 1 are listed and totalled at JP4. This figure is deducted from JP3 to give (at JP5) the net total of assets passing by survivorship where tax may not be paid by instalments. This figure is carried to box WS2 on IHT(WS)—(see **14.22.1**).

A similar process is repeated for Box 2. The value of the deceased's share of assets and liabilities in respect of joint property where the instalment option is available is totalled at JP6 and JP7 respectively and the value of net assets entered at JP8. [If this is a minus figure, JP9 should not be completed and '0' should be entered at JP10]. Any exemptions and reliefs are identified and totalled at JP9 and the net total of assets passing by survivorship where tax may be paid by instalments is entered at JP10 [and carried to box WS7 on Form IHT(WS)].

14.21.4.3 Assets owned as beneficial tenants in common

The procedure is initially similar to that described above but in Box 1, no entries should be made in JP3, JP4 or JP5. The figures from JP1 and JP2 should be carried to the appropriate boxes in Section F on Form IHT 200 and any exemptions and reliefs should be deducted on Form IHT 200 only. Similarly in box 2, no entries should be made at JP8, JP9 or JP10. The figures from JP6 and JP7 should be carried to the appropriate boxes in Section G of IHT 200 and any exemptions and reliefs again claimed on that form only.

14.21.4.4 Box 3

The details of any property that had been the subject of a statutory nomination passing on the deceased's death (see **13.18.4**) should be given here—including the identity of the nominee(s)—and the value carried to the appropriate box in Section F of IHT 200.

14.21.5 Form D5 (p 329)

Where the deceased had a right to the income from or the use or enjoyment of assets held in a trust, it will be necessary to complete this form: in practice, it is probably easier to complete a separate form for each trust under which the deceased was so entitled.

As we saw in **11.2.3**, where the deceased had such an entitlement the value of the trust assets concerned is effectively part of the estate for tax purposes—though the trustees will be primarily liable for any tax due in respect of the trust assets.

It will not be necessary to complete form D5 where the deceased was the object of a discretionary trust even if they had, in fact, received a benefit from the trust (because in such cases no one has a *right* to any benefit).

14.21.6 Form D6 (p 331)

It is necessary to complete this form where the deceased had either received or made provision for a pension (other than the State pension) from either an employer or a personal pension scheme or policy. The three questions should be answered, and any requested information given.

14.21.6.1 Box 1

In most cases, the payment of a pension or similar benefit will cease on death. However, in some cases the pension may be payable for a guaranteed period and if the death occurs before the expiry of this period it may continue to be payable to the estate. In such cases, the value of the right to receive the remainder of the payments should be identified and totalled at PA1 and this figure carried to box F15 on IHT 200.

14.21.6.2 Box 2

Some pension schemes provide for the payment of a lump sum benefit on death. If such benefit is payable to the deceased's personal representatives as of right or where the deceased could—up to death—have made a nomination that would have been *binding* on the trustees of the pension scheme, then the lump sum forms part of the deceased's estate. Details of the scheme/policy and the identity of the recipient should be given and the amount should be included at PA2. This figure is then carried to Box F15 on IHT 200.

However, if the deceased could not have so bound the trustees, the lump sum is not part of the estate (see **13.18.3**). Details should be given as before, but it should be indicated that the lump sum was payable at the trustees' discretion and the amount should *not* be included at PA2.

14.21.6.3 Box 3

The request here is for details of any gifts of benefits or other changes made by the deceased, in either case within two years of death. In certain circumstances, such gifts/changes may have a bearing on liability to inheritance tax.

14.21.7 Form D7 (p 332)

This form is required where the deceased owned stocks and shares. If the personal representatives have obtained a stockbroker's valuation, the totals for each category should be shown and a copy of the valuation attached. It is not necessary to list the holdings again on the form.

14.21.7.1 Box 1

Information is required here as to the identity and value of all stocks, shares and other securities quoted in the Stock Exchange Daily List; unit and investment trusts; Personal Equity Plans (PEPs); shares held in an Individual Savings Account (ISAs); and any foreign shares listed on the London Stock Exchange.

The total value of such holdings at the date of death is entered at SS1 and carried to Box F1 on IHT 200. The total of any dividends or interest due to the date of death is separately entered at SS1 and carried to Box F5 on IHT 200.

14.21.7.2 Box 2

In this section, similar information should be given regarding the deceased's holdings of UK government and municipal securities. The total value at the date of death and of interest due to the date of death are separately entered at SS2 and carried respectively to Boxes F2 and F5 on IHT 200.

14.21.7.3 Box 3

The process is repeated for any unquoted shares held at the date of death. The correct destination of the total value of such shares on Form IHT 200 will depend upon whether or not the shares qualify for the instalment option. If they do not, the total should be carried to box F3. If they do, then it should be entered in Box G11. The total of any dividends should be carried to box F5 on IHT 200.

14.21.7.4 Box 4

Stocks and shares that should feature in this section of the form include those listed on the Alternative Investment Market (AIM) and those traded on the Unlisted Securities Market (USM). Again, the appropriate destination on IHT 200 for the totals depends upon the availability of the instalment option: if this is not available, the entry should be made at Box F4 and if it is then at Box G12. Again, the total of any dividends should be included at Box F5.

14.21.8 Form D8 (p 334)

This form is required where there were debts owing to the deceased at the date of death. A separate form should be completed for each debt.

14.21.9 Form D9 (p 335)

This form is required if the deceased was paying premiums on any life policies whether on their own life or that of another. Whether or not the policies were for the deceased's benefit should be indicated.

The questions in each section must be answered by ticking the appropriate box, and if 'Yes' the relevant further information given.

If the policy is a mortgage protection policy and the deceased owned the property outright, the details of the life policy should be included in Box 1. If the deceased owned the property jointly, the policy (along with details of the property and the mortgage) should be included in Form D4 (see **14.21.4** above).

14.21.9.1 Box 1

In this section, details are required of policy monies payable to the estate. The information required is the name of the insurance company, the policy number and the amount (including any bonuses) paid under the policy. The total of all such policies is entered at IP1.

14.21.9.2 Box 2

Similar information is required here in relation to any joint life policy that pays out only on the death of the survivor, or where the deceased was entitled to benefit under a policy on the life of someone else who is still alive. In either case, the value of the deceased's interest is part of their estate—the amount concerned will have to be obtained from the insurance company issuing the policy, a copy of which should be attached to the form. The total value of all such policies is entered at IP2.

The values at IP1 and IP2 are totalled at IP3, and this figure is carried to Box F16 on Form IHT 200.

14.21.9.3 Box 3

In most cases, payments under a purchased life annuity will cease on death. However, if the payments are guaranteed for a fixed period and the death occurs before this has expired, they continue. The value of the right to receive the remaining payments should be included here and the total at IP4 carried to Box F15 on IHT 200.

14.21.9.4 Box 4

In some cases, a lump sum may be payable to the estate under a purchased life annuity. If so, the details should be given here and the total at IP5 carried to Box F23 on IHT 200.

14.21.9.5 Box 5

If the deceased was paying premiums on a life policy for the benefit of someone else (other than their spouse) each premium paid within seven years of the deceased's death will be a transfer of value. In many cases, there will be no tax liability because the normal expenditure exemption (see **7.6.3.4**) will apply. The necessary information should be supplied on Form D3 (**14.21.3**).

14.21.9.6 Box 6

If the deceased was entitled to a benefit from a life policy on someone else's life and held in trust, that right may be settled property in which case details must be provided on Form D5 (see **14.21.5**).

14.21.10 Form D10 (p 337)

This should be completed where the deceased owned any household or personal goods (though if such items were owned jointly, the value should be included on Form D4—see **14.21.4**).

Household and personal goods include:

(a) antiques and works of art (including paintings, drawings, sculptures, porcelain, glass, silver etc.);

(b) jewellery;

(c) collections of (e.g.) books, stamps, coins;

(d) cars, caravans, boats;

(e) TV, audio and video equipment, cameras;

(f) all other furniture, household and domestic items (including electrical goods, clothes, garden equipment, tools).

There is no need to provide details of any items passing on the death to the deceased's spouse: only an approximate value for such items need be given and spouse exemption claimed on page 4 of IHT 200.

14.21.10.1 Box 1

Where any household goods etc. have been already sold, the gross proceeds of sale should be inserted at HG1. If any items have been sold for less than market value, the figure must be increased to reflect the open market value of the items concerned.

The figure from box HG1 is carried to Box F19 on IHT 200.

14.21.10.2 Box 2

The information required here relates to unsold household goods. If a valuation has been obtained, a copy should be attached and the total value inserted at Box HG2. In other cases, the items should be listed (in the groupings above) and a total identified for each group. The grand total should then be entered in Box HG2. The figure from HG2 is carried to Box F20 on IHT 200.

14.21.10.3 Box 3

One of the boxes should be ticked in answer to the question: the personal representatives must inform the Capital Taxes Office about any sales by them or the beneficiaries within a reasonable time after death where the gross sale price differs from that included in Box HG2.

14.21.10.4 Box 4

If the unsold items have not been professionally valued, the basis upon which the values have been arrived at must be disclosed here.

14.21.11 Form D11 (p 338)

This form must be completed where the deceased had the right to a legacy or a share in the residuary estate of someone who had died before them, but had not actually received their entitlement before their death. If the deceased had more than one such entitlement, a separate form should be completed in respect of each other estate.

14.21.12 Form D12 (p 339)

This form should be used to give details of all the land, buildings and interests in land owned by the deceased. If a professional valuation has been obtained a copy should be attached.

14.21.12.1 Box 1

The Capital Taxes Office usually refers the valuation of land to the local District Valuer: the name and address of the person that the District Valuer should contact (e.g. the person who has provided any professional valuation) should be entered in this box.

14.21.12.2 Box 2

Each property should be sequentially numbered and the details requested entered in the appropriate columns—continuing over the page, or even on additional forms, if necessary. Property owned outright by the deceased and jointly with others may both be included on the same form: where jointly owned, the extent of the deceased's share should be identified in column B and its value in column F. If the property is let, a copy of the lease should be provided.

14.21.12.3 Box 3

The question concerning damage to any of the listed properties that might have affected their value must be answered, and if 'Yes' the details supplied.

14.21.12.4 Box 4

The question concerning sales/intended sales should be answered: if 'Yes' the properties concerned should be identified in column G (using the same identity numbers as in Box 2) and the present state of the sale (sold, on the market or to be sold later) indicated in column H. The remaining columns in this box need only be completed if the property has already been sold.

14.21.13 Form D13 (p 341)

This form must be completed if agricultural property relief (see **7.5.3.5** and **7.5.3.6**) is being claimed for any of the land included in the deceased's estate. The Capital Taxes Office requests that a plan of any such property is attached. In practice, if several properties qualify it may be easier if separate forms are completed for each one. A separate form must be completed if the relief is claimed for any lifetime transfer.

14.21.13.1 Boxes 1 and 2

The address of the property should be disclosed in Box 1 and the questions in Box 2a and (if the answer to 2a is 'No') in 2b should be answered. A 'No' answer to both 2a and 2b means that agricultural property relief would not normally be available. However, where the deceased had inherited the property or the property had replaced other agricultural property the relief may still be available. If either of these circumstances is relevant to the particular case, this should be disclosed in Box 2c.

14.21.13.2 Boxes 3 to 5

Details of when and how the deceased acquired the property should be given in Box 3 and the nature of the agricultural activities carried out on the land by the deceased described in Box 4. This information is required so that the Capital Taxes Office can satisfy itself that the relief is available: only property occupied for the purposes of agriculture qualifies. Box 5 need only be completed if the answer given to the question in Box 2a is 'No'.

14.21.13.3 Boxes 6 to 8

Where the deceased was entitled to vacant possession of the land at the date of death, or the property was let after 31 August 1995 the relief available is 100 per cent. If the land was let prior to 1 September 1995 it would normally only qualify for 50 per cent relief. However, in such cases it might still be eligible for the higher relief if the deceased would have been able to claim vacant possession within 24 months of the date of death (e.g. because the tenancy was due to end within that period of time). If the answer to the question in Box 6 is 'Yes' an explanation of how the deceased would have been able to claim vacant possession must be included.

As we have seen (in **14.21.13.2**) agricultural property relief is only available for property occupied for the purposes of agriculture and this applies to the farmhouse and farm cottages as well as the farmland. The information required in Box 7 is necessary to establish whether such properties will indeed qualify for relief.

In Box 8 it is necessary to indicate whether or not contracts for the sale of (any part of) the land had been exchanged prior to the death. If so, agricultural property relief would not be available for land contracted to be sold. If the answer to the question is 'Yes' details should be provided.

14.21.13.4 Box 9

This box need only be completed if relief is being claimed in connection with a lifetime transfer. The purpose of the various questions is to enable the Capital Taxes Office to determine whether the various conditions enabling the claim to be made are met.

14.21.14 Form D14 (p 343)

This form must be completed where business property relief (see **7.5.3.1–7.5.3.4**) is claimed. A separate form should be completed for each type of business interest for which relief is claimed.

14.21.14.1 Boxes 1 to 3

These boxes should be completed in all cases. In Box 1 the type of business interest concerned should be identified.

If the answer to the question in Box 2 is 'No', business property relief is not normally available because the deceased will not have owned the property long enough to qualify. However, where the deceased had inherited the property or the property had replaced other property that qualified for the relief it may still be available: if either of these circumstances is relevant to the particular case, this should be disclosed in Box 2.

In Box 3 it is necessary to disclose whether (any part of) the business interest concerned was at the date of death subject to a binding contract for sale. If so, business property relief will not be available and details of the contract should be supplied.

14.21.14.2 Box 4

This must be completed where the business interest concerned is a holding of unquoted shares or securities. The name of the company, the number and type of shares and their value should be stated, together with (if known) the company's registration number.

14.21.14.3 Box 5

This box must be completed where the business interest concerned is a business or a partnership interest.

The last set of accounts prepared before the death is the best starting point for the valuation of the business. The value of the deceased's business or partnership interest is the sum of the deceased's capital and current accounts (a copy of the last two years' accounts should be attached). The value of the deceased's business or partnership interest should be stated in Box 5a at BR1 and carried to Box G7 on Form IHT 200 in the case of a farming business, or Box G8 in the case of any other type of business.

The identity and main activity of the business should be disclosed in Box 5b (business property relief is not available for businesses or partnerships that deal in investments or properties). The way in which the value of the business or partnership interest has been calculated should also be explained here.

If the interest is a partnership interest, details of the terms of the partnership should be given in Box 5c, and a copy of any partnership agreement should be attached. The question as to sale of the business etc. in Box 5d should also be answered by ticking the appropriate box.

14.21.14.4 Box 6

This should be completed where the relief is claimed for land or buildings, plant or machinery belonging to the deceased but used by a partnership of which the deceased was a member, or by a company that the deceased controlled.

In Box 6a the relevant assets should be described and their value given. The value(s) should be carried to the appropriate box at G9 on Form IHT 200. The information requested in Box 6b enables the Capital Taxes Office to determine whether the conditions for the availability of the relief are met.

14.21.14.5 Box 7

This box need only be completed if relief is being claimed in connection with a lifetime transfer. The purpose of the various questions is to enable the Capital Taxes Office to determine whether the various conditions enabling the claim to be made are met.

14.21.15 Form D15 (p 345)

This must be completed if the deceased died domiciled in the UK and owned assets abroad.

14.21.16 Form D16 (p 347)

This form must be completed where a deduction is claimed on form IHT 200 for certain types of debts. They include loans from close friends or relatives; bank loans and overdraft facilities; where the deceased stood as a guarantor for any person; and certain debts created on or after 18 March 1986 which are the subject of anti-avoidance rules.

14.21.17 Form D17 (p 348)

This form should be used as a continuation sheet or to give additional information requested by the Capital Taxes Office. Any entries on this form should be cross-referenced to the box number on Form IHT 200 or the relevant supplementary page number to which the information given relates.

14.21.18 Form D18 (p 350)

This form must be completed in every case (other than an excepted estate) where application is being made for a grant in England and Wales (or Northern Ireland).

14.21.18.1 Sections A and B

In Section A the details of the solicitor or other contact person should be copied from Section C of IHT 200, and the name of the relevant probate registry from Section A of that form.

In Section B the required details relating to the deceased should be copied from Section B of IHT 200.

14.21.18.2 Section C

The figures are copied as indicated from the various boxes in IHT 200. The purpose of this is to identify the values to be shown for the gross and net estate for probate purposes in the appropriate form of Oath (see **14.13.9**).

The figure at PS3 is the gross estate and that at PS6 is the net estate. These figures will also appear in the grant itself when issued by the relevant probate registry, along with the figure for the total tax and interest paid on the account shown at PS7.

Section C must also be signed and dated.

For our purposes, the reference to 'any general power property' should be ignored as being an issue beyond the scope of this book.

Inland Revenue
Capital Taxes Office

The Will

Name

Date of death / /

Give details about the latest Will made by the deceased. If a Deed of Variation has been signed before applying for a grant, fill in the form to show the effect of the Will and the Deed together. You should read form D1(Notes) before filling in this form.

1 Is the address for the deceased as shown in the Will the same as the address on page 1 of form IHT200? No ☐ Yes ☐

If the answer is "No", say below what happened to the property shown in the Will.

2 Are all items referred to in the Will, for example, legacies referring to personal possessions, stocks and shares, loans or gifts made by the deceased, included in form IHT200? N/A ☐ No ☐ Yes ☐

If the answer is "No", say below why these items are not included.

3 Does the whole estate pass to beneficiaries who are chargeable to inheritance tax? No ☐ Yes ☐

If the answer is "No", deduct the exemption on form IHT200.

D1

42171 12.99 Guilbert UK R0G4113

Inland
Revenue
Capital Taxes Office

Domicile outside the United Kingdom

Name

Date of death

/ /

You have said that the deceased was not domiciled in the United Kingdom. Answer the following questions and give the further details we ask for. You should read form D2(Notes) before filling in this form.

1 Write a brief history of the life of the deceased. If the deceased was female, and had married at any time on or before 1 January 1974, include a history of the life of the deceased's husband (or husbands) while she was married and up until 1 January 1974.

2 Was the deceased domiciled in the UK at any time during the 3 years up to the date of death? No ☐ Yes ☐

3 Was the deceased resident in the UK for income tax purposes during the 3 years up to the date of death? No ☐ Yes ☐

If the answer is "Yes" give details of any periods that the deceased was treated as resident in the UK during the last 20 years.

Please turn over

42172 12.99 Guilbert UK R0H4183

D2

4 Who will benefit from the deceased's estate under the law that applies in the country of domicile?

5 Do you claim surviving spouse exemption? No ☐ Yes ☐

If you have answered "No" go on to question 6 below. If you have answered "Yes", provide the details we ask for below.

5a Give brief details of the property the surviving spouse will receive following the death.

5b Was a community of property established in the foreign country? No ☐ Yes ☐

If you have answered "No" go on to question 6. If you have answered "Yes" give full details of the rights each party to the marriage had over property.

5c Was any property under the community situated in the UK at the date of death? No ☐ Yes ☐

If you have answered "Yes" give full details of the property.

5d Has the form IHT200 been completed on the basis of the community? No ☐ Yes ☐

6 Did the deceased leave any assets of any description outside the UK? No ☐ Yes ☐

If so, give their approximate value. £

7 Do you expect the terms of a Double Taxation Convention or Agreement to apply to any or all of the foreign assets owned by the deceased? No ☐ Yes ☐

8 Is any foreign tax to be paid on assets in the UK as a result of the deceased's death? No ☐ Yes ☐

Inland Revenue
Capital Taxes Office

Gifts and other transfers of value

Name

Date of death
/ /

You have said that the deceased had transferred assets during their lifetime. Answer the following questions and give the further details we ask for. You should read form D3(Notes) before filling in this form.

1 Did the deceased within seven years of their death

1a make any gift or transfer to, or for the benefit of, another person? No ☐ Yes ☐

1b create any trust or settlement? No ☐ Yes ☐

1c pay any premium on a life insurance policy for the benefit of someone else other than the deceased's spouse? *(see also form D9, question 5)* No ☐ Yes ☐

1d cease to have any right to benefit from any assets held in trust or in a settlement? No ☐ Yes ☐

If the answer to any part of question 1 is "Yes", fill in the details we ask for below

Date of gift	Name and relationship of recipient and description of assets	Value at date of gift	Amount and type of exemption claimed	Net value after exemptions
			Total LT1	£

D3

Please turn over

42173 12.99 Guilbert UK R0H4164

Gifts with reservation

2 Did the deceased transfer any assets during their lifetime but

2a the person receiving the gift did not take full possession of it, or — No ☐ Yes ☐

2b the deceased continued to have some right to benefit from all or part of the asset? — No ☐ Yes ☐

If the answer to either part of question 2 is "Yes", fill in the details we ask for below.

Date of gift	Name and relationship of recipient and description of assets	Value at date of death	Amount and type of exemption claimed	Net value after exemptions

Total LT2 £

Earlier transfers

3 Did the deceased make any *chargeable* transfers during the 7 years before the earliest date of the gifts shown at boxes LT1 and LT2 above? — No ☐ Yes ☐

If the answer to question 3 is "Yes", fill in the details below, ***but do not include the value in any of the tax calculations.***

Date of gift	Name and relationship of recipient and description of assets	Value at date of gift	Amount and type of exemption claimed	Net value after exemptions

Inland Revenue
Capital Taxes Office

Joint and nominated assets

Name

Date of death / /

Give details of any assets that the deceased owned jointly with another person or people. If necessary use a separate form for each item. Give details of any property that the deceased had nominated during their lifetime. You should read form D4(Notes) before filling in this form.

1 Bank and building society accounts, stocks, shares, unit trusts, household effects etc

If the value of the deceased's share is **not** the **whole** value, say

- who the other joint owner(s) is or are
- when the joint ownership began
- how much each joint owner provided to obtain the item
- who received the income or interest, if there was any
- who received the benefit of any withdrawals from bank or building society accounts, if any were made
- whether the item passes to other joint owner(s) by survivorship or under the deceased's Will or intestacy.

Details of each item	Whole value	Deceased's share

- Liabilities

Total of assets JP1 £

Total of liabilities JP2 £

Net assets *(box JP1 less box JP2)* JP3 £

- Exemptions and reliefs

Total exemptions and reliefs JP4 £

Net total of joint assets ***passing by survivorship*** **where tax may not be paid by instalments** *(box JP3 less box JP4)* JP5 £

D4

Please turn over

42174 12.99 Guilbert UK R0H4165

2 Land, buildings, business assets, control shareholdings and unquoted shares

Do you wish to pay tax on these assets by instalments? **No** ☐ **Yes** ☐

If the value of the deceased's share is **not** the **whole** value, say

- who the other joint owner(s) is or are
- when the joint ownership began
- how much each joint owner provided to obtain the item
- who received the income, if there was any
- whether the item passes to other joint owner(s) by survivorship or under the deceased's Will or intestacy.

Details of each item	Whole value	Deceased's share

Total of assets JP6 £

- Liabilities

Total of liabilities JP7 £

Net assets *(box JP6 less box JP7)* JP8 £

- Exemptions and reliefs

Total exemptions and reliefs JP9 £

Net total of joint assets ***passing by survivorship*** **where tax may be paid by instalments** *(box JP8 less box JP9)* JP10 £

3 Nominated property

If the deceased nominated any assets to any person, describe the assets below and show their value.

Include the assets in the appropriate box in section F of form IHT200.

Inland Revenue
Capital Taxes Office

Assets held in trust (settled property)

Name | **Date of death** / /

You have said that the deceased had a right to benefit from a trust created by a deed or under someone else's Will or intestacy. Answer the following questions and give the further details we ask for. If necessary, use a separate form for each trust. You should read form D5(Notes) before filling in this form.

1 Give the

- full name of the person who created the trust or who died before the deceased
- date the trust was created, or date of death of the person who died earlier, and
- name(s) of the trustees and the name and address of their solicitors.

2 **Settled property where tax may not be paid by instalments**

- Assets

Total of assets SP1 £

- Liabilities

Total of liabilities SP2 £

Net assets *(box SP1 less box SP2)* SP3 £

- Exemptions and reliefs

Total exemptions and reliefs SP4 £

Net total of settled property where tax may not be paid by instalments *(box SP3 less box SP4)* SP5 £

D5

Please turn over

42175 12.99 Guilbert UK R0H4166

3 Settled property where tax may be paid by instalments

Do you wish to pay tax on these assets by instalments? **No** ☐ **Yes** ☐

- Assets

Total of assets SP6 £

- Liabilities

Total of liabilities SP7 £

Net assets *(box SP6 less box SP7)* SP8 £

- Exemptions and reliefs

Total exemptions and reliefs SP9 £

Net total of settled property where tax may be paid by instalments *(box SP8 less box SP9)* SP10 £

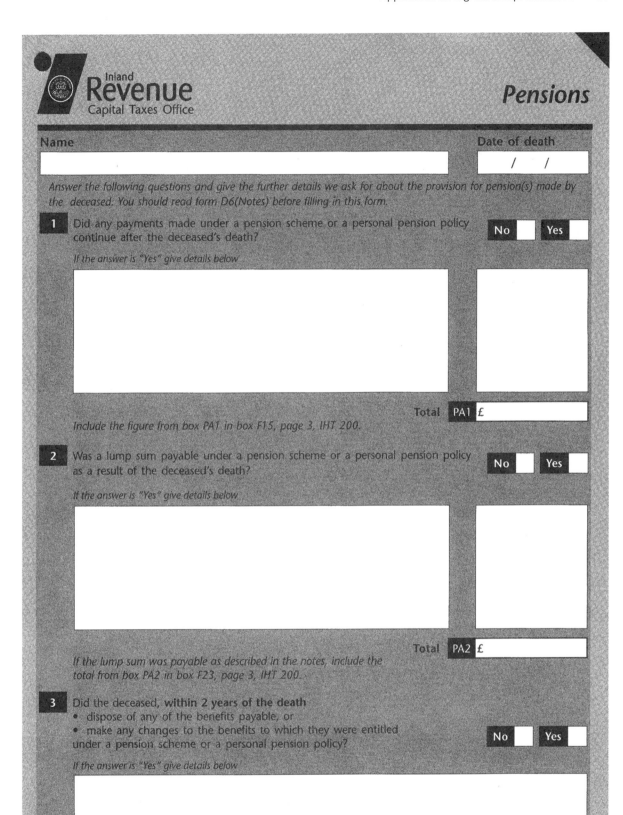

Inland Revenue
Capital Taxes Office

Pensions

Name

Date of death / /

Answer the following questions and give the further details we ask for about the provision for pension(s) made by the deceased. You should read form D6(Notes) before filling in this form.

1 Did any payments made under a pension scheme or a personal pension policy continue after the deceased's death? No Yes

If the answer is "Yes" give details below

Total PA1 £

Include the figure from box PA1 in box F15, page 3, IHT 200.

2 Was a lump sum payable under a pension scheme or a personal pension policy as a result of the deceased's death? No Yes

If the answer is "Yes" give details below

Total PA2 £

If the lump sum was payable as described in the notes, include the total from box PA2 in box F23, page 3, IHT 200.

3 Did the deceased, **within 2 years of the death**
- dispose of any of the benefits payable, or
- make any changes to the benefits to which they were entitled

under a pension scheme or a personal pension policy? No Yes

If the answer is "Yes" give details below

D6

42176 12.99 Gulbert UK R0J4121

Inland Revenue
Capital Taxes Office

Stocks and shares

Name

Date of death / /

Give details about the stocks and shares included in the deceased's estate. You should read form D7(Notes) before filling in this form.

1 Quoted stocks, shares and investments *(see box 2 for government securities)*

Name of company and type of shares or stock, or **full** name of unit trust and type of units	Number of shares or units or amount of stock held	Market price at date of death	Total value at date of death	Dividend or interest due to date of death	For CTO use only
		Total(s) SS1	£	£	

Copy the total from box SS1 to box F1, page 3, form IHT200.
Include the total of all dividends and interest in box F5, page 3.

D7

Please turn over

42177 12.99 Guilbert UK R0H4167

2 UK Government and municipal securities

Description of stock	Amount of stock £	Market price at date of death	Total value at date of death	Interest due to date of death	For CTO use only
		Total(s) SS2	£	£	

Copy the total from box SS2 to box F2, page 3, form IHT200.
Include the total of all dividends and interest in box F5, page 3.

3 Unquoted stocks, shares and investments

Name of company and type of share or stock	Number of shares	Price per share	Total value of shares	Dividend due to date of death	For CTO use only

Include the value of the shares in box F3, page 3 or box G11, page 5, form IHT200.
Include the total of all dividends in box F5, page3.

4 Traded unquoted stocks and shares

Name of company and type of share or stock	Number of shares	Price per share	Total value of shares	Dividend due to date of death	For CTO use only

Include the value of the shares in box F4, page 3 or box G12, page 5, form IHT200.
Include the total of all dividends in box F5, page 3.

Inland Revenue
Capital Taxes Office

Debts due to the estate

Name

Date of death / /

Give details about any debts owed to the deceased. Use a separate form for each loan or mortgage. You should read form D8(Notes) before filling in this form.

1 On what date was the original loan made? / /

2 What was the original value of the loan on that date? £

3 What was the value of the loan, including any interest due, still outstanding at the date of death? DD1 £

Copy the total from box DD1 to box F10 or F11, page 3, form IHT200.

4 If you do not think that the value in box DD1 should be included as part of the deceased's estate, say why in the box below. If you wish to include a reduced value in box F10 or F11, page 3, form IHT200, show how that value is calculated.

5 Give the name(s) of the borrower(s) and say whether they were related to the deceased.

6 Is there evidence to prove the existence of the loan? No Yes
If the answer is "Yes" give details below

7 Was interest charged on the loan? No Yes
If the answer is "Yes" give details below

8 Was any capital repaid to the deceased during their lifetime? No Yes
If the answer is "Yes" give details below

D8

42178 12.99 Guilbert UK R0G4112

Inland Revenue
Capital Taxes Office

Life insurance and annuities

Name

Date of death / /

Give details about the life insurance policies and annuities that the deceased paid premiums for. You should read form D9(Notes) before filling in this form.

1 Were any sums payable by insurance companies to the estate as a result of the deceased's death? No ☐ Yes ☐

If the answer is "Yes" give details below

Total IP1 £

2 Was the deceased

2a a life assured under a joint life insurance policy which continues after death, or No ☐ Yes ☐

2b entitled to benefit from a life insurance policy on the life of another person where the policy continues after death? No ☐ Yes ☐

If the answer to either part of question 2 is "Yes" give details below

Total IP2 £

Total value for life insurance policies *(box IP1 plus box IP2)* IP3 £

Copy the total from box IP3 to box F16, page 3, form IHT200.

D9

Please turn over

42179 12.99 Guilbert UK R0H4168

3 Did any payments made under a purchased life annuity continue after the deceased's death?   No ☐ Yes ☐

If the answer is "Yes" give details below

Total   IP4 £ _____

Include the total from box IP4 in box F15, page 3, form IHT200.

4 Was a lump sum payable under a purchased life annuity as a result of the deceased's death?   No ☐ Yes ☐

If the answer is "Yes" give details below

Total   IP5 £ _____

Include the total from box IP5 in box F23, page 3, form IHT200.

5 Did the deceased, within 7 years of their death, pay any premium on a life insurance policy for the benefit of someone else, other than the deceased's spouse?   No ☐ Yes ☐

6 Did the deceased have some right to benefit from a life insurance policy taken out on another person's life and held in trust for the benefit of the deceased (and others)?   No ☐ Yes ☐

If the answer to either question 5 or 6 is "Yes" you should read form D9(Notes) to find out what you should do.

Inland Revenue
Capital Taxes Office

Household and personal goods

Name

Date of death / /

Give details about the household goods or other personal property owned by the deceased. You should read form D10(Notes) before filling in this form.

1 If any household goods and other personal possessions have **already been sold**, fill in the **gross** sale proceeds below.

Gross proceeds of sale HG1 £

Copy the value from box HG1 to box F19, page 3, form IHT200.

2 If you have obtained any valuation(s) of the household goods and other personal possessions that have not been sold, enter the total figure in the box below.

If no valuation has been obtained, give brief details of the items and their value.

Total value of household and personal goods unsold HG2 £

Copy the value from box HG2 to box F20, page 3, form IHT200.

3 Are any of the unsold items going to be sold? Unknown ☐ No ☐ Yes ☐

4 Say below how the value for the unsold items has been established. If you have given a low total value, or the value is "Nil", say why this is so.

D10

42180 12.99 Quilbort UK R014120

Inland Revenue
Capital Taxes Office

Interest in another estate

Name | Date of death / /

Give details about the right the deceased had to a legacy or share in an estate of someone else who died before them, but which they had not received before they died. You should read form D11(Notes) before filling in this form.

1 Full name of the person who died earlier (the 'predecessor')

2 On what date did the predecessor die? / /

3 State CTO reference of the earlier estate, if known

4 What was the deceased's entitlement from the other estate?

5 Had the deceased received any part of their entitlement before they died? No Yes

If the answer is "Yes", give details of the assets that the deceased had received before they died

6 Details of the entitlement the deceased had still to receive

Net value UE1 £

Copy the total from box UE1 to box F21, page3, form IHT200.

D11

42193 12.99 Gulbert UK R0G4111

Inland Revenue
Capital Taxes Office

Land, buildings and interests in land

Name

Date of death / /

CTO reference

Give the details we ask for about the land included in the deceased's estate. You should read form D12(Notes) before filling in this form.

1 Name and address of the person that the Valuation Office should contact

Reference

Telephone number

2

A Item No.	B Full address (including postcode) or description of property	C Tenure	D Lettings/leases	E Agricultural, timber or heritage element	F Open market value
			Total(s) carried forward	£	£

D12

Please turn over

42181 12.99 Guilbert UK R0H4169

A Item No.	B Full address (including postcode) or description of property	C Tenure	D Lettings/leases	E Agricultural, timber or heritage element	F Open market value
			Total(s) brought forward	£	£
			Total(s)	£	£

3 Were any of the properties subject to any damage that may affect their value? **No** ☐ **Yes** ☐

If the answer is "Yes", fill in the box below using the same item number(s) that you have used in column A above.

Item No.	Details of damage

4 Have any of the properties been sold, or do you intend to sell any of them within 12 months? **No** ☐ **Yes** ☐

If the answer is "Yes", fill in table below using the same item number(s) that you have used in column A above.

G Item No.	H Present position of sale	I Sale price	J Type of sale	K Price for fixtures, carpets and curtains	L Use sale price as value

Inland Revenue
Capital Taxes Office

Agricultural Relief

Name

Date of death / /

You have deducted agricultural relief on form IHT200. Answer the following questions and give the further details we ask for. If necessary, fill in a separate form for each item of property. You should read form D13(Notes) before filling in this form.

1 What is the address of the property concerned?

2a Did the deceased own and occupy the property for the purposes of agriculture *throughout* the 2 years up to the date of death? No ☐ Yes ☐

If the answer is "Yes" go to question 3 and ignore question 5. If "No", go to question 2b.

2b Was the whole of the property occupied for agricultural purposes *throughout* the 7 years up to the date of death? No ☐ Yes ☐

If the answer is "Yes", go to question 3 and ignore question 4. If "No", go to question 2c.

2c As you have answered "No" to questions 2a and 2b, agricultural relief would not normally be available. If you feel the relief should be due, say why below.

3 When and how did the deceased acquire the property?

4 Describe the nature and extent of the agricultural operations carried out by the deceased.

5a Who occupied the property during the 7 years up to the date of death?

5b Describe the nature and extent of the agricultural operations carried out on the land

D13

Please turn over

42182 12.99 Guilbert UK R0K4135

5c Provide a copy of any lease, tenancy or other proprietary interest that applied to the property immediately before the deceased died. If there is nothing in writing, give details below. If the tenancy began after 31 August 1995, you need only give the date the tenancy started.

6 Did the deceased have the right to vacant possession immediately before the death, or the right to obtain it within 24 months? No ☐ Yes ☐

If the answer is "Yes" say how the deceased would have been able to obtain vacant possession. If the answer is "No", but you feel relief is due at the higher rate, say why below.

7 Who occupied any farmhouse or cottage at the property and what was the nature of the occupation? Provide details for each building separately.

8 Was the property, or any part of it, subject to a binding contract for sale at the date of death? No ☐ Yes ☐

If the answer is "Yes", give details of the contract below

9 ***Only answer question 9 if you are claiming agricultural relief in connection with a lifetime transfer.***

9a Was the property agricultural property immediately before the end of the relevant period? No ☐ Yes ☐

9b Was the property owned by the person who received the gift throughout the relevant period? No ☐ Yes ☐

9c Was the property occupied (by the person who received the gift or by someone else) for agricultural purposes *throughout* the relevant period? No ☐ Yes ☐

9d Was the property subject to a binding contract for sale immediately before the end of the relevant period? No ☐ Yes ☐

Inland Revenue
Capital Taxes Office

Business relief, business or partnership interests

Name

Date of death / /

You have deducted business relief on form IHT200. Answer the following questions and give the further details we ask for. If necessary, fill in a separate form for each business, holding of shares or business asset concerned. You should read form D14(Notes) before filling in this form.

1 Tick one of the boxes below to show the type of business interest concerned.

- ☐ a holding of unquoted shares *(see question 4)*
- ☐ an interest in a business *(see question 5)*
- ☐ the whole business, *(see question 5)*
- ☐ land or buildings, plant or machinery used by a business or company *(see question 6)*

2 Did the deceased own the shares or business interest *throughout* the two years up to the death? No ☐ Yes ☐

If the answer is "No", business relief would not normally be due. If you feel that business relief should still be due, say why below.

3 Was the business, interest in a business, shares, assets, or any part of them, subject to a binding contract for sale at the date of death? No ☐ Yes ☐

If the answer is "Yes", give details of the contract below

4 **Unquoted shares and securities**

What is the name of each company, the number, type and value of shares against which you have deducted business relief?

D14

Please turn over

42163 12.99 Guilbert UK R0H4170

5   **Business or interest in a business**

5a What is the value of the deceased's business or interest in a business
        at the date of death?

        BR1 £ [   ]

        Include the total from box BR1 in either box G7 or G8, page 5, IHT200.

5b What is the name and the main activity of the business? How has the value for the business
        or interest in a business been calculated?

        [   ]

5c Is the business an interest in a partnership?   No [ ]   Yes [ ]
        If the answer is "Yes" give details below.

        [   ]

5d Is the business or interest in a business to be sold as a result of the death?   No [ ]   Yes [ ]

6   **Asset(s) owned by the deceased and used by a business or company**

6a Describe the assets owned by the deceased and used by a business or a company and give their value.

        [   ]   [   ]

        Include the value(s) in the appropriate boxes at G9, page 5, form IHT200.

6b What is the main activity of the business or company concerned and what was the extent of the
        deceased's interest in the business or company?

        [   ]

7   *Only answer question 7 if you are claiming business relief in connection with a lifetime transfer.*

7a Was the business, interest in a business, shares or asset concerned owned by
        the person who received the gift throughout the relevant period?   No [ ]   Yes [ ]

7b Would the business, interest in a business, shares or asset concerned have
        qualified for business relief if *the person who received the gift* had made a
        transfer of the property at the date of death?   No [ ]   Yes [ ]

7c Was the business, interest in a business, shares or asset concerned subject
        to a binding contract for sale immediately before the end of the relevant period?   No [ ]   Yes [ ]

Inland Revenue
Capital Taxes Office

Foreign assets

Name | **Date of death** / /

Give details about any assets situated outside the UK that the deceased owned. You should read form D15(Notes) before filling in this form.

1 Assets outside the UK where tax may not be paid by instalments

- Assets

Stocks, shares and securities

Total FP1

Other foreign assets

Total FP2

Total of assets *(box FP1 plus box FP2)* FP3 £

- Liabilities

Total of liabilities FP4 £

Net assets *(box FP3 less box FP4)* FP5 £

- Exemptions and reliefs

Total exemptions and reliefs FP6 £

Net total of foreign property where tax may not be paid by instalments *(box FP5 less box FP6)* FP7 £

Please turn over

42184 12.99 Gullbert UK R0K4134

2 Assets outside the UK where tax may be paid by instalments

Do you wish to pay tax on these assets by instalments? No ☐ Yes ☐

- Assets

Total assets FP8 £

- Liabilities

Total FP9 £

Net assets *(box FP8 less box FP9)* FP10 £

- Exemption and reliefs

Total exemptions and reliefs FP11 £

Net total of foreign property where tax may be paid by instalments *(box FP10 less box FP11)* FP12 £

Inland Revenue
Capital Taxes Office

Debts owed by the estate

Name

Date of death / /

You have deducted certain types of debts against the estate. Give the details of the debts we ask for below.
You should read form D16(Notes) before filling in this form.

1 Debts due to close friends or relatives

2 Loans and overdrafts

3 Guarantee debts

4 Debts created on or after 18 March 1986

D16

42185 12.99 Guilbert UK R0G4110

Inland Revenue
Capital Taxes Office

Continuation sheet for additional information

Name

Date of death
/ /

Use this form as a continuation sheet or to give any additional information that we ask for. Show the box number on form IHT200 or the supplementary page number the information relates to. You should read form D17(Notes) before filling in this form.

Box or page number	Additional information	£

D17

Please turn over

42186 12.99 Guilbert UK R0H4171

Box or page number	Additional information	£

Inland Revenue
Capital Taxes Office

Probate summary

Fill in this page to give details of the estate that becomes the property of the personal representatives of the deceased. It is this property for which the grant of representation is to be made. You should read form D18(Notes) before filling in this form.

A Name and address

Probate registry

Date of grant
(for probate registry use)

B About the person who has died

Title

Surname

First name(s)

Last known usual address

Date of death / /

Domicile

Postcode

C Summary from IHT200

Add the value of any general power property on form D5 to boxes PS1-PS5

Gross assets, section F, box 24	PS1	£
Gross assets, section G, box 13	PS2	£
Gross value to be carried to Probate papers *(box PS1 plus box PS2)*	PS3	£
Liabilities, section F, box F27	PS4	£
Liabilities, section G, boxes G14 plus G15	PS5	£
Net value to be carried to Probate papers *(box PS3 less box PS4 less box PS5)*	PS6	£
Tax and interest paid on this account, section J, box J19	PS7	£

Signature of person or firm calculating the amount due

Contact name and /or reference

Date / /

(For CTO use only)

CTO reference

EDP

Cashier's reference

CTO Cashiers

D18

42187 12.99 Guilbert UK R0G4109

14.22 The calculation of inheritance tax

14.22.1 Inheritance tax worksheet [IHT(WS)]

In order to complete this form, it will be necessary to copy figures, as directed, from IHT 200 and the various supplementary sheets in order to calculate the value of the estate for tax purposes. When the tax and any interest due has been calculated, the various figures relating to the value of the estate and the tax etc. should be copied to Sections H and J of IHT 200. Note that although the taxable values ignore pence, this is not the case with the calculations of the tax itself or any interest.

The Capital Taxes Office has issued a Guide (IHT 213) to assist in the completion of IHT(WS) and the calculation of the tax due. It has also issued some examples of inheritance tax calculations in Form IHT 214.

Form IHT(WS) should be retained when the account is sent to the Capital Taxes Office. **Form IHT(WS) is reproduced at pp 354–357 below.**

14.22.1.1 Working out the value of the estate

The value of the taxable estate is established on IHT(WS) under three headings:

Assets where tax may not be paid by instalments

(a) The estate in the UK (Box F30 on IHT 200);

(b) Joint property passing by survivorship (Box JP5 from Form D4);

(c) Foreign assets (Box FP7 on Form D15);

(d) Settled property on which the trustees wish to pay tax on delivery of the account (Box SP5 on Form D5).

These are totalled at box WS5.

Assets where tax may be paid by instalments

(a) The estate in the UK (Box G18 on IHT 200);

(b) Joint property passing by survivorship (Box JP10 from Form D4);

(c) Foreign assets (Box FP12 on Form D15);

(d) Settled property on which the trustees wish to pay tax on delivery of the account (Box SP10 on Form D5).

These are totalled at box WS10.

Other property taken into account to calculate the total tax

(a) Settled property where the trustees wish to pay the tax later (the remaining property included in Boxes SP5 and SP10 on Form D5);

(b) Gifts with reservation (Box LT2 on Form D3).

The chargeable estate (WS5 plus WS10 plus WS11 plus WS12) is entered at WS13. To this must be added the cumulative total of lifetime transfers (from box LT1 on Form D3) to give at WS15 the deceased's aggregate chargeable transfer.

14.22.1.2 Working out the total tax that is payable

The figure for the aggregate chargeable transfer (WS15) is entered in box WS16 and the tax threshold at the date of death (currently £242,000) in box WS17. The value chargeable to tax (i.e. at a rate above nil) (WS16 less WS17) is then entered at WS18. If this is a minus figure, write '0' in this box—there is no need to complete any more of the form because no tax will be payable. Otherwise, the tax due (WS18 p 40 per cent) is then entered at WS19.

At box WS20 it is necessary to state the amount of tax (included in the total entered at WS19) that is attributable to any lifetime transfers. If the total in box WS14 is less than that shown at WS17 (so that all the lifetime transfers are covered by the Nil Rate Band) the figure '0' should be entered at WS20 and the calculation can proceed straight to Box WS21. If, however, the total of lifetime transfers exceeds the tax threshold at the date of death it will be necessary to identify the tax attributable to them by completing boxes LT3 to LT6 on IHT(WS). If the figure to be entered in box LT5 is a minus figure, the figure '0' should be entered in boxes LT5, LT6 and WS20. Otherwise, the tax on lifetime transfers (LT5 @ 40 per cent) should be entered at LT6 and WS20.

If quick succession relief (see **7.9.3.2**) is claimed, this is calculated at the middle section on the final page of IHT(WS) and the figure shown there at SC6 entered in Box WS21.

The tax payable on the chargeable estate (WS19 less WS20 less WS21) is entered at WS22. If the answer is a minus figure, the figure '0' should be entered at WS22 and there will be no need to complete any further sections of the IHT(WS) as there will be no tax to pay.

14.22.1.3 Working out the tax that is payable on delivery of the account

It is now necessary to calculate the proportion of the total inheritance tax that is due on the delivery of the account, for example:

(a) the tax (for which the personal representatives are liable) attributable to the property where tax cannot be paid by instalments;

(b) the tax on any instalment property for which they are liable where the option is not being exercised;

(c) the tax on any instalment option property (where the option is being exercised) where an instalment has fallen due or will be due within one month of the delivery of the account.

If payment is late, interest will also be payable.

To find the tax attributable to any part of the estate multiply the amount of the capital concerned by the fraction A over B, where A is the total tax payable and B is the chargeable death estate.

Thus, the tax on the non-instalment option property at TX4 is found by multiplying the total from Box WS 5 by the total from Box WS22 over the total from Box WS13. If any double taxation relief is available in relation to foreign assets this is calculated in the final section of IHT(WS) and the amount entered at TX5. This is then deducted from that at TX4 to give, at TX6, the net tax payable. If any interest is due, this is calculated using tables provided by the Capital Taxes Office in IHT 213 and entered at TX7. This is added to the figure at TX6 to give at TX8 the total tax and interest now being paid.

If the instalment option is being exercised and the account is being submitted more than one month before the first instalment is due, the figure '0' should be written in each of the boxes TX12 to TX19 inclusive and the figure at TX8 inserted at TX20.

In other cases i.e. if the option is not being exercised or an instalment is already or imminently due, the process described above is repeated for the instalment option property. Thus, the tax on the instalment option property at TX12 is found by multiplying the total from WS 10 by the total from Box WS22 over the total from Box WS13. If any double taxation relief is available for foreign assets this is calculated in the final section of IHT(WS) and the amount entered at TX13. This figure is then deducted from that at TX12 to give at TX14 the net tax payable. The number of instalments now to be paid is entered at TX15 (if the tax is being paid in full, the figure '10' should be entered) and the total tax now payable (TX14 plus TX15) is indicated at TX16. If interest is due on an instalment, this is calculated using tables provided by the Capital Taxes Office in IHT 213 and entered at TX17: if more than one instalment is due additional interest will be payable and is indicated at TX18. This is added to the figures at TX16 and TX17 to give at TX19 the total tax and interest now being paid on the instalment option property.

The total tax and interest payable on the account will be the figure at TX8 plus the figure at TX19, and this total is entered at TX20.

Inland Revenue
Capital Taxes Office

Inheritance tax worksheet

Working out the value of the estate

Assets where tax may not be paid by instalments

- Estate in the UK *(box F30, form IHT200)* — WS1 £ — Copy to box H1 on IHT200
- Joint property – ***passing by survivorship.*** Copy the figure from box JP5 on form D4. If you have filled in more than one form D4, there is space here to copy the figure off each form. Total £ — WS2 £ — Copy to box H2 on IHT200
- Foreign assets – copy the figure from box FP7 on form D15. If you have filled in more one form D15, there is space here to copy the figure off each form. Total £ — WS3 £ — *Copy to box H3 on IHT200*
- Settled property – ***on which the trustees would like to pay tax now.*** Copy the figure from box SP5 on form D5. If you have filled in more than one form D5, there is space here to copy the figure off each form. Total £ — WS4 £ — *Copy to box H4 on IHT200*

Total of assets where tax may not be paid by instalments *(WS1 + WS2 + WS3 + WS4)* — WS5 £ — Copy to box H5 on IHT200

Assets where tax may be paid by instalments

- Estate in the UK *(box G18, form IHT200)* — WS6 £ — Copy to box H6 on IHT200
- Joint property – ***passing by survivorship.*** Copy the figure from box JP10 on form D4. If you have filled in more than one form D4, there is space here to copy the figure off each form. Total £ — WS7 £ — Copy to box H7 on IHT200
- Foreign assets – copy the figure from box FP12 on form D15. If you have filled in more than one form D15, there is space here to copy the figure off each form. Total £ — WS8 £ — *Copy to box H8 on IHT200*
- Settled property – ***on which the trustees would like to pay tax now.*** Copy the figure from box SP10 on form D5. If you have filled in more than one form D5, there is space here to copy the figure off each form. Total £ — WS9 £ — *Copy to box H9 on IHT200*

Total of assets where tax may be paid by instalments *(WS6 + WS7 + WS8 + WS9)* — WS10 £ — Copy to box H10 on IHT200

IHT(WS)

R0H4162CTO11/99

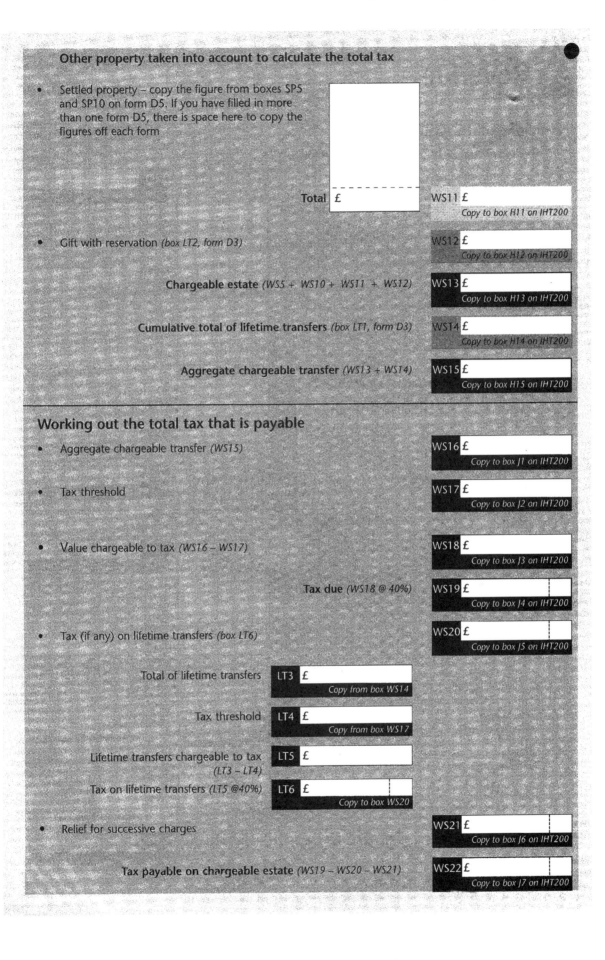

Other property taken into account to calculate the total tax

- Settled property – copy the figure from boxes SP5 and SP10 on form D5. If you have filled in more than one form D5, there is space here to copy the figures off each form

Total £ | WS11 £ *Copy to box H11 on IHT200*

- Gift with reservation *(box LT2, form D3)* | WS12 £ *Copy to box H12 on IHT200*

Chargeable estate *(WS5 + WS10 + WS11 + WS12)* | WS13 £ *Copy to box H13 on IHT200*

Cumulative total of lifetime transfers *(box LT1, form D3)* | WS14 £ *Copy to box H14 on IHT200*

Aggregate chargeable transfer *(WS13 + WS14)* | WS15 £ *Copy to box H15 on IHT200*

Working out the total tax that is payable

- Aggregate chargeable transfer *(WS15)* | WS16 £ *Copy to box J1 on IHT200*
- Tax threshold | WS17 £ *Copy to box J2 on IHT200*
- Value chargeable to tax *(WS16 – WS17)* | WS18 £ *Copy to box J3 on IHT200*

Tax due *(WS18 @ 40%)* | WS19 £ *Copy to box J4 on IHT200*

- Tax (if any) on lifetime transfers *(box LT6)* | WS20 £ *Copy to box J5 on IHT200*

Total of lifetime transfers | LT3 £ *Copy from box WS14*

Tax threshold | LT4 £ *Copy from box WS17*

Lifetime transfers chargeable to tax *(LT3 – LT4)* | LT5 £

Tax on lifetime transfers *(LT5 @40%)* | LT6 £ *Copy to box WS20*

- Relief for successive charges | WS21 £ *Copy to box J6 on IHT200*

Tax payable on chargeable estate *(WS19 – WS20 – WS21)* | WS22 £ *Copy to box J7 on IHT200*

Working out the tax that is payable on this account

Tax which may not be paid by instalments

- TX1 £ ____ (Copy from box WS5) X TX2 £ ____ (Copy from box WS22) / TX3 £ ____ (Copy from box WS13) = TX4 £ ____ (Copy to box J8 on IHT200)
- Double Taxation Relief — TX5 £ ____ (Copy to box J9 on IHT200)
- Net tax payable *(TX4 - TX5)* — TX6 £ ____
- Interest - date interest starts — IT1 / /
  - date interest ends — IT2 / /

IT3 Col 1	Col 2	Col 3	Col 4
Start and end dates for interest periods	No. of days	Daily rate	Interest payable
		Total	£

TX7 £ ____ (Copy to box J10 on IHT200)

Tax and interest now being paid *(TX6 + TX7)* — TX8 £ ____ (Copy to box J11 on IHT200)

Tax which may be paid by instalments

- TX9 £ ____ (Copy from WS10) X TX10 £ ____ (Copy from box WS22) / TX11 £ ____ (Copy from box WS13) = TX12 £ ____ (Copy to box J12 on IHT200)
- Double Taxation Relief — TX13 £ ____ (Copy to box J13 on IHT200)
- Net tax payable *(TX12 - TX13)* — TX14 £ ____
- Number of instalments being paid now — TX15 ____ / 10 (Copy to box J14 on IHT200)
- Tax payable now *(TX14 x TX15)* — TX16 £ ____ (Copy to box J15 on IHT200)
- Interest on instalments to be added

IT4 Col 1	Col 2	Col 3	Col 4
Start and end dates for interest periods	No. of days	Daily rate	Interest payable
		Total	£

TX17 £ ____ (Copy to box J16 on IHT200)

- Additional interest to be added

IT5 Col 1	Col 2	Col 3	Col 4
Start and end dates for interest periods	No. of days	Daily rate	Interest payable
		Total	£

TX18 £ *Copy to box J17 on IHT200*

Tax and interest now being paid *(TX16 + TX17 + TX18)* TX19 £ *Copy to box J18 on IHT200*

Total tax and interest now being paid on this account *(TX8 + TX19)* TX20 £ *Copy to box J19 on IHT200*

Working out Successive Charges Relief

Estate of first person to die

Net value of estate for inheritance tax SC1 £

Legacies paid out from estate SC2 £

Inheritance Tax paid on estate SC3 £

Deceased's entitlement from estate SC4 £

Rate of relief SC5 %

Formula for relief

SC3 £ / SC1 £ X SC4 £ X SC5 % = SC6 £

Working out Double Taxation Relief

Value of foreign property included in form IHT200 on which foreign tax has been paid (figure in sterling) DT1 £

Foreign tax paid (in sterling) DT2 £

Formula for relief

WS22 £ / WS13 £ X DT1 £ = DT3 £

The relief is the **lower** of boxes DT2 and DT3.

Printed in the UK by St Ives Direct, St Ives plc, R0H4162 CTO11/99

Inland Revenue
Capital Taxes Office

Checklist

Have you remembered to include, if appropriate?

The numbers refer to the forms and guides where we ask you to provide the information requested.

1 Any professional valuation of **stock and shares** - *page 13, "How to fill in form IHT200".* Yes ☐ N/A ☐

2 Any professional valuation of **household or personal goods** - *D10(Notes).* Yes ☐ N/A ☐

3 Any professional valuation of **land** - *page 22, "How to fill in form IHT200".* Yes ☐ N/A ☐

4 A copy of the **Will** if necessary - *D1(Notes).* Yes ☐ N/A ☐

5 A copy of any **insurance policy** (and **annuity,** if appropriate) where the deceased was paying the premiums for the benefit of someone else - *D3(Notes)* Yes ☐ N/A ☐

6 A copy of the **trust deed,** if the trustees are paying tax at the same time as you apply for the grant - *D5(Notes)* Yes ☐ N/A ☐

7 Any evidence of **money owed** to the deceased, including loan agreements and related trusts or policies and any evidence of debts being released - *D8(Notes)* Yes ☐ N/A ☐

8 A copy of any **joint life** insurance policy or policy on the life of another person - *D9(Notes)* Yes ☐ N/A ☐

9 A copy of any structural survey and/or correspondence with the **loss adjuster** about stucturally damaged property - *D11(Notes)* Yes ☐ N/A ☐

10 A plan of the property and a copy of the lease or agreement for letting (where appropriate) if you are claiming **agricultural relief** - *D13(Notes).* Yes ☐ N/A ☐

11 A copy of the partnership agreement (where appropriate) and the last two years' accounts if you are claiming **business relief** - *D14(Notes).* Yes ☐ N/A ☐

12 Any written evidence of **debts to close friends or family** - *D16(Notes).* Yes ☐ N/A ☐

13 Your **payment** of tax where you are calculating your own tax - *page 11, "How to fill in form IHT(WS)".* Yes ☐ N/A ☐

14 And please do not forget to sign page 8 of the **Inland Revenue Account** IHT200. Yes ☐

But do not send this checklist or form IHT(WS) to CTO.

CHK 1

42188 12.99 Gullbert UK R0G4108

14.22.2 Summary

In completing, where required to do so, Form IHT 200 and any necessary supplementary pages, you are, in effect, presenting the details of the taxable estate and (where tax is payable) the calculation of the tax in the manner which the Capital Taxes Office prefers and, indeed, requires. However, in essence, the process is that described in **7.9** to **7.11**. In summary, this involves:

(a) Identifying the chargeable value (i.e. after any available exemptions and reliefs have been claimed) of any lifetime chargeable transfers (including former PETs) within the seven years prior to the death.

(b) Identifying the value of the chargeable estate on death, which involves:
  - (i) establishing the gross value of all assets within the succession estate;
  - (ii) establishing the gross value of all property (of the kinds identified in **13.19**) which is not part of the succession estate but is part of the taxable estate;
  - (iii) deducting the value of any allowable debts, etc.;
  - (iv) deducting the value of property covered by an available exemption or relief from tax.

(c) Cumulating the chargeable estate on death with the total of lifetime chargeable transfers.

(d) Applying the current inheritance tax rate scale to that (combined) cumulative total.

(e) Identifying the tax for which the personal representatives/others are accountable:
  - (i) lifetime chargeable transfers (supplementary charge)—normally the trustees;
  - (ii) former PETs—normally the donees;
  - (iii) gifts with reservation of benefit—normally the donees;
  - (iv) trust property—normally the trustees;
  - (v) deceased's free estate—normally the personal representatives.

(f) Identifying the amount of tax to be paid by the personal representatives on delivery of the account:
  - (i) tax on the non-instalment option property in full;
  - (ii) tax on instalment option property;
    - (1) if option not being exercised, in full;
    - (2) if option being exercised, any instalment(s) already due;
  - (iii) any interest where payment late.

14.23 The Revenue's requirements: Checkpoints

1. Is the estate an 'excepted estate' (**14.19**)?
2. If not, use form IHT 200 (**14.20**) and supplementary pages as required (**14.21**).
3. Calculate any tax due (**14.22**).

14.24 Obtaining the grant: Practice

14.24.1 The early stages

We have already considered much of the practice involved in the early stages of the administration of an estate. At **14.24.2** to **14.24.4** we will endeavour to put those matters in context and consider other practical issues which may arise in the pre-grant period of the matter.

14.24.2 Early stages: Instructions

The personal representatives may (and frequently do) instruct a solicitor to act for them in the conduct of the administration. You may yourself be appointed an executor, or be a partner in a firm which has been appointed to act. In all of these cases you will have to ascertain the information you need to begin the task from the personal representatives or family members who may (especially initially) be in a distressed state. Whilst it is, of course, important that you perform your role efficiently, it is equally important that you conduct matters with sensitivity and with a proper concern for those who may not only be very upset but perhaps in temporary difficult financial circumstances resulting from the death.

14.24.2.1 What do you need to know?

Much of the information required to enable you to complete the first stage of the administration of the estate (obtaining the grant) will be apparent from the discussions in the previous sections of this chapter. In addition, you will also need to establish how and to whom the estate is to be distributed (**Chapter 13**), and whether any problems are likely to be encountered in this connection. There may, for example, be missing beneficiaries (see **15.6.2**) or the possibility of a claim under Inheritance (Provision for Family and Dependants) Act 1975 (see **13.22** to **13.29**).

14.24.2.2 Checklists

The best way to ensure the efficient collection of the information you need from the personal representatives or family members is to use a suitable checklist. Most firms will have their own version of such a checklist, which should prompt you to discover the details appropriate to any given case relating to the following matters:

(a) Full personal details relating to the deceased, the immediate family and any dependants.

(b) Full personal details relating to the proposed personal representative(s), and to beneficiaries entitled to share in the estate. In both cases, as we have seen, who these people are will very much depend upon whether or not there is a will.

(c) Details of the various assets:

- (i) in the deceased's succession estate (i.e. passing under the will or the intestacy rules);
- (ii) not in the succession estate but in the taxable estate (i.e. any property of which the deceased was a beneficial joint tenant, or in respect of which he/she had made a statutory nomination or a *donatio mortis causa*; any settled property of which the deceased had been a tenant for life);
- (iii) not forming part of the estate for either succession or taxation purposes (such as s 11 of the Married Womens' Property Act 1882 and other trust policies; certain lump sum pension scheme benefits).

(d) Details of the various liabilities due from the estate or charged upon any of the assets listed above.

(e) Details of any lifetime gifts within the seven years prior to the death (or at any time if a benefit was reserved).

14.24.3 Early stages: What else will you need?

In addition to the information identified above, you will need (as appropriate) the following:

(a) The death certificate—ideally several copies to enable you more speedily to register the death (see **14.25** below).

(b) The original will and any codicil(s). Your firm may already be holding these, or perhaps they have been lodged for safe keeping with the deceased's bank. Once obtained, it will be necessary to consider any issues of validity etc which may arise (see **13.2** to **13.7**) and whether affidavit evidence may be required to support the application (see **14.16**).

(c) Any 'paperwork' associated with the various assets and liabilities. Thus, for example, you will need the title deeds relating to any land (or at least to discover their whereabouts). Similarly, such things as share certificates, insurance policies, bank and building society account details, outstanding bills, etc. should be obtained.

(d) Details of any insurances (e.g. house and contents cover) effected by the deceased. Arrangements should be made, as soon as possible, either to have the interest of the personal representatives noted on any such policies, or for fresh cover in their name to be taken out. In the case of motor insurance, ensure (if needed) that appropriate cover is (or has been) arranged to enable family members to continue to use the vehicle.

14.24.4 Early stages: Financial difficulties?

Always check at the first interview whether the deceased's family have any immediate financial needs as a result of the death. It will be some weeks (perhaps months) before significant funds will become available from the estate: do any surviving spouse and children have access to adequate funds in the meantime?

What sources of funds might there be to assist here? Where the deceased had a joint bank or building society account with the surviving spouse, or the survivor has adequate funds of their own the problem may not be acute. Where there are funds which could be released without a grant (particularly, any s 11 of the Married Womens' Property Act 1882 or other trust policies; certain pension fund lump-sum benefits payable at the discretion of the trustees of the scheme) try to take the necessary steps to enable payment to be made as quickly as possible. Similarly, where a state or employment related 'pension' may be payable, deal with this as a matter of priority.

14.25 Registering the death

The first task upon receipt of instructions is to register the death with the various banks, building societies, insurance companies, etc. in which the deceased had investments and to establish the amounts due to the estate as at the date of death.

This is done by sending a copy death certificate (not a photocopy) to the various institutions with a request to inform you of the amount due—and to return the copy death certificate to you: however, where a special certificate has been issued by the Registrar (e.g. for National Savings or Social Security purposes) that certificate will be retained by the appropriate agency.

In the case of shareholdings, you should register the death with the various companies and ask them to confirm the extent of the deceased's holding: it may be that the personal representatives have not in fact located all the share certificates. You may then wish to instruct a stockbroker to prepare a valuation for you. Where the deceased owned land, the assistance of a surveyor may be required: it will be helpful in such a case if the surveyor can also give a valuation of the household and personal effects. Expert assistance in valuing the deceased's assets will also be necessary where, for example, the deceased was 'in business', whether as a sole trader or partner, or the business was conducted through the medium of a company.

The deceased's Inspector of Taxes should also be notified of the death: you will then usually receive a tax return to be completed in due course in respect of the pre-death period of the tax year in question and another relating to the post-death period: if the administration period stretches beyond the end of that tax year, further returns for the later years will be required.

At an early stage, you should also notify the various creditors of the death and that the estate is now responsible for the debts due to them. This will hopefully stop the family being further distressed by demands for payment.

If there is a will and there are beneficiaries other than those instructing you, you should inform them of their 'interest' under the will, and that—subject to the will being admitted to probate and the needs of the administration—you will be contacting them again as soon as you are able to deal with their legacies. It will be helpful if you give them an estimate of the timescale involved, being as realistic as possible in this. It is important to be cautious in what you say because the will might prove not to be admissible and/or there might not be sufficient funds to enable payment in full of all the legacies after the various liabilities have been discharged.

14.26 Preparing the papers to lead the grant

As confirmation of the amounts due to the estate is received, the appropriate Oath and Inland Revenue Account forms can be drafted, along with any other supporting evidence (such as affidavits and copy testamentary documents) which may be required in the particular case. Fair copies will have to be prepared for swearing or signature (as appropriate) before being lodged at the selected Registry.

14.27 Payment of inheritance tax

As we have seen, in order to obtain the grant the personal representatives will have to pay any inheritance tax due on the delivery of the Inland Revenue Account. However, they normally need the grant as evidence of their title—without which those holding the deceased's funds will be unwilling to part with them! How can the deceased's personal representatives solve this 'circular' problem? We saw in **14.4** that it is possible to obtain amounts due to the estate without production of a grant under Administration of Estates (Small Payments) Act 1965 and any such funds could be used to help pay the tax bill. However, it is likely in many cases that much more will be needed than can be raised in this way. In the following paragraphs we consider other sources of funding which may be available to the personal representatives.

14.27.1 Bank loan

Either the deceased's or the personal representatives' bank will normally be happy to lend whatever is needed to pay the inheritance tax. The bank will usually insist upon an undertaking from the personal representatives to account to it from the first proceeds of the realisation of the estate assets once the grant has been obtained. An undertaking may also be required from the solicitor acting for the personal representatives, in which event the solicitors should first obtain an irrevocable authority from the personal representatives.

The bank will of course charge interest, so that, irrespective of the terms of any undertaking the loan should be discharged as soon as possible. Provided the arrangement with the bank takes the form of a loan (rather than an overdraft facility) the personal representatives may be entitled to income tax relief for the interest payable.

14.27.2 Loan from beneficiary

A beneficiary may well be prepared (in order to mitigate or avoid the cost of bank borrowing) to lend money to help pay the inheritance tax (either interest-free or at a rate less than the commercial rate charged by the bank). (If interest is paid, it will also qualify for income tax relief in the manner described in **5.6.3**).

This approach will only work, of course, if the beneficiaries have money readily available—either from existing resources, or from monies passing to them on the death but outside of the will or the intestacy rules (such as the proceeds of a s 11 of the Married Women' Property Act 1882 or other trust policy; jointly held property accruing by survivorship; nominated property; lump-sum benefits under a superannuation scheme payable at the discretion of the trustees of the scheme).

14.27.3 Sale of assets

We saw in **14.3.1** that an executor's authority derives from the will, the grant merely confirming this: administrators, on the other hand, actually have their authority conferred by the grant. In principle, therefore, it is possible for an executor (but not an administrator) to sell estate assets prior to the issue of the grant: in practice, however, purchasers may well wish to see confirmation of the vendor's title before parting with their money! In particular, although it is possible to enter into a contract to sell land 'subject to probate', the grant will be needed to make the executor's title before the sale can be completed.

However, it may be possible for an executor to sell some assets before grant. A grant is not needed to pass title to chattels; this is achieved by delivery coupled with the necessary intention. Further, under Stock Exchange rules an executor can sell quoted shares before the grant is issued, subject to an undertaking for its production being given.

14.27.4 Direct payment to the revenue

Where the deceased's assets include monies held in a building society account or policies of life assurance whose proceeds are payable to the personal representatives, the building society or insurance company may be prepared to release some/all the monies due to the estate direct to the Revenue in payment of inheritance tax.

14.28 Swearing or affirming the oath

Remember that this must be done before an independent solicitor (or Justice of the Peace), and it will be a necessary formality also for any other affidavit evidence required. The fees payable are currently £5.00 per deponent for each Oath or other affidavit, plus £2.00 per deponent for marking each will, codicil or exhibit to any other affidavit.

14.29 Lodging the papers

When all is ready, it is necessary to lodge (by post or in person) at the selected Registry:

(a) the appropriate Oath;

(b) the Probate Summary (Form D18)—not required if an excepted estate;

(c) any further supporting documents, such as further affidavits, copy testamentary documents and renunciations;

(d) a cheque for the probate fees. Where the net estate does not exceed £5,000, no fee is payable. For larger estates, the fee is currently £50. Normally, the issue of one or more Office Copies of the grant should be requested on lodging the application. This will (*inter alia*) help to speed-up the process of registering the grant: the fee payable for each such copy is £1.

15

Post-grant practice

15.1 Duties and powers of personal representatives

As we have seen, it is generally necessary for personal representatives to obtain a grant of representation to establish title to the deceased's estate. Once the grant has been obtained, the personal representatives will need to know what duties and powers they have in the administration of the estate.

The Trustee Act 2000, which came into effect on 1 February 2001 but *in general applies to all trusts whenever created*, has significantly affected a number of the duties and powers discussed in **15.2** and **15.3** below. The 2000 Act, which by virtue of s 35 *also applies to personal representatives*, does not override any express provisions of the will or trust instrument: these may extend, modify or exclude the statutory provisions.

15.2 Duties of personal representatives

15.2.1 The fundamental duty of personal representatives

The fundamental duty of a personal representative is to 'collect and get in' the deceased's estate, and then 'to administer it according to law' (Administration of Estates Act 1925, s 25, as amended). This duty must be performed 'with due diligence'.

15.2.1.1 Duty to collect the deceased's assets

Within a reasonable time, taking such steps as may be reasonably necessary, the personal representatives must collect the monies due and other assets belonging to the deceased which vest in them. There is no absolute rule as what is a 'reasonable' in this context. Personal representatives will only be liable for loss resulting from their unreasonable conduct.

In practice, it will generally be necessary for the personal representatives to produce the original (or office copy) grant of representation to the persons who hold the deceased's assets, in order to establish entitlement to deal with such assets (see **14.3**).

15.2.1.2 Property of the deceased which does not vest in the personal representatives

The above duty only relates to the deceased's interests in property which devolve on the personal representatives. As we saw at **13.18**, certain types of property pass direct to those entitled on death and therefore does not vest in the personal representatives.

15.2.1.3 The duty to administer

Reasonable steps must be taken to preserve the deceased's estate, and within a reasonable time (*prima facie* within the 'executor's year'—the period of 12 months from the date of death) the personal representatives must realise any investments which it is not proper for them to retain.

Once the assets have been realised, administration of the estate thereafter involves the payment of debts, etc. and any legacies, and the distribution of the residue according to the terms of the will and/or the intestacy rules (see further **15.5** to the end of this chapter).

15.2.1.4 Other duties

Duties imposed by s 25 of the Administration of Estates Act 1925 relate to the preparation (when required to do so by the court) of an inventory and account, and the delivery up to the court of the grant issued (e.g. so that it can be revoked and a new grant issued) if called upon to do so. We have seen that the various forms of Oath which constitute (in effect) the application for the grant (discussed in **14.11** et seq.) contain statements acknowledging these duties.

15.2.2 The duty of care—Trustee Act 2000

Section 1 of the Trustee Act 2000 creates a new defined statutory duty of care applicable to trustees and personal representatives when carrying out their functions under the Act or equivalent functions under powers conferred by the will or trust instrument. They must act with such care and skill as is reasonable, bearing in mind any special knowledge or experience they have and, for professional trustees or personal representatives, any special knowledge or experience it is reasonable to expect them to have. This duty is in addition to the existing fundamental duties of trustees—e.g. to act in the best interests of the beneficiaries and to comply with the terms of the trust.

It is probable that the statutory duty does no more in effect than codify the common law duty of care so that the 2000 Act may make little difference in practical terms.

The statutory duty is a 'default' provision that may be excluded or modified by the trust instrument. Many professionally drafted wills and trust documents contain a clause excluding liability for breach of the standard of care, and it is anticipated that this practice will continue, with the effect that the beneficiaries of professionally drafted wills and trusts may be 'entitled' to a lower standard of care than that applicable to home-made efforts or on intestacy. The Trust Law Committee has recommended that paid trustees should not be able to rely on a clause excluding liability for negligence.

15.2.3 Statutory and equitable apportionments

Personal representatives may be under a duty to apportion income by virtue of s 2 of the Apportionment Act 1870, or under various equitable rules (such as the rules in *Howe v Earl of Dartmouth (1802)* 7 Ves 137, *Re Earl of Chesterfield's Trust* (1883) 24 ChD 643, *Allhusen v Whittell* (1867) LR 4 Eq 295. The former are designed to solve questions of ownership of, for example, dividends received after the date of death but which relate to a period partly before and partly after the death. The equitable rules only apply where property is left to persons in succession (for example, to Albert for life, remainder to Victoria) and are designed to achieve fairness between the interests of life tenants and remaindermen. You will doubtless have encountered the apportionment rules is your study of Equity and the Law of Trusts, and will perhaps be relieved to know that both the statutory and equitable rules of apportionment are commonly excluded by contrary provision in the will—it being generally considered that the inconvenience and cost of implementing them outweighs any benefit to the beneficiaries.

15.2.4 Liability of personal representatives

Having accepted office, a personal representative is liable to beneficiaries or creditors for loss resulting from his own breach of duty (whether that arises from a misappropriation of estate assets, maladministration or negligence). A personal representative is not liable for loss resulting from a breach of duty by fellow personal representatives, unless negligent in allowing such breaches to take place.

15.3 Administrative powers of personal representatives

The Administration of Estates Act 1925 confers upon personal representatives a number of powers in connection with the administration of an estate. In addition, the Trustee Act 1925, the Trusts of Land and Appointment of Trustees Act 1996 and the Trustee Act 2000 give certain powers to trustees—and since the definition of 'trustee' for the purpose of these Acts effectively includes a personal representative, personal representatives also have these powers. These statutory powers are implied in all cases, i.e. whether the deceased died testate or intestate. In some cases they are subject to awkward limitations and professionally drawn wills usually give the personal representatives wider powers. The principal statutory powers are outlined below, together with an indication, where appropriate, of the type of modification or express clause that will commonly be contained in a will.

15.3.1 Power of personal representative to sell, mortgage or lease

Section 39 of the Administration of Estates Act 1925 (as amended by the Trusts of Land and Appointment of Trustees Act 1996 and the Trustee Act 2000) confers upon personal representatives wide powers enabling them to sell or exchange any property, raise money by mortgage or charge, and grant or accept surrender of leases. These wide powers are necessary to enable the personal representatives to raise monies to pay a range of administration expenses (for instance, the payment of debts, funeral and testamentary expenses, inheritance tax and pecuniary legacies). The personal representatives must decide which assets should be sold (see further **15.8**).

15.3.2 Power to appropriate

15.3.2.1 The power

Section 41 of the Administration of Estates Act 1925 provides that personal representatives may appropriate any part of the estate in or towards satisfaction of any legacy or interest or share in the estate, provided no specific beneficiary is thereby prejudiced. The 'appropriate consents' are necessary: thus, if the beneficiary is absolutely and beneficially entitled, the consent of that beneficiary is required (or of the beneficiary's parent or guardian if a minor). The asset to be appropriated must be valued for this purpose at the date of appropriation rather than at death (*Re Collins* [1975] 1 WLR 309).

EXAMPLE 1

Tom leaves a pecuniary legacy of £5,000 to Beth. The residue includes shares now worth £3,000. Provided Beth consents, the shares can be appropriated to her in partial satisfaction of her legacy, the balance being paid in cash. However, this would not be possible if (for example) the shares concerned had been specifically bequeathed to Beatrice.

15.3.2.2 Provision in will

Wills commonly dispense with the need for the consents required by s 41 on the grounds of convenience.

15.3.2.3 Application of the 'self-dealing' rule

You will hopefully recall this rule (i.e. that a trustee may not purchase trust property) from your earlier study of the law of trusts. The justification for the rule lies in the potential conflict of interest that may arise.

In *Kane v Radley-Kane* [1998] 3 WLR 617 it was held that this rule applies equally to personal representatives. In this case, a widow took out letters of administration to her husband's estate. The assets included some shares in a private company, which she appropriated to herself in partial satisfaction of her statutory legacy. She subsequently sold the holding for almost ten times its value at the date of appropriation. It was held that the appropriation without the consent of the court or the other beneficiaries was invalid.

Thus, it will not be possible (unless authorised in the particular case by the will) for a personal representative to make an appropriation in his/her own favour in satisfaction of a pecuniary legacy—unless the assets appropriated are cash or the equivalent of cash (e.g. government stocks, plc shares).

15.3.3 Power to appoint trustees of a minor's property

Unless the will provides otherwise, a minor is unable to give a valid receipt for monies or assets transferred to the minor in satisfaction of a legacy. Neither does statute enable parents or guardians to give a valid receipt to the personal representatives on behalf a minor, although the will may authorise this. In the absence of any such provision in the will, personal representatives will normally have to hold the legacy until the minor attains 18, when of course a valid discharge can be given. To overcome this difficulty, s 42 of the Administration of Estates Act 1925 enables personal representatives to appoint trustees of the property for the minor, provided the minor has a vested interest. The personal representatives can then transfer the property to the trustees and a receipt signed by the trustees will be a valid discharge to the personal representatives.

15.3.3.1 Express provision in the will

Wills commonly provide that a parent or guardian may give a valid receipt on behalf of a minor beneficiary, or that the minor may personally give a receipt having reached a specified age (usually 16).

15.3.4 Section 15 of the Trustee Act 1925

This section gives personal representatives (and trustees) wide powers to settle claims made by or against the estate. This very useful power enables personal representatives to make a reasonable compromise instead of having to litigate in order to protect themselves against claims for breach of duty—subject to them having exercised the standard of care in Trustee Act 2000, s 1.

15.3.5 Power to insure

By s 19 of the Trustee Act 1925 (as amended by the Trusts of Land and Appointment of Trustees Act 1996 and the Trustee Act 2000, s 34) personal representatives may insure land and other property comprehensively and for its full value.

Insurance monies received under a policy of insurance are held as capital. They may be used to reinstate the property lost or damaged providing that the consent of any person whose consent is required to investment is obtained (Trustee Act 1925, s 20).

15.3.5.1 Express provision in the will

It is common for a will to provide for insurance of land and other property to full value, or reinstatement value, and against all risks. It may also provide that the property may be reinstated at the discretion of the personal representatives.

15.3.6 Power to delegate

15.3.6.1 Power to appoint agents

By s 11 of the Trustee Act 2000, personal representatives may collectively delegate all or any of their 'delegable functions' to an agent (such as a solicitor). 'Delegable functions' are any functions other than those relating to whether or in what way the estate assets should be distributed; decisions as to whether fees or other payments due should be made from capital or income; any power to appoint new trustees; and any power to delegate. By s 12, anyone (other than a beneficiary) can be appointed as agent, and if two or more people are appointed agents they must act jointly. Agents may be remunerated and employed on such terms as the personal representatives may determine (s 14) and s 15 directs that where an agent is engaged in 'asset management functions' (i.e. investment, acquisition or management of trust property) there must be an agreement evidenced in writing, to include a 'policy statement'—in effect, guidance as to how the agent should act in the best interests of the trust.

15.3.6.2 Review of and liability for agents

By virtue of s 21 of the Trustee Act 2000, the will may restrict the liability of personal representatives for the acts or omissions of their agent(s)—whether appointed under the authority of the statute or of a power in the will.

Subject to any inconsistent provision in the will, by virtue of Trustee Act 2000, s 22, personal representatives must keep under review the arrangements under which their agents act and how those arrangements are being put into effect. If asset management functions have been delegated, they have a duty to consider whether there is a need to revise or replace the policy statement (and if they consider there is such a need then to do so) and must assess whether the policy statement is being complied with by the agent(s). Further, if the circumstances make it appropriate to do so, the personal representatives must consider whether there is a need to exercise their power of intervention (in effect, to give directions to the agent(s) or to revoke the appointment), and if necessary to exercise such power.

Under s 23 of the Trustee Act 2000, personal representatives will not be liable for any act or default of the agent(s) unless they have failed to comply with the statutory duty of care applicable to them when appointing the agent or in carrying out their duties under s 22.

15.3.6.3 Section 25 of the Trustee Act 1925 (as substituted by s 5 of the Trustee Delegation Act 1999)

This allows personal representatives individually to delegate by power of attorney (on/after 1 March 2000) for a period not exceeding 12 months any of the duties, powers and discretion vested in them. In this case, however, the personal representative remains fully liable for the acts of the delegate.

15.3.7 Indemnity for expenses

By s 31 of the Trustee Act 2000, trustees and personal representatives may reimburse themselves for all expenses properly incurred when acting on behalf of the trust or estate on or after 1 February 2001.

15.3.8 Power to run the deceased's business

The position here will depend upon whether the deceased was a sole trader or ran the business through the medium of a partnership or limited company.

15.3.8.1 Where the deceased was a sole trader

The general rule is that personal representatives have no authority to carry on the deceased's business. As an exception to this rule, however, they may do so with a view to the proper realisation of the deceased's estate, for example, to enable it to be sold as a going concern. This would not enable them, normally, to carry on the business for more than the executor's year.

A power to carry on the business may be implied from the terms of the will, but it seems in such cases that personal representatives will only have authority to utilise assets used in the business at the date of death and will not be entitled to have resort to any other part of the estate for additional funds.

Personal representatives are personally liable for debts incurred in running the deceased's business after his death, though they are entitled to an indemnity from the estate.

15.3.8.2 Express provision in the will

The will may confer wider powers on the personal representatives—for instance, to run (indefinitely) the business as a going concern and to use a wider range of estate assets in running the business.

15.3.8.3 Where the deceased traded as a partner

The personal representatives will usually have no power to intervene in the business. The partnership agreement must be consulted as it will normally contain provisions relating to the succession to a deceased partner's share, which will therefore pass outside the terms of the will.

15.3.8.4 Where the deceased was a shareholder in a limited company

In such a case the company will, of course, continue despite the death of its shareholder. The Articles of Association should be consulted, as these may give other shareholders rights to purchase the deceased shareholder's shares.

15.3.9 Power to invest

15.3.9.1 The general power of investment

Like the other provisions of the Trustee Act 2000, the statutory power of investment is a default power: it is expressed to be additional to powers conferred by, but subject to any restrictions in, the trust instrument.

The 'general power of investment' contained in s 3 of the Act authorises trustees and personal representatives to make any kind of investment that they could make if they were absolutely entitled to the assets of the trust. However, it explicitly excludes investments in land other than by way of loan (though see further **15.3.9.3** below).

Most professionally drawn wills (and trust instruments) are likely to contain express powers of investment in terms similar to the default power, so that this will in practice be most beneficial to older trusts lacking appropriately wide express powers, home-made wills and cases of intestacy. It is likely that draftsmen will in future continue to use express investment clauses for a number of reasons. 'Investment' is not defined by the 2000 Act and the term will, as a result, cover whatever the common law from time to time determines. There could still, therefore, be doubt as to whether non-income producing assets constitute 'investment'. Alternatively, the testator may wish to restrict the trustees by ethical investment clauses preventing investment in, for example, the tobacco or arms industries.

15.3.9.2 The standard investment criteria

By virtue of s 4 of the Trustee Act 2000, trustees and personal representatives (whether exercising the statutory power or one conferred by the trust instrument) must have regard to 'the standard investment criteria'. They must also from time to time review the investments and consider whether, having regard to the standard investment criteria, they should be varied.

The standard investment criteria are:

(a) the suitability to the trust of the investment, and

(b) the need (to the extent that is appropriate in the circumstances) for diversification of the trust's investments.

Unless they reasonably conclude that in all the circumstances it is unnecessary or inappropriate to do so, personal representatives, before exercising the new statutory power or one conferred by the trust instrument, must (under Trustee Act 2000, s 5) obtain and consider proper advice about the way in which, having regard to the standard investment criteria, the power should be exercised. A similar requirement is imposed when reviewing the trust's investments. Proper advice is that of a person who is reasonably believed by the trustee to be qualified to give it.

15.3.9.3 Purchase of land

The purchase of land is not authorised by the general power of investment, but may be under an express power. However, the Trusts of Land and Appointment of Trustees Act 1996 effectively empowers personal representatives who are trustees of land (as defined) to purchase any legal estate in land in England and Wales for whatever purpose (including as a residence for a beneficiary). A similar default power (again expressed to be additional to powers conferred by, but subject to any restrictions contained in, the trust instrument) is given by the Trustee Act 2000, s 8, to personal representatives who are not trustees of land within the meaning of the 1996 Act.

Personal representatives are not given an express duty to take 'proper advice' when buying land, unless they are acquiring it as an investment when s 5 (**13.9.2** above) will apply.

Again, it seems likely that professional draftsmen will continue to use express clauses relating to the purchase of land containing powers to repair, improve and maintain property, matters which are not covered in the Act.

15.3.10 Power to maintain a minor

Section 31 of the Trustee Act 1925 provides that where property is held for a minor beneficiary and the gift carries the right to the intermediate income, the trustees or personal representatives may apply the income for the maintenance education or benefit of the minor, and must accumulate the income not so applied. The following points should be noted:

(a) It does not matter whether the minors's interest is vested or contingent.

(b) In exercising their discretion, the personal representatives must consider the age and requirements of the minor and the circumstances of the case generally, including what other income is applicable for the same purpose.

(c) Once the beneficiary attains the age of 18, accumulated income is normally added to capital and devolves with it (s 31(2)).

(d) If, although the minor has attained 18, the interest remains contingent, the discretion to use income for maintenance, etc. ceases, and henceforth the income *must* be paid to the beneficiary until such time as the contingency is fulfilled or the interest fails (s 31(1)).

(e) The statutory power it is only available to permit maintenance where the gift carries the intermediate income: most testamentary gifts will (in the absence of contrary provision in the will) carry such income. However, contingent pecuniary legacies generally do not, in which event s 31 will not apply: the intermediate income belongs in this case to the residuary beneficiaries.

EXAMPLE 2

In her will Tessa leaves £100,000 to her niece, Penny, contingently upon her attaining the age of 18, and the residue of her estate upon trust for her son, Rex, contingently upon his attaining the age of 25.

Both Penny and Rex are minors when Tessa dies.

The gift to Penny is a contingent pecuniary legacy, and unless it is one of the exceptional cases, or there is specific provision in the will, the statutory power to maintain is not available. The income will form part of the residue.

So far as Rex is concerned the statutory power is available, and the trustees may choose to pay the income yielded by the residue for Rex's maintenance. Any income not so paid over must be accumulated. When Rex reaches the age of 18 the power to maintain ceases, and the trustee must pay the current income to Rex until he reaches 25, or dies without having satisfied the contingency. If Rex attains the age of 25, he is then entitled to capital and accumulations.

15.3.10.1 Express provision in the will varying s 31

The statutory power may be considered to be adequate. The will may, however, commonly make the following modifications:

(a) conferring an absolute discretion on the trustees as to the amount of income available;

(b) removing the restriction as to the amount of income applicable where other funds are available.

(c) where the gift is contingent on the beneficiary attaining an age greater than 18, removing the right to receive income at 18.

15.3.11 Power to advance capital

Section 32 of the Trustee Act 1925 gives trustees and personal representatives a discretion to apply capital for the advancement or benefit of a beneficiary (whether or not a minor) who has a vested or contingent interest in capital. The following points should be noted:

(a) up to one-half of the beneficiary's vested or presumptive share may be advanced;

(b) any person with a prior interest (e.g. a life tenant) must consent in writing to the advance;

(c) any advance made must be brought into account when the beneficiary becomes absolutely entitled;

(d) if a beneficiary contingently entitled receives an advance but fails to fulfil the contingency (e.g. the beneficiary dies before attaining the age specified for vesting) the amount advanced is not recoverable from the beneficiary's estate;

(e) an advancement is a substantial payment made with a view to setting the recipient up in life: the term 'benefit' has been construed extremely widely. It may include (for example) a saving of tax: *Pilkington v IRC* [1964] AC 612.

15.3.11.1 Express provision in the will

The will may amend the statutory power by removing the first three limitations referred to in **15.3.11**. The statutory power does not of course enable advancements to be made to a life tenant, but this power may be granted by the will.

15.3.12 Exercise of personal representatives' powers

A sole personal representative (whether originally so appointed or by survivorship) has the same powers as two or more personal representatives. A sole personal representative may thus give a valid receipt for the proceeds of sale of land (Law of Property Act 1925, s 27). Joint personal representatives generally have joint and several authority, so that the act of one binds the others and the estate. However, there are statutory exceptions in relation to the conveyance of land and the transfer of shares: in these cases, the conveyance or transfer will normally require all living personal representatives (i.e. to whom a grant has been issued) to join in.

Personal representatives' powers are in nature fiduciary and, therefore, must be exercised in good faith in the interest of the estate as a whole.

15.4 Duties and powers of personal representatives: Checkpoints

1. Duties of personal representatives:
   (a) to collect the deceased's assets (**15.2.1.1**);
   (b) to administer the estate according to law (**15.2.1.3**);
   (c) statutory and equitable apportionments (**15.2.2**).
2. Powers of personal representatives:
   (a) Does the will contain modifications/additions to the statutory powers?
   (b) If not, statutory authority for power:
      (i) to sell, etc. (**15.3.1**);
      (ii) to appropriate (**15.3.2**);
      (iii) to appoint trustees of a minor's property (**15.3.3**);
      (iv) to settle claims (**15.3.4**);
      (v) to insure (**15.3.5**);
      (vi) to delegate (**15.3.6**);
      (vii) for indemnity (**15.3.7**);
      (viii) to run the deceased's business (**15.3.8**);
      (ix) to invest (**15.3.9**);
      (x) to maintain a minor (**15.3.10**);
      (xi) to advance capital (**15.3.11**).

15.5 Administering the estate

In **15.5** to **15.11**, we will begin our consideration of what happens once the personal representatives have received the grant from the issuing Registry. In **15.6** we will consider how the personal representatives may protect themselves against claims from potential beneficiaries or other claimants against the estate. In **15.7** we will outline the implications for personal representatives and solicitors acting for them of the compliance requirements under The Financial Services Act 1986 and the Solicitors' Investment Business Rules. The steps necessary to collect and realise the estates assets are then identified (**15.8**). In **15.9** we look at the rules governing the payment of debts where the estate is solvent; the position where the estate is insolvent is outlined in **15.10**. The section concludes with a brief look at ways in which post-death changes may be effected to the deceased's dispositions (**15.11**).

15.6 Protection of personal representatives

15.6.1 Against claims of unknown beneficiaries/creditors (Trustee Act 1925, s 27)

Even though they were not aware of the claims of a beneficiary or creditor at the time of distribution, the personal representatives remain personally liable to any unpaid beneficiary or creditor (*Knatchbull v Fearnhead* (1837) 3 M & C 122; 1 Jur 687). By complying with the requirements of s 27 the personal representatives can protect themselves against such liability. It is important, however, to appreciate that s 27 only affords protection to the personal representatives as such. Any disappointed beneficiary or creditor may recover from the person(s) to whom the personal representatives have distributed, including themselves if they are also beneficiaries.

In the case of an executor, whose authority derives from the will, advertisements under this section can (and to save time should) be made even before the grant is issued. Where the personal representatives are administrators they cannot properly do this, since they are authorised to act only by the grant itself. Once this has been issued, however, the placing of the required advertisements should be a matter of priority.

15.6.1.1 The advertisements

These are usually made by the solicitor acting for the personal representatives and on their behalf, requiring any person interested (as beneficiary or creditor) to send particulars to the personal representatives' solicitor within a stated time, which must not be less than two months from the date upon which the advertisement appears, after which time the estate will be distributed on the basis of claims of which the personal representatives then have notice (whether from a response to the advertisements or otherwise).

Such advertisements must be placed in:

(a) the *London Gazette*; and

(b) a newspaper circulating in the district in which any land forming part of the estate is situated (in practice, this will often be a local newspaper); and

(c) (in effect) any other newspaper, etc. (whether in this country or abroad) as might be appropriate to the particular case. Thus, for example, where the deceased had been in business it might be appropriate to advertise in a relevant trade journal. If the personal representatives are in doubt they should apply to the court for directions.

15.6.1.2 Searches

The personal representatives should also make such searches as a purchaser of land would make (s 27(2)). Searches should therefore be made in the Land Registry or Land Charges Registry; in the Local Land Charges Register; and a bankruptcy search against the deceased and the beneficiaries.

15.6.2 Against claims of missing beneficiaries/creditors

No protection, however, is afforded to personal representatives by s 27 where they are aware of the existence of claimants who simply cannot be found. In practice, the personal representatives should still make s 27 advertisements, but some further steps will be necessary to safeguard their position.

15.6.2.1 Payment into court

The personal representatives could pay the amount due to the missing beneficiary or creditor into court and distribute the rest of the estate in the normal way. The personal representatives will thereby achieve total protection, but from the viewpoint of the beneficiaries this is far from an ideal solution!

15.6.2.2 Indemnity

The personal representatives could distribute the whole of the available estate against an agreement by the beneficiaries to indemnify them in the event of the missing beneficiary or creditor subsequently appearing to claim their entitlement. This will certainly be more attractive to the beneficiaries, but is obviously risky from the standpoint of the personal representatives.

15.6.2.3 Benjamin Order

This is an order of the court giving the personal representatives leave to distribute the estate on the basis of an assumption set out in the order: in the case from which the order takes its name (*Re Benjamin* [1902] 1 Ch 723) the assumption was that a missing beneficiary had predeceased.

Before an application for such an order can be made, it will be necessary to make full enquiries for the missing claimant. In addition to the s 27 advertisements, the personal representatives should advertise for information in a newspaper circulating in the locality where the missing beneficiary was last heard of. The court may direct further enquiries and advertisements if it considers them to be necessary.

If the assumption in the order subsequently turns out to be wrong, the personal representatives are fully protected. The (no longer) missing beneficiary will have to seek his remedies against those to whom the estate has been distributed.

15.6.2.4 Insurance

As an alternative to a Benjamin Order, the personal representatives could seek cover against the risk of the missing beneficiary or creditor subsequently appearing. The insurance company will almost certainly require the same sorts of enquiries, etc. as the court might require before making a Benjamin Order. However, where the risk is not great (e.g. because the sum involved is not large or the chances of a claim being made are remote) this may be a cheaper and quicker solution than an application to the court. Indeed, the use of 'missing beneficiary insurance' in the case of small estates was specifically approved in *Evans v Westcombe* (Law Society *Gazette*, 10 March 1999) with the cost of the premium being a proper expense of the administration.

15.6.3 Other protection for the personal representatives

In relation to claims under the Inheritance (Provision for Family and Dependants) Act 1975, we have already seen at **13.24.2** that personal representatives are protected (should the court allow an 'out of time' application) if they have refrained from distributing the estate for six months after the issue of the grant. This does not, however, protect the beneficiaries to whom the the assets may have been distributed.

There are a number of situations where the personal representatives need protection against other possible claims from potential beneficiaries, creditors or other claimants. These include the following.

15.6.3.1 Future and contingent liabilities

Where personal representatives distribute with knowledge of such liabilities, they receive no protection under s 27 of the Trustee Act 1925. Where there is a known future liability, therefore, a fund should be set aside by the personal representatives to meet it.

A contingent liability might arise, for example, where the deceased had acted as a guarantor for the repayment of a loan, or there is a threat of legal proceedings against the estate. There are several possible courses open to the personal representatives to deal with such a problem:

(a) They could estimate the amount of the possible liability and set aside an appropriate amount—distributing the rest of the estate. This is really unsatisfactory on two counts:
  (i) an accurate estimate may be difficult (even impossible) to make;
  (ii) the beneficiaries will have to wait for payment of the full amount due to them until the danger of the liability arising has passed.

(b) They could distribute the whole estate subject to an agreement from the beneficiaries to indemnify them should the liability actually materialise. This (again) is not a course which should appeal to the personal representatives for (hopefully) fairly obvious reasons!

(c) If they wish to be able to distribute the whole estate (which is certainly what the beneficiaries would want) they could safely do so if they can arrange suitable (i.e. not too expensive) insurance cover.

(d) Failing this, the only other approach is an application to the court for directions.

15.6.3.2 Inheritance tax

The personal representatives can become liable for the inheritance tax on former PETs (and for the supplementary charge in respect of lifetime chargeable transfers) where the transferor dies within seven years, and the transferee has not paid the tax concerned within 12 months after the end of the month in which the transferor dies (**7.11**). A similar liability can also arise in respect of gifts with a reservation.

This potential liability is obviously something of which the personal representatives must take account. The trouble is, however, that (for example) the existence of a PET might not come to light until after they have distributed the estate (there is no obligation to report PETs in the transferor's lifetime). Further, the tax position on death may have been calculated on the assumption that there were no lifetime transfers: the discovery of the former PET may mean that the tax liability of the personal representatives in respect of the estate deemed to be transferred on death will also be increased.

The position of the personal representatives in such circumstances has been clarified by the Revenue (see statement in *The Law Society's Gazette*, 13 March 1991). Broadly, it seems that the Capital Taxes Office will not normally pursue the personal representatives for any further inheritance tax where they have made 'the fullest enquiries that are reasonably practicable in the circumstances' to discover lifetime transfers, and have obtained a certificate of discharge (see further **15.15.2.4**) and distributed the estate before the former PET comes to light.

Where the personal representative is a practising solicitor, some protection may be afforded by the Solicitors' Indemnity Fund (see *The Law Society's Gazette*, 7 March 1990).

15.6.3.3 Other cases

There are a number of other situations in which the personal representatives may be afforded protection; these are described in various practitioner works which you will need to consult in appropriate circumstances. These include:

(a) s 45 of the Adoption Act 1976 (distribution of estate in ignorance of an adoption order of which they do not have notice);

(b) liability for rent and breaches of covenant where the estate includes leasehold interests;

(c) where the court grants an application for rectification of a will under s 20 of the Administration of Justice Act 1982.

15.7 Financial services

We do not propose here to examine in any detail the framework of the Financial Services and Markets Act (FSMA) 2000 and the Financial Services and Markets Act 2000 Regulated Activities Order 2001 (RAO) discussed in **Chapter 2**. Remember that, in the case of solicitors who are exempt (under Pt XX of the FSMA 2000) as members of a profession regulated by a Designated Professional Body (DPB), the Act must be read in conjunction with the Solicitors' Financial Services (Scope) Rules 2001 (the Scope Rules) and the Solicitors' Financial Services (Conduct of Business) Rules 2001 (see **Appendix 2** and **Appendix 3**).

Our purpose here is to consider briefly the impact of the regime upon personal representatives and the solicitors acting for and advising them.

15.7.1 Personal representatives

Under s 19, FSMA 2000, there is a general prohibition against undertaking a 'regulated activity' (dealing, arranging, managing, or advising) in relation to investments unless the person carrying out the activity is authorised by the Financial Services Authority (FSA) or is exempt. Under the RAO, Article 66 exempts personal representatives (and trustees), provided that they receive no separate remuneration for such investment business and provided (in some cases involving professional personal representatives/trustees) that they do not advertise investment services. (Note, however, that Article 66 does not apply where solicitors are not themselves personal representatives/trustees but are merely acting for them.)

15.7.2 Solicitors

In practice, it is highly unlikely that any firm of solicitors engaging in probate and administration work could avoid carrying out investment business as defined by the FSMA 2000.

Thus, whether partners or employees of a firm are themselves the personal representatives, or are simply acting for the personal representatives, it is virtually impossible for them not to be managing investments—unless the particular estate comprised only assets that are not 'investments' for the purposes of the FSMA 2000 (e.g., land, works of art). Similarly, in whatever capacity partners or employees of the firm are involved, it is more likely than not that at some stage they may be called upon to give investment advice (e.g., as to whether to sell certain investments), or to arrange deals in investments (e.g., by arranging for the sale of certain shares by a stockbroker). It should be stressed that there is no bar on solicitors giving purely generic advice on investments (as opposed to advising in relation to a specific investment).

The question then arises as to whether the investment business is 'mainstream investment business'—such as advising a beneficiary on what investments to make with an inheritance received—or is 'non-mainstream investment business'. This is business that is incidental to the solicitor's main work, such as selling shares in an estate that the solicitor is administering. Mainstream investment business requires regulation by the FSA. Subject to certain conditions, solicitors carrying out only non-mainstream investment business can avoid this requirement provided they fall within the exemption in Pt XX of the 2000 Act for members of a profession regulated by a Designated Professional Body (DPB)—in the case of solicitors, The Law Society. For this exemption to apply:

(a) the investment business must be incidental to other services being provided by the solicitors which do not themselves constitute mainstream investment business;
(b) the solicitor accounts to the client for *all* commission received;
(c) the solicitor does not hold himself/herself out as offering investment services to clients.

Further, to avoid the need for regulation by the FSA, if the solicitor does in fact arrange or advise investments, this must be on the advice of an authorised person (such as a stockbroker or an independent financial adviser).

Rule five of the Scope Rules sets out further restrictions. For example, solicitors relying on the DPB exemption cannot recommend clients to buy packaged products (unit trusts, life policies, and stakeholder pensions), though it is possible to arrange such a transaction where the client is relying on independent advice from an authorised person. In addition, a solicitor managing the administration of an estate/trust must be careful to delegate the day-to-day decision-making in relation to investments to an authorised person (such as a stockbroker).

15.8 Collecting/realising the assets

15.8.1 Registering the grant

On the issue of the grant, the personal representatives now have their evidence of title and should proceed apace to register the grant with the various institutions (banks, building societies, insurance companies, etc.) holding the deceased's assets and obtain from them the sums due to the estate.

Office copies of the grant, bearing the seal of the Registry, should be used rather than the original: photocopies are not acceptable evidence! The original is an important document of title and therefore should so far as possible be protected from the risk of loss and kept in the file. However, the Inland Revenue certainly like to see the original.

Hopefully, you will have obtained enough office copies of the grant to enable this process to be completed swiftly. The absolute priority should be the release of sufficient funds to discharge any loan to pay the inheritance tax (**14.27**). After this has been done, normally you should aim to discharge interest bearing liabilities first so as to minimise the 'cost' to the estate.

As we have seen, the personal representatives' duty is to 'collect and get in' all the deceased's real and personal estate (and then administer it according to law). This must be done with 'reasonable diligence'. Unsecured debts due to the deceased should be collected as soon as practicable—the personal representatives taking proceedings for their recovery if necessary. There is no need to call in or realise loans secured on mortgages of land which are authorised investments, unless the money is needed to discharge the funeral, testamentary and administration expenses, debts and pecuniary legacies.

Where the estate's assets include a reversionary (i.e. future) interest under a trust, this should not be sold unless there is some special reason for doing so (e.g. that there are no other funds available for the payment of the various expenses and debts of the estate).

Generally, causes of action vested in the deceased at the date of death survive for the benefit of the estate (as do those subsisting against the deceased against the estate) (Law Reform (Miscellaneous Provisions) Act 1934, s 1(1)). The main exceptions relate to contracts for the provision of personal services and the tort of defamation.

The personal representatives may also have an action to recover damages on behalf of certain dependants where the deceased's death has been caused by a wrongful act in respect of which the deceased could have sued if still alive (Fatal Accidents Act 1976). Any damages recovered under this Act do not form part of the deceased's estate for any purpose, but 'belong' to the dependant's concerned.

The personal representatives (as we saw at **15.3.4**) have wide powers of settling claims made by or against the estate, so that they are not obliged to litigate every possible point or risk being held liable for not doing so.

15.8.2 Sales of assets

In order to be able to pay taxes and other liabilities, the personal representatives may have to sell assets in the estate. In principle, they are at liberty to use any assets coming into their hands for this purpose (see further **15.9** below). However, in practice there are a number of 'constraints' which they should bear in mind.

15.8.2.1 The will

The terms of any will should very much influence their decision. Thus, if the will makes specific gifts the property so given should not be sold unless other assets have been exhausted. Further, beneficiaries may have indicated a wish to receive particular assets in partial or total satisfaction of (as the case may be) a pecuniary legacy or share of residue. The personal representatives should endeavour to respect those wishes and avoid selling the assets concerned, if possible to do so.

15.8.2.2 Tax implications

You will have already encountered (in **7.9.1.7** and **7.9.1.8**) what are sometimes called 'loss on sale' reliefs for land and quoted securities sold within the prescribed statutory periods for less than their probate values. Where there are assets which might qualify for such relief, the personal representatives should consider whether to sell them and thus be able to reclaim any inheritance tax paid on the 'difference'. (If this relief is claimed, remember that no loss relief is available for capital gains tax purposes.)

Where personal representatives sell any assets during the course of the administration, there will *prima facie* be a charge to capital gains tax on gains accruing since the date of death. Such gains may be relieved from charge by the annual exempt slice: personal representatives have the same exemption as an individual (currently £7,100) for gains made on disposals in the tax year in which the death occurs and in the following two tax years. Thus, for example, if in March they are contemplating selling shares which show a gain of £10,000 since the date of death, they would be well advised to consider selling immediately sufficient to utilise the current year's exemption and the rest after 6 April.

Where personal representatives realise an allowable loss on a sale of estate assets, it may be set against their gains of that year and any amount not thereby absorbed is carried forward to be set against their gains in future tax years. Their loss cannot be passed on to the beneficiaries, so if it is possible that the personal representatives will not have sufficient gains to absorb any loss an alternative strategy should be considered. Where the asset concerned, instead of being sold, is vested in a beneficiary this is not a chargeable event and the beneficiary acquires at the value at the date of death. The beneficiary can then sell realising a loss to be set against any chargeable gains of the beneficiary.

15.9 Payment of debts (solvent estate)

A solvent estate is one where the assets are sufficient to cover in full the funeral, testamentary and administration expenses, debts and other liabilities. It is immaterial whether or not legacies can also be paid in full.

So far as the creditors (including secured creditors) are concerned, they are entitled to be paid what is due to them from any part of the estate available for the payment of debts. As long as they are paid, it does not matter to them upon what part of the estate the burden of the payment falls. However, this is a matter of considerable importance from the viewpoint of the beneficiaries. Thus, to take a simple example, if the will leaves Blackacre to Beatrice and the residue of the estate to Rosalind, it will matter very much to them who has to bear the burden of the debts—particularly if Blackacre is subject to a mortgage at the date of the testator's death. It is with the resolution of such problems that this section is concerned: as we shall see, the answer will depend upon whether (and what) provision is made in any will.

15.9.1 Secured creditors

We are here concerned with the situation where a debt has been charged on the deceased's property during the deceased's lifetime (for example, a mortgage on Blackacre).

Subject to the testator showing contrary intention (see **15.9.4**), by s 35 of the Administration of Estates Act 1925 the property so charged is liable for the payment of that debt. So, in the example above, Beatrice will *prima facie* take Blackacre subject to the mortgage debt. If the value of Blackacre is insufficient to cover the mortgage debt, the 'deficit' would have to be met by the residuary estate, so that Rosalind's entitlement would be correspondingly reduced.

15.9.2 Other debts: The statutory order, etc.

So far as unsecured creditors are concerned (again, subject to any express provision in the will (see **15.9.4**) the order in which the estate's assets should be used is laid down by s 34(3) and Part II of the First Schedule to the Administration of Estates Act 1925. These provisions draw no distinction between realty and personalty.

The order is as follows: if there is nothing in a given 'category', or what there is proves insufficient, you move on down the list.

(a) Property undisposed of by the will (subject to the setting aside of a fund from which to pay any pecuniary legacies). Thus, where a partial intestacy arises (because the deceased's will contains no residuary gift, or where such residuary gift has totally or partially failed) the property not disposed of by the effective provisions of the will is primarily liable for the payment of the unsecured debts of the deceased. However, it is only so much of such undisposed of property as is not set aside to pay any pecuniary legacies (see **15.14.2**) that is so liable.

(b) Residue (again, subject to the setting aside of a fund from which to pay any pecuniary legacies, i.e to the extent that these are not fully covered by the retention made under (a) above).

In most cases, this is as far down the order as you will need to go. However, if the assets comprised in (a) and (b) are insufficient, the list continues:

(c) Property specifically given for the payment of debts. Property is within this category if the will contains a direction that the identified property (e.g. Greenacre) is to be used to fund the payment of debts, but nothing is said as to what is to happen to any surplus.

(d) Property specifically charged with the payment of debts. Property falls within this category where the will contains a direction as in (c) above, but goes on to provide what is to happen to any surplus.

You may be pardoned for thinking that where the deceased has taken the trouble to identify specific property in the estate to fund the payment of debts, this would place such property firmly at the head of the list! Faced with the problem of reconciling logic with the statutory order, the courts have concluded that such a provision can only make the specifically given or charged property primarily liable where the will shows an intention to exonerate any property falling within categories (a) and (b) above (see further **15.9.4**).

(e) The pecuniary legacy fund (retained under (a) and/or (b) above). At this point, any such fund will be used to help pay the debts. Unless the testator has indicated that any such legacies are to be paid in priority, they will abate proportionately, so that each legatee bears a share of the burden of the payment.

(f) Property specifically devised or bequeathed, rateably according to the property's value (i.e. to the deceased) at the date of death. Thus, if Whiteacre (the subject of a specific gift in the will) is worth £100,000 and is subject to an outstanding mortgage of £25,000, its value for the purposes of this exercise will be £75,000.

(g) Property expressly appointed under a general power of appointment (again, rateably according to value). This category is rarely encountered in practice.

If needed, certain other categories of property may also be available for the payment of debts, but only after all the above categories have been exhausted. The categories include:

(a) *donationes mortis causa*;

(b) nominated property;

(c) property in respect of which an option to purchase has been given by the will (*Re Eve* [1956] Ch 479; 3 WLR 69; 3 All ER 321).

15.9.3 Marshalling

Where (as they are entitled to do) the personal representatives discharge a debt out of property within a category which is not—as between the beneficiaries—liable to bear the burden of that debt, the equitable doctrine of marshalling can be invoked by the disappointed beneficiary so as to ensure that the debt is (at the end of the day) born by the appropriate property. Thus, if the will makes a specific gift of some shares (within (f) in the list in **15.9.2** to Peter and these are in fact sold to pay the debts (although the residuary estate (which is listed at (b) in **15.9.2**) is sufficient to cover them), Peter will be entitled to 'compensation' from the residue.

15.9.4 Contrary provision

The above rules only apply in the absence of contrary provision in the will. What constitutes such provision?

15.9.4.1 Secured creditors

The effect of s 35 of the Administration of Estates Act 1925 can be avoided in several ways. Thus, the gift of Blackacre in our earlier example (in **15.9**) might have been expressed to be 'free of mortgage', in which event the mortgage would be repayable out of the residue. Alternatively, the will might have contained a direction to pay debts 'including any mortgage charged on Blackacre' out of residue. It is important to appreciate, however, that a simple direction to pay 'debts' from residue without specifically mentioning the charge on Blackacre would not oust s 35. On the other hand, where the testator has identified a particular fund other than residue for the payment of 'debts', this is *prima facie* sufficient to cover all debts including the mortgage on Blackacre. However, Blackacre would remain charged with the payment of any deficit if the particular fund proved insufficient to discharge the debt completely.

15.9.4.2 Unsecured creditors

There are three formulae likely to be met in practice for varying the statutory order, the first two being most commonly encountered. They are:

(a) gift of residue on trust or trust for sale with a direction for payment of debts out of the proceeds (before division amongst the beneficiaries);

(b) gift of residue 'subject to' or 'after' payment of debts.

In both of these cases, the effect will be to make the residue as a whole, including the property undisposed of by the will in the case of a partial intestacy, primarily liable for the payment of the debts.

(c) property 'given for' or 'charged with' payment of debts with intention to exonerate residue.

As we saw in **15.9.2** above, without some evidence of intention to exonerate residue such property remains in the third and fourth categories in the Statutory Order. However, provided this intention is clear, the property given or charged will become primarily liable.

15.10 Payment of debts (insolvent estate)

An estate is insolvent if the assets are insufficient to pay in full all the funeral, testamentary and administration expenses, debts and liabilities. Clearly, in such a case, the beneficiaries can receive nothing, and the creditors will not be paid in full. In what order are the creditors entitled to be paid?

This is a question of crucial importance for the personal representatives because if they pay 'out of order' they will *prima facie* incur personal liability for debts in a higher category that have not been paid (see further **15.10.3**). As a result, if there is any risk that the estate may prove to be insolvent it is necessary to be extremely careful strictly to observe the prescribed order for payment.

15.10.1 Secured creditors

Such creditors will in practice have a choice:

(a) They may simply rely on their security. Thus, for example, the mortgagee will rely on the (eventual) proceeds of sale of the mortgaged property to obtain repayment of the loan.

(b) They may realise their security (i.e. sell the property) and to the extent that this proves inadequate to join the 'queue' of unsecured creditors (see further **15.10.2**).

(c) They may (without selling) place a value on their security and seek payment of any deficit as unsecured creditors.

There is, in principle, a fourth choice—unlikely in practice often to be adopted: they could surrender their security and simply be treated as unsecured creditors!

To the extent that secured creditors rely upon their security to obtain repayment, they enjoy priority over the unsecured creditors.

15.10.2 Unsecured creditors

The order of priority—which cannot be varied by the testator—is governed by Administration of Insolvent Estates of Deceased Persons Order 1986.

The order of priority is:

15.10.2.1 Reasonable funeral, testamentary and administration expenses

By tradition, reasonable funeral expenses take precedence.

15.10.2.2 The bankruptcy order

Within each of the categories identified below debts rank equally. Personal representatives have no right to 'prefer' one creditor above the others in the same category, so that if there is insufficient to pay all the creditors in the given category in full, those debts abate proportionately, so that everyone receives (for example) 50p in the £ (see further **15.10.3**).

Under the bankruptcy order, debts rank as follows:

(a) Preferred debts. These include:

(i) Amounts due to the Inland Revenue in respect of PAYE deductions which the deceased was liable to make from wages or salaries of employees paid during the 12 months prior to the death.

(ii) Certain Social Security contributions which became due in the like period.

(iii) VAT referable to the period of six months prior to the death and certain Excise Duties due in the 12 months prior to death.

(iv) Wages and salaries of the deceased's employees in the period of four months prior to the death, up to a maximum in the case of each employee of (currently) £800.

(b) Ordinary debts. These are all other debts (except deferred debts) including the balance of any claim that does not rank as a preferred debt. Thus, for example, an employee who was owed wages of £1,000 could (subject to meeting the conditions above) claim £800 as a preferred creditor and the balance as an ordinary creditor.

(c) Interest on preferred and ordinary debts. The rate of interest will be the greater of the rate specified in s 17 of the Judgments Act 1838 at the date of death (currently 8 per cent) or the contractual rate applicable to the particular debt. Interest is payable from the date of death until payment, and the two categories rank equally for this purpose.

(d) Deferred debts. These are loans from the deceased's spouse, i.e. spouse at the date of death (the position at the date of the loan is irrelevant).

15.10.3 Protection of the personal representatives

If personal representatives pay (say) an ordinary debt having knowledge that there are preferred debts, the payment is an implied 'warranty' that there are sufficient assets to meet all the preferred debts of which they have notice (whether as a result of s 27 of the Trustee Act 1925 advertisements (**15.6.1**) or otherwise). If there are not sufficient funds to do this, the personal representatives are personally liable.

However, it has long been settled that they will not be personally liable where, without undue haste, they have paid an inferior debt without notice of a debt in a higher category (*Harman v Harman* (1686) 2 Show 492; 3 Mod Rep 115; Comb 35).

We have seen that personal representatives must not 'prefer' one creditor in a given category above any other in the same category. By s 10(2) of the Administration of Estates Act 1925, personal representatives are protected from liability to creditors of the same class where payment to others in that class has been made in full should the estate subsequently prove to be insolvent, provided that at the time of the payment the personal representatives were acting in good faith and had no reason to believe that the estate was insolvent. This protection is available even where a personal representative has paid a debt due to himself, unless the grant was taken as a creditor.

15.11 Post-death changes

At the beginning of the chapter we saw that the devolution of a person's estate will largely depend on whether that person has left a valid will or not. It may be, however, that when that person dies the dispositions effected by the will or intestacy, or otherwise, are unsuitable in some way. For example, they may fail to make adequate provision for the surviving spouse or another relative or dependant of the deceased; or it may be that the person entitled does not want the property which is left to them. Another possibility is that tax-saving opportunities will be wasted if the estate is distributed in accordance with the will or intestacy rules.

We have already noted (at **13.22** to **13.29**) the provisions of Inheritance (Provision for Family and Dependants) Act 1975. There are two further methods whereby alterations can be made to the dispositions of a deceased person's property after that person's death, and generally such alterations can be achieved without adverse inheritance and/or capital gains tax consequences.

15.11.1 Disclaimers

In the much quoted words of Abbot C.J. 'the law is not so absurd as to force a man to take an estate against his will' (*Townson v Tickell* [1819] B & Ald 31). A beneficiary under a will or intestacy can disclaim an interest that is not wanted provided no benefit has been taken from the gift. The right to disclaim is lost once any benefit has been accepted by the beneficiary, who cannot generally disclaim part only of a single gift (but may disclaim one of several gifts). All that is necessary for a disclaimer to be effective is for disclaiming beneficiaries to indicate their intention to refuse the gift either orally or in writing to the deceased's personal representatives. However, if the disclaimer is to be effective for inheritance tax or capital gains tax purposes, it must be in writing. The effect of a disclaimer is that the property will pass as if the disclaiming beneficiary had predeceased the testator or the intestate. In the case of a specific or pecuniary gift in a will, on disclaimer this will normally fall into residue. In the case of a residuary gift, the subject matter will pass under the intestacy rules (except in the case of a class gift or gift to joint tenants, when it will accrue to the other class members/joint tenants as appropriate). In both cases this is subject to contrary intention in the will.

A disclaimer of a gift under a will does not operate so as to prevent the person disclaiming receiving the property under the intestacy rules.

EXAMPLE 3

If residue is left by Tom, a widower, to his two children Ann and Ben in equal shares and Ann disclaims her share under the will, one-half of the residue will pass on Tom's intestacy. Ann's disclaimer of her entitlement under the will does not operate to prevent her taking under the intestacy, however, and if this is desired she will also have expressly to disclaim her entitlement on intestacy.

The disadvantage of a disclaimer is, then, that the original beneficiary has no control over the ultimate destination of the gift. If the intention is to benefit someone other than the person next entitled under the will or intestacy rules, a 'variation' (see **15.11.2**) will be more appropriate.

15.11.2 Variations

A variation is a direction by the original beneficiary to the personal representatives to transfer property that would otherwise be taken by the beneficiary to someone else. Normally a variation will be in writing, and commonly by deed.

Unlike a disclaimer:

(a) a variation is possible even though the original beneficiary has accepted a benefit;

(b) a partial variation of a gift is possible;

(c) the original beneficiary can control the destination of the property following the variation. Those taking under the variation do not have to be other beneficiaries or members of the deceased's family.

15.11.3 Inheritance tax and capital gains tax consequences

Prima facie, a disclaimer or a variation will constitute a transfer of value (usually a PET) for inheritance tax purposes and a disposal for capital gains tax. However, under s 42 of the Inheritance Tax Act 1984 and s 62 of the Taxation of Chargeable Gains Act 1992, it is possible to effect a disclaimer or variation without either of these consequences.

The conditions to be met are:

(a) the disclaimer/variation must be:
   (i) in writing;
   (ii) made within two years of death;

(iii) not made for any consideration (other than another disclaimer/variation) in money or money's worth;

(b) in the case of a variation only:

(i) notice claiming s 142 and/or s 62 relief(s) is given to the Revenue within six months of the variation (the Finance Bill 2002 contains proposals that will remove the need to give such notice in relation to variations made after 1 August 2002—provided the instrument of variation itself contains a statement of intent that the relief(s) should apply);

(ii) if the variation results in more inheritance tax being payable, the personal representatives must join in the election.

If all the relevant conditions are met, then:

(a) the disclaimer/variation is not itself a transfer of value and/or disposal;

(b) the inheritance tax and/or capital gains tax position will be determined as if the deceased had made the disposition now effected.

15.12 Administering the estate: Checkpoints

1. Protection of personal representatives:
   (a) Against claims of unknown beneficiaries/creditors (**15.6.1**).
   (b) Against claims of missing beneficiaries/creditors (**15.6.2**).
   (c) Against future or contingent liabilities (**15.6.3.1**).
   (d) Against liability for inheritance tax (**15.6.3.2**).
   (e) Against claims of unknown, adopted/illegitimate beneficiaries (**15.6.1**, **15.6.3.3**).
   (f) Against liability for rent and other breaches of leasehold covenants (**15.6.6.3**).
   (g) Against claims under the Inheritance (Provision for Family and Dependants) Act 1975 (**13.24.2**).
2. Financial services issues:
   (a) For personal representatives (**15.7.1**).
   (b) For solicitors acting as, or advising, personal representatives (**15.7.2**).
3. Collecting/realising the assets:
   (a) Registering the grant (**15.8.1**).
   (b) Which assets to sell (**15.8.2**).
4. Payment of debts—solvent estate
   (a) secured creditors (**15.9.1**);
   (b) unsecured debts—the statutory order and other property (**15.9.2**);
   (c) marshalling (**15.9.3**);
   (d) contrary provision in will (**15.9.4**).
5. Payment of debts—insolvent estate:
   (a) secured creditors (**15.10.1**);
   (b) unsecured creditors (**15.10.2**);
   (c) protection of personal representatives (**15.10.3**).

6. Post-death changes:
   (a) Inheritance (Provision for Family and Dependants) Act claims (**13.22** to **13.29**);
   (b) disclaimers (**15.11.1**);
   (c) variations (**13.28.2** and **15.11.2**);
   (d) inheritance tax and capital gains tax consequences (**15.11.3**).

15.13 Distributing the estate

In **15.5** et seq., we examined various practical issues surrounding the early and 'middle' stages of the administration of an estate once the grant has been issued—to the point where the various debts and liabilities were discharged. We also considered how personal representatives might protect themselves against claims for breach of their duty, and how changes might be effected to the deceased's dispositions otherwise taking effect on death.

In the remainder of this section, we will now consider the 'endgame'—the distribution of the estate to those entitled under the terms of the will or the operation of the intestacy rules.

Although we have arbitrarily divided up our consideration in this way, it is of course an artificial division: the process of winding-up an estate is a continuum with no 'natural breaks' or (necessarily) clearly definable stages (except, perhaps, 'pre-grant' and 'post-grant').

We will first look at some practical issues concerning the payment of the various legacies in any will (**15.14**). We will then consider how the residue (to which the residuary beneficiaries are entitled) is ascertained (**15.15**). Next, we will discuss estate accounts (**15.16**), assents (**15.17**) and financial services issues (**15.18**). Lastly, we will briefly discuss beneficiaries' rights and remedies (**15.19**).

15.14 Payment of legacies

Once the personal representatives are satisfied that assets are not needed for administration purposes (i.e. to pay the debts, etc.), they can give effect to the various specific, general and pecuniary gifts made by the will. An indication by them that a particular asset is not needed for the purposes of the administration is technically 'an assent' (see further **15.17**).

15.14.1 Specific legacies and devises

The property which has been specifically given by the will is vested in the beneficiaries entitled by the method appropriate to the assets concerned. Thus, for example, chattels will be transferred by delivery, and company shares by the completion of the appropriate stock transfer form—which with the share certificate(s) is lodged with the company's Registrar for registration of the change of ownership and the issue of a new share certificate. In the case of land, an assent in writing will be needed (see further **15.17.2**).

Unless the will otherwise provides, beneficiaries entitled to specific gifts will have to bear the costs of the transfer of the gifted property, and also the cost of its preservation and upkeep between the date of death and assent or actual transfer (*Re Rooke* [1933] Ch 970; *Re Pearce* [1909] 1 Ch 819).

However, specific beneficiaries are entitled to the income (if any) produced by the asset since the date of death. Thus, for example, on a specific gift of shares or land, the assent retrospectively passes to the beneficiary concerned any dividends or rent arising since the date of death.

15.14.2 Pecuniary legacies

In s 55(1)(ix) of the Administration of Estates Act 1925 the term 'pecuniary legacy' is defined so as to include general legacies; demonstrative legacies in so far as they cannot be paid from the designated fund; and any general direction for the payment of money (such as the inheritance tax on a specific gift which is to be free of tax). In this section we will use the term 'pecuniary legacy' as so defined.

The problem for the personal representatives in all these cases is essentially the same: from what part of the estate should they take the money to pay the beneficiary, or to purchase the subject matter of the general legacy, or to pay the inheritance tax? We have seen that there is a similar problem for the personal representatives in relation to the payment of the various debts and liabilities of the estate (see **15.9** and **15.10**.).

Unfortunately, the general law regarding the incidence of pecuniary legacies is sometimes far from clear. The problems centre upon the extent to which the pre-1926 rules have been displaced by the provisions of s 33 of the Administration of Estates Act 1925—an issue still not entirely resolved more than 70 years on!

The rules can be briefly summarised as follows.

15.14.2.1 Provision in the will

The will may (and if you ever have to grapple with the complexities which can arise you will doubtless (rightly!) conclude should) contain express provision as to the property to be used to fund the payment of pecuniary legacies. In practice, the formulae usually adopted for dealing with the payment of debts (**15.9.4.2**) are simply adapted to include legacies as well. So, if residue is to be the chosen source, the trust or trust for sale of the residuary estate will direct the payment out of the proceeds of 'debts and legacies' before division. Alternatively, the residue may be given 'subject to' or 'after payment of' the 'debts and legacies'. Any of these provisions will make the residue as a whole (including any lapsed share) primarily liable. Where a specific fund is identified, it can similarly be made liable for the payment of the legacies in addition to the debts.

15.14.2.2 No provision in the will

In practice, you will usually find that the rules effectively identify the residuary estate as the fund from which pecuniary legacies should be paid. However, the situation is not quite as simple as this statement implies, and there can be especially difficult problems where there is a partial intestacy. In any case where the will does not provide for which part of the estate should bear the burden of pecuniary legacies you will need to consult appropriate practitioner works to make sure you get it right!

15.14.3 Abatement

If the property identified under the rules discussed in **15.14.2** is insufficient to meet the pecuniary legacies in full, they will abate proportionately.

15.14.4 Appropriation

If a beneficiary wishes to have a particular asset from the estate in total or partial satisfaction of a pecuniary legacy given by the will, the personal representatives will normally be able to accede to the request by exercising the power of appropriation in s 41 of the Administration of Estates Act 1925, or that conferred by the will (see **15.3.2**).

15.14.5 Receipts

The personal representatives are entitled to a discharge from the beneficiaries, which normally is obtained by getting them to sign a receipt.

Beneficiaries who are under 18 cannot (unless the will otherwise provides) give a good receipt, nor can their parent, guardian or spouse do so for them. In such cases, it will be necessary for the personal representatives to adopt one of the following solutions:

(a) Hold the gifted property until the infant attains the age of 18 (in the case of a pecuniary legacy in the meantime investing in an authorised investment).

(b) Use the power of appropriation (in s 41 of the Administration of Estates Act 1925 or the will), with the infant's parent, guardian or (if none) the court giving any necessary consent (see **15.3.2**).

(c) Use the power in s 42 of the Administration of Estates Act 1925 to appoint trustees to receive and hold the property for the infant until 18 (see **15.3.3**).

(d) Obtain their discharge by payment of the legacy into court under s 63 of the Trustee Act 1925.

15.15 Ascertainment of residue

Once the various legacies have been paid, the personal representatives can direct their attention to establishing the amount available for distribution to the residuary beneficiaries. In order to do this, they will have to finalise the tax position and deal with the expenses of the administration.

15.15.1 Income tax and capital gains tax

The personal representatives will need to have dealt with two matters here.

15.15.1.1 The deceased's tax affairs

The deceased's income tax and capital gains tax liability must be finalised—with any further tax payable being paid, or any repayment due being recovered. In either event, an inheritance tax Corrective Account may be required (see **15.15.2.3** below).

15.15.1.2 The administration period

The personal representatives must make tax returns for each of the tax years which the administration spans and discharge any assessments.

15.15.2 Inheritance tax

Various issues concerning this tax will also need to be resolved.

15.15.2.1 The deceased's liability

Where the deceased at the date of death had an outstanding liability to inheritance tax, this will need to be discharged—and if met by the estate is an allowable deduction in arriving at the taxable estate on the death.

15.15.2.2 Recovery of tax

The personal representatives may be liable to pay tax on property where the burden of the tax is in fact to be borne by the beneficiary to whom the property passes on the death. This may happen, for example, because the will expressly makes the beneficiary responsible for the tax attributable to the value of the gifted property. It may also happen where the property passes outside of the will (for example, where the deceased's interest as a beneficial joint tenant accrues by right of survivorship to the surviving joint tenant(s)—though this is not a problem, of course, where it accrues to a surviving spouse). How can the personal representatives ensure that they recover for the benefit of the residuary estate the tax ultimately to be borne by others?

Where a pecuniary legacy is given 'subject to tax' the problem is easily resolved: the personal representatives simply withhold the appropriate amount and pay the net legacy to the beneficiary.

That solution is clearly not appropriate where there has been a specific legacy of, for example, Blackacre or a diamond necklace. In such cases, the personal representatives should not vest the asset in the beneficiary concerned until the tax has been paid or satisfactory arrangements have been made for their reimbursement.

If the property has passed by survivorship, the personal representatives may have a ready solution if other assets are due to the beneficiary concerned under the will or the intestacy rules: before they part with any such assets, they should ensure that they are paid, e.g. by deducting the amount due. Where there are no other amounts due to the beneficiary concerned, they may ultimately have to sue to recover the amount due.

15.15.2.3 Corrective accounts

Any variations in the value or content of the estate will need to be reported to the Capital Taxes Office on a Corrective Account (or by letter if the adjustments are minor). Any further inheritance tax then due will have to be paid, or any repayment due claimed.

15.15.2.4 Certificates of discharge

When the inheritance tax position has been finalised, the personal representatives should seek a discharge from any further liability to inheritance tax on Form IHT 30. This requests the issue of a Certificate of Discharge of the property in the estate and all persons liable from any further claims to inheritance tax. When given, the Certificate is an effective discharge except in the case of fraud, failure to disclose material facts, the subsequent discovery of further assets, or changes in the 'tax bill' arising as a result of any variations etc. discussed at **15.11**.

If the personal representatives have paid all the tax other than that attributable to instalment option property, a limited form of Certificate may be issued, expressed to be a complete discharge except for the outstanding tax on the instalment option property. In such cases, the personal representatives will need to ensure that there are appropriate arrangements to protect them against claims for future instalments. No Certificate of Discharge is necessary (nor should it be sought) where the estate is an 'excepted estate' (see **14.19**) so that no Inland Revenue Account was required to be submitted. In such cases, there is, as we saw, normally an automatic discharge 35 days after the issue of the grant, unless the Revenue calls for an account or it is subsequently discovered that the estate is not, after all, an excepted estate.

15.15.3 Administration expenses

The expenses of the administration, i.e. (in addition to reasonable funeral expenses) the properly incurred expenses of the personal representatives themselves in the carrying out of their duties, will have to be ascertained and met.

15.15.3.1 Reasonable funeral expenses

The estate is only liable for 'reasonable funeral expenses': any excess will be the personal responsibility of the person incurring those expenses. What is reasonable is a question of fact: matters to be taken into account would include the deceased's position in life, religious beliefs and expressed wishes as to funeral arrangements.

15.15.3.2 Legal costs

The personal representatives are, as we have seen, at liberty to instruct solicitors to act for them in the administration of the estate. The costs (including disbursements) of such solicitors are part of the expenses of the administration.

Solicitors' charges in non-contentious probate matters are governed by the Solicitors' (Non-Contentious Business) Remuneration Order 1994. Under the Order, a solicitor is entitled to charge and be paid 'such sum as may be fair and reasonable' having regard to all the circumstances of the case, and in particular to:

(a) the complexity of the matter or the difficulty or novelty of questions raised;
(b) the skill, labour, specialised knowledge and responsibility involved on the part of the solicitor;
(c) the number and importance of the documents prepared or perused, without regard to length;
(d) the place where and circumstances in which the business or any part of it is transacted;
(e) the time expended by the solicitor;
(f) the nature and value of the property involved;
(g) the importance of the matter to the client.

15.15.3.3 Fees of other professionals

Where, for example, stockbrokers or surveyors are employed to assist with valuations of the deceased's assets their fees are also part of the expenses of the administration. Where such professionals have been instructed by the solicitors acting for the personal representatives, the solicitors will—as a matter of professional conduct—incur liability to meet their proper fees, which will then feature as disbursements in the solicitors' bill of costs.

15.15.4 Remuneration

Personal representatives, like trustees, are not entitled to remuneration for their services unless in some way this is authorised.

15.15.4.1 Legacy to proving executors

There is a presumption that any specific or general legacy (but not a gift of residue) given to someone appointed as executor is intended to be conditional upon that person accepting the office (*Re Appleto* (1885) 29 Ch D 893). The presumption is rebuttable (e.g. by the testator indicating some other motive for the legacy, such as 'in recognition of a lifetime's friendship', or making it clear that the legacy should be payable whether or not the beneficiary proves the will).

15.15.4.2 Charging clause in the will

In practice, this will be the usual means by which authority to charge for their services will be conferred upon the personal representatives. Such clauses are routinely included where professionals (such as solicitors and accountants) or institutions (such as banks) are appointed.

Section 28 of the Trustee Act 2000 introduces new rules for the interpretation of charging clauses in favour of trust corporations or personal representatives acting in a professional capacity. They include:

(a) The services for which charge may be made include those that could be provided by a lay trustee and are not confined to strictly professional services (as in the past).

(b) In the case of deaths on or after 1 February 2001, an express charging clause is not treated as a gift for the purposes of the Wills Act 1837, s 15 (see **13.6.5**).

Further, s 29 creates an 'implied' professional charging clause in certain circumstances. Trust corporations are generally entitled to receive 'reasonable remuneration' for services provided on behalf of a trust even if they could have been provided by lay trustees. Other professional trustees (but not a sole trustee) may be entitled to such remuneration provided each of the other trustees has agreed in writing.

It seems likely that draftsmen will continue to include express charging clauses both to cover sole professional trustees and to remove the need for agreement to payment by the other trustees where the professional is one of several trustees.

15.15.4.3 Agreement with beneficiaries

Remuneration can be paid to the personal representatives as a result of an agreement with the beneficiaries (being *sui juris*) out of assets to which they are entitled. There must, of course, be no hint of undue influence.

15.15.4.4 The court

The court, as part of its inherent jurisdiction, has power to authorise remuneration for the personal representatives, whether for past, present or future services. There are also various statutory provisions which enable the court to authorise a personal representative to charge e.g. s 42 of the Trustee Act 1925 (trustees to hold minor's legacy); s 50 of the Administration of Justice Act 1985 (substituted personal representative).

15.15.4.5 Rule in *Cradock v Piper* (1850) 1 Mac & G 664

This rule applies where a solicitor (being one of two or more personal representatives) acts in connection with litigation on behalf of all the personal representatives. Such a solicitor (or his/her firm) may charge for such work provided the bill is not 'inflated' by virtue of the solicitor being one of the parties.

15.15.4.6 Foreign remuneration

Where the law of a foreign jurisdiction entitles the personal representatives to remuneration, they will it seems be entitled to receive it (*Re Northcote's Will Trust* [1949] 1 All ER 442).

15.16 Estate accounts

If beneficiaries are left, for example, 'Blackacre' or '£1,000' by the will, they are clearly able to identify their entitlement. Unlike pecuniary or specific beneficiaries, the residuary beneficiaries have no ready means of knowing what they are entitled to receive. The estate accounts are, in effect, the means whereby the personal representatives identify the property available for distribution to the residuary beneficiaries, and they will also show how that entitlement is to be met.

15.16.1 Form

There are no particular rules, save that the accounts should be clear and easy to follow.

15.16.1.1 The accounts

Three accounts will, in practice, be needed: an income account (**15.16.2**), a capital account (**15.16.3**) and a distribution account (**15.16.4**). In the case of small estates, the income and capital accounts will often be combined; indeed, sometimes all three are combined in a single account: this is perfectly acceptable as long as the end result is clear and easy to follow.

15.16.1.2 Apportionments

Separate income and capital accounts will certainly be needed where there is (under the will or the intestacy rules) a life interest in the residue. Unless excluded by the terms of the will, the Apportionment Act 1870 (**15.2.2**) will require the apportionment of income received after death which relates partly to a period before and partly to a period after the death: the former will be shown in the capital account and the latter in the income account. The equitable apportionment rules (unless excluded) will also affect the entries to be made in the income and capital accounts.

15.16.1.3 Commentary

The accounts are in practice often accompanied by a commentary to explain the various entries, so as to assist the beneficiaries to understand how their entitlement has been arrived at. Thus, for example, the commentary will:

(a) identify the gross and net values of the estate;

(b) indicate its disposition (whether under the terms of the will or under the intestacy rules);

(c) deal with any other relevant matters, such as interim distributions and distributions *in specie* (e.g. as a result of the personal representatives exercising a power of appropriation).

15.16.2 Income account

This should essentially do three things:

(a) give details of income receipts, itemising receipts from different sources (e.g. building society interest, bank interest, dividends, rent, etc.);

(b) itemise details of expenditure from income (e.g. income tax, interest paid on legacies, legal costs properly attributable to income such as the cost of preparing income tax returns);

(c) show the net amount available for distribution.

15.16.3 Capital account

This will in practice need to do four things:

(a) itemise all the assets of the estate at their probate values: it may be more convenient to give the details required in a schedule or schedules to the account, simply bringing in the total(s);

(b) show realisations by the personal representatives during the course of the administration. The proceeds of sale may well differ from the probate valuation of the asset(s) concerned and any such variations have to be taken on board when accounting to the residuary beneficiaries;

(c) give details of all the liabilities discharged, pecuniary and specific legacies and expenses paid, including inheritance tax, capital gains tax and income tax; and legal costs properly attributable to capital;

(d) show the balance available for distribution.

15.16.4 Distribution account

This should show how the beneficiary's entitlement (whether this be to income or capital) is to be met. It should show details of any interim distribution(s) and indicate how the balance is to be paid (perhaps partly *in specie* and partly in cash).

15.16.5 Discharge

The estate accounts are the personal representatives' accounts and where you or your firm are not yourselves the personal representatives they should, therefore, first be presented to them for their approval. The personal representatives' acceptance of the accounts is usually signified by an endorsement to that effect signed by them.

The approved accounts are then presented (usually in duplicate) to the residuary beneficiaries, from whom the personal representatives are entitled to a discharge. Again, this is achieved by requesting the beneficiaries to return one of the copies of the accounts sent to them with an appropriate endorsement, such as 'I ... agree to accept the amount due to me as shown by the within written accounts', duly signed. The endorsement will usually also contain a formal discharge of the personal representatives and an agreement to indemnify them against all claims and demands.

If a beneficiary refuses to approve the accounts, there are in practice ultimately only two possible solutions:

(a) an administration action for the examination of the accounts by the court may be commenced

(b) the personal representatives may pay the beneficiary's share into court under s 63 of the Trustee Act 1925.

It may not be possible for acceptance to be signified because the beneficiary is a minor or suffering from some other disability (e.g. mental incapacity).

In the case of a minor beneficiary, the solution may be the appointment of trustees under s 42 of the Trustee Act 1925 (**15.3.3**). If this section cannot be used (because the beneficiary's interest is contingent only) the personal representatives will in practice have to continue to hold the assets concerned until the beneficiary concerned attains the age of 18.

If the beneficiary is suffering from mental disability, the personal representatives should inform any receiver appointed by the Court of Protection to manage the beneficiary's affairs of the entitlement, and then proceed in accordance with the court's directions. If no receiver has been appointed, ideally application should be made for this to be done (usually by a close relative of the person concerned). If not, the personal representatives may be forced to consider payment into court to obtain their discharge.

If approval cannot be obtained because a beneficiary is missing, we saw (in **5.66**) that the personal representatives should (at an earlier stage of the administration) have taken steps to overcome this difficulty. In practice, this will have probably involved either obtaining a 'Benjamin Order' or some insurance cover, so that the full amount of the residue can be distributed to the other beneficiaries.

15.16.6 Transfer of assets

Once the personal representatives have obtained their discharge, they can arrange for the transfer of the assets to the residuary beneficiaries. As we saw in **15.14** above, the method of doing this will depend upon the nature of the assets concerned (see also **15.17**).

15.17 Assents

An assent occurs when the personal representatives acknowledge that they do not require an asset for the purposes of the administration (see **15.24**). Prior to this, the beneficiaries do not generally have any legal or equitable proprietary interest in the asset, but merely the right to have the deceased's estate duly administered (see further **15.19**).

15.17.1 Pure personalty

At common law, an assent may be in writing, made orally or implied from conduct. Although the equitable title passes by virtue of such assent, if there are particular formalities needed to transfer the legal title, these must also be complied with—the personal representatives holding in the meantime as trustees for the beneficiary concerned.

15.17.2 Land

Here, the position is governed by s 36 of the Administration of Estates Act 1925. All assents relating to unregistered land are now subject to compulsory first registration under the terms of the Land Registration Act 1997 under which the duty to register (within two months of the disposition) lies with the transferee. However, if the application for registration is not made within this period, the disposition is void and the title will revert to the personal representatives who will (pending re-execution of the assent) hold it on trust for the transferee. In practice, therefore, the personal representatives should ensure that first registration takes place with the cost being a testamentary expense.

15.17.2.1 The power to assent

By s 36, Administration of Estates Act 1925 personal representatives are enabled to vest any interest in freehold or leasehold land in any person entitled to it—whether beneficially, as trustee, as personal representative of a beneficiary who has died before the assent can be made, or otherwise (such as a purchaser under a contract made by the deceased: *GHR Co. Ltd v IRC* [1943] KB 303). An assent should not, in practice, be used where the personal representative is selling, or is asked to give effect to a contract for sale entered into by a beneficiary.

15.17.2.2 Form

By s 36(4), an assent must be in writing, signed by the personal representative(s) and naming the person(s) in whose favour it is given. Although technically a form of conveyance, an assent does not bear *ad valorem* stamp duty (except where being used to give effect to a contract).

Sometimes, a deed will in practice be needed, e.g. because indemnity covenants are required from the beneficiary.

It has been held that an assent complying with the requirements of s 36(4) is needed even where the personal representative is the person in whose favour the assent is being made, whether as beneficiary, trustee or as personal representative of a deceased beneficiary: *Re King's Will Trusts* [1964] Ch 542.

15.17.2.3 Effect

By s 36(2), unless there is evidence of a contrary intention, an assent relates back to the date of the deceased's death. Thus, the beneficiary will now be entitled to rents or profits produced by the land since the date of the deceased's death.

15.17.2.4 Protection of beneficiaries

Anyone in whose favour an assent is made is entitled to require (at the expense of the estate) a memorandum of the assent to be endorsed upon the (original) grant of representation—and to call for the production of the grant to prove that this has been done (s 36(5)).

15.17.2.5 Protection of purchasers

There are two provisions affording protection to purchasers from personal representatives:

(a) Section 36(6): If a purchaser takes in good faith a conveyance from personal representatives containing a statement that the personal representatives have not previously made any assent or conveyance relating to the legal estate, the purchaser will take priority over any beneficiary in whose favour a prior assent or conveyance had been made unless notice of the earlier transaction had been endorsed upon the (original) grant. It is essential, therefore, that the purchaser ensures that the conveyance contains such a statement and that the grant is inspected to check for previous memoranda. Further, an endorsement on the grant relating to the conveyance to the purchaser should also be insisted upon.

(b) Section 36(7): The protection here is, again, afforded to the purchaser in the absence of any memorandum relating to a previous assent or conveyance endorsed on the grant. Subject to this, an assent or conveyance by a personal representative is sufficient evidence that the person in whose favour it is given or made is the person entitled to the legal estate. Thus the purchaser is not concerned, for example, to see the terms of the will to check that the recipient of the property was indeed entitled to it. However, the section does not provide that the assent or conveyance is 'conclusive' evidence, so that a purchaser in possession of information which indicates that the assent or conveyance was given or made to the wrong person will not be protected: *Re Duce and Boots Cash Chemists (Southern) Ltd's Contract* [1937] Ch 642.

15.17.2.6 Protection of personal representatives

By s 36(10), personal representatives may—as a condition of giving an assent or conveyance—require security for the discharge of any debts or liabilities to which the property is subject (such as a mortgage or liability to instalments of inheritance tax). However, personal representatives cannot refuse to give an assent once 'reasonable arrangements' have been made.

15.18 Financial services

We have seen (in **15.17**) that, in the context of probate and administration most investment business will in practice be non-mainstream investment business. However, where solicitors advise beneficiaries as to, for example, the investment of their inheritance, such advice will be *prima facie* mainstream business. Avoiding this consequence will normally involve taking the advice of, and making arrangements through, an authorised person.

15.19 Beneficiaries' rights and remedies

The beneficiaries will want to know that the estate is being efficiently administered by the personal representatives, and will be concerned to receive their entitlements under the will or intestacy as quickly as possible. In this section we will consider the nature of the beneficiaries' rights, and how they may be enforced.

15.19.1 The beneficiaries' right to compel due administration

The deceased's assets vest in the personal representatives 'in full ownership without distinction between legal and equitable interests' (*Commissioner of Stamp Duties (Queensland) v Livingston* [1965] AC 694).

Thus, until the administration is complete the beneficiary (whether under the will or intestacy rules) has neither a legal or equitable interest in the deceased's assets. It is only at this point that the personal representatives will know which of the deceased's assets have had to be sold to pay debts and administration expenses, and which are available for distribution to beneficiaries.

The beneficiary does, however, have a chose in action, the right to have the deceased's estate properly administered.

15.19.2 Date for payment of entitlement under will or intestacy

We have seen that personal representatives cannot be compelled to distribute the estate before the end of the executor's year (**15.2.1.3**). Beneficiaries will want to know whether they are entitled to income or interest between the date of death and the date of distribution. Whether the beneficiary is entitled to income from, or interest on, the value of the asset(s) during this period will depend on the provisions of any will, on the nature of the asset (i.e. whether or not it is income producing) and on the nature of the gift.

15.19.2.1 Specific gifts

Where the entitlement of the beneficiary is immediate, such gifts carry the right to any income accruing between the date of death and the vesting of the property in the beneficiary. The assent by the personal representatives vesting the property in the beneficiary (see **15.17**) operates retrospectively to give the beneficiary the right to such income. If the beneficiary has a contingent or future (deferred) entitlement, again such gifts carry the intermediate income which will be added to capital (and devolve with it) for so long as the rules against indefinite accumulation permit. (Thereafter, the income either falls into residue or passes under the intestacy rules.)

15.19.2.2 Residuary gifts

Whether the beneficiary's entitlement is immediate or contingent, and whether of personalty or realty, such gifts carry the intermediate income. Where the beneficiary has a future (deferred) interest, devises (i.e. gifts of realty) probably carry the intermediate income: bequests (i.e. gifts of personalty) do not carry such right and the income passes under the intestacy rules.

15.19.2.3 Contingent pecuniary legacies

Where the will contains such a legacy, so that the sum involved has to be invested pending the fulfilment of the contingency, the gift does not normally carry the intermediate income; the income from the investment therefore belongs to the residuary beneficiaries. There are exceptions to this rule where the gift is to the child or person to whom the testator stands *in loco parentis*, and the contingency is attaining an age not greater than 18 (or earlier marriage); or where the gift is to any child made with the intention of providing for that child's maintenance.

All the rules stated above apply in the absence of provision to the contrary in the will.

15.19.2.4 Pecuniary legacies

As a general rule, a pecuniary legatee, general legatee, or demonstrative legatee (if the designated fund is exhausted) is entitled to interest at 6 per cent only from the date upon which such legacy is payable. In the absence of any direction to the contrary in the will, such a legacy is payable at the end of the executor's year. Any interest payable is regarded as an administration expense, payable therefore normally from residue.

Exceptionally, however, interest on such legacies is payable from the date of death (unless the will otherwise provides). For example:

(a) if the legacy is in satisfaction of a debt;

(b) if the legacy is charged on realty;

(c) if the legacy is to testator's infant child or to an infant to whom he stands *in loco parentis*;

(d) if the legacy is to any infant with the intention to provide for that child's maintenance.

15.19.3 Remedies available to beneficiaries

Where difficulties arise during the administration of an estate, there are a number of formal remedies available to a beneficiary. Essentially, they fall into two categories:

(a) 'Administration proceedings', designed to ensure that the administration of the estate is properly conducted. Such actions may be general, or for specific relief, and need not necessarily be 'contentious', in that the personal representatives are equally entitled to seek the court's assistance in this way.

(b) Actions to 'recover loss' suffered. These include:

15.19.3.1 Personal action against the personal representatives

Instead of commencing administration proceedings a personal action may be brought against the personal representatives. A failure by a personal representative to carry out the duties of the office is a *devastavit*, for which the personal representative is personally liable to the beneficiaries or creditors, unless they have acquiesced in or encouraged the breach. Personal representatives may, however, be relieved from liability:

(a) by provisions in the will relieving personal representatives from liability, e.g. where mistakes are made in good faith;

(b) by s 61 of the Trustee Act 1925 the court may wholly or partly relieve the personal representative from personal liability where it is satisfied that the personal representative acted 'honestly, reasonably and ought fairly to be excused;

(c) by agreement with the beneficiaries, being *sui juris* and fully aware of the breach, the personal representatives may be released from liability.

15.19.3.2 Tracing

A beneficiary (whether under a will or the intestacy rules) or a creditor may have the right to trace and recover property of the estate (or property representing such property) from the personal representatives or any other recipient of it, other than a *bona fide* purchaser for value or person deriving title from such purchaser. The right to trace is also lost if the property has been dissipated, or where to allow tracing would be inequitable. This remedy may be sought whether or not a personal action has been brought against the personal representative, though in so far as such action has been 'successful' the right to trace is clearly not also going to be available.

15.19.3.3 Personal action against recipients of estate assets

Where all other remedies of a beneficiary (whether under the will or intestacy rules) or creditor have been exhausted, a personal action may be brought against a person who has wrongly received the assets of the estate (*Ministry of Health v Simpson* [1951] AC 251).

15.20 Distributing the assets: Checkpoints

1. Payment of legacies:
   (a) Specific legacies/devises (**15.14.1**).
   (b) Burden of pecuniary legacies (**15.14.2**):
      (i) provision in the will (**15.14.2.1**);
      (ii) no provision in the will (**15.14.2.2**).
   (c) Abatement (**15.14.3**).
   (d) Appropriation (**15.14.4**).
   (e) Receipts (**15.14.5**).
2. Ascertainment of residue:
   (a) Finalising the tax position:
      (i) income tax and capital gains tax (**15.15.1**);
      (ii) inheritance tax (**15.15.2**):
         (1) corrective accounts (**15.15.2.3**);
         (2) certificates of discharge (**15.15.2.4**).
   (b) Administration expenses:
      (i) funeral expenses (**15.15.3.1**);
      (ii) legal costs (**15.15.3.2**);
      (iii) other professionals' fees (**15.15.3.3**).
   (c) Remuneration of personal representatives:
      (i) legacy to proving executor (**15.15.4.1**);
      (ii) charging clause in will (**15.15.4.2**);
      (iii) other possibilities (**15.15.4.3** to **15.15.4.6**).
3. Estate accounts:
   (a) Income account (**15.16.2**).
   (b) Capital account (**15.16.3**).
   (c) Distribution account (**15.16.4**).
   (d) Discharge of personal representatives (**15.16.5**).

4. Assents:
   (a) Pure personalty (**15.17.1**).
   (b) Land (**15.17.2**).

5. Beneficiaries' rights and remedies:
   (a) Right to compel due administration (**15.19.1**).
   (b) Date for payment of entitlement under will/intestacy (**15.19.2**).
   (c) Remedies:
      (i) personal action against the personal representatives (**15.19.3.1**)
      (ii) tracing (**15.19.3.2**)
      (iii) personal action against recipients of estate assets (**15.19.3.3**)

Human rights

16

Human rights

16.1 Introduction

The Human Rights Act 1998 came into force on 2 October 2000 and effectively incorporated the European Convention on Human Rights into UK legislation.

The Convention is made up of various Articles and Protocols which need to be applied by the judiciary when reaching decisions in our courts. All areas of UK law are affected by the incorporation—in particular the areas of criminal, family, and employment law. All courts, from the magistrates' court to the Court of Appeal, require a thorough working knowledge of the contents of the Articles and Protocols, and their application.

Lawyers must do more than have an understanding of the contents of the Convention and the Act. European case law plays a significant part in the application of the Convention and must be integrated into legal practice. To interpret and apply case law effectively, lawyers and courts alike must have a grasp of the European jurisprudence that exists when the European Court comes to a decision.

This chapter aims to provide an introduction to the Convention and the Human Rights Act 1998, by taking into account the origins of the Convention and how it came to be incorporated into UK legislation. The chapter then discusses general principles of European jurisprudence before moving on to deal with the contents of the Articles and Protocols themselves. Commentary is provided, where appropriate, for each of the Articles although this is merely an overview of the potential ramifications of the Act. Recent case law and legislation, where appropriate, is referred to within the main body of the text. However, as you will see, the case law is piecemeal and some of the judgments that have been handed down do not provide a definitive guide, for practitioners, for the application of the 1998 Act within UK legislation. What is clear, however, is that not only can legislative provisions be challenged, but also the way in which they have been applied. Defence practitioners should be clear about whether they are arguing that the relevant law is incompatible, and therefore attempting to invoke s 3 or s 4 of the Act, or whether they are arguing that the relevant law is compatible of itself but the way in which it has been applied contravenes the defendant's rights under the Convention.

16.2 History

16.2.1 Origins of the Convention

As a direct response to the atrocities committed in World War II, the Council of Europe, which was set up by Western European governments, created the European Convention on Human Rights which contained a basic set of guidelines for human rights that would protect all individuals. In 1950 the Council of Europe proclaimed these rights in the European Convention on Human Rights and Fundamental Freedoms. This document was largely based upon the Universal Declaration of Human Rights which had been issued by the United Nations in 1948. The European Convention on Human Rights came into force in international law in 1953.

Initially, one state *could* take action against another only if it believed an individual's rights were being violated. These actions were brought before the European Court of Human Rights which sits in Strasbourg. The Court consists of judges from the member states of the Council of Europe. The Convention also allows for an individual to petition the court in respect of breaches of Convention rights by their respective governments. The United Kingdom recognised the individual's right to petition in 1966.

Individuals still had to exhaust all national remedies available to them before availing themselves of the rights conveyed under the Convention. Even if an individual was successful in Strasbourg the decision was not then binding upon the UK as the UK took the view that our national laws and procedures did in fact give effect to the rights enjoyed by an individual under the Convention. However, the number of applications to Strasbourg belied this way of thinking.

In response to this underlying need to protect an individual's rights more effectively under the Convention, it was finally decided to incorporate the Convention into our legislation under the umbrella of the Human Rights Act 1998.

Prior to the introduction of the Human Rights Act 1998, the Convention had limited application and was really used by national courts only in the following circumstances:

(a) as an aid to the construction of legislation in cases of ambiguity—*R v Secretary of State for the Home Department, ex parte Brind* [1991] 1 AC 696;

(b) to inform the exercise of judicial (as opposed to administrative) discretion—*Attorney-General v Guardian Newspapers Ltd* [1987] 1 WLR 1248;

(c) to establish the scope of common law—*Derbyshire County Council v Times Newspapers Ltd* [1992] QB 770.

Following the implementation of the Human Rights Act 1998 the Convention is applied by our national courts at grass roots level.

16.2.2 The Human Rights Act 1998

The Human Rights Act 1998 has made the Convention central to the practice of law in the United Kingdom.

Section 2(1) of the Act requires all courts and tribunals to take into account the Convention and decisions by the institutions of the Convention, whether the European Court of Human Rights, the Commission of Human Rights or the Council.

The Act creates a general statutory requirement that all legislation (past or present) be read and given effect in a way which is compatible with the Convention. It does this by providing, in s 3, that all legislation, primary and secondary, whenever enacted, must be read and given effect in a way which is compatible with Convention rights wherever possible.

Section 6(1) and (3) require public authorities to act in compliance with the Convention unless they are prevented from doing so by statute. This means that the courts have their own primary duty to give effect to the Convention unless a statute positively prevents this. It would therefore be unlawful for public authorities to act in a way which is incompatible with a Convention right. Courts themselves are included in the definition of public authorities.

It is generally perceived that it is only the actual decision of a court in a criminal or civil case that is subject to the right of appeal. This is true, but under the 1998 Act it is not just the decision of a court that is open to challenge but the way in which the courts actually function. For example, the administrative element of the Magistrates' Court Service or clerks who are exercising judicial functions conveyed upon them by national legislation are open to challenge. Clearly the management of the court itself by the Chief Executive and the Magistrates' Courts Committee has a direct effect upon the public and public funds and those decision-making processes are also open to scrutiny. As a result, any court, committee or individual must act compatibly with the Convention both in the decisions that it comes to and the process that it uses.

All courts and tribunals must have a working knowledge of the content of the Convention and the relevant case law to any given article in order to be able to apply it correctly in accordance with UK legislation. To apply the decisions of cases brought down by Strasbourg, the courts and tribunals need to understand how decisions at Strasbourg are actually reached, so as to give the appropriate weight to any decision. In order to be able to effectively interpret Convention legislation and case law, the courts must understand the 'European jurisprudence' that exists when the judges come to a decision in Strasbourg.

16.3 European and International Doctrines

A common misconception about the rights conveyed by the Convention is that if there is a breach by a public authority or member state, the acts of that authority or member state must be amended to bring them within the Convention. This is too draconian and would throw national law and procedures into a state of confusion. Although rights are conveyed to individuals, the rights contained within the articles are rarely absolute and can be limited or qualified. The majority of rights are subject to limitations and qualifications; however, the right to freedom from torture is an absolute right and an act of torture could never be justified by acting in the interests of the state.

16.3.1 Limited rights

Some of the rights conveyed under the articles of the Convention have limitations placed upon them so that in some circumstances an infringement of a guaranteed right does not amount to an infringement. For example, Article 2 contains the right to life. This right is limited by Article 2(2) which allows the use of force, but the amount used cannot be more than is absolutely necessary in the defence of a person from unlawful violence, to prevent escape from lawful detention, or to effect an arrest or quell a riot or insurrection. See the case of *McCann v United Kingdom* (1995) 21 EHRR 97, where suspected terrorists were shot dead in Gibraltar by British security agents. The Court held that there had been a breach of Article 2 as the state had failed to give adequate training or instructions to agents likely to use lethal force. This failure to plan and control was the central issue in deciding whether the force used had been absolutely necessary.

16.3.2 Qualified rights

Some articles contain qualified rights, and as such the Convention permits them to be infringed in certain circumstances.

Once a victim has been shown to have established a primary right, the Convention seeks to balance the rights of the individual against other public rights. However, rights such as the right to respect for private life and the right to freedom of expression may sometimes compete with one another. Equally, some rights may be in direct conflict with public interest considerations. These sorts of rights, which impinge on the rights and freedoms of others, are necessarily qualified, and the Convention permits them to be limited by the state.

16.3.3 How far can a state limit the rights contained within the Convention?

The Convention permits these limitations only where they are:

(a) prescribed by law;

(b) intended to achieve a legitimate objective; and

(c) necessary in a democratic society (that is, proportionate to the ends to be achieved).

For example, Article 8 states that, 'Everyone has the right to respect for his private and family life, his home and his correspondence.' This is a presumed right, but a number of limitations and exceptions to it are set out in Article 8(2):

> There shall be no interference by a public authority with the exercise of this right except such as is in accordance with the law and is necessary in a democratic society in the interests of national security, public safety or the economic well-being of the country, for the prevention of disorder or crime, for the protection of health or morals, or for the protection of the rights and freedoms of others.

The precise terms of the limitations in respect of the articles vary but the judicial method for considering them is the same:

(a) Is the interference prescribed by law?

(b) Does it serve a legitimate objective?

(c) Is it necessary in a democratic society?

16.3.3.1 Is the interference prescribed by law?—the rule of law

No interference with a right protected under the Convention is permissible unless the citizen knows the basis for the interference because it is set out in ascertainable law. In the absence of any such detailed authorisation by the law, any interference, however justified, will violate the Convention—see *Malone v United Kingdom* (1984) 7 EHRR 14 where the applicant's telephone was tapped by the police. When this took place the only authorisation was an internal code of guidance produced by the police which was not available to the public. The European Court took the view that Mr Malone was unable to assess whether or not his telephone would be listened to, or what the basis in law for the surveillance might be. The common law position was inadequate, as could be seen from his failure in the High Court. The interference violated the Convention because it was not prescribed by law.

16.3.3.2 Does it serve a legitimate objective?

Legitimate objectives are:

(a) the interests of public safety;

(b) national security;

(c) the protection of health and morals; and

(d) the economic well-being of the country, or the protection of the rights and freedoms of others.

16.3.3.3 Is it necessary in a democratic society?—proportionality

The Convention's approach is to decide whether a particular limitation from a right is justified in the sense of being 'proportionate to the legitimate aim pursued'.

This means that even if a policy which interferes with a Convention right might be aimed at securing a legitimate social policy, for example, the prevention of crime, this will not in itself justify the violation if the means adopted to secure the aim are excessive in the circumstances. *Soering v United Kingdom* (1989) 11 EHRR 439 stated:

> inherent in the whole of the Convention is a search for the fair balance between the demands of the general interest of the Community and the requirements of the protection of the individual's human rights. (para 89)

16.3.4 The margin of appreciation

A state is allowed a certain freedom to evaluate its public policy decisions, but this is subject to review by the Strasbourg institutions. The court has to ensure that the member states' own political and cultural traditions are respected. When determining whether a social policy aim is legitimate therefore, or whether the means adopted to achieve it are 'necessary in a democratic society', the Commission and the Court have recognised limits as to their own competence to judge the issue. They have done this by giving the state a so-called 'margin of appreciation' when assessing the extent to which a signatory has violated the Convention.

The most notable case in this area is *Handyside v United Kingdom* (1976) 1 EHRR 737. This case arose because of the intention to publish *The Little Red Schoolbook*, intended for children, but which included a chapter on sex. The books were seized by the police under the Obscene Publications Act 1959 and a forfeiture order obtained against the publishers. The publishers claimed a breach of their right to freedom of expression under Article 10.

Was the seizing of the books proportionate to the legitimate aim that the state sought to protect? The Court recognised that there was a margin of appreciation in this case which justified the interference with Article 10. It stated:

> By reason of their direct and continuous contact with the vital forces of their countries, state authorities are in principle in a better position than the international judge to give an opinion on the exact nature of these requirements as well as on the necessity of a restriction or penalty intended to meet them. ... Nevertheless Article 10(2) does not give the contracting state an unlimited power of appreciation. The Court which is responsible for ensuring the observance of those states' engagements is empowered to give the final ruling on whether a restriction or penalty is reconcilable with the freedom of expression as protected by Article 10. The domestic margin of appreciation thus goes hand in hand with a European supervision.

16.3.5 Derogations and reservations

In times of war or other public emergency it is open to a member state to enter into derogation in respect of certain obligations. These cannot be general derogations. A derogation simply allows a state not to comply with the article in question to the legitimate extent of the derogation. However, derogations in respect of the right to life (except arising from the lawful prosecution of war) or from the prohibitions against torture are not permitted.

Reservations differ from derogations in that they are merely conditions upon acceptance of a particular article.

16.3.6 Equality of arms

This principle, laid down in the case of *Neuminster v Austria* (1968) 1 EHRR 91, was created in order to ensure that both parties to a case, whether in civil or criminal proceedings, were not placed at a procedural disadvantage. The principle can be more easily explained with reference to a practical example.

In the case of a summary-only offence which must be tried in the magistrates' court, the defence has no right to advance information from the prosecution. This differs from an either-way offence where such information is readily available. The defence must conduct its case ignorant of evidence in the prosecution's possession and it is therefore deprived of the opportunity of investigating and testing the strength of the prosecution's case. This may well have given rise to an application in the magistrates' court that there has been a breach of Article 6 of the Convention because the principle of equality of arms has been infringed (given that the majority of summary-only offences do carry the threat of a custodial sentence). However, this potential breach is effectively dealt with by para 43 of the Attorney-General's Guidelines: Disclosure of Information in Criminal Proceedings, where such advance information is now provided.

16.3.7 Horizontality

As mentioned earlier, s 6 of the Human Rights Act 1998 incorporates courts and tribunals into the definition of public bodies. When two individuals come to court for a decision to be made about their dispute, the court needs to act compatibly with the Convention. This will therefore have an indirect effect upon the two individuals who are not themselves covered by the Convention. The court's adherence to the Convention will have a *horizontal* effect on their relationship. In *Hokkanen v Finland* (1994) 19 EHRR 139, the European Court held that where grandparents failed to abide by court orders for contact and custody in favour of the father, Article 8 imposed upon the state a positive obligation to assist, so far as possible, the father's relationship with his child.

A recent case *Douglas and Others v Hello! Ltd* CA: Brooke, Sedley and Keene LJJ; reported: 21st December 2000 [2001] QB 467 involving Michael Douglas and Catherine Zeta Jones again illustrated that the court had a duty under s 6 to protect their private life. The case involved proceedings against *Hello* magazine which threatened to publish unauthorised photographs from the couple's wedding when they had in fact sold the exclusive rights to *OK* magazine. While all three judges agreed that an injunction should be refused because the couple had in fact traded their right to private life like a commodity, the judgment is notable in confirming the effect the Human Rights Act 1998 has had upon legal relations between individuals as opposed to legal relations between individuals and the state.

16.3.8 Living instrument

The Convention was drafted more than 40 years ago and, unlike usual pieces of legislation, it has not been amended, repealed or replaced by more up-to-date legislation. To use the UK model of precedent would bind the court to adhere to decisions which are outmoded and probably unfair. It is primarily for this reason that the doctrine of precedent is not a main feature of Convention case law. The Convention is a 'living instrument' and cases are decided in line with the up-to-date and economic and moral conditions of the member states. Although this creates some uncertainty when relying on previous decisions handed down, it at least ensures that the decisions are modern in their approach.

16.3.9 Protocols

Protocols can be thought of as extensions to the Convention where member states can agree to add to the rights contained within it. The procedural method for doing this is to draw up a protocol setting out the additional rights. The First Protocol provides for rights to the peaceful enjoyment of property, to education and to free elections. The Human Rights Act 1998 allows the government to incorporate future protocols into national law using rules of Parliament. The rights contained within the protocols carry as much weight as the provisions contained in the articles themselves.

16.3.10 Where to find Convention case law

The Council of Europe publishes individual judgments and decisions under the title *Publications of the European Court of Human Rights*. Court judgments are published in Series A and the pleadings, oral arguments and documents are published in Series B.

Decisions of the Commission and judgments of the Court can be found at **www. echr.coe.int**.

Another source is the European Human Rights Reports (EHRR), which publishes all judgments and important decisions. The European Human Rights Law Review (EHRLR) appears six times a year, and has a case law section which highlights interesting cases and recent decisions.

16.4 The Convention rights

This section contains commentary on the main articles of the Convention which affect legal practice. It should be viewed only as an introduction to some of the possible effects of the Convention and is no substitute for empirical research.

Schedule 1 to the Human Rights Act 1998 lists the Convention rights by reference to the relevant articles of, and protocols to, the European Convention on Human Rights, as follows.

16.4.1 Article 2—right to life

1. Everyone's right to life shall be protected by law. No one shall be deprived of his life intentionally save in the execution of a sentence of a court following his conviction of a crime for which this penalty is provided by law.
2. Deprivation of life shall not be regarded as inflicted in contravention of this Article when it results from the use of force which is no more than absolutely necessary:
   (a) in defence of any person from unlawful violence;
   (b) in order to effect a lawful arrest or to prevent the escape of a person lawfully detained;
   (c) in action lawfully taken for the purpose of quelling a riot or insurrection.

This is a limited right: see *McCann v United Kingdom* (1995) 21 EHRR 97.

16.4.2 Article 3—prohibition of torture

No one shall be subjected to torture or inhuman or degrading treatment or punishment.

This is an absolute right although there is a minimum level of severity required before Article 3 will be contravened. The case of *Ireland v United Kingdom* (1978) 2 EHRR 25 gave guidelines as to what constituted prohibited treatment. Torture was defined as deliberate inhuman treatment causing very serious and cruel suffering; inhumane treatment or punishment as treatment or punishment which causes intense physical and mental suffering; degrading treatment or punishment as treatment or punishment that arouses in a victim a feeling of fear, anguish and inferiority capable of humiliating and debasing the victim and possibly breaking his or her physical or moral resistance.

16.4.3 Article 4—prohibition of slavery and forced labour

1. No one shall be held in slavery or servitude. [This is an absolute right.]
2. No one shall be required to perform forced or compulsory labour. [This is a limited right.]
3. For the purpose of this Article the term 'forced or compulsory labour' shall not include:
   (a) any work required to be done in the ordinary course of detention imposed according to the provisions of Article 5 of this Convention or during conditional release from such detention;
   (b) any service of a military character or, in case of conscientious objectors in countries where they are recognised, service exacted instead of compulsory military service;
   (c) any service exacted in case of an emergency or calamity threatening the life or well-being of the community;
   (d) any work or service which forms part of normal civic obligations.

16.4.4 Article 5—right to liberty and security

1. Everyone has the right to liberty and security of person. No one shall be deprived of his liberty save in the following cases and in accordance with a procedure prescribed by law:
   (a) the lawful detention of a person after conviction by a competent court;
   (b) the lawful arrest or detention of a person for non-compliance with the lawful order of a court in order to secure the fulfilment of any obligation prescribed by law;
   (c) the lawful arrest or detention of a person effected for the purpose of bringing him before the competent legal authority on reasonable suspicion of having committed an offence or when it is reasonably considered necessary to prevent his committing an offence or fleeing after having done so;
   (d) the detention of a minor by lawful order for the purpose of educational supervision or his lawful detention for the purpose of bringing him before the competent legal authority;
   (e) the lawful detention of persons for the spreading of infectious diseases, of persons of unsound mind, alcoholics or drug addicts or vagrants;
   (f) the lawful arrest or detention of a person to prevent his effecting an unauthorised entry into the country or of a person against whom action is being taken with a view to deportation or extradition.
2. Everyone who is arrested shall be informed promptly, in a language which he understands, of the reasons for his arrest and of any charge against him.
3. Everyone arrested or detained in accordance with paragraph 1(c) of this Article shall be brought promptly before a judge or other officer authorised by law to exercise judicial power and shall be entitled to trial within a reasonable time or to release pending trial. Release may be conditioned by guarantees to appear for trial.
4. Everyone who is deprived of his liberty by arrest or detention shall be entitled to take proceedings by which the lawfulness of his detention shall be decided speedily by a court and his release ordered if the detention is not lawful.
5. Everyone who has been the victim of arrest or detention in contravention of the provisions of this Article shall have an exercisable right to compensation.

This is a limited right and will have most relevance in a magistrates' court, particularly in relation to the granting of bail. When a defendant is charged with a criminal offence he must appear before the magistrates who will decide whether or not there should be a release pending trial, with or without conditions, or a remand into custody. Article 5(3) states that he should be entitled to trial within a reasonable time or to release pending trial. The case of *Wemhoff v Germany* (1968) 1 EHRR 55 stated that the defendant was entitled to both things notwithstanding the wording and also that the defendant should be released pending trial unless there are *'relevant and sufficient'* reasons to justify continued detention. Clearly the Bail Act 1976 provides that the magistrates must be satisfied that there are substantial grounds for believing that a person should be deprived of his liberty and the exceptions to the *prima facie* right to bail are clearly set out in the Schedule to the Act. However, there are several areas where our legislation may still fall foul of the requirements in Article 5(3).

(a) The reasons that are given by the magistrates to justify a refusal of bail must be *clearly stated* and there can be no stereotyped reason for refusal—*Yagei and Sargin v Turkey* (1995) 20 EHRR 505. The case of *Letellier v France* (1991) 14 EHRR 83 was quite clear when it stated that the function of any court considering the question of bail is to:

> examine all the facts arguing for or against the existence of a genuine requirement of public interest justifying, with due regard to the presumption of innocence, a departure from the rule in respect of individual liberty and set them out in their decision on application for release.

In addition the courts should be careful when providing their reasons that they adhere to the presumption of innocence which is enshrined in Article 6(2).

(b) Once a defendant has had his two applications for bail refused and has exhausted all alternatives available to him in the higher courts, it is not usual for a further bail application to be heard unless there has been a material change in circumstances. However, it may well be the case that the elapse of time between detention and trial of itself will give rise to grounds to put forward a material change in circumstances application.

16.4.4.1 Disclosure and bail

Disclosure is an area which requires some consideration in relation to Article 6: the right to a fair trial and the equality of arms. However, disclosure will also be very relevant to bail applications where the prosecution is in possession of information which is not readily available to the defence. This may well prove to be a breach of the principle of equality of arms, placing the prosecution in breach of Article 5(4). Authority for this can be found in *Lamy v Belgium* (1989) 11 EHRR 529 where the applicant had been refused access to the prosecution file at both applications for bail and had had bail refused. He merely had access to some information disclosed on the face of the warrant for his arrest. The European Court held that there had been a breach of Article 5(4) even though the national law at the time only allowed for disclosure 30 days after arrest. The Court then took the matter a stage further and said that not only should the information be disclosed but the applicant should have had sufficient time to consider and evaluate the material.

16.4.4.2 Right to review

Note the case of *T and V v United Kingdom*, Applications 24724/94 and 24888/94, 16 December 1999, which held that the two applicants had been denied the opportunity to have the lawfulness of detention reviewed by a judicial body.

16.4.5 Article 6—right to a fair trial

1. In the determination of his civil rights and obligations or of any criminal charge against him, everyone is entitled to a fair and public hearing within a reasonable time by an independent and impartial tribunal established by law. Judgment shall be pronounced publicly but the press and public may be excluded from all or part of the trial in the interest of morals, public order or national security in a democratic society, where the interest of juveniles or the protection of the private life of the parties so require, or to the extent strictly necessary in the opinion of the court in special circumstances where publicity would prejudice the interests of justice.
2. Everyone charged with a criminal offence shall be presumed innocent until proved guilty according to law.
3. Everyone charged with a criminal offence has the following minimum rights:
   (a) to be informed promptly, in a language which he understands and in detail, of the nature and cause of the accusation against him;
   (b) to have adequate time and facilities for the preparation of his defence;
   (c) to defend himself in person or through legal assistance of his own choosing or, if he has not sufficient means to pay for legal assistance, to be given it free when the interests of justice so require;
   (d) to examine or have examined witnesses against him and to obtain the attendance and examination of witnesses on his behalf under the same conditions as witnesses against him;
   (e) to have the free assistance of an interpreter if he cannot understand or speak the language used in court.

This article will affect proceedings in both civil and criminal trials.

16.4.5.1 Criminal proceedings

Article 6(1) provides the right to a trial within a reasonable time and guarantees the expedition in the conduct of the proceedings themselves in order to prevent a defendant from remaining uncertain about the outcome of his fate for too long.

This has changed our approach to abuse of process proceedings. Under common law, the defence must show that the defendant has been prejudiced by the delay in order to make a successful application. However, since October 2000, there is no requirement to show prejudice as the delay, of itself, will be sufficient. In extreme circumstances the European Court may adjudge that a long delayed trial amounts to oppression.

16.4.5.2 Article 6(2)—reverse burden of proof

The case of *Salabiaku v France* (1991) 13 EHRR 379 was notable in that it stated that:

> Article 6(2) does not therefore regard presumptions of fact or law provided for in criminal law with indifference. It requires states to confine them within reasonable limits which take into account the importance of what is at stake and maintain the rights of the defence.

Article 6(2) and the presumption of innocence has already been raised as an issue in UK proceedings, in particular the case of *R v Director of Public Prosecutions, ex parte Kebilene* [1999] 3 WLR 972. This case concerned ss 16A and 16B of the Prevention of Terrorism Act 1989 which carries with it a reverse burden of proof. The House of Lords held, in relation to the particular provision, that it was not clear that these sections were necessarily going to be contrary to Article 6(2). Two of their Lordships thought that the offence of possessing an article reasonably suspected of being possessed for terrorist purposes might well violate Article 6(2), since it required the accused to prove that the article was not in his possession for those purposes, and they proposed reinterpreting the burden on the accused as evidential only. Other members of the Court disagreed and said it was sufficient that the prosecution has the burden of showing *'circumstances giving rise to a reasonable suspicion'* of terrorist purposes.

Two issues relating to the burdens which may be imposed upon a defendant in respect of certain criminal offences rose in the case of *R v Lambert* [2001] 2 WLR 211. First, the Court of Appeal decided that the defendant's burden of proof in relation to establishing a defence of diminished responsibility does not violate Article 6(2). The Court found that this 'special defence' had been introduced by s 2 of the Homicide Act 1957 for the benefit of a defendant who may then be able to avail himself of this defence or exception to the rule. Secondly, the court turned its attention to ss 5 and 28 of the Misuse of Drugs Act 1971, which imposed on the accused the burden of proving lack of knowledge or mistake. The Court held that 'they do not impose additional ingredients which have to be proved to complete the offence but a way of avoiding liability that would otherwise be an offence'.

Unfortunately this does not give clear guidance at to how the courts are going to deal with the wide variety of offences that carry a reverse burden of proof. Careful note should, however, be taken of the 'essential elements test' repeated by Lord Woolf in *Lambert* where he said 'if the defendant is being required to prove an essential element of the offence this will be more difficult to justify'. If the prosecution have to prove facts which are not of themselves incriminating, leaving the defence to disprove essential elements of the offence, this may well fall foul of Article 6(2).

16.4.5.3 Article 6(3)(b)—disclosure

Our present system of disclosure contains various anomalies which contravene a defendant's right to disclosure under the Convention. The main piece of legislation to be affected here is the Criminal Procedure and Investigations Act 1996 which deals with primary and secondary disclosure of unused material.

The Attorney-General's Guidelines: Disclosure of Information in Criminal Proceedings sought to deal with some of the unfairness that had been created by the 1996 Act and by disclosure provisions in general. Indeed, in its introduction it states that the guidelines are designed to:

> ensure that there is fair disclosure of material which may be relevant to an investigation and which does not form part of the prosecution case ... Disclosure which does not meet these objectives risks preventing a fair trial taking place.

Areas of note are as follows:

Summary only offences

Previously there has been no requirement that the prosecution disclose their case to the defence. This situation has been remedied by para 43 of the Attorney-General's Guidelines which states that:

> The prosecutor should, in addition to complying with the obligations under the Criminal Procedure and Investigations Act 1996, *provide to the defence all evidence upon which the Crown proposes to rely in a summary trial*. Such provision should allow the accused or their legal advisers sufficient time properly to consider the evidence before it is called. Exceptionally, a statement may be withheld for the protection of witnesses or to avoid interference with the course of justice.

Defence statement

Paragraph 18 of the Attorney-General's Guidelines deals with the scenario envisaged by most defence practitioners when the 1996 Act came into force. If a defence statement had to be filed in a case where its contents, such as self-defence, would make up for the inherent defects in the prosecution's case, such as weak identification evidence, did the statement have to set out the actual defence or could it be limited to relying upon the defects in the prosecution's case in the hope of making a successful submission of no case to answer? The situation is now quite clear. Paragraph 18 states that:

> Prosecutors should *not* adduce evidence of the contents of a defence statement ... There may be occasions when a defence statement points the prosecution to other lines of enquiry. Further investigation in these circumstances is possible and evidence obtained as a result of inquiring into a defence statement may be used as part of the prosecution case or to rebut the defence.

Paragraph 27 attempts to clarify the position of the defence statement in the procedure leading up to and including trial and barely conceals its plea for fuller and more detailed information to be provided by the defence.

Clearly the amount of secondary disclosure provided by the Crown Prosecution Service depends upon the clarity of information provided by the defence in their statement. Prosecuting bodies complain that defence statements do not comply with the spirit of the 1996 Act and do not disclose enough detail. Paragraph 27 tries to peddle the line that a comprehensive statement assists the participants in the trial to ensure that it is fair; the more detail a defence statement contains the more likely it is that the prosecutor will make a properly informed decision about whether any remaining material may assist the defence case. This clearly begs the question whether if the defence statement contains little detail the prosecutor will endeavour to make an *improperly* informed decision!

It is not quite clear which piece of legislation the prosecuting authorities are seeking to rely upon in their plea for more detailed disclosure from the defence at this early stage. The only authority that exists is that which is contained within the 1996 Act and that is limited to the defence setting out the nature of the defence, what the defence takes issue with and the reasons why the defence takes issue. If a defence practitioner chooses to disclose more information than is required under the Act, in line with para 27 of the Guidelines, in an attempt to obtain further and better secondary disclosure as promised, he may, in some cases, be sadly disappointed.

What is worthy of note is 'Points for Prosecutors' published, just prior to the implementation of the Human Rights Act 1998, by government law officers 'to assist prosecutors in providing a consistent response to challenges to a selection of legislative provisions where Convention issues are likely to be raised'. In essence this document is an attempt to help prosecutors consistently refute human rights points made by defence practitioners. However, it does contain one or two elements which all defence practitioners should be pleasantly aware of. First, in relation to defence statements the document, in attempting to protect defence statements from challenge asserts that 'disclosure of material which might assist the defence is not contingent upon a [defence] statement being provided'. Secondly, in relation to disclosure at time of bail, it is asserted that 'the prosecution is under a duty to disclose any material which might assist the defendant to make a bail application, irrespective of the stage the proceedings have reached and whether or not the Criminal Procedure and Investigations Act 1996 applies'.

Disclosure prior to primary disclosure under the 1996 Act

Paragraph 34 has been inserted into the Guidelines to deal, in some way, with the ruling laid down in the case of *R v Director of Public Prosecutions, ex parte Lee* [1999] 1 WLR 1950. *Ex parte Lee* was concerned with the inherent unfairness of a system which only allowed for primary prosecution disclosure at committal when the nature of some of the information then disclosed had long outlived its usefulness, to the detriment of the defendant, i.e. the identity of a material witness who the prosecution do not seek to rely upon who, in the intervening six to eight week period may well have either disappeared, forgotten the incident itself or forgotten such detail as to render his statement of very little value and bring his credibility as a witness open to question. This paragraph effectively brings forward the prosecution's duty of disclosure from committal stage to that of a bail application, for example. The test to be applied at a bail hearing is that 'disclosure ought to be made of significant information that might affect a bail decision or that might enable the defence to contest the committal proceedings'.

This extension of primary prosecution disclosure is qualified by para 35 which dispenses with the prosecution's duty of disclosure under para 34 where the '*need for such disclosure is not apparent to the prosecutor*' a qualification that does not instil the greatest of confidence that even where such relevant material does in fact exist it will actually be disclosed. If the need for disclosure is not apparent to the prosecutor, the burden then shifts to the defence to provide details surrounding the defence case in order to provoke the 'chance' that some relevant disclosure may be forthcoming.

Note: As ss 50 and 51 of the Crime and Disorder Act 1998 are now in force, at least the potential prejudice to those charged with an indictable-only offence is limited as committal proceedings will rapidly come upon them; but this still leaves a large number of either way offences, where summary jurisdiction has been refused, that are vulnerable to delay unless the prosecutor's duty under para 34 is properly discharged.

Extending the application of primary prosecution disclosure

Paragraph 37 of the Guidelines provides a helpful list of the types of information which may undermine the prosecution's case the most notable of which can be found at subparagraph (v):

> Any material that might support a defence that is either raised by the defence or apparent from the prosecution papers. If the material might undermine the prosecution case it should be disclosed at this stage even though it suggests a defence inconsistent with or alternative to one already advanced by the accused or his solicitor.

This is a welcome addition from the defence point of view not least because it should ensure that all interview tapes where the suspect has put forward an account are listened to, in their entirety, by the prosecutor reviewing the case.

Miscellaneous

Other concerns with the 1996 Act are that many important disclosure issues in relation to unused material rely heavily upon the disclosure/investigating officer's subjective interpretation of what is 'relevant' and what would 'undermine the prosecution's case' or 'assist' the defence case. There is no method of early judicial intervention in this present system except in public interest immunity cases and it may well be that the failure to provide judicial scrutiny of all of the material would result in a breach of Article 6. Again the Attorney-General's Guidelines seeks to address these concerns by extending the duties of Investigating and Disclosure Officers and Prosecutors generally. Even so, however welcome these extensions may be, they do not allay the very real fears of defence practitioners whose clients are still reliant upon a flawed system of disclosure which is based on limited access to material on the part of the Crown Prosecution Service and the subjective nature of the decisions taken by both the police and Crown Prosecution Service alike.

16.4.5.4 Article 6(3)(c)—public funding

Our present provisions in relation to the granting of public funding may result in minor cases being refused legal aid. However, even minor cases may result in a term of imprisonment being imposed and in these cases a refusal of public funding would lead to a breach of this part of Article 6.

16.4.5.5 Hearsay

Our legal system, while accepting that hearsay evidence is inadmissible, provides a number of common law and statutory exceptions to the hearsay rule. Article 6(d) deals with the individual's right to cross-examine witnesses against him. It is possible that the provisions contained in s 23 of the Criminal Justice Act 1988, which allow for witness statements to be admitted into evidence in particular circumstances, could fall foul of this particular section of Article 6. This has already been raised in the case of *R v Gokal* [1998] 1 Cr App R 206 and *R v Radak* [1999] 1 Cr App R 187.

In the latter case Lord Bingham stated that when the court was exercising its discretion under s 26, it must have regard to the accused's rights in accordance with Article 6(3)(d) and that when one party sought to admit a statement on the grounds that the witness was overseas, a relevant consideration would be whether that evidence could have been obtained on commission in the witness's country of residence.

Clearly a party to criminal proceedings should try to anticipate, as far as possible, the non-availability of a witness and attempt to offer pre-trial facilities for examination, perhaps by using a pre-recorded video under s 23 (a 'Special Measure Direction' under Part II of the Youth Justice and Criminal Evidence Act 1999 (not yet in force)).

16.4.5.6 Article 6 and inferences from silence

The Criminal Justice and Public Order Act 1994 introduced various inroads into the right to silence which had hitherto been absolute. Under s 34, in particular, if an accused failed to mention when questioned, or charged, a fact which he later relied upon in court then such inferences as appeared proper could be drawn from that earlier silence, most notably the inference of recent fabrication. It is accepted that the mere fact of drawing inference from an accused's silence will not, of itself, involve a breach of Article 6. However, the procedural safeguards involved in situations where inferences may be drawn have been subject to close scrutiny in our national courts and more recently have been challenged in the European Court (most notably in *Condron v United Kingdom*, Application 35718/97, 2 May 2000).

The Court held that there had in fact been a breach of Article 6 in that the direction given to the jury in respect of the s 34 inference had been incomplete. As a matter of fairness the judge should have directed them that if they were satisfied that the applicant's silence at the police interview could not sensibly have been attributed to their having no answer or none that would stand up to cross-examination it should not draw an adverse inference.

The problem in this case is that the Court of Appeal also accepted a defect in the summing up and also accepted that they could not know how much account the jury had taken of the defendant's silence when reaching their verdict. However, they were happy that, having looked at the other evidence before the court, the conviction of the defendants was not unsafe. This, in effect, seems to be suggesting that the Court of Appeal feels able to superimpose its own reasoning onto the trial process. It remains to be seen whether or not this attempt to override the jury's actual thought process in coming to a decision is in fact a breach of Article 6 itself.

Inferences under s 34 are clearly not going to invalidate a trial procedure but there are procedural issues involved which will need to be carefully scrutinised.

Sections 36 and 37 of the Criminal Justice and Public Order Act 1994 deal with a situation where the accused, in interview, fails to provided a reasonable explanation for his presence at the scene of the crime or for his possession of incriminating objects such as drugs, or a weapon.

In these circumstances, provided the appropriate special warning is administered by the investigating officers in interview, a court may draw such inference as appears proper. The difference between ss 36 and 37 and s 34 is that there is no requirement for the court to look at whether or not it was *reasonable* in the circumstances to have expected the accused to provide an explanation. It is possible that this fetter upon the judge's discretion could well give rise to an application that these sections infringe Article 6.

16.4.5.7 Article 6 and public interest immunity

Public interest immunity (PII) is an exclusionary rule of evidence which allows for material falling within the definition of public interest immunity to be withheld from the defence.

Procedure

The procedural requirements that govern the way in which the prosecution should claim such immunity have been quite vigorously challenged in Strasbourg in the case of *Rowe and Davis v United Kingdom* (2000) 30 EHRR 1. At trial, the prosecution decided, without informing the judge, to withhold relevant material on the grounds that it fell within the definition of PII. The court felt that:

> Such a procedure, whereby the prosecution itself attempts to assess the importance of concealed information to the defence and weigh this against the public interest in keeping the information secret, cannot comply with ... Article 6(1).

The subsequent review of the material by the Court of Appeal could not cure the inherent unfairness arising from the initial trial. The trial judge had never seen the material and he would have been the person in the best possible position to assess the material in the light of the evidence being given as opposed to the Court of Appeal attempting artificially to manufacture the live trial situation from a set of lifeless manuscripts.

The generic issue that the Court was concerned with was the fact that in the UK the prosecution may make an *ex parte* application without notice to the judge in order to obtain PII status without the defence ever being involved in the decision-making process. This is as opposed to an *inter partes* hearing, or an *ex parte* hearing with notice, where the defence are allowed to make representation in writing or in person. Whilst the latter two options are clearly quite fair, the former *ex parte* without notice application has been severely criticised by Strasbourg and the position has yet to be clarified.

A later case of *Fitt v United Kingdom* (2000) 30 EHRR 480 held that the procedures adopted with regards to disclosure, in this particular case, were Article 6(1) compliant. This was because, although the prosecution were heard *ex parte*, the defence were kept informed and permitted to make submissions and participate in those decisions as far as possible without disclosing the material the prosecution sought to withhold on PII grounds. The Court also had regard to the judge's continuing duty to monitor the situation, which it felt was an important safeguard from a defence point of view. The Court came to the same conclusion in similar terms in *Jasper v United Kingdom* (2000) 30 EHRR 441.

Consequently, care should always be taken to ensure that the trial judge is complying with the spirit of Article 6 by allowing the defence to have a role in the decision-making process, especially in cases where the prosecution adopt the *ex parte* method of application for claiming PII status. These representations can only be made, of course, where the defence is actually made aware of the fact of the application in the first place—a position that did clearly not exist in *Rowe and Davis*. Indeed, even where the defence are involved in some way in the decision-making process this will not always guarantee that the individual's rights are protected. In *R v Doubtfire* (2000) *The Times*, 28 December the defence had been given the opportunity to explain its case to the judge, after a prosecution *ex parte* application, before he ruled, in the prosecution's favour, upon the issue of PII. Allowing the appeal, after a referral from the Criminal Cases Review Commission, the court held that it was sufficient to state that the trial had been materially unfair because there had been a failure in respect of disclosure in the context of submissions made at the *ex parte* PII application during trial, and the material in the confidential annex which the court had considered in private had not been available to the trial judge or at the earlier appeal hearing, confirming there had been unfairness.

16.4.5.8 Article 6—unfairly obtained evidence

Traditionally, unfairly obtained evidence may be excluded under s 78 of the Police and Criminal Evidence Act 1984; and, following the implementation of the Human Rights Act 1998, it could also be held to be a violation of an individual's rights under Article 6 or Article 8, the latter sometimes resulting in the courts determining that there had consequently been a breach of Article 6.

Section 78(1) of the Police and Criminal Evidence Act 1984 provides that the court:

> may refuse to allow evidence on which the prosecution proposes to rely to be given if it appears to the court that, having regard to all the circumstances, *including the circumstances in which the evidence was obtained*, the admission of the evidence could have such an adverse effect on the fairness of the proceedings that the court ought not to admit it. (emphasis added)

Where the evidence under s 78 it did not automatically follow that the prosecution came to an end, or that conviction, upon appeal, was necessarily unsafe. Similarly, even where a breach of Article 6 and/or Article 8 was found, it was still possible for the Court of Appeal safely to uphold a conviction.

The case of *Teixera de Castro v Portugal* (1998) 28 EHRR 101, while notable for its decision regarding unfairly obtained evidence, also states:

> The Court reiterates that the admissibility of evidence is primarily a matter for regulation by national law and as a general rule it is for the courts to assess the evidence before them. The Court's task under the Convention is not to give rulings as to whether the statements of witnesses were properly admitted as evidence, but rather to ascertain whether the proceedings as a whole, including the way in which evidence was taken, were fair.

The practical consequences of evidence obtained primarily as a result of intelligence-led policing have been clarified in the House of Lords, in the *Attorney-General's Reference (No. 3 of 2000)*, [2002] 1 Cr.App.R 29 which dealt with the conjoined appeals of *R v G* and *R v Looseley*. What the House of Lords provides is a rationale for the courts to stay prosecutions based upon entrapment, described by Lord Hoffman as a 'jurisdiction to prevent abuse of executive power' and which Lord Nicholls pronounced in greater detail as follows:

> It is not simply acceptable that the state through its agents should lure its citizens into committing acts forbidden by the law and then seek to prosecute them for doing so. That would be entrapment. That would be a misuse of state power, and an abuse of process for the courts. The unattractive consequences, frightening and sinister in extreme cases, which state conduct of this kind could have are obvious. The role of the courts is to stand between the state and its citizens and make sure this does not happen.

The House of Lords held that in *Looseley* the trial judge had been correct to refuse the application to stay the proceedings for abuse of process, as the police had reasonable grounds to suspect that the defendant was involved in the supply of Class A drugs and all the undercover officer had done was provide an opportunity for him to commit the offence; in contrast their Lordships found that the trial judge in the *Attorney-General's Reference* had been correct in staying the proceeding because there were no reasonable grounds to suspect that the defendant was involved in the supply of Class A drugs and the officer had repeatedly phoned his mobile phone number offering cheap cigarettes in return for the supply of such drugs.

The approach adopted by the House of Lords is consistent with the reasoning of the European Court in *Teixera de Castro v Portugal*, which stated that where there was conduct amounting to entrapment, the defendant would be denied the right to a fair trial from the outset.

From a prosecution point of view this is clearly the most serious consequence resulting from an abuse of state power; but it is not the only consequence. In cases where the court feels that a stay is inappropriate, it will still be open to the defence to make an application to exclude the evidence of the undercover officer under s 78 of the 1984 Act either because to admit it would have an adverse effect on the trial as a whole, or on grounds that could have been submitted to support an application for a stay. Even if the evidence remains, it may still be appropriate to refer to how it was obtained in the plea in mitigation.

How should the court determine what conduct should lead to the exclusion of evidence, or indeed the stay of proceedings for abuse of process? The case of *R v Smurthwaite and Gill* [1994] 1 All ER 898 has long since provided the courts with guidelines to apply in these cases in order to determine whether or not evidence ought to be excluded. Smurthwaite was convicted of soliciting to murder. The person solicited was in fact an undercover police officer who had posed as a contract killer. The prosecution's case relied upon covertly recorded conversations of meetings between the undercover officer and the defendant. The defendant appealed on the basis that this evidence should have been ruled inadmissible. The Court of Appeal held that the relevant factors to consider when applying s 78 to such circumstances included:

(a) whether the undercover officer was acting as an *agent provocateur*;

(b) the nature of any entrapment;

(c) whether the evidence consists of admissions to a completed offence, or relates to the actual commission of the offence;

(d) how active or passive the officer's role was in obtaining the evidence;

(e) whether there is an unassailable record of what occurred, or whether it is strongly corroborated;

(f) whether the officer abused his (undercover) role to ask questions which ought properly to have been asked as a police officer in accordance with Code C of the Police and Criminal Evidence Act 1984.

In Smurthwaite's case, although there was an element of entrapment and trick, the officer had not acted as an *agent provocateur*. The tapes recorded the actual commission of the offence rather than an offence committed in the past, and they made it clear that it was the accused who was the instigator. The officer had very much taken a back seat and used no persuasion.

Both the *Attorney-General's Reference* and *Nottingham City Council v Amin* [2000] 1 WLR 1071 (see below) abandon the test of whether the officer's role is active or passive, in that they regard it as unhelpful. The basis of the distinction was not whether the officer had acted or not acted, but whether or not the extent of his involvement was acceptable to the court; but as Lord Bingham in *Amin* stated, 'there was nothing to suggest that without [the police officers'] intervention [the offence] would have been committed'.

The decision in *Nottingham City Council v Amin* [2000] 1 WLR 1071, where a driver was prosecuted for plying for hire without a licence provides the modern approach to cases involving undercover officers. The defendant's cab was licensed for an adjoining area, but not the city centre where he was driving when stopped by two plain-clothes police officers. The light on his cab was not illuminated, but when the officers asked him to convey them to a specified destination he agreed, and did so for a fare. He argued that the evidence was obtained unfairly and should be excluded under s 78 of the 1984 Act. The Divisional Court held that the facts could not be construed as showing the defendant in any way being pressurised into committing the offence and that the evidence should be admitted. Confirming that it was the fairness of the proceedings as a whole that had to be looked at, the court identified two conflicting public interest points. On the one hand, it was recognised as deeply offensive to ordinary notions of fairness if a defendant were to be convicted and punished for committing a crime only because he had been incited, persuaded or pressurised into doing so by a law enforcement officer. On the other hand, it had been recognised that law enforcement agencies had a general duty to the public to enforce the law, and it had been regarded as unobjectionable if such an officer gave a defendant an opportunity to break the law, of which he freely took advantage, in circumstances where it appeared that he would have behaved in the same way if the opportunity had been offered by anyone else. The court drew a distinction between creating an opportunity to commit an offence and inducing the commission of the offence. It would seem that positive action, beyond merely providing the opportunity to commit the offence, will be required before any breach of Article 6 becomes imminent.

European perspective

The use of participating informants was challenged in *Ludi v Switzerland* (1992) 15 EHRR 173 where the court refused to find that the use of an undercover agent infringed the applicant's Article 8 rights as he was a suspected member of a large group of drug traffickers in possession of five kilos of cocaine and 'must therefore have been aware from then on that he was engaged in a criminal act ... and that consequently he was running the risk of encountering an undercover police officer whose task would in fact be to expose him'. In *Ludi* the drug trafficking was already under way when the undercover officer came on the scene and so the admission of evidence gathered in the course of the operation did not violate Article 6. Notable in this case was that the operation had been judicially sanctioned, and it is a weakness of our statutory scheme that certain types of covert activity do not require prior independent authorisation.

However, some cases are illustrative of the fact that covert human intelligence can be taken a stage too far, a classic example being found in the case of *Teixera de Castro v Portugal* (1998) 28 EHRR 101, where the court ruled that the admissibility of evidence where there had been entrapment of a person not predisposed to that type of offence will not be left to regulation by national law. The applicant in this case, who had no record of drug dealing, was introduced to a third party by two police officers posing as drug addicts. They asked him to supply them with heroin. Initially he refused, but complied with a second request and supplied the officers with heroin at a profit. He maintained in his defence that he had been incited to commit an offence which, but for the intervention of the two officers, he would not have committed. The Court agreed, saying that '... the two police officers did not confine themselves to investigating criminal activities in an essentially passive manner, but exercised an influence such as to incite the commission of the offence'. The prosecution were unable to prove any predisposition to commit such a type of offence on the part of the applicant, and not even the public interest in fighting drug trafficking could justify relying on evidence obtained as a result of police incitement.

16.4.5.9 Civil proceedings

The Woolf Reforms in respect of civil procedure have been in force for sometime now and were designed with the Human Rights Act 1998 in mind. This was certainly the intention of Lord Woolf who has made his views known, most recently in the case of *Daniels v Walker*

(2000) *The Times*, 17 May, CA, where he stated that:

> The provisions of the Civil Procedure Rules 1998 make it clear that it is the obligation of the court to deal with cases justly ... it is highly undesirable for the consideration of issues to be made more complex by the injection of Article 6 arguments and it is hoped that judges will be robust in resisting such arguments.

Clearly, there is a danger that human rights points will be overused by practitioners and incur the displeasure of the court, most likely in costs penalties, but there are still genuine areas of concern with the Civil Procedure Rules which may justify a valid application before the court. Where cases are allocated to the fast track and there is a limited time period within which to prepare for trial, it may be possible to argue that such strict adherence to a time limit is unfair, especially where the preparation of the case involves complex issues and has necessitated the use of experts. This would have to be balanced against the applicant's right to a speedy trial but it would be a valid point to make.

Similarly there is the right to 'a public hearing' which is embodied in Article 6. The recent case of *Roger Storer v British Gas plc* (2000) *The Times*, 1 March, provides an illustration of the problems that may arise for the court service in this area. In this case the employment tribunal took place in a courtroom the only means of access to which were by a combination lock (a system not unusual in courtrooms in the United Kingdom). The Court of Appeal held that this did not constitute a hearing in 'open court' and therefore the proceedings were flawed. Family proceedings at the present time are conducted in 'Chambers' hearings and not in public, so changes may have to be made there as well.

Lastly, the court fees imposed under the Rules may well be subject to scrutiny. The right to a fair trial implies reasonable access to the courts. If court fees are proscriptive, i.e. disproportionate or unfair, and as a result prevent an individual from seeking legal redress, there may well be an infringement of Article 6. Certainly the rules involved refer to the principle of proportionality, and this is reflected in the principles that Strasbourg applies as well.

Despite the advance warnings that human rights points will be met with a robust approach from the judiciary, there are areas in civil proceedings where human rights points can be argued effectively, but they should be chosen with care and well argued to avoid the judge taking the view that the court is being led down a 'blind alley'.

16.4.6 Article 7—no punishment without law (no retrospective criminal offences or penalties)

1. No one shall be held guilty of any criminal offence on account of any act or omission which did not constitute a criminal offence under national or international law at the time when it was committed. Nor shall a heavier penalty be imposed than the one that was applicable at the time the criminal offence was committed.
2. This article shall not prejudice the trial and punishment of any person for any act or omission which, at the time it was committed, was criminal according to the general principles of law recognised by civilised nations.

There is the presumption in relation to criminal offences that there will be no retro-activity and that provisions of criminal law may be argued against if they are not clear. There are various changes in our domestic legislation which may cause a problem in relation to retro-activity which can be more clearly explained in relation to case law. In *SW and CR v United Kingdom* (1995) 21 EHRR 363 the defendant was charged with raping his wife. He argued that that the change in the law making rape within marriage a crime was a violation of Article 7. It was held that there was no violation of Article 7 as it was sufficiently foreseeable.

Other changes to our legislation may give rise to an application under Article 7 as well. For example, the Criminal Evidence (Amendment) Act 1997 allows the police to take DNA samples from offenders convicted before the Act came into force. This could be viewed as retroactivity and in breach of Article 7.

16.4.7 Article 8—right to respect for private and family life

1. Everyone has the right to respect for his private and family life, his home and his correspondence.
2. There shall be no interference by a public authority with the exercise of this right except such as is in accordance with the law and is necessary in a democratic society and in the interests of national security, public safety or the economic well being of the country, for the prevention of disorder or crime, for the protection of health and morals, or for the protection of the rights and freedoms of others.

Note that in the case of *X and Y v Netherlands* (1985) 8 EHRR 235 the European Court stated that Article 8:

> does not merely compel the state to abstain from interference: in addition to this primarily negative undertaking, there may be positive obligations inherent in an effective respect for private and family life. These obligations may involve the adoption of measures designed to secure respect for private life even in the sphere of relations of individuals between themselves.

This imposes a secondary duty quite separate to the main function of the Article which refers to interference by a public authority.

16.4.7.1 Article 8—intrusive surveillance

It is accepted that certain forms of intrusive surveillance adopted by the police prior to the implementation of the 1998 Act were incompatible with the rights conveyed under Article 8, not least because there was no legislative regulation of such conduct and therefore the requirement under Article 8(2) that the surveillance be legal could not be satisfied. However, following the implementation of the Police Act 1997, Pt III, and the Regulation of Investigatory Powers Act 2000, Pt II, such regulation is thought to exist. However, it is feared that the potential for challenge still exists, not perhaps in terms of the validity of the procedures as a compatible piece of legislation but in relation to the doctrine of proportionality, i.e. that that surveillance adopted is not a proportionate response to the actions complained of having regard to the legitimate aim under Article 8(2) of preventing crime.

Note that regard should be had to those undercover operations which do not fall under the umbrella of the Regulation of Investigatory Powers Act 2000 as they run the risk of being held to be prima facie unlawful.

The Regulation of Investigatory Powers Act 2000 is essentially a vehicle designed to ensure a valid legal basis is established for the use of covert human intelligence sources—be this a participating informant or an undercover police officer.

The position at common law is that the use of participating informants has always been recognised as a necessary evil by the courts. Indeed Lord Parker stated in *R v Birtles* [1969] 1 WLR 1047:

> ... whilst the police are entitled to make use of information concerning an offence already laid on, and while with a view to mitigating the consequences of the proposed offence, e.g. to protect the proposed witness, it may be perfectly proper for the police to encourage the informer to take part in the offence, or indeed for the police officer himself so do so, the police must never use an informer to encourage another to commit an offence he would not otherwise commit.

Clearly the source should not overstep the boundaries contained in *Smurthwaite and Gill*, and when applying the position at common law regard will now have to be had to relevant European case law (see **16.4.5.8**).

16.4.8 Article 9—freedom of thought, conscience and religion

1. Everyone has the right to freedom of thought, conscience and religion; this right includes freedom to change his religion or belief and freedom, either alone or in community with others and in public or in private, to manifest his religion or belief, in worship, teaching, practice and observance.
2. Freedom to manifest one's religion or beliefs shall be subject only to such limitations as are prescribed by law and are necessary in a democratic society in the interests of public safety, for the protection of public order, health or morals, or for the protection of the rights and freedoms of others.

16.4.9 Article 10—freedom of expression

1. Everyone has the right to freedom of expression. This right shall include freedom to hold opinions and to receive and impart information and ideas without interference by public authority and regardless of frontiers. This Article shall not prevent States from requiring the licensing of broadcasting, television or cinema enterprises.
2. The exercise of these freedoms, since it carries duties and responsibilities, may be subject to such formalities, conditions, restriction or penalties as are prescribed by law and are necessary in a democratic society, in the interests of national security, territorial integrity, or public safety, for the prevention of disorder or crime, for the protection of health and morals, for the protection of the reputation or rights of others, for preventing the disclosure of information received in confidence, or for maintaining the authority and impartiality of the judiciary.

This is a qualified Article which has dealt primarily with political and journalistic expression. In all cases the courts must look at the restriction on the freedom of expression, and decide whether or not there is a legitimate aim which has been prescribed by law and whether or not the restriction is proportionate to the legitimate aim.

Freedom of expression was defined in *Handyside v UK* (1976) 1 EHRR 737:

> Freedom of expression constitutes one of the essential foundations of [a democratic] society, one of the basic conditions for its progress and for the development of every man. Subject to paragraph 2 of Article 10, it is applicable not only to 'information' or 'ideas' that are favourably received and regarded as inoffensive ... but also to those that offend, shock or disturb that State or any sector of the population. Such are the demands of pluralism, tolerance and broadmindedness without which there is no 'democratic society'.

In *Observer and Guardian v United Kingdom* (1991) 14 EHRR 153, the government obtained an interlocutory injunction against two newspapers from publishing extracts from *Spycatcher* written by former MI5 agent Peter Wright. However, once the book had been published in the US and could therefore be transported to the UK, the European Court held that the injunctions could no longer be justified because from that time confidentiality of the material had been destroyed.

There is strong protection of journalistic sources, as evidenced by the case of *Goodwin v UK* (1996) 22 EHRR 123 where the European Court stated:

> Protection of journalistic sources is one of the basic conditions for press freedom. Without such protection, sources may be deterred from assisting the press in informing the public on matters of public interest ... [An order to disclose] cannot be compatible with Article 10 unless it is justified by an overriding requirement in the public interest.

Clearly issues of privacy arise here and may cause our courts some problems in the future. In the UK there has never been a right of privacy, but Article 8 quite clearly affords the individual some form of protection and the development of case law in this area will be quite drastic.

One of the most recent cases in relation to Article 8 is that of *Khan v UK* [2000] Crim LR 684. There, the Court allowed evidence to be heard from a concealed listening device installed in the premises of another suspect in accordance with the Home Office guidelines on the use of equipment in police surveillance operations. K was convicted on the basis of this evidence. The Court held that the tape-recording was an infringement of the right to private life guaranteed by Article 8(1) but that the interference could not be justified under Article 8(2). At the time there was no statutory framework to regulate the police. The Court was not happy to accept the guidelines as they were not legally binding, neither were they directly accessible to the public. The comment was also made that they were of themselves insufficient to protect against arbitrary interference with an individual's rights under Article 8. The Court was also concerned to point out that although there had been a breach of Article 8, this did not render the trial unfair under Article 6 as it was not the function of the European Court to correct legal or factual errors made by national courts.

16.4.10 Article 11—freedom of assembly and association

1. Everyone has the right to freedom of peaceful assembly and to freedom of association with others, including the right to form and to join trade unions for the protection of his interests.
2. No restrictions shall be placed on the exercise of these rights other than such as are prescribed by law and are necessary in a democratic society in the interest of national security or public safety, for the prevention of disorder or crime, for the protection of health or morals or for the protection of the rights and freedoms of others. This Article shall not prevent the imposition of lawful restrictions on the exercise of these rights by members of the armed forces, of the police or of the administration of the State.

16.4.11 Article 12—right to marry

Men and women of marriageable age have the right to marry and to found a family, according to national laws governing the exercise of this right.

16.4.12 Article 14—prohibition of discrimination (as regards the enjoyment of the rights and freedoms set out in the Convention)

The enjoyment of the rights and freedoms set forth in this Convention shall be secured without discrimination on any ground such as sex, race, colour, language, religion, political or other opinion, national or social origin, association with a national minority, property, birth or other status.

16.4.13 Article 16—restrictions on political activity of aliens

Nothing in Articles 10, 11 and 14 shall be regarded as preventing the High Contracting Parties [the States] from imposing restrictions on the political activities of aliens.

16.4.14 Article 17—prohibition of abuse of rights

Nothing in the Convention may be interpreted as implying for any State, group or person any right to engage in any activity or perform any act aimed at the destruction of any rights and freedoms set forth herein or at their limitation to a greater extent than is provided for in the Convention.

16.4.15 Article 18—limitation on use of restriction on rights

The restrictions permitted under this Convention to the said rights and freedoms shall not be applied for any purpose other than those for which they have been prescribed.

The Human Rights Act 1998 also incorporates two existing protocols in UK legislation, the first and the sixth. They are set out as follows.

16.4.16 The First Protocol: Article 1—protection of property

Every natural or legal person is entitled to the peaceful enjoyment of his possessions. No one shall be deprived of his possessions except in the public interest and subject to the conditions provided for by law and by general principles of international law.

The preceding provisions shall not, however, in any way impair the right of a State to enforce such laws as it deems necessary to control the use of property in accordance with the general interest or to secure the payment of taxes or other contributions or penalties.

16.4.17 The First Protocol: Article 2—right to education

No person shall be denied the right to education. In the exercise of any functions which it assumes in relation to education and to teaching, the State shall respect the right of parents to ensure such education and teaching in conformity with their own religious and philosophical convictions.

16.4.18 The First Protocol: Article 3—free elections

The High Contracting Parties [the States] undertake to hold free elections at reasonable intervals by secret ballot, under conditions which will ensure the free expression of the opinion of the people in the choice of the legislature.

16.4.19 The Sixth Protocol

This was ratified in 1999 and effectively outlaws the death penalty.

16.5 Judicial remedies

Section 8(1) of the Human Rights Act 1998 states that:

In relation to any act (or proposed act) of a public authority which the court finds is (or would be) unlawful, it may grant such relief or remedy, or make such order, within its powers as it considers to be just and appropriate.

But note that damages may be awarded only by a court which has powers to award damages, or to order the payment of compensation, in civil proceedings.

Where the court is required to remedy a Convention violation in relation to criminal proceedings it will be required to consider:

(a) directions in relation to the trial process;

(b) disclosure applications;

(c) an application for a stay of proceedings;

(d) arguments in relation to the admissibility of evidence.

Where a court fails to take account of Convention provisions, individuals will be able to make use of judicial review and appeal mechanisms available under the Act and at common law. The Court of Appeal will have the right to quash a conviction in relation to an offence which of itself violates Convention rights, or where there has been a violation of an Article 6 right.

While a court may not strike down an Act of Parliament it may interpret it so as to give effect to Convention rights. Where it is not possible to construe a section to bring it within the Convention, the lower courts will have to apply the offending piece of legislation. The higher courts, including the High Court and Court of Appeal, will have the power to issue a 'declaration of incompatibility'. The government then has the power to either amend legislation or make a 'remedial order' under s 2 and sch 2. Such a declaration would give rise to a ground for appeal against the conviction although it is only the Court of Appeal who has the power to quash a conviction.

16.6 Conclusion

The effect of the Convention has already had wide-ranging ramifications which are continuing to gather speed. Legislation has been changed and will be changed in the future, guidelines have come into existence, and case law is developing on a daily basis. All lawyers will need to keep abreast of developments and use the Convention as part of their approach to advising and representing clients. As previously mentioned, however, it should be used with care. Randomly invoking the Convention may provoke a considerable backlash against lawyer and client alike.

16.7 BIBLIOGRAPHY

Ashcroft, P. *et al.*, *Human Rights and the Courts* (Winchester: Waterside Press, 1999).

Starmer, K., *European Human Rights Law* (London: Legal Action Group, 1999).

Wadham, J. and Mountfield, H., *Blackstone's Guide to the Human Rights Act 1998* (London: Blackstone Press, 1999).

APPENDIX 1
INVESTMENTS

INVESTMENT money invested for income or profit, for a return of income or capital

INCOME	Of a recurring nature
CAPITAL	One-off benefit
JARGON	
Gross interest	Taxable but not subject to direct taxation
Variable rate	Rate of interest paid may change—usually in line with other interest rates
Fixed rate	Rate of interest quoted at the outset doesn't change—even if other interest rates do
Index-linked	Value of the capital invested is inflation proofed, (its purchasing power remains the same from beginning to end of the investment period). The value of the capital changes in line with the Retail Prices Index (RPI).
Base rate (Official name—Minimum Lending Rate)	Controlled by the Bank of England. It sets the general level of UK interest rates and is a valuable tool in managing the economy
Tax-free	Excluded income for income tax purposes. No tax is charged either by direct assessment or deduction at source
Tax-paid	Tax is deducted at source at the basic rate. There may be an additional liability if the taxpayer is a higher rate payer. Non-taxpayers or lower rate taxpayers can apply to the Inland Revenue for a tax refund
Share	The proprietorship element in a company usually represented by transferable certificates, share certificates
Equity/equities	A share or shares which do not bear fixed interest
Quoted shares	Shares in companies listed on a stock market
Unquoted shares	Shares in companies **not** listed on a stock market
Warrant	Evidence that the holder has the right to subscribe for shares or stock.
Stock	A debt due for money loaned to a company or public body (Government or Local Authority) usually with interest being paid from the company or public body to the investor
Gilts 'Gilt-edged' Securities	Stocks issued by the Government to finance its borrowing. They are issued on the National Savings Register or through the Bank of England and can be bought and sold on The Stock Market

Investment trust	A company whose assets are solely shares in other companies
Unit trust	Various banks and institutions offer unit trusts. The investor hands money to the institution and is issued with a number of units. The institution uses the money to invest in shares in other companies. The units can be sold back to the institution at any time
Bid price	The price received if the investor sells his investment (usually units in a unit trust)
Offer price	The price an investor has to pay to buy units
Bid/offer spread	The difference in the bid price and offer price
Par	Nominal or face value
Repayable at par	Nominal or face value is the amount paid to the investor on maturity
Life assured	Is the person on whose life a policy is taken out. The policy will be payable on the life assured's death if it does not mature earlier
Joint lives	Two lives are insured under one policy and the policy will pay out either on the death of the first to die or on the second death. It is agreed at the outset which is to occur

Types of investments:

WITHOUT RISK or LOW RISK:

BANK ACCOUNTS	Current:	money available immediately no interest or very little (due to immediate access) transactions recorded on statements
	Deposit	money available on specified period of notice differing rates of interest linked to notice period transactions recorded on statements
BUILDING SOCIETY ACCOUNTS	Deposit	money available immediately priority on repayment if society faces difficulties low interest (due to security of investment) transactions recorded in pass books
	Share	money available on specified period of notice differing rates of interest linked to notice period and/or balance invested (tiered rates) transactions recorded in pass books
TESSAs	Tax Exempt Special Savings Accounts [No new accounts after 5 April 1999]	tax-free income limit of £9,000 capital 5 year period
NATIONAL SAVINGS	Schemes offered by the Government Security of the money invested is guaranteed by the Government Return is known at the outset	

Bank Accounts	Ordinary	up to £100 available on demand low interest (due to immediate access and security of investment) operated through the post or Post Office transactions recorded in pass book
	Investment	money available on one month's notice operated through the post or Post Office differing rates of interest depending on balance invested (tiered rates)

Savings Certificates

Tax-free interest
Invested for a five-year term
Rate of interest increasing each year of the five-year term but rate fixed at outset
If Bank of England interest rate changes the Government usually make available savings certificates on new terms (a new 'issue')
Existing 'issues' continue to the end of their five year term
Can be index-linked

Income Bonds

Repayable on three months notice
Penalties if withdraw before end of first year
Interest paid monthly
Rate of interest is variable

Premium Bonds

Repayable on demand
No interest paid
Chance of winning a cash prize in the monthly draw

LOCAL AUTHORITY BONDS

Repayable only at end of term
Fixed-rate of interest
Interest usually paid monthly

GILTS

Repayable at par at end of term **but** can be sold before maturity
Fixed-rate of interest
Interest usually paid half yearly

ISA

Individual Savings Account
risk depends on category invested in
tax free investment income and capital gains
limit of £7,000 capital invested in any one tax year (up to and including 2005/06, then £5,000)
maximum of £3,000 (then £1,000) in cash, maximum of £1,000 in life insurance, balance in stocks and shares
no minimum or maximum holding periods
Possibility of income—interest and dividends
Possibility of capital gain—on selling stocks or shares
Possibility of capital loss—on selling stocks or shares

WITH RISK:

QUOTED SHARES

With-risk investment
Money available on sale of the holding, delay in monies reaching investor
Possibility of income—dividends and/or capital gain/loss on selling shares

INVESTMENT TRUSTS	With-risk investment Money available on sale of the holding, delay in monies reaching investor Possibility of income—dividends and/or capital gain/loss on selling shares
UNIT TRUSTS	With-risk investment Money available on sale of the holding, delay in monies reaching investor Possibility of income—dividends and/or capital gain/loss on selling shares
PEP	Personal Equity Plan [no new investments after 5 April 1999] with risk investment tax free investment (income and capital gains) limit of £6,000 capital invested in any one tax year Possibility of income—dividends Possibility of capital gain—on selling shares Possibility of capital loss—on selling shares
LIFE ASSURANCE	
Whole life	No return until death of life assured Life assured or policy holder pays regular premiums Fixed sum is paid out on the death of the life assured
Term assurance	No return unless life assured dies within specified period Life assured or policy holder pays regular premiums Fixed sum is paid out if life assured dies within a fixed period of time
Endowment assurance	No return until specified date or death if earlier Life assured or policy holder pays regular premiums Sum is paid on a specified date or earlier if life assured dies before that date If 'with profits' sum paid is greater of fixed sum assured or value of fund in which premiums are invested
ANNUITIES	No return of capital Capital sum is paid to the insurance company Guaranteed income will be paid to the investor for life or until agreed period ends Usually ceases on death but can be guaranteed for a fixed period notwithstanding death

Stock market terminology:

AIM	Alternative Investments Market
Emerging Markets	It is generally thought that the biggest stockmarket returns in the future will not be in the established markets but in cities such as Manila, Caracas, Lima and Mexico City. Their economies are expected to grow faster than more mature economies

Indices	**FT-SE 100:** An index jointly sponsored by the Financial Times, the London Stock Exchange and the Institute and Faculty of Actuaries. It contains shares of the top **100** UK companies ranked by market capitalisation. It is calculated every minute during the working day and shares enter and leave the index every quarter **FT-SE Eurotrack 200:** It contains the shares of 100 companies from Continental Europe and the constituents of the FT-SE 100 index. The weighting of the 100 shares from the UK are adjusted so as not to take up an inappropriate proportion of the index. It is calculated every minute **DAX:** This is the German share index and is published by the Frankfurt Stock Exchange. It contains 30 stocks from the main German markets. It is calculated every minute **NIKKEI 225:** This is the original Japanese share index published by Nihon Keizai Shimbun. It is calculated every minute and contains shares from 225 companies **DOW-JONES INDUSTRIAL AVERAGE:** The grandfather of all indices. First calculated in January 1897. It contains 30 stocks chosen by Dow-Jones and Wall Street. It is also calculated every minute
Insider Dealing	When someone trades in a company's shares using specific information that has not been made public but which would seriously affect the company's share price if it were known. It can be done by a director or a receptionist
Derivatives	High risk investments. Can make or break an investor or a bank. They use futures and options. An option is a bet on the future price of anything—pork bellies to ordinary shares. An investor who takes an option retains the right to buy or sell a share within a set period with the price fixed at the outset. In a futures contract the investor has to exercise the option even if the market goes against him and, as Nick Leeson and Barings know, the losses can be unlimited
Bulls & Bears	Terms describing different types of investor Bulls are optimists about market prices and believe that they will rise in a **bull** market. There was bull market in the mid-1980s which ended in the crash on Black Monday, 19th October 1987 Bears are pessimists and believe that market prices will fall. There was a bear market after the 1929 Wall Street Crash

APPENDIX 2
SOLICITORS' FINANCIAL SERVICES (SCOPE) RULES 2001

These rules, dated 18 July 2001, are made by the Council of the Law Society with the concurrence of the Master of the Rolls under section 31 of the Solicitors Act 1974, section 9 of the Administration of Justice Act 1985 and for the purposes of section 332 of the Financial Services and Markets Act 2000, regulating the practices of:

- *solicitors and recognised bodies in any part of the world,*
- *registered European lawyers in any part of the United Kingdom, and*
- *registered foreign lawyers in England and Wales,*

in carrying out 'regulated activities' in, into or from the United Kingdom.

1 Purpose

(1) The Law Society is a designated professional body under Part XX of *the Act*, and *firms* may therefore carry on certain *regulated activities* without being regulated by the *FSA*, if they can meet the conditions specified in section 327 of *the Act*. As a designated professional body the Law Society is required to make rules governing the carrying on by *firms* of *regulated activities*. The purpose of these rules is to set out the scope of the *regulated activities* which may be undertaken by *firms* which are not regulated by the *FSA*.

(2) These rules:

- prohibit *firms* which are not regulated by the *FSA* from carrying on certain *regulated activities*;
- set out the basic conditions which those *firms* must satisfy when carrying on any *regulated activities*;
- set out other restrictions on *regulated activities* carried on by those *firms*.

2 Application

These rules apply only to *firms* which are not regulated by the *FSA*.

3 Prohibited activities

A *firm* must not carry on, or agree to carry on, any of the following activities:

(a) *market making* in *investments*;

(b) *buying*, selling, subscribing for or underwriting *investments* as principal where the *firm:*
   (i) holds itself out as engaging in the business of *buying* such *investments* with a view to selling them;
   (ii) holds itself out as engaging in the business of underwriting *investments* of the kind to which the *transaction* relates; or
   (iii) regularly solicits members of the public with the purpose of inducing them, as principals or agents, to enter into *transactions* and the *transaction* is entered into as a result of the *firm* having solicited members of the public in that manner.

(c) *buying* or selling *investments* with a view to stabilising or maintaining the market price of the *investments*;

(d) acting as a *stakeholder pension scheme* manager;

(e) entering into a *broker funds arrangement*;

(f) effecting and carrying out *contracts of insurance* as principal;

(g) establishing, operating or winding up a *collective investment scheme*;

(h) establishing, operating or winding up a *stakeholder pension scheme*;

(i) managing the underwriting capacity of a Lloyd's syndicate as a managing agent at Lloyd's;

(j) advising a person to become a member of a particular Lloyd's syndicate;

(k) entering as provider into a *funeral plan contract*; or

(l) entering into a *regulated mortgage contract* as lender or administering a *regulated mortgage contract*.

4 Basic conditions

A *firm* which carries on any *regulated activities* must ensure that:

(a) the activities arise out of, or are complementary to, the provision of a particular *professional service* to a particular *client*;

(b) the manner of the provision by the *firm* of any service in the course of carrying on the activities is incidental to the provision by the *firm* of *professional services*;

(c) the *firm* accounts to the *client* for any pecuniary reward or other advantage which the *firm* receives from a third party;

(d) the activities are not of a description, nor do they relate to an investment of a description, specified in any order made by the Treasury under section 327(6) of *the Act*;

(e) the *firm* does not carry on, or hold itself out as carrying on, a *regulated activity* other than one which is allowed by these rules or one in relation to which the *firm* is an *exempt person*;

(f) there is not in force any order or direction of the *FSA* under sections 328 or 329 of *the Act* which prevents the *firm* from carrying on the activities; and

(g) the activities are not otherwise prohibited by these rules.

5 Other restrictions

(1) Packaged products (except personal pension schemes)

A *firm* must not recommend, or make arrangements for, a *client* to *buy a packaged product* **except where**:

(a) recommending, or arranging for, a *client* to *buy* a *packaged product* by means of an assignment;

(b) the arrangements are made as a result of a *firm* managing assets within the exception to rule 5(4) below; or

(c) arranging a *transaction* for a *client* where the *firm* assumes on reasonable grounds that the *client* is not relying on the *firm* as to the merits or suitability of that *transaction*.

(2) Personal pension schemes

(a) A firm must not recommend a *client* to *buy* or dispose of any rights or interests in a *personal pension scheme*.

(b) A *firm* must not make arrangements for a *client* to *buy* any rights or interests in a *personal pension scheme* **except where** the *firm* assumes on reasonable grounds that the *client* is not relying on the *firm* as to the merits or suitability of that *transaction* but this exception does not apply where the *transaction* involves:

(i) a *pension transfer*; or

(ii) an *opt-out*.

(3) Securities and contractually based investments (except packaged products)

(a) A *firm* must not recommend a *client* to *buy* or subscribe for a *security* or a *contractually based investment* where the *transaction* would be made:

(i) with a person acting in the course of carrying on the business of *buying*, selling, subscribing for or underwriting the *investment*, whether as principal or agent;

(ii) on an investment exchange or any other market to which that *investment* is admitted for dealing; or

(iii) in response to an invitation to subscribe for an *investment* which is, or is to be, admitted for dealing on an investment exchange or any other market.

(b) This rule does not apply where the *client* is:-

(i) not an individual;

(ii) an individual who acts in connection with the carrying on of a business of any kind by himself or by an undertaking of which the *client* is, or would become as a result of the *transaction* to which the recommendation relates, a *controller;* or

(iii) acting in his capacity as a trustee of an occupational pension scheme.

(4) Discretionary management

A *firm* must not manage *assets* belonging to another person in circumstances which involve the exercise of discretion **except where** the *firm* or a *partner, officer* or *employee* of the *firm* is a trustee, personal representative, donee of a power of attorney or receiver appointed by the Court of Protection, and either:

(a) all routine or day to day decisions, so far as relating to that activity, are taken by an *authorised person* with permission to carry on that activity or an *exempt person*; or

(b) any decision to enter into a transaction, which involves *buying* or subscribing for an *investment*, is undertaken in accordance with the advice of an *authorised person* with permission to give advice in relation to such an activity or an *exempt person*.

(5) Corporate finance

A *firm* must not act as any of the following:

(a) sponsor to an issue in respect of securities to be admitted for dealing on the London Stock Exchange; or

(b) nominated adviser to an issue in respect of securities to be admitted for dealing on the Alternative Investment Market of the London Stock Exchange.

6 Effect of a breach of these rules

(1) The Law Society may exercise its statutory powers in respect of any *firm* which breaches these rules.

(2) In determining whether or not there has been a breach of these rules the Law Society will take account of whether the *firm* has given due regard to the guidance issued by the Law Society on how to determine whether *regulated activities* are carried on in accordance with these rules.

(3) A *firm* which breaches these rules may:

(a) be committing a criminal offence under section 23 of *the Act*;

(b) be made subject to an order by the *FSA* under section 329 of *the Act* which could prevent the *firm* from carrying on any *regulated activities*.

7 Repeal and commencement

(1) These rules repeal the Solicitors' Investment Business Rules 1995.

(2) These rules come into force on 1 December 2001.

8 Interpretation

(1) In these rules unless the context otherwise requires:

the Act means the Financial Services and Markets Act 2000;

AIM means The Alternative Investment Market of the London Stock Exchange;

asset means an *investment;*

authorised person has the meaning given in section 31 of *the Act;*

broker funds arrangement means an arrangement between a *firm* and a *life office* (or operator of a *regulated collective investment scheme*) under which the *life office* (or operator of the *regulated collective investment scheme*) agrees to establish a separate fund whose composition may be determined by instructions from the *firm* and in which it is possible for more than one *client* to invest;

buy or buying includes acquiring for valuable consideration;

client, in relation to any *regulated activities* carried on by a *firm* for a trust or the estate of a deceased person (including a controlled trust), means the trustees or personal representatives in their capacity as such and not any person who is a beneficiary under the trust or interested in the estate;

collective investment scheme means (in accordance with section 235 of *the Act* (Collective investment schemes)) any arrangements with respect to property of any description, including money, the purpose or effect of which is to enable persons taking part in the arrangements (whether by becoming owners of the property or any part of it or otherwise) to participate in or receive profits or income arising from the acquisition, holding, management or disposal of the property or sums paid out of such profits or income, which are not excluded by the Financial Services and Markets Act (Collective Investment Schemes) Order 2001 (SI 2001/1062);

contract of insurance has the meaning given by article 3(1) of the *Regulated Activities Order;*

contractually based investment has the meaning given by article 3(1) of the *Regulated Activities Order* but does not include an investment which falls within the definition of a *packaged product;*

controller has the meaning given in section 422 of *the Act*;

employee means an individual who is employed in connection with the *firm's regulated activities* under a contract of service or under a contract for services such that he or she is held out as an employee or consultant of the *firm*;

exempt person means a person who is exempt from the *general prohibition* as a result of an exemption order made under section 38(1) or as a result of section 39(1) or 285(2) or (3) of *the Act* and who, in engaging in the activity in question, is acting in the course of business in respect of which that person is exempt;

firm means:

(a) a sole solicitor or *registered European lawyer*,

(b) a lawyers' *partnership* which includes at least one solicitor, *registered European lawyer* or *recognised body*, and which is permitted by rule 7(6)(a)–(c) of the Solicitors' Practice Rules 1990; or

(c) a *recognised body;*

FSA means the Financial Services Authority;

funeral plan contract has the meaning given in article 59 of the *Regulated Activities Order*,

general prohibition has the meaning given in section 19(2) of *the Act;*

individual pension contract means a *pension policy* or *pension contract* under which contributions are paid to:

(a) a personal pension scheme approved under section 630 of the Income and Corporation Taxes Act 1988, whose sole purpose is the provision of annuities or lump sums under arrangements made by individuals in accordance with the scheme;

(b) a retirement benefits scheme approved under section 591(2)(g) of the Income and Corporation Taxes Act 1988, for the provision of relevant benefits by means of an annuity contract made with an insurance company of the employee's choice;

Individual Savings Account means an account which is a scheme of investment satisfying the conditions prescribed in the *Individual Savings Account* Regulations 1998 (S.I. 998/1870);

investment means any of the investments specified in Part III of the *Regulated Activities Order;*

investment trust means a closed-ended company which is listed in the United Kingdom or another member state and:

(a) is approved by the Inland Revenue under section 842 of the Income and Corporation Taxes Act 1988 (or, in the case of a newly formed company, has declared its intention to conduct its affairs so as to obtain approval); or

(b) is resident in another member state and would qualify for approval if resident and listed in the United Kingdom;

investment trust savings scheme means a dedicated service for investment in the securities of one or more *investment trusts* within a particular marketing group (and references to an *investment trust savings scheme* include references to securities to be acquired through that scheme);

ISA means an *Individual Savings Account*;

life office means a person with permission to effect or carry out *long term insurance contracts*;

life policy means a *long term insurance contract* other than a *pure protection contract* or a reinsurance contract, but including a *pension policy*;

long term insurance contract has the meaning given in Part II of Schedule 1 to the *Regulated Activities Order*,

market making means where a *firm* holds itself out as willing, as principal, to buy, sell or subscribe for *investments* of the kind to which the *transaction* relates at prices determined by the *firm* generally and continuously rather than in respect of each particular *transaction*;

occupational pension scheme means any scheme or arrangement which is comprised in one or more documents or agreements and which has, or is capable of having, effect in relation to one or more descriptions or categories of employment so as to provide benefits, in the form of pensions or otherwise, payable on termination of service, or on death or retirement, to or in respect of earners with qualifying service in an employment of any such description or category;

officer means a director or secretary of a *recognised body* which is a company, or a member of a *recognised body* which is a limited liability partnership;

opt-out means a *transaction* resulting from a decision by an individual to opt out of or decline to join a final salary or money-purchase *occupational pension scheme* of which he or she is a current member, or which he or she is, or at the end of a waiting period will become, eligible to join, in favour of an *individual pension contract* or contracts;

packaged product means a *life policy*, a unit or share in a *regulated collective investment scheme*, or an *investment trust savings scheme* whether or not held within an *ISA* or *PEP*, or a *stakeholder pension scheme;*

partner and *partnership* refer only to an unincorporated *firm* and not to a *firm* which is incorporated as a limited liability partnership;

pension contract means a right to benefits obtained by the making of contributions to an *occupational pension scheme* or to a *personal pension scheme*, where the contributions are paid to a *regulated collective investment scheme*;

pension policy means a right to benefits obtained by the making of contributions to an *occupational pension scheme* or to a *personal pension scheme*, where the contributions are paid to a *life office*;

pension transfer means a *transaction* resulting from a decision by an individual to transfer deferred benefits from a final salary *occupational pension scheme*, or from a money-purchase *occupational pension scheme*, in favour of an *individual pension contract* or contracts;

PEP means a personal equity plan within the Personal Equity Plan Regulations 1989;

personal pension scheme means a scheme of investment in accordance with section 630 of the Income and Corporation Taxes Act 1988;

professional services means services provided by a *firm* in the course of its practice and which do not constitute carrying on a *regulated activity*;

pure protection contract means a *long term insurance contract*:

(a) under which the benefits are payable only in respect of death or of incapacity due to injury, sickness or infirmity;

(b) which provides that benefits are payable on death (other than a death due to accident) only where the death occurs within ten years of the date on which the life of the person in question was first insured under the contract, or where the death occurs before that person attains a specified age not exceeding 70 years;

(c) which has no surrender value or the consideration consists of a single premium and the surrender value does not exceed that premium; and

(d) which makes no provision for its conversion or extension in a manner which would result in its ceasing to comply with (a), (b) and (c);

recognised body means a body corporate recognised by the Council under the Solicitors' Incorporated Practice Rules 2001;

registered European lawyer means a person whose name is on the register of European lawyers maintained by the Law Society under regulation 15 of the European Communities (Lawyer's Practice) Regulations 2000;

Regulated Activities Order means the Financial Services and Markets Act 2000 (Regulated Activities) Order 2001;

regulated activity means an activity which is specified in the *Regulated Activities Order;*

regulated collective investment scheme means:

(a) an investment company with variable capital;

(b) an authorised unit trust scheme as defined in section 237(3) of *the Act*; or

(c) a scheme recognised under sections 264, 270 or 272 of *the Act;*

regulated mortgage contract has the meaning given by article 61(3) of the *Regulated Activities Order*;

security has the meaning given by article 3(1) of the *Regulated Activities Order* but does not include an *investment* which falls within the definition of a *packaged product;*

stakeholder pension scheme means a scheme established in accordance with Part I of the Welfare and Pensions Reform Act 1999 and the Stakeholder Pension Scheme Regulations 2000; and

transaction means the purchase, sale, subscription or underwriting of a particular *investment.*

(2) In these rules references to statutes, rules, codes or regulations, statements or principles etc. other than these rules include any modification or replacement thereof.

(3) As the context requires, other words and expressions shall have the meanings assigned to them by the Interpretation Act 1978, *the Act* and the Solicitors Act 1974.

(4) References in these rules to activities carried on by a *firm* include activities carried on by an individual as a principal, *officer* or *employee* of the *firm.*

GUIDANCE ON THE BASIC CONDITIONS

The Scope rules set out basic conditions which firms wishing to undertake *exempt regulated activities* must satisfy. These conditions are derived from sections 327 and 332(4) of the Act. The conditions are as follows:

1 The activities arise out of, or are complementary to, the provision of a particular professional service to a particular client (rule 4(a)).

1.1 This is the overriding condition which must be satisfied before a firm, which is not authorised by the FSA, may undertake a *regulated activity*. The effect of this is that it is not possible to undertake a *regulated activity* in isolation for a client, as the basic condition will only be satisfied where the activity in question **arises out of or is complementary to** other professional services provided to a particular client. These professional services must be services which are provided by a firm in the course of its practice and which do not themselves constitute carrying on a *regulated activity*. To satisfy this basic condition, the firm must be able to identify the relevant professional services.

1.2 Listed below are examples of the types of services which *regulated activities* may arise out of or be complementary to:

- Conveyancing work—giving legal advice, drafting documents, dealing with the Land Registry and undertaking the conveyancing transaction.
- Corporate work—giving legal or tax advice, drafting documents, dealing with regulatory or other quasi-legal matters.
- Matrimonial work—giving legal or tax advice, drafting documents, dealing with court proceedings and other related matters.
- Probate work—winding up the estate, giving legal or tax advice, drafting documents and dealing with court procedures.
- Trust work—giving legal or tax advice, dealing with trust property, preparing trust accounts and drafting legal documents.
- Acting as an attorney or as a receiver appointed by the Court of Protection.

1.3 This test is similar to the 'incidental' exception to discrete investment business in the SIBR. Therefore anything which met that exception will meet this test. Otherwise it should not be difficult for firms to apply a common sense approach to this test.

2 The manner of the provision by the firm of any service in the course of carrying on the activities is incidental to the provision by the firm of professional services (rule 4(b)).

2.1 To satisfy this condition, the *exempt regulated activities* cannot be a major part of the practice of the firm. The FSA considers that the following factors are relevant to this condition:

- the scale of regulated activity in proportion to other professional services provided;
- whether and to what extent activities that are *regulated activities* are held out as separate services; and

- the impression given of how the firm provides *regulated activities*, e.g. through its advertising or other promotion of its services.

2.2 This condition is required because of the Investment Services Directive (ISD) which defines those 'investment firms' which are subject to the ISD, and capital adequacy requirements, but exempts *'persons providing an investment service where that service is provided in an incidental manner in the course of a professional activity'*. This test is different to the **arising out of or complementary** test, as it depends on a qualitative judgement about the way in which the services are provided. For example, even if the services can be shown to contribute a minor part of the services provided by the practice as a whole, the way in which the *regulated activities* are advertised and/or presented as a separate business within the overall practice, could be relevant. Firms should, therefore, take care that any advertisement or promotion does not have the effect of holding out the *regulated activity* as a separate business.

2.3 Under the FS Act the Law Society, as a Recognised Professional Body, was not allowed to authorise firms which did not meet the equivalent test. Therefore it is unlikely that this condition will cause any difficulty to firms within the DPB regime. In addition, any advertising or promotional activity which could lead to a breach of this condition may also be a financial promotion under the FPO and therefore could not be issued by a solicitor's firm which is not authorised by the FSA unless it is approved by an authorised person.

3 The firm accounts to the client for any pecuniary reward or other advantage which the firm receives from a third party (rule 4(c)).

3.1 This condition means that if a firm receives commission (or any financial benefit) from a third party because of acting for or giving advice to a client, the firm must account for the commission (or other financial benefit) to the client. Accounting to the client does not mean simply telling the client that the firm will receive commission. It means that the commission or reward must be held to the order of the client. This is similar to the requirement under rule 10 of the Solicitors' Practice Rules 1990, (see the Guide to the Professional Conduct of Solicitors 8th edition). The Society believes that solicitors will still account to the client if they have the client's **informed consent** to keep the commission.

3.2 If a firm is charging the client on a fee basis, the firm can off-set the commission against the firm's fees. The firm must send the client a bill or some other written notification of costs to comply with the Solicitors' Accounts Rules 1998.

3.3 The requirement for informed consent would not be met if a firm were to:

- seek blanket consent in terms of business to the keeping of all unspecified commissions, or
- seek negative consent.

The firm must be able to demonstrate that the client has given informed consent to any retention of the commission, having had full disclosure of the amount. The FSA Perimeter Guidance (Section 1.9) indicates that the firm should also inform the client, in effect, that the commission belongs to the client.

3.4 There is one important difference between Practice rule 10 and the condition in rule 4(c) of the Scope rules in that Practice rule 10 includes a *de minimis* provision whereby firms are allowed to keep commissions of £20 or less. **This £20 de minimis provision does not apply in relation to rule 4(c)**. Therefore commissions of £20 or less, which arise out of *regulated activities*, must be treated in the same way as commissions of more than £20.

4 The activities are not of a description, nor do they relate to an investment of a description, specified in any order made by the Treasury under section 327(6) of the Act (rule 4(d)).

4.1 Under s327(6) of the Act, the Treasury has made the Financial Services and Markets Act 2000 (Professions) (Non-Exempt Activities) Order 2001 (NEAO) which specifies certain *regulated activities* which do not fall within the exemption under Part XX of the Act. The provisions of the NEAO have been incorporated into the Scope rules and therefore a firm which complies with the Scope rules will also be complying with the NEAO.

5 The firm does not carry on or hold itself out as carrying on any regulated activity other than one which is allowed by these rules or one in relation to which the firm is an exempt person (rule 4(e)).

5.1 This condition makes it clear that a firm must not hold itself out as carrying on *regulated activities* which do not fall within the Scope rules other than activities in relation to which the firm is exempt, for example, activities undertaken whilst acting as an insolvency practitioner (see FSA Perimeter Guidance Section 1.24). The effect of this condition is that a firm which is regulated by the FSA would not be able to be an *exempt professional firm* for the purposes of Part XX of the Act.

6 There is not in force any order or direction of the FSA under s328 or s329 of the Act which prevents the firm from carrying on the activities (rule 4(f)).

6.1 This refers to the FSA's powers under s328 and s329 of the Act.

Section 328—This enables the FSA to make a direction in relation to classes of person or descriptions of *regulated activity* whereby a person within a particular class (or carrying on a particular *regulated activity*) will not be an *exempt professional firm* for the purposes of Part XX of the Act.

Section 329—This gives the FSA power to make an order disapplying the Pt XX exemption from a person named in the order.

7 The activities are not otherwise prohibited by these rules (rule 4(g)).

7.1 This refers to the other restrictions contained in rule 5 of the Scope rules. Further guidance on the effect of these other restrictions in relation to particular areas of work is contained in Section 5.

APPENDIX 3
SOLICITORS' FINANCIAL SERVICES (CONDUCT OF BUSINESS) RULES 2001

These rules, dated 18 July 2001, are made by the Council of the Law Society with the concurrence of the Master of the Rolls under section 31 of the Solicitors Act 1974 and section 9 of the Administration of Justice Act 1985, regulating the practices of:

- *solicitors and recognised bodies in any part of the world,*
- *registered European lawyers in any part of the United Kingdom, and*
- *registered foreign lawyers in England and Wales,*

in carrying out 'regulated activities' in, into or from the United Kingdom.

1 Purpose

(1) The Law Society is a designated professional body under Part XX of *the Act*, and *firms may* therefore carry on certain *regulated activities* without being regulated by the *FSA*.

(2) The Solicitors Financial Services (Scope) Rules 2001 set out the scope of the *regulated activities* which may be undertaken by *firms* which are not regulated by the *FSA*. These rules regulate the way in which *firms* carry on such exempt *regulated activities*.

2 Application

Apart from rule 3 (status disclosure), these rules apply to:

(a) *firms* which are not regulated by the *FSA*; and

(b) *firms* which are regulated by the *FSA* but these rules only apply to such firms in respect of their *non-mainstream regulated activities*.

3 Status disclosure

(1) This rule applies only to *firms* which are not regulated by the *FSA*.

(2) A *firm* shall give the *client* the following information in writing before the *firm* provides a service which includes the carrying on of a *regulated activity*:

(a) a statement that the *firm* is not authorised by the *FSA*;

(b) the nature of the *regulated activities* carried on by the *firm*, and the fact that they are limited in scope;

(c) a statement that the *firm* is regulated by the Law Society; and

(d) a statement explaining that complaints and redress mechanisms are provided through Law Society regulation.

GUIDANCE NOTE

1 There is no prescribed form in which this information must be given to the client. It may be included in the firm's client care letter or in a separate letter.

2 A statement on the firm's stationery to the effect that the firm is regulated by the Law Society would assist in meeting the requirements of this rule.

4 Execution of transactions

A *firm* shall ensure that where it has agreed or decided in its discretion to effect a *transaction*, it shall do so as soon as possible, unless it reasonably believes that it is in the *client's* best interests not to do so.

GUIDANCE NOTE

1 Rule 1 of the Solicitors' Practice Rules 1990 emphasises a solicitor's duty to act in the best interests of the client. Accordingly, in cases where there is any doubt on the point, firms should ensure that transactions are effected on the best terms reasonably available.

2 Rule 15 of the Solicitors' Practice Rules 1990 provides that clients should be kept fully informed of transactions effected on their behalf, unless clients have indicated to the contrary.

5 Records of transactions

(1) Where a *firm* receives instructions from a *client* to effect a *transaction*, or makes a decision to effect a *transaction* in its discretion, it shall keep a record of:

(a) the name of the *client*;

(b) the terms of the instructions or decision; and

(c) in the case of instructions, the date when they were received.

(2) Where a *firm* gives instructions to another person to effect a *transaction*, it shall keep a record of:

(a) the name of the *client*;

(b) the terms of the instructions;

(c) the date when the instructions were given; and

(d) the name of the other person instructed.

GUIDANCE NOTE

It is not necessary for the firm to make a separate record. Normal file notes or letters on the file will meet the requirements of this rule provided that they include the appropriate information. If instructions are given or received over the telephone, an appropriate attendance note would satisfy this rule.

6 Record of commissions

Where a *firm* receives commission which is attributable to *regulated activities* carried on by the *firm*, it shall keep a record of:

(a) the amount of the commission; and

(b) how the *firm* has accounted to the *client*.

GUIDANCE NOTE

1 Any commission received by the firm has to be dealt with in accordance with Rule 10 of the Solicitors' Practice Rules 1990. However, firms should bear in mind that in the case of commissions attributable to regulated activities, the exception for commissions received of £20 or less, does not apply because it is overridden by the condition in section 327(3) of the Act.

2 The record could be a letter or bill of costs provided the information is clear.

7 Safekeeping of clients' investments

(1) Where a *firm* undertakes the *regulated activity* of safeguarding and administering investments, the *firm* must operate appropriate systems, including the keeping of appropriate records, which provide for the safekeeping of *assets* entrusted to the *firm* by *clients* and others.

(2) Where such *assets* are passed to a third party:

(a) an acknowledgement of receipt of the property should be obtained; and

(b) if they have been passed to a third party on the *client's* instructions, such instructions should be obtained in writing.

8 Packaged products—execution-only business

If a *firm* arranges for a *client* on an *execution-only* basis any *transaction* involving a *packaged product*, the *firm* shall send the *client* written confirmation to the effect that:

(a) the *client* had not sought and was not given any advice from the *firm* in connection with the *transaction; or*

(b) the *client* was given advice from the *firm* in connection with that *transaction* but nevertheless persisted in wishing the *transaction* to be effected;

and in either case the *transaction* is effected on the *client's* explicit instructions.

9 Retention of records

Each record made under these rules shall be kept for at least six years.

GUIDANCE NOTE

The six years shall run from the date on which the relevant record has been made.

10 Waivers

(1) In any particular case or cases the Council shall have power to waive in writing any of the provisions of these rules, but shall not do so unless it appears that:

(a) compliance with them would be unduly burdensome having regard to the benefit which compliance would confer on investors; and

(b) the exercise of the power would not result in any undue risk to investors.

(2) The Council shall have power to revoke any waiver.

11 Commencement

These rules come into force on 1 December 2001.

12 Interpretation

(1) The interpretation of these rules is governed by rule 7(1)–(4) of the Solicitors' Financial Services (Scope) Rules 2001.

(2) In these rules:

execution-only (transaction) means a *transaction* which is effected by a *firm* for a *client* where the *firm* assumes on reasonable grounds that the *client* is not relying on the *firm* as to the merits or suitability of that *transaction*;

GUIDANCE NOTE

1 Whether a transaction is 'execution-only' will depend on the existing relationship between the client and the firm and the circumstances surrounding that transaction. Generally, a transaction will be 'execution-only' if the client instructs the firm to effect it without having received advice from the firm. Even though this is the case, however, the transaction may still not qualify as 'execution-only' because, in view of the relationship, the client may reasonably expect the firm to indicate if the transaction is inappropriate. In any event, a firm may be negligent (and possibly in breach of Rule 1 of the Solicitors' Practice Rules 1990) if it fails to advise on the appropriateness or otherwise.

2 A transaction will also be 'execution-only' if the firm has advised the client that the transaction is unsuitable, but the client persists in wishing the transaction to be carried out. In those circumstances it is good practice (and in some cases a requirement) for the firm to confirm in writing that its advice has not been accepted, and that the transaction is being effected on an 'execution-only' basis.

3 Where the transaction involves a packaged product, there is a specific requirement to confirm in writing the 'execution-only' nature of a transaction (see Rule 8 above).

non-mainstream regulated activity means a *regulated activity* of a *firm* regulated by the *FSA* in relation to which the conditions in the Professional Firms Sourcebook (5.2.1R) are satisfied.

(3) These rules are to be interpreted in the light of the guidance notes.

GUIDANCE ON THE CONDUCT OF BUSINESS RULES

1 Introduction

1.1 The detailed conduct of business rules contained in the SIBR are repealed on 1 December 2001. Most of those rules applied to discrete investment business, i.e. mainstream investment business. However, some rules applied to non-discrete investment business, and some of those have been retained, in an amended form, in the Conduct of Business rules.

1.2 The Society has concluded that the number of special rules which only apply to *exempt regulated activities* should be kept to a minimum as those activities should, as far as possible be covered by the same rules as all other services provided by firms.

1.3 These rules would not apply where firms are operating under an **exclusion** in the RAO. However there may sometimes be a fine line between operating under an **exclusion** and providing services within the DPB regime. It may therefore be easier for firms to apply these rules to all such activities.

2 Application

2.1 These rules apply to all firms within the DPB regime and regulate the way in which they carry on *exempt regulated activities*. However, most of the rules also apply to firms who are authorised by the FSA, in respect of their *non-mainstream regulated activities*. FSA rules distinguish between mainstream activities of solicitors' firms and *non-mainstream regulated activities*. Most FSA rules are disapplied to firms' *non-mainstream regulated activities*—which are the same as the services that non-FSA authorised firms can provide as an *exempt regulated activity* under the DPB regime. The FSA relies on the relevant professional body (i.e. the Law Society) to regulate *non-mainstream regulated activities* and it is, therefore, appropriate that the Conduct of Business rules are applied to all firms.

3 Status disclosure (rule 3)

3.1 The FSA Professional Firms Sourcebook (4.1.2R) provides that DPB firms must avoid making any representation to a client that:

(i) it is authorised under the Act or regulated by the FSA; or

(ii) the regulatory protections provided by or under the Act to a person using the services of an authorised person are available.

This means that firms who are not authorised by the FSA must remove any statement on letterheads that the firm is authorised for the conduct of investment business by the Law Society. The FSA have indicated that firms may use up old stocks of pre-printed stationery provided that the statement is crossed through.

3.2 The Professional Firms Sourcebook (4.1.3R) also requires firms in the DPB regime, before providing a regulated activity, to disclose in writing to a client, in a manner that is clear, fair and not misleading, that it is not authorised under the Act. The guidance makes it clear that this information does not have to be contained on stationery and the Society does not consider that such a statement on stationery would be helpful. However, the information can be contained in client care/terms of business/retainer letters.

3.3 The FSA also considers that clients should understand the implications of receiving *exempt regulated activities* from a non-FSA authorised firm and have required the Society, as a DPB, to provide for further status disclosure in the Conduct of Business rules. Therefore, rule 3(2) provides that firms should give clients the following information in writing before carrying out an *exempt regulated activity*:

(a) that the firm is not authorised by the FSA;

(b) information on the nature of the *regulated activities* carried on by the firm and the fact that they are limited in scope;

(c) a statement that the firm is regulated by the Law Society; and

(d) a statement explaining that complaints and redress mechanisms are provided through Law Society regulation.

3.4 Many firms already carry a statement that they are regulated by the Law Society on their stationery, as it is a requirement of rule 11 of the Solicitors' Practice Rules in cases where firms do not have the word 'solicitors' on their notepaper. Having this statement on stationery will ensure compliance with **rule 3(2)(c)**. Suggested paragraphs that could be included in terms of business to deal with **rule 3(2)(a)(b) and (c)** would be as follows:

Sometimes conveyancing/family/probate/company work involves investments. We are not authorised by the Financial Services Authority and so may refer you to someone who is authorised to provide any necessary advice. However we can provide certain limited services in relation to investments, provided they are closely linked with the legal services we are providing to you, as we are regulated by the Law Society.

If during this transaction you need advice on investments, we may have to refer you to someone who is authorised by the Financial Services Authority, as we are not. However, as we are regulated by the Law Society, we may be able to provide certain limited investment services where these are closely linked to the legal work we are doing for you.

Sometimes family etc. work involves investments. We are able to provide a limited range of advice and arrangements for which we are regulated by the Law Society. For more complicated matters we may refer you to someone who is authorised by the Financial Services Authority, as we are not so authorised.

3.5 The Financial Promotions Order, as referred to in Section 1, para 8.2 above, can apply to a firm's own advertising material if the material refers to, broadly, *regulated activities*. However, article 55A contains an exemption for DPB firms, a condition of the exemption requires a certain statement to be included in the advertising material. This statement would also comply with rule **3(2)(a) and (b)**, but the firm must ensure that the client has received a copy of the statement. The statement is:

The firm is not authorised under the Financial Services and Markets Act 2000 but we are able in certain circumstances to offer a limited range of investment services to clients because we are members of the Law Society. We can provide these investment services if they are an incidental part of the professional services we have have been engaged to provide.

3.6 **Rule 3(2)(d)** does go further than the requirements in the Solicitors' Costs Information and Client Care Code relating to the information that should be given to clients on complaints handling. Firms can ensure compliance with this rule by expanding the paragraph in all client care letters on complaints handling, or will have to identify those clients who are most likely to receive *exempt regulated activities* and give a special retainer letter to those clients. A suggested paragraph which could be included in such letters is:

If you have any problem with the service we have provided for you then please let us know. We will try to resolve any problem quickly and operate an internal complaints handling system to help us to resolve the problem between ourselves. If for any reason we are unable to resolve the problem between us, then we are regulated by the Law Society which also provides a complaints and redress scheme.

4 Execution of transactions (rule 4)

4.1 Under the DPB regime, solicitors may often be effecting transactions and this rule, therefore, repeats the requirements of the current SIBR that firms should execute transactions as soon as possible unless it believes that would not be in the client's best interests.

5 Records of transactions (rule 5)

5.1 Rule 5 requires that firms keep certain basic information when dealing with transactions involving *exempt regulated activities*. This obligation applies where the firm instructs another person to effect a transaction, in that the firm should also keep details of the terms of the instructions, the date when they were given and the name of the other person instructed. It is likely that this information will be contained in most files in any case. The rule does not require a separate record to be made nor for it to be kept centrally.

6 Record of commissions (rule 6)

6.1 Again, rule 6 repeats broadly what is contained in the current SIBR in that firms are required to keep a record of the amount of commission but this rule also requires a record of how the firm has accounted to the client. It is a basic condition of the DPB regime that firms account to clients for commission (see Section 4). It is also a condition of some of the exclusions in the RAO. Compliance with this Conduct of Business rule should, therefore, help firms to demonstrate compliance with these conditions. The rule is not prescriptive as to how the record should be kept and it is likely that the normal information on the file, e.g. letters to the client, would provide the relevant record. Where the firm has accounted to the client by setting off the commission against the bill, the bill itself may amount to a record for the purposes of this rule.

7 Safekeeping of clients' investments (rule 7)

7.1 The SIBR contained fairly detailed provisions about the safekeeping (custody) of clients' investments. These provisions are now replaced by this rule which simply requires firms to operate appropriate systems (including the keeping of appropriate records) to ensure the safekeeping of assets entrusted to the firm by clients and others. Most firms of solicitors will operate such systems for all assets and deeds held on behalf of clients whether or not they are investments.

7.2 The rule also contains the sensible requirement that where assets are passed to a third party, the firm should obtain a receipt and that where such assets are being passed to a third party on the client's instructions, the instructions are also obtained in writing.

8 Packaged products—execution-only business (rule 8)

8.1 The Guidance on avoiding FSA authorisation (Section 5) refers to a number of situations where solicitors can, for example, make arrangements for the disposal of a packaged product on an execution-only basis. The condition attached to those exclusions/exceptions requires that it must be clear that the client has not sought advice from the firm as to the merits of entering into the transaction or that if the client has sought such advice and the firm has declined to give it that the firm has suggested that the client seeks advice from an authorised person. Compliance with rule 8 will assist firms in demonstrating that the conditions in the exclusions/exceptions have been met. The rule requires the firm to send to the client written confirmation to the effect that the client has not sought and was not given advice by the firm, or that the client was given negative advice by the firm, but nevertheless wishes to persist in effecting the transaction. The letter should clarify the fact that the transaction is effected on the client's explicit instructions.

8.2 This rule again replicates, more or less, the requirements in the current SIBR and is retained as it will help in clarifying the position for clients and in establishing that the solicitor is acting within the terms of the exclusions/exceptions.

INDEX

D

U

V